ORIGINS OF THE KABBALAH

GERSHOM SCHOLEM

Originally published in German under the title *Ursprung und Anfänge der Kabbala*

First English edition
Manufactured in the United States of America
Library of Congress Cataloging in Publication Data

Scholem, Gershom Gerhard, 1897–1982
Origins of the Kabbalah.

Translation of: Ursprung und Anfänge der Kabbala.
Bibliography: p.
Includes index.
1. Cabala—History. 2. Sefer ha-bahir. I. Werblowsky, R. J. Zwi (Raphael Jehudah Zwi), 1924– . II. Title.
BM526.S363513 1987 296.1′6 86–7381
ISBN 0–691–07314–7
ISBN 0–691–02047–7

Third printing and First Princeton Paperback printing, 1990

Designed by ADRIANNE ONDERDONK DUDDEN

9 8 7 6 5 4 3 2

Contents

CHAPTER 3

THE FIRST KABBALISTS IN PROVENCE · 199

CHAPTER 4

THE KABBALISTIC CENTER IN GERONA · 365

Sources

Ar.Or.	*Archiv Orientalni*
HTR	*Harvard Theological Review*
HUCA	*Hebrew Union College Annual*
JAOS	*Journal of the American Oriental Society*
JBL	*Journal of Biblical Literature*
JJS	*Journal of Jewish Studies*
JQR	*Jewish Quarterly Review*
JRAS	*Journal of the Royal Asiatic Society*
MGWJ	*Monatsschrift für die Geschichte und Wissenschaft des Judentums*
PAAJR	*Proceedings of the American Academy for Jewish Research*
REJ	*Revue des études juives*
RHR	*Revue de l'Histoire des Religions*
ZMRW	*Zeitschrift für Missionskunde und Religionswissenschaft*

Editor's Preface

It is idle to question which of a great scholar's great works is his greatest. In the case of Gershom Scholem, also the *opera minora,* articles, and essays were "great." But three works stand out not only by virtue of their size, but also by virtue of their impact. Each exhibits different qualities. *Major Trends in Jewish Mysticism* (1st ed. 1941) is the first great and still classic attempt to view the whole history of Jewish mysticism in one wide sweep, combining synthetic power with analytical precision and attention to philological detail. *Sabbatai Sevi: The Mystical Messiah* (original Hebrew ed. 1956; revised English version 1973) became a best seller not only because of the fascination with its exotic subject matter. Rarely before had such erudition, quantity and breadth of the sources, minute textual analysis, and profound historical insight been brought to bear on a relatively short—but nevertheless bizarre, spectacular, and, withal, significant—episode in Jewish history (and the history of messianic movements in general for that matter). Yet in many ways *Ursprung und Anfänge der Kabbalah* (1962) is the most impressive of all, for here Scholem dealt with a major yet enigmatic phenomenon in the history of Jewish spirituality. The very specific form of Jewish mysticism (or mystical theosophy) known as Kabbalah appeared suddenly, as if out of the blue, in the late Middle Ages. What were its antecedents? Was it really as ancient as it purported to be? Exactly where, when, and in what circles did it originate? What were the influences (Oriental, Western, philosophical, gnostic, early, late) that went into its making? The wealth of source material marshaled, the penetrating philological accuracy with which it was analyzed, and the scope of historical insight with which it was evaluated all made this study, first published in German in 1962, a *maximum opus.*

The book was a first synthesis of research that had been presented as a draft, as it were, in a small Hebrew book *Reshith ha-Qabbalah* (1948). The author, in his Preface (see p. xv), describes his German publication of 1962 as "more than double the size of the earlier Hebrew publication." In a letter written in the summer of 1961 from London to his lifelong friend S.Y. Agnon, the Hebrew writer and Nobel laureate, and preserved in the Agnon Archive at the National and Hebrew University, Scholem referred to his fruitful year, praised the cold London winter that had kept him indoors and hard at work, and mentioned that the size of the book he was finishing was about three times that of the Hebrew publication. In actual fact the Hebrew book had 262 pages octavo size, whereas the German publication of 1962 ran to 464 pages quarto size. After the publication of *Ursprung,* research continued with growing intensity, and in due course Scholem's graduate and postgraduate students began to contribute to it in increasing measure. Additional sources came to light, necessitating a reexamination and reevaluation of the known sources and texts. Scholem's developing views were voiced in his course lectures at the Hebrew University, and some of those notes were subsequently edited by his students and circulated in stenciled copies. Thus his lecture courses on "The Origins of the Kabbalah and the Book Bahir" (1961/1962) and on "The Kabbalah in Provence: the circle of RABAD and his son R. Isaac the Blind" (1962/1963) were edited by his student, now Professor Rivkah Schatz-Uffenheimer, and published in 1966. The lecture course on "The Kabbalah of the Book Temunah and of Abraham Abulafia" (1964/1965) was edited by another student, now Professor J. Ben-Shlomoh, and published in 1965. A French translation of *Ursprung* appeared in 1966 *(Les origines de la Kabbale);* although it made the work accessible to the French reader, it did not add to the state of knowledge as represented by the original.

Several years ago the Jewish Publication Society conceived the happy idea of bringing out an English version of this seminal work.

The translator, Dr. Allan Arkush, who rendered the German original into English, had to struggle with the extreme difficulty of the subject matter and the equally extreme difficulty of the author's German style. And when the translation was ready a new problem became apparent. The accumulation of the results of more than twenty years of intensive research rendered very questionable the value of a simple "reprint" (albeit in English) of a study reflecting the state of knowledge in 1962. The editor therefore decided to bring the book up-to-date.

But here the difficulty was compounded by the death of Professor Scholem early in 1982. By contrast, in the late sixties, when the present editor translated and to some extent rewrote *Sabbatai Sevi* in the light of newly discovered texts and sources, it was with Scholem's permission and under his watchful eye. In fact, knowing that the author would carefully scrutinize the product, accepting or rejecting the translator's changes, the editor felt free to revise the text and add or delete according to his judgment. Professor Scholem's death laid a heavy burden of responsibility on the editor of the present, posthumous, English version.

The editor solved his problem by making only those changes that he was confident the author would have made himself. (The few exceptions are marked by square brackets and the addition of the editor's initials). To this end the editor had no need of special occult powers. One of Scholem's scholarly habits was to have every work of his bound in a special interleaved volume. Thus he had not only the margins but also a full blank page facing every page of text on which to add notes, queries, references, corrections, additions, and so forth. Whenever he read anything that had a bearing on his research, he immediately entered a note on the relevant page of his working copy of the relevant book. Scholem's interleaved working copy of *Ursprung,* into which he made entries until shortly before his last illness, shows the enormous amount of research done since 1962. On many points Scholem was confirmed in his original judgment; on many others he came to express doubts or even to repudiate opinions held earlier. The basic thesis that the Kabbalah originated in one chronologically limited time-span and in one geographically limited area is, however, still upheld. It may become the subject of debate in the future.

On one important point the editor was faced with a major quandary. In his discussion of Gerona, the most important kabbalistic center on the eve of the composition of the *Zohar,* Scholem devotes a whole section to the Book *Temunah* and its doctrine of cosmic cycles. At the time of writing Scholem was convinced that the *Temunah* was composed during the first half of the thirteenth century. Subsequent research, especially by Scholem's students, led him to revise this opinion and to date the book after 1300, i.e., decades after the composition of the *Zohar.* I inserted the relevant remarks from Scholem's interleaved copy, but did not radically tamper with the text, especially as Scholem seems to have held to the belief that, however late the date of the composition of the book, some of its basic ideas and doctrines had developed in the thirteenth century and should therefore form part of any discussion of pre-Zoharic Kabbalah. In this English edition, part of the material taken from Scholem's interleaved working copy has been incorporated in the main text and part has been presented in the form of additional notes.

Biblical quotations are rendered according to the new translation of The Jewish Publication Society (1962–1982), except in cases where the rabbinic or kabbalistic exegesis of the verse necessitated a different rendering.

The editor hopes that in performing his delicate task he has not betrayed Scholem's views and intentions and that his labors would have met with the approval of the author אשר שפתותיו דובבות בקבר.

R. J. Zwi Werblowsky
The Hebrew University of Jerusalem

Author's Preface to the First (German) Edition

The present work contains the result of studies that I began forty years ago. At that time my first substantial publication was devoted to the Book *Bahir,* the oldest extant kabbalistic text. The further treatment of the problems resulting from that study, which I then promised in a mood of youthful rashness, had to wait for many more years and is now, in the present work, submitted in its definitive form. It is not my first attempt to tackle the problem of the origin of the Kabbalah. A first draft of my ideas concerning this problem and its solution was presented in 1928, in an article entitled "Zur Frage der Entstehung der Kabbala" and published in the *Korrespondenzblatt des Vereins für die Begründung einer Akademie für die Wissenschaft des Judentums.* My studies of the kabbalistic manuscripts of the earlier period, which I continued for many years and which proved extremely fruitful, resulted in further clarifications, the results of which I first presented in a Hebrew book, published under the title *Reshith ha-Qabbalah* (Jerusalem, 1948). The essential theses proposed at that time are also maintained in the present study, which is more than double the size of the earlier Hebrew publication. But the arguments are elaborated in greater detail (to the extent possible within the limits of this volume), and the relevant material is described and analyzed. Historians of religion should therefore be able to form their own judgments regarding the views presented here. Although it seems unlikely that the discovery of further Hebrew manuscripts will yield more and decisive material that has escaped my thorough study of this literature over the course of decades, I entertain the hope that new perspectives may fecundate the discussions concerning our understanding of the problem and the interpretation of the material. Once the ice of ignorance has been broken and the charlatanism that dominated the field has been overcome, the way will be open to further fruitful research. Jewish studies as well as the history of Oriental and Western religions will benefit equally from a more penetrating study and discussion of the problem of the Kabbalah.

The termination of this work was greatly facilitated by a Research Fellowship of the Institute of Jewish Studies in London, which enabled me to devote the greater part of the year 1961 to this undertaking. The hospitality of the Warburg Institute in London with its rich library was of the utmost assistance and value. I also gratefully record the necessity that compelled me again and again, in my courses at the Hebrew University since 1925, to confront myself and my students with the problems discussed in this book. If the present work can lay any claim to a certain maturity, it is due to the constantly renewed critical rethinking of those problems in my academic lecture courses. In the light of this experience I can confirm the dictum of an ancient talmudic sage who declared: from all who could teach me I have learned, but most of all from my pupils.

Jerusalem
The Hebrew University — Gershom Scholem

ORIGINS OF THE KABBALAH

CHAPTER ONE

THE PROBLEM

1. The State of Research: The Views of Graetz and Neumark

The question of the origin and early stages of the Kabbalah, that form of Jewish mysticism and theosophy that appears to have emerged suddenly in the thirteenth century, is indisputably one of the most difficult in the history of the Jewish religion after the destruction of the Second Temple. Just as indisputably, it is one of the most important. The significance acquired by the kabbalistic movement within the Jewish world was so great and its influence at times so preponderant that if one wishes to understand the religious possibilities inherent in Judaism, the problem of the specific historical character of this phenomenon appears to be of primary importance. Researchers, therefore, have justly devoted a great deal of attention to this problem and have made diverse attempts to find a solution.

The difficulty does not lie only in the prejudices with which many scholars have approached this problem, although such prejudices—whether of an apologetic or of an explicitly hostile nature—are in no small measure responsible for the prevailing confusion. Two circumstances, in particular, have impeded research in this area. Above all, the original sources, the oldest kabbalistic texts—

those best suited to shed light on the circumstances under which the Kabbalah made its appearance—have by no means been sufficiently studied. This is not surprising, for these documents contain hardly any historical accounts that could clarify by means of direct testimony either the milieu into which the Kabbalah was born or its origin. To the extent that such accounts do exist, they are mostly pseudepigraphical stories and inventions. Nor is the task of the historian of religion rendered easier by an abundance of detailed mystical texts whose analysis could compensate for this paucity of historical documents. On the contrary, he faces texts that are preserved only in a fragmentary state, rendering them extremely difficult to understand, and that employ concepts and symbols so strange that often they are simply incomprehensible. These difficulties in deciphering the oldest texts are further increased by the style in which they are written; the syntax alone can often drive the reader to despair.

Moreover, these primary sources are few. We are not dealing here with either voluminous works or personal documents that include exchanges of letters or biographical records of the kind that are of such invaluable assistance to the historian of Christian or Islamic mysticism. Nearly all documents of this nature have been lost in the storms of Jewish history. When I was fortunate enough to discover one such letter written by a central figure of the early days of the Provençal Kabbalah, this came as a great and pleasant surprise.

Since the kabbalistic literature appears to turn only its most forbidding face toward researchers, few of them have taken the pains to rescue the manuscripts from the dust of the libraries, publish them, and attempt to uncover their meaning. Adolph Jellinek was the only nineteenth-century scholar to publish at least some texts that bear on the investigation of the Kabbalah of the thirteenth century, and of these only a few relate to the earliest period or to that which immediately followed. The authors who wrote about the Kabbalah were content to study only what the kabbalists themselves had chanced to publish. It does not require much imagination to conceive how unsatisfactory these editions of difficult texts are to the modern researcher and how liable they are to lead him to false conclusions through incorrect readings and other deficiencies. On this difficult terrain, the absence of any painstaking philological spadework whose conclusions could supply the basis for a comprehensive structure has led to disastrous results.

If I have discussed at some length the difficulties with which the researcher of the Kabbalah must grapple, it has been in order to emphasize that we cannot expect any easy and elegant solution of problems that by their very nature defy elementary and simplistic treatment. Nevertheless, we must stake out a path and unravel with the greatest possible clarity and care the knotty problems along the way. This task is not as impossible as it may appear at first or even second glance. Much more of the kabbalistic literature of the first half of the thirteenth century has survived than had been assumed earlier. Even if these writings do not contain very many of the original sources that antedate the period, they at least make it possible for us to form a precise idea of the state of the Kabbalah in the generation following its entrance upon the scene. The analysis of the different tendencies that then arose and took shape within the Kabbalah can also teach us a few things about what preceded them. Moreover, it was precisely these developments in the first half of the thirteenth century that proved particularly productive for kabbalistic Judaism and that profoundly influenced the following generations.

Unfortunately, the most voluminous kabbalistic work of the thirteenth century, the *Zohar,* namely, the complex of writings included within it, must be entirely eliminated from this discussion of the origin and early stages of the Kabbalah. The contention has often been made, and is still frequently repeated, that this book contains in part, if only in the form of a later redaction or revision, texts of great antiquity whose identification and analysis would thus be of the greatest relevance for our investigation. Most of the writings on the Kabbalah have taken practically no account of the sources and the points of reference of scientific discussion that will be treated here, but have relied almost exclusively upon the *Zohar.* In the chapter of my book *Major Trends in Jewish Mysticism* in which I touch upon this point, I presented the results of an extensive and detailed investigation of this work and demonstrated that there is unfortunately no basis for assuming that the *Zohar* contains any ancient texts. The entire work belongs to the last quarter of the thirteenth century and is of no use to us in the discussion that follows. Efforts are still being made in our day to sift out ancient elements of one kind or another, but they cannot withstand philological analysis and rather belong to the realm of fantasy.[1] The *Zohar* is based entirely upon rabbinic and kabbalistic literature composed before 1275. If it were possible to prove otherwise in a truly convincing manner, our task would, of course, be greatly facilitated. I once made a serious attempt to do so myself, but this endeavor, to which I devoted a number of years, thoroughly persuaded me that this thesis was untenable. As things stand, we must turn aside from this high road and make do on the thornier path of historical analysis of the texts that are nearer to the origin and first stages of the Kabbalah.

This automatically excludes from consideration certain theories that readily trace the kabbalistic doctrines back to antiquity. These theories in the form in which they have been presented until now—for example, in the widely read book of Adolphe Franck[2]—no longer merit serious scholarly discussion. Nor is it possible to take seriously Tholuck's attempt to show that the Kabbalah is historically dependent upon Muslim Sufism.[3] The philological and historical foundations of these investigations were much too weak to justify their authors' far-reaching results and conclusions. It is thus not surprising that scholarship soon turned its back upon these views. On the other hand, the forms of Jewish mysticism that appeared in the Middle Ages from around 1200 onward under the

---

1. The earlier literature is noted in the bibliography to chapter 5 of my book *Major Trends in Jewish Mysticism,* 430–432. The most recent attempt to demonstrate the presence of old sources in the *Zohar* was made by Professor Samuel Belkin in his Hebrew article "The *Midrash ha-Ne 'elam* and its Sources in the Old Alexandrian Midrashim," in the annual *Sura* 3 (1958): 25–92. Unfortunately, his argument is completely wanting in its methods as well as its results and represents a definite regression in scholarship, as R. J. Zwi Werblowsky has demonstrated in a detailed critique of Belkin's thesis in "Philo and the Zohar," *JJS* 10 (1959): 23–44, 113–135. Finkel's "reply" to Werblowsky (see below ch. 4, n. 111) hardly deserves to be taken seriously.

2. Adolphe Franck, *La Kabbale ou la philosophie religieuse des Hébreux* (Paris, 1843; 3rd ed., 1892). Franck arrives at the conclusion (I am citing according to the German translation by Adolph Jellinek [Leipzig, 1844], 287) that "the materials of the Kabbalah were drawn from the theology of the ancient Persians," but that this borrowing did not detract from the originality of the Kabbalah, for it replaced the dualism in God and in nature with the absolute unity of cause and substance. (Franck took the Kabbalah to be a pantheistic system.)

3. F. A. Tholuck, *Commentatio de vi, quam graeca philosophia in theologia tum Muhammedanorum tum Judaeorum exercuerit. II. Particula: De ortu Cabbalae* (Hamburg, 1837).

name "Kabbalah" are so different from any earlier forms, and in particular from the Jewish gnosis of Merkabah mysticism and German Hasidism of the twelfth and thirteenth centuries, that a direct transition from one form to the other is scarcely conceivable. This difference has not escaped the notice of scholars, who have tried to account for it, each in his own manner. Precisely because the structure of kabbalistic thought was completely unlike that of older or contemporary currents, it engendered explanations that were forced to take that state of affairs into consideration. Two theories, in particular, have been advanced with regard to the formation of the Kabbalah. Their authors undertook to prove their validity as best they could and exerted a considerable influence over the past few generations. I refer here to Graetz and Neumark, about whose conceptions I wish to make a few remarks, even though, or perhaps precisely because, they are so utterly different in both principle and method from those presented in this book.

Graetz[4] proposed an historical explanation based upon the great events and controversies of Jewish history. According to him, the Kabbalah was essentially nothing but a reaction against the radical rationalism of the Maimonideans—the adherents of the philosophy of Maimonides, who died in Fostat (Old Cairo) in 1204 but had enthusiastic followers throughout the Orient and in Provence as well. There, his principal work, *The Guide of the Perplexed,* appeared in the year of his death, translated from the original Arabic into Hebrew. The appearance of the Kabbalah upon the historical scene in Provence at the beginning of the thirteenth century coincides with the birth of this philosophy. Obscurantists who hated the light that shone forth from the school of the new rationalists raised against it a system they called "Kabbalah," which literally means "tradition." Its fantastic and extravagant doctrines, elaborated in overheated brains, were essentially superstitious and contrary to the spirit of Judaism. In their battle against enlightenment these obscurantists were not particularly discriminating and therefore did not hesitate to draw upon foreign, imprecisely identified sources for their fundamental ideas. The Kabbalah is not historically continuous with the older mystical movements in Judaism, in particular the

---

4. Graetz expounded his conception, for the first time, in 1862 in vol. 7, n. 3 of his *Geschichte der Juden;* cf. the 4th ed. (Leipzig, 1908), 385–402: "Ursprung der Kabbala."

mysticism of the Merkabah. The crude anthropomorphisms of the adepts of the *Shi'ur Qomah,* the doctrine of the mystical figure of the Godhead,[5] merely furnished the kabbalists with a symbolic vocabulary. Graetz does not exclude the possibility that older materials may have been absorbed into this mystical symbolism, but he never enters into a more direct discussion of this problem, whose importance is nevertheless evident. "It can no longer be said with complete certainty whence the first kabbalists . . . acquired their basic principles, borrowed from Neoplatonism."[6] But in their struggle against the sublimation of the Talmudic Aggadah and the Jewish ritual law by the adherents of the philosophy of Maimonides, the new "enemies of the light" developed their own theory. It was based upon the supposition that the rituals had a magical effect; its details were drawn from the kabbalistic revelations to which the initiators of this tendency laid claim. It is interesting to note that the possibility of a filiation linking the Kabbalah with ancient Gnosticism, which had appeared so plausible to other authors because it supported their belief in the great antiquity of the Kabbalah, does not play the slightest role in Graetz's theory.

David Neumark's theory in his *Geschichte der jüdischen Philosophie des Mittelalters*[7] is completely different. He, too, proposed an explanation based upon an immanent process. But according to him this process was not associated with the struggle between the adher-

5. Cf. *Major Trends,* 63–67, as well as section 3 of this chapter.

6. Graetz, *Geschichte der Juden,* vol. 7, 401.

7. Vol. 1 (Berlin, 1907), 179–236. In the Hebrew edition of this work (New York, 1921), 166–354, Neumark more than doubled the length of the chapter entitled "The Kabbalah," thus making it one of the most extensive monographs on the old Kabbalah up to the *Zohar* but also, to be sure, one of the most misleading. A playful but truly uncommon perspicacity proceeding on the basis of fanciful assumptions combines with an astonishing lack of historical sense and sound judgment. Nevertheless, here and there one encounters profound views, which is doubly surprising, as the method is completely untenable. Solemn babble combines with keen insight, which the author by no means lacks. In many places he completely misunderstands the literal meaning of the kabbalistic texts as well as decisive points of the kabbalistic symbolism; and even where this is not the case, he indulges in arbitrary interpretations and establishes philosophic relations of which the critical reader can find no trace in the texts. But it is not inconceivable, I think, that some future rationalist, possessing a greater knowledge of the texts that Neumark treated in such an arbitrary manner and a better understanding of their symbolism, may once again take up this scholar's approach with greater success and in better accord with the demands of philological criticism; for, in itself, his dialectic and manner of thinking offer fruitful possibilities.

ents of Maimonides and his opponents. Rather, he sees the Kabbalah as a product of the internal dialectic that governs the development of philosophical ideas in Judaism. The great events of history play no essential role, and everything is attributed solely to internal processes within philosophic thought. Contrary to Graetz, Neumark assigns an early date to the Kabbalah, which he regards as an intrinsic development within Judaism, requiring no borrowings from foreign sources. This process was a "remythologizing" of philosophic conceptions. In his opinion, the philosophic movement in Judaism issued, on the one hand, from the cosmogonic speculations *(Ma'aseh Bereshith)* of the talmudists, which raised the problem of the primal substance and developed the doctrine of ideas, and, on the other hand, from the Merkabah speculations concerning the world of the divine Throne, in which doctrines of emanations and angelology, that is, of intermediary beings in the process of the creation, were evolved. These two disciplines, esoteric in origin, were engaged in a permanent and increasingly hostile controversy. As the genuinely philosophic contents of these early secret doctrines were formulated they also served as the point of departure for a countermovement, the Kabbalah, which, in this manner, represents a "latent parallel" to philosophy.

> The philosophers struggle against the mystical elements and overcome them, but in the intermediate stages of this combat many ideas were conceived, many images were projected and many phrases were polished. These crumbs were gathered up by mystically disposed spirits and mixed with other elements, coming from the old hearth of the doctrine of the Merkabah, to form a new creation. Slowly but surely, this new creation intruded itself into the framework of the old mysticism until it filled all of its enormously expanded dimensions and ornamental twists and turns.[8]

Neumark believed that he could detail this process by means of a demonstrable philosophic chain of literature that reveals the transition from philosophic to kabbalistic conceptions. Many writers still employing the terminology of philosophy really belonged to that latent parallel movement, which gave birth in the thirteenth century to the speculative form of the Kabbalah.

Methodologically, both Graetz and Neumark began by asking

8. Ibid., 181.

what kind of relationship existed between the Kabbalah and medieval Jewish philosophy, each in his own way placing the Kabbalah in the context of that relationship. The two of them shared a rigorously rationalistic evaluation of the phenomenon; but as a result they also rejected the significance of the role played by the Kabbalah in this connection (without, however, suggesting any alternative links). This may explain the lack of interest, not to say incomprehension, which marks their attitude toward the specifically religious concerns expressed in the Kabbalah.

Each of these theories contains, as far as I can judge, a kernel of truth, but nothing more. It may be said, in particular, that Neumark's thoughtful conception appears to be far superior to Graetz's overly simplistic theory; it deserves attention even though it must be judged a total failure—as appears to me beyond any doubt, since his argumentation is in large part extremely dubious and does not withstand examination. Above all, it does not at all follow from the evidence he adduces how, by this methodology, we are to imagine the birth of the fundamental ideas of the Kabbalah. Besides, in his almost inconceivable naïveté, Neumark relied almost exclusively upon printed texts and adopted, uncritically, the utterly baseless and completely arbitrary hypotheses of earlier authors with regard to the dating of certain kabbalistic texts. Nevertheless, within the philosophic movement there undoubtedly existed currents of the sort he characterized and which, in fact, flowed into the Kabbalah after its emergence, above all in the thirteenth and fourteenth centuries.[9] No legitimate history of the Kabbalah can afford to overlook these currents. And yet, as is proven by an impartial analysis of the kabbalistic literature, to which Neumark all too often does great violence in his interpretations, it is not in this direction that we will find the true solution to the problem of the birth of the movement. Both Graetz and Neumark fell victim to the nineteenth-century illusion of an enlightened conception of religion. Neumark drew far-reaching conclusions from this prejudice and was led to view the Kabbalah as

9. Above all the highly valuable studies of Georges Vajda (Paris) have in recent years shed a great deal of light upon many currents and figures in whom the philosophic and kabbalistic tendencies meet, unite, or enter into controversy between 1270 and 1370. Cf., above all, the following studies: *Juda ben Nissim ibn Malka, philosophe juif marocain* (Paris, 1954); *Recherches sur la philosophie et la Kabbale dans la pensée juive du moyen âge* (Paris, 1962), as well as his articles in the *REJ* and the *Archives d'histoire doctrinale et littéraire du moyen âge* (1954 to 1961).

the product of a philosophical and rational process, not as the product of a religious process in which factors of an entirely different nature were at work. He went so far as to found his explanations, in all seriousness, upon this strange supposition: in the early kabbalistic literature there appeared texts of a programmatic character that were meant to be "filled in," as indeed they were, in the course of subsequent development. It is one of the ironies of research that precisely the "Treatise on Emanation" *(Massekheth 'Aṣiluth),* which in his opinion fulfilled such a programmatic function, was by no means composed in the middle of the twelfth century, as Neumark thought, but at the beginning of the fourteenth century, after the development of the Spanish Kabbalah had already reached its peak.[10]

The following investigation and the views that find expression in it are based upon an assumption that is in itself quite simple, but that will nevertheless direct us toward important conclusions in matters of detail: the kabbalistic movement in Judaism cannot be described adequately according to the categories of the history of philosophy; it can only be explained in terms of the history of religions, however close its connection with philosophy may here and there turn out to be. Many researchers have succeeded only in obscuring the fundamental fact that it was religious motifs and no other kind that decisively determined the development of the Kabbalah, even in its confrontation with philosophy. To be sure, the history of the Jewish religion did not unfold in a vacuum. The revelations made to the earliest kabbalists, according to their tradition, by the prophet Elijah, also have an historical background and specific terminology into which it is surely legitimate to inquire. However, it is not the history of philosophy that will enable us to understand them; they grew in a different historical humus and originated in circles other than those of the philosophers. In this investigation, we must never lose sight of this simple yet highly important truth. There will be hardly any discussion here of the kind of evidence adduced by Neumark in explanation of the birth of the Kabbalah, and where there is, it will be from an altogether different perspective. We shall be concerned, instead, with arguments for which one

10. Neumark was misled by Jellinek, who ascribed this small work, without the slightest reason, to Jacob the Nazirite. Cf. my article on this tract in the *Encyclopaedia Judaica* 3 (Berlin, 1929), cols. 801–803. This tract was undoubtedly composed after the *Zohar.*

searches in vain in his work or that of Graetz. The examination of the correct chronological order of the oldest kabbalistic texts and of the conceptions that can be discerned in them forces us to take a different path. The history of the mystical terminology, neglected by earlier researchers in favor of general ideas, provides the authentic signposts by which research must orient itself; it played a very large part in the elaboration of the views presented in the following pages.

2. Southern France in the Twelfth Century: The Catharist Movement—The Jews of Languedoc

The following questions may serve as a natural point of departure for this investigation: under what circumstances did the Kabbalah step into the light of history, and what was the character of the age in which we first learn of its appearance? As an historical phenomenon in medieval Judaism, the Kabbalah was born in Provence, or more precisely in its western part, known as the Languedoc. It is in this sense that the term Provence will be used in the following text. From there it was transplanted in the first quarter of the thirteenth century to Aragon and Castile in Spain, where most of its classical development took place. It thus constitutes a phenomenon of Jewish life in the Christian Occident; we possess no historical information or direct testimony to its existence or propagation in the lands of Islam. However, we do have an important piece of negative evidence. Abraham, the son of Maimonides, in contrast to his father, had an inclination toward mysticism, as is evident from his work *Kifayat al 'abidin,* preserved in Arabic, which has now been partially translated into English under the title *The High Ways to Perfection.* Writing around 1220–1230, he evidently knew nothing of the Kabbalah, and it was the Sufism of Islam that served as his source of illumination and edification. In connection with the adoption of Sufi rites, he laments that "the glory of Israel has been taken away from him and given to the non-Jews." The mystical treasure held by Islam was originally destined to be the glory and the special possession of Israel, but it was lost—a conception that is certainly worthy of note. What brought his friend Abraham the Hasid to Sufism and made him adapt it to Judaism were precisely the motifs of theosophical mysticism and Hasidic illumination that were also at work among the contemporary circles of Hasidim and *perushim* in Provence, though in his case, nothing kabbalistic resulted of it.[11] It was only three or four generations later that kabbalistic influence began to be felt in the Muslim lands as well. In Muslim Spain, the Kabbalah played no demonstrable role before it reached its peak around 1300.

In our investigation, we shall therefore not focus our attention upon the developments of the Kabbalah after its passage to Spain. Here, we shall discuss only the initial stage of the process. On the other hand, we shall examine all the more closely the form it had before being taken up and taught by Isaac the Blind and the character it assumed in his circle. To what extent can we draw a posteriori conclusions with regard to older sources? Whatever we know about the earliest kabbalists and their circles comes from the Languedoc. It is in cities like Lunel, Narbonne, Posquières, and perhaps also in Toulouse, Marseilles, and Arles that we find the first personalities known to us as kabbalists. Their disciples then transplanted the kabbalistic tradition to Spain, where it took root in such localities as Burgos, Gerona, and Toledo, and whence it spread to other Jewish communities. Concerning Isaac the Blind as well as the kabbalistic circles intimately connected with him we now have in our possession from an examination of the available manuscripts, sufficient and by no means negligible material that offers a solid basis for research. In the following chapters we shall have to concern ourselves with this material. On the other hand, the problem of the origin of the Kabbalah and its "prehistoric" beginnings, which takes us back to the Orient, remains in all its complexity. It requires—as we shall see in the next chapter—closer examination; and despite the precision of certain results, we cannot entirely renounce the formulation of hypotheses.

Southern France, during the period that interests us here—that is, between 1150 and 1220—was a region replete with cultural and religious tensions. It was one of the chief centers of medieval culture. In order to understand the Judaism of this region, we must see it within its environmental context and not remain content with an analysis of the internal factors active at the time. Provence, and especially Languedoc, was the seat of a developed courtly and feudal culture. An intimate contact was established there (through chan-

11. Cf. N. Wieder, *Melila* 2 (Manchester, 1946): 60–65. S. Rosenblatt's edition and translation of a part of Abraham's work appeared in Baltimore in 1927 and 1938.

nels that are often no longer perceptible or that have only today come within the purview of serious scholarship) between Islamic culture penetrating from Spain and North Africa and the culture of chivalry of the Christian Middle Ages. There, during this same period, the poetry of the troubadours reached its peak. But beyond that, southern France was an area particularly characterized by strong religious tension unparalleled in other lands of Christian culture. In this period, among many circles of Languedoc, especially in the area between Toulouse, Albi, and Carcassonne, it was no longer Catholic Christianity that reigned, but the dualistic religion of the Cathars or Albigenses, whose fundamental character has, not without reason, long been a subject of controversy. Judging from the external forms, one would think that it was a matter of a Christian sect seeking to oppose the corruption of the clergy and of contemporary society by means of ideals held to be more or less those of primitive Christianity. An alternative line of thought, increasingly accepted today, holds that we are dealing here with a religion that, while utilizing certain Christian notions, undermined the very foundations of Christianity. That surely was already the opinion of the Catholic opponents of this powerful heresy, which was brutally extirpated only after a long and extremely bitter crusade by the Inquisition, which, as is well known, was originated in order to repress it.

There is no longer any doubt that this movement was not autochthonous to southern France. It stood in direct historical relationship with the religion of the Bulgarian Bogomils and their dualistic predecessors; however it is still a matter of debate whether there is any direct historical filiation leading back to ancient Manichaeism (as the Church claimed) or whether the dualistic teaching and the specific organizational forms of this medieval neo-Manichaeism derived from other sources. Another difficult problem that has still not been resolved is that of the possible survival of gnostic, other than Manichaean, influences and ideas in the religion of the Cathars. It is not our task to enter into this discussion, which has had a vigorous revival as a result of the important discoveries of recent years.[12] However, the existence of this extremely strong religious movement whose anti-Catholic tendencies cannot be doubted is also important for our investigation. The Judaism of Provence like-

12. See the presentation of the current state of research in Arno Borst, *Die Katharer* (Stuttgart, 1953), which contains a full critical discussion of the literature. Cf. also chap. 3, p. 234ff., herein.

wise went through a highly fruitful period in the twelfth century. It thus developed in an environment where Catholic Christianity in its orthodox form had to fight for its bare existence and where it had effectively lost much of its influence over wide circles of the dominant feudal and chivalric class and their cultural spokesmen, as well as in the broader social strata of peasants and shepherds. Nevertheless, more recent attempts (since the appearance of the first German edition of the present work) to demonstrate direct Cathar influences on the earliest sources of the Kabbalah are totally unconvincing.[13]

This was a phenomenon unique in Occidental Europe. There appear to have been close ties between many spokesmen of the secular culture—which reached its zenith in the lyrical poetry of the troubadours, seemingly devoid of religious tension—and this radical movement, which touched the hearts of the masses and attacked the foundations of the Church's authority and its hierarchy. Tolerated or even actively encouraged by many of the great feudal rulers and by a majority of the barons, the movement took root; and it required the intervention of the kings of France, here pursuing their own special interests, to bring the Crusade against the Cathars to a victorious conclusion and to break the power of the movement. In the heart of the Occident, a sect linked at least by its structure and perhaps also by its history to the world of Gnosticism and Manichaeism was able not only to gain a foothold but also to come close to a position of dominance in society.

The old issues that once had determined the physiognomy of the Marcionite gnosis returned to the surface, revealing an indestructible vitality. With varying degrees of radicalism, the Cathars contrasted the true God, creator of the intelligible and of the soul, to Satan, creator of the visible world. In their propaganda, nourished by a profound pessimism with regard to the visible creation, they sought to show to the "perfect" *(perfecti)* a path leading to deliverance of the soul. It is interesting to observe, as more than one historian of culture has noted, that the uncompromising radicalism of the sect built a more solid bridge to the secular culture, which was positively oriented toward life in this world, than had the Catholic Church, with its gradualist system so receptive to compromise. These dialectical relations have attracted the attention of many observers of the domestic situation then prevailing in Provence, and

13. Cf. chap. 3, n. 73, herein.

they may also throw light on the problems connected with the rise of the Kabbalah. It is quite conceivable that the influence exerted by a great movement like Catharism might be reflected in phenomena that, at first glance, appear to be far removed from it.

At that time, Cathar heresy was not, as we have seen, the affair of closed conventicles. The entire land was in commotion. In the streets and markets, the *bonshommes*—called the *perfecti,* those who took upon themselves the yoke of the Cathar demands in all its severity, and thus served as living examples—preached against the corruption of the Catholic clergy, against its social privileges, and against many dogmas of the Church. Following in the footsteps of Marcion, many of them dug an abyss between the Old and the New Testaments, which they regarded as mutually exclusive revelations. Their metaphysical anti-Semitism did not necessarily prevent them from engaging, on occasion, in an exchange of ideas with Jews, who were, like themselves, adversaries of Catholicism.[14] It is nevertheless difficult to judge how much truth there is in the accusations of several thirteenth-century Catholic polemicists who reproached the heretics for their relations with the Jews.[15] However, reading the interesting description of the spiritual state of Provence during that period presented by Jean Giraud in the first volume of his great *Histoire de l'Inquisition au moyen âge,*[16] one becomes convinced that it is inconceivable that the Provençal Jews had seen and observed nothing of the profound agitation that shook the land. In Narbonne and Toulouse, important Jewish centers at that time, there were stormy disputes and incessant clashes between the hostile camps. It

14. L. J. Newman, *Jewish Influences on Early Christian Reform Movements* (New York, 1925), 131–207, "Jewish Influence on the Catharist Heresy," made some far-reaching assertions concerning the participation of Jews in the Cathar movement or their influence on the Cathars, but they hardly withstand examination; cf. Borst, *Die Katharer,* 99, 105, 125. Neumark's discussion of the Kabbalah and the Catharist doctrine is, I regret to say, completely irrelevant. With regard to the Passagians, a Jewish-Christian sect that some authors (erroneously) include among the Cathars, see the literature in Borst, *Die Katharer,* 112.

15. Cf. Newman, *Jewish Influences,* 140, extract from Lucas of Tuy, *Adversus Albigenses* (Ingolstadt, 1612), 189–190.

16. Jean Giraud, *Histoire de l'Inquisition au moyen âge,* vol. 1, *Cathares et Vaudois* (Paris, 1935). With regard to the relationship between the ascetic Catharism and the secular culture flourishing at that time in Provence, cf. the bibliographical references in Borst, *Die Katharer,* 107–108. There it is a question of "a confused mesh of Bogomilian doctrine and Occidental life."

was precisely in these regions that the Kabbalah made its first appearance. However, in this connection it should be noted that the Cathar heresy did not obtain a firm foothold in the major Jewish centers such as Narbonne and Montpellier.[17]

The Jewish communities of Languedoc, at least their upper strata, had attained a high degree of cultural flowering. The persecutions of the Crusades had not touched them. In Marseilles, Lunel, Béziers, Narbonne, Perpignan, Carcassonne, and Toulouse the study of the Torah and the Talmud flourished. Narbonne especially could point to a great tradition of Jewish scholarship that spanned several generations. Even before the appearance of the Kabbalah, since the eleventh century, the latest midrashim had their origin or were revised in this city or in the neighboring centers. This was the case for large parts of the *Midrash Rabbah* on Numbers, the *Midrash Bereshith Rabbathi,* and the *Midrash Tadshe,* of particular interest from the point of view of the history of religions. Not only do they show a marked penchant for ideas that are close to or continue the esoteric doctrines of the Talmud in their older forms, but some of their authors, above all that of the *Midrash Tadshe,* were also still acquainted with ancient literary sources that were no longer known elsewhere. Thus it can be shown that the apocryphal *Book of Jubilees* exercised a significant influence upon the *Midrash Tadshe,* without it being possible for us, at present, to decide whether the author drew on an internal Jewish tradition that has otherwise left very few traces in the Occident or upon Christian sources.[18] However, it is evident that the aggadic production in southern France in the eleventh and twelfth centuries, the substance of which has been deposited in those works, could serve as a kind of vestibule to the subsequent development of the Kabbalah. We still lack a clearer and more

---

17. Cf. E. Griffe, *Les débuts de l'aventure cathare en Languedoc (1140–1190)* (Paris, 1963), 168.

18. On the *Midrash Tadshe,* also known as the "Baraitha of R. Pinḥas ben Yair," cf. the research of Abraham Epstein and his edition of the text, with separated pagination, in his (Hebrew) *Beiträge zur Jüdischen Alterthumskunde,* pt. 1 (Vienna, 1887), as well as his examination of the relationships between this text, the *Book of Jubilees,* and Philo in *REJ* 21 (1890): 88–97, and 22 (1891): 1–25. Epstein assumed that the author (Moses ha-Darshan, around the year 1000, in Narbonne?) had a certain familiarity with the writings of Philo, which is less convincing. I also consider the supposed relationship with Essene traditions as extremely doubtful. August Wünsche translated this midrash into German in *Aus Israels Lehrhallen,* vol. 5 (1910), 85–138.

precise elucidation of the contribution of those older generations of Languedoc to the religious culture of Judaism. Even if internal factors were at work independently, we must nevertheless consider it certain that they were at the same time stimulated and supported by other Jewish groups. The threads of tradition extended not only from Narbonne to northern France and the Rhineland, with their important centers of Jewish productivity, but also—and this seems to me to deserve particular emphasis—to the Orient, with which there existed close commercial relations. And who can say which ideas or bits of ideas, what kind of notebooks or fragments, were conveyed along these paths and channels, carrying with them the vestiges of old literary materials?

We may affirm, then, that the Kabbalah did not make its appearance in a stagnant milieu, but in one full of strife and tension. Nor was it a backward milieu with respect to the general development of Judaism. Openly or invisibly it had absorbed a rich store of traditions.

3. The Esoteric Doctrine of the Creation and the Merkabah in Pre-kabbalistic Judaism: The Literature of the Hekhaloth and Jewish Gnosticism

Having arrived at this point, we must inquire into the situation of Jewish esotericism and mysticism before the appearance of the Kabbalah upon the stage of history. We have already mentioned previously the ancient cosmogonic speculations of the talmudists as well as their throne-mysticism. It is now necessary to determine to what extent these speculations were still known to the Jewish tradition of the twelfth century and which literary or direct oral sources it had at its disposal. For, as has already been remarked, however great the distance between these ancient ideas and the Kabbalah, the latter nonetheless not only claimed to be the legitimate successor of these ancient esoteric doctrines of the Creation and the Merkabah but also pretended to represent their actual content in its own teaching.

On this point, too, research has made substantial progress in the course of the past generation. Until several decades ago, most researchers supposed—with the notable exception of Moses Gaster—that two completely different stages of development should be assumed. On the one hand, there existed between the first and the third centuries, above all in the circles of the talmudists, the two esoteric disciplines attested to in the Mishnah *Ḥagigah* 2:1, concerning the Creation, *bereshith,* and the divine chariot of Ezekiel 1, the Merkabah. We possess some scattered and fragmentary information, in large part unintelligible, about these doctrines in certain passages of the talmudic literature and in old midrashim.[19] These traditions were held to have fallen more or less into oblivion and to have disappeared. On the other hand, during post-talmudic times, in the Gaonic period (from the seventh until the beginning of the eleventh century), a new mystical wave is said to have swept over Judaism, particularly in Babylonia, and stimulated a broad literature of Merkabah-mysticism and kindred texts. This literature—it was averred—had not very much more in common with the old doctrines than the name and a certain number of talmudic traditions of which it made literary use.

Today we can state with certainty that this separation that places the late mysticism of the Merkabah very close to the formative period of the medieval Kabbalah cannot be maintained. I have elsewhere dealt at length with this Merkabah-mysticism of the so-called Hekhaloth literature, and shown that a genuine and unbroken chain of tradition links these writings to the secret doctrine of the Talmud. Large parts of this literature still belong to the talmudic period itself, and the central ideas of these texts go back to the first and second centuries. They are thus directly connected with the productive period during which rabbinic Judaism crystallized in the midst of great religious ferment, asserted itself, and prevailed over other currents in Judaism.[20] To be sure, these texts, which in their

---

19. Much but by no means all the material was collected by Strack and Billerbeck, *Kommentar zum Neuen Testament aus Talmud und Midrash;* see the references in the index, vol. 4, s.v. "Merkaba," "Thron." In addition, cf. also the monographs of H. Graetz, *Gnosticismus und Judenthum* (Krotoshin, 1846); M. Joël, *Blicke in die Religionsgeschichte zu Anfang des zweiten christlichen Jahrhunderts,* vol. 1 (Breslau, 1880), 103–170; M. Friedländer, *Der vorchristliche jüdische Gnosticismus* (Göttingen, 1898); Erich Bischoff, *Babylonisch-Astrales im Weltbilde des Thalmud und Midrasch* (Leipzig, 1907); G. Castelli, *Gli antecedenti della Cabbala nella Bibbia e nella Letteratura Talmudica, Actes du 12me Congrès des Orientalistes 1899,* vol. 3 (Turin, 1903), 57–109.

20. Cf. my exposition in *Major Trends,* 40ff. and 355ff., as well as, above all, my more recent investigations in *Jewish Gnosticism, Merkabah Mysticism and Talmudic Tradition* (New York, 1960; revised and [in the appendix] enlarged ed., 1965). Further progress in this area has been made by Ithamar Gruenwald, *Apocalyptic and Merkavah*

present form belong in part to the genre of apocalyptic pseudepigraphy, are not always as old as they pretend to be. But even in these later adaptations, the underlying traditional material dates back to the period indicated. The mystical hymns found in several of the most important texts may definitely be traced back at least to the third century; here it is the literary form itself that militates against the idea of a later revision. The conceptions that find expression here surely were not developed later; in fact, the may date from a much earlier time.[21]

These writings contain instructions for obtaining the ecstatic vision of the celestial regions of the Merkabah. They describe the peregrinations of the ecstatic through these regions: the seven heavens and the seven palaces or temples, Hekhaloth, through which the Merkabah mystic travels before he arrives at the throne of God. Revelations are made to the voyager concerning the celestial things and the secrets of the Creation, the hierarchy of the angels, and the magical practices of theurgy. Having ascended to the highest level, he stands before the throne and beholds a vision of the mystical figure of the Godhead, in the symbol of the "likeness as the appearance of a man" whom the prophet Ezekiel was permitted to see upon the throne of Merkabah. There he receives a revelation of the "measurement of the body," in Hebrew *Shi'ur Qomah,* that is, an anthropomorphic description of the divinity, appearing as the primal man, but also as the lover of the Song of Songs, together with the mystical names of his limbs.

The age of this *Shi'ur Qomah* mysticism, which scandalized the consciousness of later, "enlightened" centuries, may now be fixed with certainty. Contrary to the views that once prevailed, it must be dated to the second century, and certainly not later.[22] It is undoubtedly connected with the interpretation of the Song of Songs as a mystical allegory of God's relation with Israel. Just as in the earliest days God revealed himself to the entire community of Israel, as was the case at the time of the Exodus from Egypt, where he was

---

Mysticism (Leiden, 1980), who has made use of newly discovered material and has posed new questions for the research agenda. Among these, the problem of Jewish elements in Gnosticism figures prominently. On this issue, lively discussions have been taking place since the discovery of the Nag Hammadi texts.

21. *Jewish Gnosticism,* sec. 4, 20–30.

22. Cf. with respect to this important new conclusion ibid., 36–42, 129–131, as well as appendix D; *Eranos-Jahrbuch* 29 (1960 [Zurich, 1961]): 144–164.

visibly manifest upon his Merkabah (this idea is attested in midrashic interpretations that undoubtedly go back to the tannaim),[23] so is this revelation repeated in the relations between God and the mystic initiated into the secrets of the Merkabah. The most important fragments of these descriptions transmitted in the *Shi'ur Qomah* make explicit reference to the depiction of the lover in many passages of the Song of Songs; this depiction thus offers a biblical veneer for what are evidently theosophic mysteries whose precise meaning and exact connections still escape us. There can be little doubt that we are dealing here, in stark contrast to the notion of an imageless and invisible God always so energetically maintained by Jewish tradition, with a conception that knows the projection of this God as a mystical figure. In this figure there reveals itself, in the experience of a theophany, the "great Glory" or "great Power" mentioned in several of the Jewish apocryphal books and apocalypses as the highest manifestation of God. To be sure, this Glory or Power is not directly identical with the essence of God itself but rather radiates from it. It is not possible, for the moment, to determine with certainty to what extent foreign influences derived from speculations on the heavenly primordial man acted on those ideas, which apparently could be held at that time even in strictly rabbinical circles. Impulses from the outside are, of course, entirely conceivable; they are already proven by the symbolism of the chapter of the Merkabah, Ezekiel 1, for the time of the prophet himself, and there certainly was no lack of channels through which similar influences could make their way to Palestine. On the other hand, we must reckon far more seriously with the possibility of an immanent development and elaboration of such impulses that may have been much more intense than is generally assumed.

The historian of religion is entitled to consider the mysticism of the Merkabah to be one of the Jewish branches of Gnosticism.[24] However rare the references in the extant texts to gnostic myths, or

---

23. Cf. Saul Lieberman's exposition in *Jewish Gnosticism,* appendix D, 118–126.

24. The discussion as to what exactly is to be understood by "gnosis" has gained in prominence in scholarly literature and at conferences during the last decades. There is a tendency to exclude phenomena that until 1930 were designated gnostic by everyone. To me it does not seem to matter greatly whether phenomena previously called gnostic are now designated as "esoteric," and I for one cannot see the use or value of the newly introduced distinctions (for example, gnosis—Gnosticism and the like).

abstract speculations on the aeons and their mutual relations, certain fundamental characteristics of Gnosticism are nevertheless fully congruent with the kind of mysticism we find in the Merkabah writings: the possession of a knowledge that cannot be acquired by ordinary intellectual means but only by way of a revelation and mystical illumination; the possession of a secret doctrine concerning the order of the celestial worlds and the liturgical and magical-theurgical means that provide access to it. According to Anz,[25] the central teaching of Gnosticism consists of methodical instructions for the ascent of the soul from the earth through the spheres of the hostile planet-angels and rulers of the cosmos to its divine home. Even if, taking into account more recent research on Gnosticism we do not go as far as Anz, the fact remains that precisely these ideas were affirmed in the heart of an esoteric discipline within the Jewish tradition, and not only among Jewish heretics, even though the role of the pagan planet-angels is here assumed by other archons. These archons threaten the ecstatic visionary at the gates of the seven celestial palaces, and—entirely in keeping with the doctrines of various gnostic writings of the same period—can only be overcome and compelled to permit him to pass by the display of a magic "seal," through the recitation of hymns, prayers, etc. One can still discern plainly the relation to late Jewish apocalyptic writings, whose ideas evidently form a plausible transition to both Jewish monotheistic Gnosticism and the heretical Gnosticism that tended toward dualism.[26]

In the *Shi'ur Qomah* speculation, the mystical figure appears upon the throne as the creator of the world, *yoṣer bereshith;* from his cosmic mantle, which is frequently spoken of here, the stars and the firmament shine forth.[27] But this representation of the demiurge proceeds from a thoroughly monotheistic conception and completely lacks the heretical and antinomian character it assumed when the Creator God had been opposed to the true God. Here the throne of God is, in Jewish terminology, the home of the soul; it is there that the ascent of the ecstatic is completed. The world of the Merkabah

25. Wilhelm Anz, *Zur Frage nach dem Ursprung des Gnostizismus* (Leipzig, 1897).

26. Cf. R.M. Grant, *Gnosticism and Early Christianity* (New York, 1959). Grant strongly emphasized these relations in the face of the zealousness with which hypotheses of direct pagan influences have been maintained.

27. Cf. *Jewish Gnosticism,* sec. 8, 57–64.

into which he "descends" is closely related to the world of the pleroma of the Greek gnostic texts. However, in place of abstract concepts personified as aeons, we find the entities of the throne-world as they have entered into this tradition from the book of Ezekiel. At the same time, there are direct contacts between these texts of Merkabah Gnosticism and the syncretistic world of the magical papyri. We possess Hebrew Merkabah texts that read as if they belonged to the literature of magical papyri.[28] The boundaries, at least regarding Judaism, were not as well defined as those drawn by many recent authors writing on Gnosticism who were bent on differentiating between Christian Gnosticism and the syncretistic magic under discussion.

We have no reason to believe that this gnostic theosophy still possessed any creative impulses of a decisive character after the third century. The productive development of these ideas evidently occurred on Palestinian soil, as the analysis of the Hekhaloth texts proves. At a later date in Palestine as well as in Babylonia, we still encounter literary elaborations of this old material, some of which underwent metamorphosis into edifying tracts. But we no longer find any new ideas. The practical realization of these heavenly voyages of the soul and the "vision of the merkabah," *ṣefiyyath merkabah,* maintained itself also in the post-talmudic period, and some scattered reports concerning practices of this kind, which are by no means to be regarded as mere legends, have come down to us from as late as the twelfth and the thirteenth centuries from France and Germany.[29] These old texts, augmented by all kinds of later additions, were known to the Middle Ages in the form given to them in the late talmudic and early post-talmudic periods as "Greater Hekhaloth," "Lesser Hekhaloth," *Shi'ur Qomah, Book of the Merkabah* and under other titles as well as in different versions. These texts were considered to be ancient, esoteric paragraphs of the Mishnah, and in the superscriptions of the oldest manuscripts they are here and there designated as "halakhoth concerning the Hekhaloth."[30]

---

28. I published one of these texts in *Jewish Gnosticism,* appendix C, 101–117, on the basis of two manuscripts.

29. For authentic reports on Merkabah-mysticism type of celestial voyages by the French talmudists, see chap. 3, n. 86, herein.

30. As, for example, in the manuscripts that Yehudah ben Barzilai had before him the beginning of the twelfth century, as he attests in his commentary on the Book *Yeṣirah,* 101. In many thirteenth- and fourteenth-century manuscripts from Germany the various paragraphs of the "Greater Hekhaloth" are designated as halakhoth.

They enjoyed great authority and were in no way suspected of heresy. Manuscripts of these texts and the related theurgical literature were known in the Orient, as is proven by many fragments in the Cairo Genizah, but also in Italy, in Spain, in France, and in Germany.[31] In the twelfth century, texts of this kind circulated precisely in learned circles, where they were considered authentic documents of the old esoteric doctrines.[32] It was therefore only to be expected that the earliest kabbalists would seek to establish a relationship with the traditions that enjoyed such high esteem.

4. *The "Book of Creation"*

Besides these literary monuments of the Merkabah gnosis, there was another, extremely curious text which circulated widely during the Middle Ages, excercising a great influence in many lands and in diverse circles: the "Book of Creation," *Sefer Yeṣirah.* Concerning the origin and spiritual home of this work, which numbers only a few pages, divergent opinions have been voiced, although to date it has been impossible to come to any reliable and definitive conclusions.[33]

31. Thus Ms. Oxford Heb. C 65 contains a large fragment of the *Shi'ur Qomah;* Ms. Sassoon 522 contains a fragment of an unknown and very ancient Merkabah midrash and a folio of the *Shi'ur Qomah.* The extant remains of the "Visions of Ezekiel," *Re 'iyyot Yeḥezqel,* of the fourth century, which I discussed in *Jewish Gnosticism,* 44–47, all come from the Genizah. A new critical edition and commentary have been published by Ithamar Gruenwald in *Temirin,* vol. 7 (Jerusalem, 1972), 101–139; see also Gruenwald's *Apocalyptic and Merkavah Mysticism,* 134–141. At the beginning of the twelfth century, mystical and theurgical texts could also be bought from a bookseller in Cairo whose catalogue has been partly preserved in the Genizah; cf. the text in Elkan Adler, *About Hebrew Manuscripts* (Oxford, 1905), 40 (nos. 82 and 83). Most of the manuscripts of this type of literature originate, however, in Italy and Germany.

32. These writings are frequently cited in the responsa of the geonim, the heads of the Babylonian academies, as well as in the rabbinic and philosophic works of the early Middle Ages. The Karaites took special delight in making them the targets of their attacks, without the rabbinic apologists' disavowing them. The most important Gaonic materials concerning the traditions of the Merkabah, etc., were collected by Benjamin M. Lewin, *Otzar ha-Geonim, Thesaurus of the Gaonic Responsa and Commentaries,* vol. 4, fasc. 2, *Ḥagigah* (Jerusalem, 1931), 10–27, 53–62.

33. The older literature on the "Book of Creation" is collected in the articles of L. Ginzberg, *Jewish Encyclopedia* (1906), s.v. "Yezira," and G. Scholem, *Kabbalah* (Jerusalem, 1974), 23–30. To this must be added A. M. Habermann, " 'Abhanim le-Ḥeqer Sefer Yeṣirah," Sinai 10 (Jerusalem, 1947); Leo Baeck, *Sefer Jezira, Aus drei*

This uncertainty is also reflected in the various estimates of the date of its composition, which fluctuate between the second and the sixth centuries. This slender work is also designated in the oldest manuscripts as a collection of "halakhoth on the Creation," and it is not at all impossible that it is referred to by this name in the Talmud. In the two different versions that have come down to us, it is divided into chapters whose individual paragraphs were likewise regarded by medieval tradition as mishnaic.[34]

The book contains a very compact discourse on cosmogony and cosmology. The verbose and solemn character of many sentences, especially in the first chapter, contrasts strangely with the laconic form in which the fundamental conceptions and the cosmological scheme of things are presented. The author undoubtedly wished to bring his own views, clearly influenced by Greek sources, into harmony with the talmudic disciplines relating to the doctrine of the Creation and of the Merkabah, and it is in the course of this enterprise that we encounter for the first time speculative reinterpretations of conceptions from the Merkabah. The attempts by a number of scholars to present this book as a kind of primer for schoolchildren[35] or as a treatise on the grammar and structure of the Hebrew language[36] cannot be taken seriously. The book's strong link with Jewish speculations concerning divine wisdom, *ḥokhmah* or Sophia, is evident from the first sentence: "In thirty-two wondrous paths of

---

Jahrtausenden (Tübingen, 1958), 256–271; Georges Vajda, "Le Commentaire kairouanais sur le 'Livre de la Création,' " *REJ,* n.s., (1947–1954): 7:7–62; 10:67–92, 12:7–33, 13:37–61.

34. The title *Hilkhoth Yeṣirah* is attested by Saadya and Yehudah ben Barzilai. Habermann published the oldest manuscript text that has been preserved to this day, basing himself upon a tenth-century Genizah manuscript. The version Saadya took as the basis for his Arabic commentary, ed. Mayer Lambert (Paris, 1891), deviates appreciably from most of the later texts. The first edition (Mantua, 1562), contains the two most important recensions. A critical revision of the text is a very difficult desideratum of research. The so-called "critically edited text" in the edition and translation of Lazarus Goldschmidt (Frankfurt, 1894) is patched together in a completely arbitrary manner and devoid of any scientific value. Considerable progress, however, is represented by the publications of Ithamar Gruenwald in *Israel Oriental Studies* 1 (1971): 132–177, and *REJ* 132 (1973): 473–512.

35. As, for example, in S. Karppe, *Étude sur les origines et la nature du Zohar* (Paris, 1901), 164.

36. Phineas Mordell, *The Origin of Letters and Numerals according to the Sefer Yetzirah* (Philadelphia, 1914).

wisdom[37] God . . . [there follows a series of biblical epithets for God] engraved and created His world." These thirty-two paths of the Sophia are the ten primordial numbers, which are discussed in the first chapter, and the twenty-two consonants of the Hebrew alphabet, which are described in a general way in chapter 2 and more particularly in the following chapters as elements and building blocks of the cosmos. The "paths of the Sophia" are thus fundamental forces that emanate from her or in which she manifests herself. They are, as in the old conception of the Sophia herself, the instruments of creation. In her or through her—the Hebrew preposition permits both translations—God, the master of the Sophia, "engraved" Creation. The symbolism of the number thirty-two reappears also in some Christian gnostic documents,[38] but it is in this text that it seems to be established for the first time and in the most natural manner. Mention should, however, be made of Agrippa von Nettesheim, who informs us (*De occulta philosophia* 2:15) that thirty-two was considered by the Pythagoreans as the number of righteousness because of its well-nigh unlimited divisibility. More recently Nicholas Sed[39] has discussed in a remarkable essay the relationship of the symbolism of the Book *Yeṣirah* with the Samaritan *Mēmar* of Marqah.

The ten primordial numbers are called sefiroth—a Hebrew noun, newly formed here, that bears no relation to the Greek word *sphaira,* but is derived from a Hebrew verb meaning "to count." Steinschneider's contention (*Mathematik bei den Juden* [Hildesheim, 1965], p. 148) that the original term acquired its specific kabbalistic meaning as a result of the similarity to the Greek word is not borne out by an analysis of the oldest kabbalistic texts. By introducing a new term, sefirah, in place of the usual *mispar,* the author seems to

---

37. *Nethibhoth pil'oth ḥokhmah.* Proverbs 3:17 knows of the *nethibhoth* ("paths") of Wisdom. Here, however, we have the paths of the "mysteries" of *ḥokhmah,* or the "mysterious paths" of the *ḥokhmah*—both translations can be defended. There is no connection between the *Yeṣirah* and the linguistic usage in the Qumran texts. The combinations *pil'oth ḥokhmah* or *raze ḥokhmah* are not found in the texts that have become known so far

38. Cf. the epithalamium of the Sophia in Preuschen, *Zwei gnostische Hymnen* (Giessen, 1904), 10. Preuschen says: "It is therefore impossible to interpret the number thirty-two, to which one finds no parallel" (p. 41). I shall return later, pp. 92 and 96, to this number in the nuptial mysticism of the Book *Bahir.*

39. "Le Mémar samaritain, le Sepher Jeṣīrā et les trente-deux sentiers de la Sagesse," *RHR* 170 (1966): 159–184.

indicate that it is not simply a question of ordinary numbers, but of metaphysical principles of the universe or stages in the creation of the world. The possibility that the term refers to emanations from God himself can be excluded in view of both the wording and the context; it could only be read into the text by later reinterpretation. Each of these primordial numbers is associated with a particular category of creation, the first four sefiroth undoubtedly emanating from each other. The first one is the pneuma of the living God, *ruaḥ 'elohim ḥayyim* (the book continues to use the word *ruaḥ* in its triple meaning of breath, air, and spirit). From the *ruaḥ* comes forth, by way of condensation, as it were, the "breath of breath," that is, the primordial element of the air, identified in later chapters with the ether, which is divided into material and immaterial either. The idea of an "immaterial ether," *'awir she'eno nithpas,* like the other Hebrew neologisms in the book, seems to correspond to Greek conceptions. From the primordial air come forth the water and the fire, the third and the fourth sefiroth. Out of the primordial air God created the twenty-two letters; out of the primordial fire, the Throne of Glory and the hosts of angels.[40] The nature of this secondary creation is not sufficiently clear, for the precise terminological meaning that the author gave to the verbs *ḥaqaq* and *ḥaṣab,* which belong to the vocabulary of architecture, can be interpreted in different ways. He does not utilize the Hebrew word for "create," but words that mean "engrave" (is this to designate the contours or the form?) and "hew," as one hews a stone out of the rock. The Aristotelian element of the earth is not known to the author as a primordial element.

The last six sefiroth are defined in an entirely different way; they represent the six dimensions of space, though it is not expressly stated that they emanated from the earlier elements. Nevertheless, it is said of the totality of these sefiroth that their beginning and their end were connected with each other and merged one into the other. The primal decade thus constitutes a unity—although its nature is not sufficiently defined—but is by no means identical with the deity. The author, no doubt intentionally, employs expressions borrowed from the description of the *ḥayyoth,* the animals bearing the Throne in Ezekiel's vision of the Merkabah. *Ḥayyoth* means literally "living

40. The author thus combines the doctrines, and interpretations concerning both esoteric disciplines, *bereshith* and Merkabah.

beings," and it can be said of the sefiroth that they are the "living numerical beings," but nonetheless creatures: "Their appearance is like that of a flash of lightning[41] and their goal is without end. His word is in them when they come forth [from Him] and when they return. At His bidding do they speed swiftly as a whirlwind, and before His throne they prostrate themselves" (1:6). They are the "depths" of all things:[42] "The depth of the beginning and the depth of the end, the depth of good and the depth of evil, the depth of above and the depth of below—and a single Master, God, the faithful king, rules over all of them from His holy abode" (1:5).

The fact that the theory of the significance of the twenty-two consonants as the fundamental elements of all creatures[43] in the second chapter partly conflicts with the first chapter[44] has caused some scholars (for example, Louis Ginzberg) to attribute to the author the conception of a kind of double creation: the one ideal and pure brought about by means of the sefiroth, which are conceived in a wholly ideal and abstract manner; the other one effected by the interconnection of the elements of speech. According to some views, the obscure word *belimah,* which always accompanies the word sefiroth, is simply a composite of *beli mah*—without anything, without actuality, ideal. However, judging from the literal meaning, it would seem that it should be understood as signifying "closed," that is, closed within itself. I am inclined to believe that here, too, an as yet unidentified Greek term underlies the expression. The text offers no more detailed statement of the relationship between the sefiroth and the letters, and the sefiroth are not referred to again. While the numerical-mystical speculation on the sefiroth probably has its origin in neo-Pythagorean sources—Nikomachos of Gerasa, the celebrated author of a mystical arithmology who lived around 140 C.E.,

41. The image *ke-mar'eh ha-bazaq,* as well as the *raṣo' wa-shobh,* employed immediately afterward but reinterpreted in a speculative sense, are evidently derived from Ezekiel 1:14.

42. Depth probably has the meaning of "extending itself in the depth" that is, dimension. But the word could also signify "hidden depth" (cf. Daniel 2:22), or perhaps also "deep foundation, principle." The expression "depth of good and evil" would only correspond to dimension in a very figurative manner. The "depth of evil" also makes one think of the "depths of Satan" in the book of Revelation 2:24.

43. The text speaks of *'othiyyot yesod;* each of the two nouns renders one of the two meanings of the Greek *stoicheia,* which denotes letter as well as element.

44. Cf. Neumark, *Geschichte der jüdischen Philosophie,* 1:115.

came from Palestine east of the Jordan—the idea of "letters by means of which heaven and earth were created" may well come from within Judaism itself. In the first half of the third century it is encountered in a statement of the Babylonian amora, Rab, originally of Palestine.[45] It is perfectly conceivable that two originally different theories were fused or juxtaposed in the author's doctrine concerning the thirty-two paths. This range of ideas would fit well in the second or third century in Palestine or its immediate environs.[46]

All reality is constituted in the three levels of the cosmos—the world, time, and the human body, which are the fundamental realm of all being[47]—and comes into existence through the combination of the twenty-two consonants, and especially by way of the "231 gates,"[48] that is, the combinations of the letters into groups of two

---

45. *Berakhoth* 55a; cf. *Jewish Gnosticism,* 78–79.

46. There is no compelling linguistic evidence for assigning a later date to this book. In the otherwise complete absence of early philosophical writings in Hebrew we naturally have nothing to compare to its technical terminology. The language shows many points of contact with that of the tannaim and the oldest Merkabah texts. An analytical study that remains to be made of the concrete relationship between this work and late Greek speculation would no doubt permit a better determination of its age. Leo Baeck's hypothesis that the author wished to reproduce in Hebrew garb Proclus's doctrine of Henads, seems unsubstantiated, and its author has to resort to forced interpretations. Nevertheless, on some points of detail Baeck's interpretations appear plausible and valuable.

47. It is certain that this division and the exactly corresponding division into *mundus, annus, homo* in cosmological statements and illustrations of Latin authors of the early Middle Ages such as Bede go back to a common source. Harry Bober collected interesting material on this subject; cf. *Journal of the Walters Art Gallery* 19–20 (1957): 78 and illustration 11. The sources utilized by Bede and Isidore of Seville remain to be identified.

48. "Through 231 gates everything goes forth. It is found therefore, that every creature and every speech [language] goes forth out of *one* name" (2:5). Does this mean that the alphabet, in its sequence, constitutes a mystical name? Of such a conception of the alphabet, Franz Dornseiff (*Das Alphabet in Mystik und Magie,* 2d ed. [Leipzig, 1925], 69–80) collected abundant testimonies from the Greek and Latin sources; cf. also A. Dieterich, *ABC—Denkmäler, Rheinisches Museum für Philologie* 56 (1900): 77–105. In the *Wiener Jahreshefte* 32 (1940): 79–84, Joseph Keil published an important Hebrew-Greek amulet that contains, with an obviously magical intention, the Hebrew alphabet in Greek transcription in the so-called *at-bash* order. In this order the alphabet is written in two rows boustrophedon and two letters are vertically connected in pairs. The amulet should be dated between the second and fourth centuries, but certainly no later. (I was able to identify clearly, though with some effort, the Hebrew text of Deuteronomy 28:58, which was in one of the three lines that neither Keil nor Ludwig Blau—to whom he showed the amulet in 1926—was able to decipher. It is only natural that the view that the alphabet constitutes "*One* name, to wit the name of 22 letters" should have passed into the early Kabbalah, as is attested

(the author apparently held the view that the roots of Hebrew words were based not on three but on two consonants). Among the three realms there exist precise correlations, which no doubt also expresses relations of sympathy. The twenty-two consonants are divided into three groups, in accordance with the author's peculiar phonetic system. The first contains the three "matrices,"[49] א, מ, ש *'alef, mem,* and *shin.* These in turn correspond to the three elements deduced in the first chapter in connection with the sefiroth—ether, water, fire—and from these all the rest came into being. These three letters also have their parallel in the three seasons of the year (again an ancient Greek division!) and the three parts of the body: the head, the torso, and the stomach.[50] The second group consists of the seven "double consonants" that in the Hebrew phonology of the author have two different sounds.[51] They correspond, above all, to the seven planets, the seven heavens, the seven days of the week, and the seven orifices of the body. At the same time, they also represent the seven fundamental opposites in man's life: life and death, peace and disaster, wisdom and folly, wealth and poverty, charm and ugliness,

---

by the *Commentary on the Prayer Book,* composed about 1260, by the (anonymous?) commentator *Sefer ha-Manhig* on the *Pirqe Rabbi Eliezer,* Ms. British Museum, Margoliouth 743, fol. 96b.

49. This is how the word has generally been read *('immoth)* and understood at a later date. Saadya and the Genizah manuscript, on the other hand, did not read *'immoth* but *'ummoth,* a relatively rare noun attested in the Mishnah, where it signifies "foundation;" cf. Lambert's translation, p. 44. The choice of these three consonants seems to reflect an ancient division related to the quantitative force of articulation of the consonants, in explosives, aspirates, and nasals. In ', the passage of air is completely interrupted by the vocal chords; in *sh* it is obstructed in a "whistling" manner, as the book says, by an effect of contraction, and in *m* the air passes freely through the nose. On the phonetics of the Book *Yeṣirah,* cf. M. Z. Segal, "Principles of Hebrew Phonetics" *(Yesode ha-Phonetica ha-'Ibhrith)* (Jerusalem, 1928), 96–100. From the phonetics of the book, as from its Hebrew, one can conclude with a considerable degree of certainty that it had a Palestinian origin.

50. *Gewiyah* must here signify the upper part of the torso, namely, breast. In his division of the body into parts, Philo too distinguishes between the head, the torso, and the stomach, *De opificio mundi,* 118. On the three seasons cf. Robert Eisler, *Weltenmantel und Himmelszelt,* vol. 2 (Munich, 1910), 452, where the author also refers to *Yeṣirah.*

51. On the much discussed inclusion of *r* among the consonants with a double pronunciation, cf. now the valuable study of S. Morag, "Sheba' Kefuloth B G D K P R T," in the jubilee volume for Professor N. H. Tur-Sinai, *Sefer Ṭur-Sinai* (Jerusalem, 1960), 207–242. J. Weiss drew my attention to the fact that in the Stoic theory of language the consonants *b g d k p t* were likewise thrown into relief; cf. Pauly-Wissowa, *Real-Encyclopädie der klassischen Altertumswissenschaften* 6:col. 1788.

sowing and devastation, domination and servitude. To these correspond, in addition, the six directions of heaven and the Temple in the center of the world, which supports all of them (4:1–4). The twelve remaining "simple" consonants correspond to man's twelve principal activities, the signs of the zodiac,[52] the twelve months, and the twelve chief limbs of the human body (the "leaders"). The combinations of all of these elements contain the root of all things, and good and evil, "pleasure and sorrow" (*'oneg* and *nega'*, which have the same consonants) have their origin in the same process, only according to a different arrangement of the elements (2:4).

This cosmogony and cosmology, based on language-mysticism, betray their relationship with astrological ideas. From them, direct paths lead to the magical conception of the creative and miraculous power of letters and words. It is by no means absurd to imagine that our text not only pursued theoretical aims, but was intended for thaumaturgical use as well. That is how the tradition of the early Middle Ages understood it, at least in part, and it would not have been wrong, in this case, to establish a connection between our text (or its prototype) and the story of the two masters of the Talmud, Rabbi Ḥanina and Rabbi Oshayah, who every Friday studied the "halakhoth concerning Creation" and by means of it created a calf that they then proceeded to eat.[53] Also related to the magic of language mysticism is the author's view that the six dimensions of heaven are "sealed" (1:13) by the six permutations of "His great name Yaho" (Hebrew YHW). These three consonants, utilized in Hebrew as matres lectionis for the vowels *i, a,* and *o,* which are not written, make up the divine name Yaho, which contains the three consonants of the four-letter name of God, YHWH, as well as the form Yao, which penetrated into the documents of Hellenistic syncretism where its permutations likewise play a role.[54] The signs that

52. The technical term *galgal,* always employed in this book for the sphere of the zodiac, is also of tannaitic origin.

53. *Sanhedrin* 65b, 67b. According to *Berakhoth* 55a, Bezalel the architect of the Tabernacle "knew the combination of letters by means of which heaven and earth were created." This could link up with the idea of the creation of a golem, which I examined at length in chapter 5 of my book *On the Kabbalah and its Symbolism* (New York, 1965).

54. Examples of the magical use of the six permutations of Iao can be found in Preisendanz, *Die griechischen Zauberpapyri,* 2d ed. (Stuttgart, 1973–4) 1:108 (1. 1045); 2.14.

were subsequently developed to designate vowels were still unknown to the author.

This idea concerning the function of the name Yaho or Yao suggests important parallels. In the system of the Gnostic Valentinus, Iao is the secret name with which the Horos (literally: the limit, the limitation!) frightens away from the world of the pleroma the Sophia-Akhamoth who is in pursuit of Christ. Does not the cosmos (as distinct from the pleroma), sealed by means of the six permutations of Yao in the Book *Yeṣirah,* constitute a sort of monotheistic parallel, perhaps even inspired by polemical intentions, to this Valentinian myth? In another text of a manifestly Jewish-syncretistic character, we similarly find the name Iao, as an invocation that consolidates the world in its limits, a perfect analogy to the sealing in *Yeṣirah:* in the cosmogony of the Leiden magical papyrus the earth writhed when the Pythian serpent appeared "and reared up powerfully. But the pole of heaven remained firm, even though it risked being struck by her. Then the god spoke: Iao! And everything was established and a great god appeared, the greatest, who arranged that which was formerly in the world and that which will be, and nothing in the realm of the Height was without order any more." The name Iao appears again among the secret names of this greatest god himself.[55] It is difficult not to suspect a relation here

55. Ibid., vol., 2, 113. On the use of the name Iao in the magic of the age of syncretism there is an abundance of material. Most of the older examples have been collected by W. von Baudissin, *Studien zur Semitischen Religionsgeschichte,* vol. 1 (Leipzig, 1876), 179–254. The passage from *Yeṣirah* is not referred to by Baudissin, nor did R. Reitzenstein make use of it in his treatment of the Book *Yeṣirah,* for which he assumes an ultimately Hellenistic origin reaching back to the second century; his arguments are based on a comparative study of letter-mysticism in late antiquity; see Reitzenstein, *Poimandres* (Leipzig, 1904), 291. As an historian with a broad perspective, Reitzenstein perhaps had a clearer view than many other Jewish scholars, who often regarded the Book *Yeṣirah* as if it were suspended in a vacuum in the midst of the history of religions. It should also be noted, in this connection, that in the Coptic *Pistis Sophia,* chap. 136, Iao appears in a similar context: Jesus calls out his name as he turns toward the four corners of the world. The sealing of the six directions of space by means of the permutations of Iao corresponds to the idea that this name is the master of the four directions of the world, that is, the master of the cosmos. Cf. the material assembled by Erik Peterson, *Heis Theos* (Göttingen, 1926), 306–307. Peterson's interpretation of the magical name Arbathiao as "the four Iao" is, however, utterly unconvincing. The magical name is nothing other than a syncretistic transcription of the Tetragrammaton as "the tetrad [of the four letters of the name YHWH upon which is based the name] of Iao." This is proven by the corresponding form *Tetrasya,* which we find in the Hebrew writings of the Hekhaloth and

between Jewish conceptions and those of Gnosticism and syncretism. This "sealing" of the Creation by means of the divine name belongs to the old stock of ideas of the Merkabah gnosis; it is attested in chapter 9 of the "Greater Hekhaloth." What is said in the "Book of Creation" of the "six directions" of space is here said of the "orders of the Creation," therefore, of the cosmos in general, whose preservation within its established arrangements, *sidre bereshith,* is due to its "sealing" by the great name of God.

I have briefly developed here some of the fundamental concepts of the Book *Yeṣirah* because they are of essential importance for the understanding of what follows and because this book was later read and interpreted by the kabbalists as a vade mecum for the Kabbalah. In contrast to later interpretations, the special charm of this text consists in the frequently felicitous and in any event ever-vivid imagery and fullness of meaning it lends to most of the concepts newly created in order to express abstractions. The author finds concrete and appropriate designations for notions that, until then, Hebrew did not know how to render in adequate terms.

That he failed on certain points and that his images sometimes remain obscure for us—which only encouraged their subsequent reinterpretation—is a clear sign of the difficulty of his efforts and of the energy with which he undertook them. The book's solemn and enigmatic manner of speaking made it possible for the Jewish philosophers as well as the kabbalists of the Middle Ages to appeal to its authority. Saadya, in the earliest extant (although certainly not the oldest) commentary interpreted it around 933 in accordance with his philosophic conception of the doctrine of Creation and his Jewish theology in general. Since then, a complete series of more or less detailed Hebrew and Arabic commentaries continued to be writ-

---

which was still unknown to Peterson; cf. my *Major Trends,* 56, 363. The terminology employed in the *Yeṣirah* for these three directions of space is also very ancient: the phrase "above and below, in front and behind, right and left" is used in exactly the same manner in Akkadian, and is evidently also behind the wording of the Mishnah *Ḥagigah* 2:1 (first century), where "in front" and "behind" are to be understood spatially. This usage was no longer understood by the amoraim, and was in any case transferred from the spatial to the temporal, as S. E. Löwenstamm, "On an Alleged Gnostic Element in Mishnah Hagiga II, 1" (in Hebrew) in M. Haram (ed.), *Yehezkel Kaufmann Jubilee Volume* (Jerusalem, 1960), 112–121, has shown, drawing upon Akkadian material. His explanations furnished additional linguistic evidence in support of the antiquity of the Book *Yeṣirah,* although precisely the passage under consideration here escaped his attention.

ten down to the thirteenth and fourteenth centuries. Everyone found in the book more or less what he was looking for, and the fact that Yehudah Halevi devoted extensive attention to it, almost a complete commentary, in the fourth tractate of his principal work of philosophy and theology, *Sefer ha-Kuzari* (around 1130), may serve as an indication of the great authority the book enjoyed.[56]

But at the same time, this text also remained influential in entirely different circles, those who saw in its theory of language some sort of a foundation of magic, or those for whom the doctrine of the book included authentic elements of the Merkabah gnosis and of cosmogony. The Book *Yeṣirah* was studied in the schools of the sages of Narbonne as well as among the French rabbis of the school of the tosafists and among the German Hasidim of the same period, and many commentaries have come down to us from these circles, which were generally averse to philosophic speculation.[57] It offers remarkable parallels, to say the least, to the turn which the Kabbalists gave to the doctrine of the sefiroth. It is no longer possible to say with certainty to what extent the study of the Book *Yeṣirah* was re-

---

56. Around the middle of the eleventh century the head of a Palestinian school, R. Yehudah ben Yosef Cohen, *rosh ha-seder,* also composed an Arabic commentary on the *Yeṣirah,* a fragment of which is preserved in Leningrad; cf. Jacob Mann, *Texts and Studies in Jewish History and Literature,* vol. 1 (Cincinnati, 1931), 456–457. Commentaries presumably older than Saadya's were still known to Yehudah ben Barzilai, who saw them in old manuscripts and cites them in several places. On Saadya's commentary, cf. the analysis of G. Vajda in "Sa'adja commentateur du 'Livre de la Création,' " *Annuaire de l'École pratique des Hautes Études* (1959–1960).

57. Moses Taku of Bohemia had before him, around 1230, a commentary by the "scholars of Narbonne." It is unclear whether this commentary dates from the eleventh or the twelfth century; cf. *'Oṣar Neḥmad* 3 (Vienna, 1860): 71. The renowned tosafist Isaac of Dampierre explained the book orally, and we possess a commentary that Elḥanan ben Yaqar of London composed in accordance with the traditions transmitted by someone who had studied the book with this R. Isaac "the Elder." As G. Vajda has shown in *Archives d'histoire doctrinale et littéraire du moyen âge* 28 (1961): 17–18, the author also used Latin sources! Isaac died toward the end of the twelfth century. Cf. M. Weinberg concerning the manuscript A4 in the Landesbibliothek of Fulda, *Jahrbuch der Jüdisch-Literarischen Gesellschaft* 20 (Frankfurt-am-Main, 1929): 283. From the circles of the German Hasidim of the thirteenth century we have the commentary of Eleazar of Worms, of which there exists in print only one complete text (Przemyśl, 1888); a commentary falsely attributed to Saadya Gaon and printed in the editions of the book; and another commentary of the abovementioned Elḥanan of London that I found in New York, Jewish Theological Seminary, in a parchment manuscript of the fourteenth century, fol. 62–78. (The manuscript figures in the report of the library, in the *Register of the Seminary* for 1931-1932.)

garded in these circles as an esoteric discipline in the strict sense of the term. Perhaps one could view the text as situated at the limits of esotericism, partly within it, but partly already beyond it.

5. The Oldest Documents Concerning the Appearance of the Kabbalah and the Publication of the Book Bahir

In the preceding pages, we characterized the historical circumstances under which the Kabbalah saw the light of day and attempted to give an account of the kind of literary material deriving from older tradition that may have been known at that time. We may now proceed to the next question regarding the kind of information available to us concerning the initial stages of the Kabbalah and its appearance among the Jews of Provence. We have at our disposal two kinds of reports: those supplied by the kabbalists themselves and those that came from their earliest opponents. To be sure, only very little of these reports has been preserved, but even the little we have is of great importance.

The first type of report goes back to traditions preserved among the third generation of the Spanish disciples of the Provençal kabbalists. Their accounts emphasize the mystical inspiration, namely, the "appearance of the Holy Spirit," in one of the most distinguished families representing the rabbinic culture of Provençal Jewry. These sources name several historical personalities to whom the prophet Elijah is said to have revealed himself *(gilluy Eliyahu)*; that is, they were the recipients of celestial mysteries of which earlier tradition knew nothing until then, and which came to them as revelations from above. These revelations may have been of a purely visionary character, or they may have been experiences of illumination sustained while in a state of contemplation. I have expressed my opinion elsewhere on the meaning of this category of *gilluy Eliyahu*,[58] which is of considerable importance for an understanding of the relationship between religious authority and mysticism in Judaism. The prophet Elijah is for rabbinic Judaism the guardian of the sacred tradition. In the end, with the arrival of the

58. Scholem, *On the Kabbalah*, 19ff.

Messiah, he will bring the divergent opinions of the teachers of the Torah into harmony. To the pious, he now reveals himself on diverse occasions in the marketplace, on the road, and at home. Important religious traditions of the Talmud and even an entire midrashic work are attributed to his instruction.[59] He is present every time a child is admitted into the Covenant of Abraham—that is, at the establishment of the sacral connection between the generations by means of circumcision. It is by no means the mystics alone who encounter him; he may just as well reveal himself to the simple Jew in distress as to one perfect in saintliness and learning. As the zealot of God in the Bible, he is the guarantor of the tradition. He is, as I have written, "not the kind of figure of whom it could be supposed that he would communicate or reveal anything whatsoever which stood in fundamental contradiction to such a tradition."[60] A tradition that was acknowledged to have come from the prophet Elijah therefore became part, in the consciousness of the faithful, of the main body of Jewish tradition, even if it brought something new; and it stood above any possible suspicion of foreign influence or heretical attitude. It is no wonder, then, that at important turning points in the history of Jewish mysticism—precisely at those times when something new appeared—constant reference was made to revelations of the prophet Elijah. Understood in this sense, "tradition" included not only that which was transmitted on earth and in history, but also that which was received from the "celestial academy" above.

In the literature that has been preserved, these traditions relating to the appearance of the prophet Elijah among the earliest kabbalists first appear around the year 1300, yet everything indicates that they are drawn from a solid stock of traditional material going back to the first Spanish kabbalists. They are found in the writings composed by several disciples of Solomon ibn Adreth, and they largely reproduce kabbalistic traditions of the kind taught in his school in Barcelona between 1270 and 1310. Ibn Adreth was the

---

59. Cf. the article *Elija,* in the English *Encyclopaedia Judaica* (1971); Moses W. Levinsohn, "Der Prophet Elia nach den Talmudim- und Midraschimquellen" (diss. Zurich-New York, 1929); Robert Zion, *Beiträge zur Geschichte und Legende des Propheten Elia* (Berlin, 1931); Eliezer Margaliouth, *Eliyahu ha-Nabi* (Jerusalem, 1960); A. Wiener, *The Prophet Elijah in the Development of Judaism* (London, 1978).

60. Scholem, *On the Kabbalah,* 20.

most important disciple of Moses ben Naḥman (Naḥmanides), who was himself still in contact, as we shall see, with the kabbalistic masters of Provence, and who represents the kabbalistic school of Gerona. There is no reason to doubt that it is this tradition we have before us.

These sources claim that revelations of this kind came to three or four of the leading men of Provence: Abraham ben Isaac (d. around 1179), president of the rabbinical court (in Hebrew *'ab beth-din*) and master of a school in Narbonne; his son-in-law Abraham ben David of Posquières (d. 1198); his colleague, Jacob ha-Nazir (the Nazirite); as well as, finally, the son of Abraham ben David, who became known as Isaac the Blind. The latter lived, it seems, until around 1232–1236 in Posquières or Narbonne. Traditions differ in matters of detail.[61] According to some, it was Rabbi David, the father of Rabbi Abraham ben David (known in Hebrew literature by the acronym Rabad) and not Abraham ben Isaac, his father-in-law, who was the first to receive this Kabbalah. Albeck assumed Isaac the Blind was the son and not the grandson of Abraham ben Isaac, but the analysis of the oldest sources does not confirm this assumption.[62] Around these scholars, but especially around Isaac the Blind, there crystallized the oldest groups of Provençal kabbalists that we are still able to identify. The pupils of Rabad and his son, coming from Spain to study in the talmudic academies of Provence, were the principal agents of the Kabbalah's transplantation to

---

61. Cf. the passages in Jellinek, *Auswahl kabbalistischer Mystik* (Leipzig, 1853), 4–5. Here is what Menaḥem Recanati recounts, around 1300: "For he [Elijah] revealed himself to Rabbi David *'ab beth-din* and taught him the science of the Kabbalah. He transmitted it, for his part, to his son, the Rabad, and he also revealed himself to him, and he transmitted it to his son, Isaac the Blind and to him, too, he revealed himself." Another old tradition says: "R. Isaac Nazir [a reference, no doubt, to Isaac ben Abraham of Narbonne] received from the prophet Elijah and after him, R. Jacob Nazir, and from him the Rabad and his son Isaac the Blind, who was the fourth [recipient] after Elijah." The Hebrew expression "the fourth after Elijah" probably means the fourth in the chain of tradition since Elijah revealed himself. However, it could also mean the fourth person who himself had a revelation from Elijah. Shemtob ibn Gaon, a pupil of Solomon ibn Adreth, called Isaac the Blind the "third after Elijah." Cf. *Ma'or wa-Shemesh* (Livorno, 1839), fol. 35b. According to a tradition recorded by ibn Gaon, *'Emunoth* (Ferrara, 1556), fol. 36b, only the Rabad's father-in-law (who is there mistakenly called Abraham and not Isaac) received a revelation from the prophet Elijah.

62. Cf. Albeck in his introduction to the edition of Abraham b. Isaac 'Abh Beth-Din, *Sefer ha-'Eshkol* (Jerusalem, 1935), 5.

Spain and its propagation in that country. Nothing permits us to suppose that the Kabbalah, in the precise sense of the term, became known in Spain other than through this channel or by way of a parallel path that would point to Provence.

Here, to be sure, we must ask what the exact significance of the word Kabbalah was at this time in the circle of the kabbalists themselves. Kabbalah is a fairly common word in rabbinic Hebrew: it simply means "tradition." In the Talmud, it served to designate the non-Pentateuchal parts of the Hebrew Bible. Later, every tradition was called by this name, without its entailing any specifically mystical nuance. That it was already employed by the philosopher Solomon ibn Gabirol in the sense it would acquire among the kabbalists is a widespread but completely false assumption.[63] It has just a little to do with the Aramaic word *qibhla,* "amulet."[64] The Spanish kabbalists still knew very well several generations later what original notion their predecessors had in mind when they employed the term Kabbalah. As late as the year 1330, Meir ben Solomon ibn Sahula, a pupil of Solomon ibn Adreth, expressed himself clearly and directly on the origin and meaning of this new discipline. "It is incumbent upon us," he writes in the preface to his commentary on the Book *Yeṣirah,* "to explore all of these things according to the measure of our understanding, and to follow, in what concerns them, the path taken by those who, in our generation and in the preceding generations, for two hundred years, are called kabbalists, *mequbbalim,* and they call the science of the ten sefiroth and some of the reasons for the [biblical] commandments by the name Kabbalah.[65] It follows,

---

63. M. H. Landauer, *Literaturblatt des Orients,* vol. 6 (1845), cols. 196–197; Jellinek, *Beiträge zur Geschichte der Kabbala,* (Leipzig, 1852), 1:71, 2:27 (plagiarized by J. Günzig, *Die "Wundermänner" im jüdischen Volke* [Antwerp, 1921], 89). This entire hypothesis, founded on a false interpretation already present in the Hebrew text, is now shown to be totally untenable by the original Arabic text in Stephen S. Wise, ed., *The Improvement of the Moral Qualities* (New York, 1901), cf. 34.

64. Contrary to Tur-Sinai's suppositions in the *Lexicon of Ben Yehudah,* vol. 11 (1946), 5700, according to which the notion Kabbalah in its later sense would owe its origin to a popular etymology of *qibhla.* The magical term would then have been applied to the esoteric doctrine in general and been confused with *qabbalah.* The same erroneous hypothesis with regard to a connection of this kind had already been formulated by David Kaufmann in *MGWJ* 41 (1897): 186. In fact, this usage of the term definitely stems from learned circles and is always unequivocally associated with the idea of tradition. Nowhere in the old texts does one find such a confusion of the words *qabbalah* and *qibhla.*

65. Ms. in the Biblioteca Angelica in Rome, A.6, 13, fol. 2b.

then, that in the eyes of these kabbalists the new theosophic conception of God, based upon the doctrine of the ten sefiroth of the Book *Yeṣirah* as well as upon the mystical reasons founded on this doctrine for certain ritual precepts of the Torah, constitute the original content of the Kabbalah. In the author's own opinion, this teaching is by no means ancient; it does not go back many centuries. Rather, it is about two hundred years old, which brings us back, for its initial stage, to the period of the first revelations of the prophet Elijah—that is, in Provence, toward the middle of the thirteenth century. The chain of kabbalistic traditions that contains the names mentioned previously accords perfectly with this information. It should be noted, also, that the clear awareness on the part of this later kabbalist of the relative youth of the Kabbalah in no way prevents him from considering it a path to knowledge that is "incumbent upon us" to follow.

The second category of sources at our disposal does not mention individuals and the manifestation of the Holy Spirit or the prophet Elijah in the academies of important rabbinical figures. It concerns, rather, the publication of a kabbalistic book that came into the hands of the scholars we have mentioned or certain of their Provençal colleagues who are unknown to us. This literary document, the oldest of the Kabbalah if one understands that term as ibn Sahula defined it, is the Book *Bahir,* which is also called, after the second-century master of the Mishnah named in the opening words of the text, the "Midrash of Rabbi Neḥunya ben Haqqanah." The title *Bahir,* "bright," is taken from the first biblical verse (Job 37:-21) cited in the text, whose interpretation is ascribed to that rabbi: "Now, then one cannot see the sun, though it be bright in the heavens." The kabbalists do not say that this book was revealed by the prophet Elijah to the aforementioned scholars or to any of their unknown colleagues. According to them, it is an autonomous document independent of these revelations. A closer analysis of the book will prove their judgment correct on this point. For the content of the new speculative tradition deriving from the aforementioned recipients of mystical illuminations is far from simply identical with the content of the Book *Bahir.*

Concerning the origin of this book, we have the testimony of the Spanish kabbalist Isaac ben Jacob Cohen of Soria (about 1260–1270), who in the course of his kabbalistic travels in search of old traditions also sojourned for a prolonged period in Provence and undoubtedly reproduced the tradition he heard from the kabbalists of Narbonne, Arles, and other places. The work in which this testimony was originally included has not been preserved, but a kabbalist of unquestionable reliability writing one hundred years later still had it before his eyes. The author in question, Shemtob ben Shemtob, quoted many passages from this book, texts whose content is perfectly consistent with other writings that can certainly be attributed to Isaac Cohen.[66] The latter writes: "Of the [kabbalistic] allusions which they [the old sages] mentioned in the haggadoth in the Talmud and in the midrashim, this is the greatest and the most important among the kabbalists, those men gifted with understanding, who penetrated the depths of the Bible and the Talmud[67] and were experienced in the depths of the great sea [the Talmud]; and that is the Book *Bahir,* which is also designated,[68] particularly, by

---

66. I have assembled in *Madda 'e ha-Yahaduth* 2 (Jerusalem, 1927): 276–280, the citations in question from the *'Emunoth* of Shemtob. I was able partly to correct the passage on the *Bahir* (*'Emunoth,* fol. 94a) by using a parchment manuscript at the Jewish Theological Seminary, New York [no. 882 in the handwritten list of Professor A. Marx], fol. 112b. While the original German edition of this book was in press, Israel Weinstock, in a Hebrew article entitled "When was the Bahir composed according to the tradition?" *Sinai* 49 (1961): 370–378 and 50 (1961): 28–34, made some assertions that are completely without foundation. In his opinion, the kabbalists themselves possessed an ancient tradition according to which the *Bahir* was composed by one of the geonim. His assertions completely contradict the testimony of the old kabbalistic literature and do not withstand examination. The only source he can invoke is an incidental remark, altogether imprecise in its language, made by an opponent of the Kabbalah in the seventeenth century! It should be noted, however, that even Moses Cordovero (ca. 1569) thought it possible that the book was composed before (!) the destruction of the Temple, cf. his commentary *'Or Yaqar* on the *Zohar* (1967 ed.), 4:138. In the sequel I shall ignore Weinstock's publications, collected in *Be-Ma 'agale ha-Nigleh veha-Nistar* (Jerusalem, 1970), as they are based on wrong assumptions and offend against all scholarly methods and criteria. Cf., A. Goldreich, in *Kiryath Sefer* 47 (1972): 199–209, who took the trouble, and wasted precious time, to re-examine the sources and demolish Weinstock's cobwebs.

67. Hebrew: *be 'omeq pilpul ha-Miqra weha-Talmud. Pilpul* signifies an ingenious and penetrating comprehension, and is often mentioned, as in the continuation of this text, along with erudition as a praiseworthy quality of the great scholar.

68. In the manuscript: *ha-meyuḥad bi-leshon Yerushalmi,* which can also mean "composed in the language of the Yerushalmi," that is, in Aramaic, a statement that, to be sure, does not apply to our text. Another possible translation is "the eminent Book *Bahir* [composed] in the Jerusalemite language [that is, dialect]." *Meyuḥad* often has the meaning "eminent, outstanding"; cf. the medieval expression *meyuḥad bedoro.* The printed text has *ha-meyusad,* which would not permit the second translation. The version *ha-meyuḥas* in *Madda 'e ha-Yahaduth* 2:277 rests on a mistaken reading. The *Bahir* is already cited by the pupils of Isaac the Blind under the name of

the term 'Yerushalmi' [that is, as a Palestinian source]. This is the book, more precious than gold, which Rabbi Neḥunya ben Haqqanah revealed through mysterious and concealed allusions to those 'gifted with understanding' [that is, the mystics] of Israel, the group of sages and the academy of old and holy men. And this book came from Palestine to the old sages and Hasidim, the kabbalists in Germany [Allemannia], and from there it reached[69] several of the old and eminent scholars among the rabbis of Provence, who went in pursuit of every kind of secret science,[70] the possessors of a higher knowledge.[71] However, they only saw a part of it and not the whole of it, for its full and complete text did not come into their hands. In any case, it came to them from a distant land, whether from Palestine or from abroad, from old sages and holy kabbalists, who possessed a well-ordered tradition [Kabbalah] transmitted to them orally by their fathers and forefathers."

This testimony is remarkable, and we shall see further on that at least in its essentials it is not a fabrication. Nevertheless, we must draw a clear distinction between the very specific statements concerning the origin of the Book *Bahir* and its appearances in Provence and the assurances of a more general nature that those earliest kabbalists had been the guardians of an immemorial tradition passed along from "mouth to mouth" throughout the generations.

"Yerushalmi," which in medieval usage often means nothing other than "a written work coming from Palestine." Such citations of the *Bahir* as "Yerushalmi" are found, for example, in Ezra ben Salomon's commentary on the Song of Songs, fols. 12a, 20d, as well as in his *Sod Eṣ ha-Da 'ath,* Ms. Casanatense, Sacerdoti 179, fol. 96a; Moses of Burgos, in his explication of the divine name in forty-two letters, in the collection *Liqquṭim me-Rab Hai Gaon* (Warsaw, 1798), fol. 9b; Baḥya ben Asher, *Kad ha-Qemaḥ,* s.v. "'Orḥim"; Menaḥem Recanati, *Ta 'ame ha-Miṣwoth* (Basel, 1580), fol. 12a; Isaac of Acre, *Me'irath 'Enayim,* Ms. Munich 17, fol. 59a.

69. Hebrew: *hofia' we-higgia'. Hofia'* means "appear," not only in the technical sense of a book that appears, but "it shines forth, its brightness is spread abroad." From the combination of these two verbs, however, something close to the modern significance of the word results.

70. Hebrew: *ḥokhmoth reshumoth.* The kabbalists of the thirteenth century readily made use of the adjective *reshumoth* in this particular sense. Many authors of the Middle Ages read this meaning into the category of *dorshe reshumoth* mentioned in the Talmud. Cf. Ben Yehudah's *Lexicon* 14:6745, and Jacob C. Lauterbach, "The ancient Jewish allegorists in Talmud and Midrash," *JQR,* n.s., 1 (1910/1911): 291–333, 503–531.

71. Hebrew: *yod'e da'ath 'elyon,* after Numbers 24:26; the kabbalists readily employed it in the specific sense of "possessors of the gnosis." (A similar designation: *ba 'ale sod ha-madda'* in Moses of Burgos; cf. *Tarbiz* 4 [1933]: 56).

The belief in the existence of such long chains of tradition was an integral part not only of the kabbalistic *communis opinio,* but also of the Hasidic tradition in Germany. As far as the latter is concerned, we have here examples of such chains, complete with all the names, whose fictitious character cannot be doubted.[72] For our purposes, it is particularly important to note that Isaac Cohen by no means affirms the existence of an unbroken chain of oral tradition between the scholars of Provence and those ancient circles where the Kabbalah is said to have had its origin. On the contrary, he expressly declares that the book came to them *in writing* "from a distant land, whether from Palestine or from abroad." Only those men, remaining anonymous, who brought or sent the book to Provence were in possession of a Kabbalah transmitted by their fathers—an assurance that, as we noted, was strictly a formality and consistent with what the kabbalists considered to be correct usage.

Isaac Cohen's account of the old sources from which the Kabbalah came must now be contrasted with the completely different testimony of a very early opponent of the kabbalists. Meir ben Simon, a contemporary of Isaac the Blind, is rather inclined to ascribe the book to authors of his own time, and his testimony is of considerable importance for us. He was an energetic opponent of the Kabbalah, which in his time was being propagated in Provence. In an epistle that he incorporated into his anti-Christian apologetic work *Milḥemeth Miṣwah,* he came out very sharply, around 1230–1235, "against those who speak blasphemously of God and of the scholars who walk in the ways of the pure Torah and who fear God, while they themselves are wise in their own eyes, invent things out of their own minds, lean toward heretical opinions and imagine that they can bring proof for their opinions from the words of the haggadoth, which they explain on the basis of their own erroneous assumptions.[73] In this letter, which is directed against the agitation of the kabbalists and which will engage our attention again in another connection, he relates, among other things, in the slightly inflated style of contemporary rhymed prose that can hardly be imitated in translation: "They boast in mendacious speeches and statements of hav-

72. Characteristic, in this regard, are the "two chains of kabbalistic tradition of R. Eleazar of Worms," which H. Gross published and discussed in *MGWJ* 49 (1905): 692–700.

73. I presented the text of the original in *Sefer Bialik* (Tel Aviv, 1934), 146.

ing found confirmation and encouragement [for their ideas, evidently] in the lands of sages and scholars . . . But God save us from the sin of heeding such heretical words, concerning which it would be better to keep silence in Israel. And we have heard that a book had already been written for them,[74] which they call *Bahir,* that is 'bright' but no light shines through it. This book has come into our hands and we have found that they falsely attribute it to Rabbi Neḥunya ben Haqqanah. God forbid! There is no truth in this. That righteous man, as we know him, did not come to ruin [by editing such a work] and his name is not to be mentioned in the same breath as sacrilege. The language of the book and its whole content show that it is the work of someone who lacked command of either literary language or good style, and in many passages it contains words which are out and out heresy."[75]

The tone here is therefore very different from that of the enthusiastic encomia of Isaac Cohen. But even though Meir ben Simon is aware of the pseudepigraphical character of the book, he by no means attributes it, any more than does Isaac Cohen, to the circle of the family of Rabad, of whom it certainly could not be said that they lacked command of either literary language or good style. The author of the epistle leaves unanswered the question of whence the book came to the Provençal kabbalists. Yet it follows from his emphasis upon the imperfections of the language and style of the book that in his opinion its origin should be sought in circles that were far removed from the rabbinical culture of those generations and that were susceptible to heretical influences, from whatever side.

The two documents we have been discussing are, in effect, the only historical testimonies that specifically mention the publication of the book; and in spite of the differences of opinion, they agree upon one point: it was published in Provence. As we shall see in the following chapter, both testimonies contain part of the truth. In the

74. The only extant manuscript, Parma de Rossi 155, utilizes a defective Hebrew orthography almost throughout. The word חבר is therefore to be read, as is often the case here, as *pu'al: ḥubbar.* A. Neubauer, the first to publish this text, concluded from his faulty reading of the word as *pi'el: ḥibber,* "he composed," the erroneous understanding that the author wished to designate as the author of the Book *Bahir* R. Azriel, who is named previously. Naturally this error was possible only as long as the writings of Azriel himself were largely unknown.

75. Cf. the text of the original in Neubauer, "The Bahir and the Zohar," *JQR* 4 (1892): 357–368.

circle of Isaac the Blind, the book was without a doubt already regarded as an old and authentic source that had the same value as the aggadic midrashim and the writings of the Merkabah mystics. Among the extant fragments of Isaac the Blind himself, there are some that cite the Book *Bahir* by this name. Throughout the entire thirteenth century the Book *Bahir* represented the canonical text upon which the Spanish kabbalists based themselves and to which they made constant reference. It was only after the acceptance of the *Zohar* that the kabbalists of the following generations were in a position to replace the few leaves of the *Bahir,* which in Hebrew did not number more than forty pages, with a complex and extensive literature that could serve as an authority. Instead of the fragmentary and obscure sentences of the *Bahir* they had in the *Zohar* relatively well developed and systematic homilies that far better expressed the state of mind of the kabbalists of those later generations. It is no wonder, then, that the later literary production soon surpassed these older texts in influence and importance.

In the thirteenth century, the Book *Bahir,* as would later be the case for the *Zohar,* was seen as the work of the teachers of the Talmud. This is expressly attested by Jacob ben Jacob Cohen, the older brother of Isaac Cohen. In his commentary on Ezekiel's vision of the Merkabah, he speaks of the "Book *Bahir,* which was composed by the sages of the Talmud, the kabbalist elect [*ha-mequbbalim ha-yeḥidim*]."[76] The judgments of nineteenth-century scholars still conformed to these two opinions with regard to the origin and age of the Book *Bahir.* Among more recent scholars, the only one who held that the book was ancient and therefore evidently of Oriental origin was, as far as I know, Moses Gaster, who declared in 1881—without, however, offering any arguments—that it perhaps "went back further than the tenth century."[77]

---

76. Cf. the passage in my catalogue of the kabbalistic manuscripts of the University library in Jerusalem, (in Hebrew) (Jerusalem, 1930), 208. It is only since the publication of this work that I have been able to prove conclusively that Jacob ben Jacob Cohen is the author of this important book, transmitted anonymously in all the manuscripts. In a commentary on the same vision of the Merkabah, Moses of Burgos, Jacob's pupil, quotes numerous passages from the commentary of his master that can all be found in the aforementioned anonymous work. Cf. Ms. Enelow Memorial Collection 711 in the Jewish Theological Seminary, which is partly identical with a better and much older manuscript in the Mussajof Collection in Jerusalem.

77. Cf. Gaster, *Studies and Texts,* vol. 2; 1076; Steinschneider asserted, on the contrary, that the book "was no doubt composed only in the thirteenth century."

Naturally, we should not expect to find a critical historical sense among the mystics of the thirteenth century, least of all when it is a question of texts that had, at that juncture in time, a decisive influence upon their own spiritual world. Nevertheless, the clarity with which the fundamental attitudes emerge from these two types of very old documentation is something of a surprise for us. Here we can still recognize very clearly the contradiction between two tendencies that had either to unite or to engage in controversy in order for the Kabbalah to come into being as an historical phenomenon and factor. On the one hand, we are dealing here with something really new, with revelations of the prophet Elijah "and the appearance of the holy spirit in our academy"; revelations of this kind were by no means lacking even among the Spanish kabbalists of the period after 1250, as is shown by such notable illuminati as Jacob Cohen and Abraham Abulafia. On the other hand, we are also dealing with the vestiges of an unarticulated tradition that survived in the form of old notebooks and fragmentary leaves; and these came from distant lands or from subterranean levels of the Jewish societies in which they emerged into the light of day. In other words, we seem to have a current from above and one from below; their encounter produced the Kabbalah as an historical phenomenon. The mysticism of individuals who through their vision or in their contemplation express more or less completely the yearnings of their own souls and perhaps also in some measure those of the age—in brief, an aristocratic and individualistic form of religion—here combines itself with impulses emanating from anonymous sources. Historical analysis must attempt to identify these sources or at least determine their character. That is the first impression that emerges from an examination of the oldest information about the appearance of the Kabbalah. From here we can go a step further and ask what there is to be learned from an analysis of the contents of the kabbalistic tradition. What does an investigation of the Book *Bahir* tell us and what information can we glean from the extant fragments of the kabbalistic mysticism of the circle of Abraham ben David and Isaac the Blind? These are the questions that will occupy us in the following chapters.

Our investigation of the first stages of the Kabbalah is advanced by a stroke of good luck. An extremely important work has been preserved that sheds light upon the kind of ideas, which in the generation that preceded the first appearance of this new inspiration would have been considered to be part of the speculations regarding the Merkabah. The Mishnah (*Ḥagigah* 2:1 and the related explanations in both Talmuds) prohibited discourse on the doctrine of Creation in the presence of two pupils and on the Merkabah even in the presence of one unless he fulfilled certain preconditions. Literary evidence of this tradition certainly survived until the Middle Ages, as we saw earlier. But at this time it was no longer clear what had been the original and authentic content of these traditions; what exactly came within their purview and what did not. Consequently, the various spiritual currents in the Judaism of that time attempted, each in its own way, to fill the framework of the so-called doctrine of the Merkabah, the celestial reality, with metaphysics and ontology, and that of the doctrine of Creation with physics and astronomy.[78] When the Kabbalah stepped into the light of history in Provence, this identification was already very widespread in cultured circles. Other groups held onto the "Book of Creation" and attempted to read into the enigmatic words of that old esoteric text either the science of their time or their own ideas. In this regard there is, as I have already said, no difference in principle between rationalists like Saadya on the one hand and the kabbalists and mystics on the other. In the first third of the twelfth century Yehudah ben Barzilai, one of the more eminent rabbinical authorities of his generation, composed a very detailed commentary on the Book *Yeṣirah,* of which a single manuscript has survived to this day.[79] The author, as we now know, was also one of the teachers of Abraham ben Isaac of Narbonne, that is, of the scholar in Provence whom the kabbalistic tradition itself designates as the first to receive the new kabbalistic revelations.[80]

This book occupies a controversial position in the history of the Kabbalah. According to Neumark, it is "an indispensable link for the understanding of the evolution which led to the Kabbalah . . . Barzilai signifies the *internal* factor of development. Saadya, like Baḥya after him [in his work "On the Nature of the Soul"] cites . . . many passages of the rabbinic and Talmudic literature, but it is [Yehudah ben] Barzilai who systematically arranged his book in

78. This identification is known chiefly through Maimonides and his school, but it undoubtedly goes back further.

79. It is according to this manuscript that S. J. Halberstam edited the text (Berlin, 1885).

80. Cf. S. Assaf, *Sifran shel Rishonim* (Jerusalem, 1935), 2–3.

such a way as to explain all the important passages concerning *bereshith* and Merkabah . . . And in fact, from our point of view, Barzilai's *Yeṣirah* commentary can be regarded as the decisive turning point between the doctrine of the ideas and that of the Merkabah, which constitutes the very foundation of the Kabbalah."[81] Neumark even suggests that the term Kabbalah, in its later customary signification may have been coined by Yehudah ben Barzilai.[82] Having said that much, it is almost obvious that Neumark should also be convinced that this work was known to the earliest kabbalists and copiously utilized by them.

Unfortunately, these assertions of Neumark are completely without foundation. It has been impossible for me to discover in the book any element that could be construed as playing a role in the development of the Kabbalah. Nor have I been able to find traces of the profound influence that, in Neumark's opinion, this work was supposed to have exercised upon the kabbalists of the thirteenth century. The proofs he offers consist of very arbitrary comparisons and are utterly fantastic. On the contrary, what seems so curious about this book is that it appears to have been unknown to the thirteenth-century kabbalists who wrote after the *Bahir.* Only a few weak echoes suggest some acquaintance with it. Not even Abraham Abulafia, who in 1270 studied and enumerated all the commentaries on the *Yeṣirah* to which he had access, knew of this book,[83] although he resided at the time in Barcelona, where the commentary had been written.

The undeniable interest of this book therefore lies not in any direct connection with kabbalistic speculation, but precisely in the contrast between the two. It shows that even an author who admittedly felt himself drawn toward mysticism and sometimes went so far as to give expression to this inclination in his halakhic works[84]

---

81. Neumark, *Geschichte des jüdischen Philosophie,* vol. 1, 192.

82. Ibid., 194.

83. Cf. Jellinek, *Beth ha-Midrash,* vol. 3 (Leipzig, 1855), 42, where this passage concerning the commentaries on the *Yeṣirah* studied by Abulafia is presented. As Abraham Epstein has proved, basing his argument on the commentary on the *Yeṣirah* by Eleazar of Worms, the German Hasidim were the only ones who had knowledge of this book. Without giving the name of the author, he copied it in many places. I did not find any literal borrowings of this kind in the writings of the Spanish kabbalists.

84. This is the opinion of such an eminent expert on halakhic literature as S. Bialoblocki in the German *Encyclopaedia Judaica* (1931), 8: col. 940.

was completely ignorant of a distinct mystical or gnostic tradition that could have existed at this time and in his country. The ideas that characterized the Kabbalah, above all the theosophic concept of God and the doctrine of the aeons, are completely absent from his writings. The author expressly attests that even the speculations, influenced by Saadya, on the Glory of God, *kabhod,* though perfectly familiar to the German Hasidim in the twelfth century,[85] had not taken root in his own country, and he apologizes for his lengthy and repetitious treatment of these doctrines with the observation that "it is not the custom of our contemporaries to discuss these subjects."[86] His work shows, therefore, the state of nonkabbalistic speculations on these subjects as they presented themselves immediately before the appearance of the Kabbalah.

In the first part of his book he offers a sort of anthology of talmudic and midrashic passages that can in some way be brought within the scope of the doctrines of the Merkabah, of the Book *Yeṣirah,* and of cosmology. This part is interesting enough in itself. It can hardly be doubted that if the author had possessed any knowledge of the kabbalistic theosophy he would have been favorably disposed toward it and would have assimilated it to his own expositions and commentaries. But this he signally fails to do. His work thus proves in the most conclusive manner the magnitude of the difference between the situations in the north of France and in Provence wrought in the period between about 1130 and about 1180–1200. This difference is due to the reappearance, in the heart of Judaism, of the *gnostic tradition.*

---

85. For the ideas of the *kabhod* among the Hasidim, cf. *Major Trends,* 110–115.
86. Yehudah ben Barzilai's commentary, 234.

CHAPTER TWO

THE BOOK *BAHIR*

1. Literary Character and Structure of the Book: Its Different Strata

The Book *Bahir,* whose few pages seem to contain so much that is pertinent to the mystery of the origin of the Kabbalah, has the form of a midrash, namely, a collection of sayings or very brief homiletical expositions of biblical verses.[1] These are not set forth according

1. In the following pages, I cite according to the numeration of the paragraphs in my translation and commentary *Das Buch Bahir, Ein Schriftdenkmal aus der Frühzeit der Kabbala* (Leipzig, 1923). This translation is essentially based upon the oldest and relatively best extant manuscript, the Cod. Monac. 209 from the year 1298, which, as subsequent research by O. Hartig on the foundation of the Hof-Bibliothek of Munich (*Abhandlungen der Bayrischen Akademie der Wissenschaften, philosophisch-historische Klasse* Bd. 28, fasc. 3 [München, 1917]) have shown, was one of the codices used by Giovanni Pico della Mirandola when he began his kabbalistic studies in 1486. (In fact, the oldest translation of the *Bahir* into Latin, made for Pico by Guiglelmus Raimundus Moncada, alias Flavius Mithridates, and preserved in Cod. Ebr. 191 of the Vatican Library, was based upon the very same manuscript that is found in Munich today.) For many passages, however, I have preferred the readings to be found in quotations contained in the works of thirteenth-century kabbalists. Older citations from the book are indicated in each paragraph in my aforementioned translation. Needless to say, my understanding of many passages in the text has deepened, and the translations given in the present work reflect that better understanding. Num-

to any particular organizational principle. Thus the book is devoid of a literary structure. Furthermore, as we shall see, it is only with the greatest reservations that one can speak of a uniform development of thought in the various paragraphs of the text. Everything seems to have been jumbled together haphazardly. Utilizing a mystical terminology that was not known in the ancient midrashim, the book interprets all sorts of biblical passages and aggadoth, showing a preference, of course, for those of a cosmogonic and cosmological nature. Moreover, it makes the letters and the vowels of the Hebrew language, and even certain accents of the Hebrew script, the object of its speculation. Alongside fragments concerned with ritual symbolism and the mysticism of prayer that are scattered throughout the text, one finds explanations that obviously derive from the Book *Bahir* and that interpret its ideas or develop them in new ways. To these are added passages with a psychological content as well as

---

erous fourteenth- and fifteenth-century manuscripts have been preserved, but their value cannot be compared to that of old quotations in the extant manuscripts of the school of Gerona and its successors, especially from about 1220 onward. The printed editions represent an exceptionally corrupt text. It is a curious fact, as we may conclude from a note by Johann Christoph Wolf, *Bibliotheca Hebraea,* vol. 3 (1727): 796, that the first edition (Amsterdam, 1651) was probably arranged by a Christian, Jacob Bartholinus. This would explain the striking absence of rabbinical approbations in the edition. The title page claims that the book was edited "at the wish of several men from Poland who, in their modesty, wish to remain unnamed." But the kabbalistic *Ma 'yan ha-Ḥokhmah,* which was printed at the same time as the *Bahir* and carries an almost identical notice, is the very same book that was anonymously published by Bartholinus and erroneously registered by Wolf as *Ma 'ayan Gannim.* Later editions further corrupted the text (Berlin, 1706; Shklow, 1784; Lemberg, 1800 and 1865). In 1883 in Vilna a somewhat better text appeared together with an anonymous commentary, *'Or ha-Ganuz,* by a disciple of Solomon ibn Adreth; it can now be proved that its author is Meir ben Solomon ibn Sahula (or ben Sahula), under whose name the commentary was still known in the sixteenth and seventeenth centuries; cf. my book *Kithbe Yad be-Kabbala* (Jerusalem, 1930), 147. In the preface to his commentary on the *Yeṣirah,* which I have since been able to study in a manuscript in the Angelica in Rome, he reports that he finished his commentary on the *Bahir* in the year 1331, after six years of work, at the age of seventy. [Although counter-arguments and doubts have been voiced on this point, Scholem held fast to the ascription of the authorship of the commentary to Abi-Sahula. The most recent summary of the present state of the discussion is Ze'ev Galili, "The author of the commentary *'Or ha-ganuz* on the *Bahir* ascribed to Me'ir ben Solomon Abi-Sahula" in *Meḥqerey Yerushalayim be-maḥsheveth Yisra'el* (1985) 4:83–96. R.J.Z.W.] The most recent edition of the *Bahir* is that of Ruben Margalioth (Jerusalem, 1951), who consulted four manuscripts—although not the best ones, as his text proves. These manuscripts, which he does

fragments related to various mystical names of God whose magical tendency is unmistakable.

We have here, in fact, a potpourri of many motifs that could be of interest to the adepts of the old esoteric doctrine. But the exposition is hardly ever brought to a conclusion. Most of the time it is interrupted by other topics and then taken up again, without, however, being pursued consistently. There is nothing to support Neumark's thesis that an author with a theoretical or speculative tendency clothed his ideas, very artificially and consciously, in the form of a midrash, which really did not suit these ideas at all. On the other hand, this manner of exposition seems perfectly adequate to the author's (or authors') aggadic type of thought. Another of Neumark's contentions is just as ill-founded: According to him,[2] the book is entitled *Bahir* because it is concerned with the doctrine of the primordial substance of creation, the *'or bahir,* a term the philosophic exegetes of the *Book of Creation,* as well as Yehudah ben Barzilai, readily employed when they spoke of the first-created light that represents the primordial spiritual substance of creation. In

---

not identify, probably come in part form the Jewish Theological Seminary in New York. The author went so far as to omit any mention of my works, which were certainly known to him but whose historical and critical orientation incurred his displeasure. In this edition the text is divided into 200 paragraphs. Forty years ago D. N. Kotow of New York had the intention of reediting the *Bahir* on the basis of the New York manuscripts; but while still engaged in his preparatory work he was murdered in an armed robbery. His collection of manuscripts was kindly put at my disposal by his teacher, Professor Alexander Marx. The literature on the book is listed at the end of my article *Bahir* in the German *Encyclopaedia Judaica* (1929); particularly deserving of mention is David Neumark's Hebrew version of his history of Jewish philosophy in the Middle Ages, *Toldoth ha-Pilosofia be-Jisrael* (1921), 181–185, 261–268. To this must now be added Baeck, *Aus drei Jahrtausenden* (1958), 272–289, an attempt at a coherent interpretation of the first twenty-five paragraphs of the book, however, seems to me to be too homiletical and harmonistic. Another Latin translation (sixteenth century by G. Postel) is preserved in the public library in Basel (A IX aa, fol. 36–98v) but has not yet been properly studied. I. Weinstock has published two articles in Hebrew on the *Bahir* and its compositional and textual problems, in *Sinai* 50 (1962): 441–451 and in *Ch. Albeck Jubilee Volume* (Jerusalem, 1963), 188–210. Aryeh Kaplan, *The Bahir: Translation, Introduction and Commentary* (New York, 1979) is worthless and does not contribute anything to an understanding of the book. Equally insignificant is S. H. Lehmann, "The Theology of the Mystical Book Bahir and its Source," *Studia Patristica* 1 (1957): 477–483, which claims to find in the *Bahir's* "anti-manichaean polemic" (sic) indications of its Mesopotamian origins but in fact merely deals with commonplace irrelevancies.

2. Neumark, *Geschichte der jüdischen Philosophie,* vol. 1 (1907), 10, 197.

fact, the book is not particularly concerned with this teaching, and the notion of the *'or Bahir* does not reappear again after the citation in section 1 of the biblical verse from which it is taken. And it is precisely the doctrine that usually went under this heading that is not dealt with in this paragraph.[3]

The Mishnaic teacher Neḥunya ben Haqqanah reappears in the book, at the most, one more time.[4] If his name is placed at the very beginning of the work in a paragraph that has hardly any connection with what follows it is undoubtedly because this rabbi figures as one of the chief authorities of the pseudepigraphic Merkabah literature. In the Hekhaloth he appears as the teacher of the other two chief authorities, R. Akiba and R. Ishmael. The book is thus identified, as it were, as a Merkabah text, yet its two principal speakers are teachers whose names are obviously fictitious. One is called Rabbi Amora or Amorai, which in the old sources is never the name of a person. The designation of amoraim, that is, "speakers," is used in talmudic tradition for teachers who were active after the completion of the Mishnah, in order to distinguish them from the tannaim. R. Amora therefore means nothing more than "Rabbi Speaker." The second speaker is called R. Raḥmai or Reḥumai (the oldest tradition employs the first form of the name), which may be an allusion to the name of the amora Reḥumi, a fourth-century Babylonian master.[5]

---

3. The first paragraph, a sort of preamble, treats only of the identity, before God, of light and darkness. "R. Neḥunya ben Haqqanah said: A verse of Scripture [Job 37:21] says: 'Now, then, one cannot see the light, though it be bright [*bahir hu'*] in the heavens,' and another verse of Scripture [Ps. 18:12] says: 'He made darkness His screen.' [Here is] a contradiction, [but] a third verse comes and brings things into accord [Ps. 139:12]: 'darkness is not dark for you; night is as light as day; darkness and light are the same.' " Baeck thought to find in this sentence the guarantee of all mysticism, "the final hiddenness is at the same time the final knowledge, that which from below . . . appears as darkness, is seen from above as transparent light" (p. 273). The word *Bahir* appears once more in the book, in section 97, in a passage concerning the hidden primordial light that God saw shining and radiating. It is perhaps from here that Neumark derived his hypothesis.

4. He is probably the R. Neḥunya named in section 45, according to Mss. Munich 209 and Paris 680, whose name is replaced by that of Reḥumai in later texts. Here he expounds a mystical symbolism on the sefiroth. Section 106 is also mentioned by a philosophic author around 1290, not in the name of R. Berahya, as in all manuscripts, but in the name of R. Neḥunyah. But perhaps the author merely wished to introduce a quotation from the *Midrash of R. Neḥunya,* as indeed the Book *Bahir* is also known. Cf. my commentary on the passage.

5. The historical Reḥumi, however, was not concerned with esoteric doctrine as far as we can tell from the sources.

These two protagonists correspond here to Akiba and Ishmael of the Hekhaloth. Besides them, we find names that are known to us from the aggadic midrashim, such as R. Beraḥya, R. Bun, R. Eliezer, R. Yannai, R. Yoḥanan, R. Meir, R. Papias.[6] Akiba and Ishmael, whom we would expect to encounter, appear only occasionally. In section 22 they conduct a dialogue, the same dialogue that originally appears in *Midrash Bereshith Rabba* on Genesis 1:1. But these utterances are only rarely authentic citations; for the most part they are texts of a pseudepigraphic nature. However, large sections of the book remain anonymous. The paragraphs follow one another without mention of any name, even though discussions often take place between the unnamed speakers. It is doubtful whether the dialogue form or, indeed, the attribution of statements to definite persons is always original. Often it appears as if they were the result of a later redaction in which names were added or altered.[7] Nevertheless the literary form of the Midrash, that is, questions concerning the meaning of difficult or contradictory biblical verses, is preserved or imitated. However, the anonymous pieces distinctly recall, in part at least, a manner of exposition close to the anonymous Mishnah or the Book *Yeṣirah.*

That the text before us is in fact fragmentary, as Isaac Cohen already attested, is beyond doubt. We are dealing with a collection or a redactional adaptation of fragments. Sometimes the text even

6. Papias and Akiba, who in the early Aggadah are mentioned together in other circumstances (Bacher, *Agada der Tannaiten,* vol. 1, 324–327), also appear together in section 86. The scriptural interpretations transmitted in the name of Papias are known for their mystical overtones and "aggadic boldness" (Bacher). R. Ahilai, who in section 80 interprets in a magical mode a phrase from the hymns of the Merkabah mystics (concerning the twelve-letter divine name) is also unknown. The sentence attributed in section 14 to R. Levitas ben Tiburia, is given in the name of Lulliani bar Tabri, that is, Julianus the son of Tiberius, in *Bereshith Rabba.* In section 18 there is a discussion between Rabbi Amora and Mar Raḥmai bar Kibhi, who is otherwise unknown. Could this be the full name of R. Raḥmai? In place of כיבי, one should no doubt read ביבי (Bebai), a name that appears frequently in Jewish Aramaic.

7. In our discussion of the relations between the *Bahir* and the *Raza Rabba,* we shall find more examples of such modifications of names. While the beginning of the table of the ten logoi, which we have yet to consider, is presented anonymously and not in dialogue form, its latter part, from section 114 on, is abruptly changed into a dialogue, without the speakers being named. Other pieces in the second part of the book likewise give the impression of a rather artificial revision of coherent expositions into dialogues.

breaks off in the middle of one sentence and continues with the middle of another, which can hardly be explained otherwise than by the loss of a page in the oldest manuscript that served as a *Vorlage.*[8] Other lacunae are clearly recognizable: thus, in section 30, the answer to a question is missing; in section 88 and at the end of section 115, important enumerations are not brought to a conclusion. Sections 107–115 present a lengthy, anonymous exposition, while section 116 begins: "His pupils said to him," without any previous reference having been made to the teacher and his words. On the other hand, some connection with the preceding is evident, since both passages have their source in two consecutive sentences in the *Baraitha de-ma'aseh bereshith;* see *Seder Rabbah de-bereshith* in S. Wertheimer, ed., *Beth ha-Midrash,* vol. 1 (2d ed., 1950), 30. Furthermore, in many places the kabbalists may have censored themselves, for already in Provence protests were raised against the heretical character of many passages. Thus Meir ben Simon of Narbonne quotes a passage he himself read in the *Bahir* that is missing in all our manuscripts. Meir ben Simon writes:

> And why should we waste time on the words of fools whose prayers, hymns and benedictions are addressed to gods who, according to them, were created and emanated and who have a beginning and an end. For in their foolish argumentation they assert that everyone named "first" and "last" must also have a beginning and an end, invoking the verse [Isa. 44:6]: "I am the first and I am the last, And there is no God but Me." This is what we found in one of the books of their error, which they call *Bahir,* and some scholars have also heard this from their mouths."[9] (cf. also pp. 398–400 following)

---

8. This explains, for example, the rupture between sections 43 and 44, as well as between sections 66 and 67. Sections 67–70 constitute an interpolation, the beginning of which is missing, but that links up with section 64, while section 71, for its part, continues section 66, even if the connection by no means conforms to syntax.

9. I published the Hebrew text in *Sefer Bialik* (Tel Aviv, 1934), 149. I am inclined to suppose that the eliminated passage dealt with the demiurge, *Yoṣer bereshith,* in whose mouth this verse could most easily be placed. As in the old *Shi'ur Qomah,* with which this quotation might very well have some connection, the Creator God has a beginning and an end—in contrast to the Godhead that is above it, the *deus absconditus* subsequently designated by the term *'en-sof.* Did the author distinguish, perchance, between the Creator who manifests himself in the logoi or sefiroth and the God who is above the sefiroth?

Whatever idea one may have of the redaction of this book, it can be clearly shown that interpolations confused the text in many places.[10] Thus, the important table of the ten cosmogonic primordial categories, or logoi, which we shall discuss more fully below and which was certainly all of one piece originally, was badly mutilated in its second part, as much by the subsequent imposition of a dialogue form as by different interpretations and parallel recensions.

The language of the book is often chaotic and confused, and that in a greater measure than can be explained by the corruption resulting from the manuscript transmission. In many passages the syntax is almost incomprehensible. Meir ben Simon's charges with respect to the book's bad style are indeed well grounded. Many passages are distinguished by a lofty style and a solemn language, and the images are not without a certain exaltation—we will see several examples—but then again one finds oneself reading a clumsy and awkward Hebrew that had long ago lost the Midrash's genius for nuance. The language is not that of the Talmud, although the discussions imitate talmudic terminology;[11] it is rather that of the later

10. Thus we find side by side texts that presuppose completely different conceptions of the same subject and offer explanations that cannot be harmonized and unified without doing them violence. Sections 77 and 78 are a characteristic example: this is an addition that interrupts the direct sequence of sections 76 and 79 and represents an interpretation of section 76 that in no way corresponds to its original meaning. The notion of the "holy forms" in section 77, where they signify angels, contradicts the same notion as it is employed in sections 67, 69, and 116, where it refers to the manifestation of God himself in the limbs of the primordial man. The expression "holy forms" is indeed found in the *Mishneh Torah* of Maimonides, completed around 1180, but this fact does not necessarily establish a relationship of dependence or of sources between the two texts, the expression being one that readily lends itself to "numinous" differentiation. In *Hilkhoth Yesode ha-Torah* 7:1, Maimonides states that the prophet whose mind is freed from all earthly concerns and who sojourns in the upper world, in communication with the realm that extends beneath the throne, learns to grasp "those holy and pure forms," from the first form to the navel of the earth. In the *Bahir,* the expression probably derives from other, more ancient sources. Similarly, Section 88 continues the ideas of section 76, while the preceding texts, especially in sections 84–87, have an entirely different character. Evidently texts relating to the divine names and to matters concerning the Merkabah are interrupted by kabbalistic symbols of an entirely different kind. Similarly, in the enumeration of the ten logoi various texts that have a connection with the subject are interpolated after section 96; the enumeration is resumed only in section 101.

11. Expressions of this kind, taken from the terminology of talmudic discussions, are, for example, *la qashya,* "this is not difficult"; *mna'lan,* "whence do we know"; *'i ba'ith 'ema,* "if you wish, I shall say"; *la tibb'i lakh,* "this should not be a problem for you"; *qayma lan,* "we take it as established," etc. They are found

Aggadah. The greater part of the book is written in Hebrew, with several passages also in a rather poor Aramaic, and others again in a mixture of the two languages, the proportion of Hebrew and Aramaic varying in the different manuscripts. Here and there the linguistic usage recalls the later midrashim composed in southern France, as in the preference given to the use of the verb *sim* "to place," instead of *nathan* "give" (especially in the parables). It should be noted, however, that *la-sum* in the sense of *la-'asoth* is current in mishnaic Hebrew; cf. *Yoma* 4b. The few instances of evident arabisms, however, are cause for reflection.[12] In Provence at this time Arabic was not understood; it was certainly not understood in groups like those of the authors or redactors of the Book *Bahir,* who obviously devoted little effort to cultivating the knowledge of languages. The philosophic phrases one finds here and there do not permit any clear localization, quite apart from the fact that they probably belong to the latest redactional stratum.

There seems to me little doubt that the book contains deposits of different strata that perhaps also derive from different sources. The unified system that Neumark, in particular, attempted to con-

---

throughout the entire book, insofar as it maintains the form of a dialogue. *Kema de'at 'amer,* "as you say," employed in general to introduce citations from the Bible, is sometimes used here in a broader sense for quoting not merely the wording of the text but also some thesis or paraphrase deduced from it; cf. W. Bacher, *Exegetische Terminologie der Jüdischen Traditionsliteratur,* vol. 2 (1905), 11, and here sections 37 and 39.

12. At least four Arabisms of this kind are found in sections 24–38, which perhaps constitute a unit (for sections 24–28 this is certain): section 25, in an explanation of the form of the consonant *daleth: u-bha'a 'abha,* "it became thick," the verb *ba',* literally: "he came," is employed in the same way as the Arabic *ga'a* for "become"; section 27, where *be-roshah,* said of the soul, can only have the sense of "herself," like the Arabic *rasiha;* section 28, where it is necessary to translate: "And what does the name of the vowel *hireq* signify? An expression for 'burn.' " In fact, the word for "burn" in Arabic (but not in Hebrew or Aramaic) is *haraqa;* the pun in section 38, based on the words *zahabh,* gold, and a verb *nizhabh,* which does not exist in Hebrew, makes sense only on the basis of the Arabic radical *dahaba,* "going away"; section 122, the verb *messabbeb* is employed in the sense of "cause," a meaning that the word acquired only in medieval Hebrew under the influence of Arabic. However, this word appears precisely in an epigram on the relations between the ten spheres of the astronomers and the ten logoi, alleged to be a sentence from the Mishnah. The phrase *halo' tir'eh,* "surely you see," which is not found in the old Midrash, is probably an Arabism, too. From all this one may conclude with certainty that the paragraphs making use of the mysticism of vowels have their origin in the Arab-speaking Orient.

struct in the Hebrew edition of his work does not exist. It seems as if an effort had been made in the final redaction to establish some sort of general unification of the kabbalistic symbolism employed, but without thereby eliminating the frequent and obvious contradictions one still encounters. Rather, it appears that we have before us evidence of the gradual evolution of the kabbalistic symbolism. We shall encounter many examples of this process. The movement from one paragraph to another or from one group of passages to the next is often effected by means of purely extraneous associations. A verse of the Bible that has just been cited is seized en passant to become in turn the subject under consideration; a notion or an image that has just been mentioned is picked up and discussed more fully. These threads that extend through large parts of the book evidently furnished only a very superficial principle of organization for the assemblage of old and new materials. It is curious to note here that the first half of the book, or rather the first third, seems deliberately to include simpler texts, a large number of which find their explanation only in the light of the mystical symbolism that appears with greater clarity in the later parts of the work.

However, the book does not develop its conceptions in an orderly and progressive manner. In general one can say that many texts do not really explain basic concepts, but presuppose and utilize them in raising and elucidating a concrete problem. To this end, the book resorts unabashedly to a mythological mode of expression and to mythical images that are nothing less than a "dressing up" of philosophical ideas. The total unconcern with which this manner of speaking is employed, without the slightest need to offer apologies to the more timorous spirits and without formulating any reservations, is highly characteristic of the Book *Bahir.* In this it differs significantly from later works of kabbalistic literature, which almost always surround their anthropomorphic and mythical imagery with apologies and reservations as if to pay their respects to orthodox theology. Neither the authors nor the redactors of the *Bahir* had such scruples. These notions, no matter how we explain their origin, seemed to them to be legitimate images of the divine world. They treated them as a matter of course, just as the old aggadists did when they spoke of divine things in anthropomorphic images. This attitude proves conclusively that the book cannot be explained on the basis of the tradition of philosophic thought in Judaism or as a product of its decline. It has its roots in an entirely different world.

The aggadic and midrashic forms of discourse, often also presented more pointedly as questions and answers between master and pupil, expound subjects that one would seek in vain in the ancient texts of this literature; however, the earlier literature cannot have been unknown to the circles from which the Book *Bahir* issued, thus implying that they must have referred to it. What matters is that the interpretations and paraphrases of the *Bahir* have as their object not only biblical verses, but also sayings from the Talmud and the Aggadah. One must ask whether such an attitude does not ipso facto presuppose a long interval between the book and the sources it utilizes, the latter having already become canonical and subject to being read with a mystical eye. In the aggadic literature otherwise known to us, we have no example of the words of the masters of the Talmud being mystically or allegorically reinterpreted by their colleagues. No such relation can be found between the writings of the Merkabah and the exoteric Aggadah. Passages from exoteric sources are occasionally also found in the former, but they do not lose their original meaning, and certain dicta that appeared to many modern scholars to be reinterpretations of talmudic sayings are in reality more detailed explications based upon an entirely correct understanding or a perfectly reliable tradition.[13] Never does this old mystical literature appropriate passages from other writings in order to transform them into symbols, as is the case in the *Bahir.* For in this book everything is already a symbol. Every word, every phrase it introduces becomes an allusion to some secret, and this secret remains unexplained as often as on other occasions or in other passages of the book it is deciphered as soon as it is stated. We find ourselves in the presence of a typical gnostic exegesis—a fact that, of course, has no bearing on the question of the historical relation to the old gnostic tradition. The words and the concepts that are emphasized in the text become symbolic words and names for a celestial reality, indicative of the events that take place there. It would never occur to the old Merkabah mystics of the Hekhaloth tradition to relate verses from Genesis, the Prophets, or Psalms to objects of the world of the Merkabah in order to obtain a more exact representation or description of these celestial entities. The Gnostics, on the

13. Cf. my *Major Trends,* 52–53 as well as *Jewish Gnosticism,* 14–19, on the talmudic account of the four masters who entered paradise and on the parallel accounts in the Hekhaloth texts.

other hand, followed this very procedure without any difficulty, as we can see from the history of the gnostic interpretation of Scripture. They were able to discover in every word of Scripture an indication or a name of one of the "spiritual places" or aeons, whose mutual relations determine the law of the celestial world, and especially that of the pleroma. By means of such exegesis they went far beyond the Philonic method of reading the Bible. And it is precisely this method that we find again abundantly applied in the mystical midrash of the *Bahir.*

Attention should also be paid to another element. Mystical parables occupy an important place in the *Bahir.* No fewer than fifty such parables are scattered throughout the book, some of them simple and naïve, but others of a more complex texture. It is evident from section 129 that besides parables taken or adapted from the Talmud and the Midrash, there are others, unknown elsewhere, whose reference to concrete details of life in the East clearly indicate their Oriental origin. Elaborating on the mystical term, "treasure of the Torah," our text says:

> Thus a man must [first] fear God and [only] then study Torah. It is like a man who went to buy date honey and who did not take with him a container to carry them home. He said: I will carry them upon my breast, but they were too heavy for him. He was afraid that they would break open and soil his clothes, so he threw them away. Then he was doubly punished: once for the spoiling of the food and once for the loss of his money.

These lines may well be taken from a thoroughly unmystical source, but they could have been written only in a country where the culture of the date palm flourished and the date was an object of daily use, as in the warmest parts of Palestine or in Babylonia.[14] In southern Europe—in Provence, for example—the date palm was only an ornamental plant. This detail concerning date honey suggests that other passages of the *Bahir,* which presuppose and interpret mystically the bisexual character of the palm and its artificial fecundation, may also similarly go back to an Oriental origin. I shall again take up the question of this symbolism at the end of this chapter.

Many of these parables present a very bizarre and paradoxical

---

14. Cf. Immanuel Loew, *Die Flora der Juden* 2:348.

aspect. One could almost say that they seem to be intended to obscure the theme treated rather than to clarify it. Often the essential thought is developed only in the parabolic form, in which old images and concepts frequently seem to have taken refuge. Parables of this kind are unknown elsewhere in Jewish literature; later kabbalists, such as the author of the *Zohar,* always employ "meaningful" and not strikingly paradoxical parables.

Section 25, for example, is characteristic of this genre. The passage inquires into the mystical significance of the vowel *a,* in Hebrew *pathaḥ,* a word that means "opening" [of the mouth] but also "door."

> And which door? This refers to the north side, which is the door for the entire world: by the door through which evil goes forth, good also goes forth. And what is good? Then he [the master] scoffed at them and said: Didn't I tell you? The small *pathaḥ.*[15] They replied: we forgot it. Repeat it to us. He said: the thing is like a king who had a throne. Sometimes, he took it in his arms, sometimes he put it on his head. They asked him: why? Because it was beautiful, and it saddened him to sit upon it. They asked him: and where does he put it on his head? He said: in the open letter *mem,* as it is written: [Ps. 85:12] Truth springs up from the earth; justice looks down from heaven.

The open *mem* is, as we learn in section 58, a symbol of the feminine. The entire passage remains utterly enigmatic, although it is evident that the parable suggests a ritual mysticism in which the throne is compared to the tefillin of the Jewish prayer ritual, which are attached partly to the arm and partly to the head. According to a passage of the Talmud (*Berakhoth* 6a) that has been given many interpretations, God also wears tefillin. But the parable does not thereby gain in meaning, and the answer apparently does nothing to satisfy the curiosity of the questioners. The Book *Bahir* is not composed solely of texts of this kind, which seems to mock the reader, but they are not rare, and they show how far removed we are here from the usual forms of communication.

Nevertheless, and with all the novelty that this book constitutes in Hebrew literature, it is clear that the "author" intended to

---

15. *Pathaḥ qaṭan* is the oldest name of the vowel *segol.* Our passage deals with the vowels *a* and *e* in the name of the consonant *daleth.* In section 24 this vowel, *pathaḥ qaṭan,* is interpreted as indicating the south side of the world, open to good as it is to evil.

expound a mysticism of the Merkabah. He does not see any difference between the "descent" to the Merkabah and the domain toward which his speculation tends. He frequently speaks of the doctrine of the Merkabah,[16] whereas the use of the term "Kabbalah" for the doctrines that he expounds is still completely unknown to him.[17] But it is no longer the doctrine of the Merkabah as taught in the old writings, which were obviously known to him; it is a gnostic reinterpretation of that doctrine. He was familiar with the expression "to descend to the Merkabah" and sought a mystical explanation for that striking locution (section 60). In doing so, he had recourse to the new mystical symbolism of the *ennoia* of God, the *maḥshabah* that we shall discuss later. Immersion in the Merkabah without danger or error is impossible, as the Talmud already deduced from Isaiah 3:6.[18] Section 46 evinces knowledge of an interpretation of Habakkuk 3:1 as the "prayer of the prophet Habakkuk on the Merkabah," that is, on the area of study through which one cannot pass without erring, *shiggayon* (as the *'al shigyonoth* of the verse is interpreted). According to our text, this means: "everyone who frees his heart from the matters of this world and becomes immersed in the contemplation of the Merkabah is accepted by God as if he had prayed the whole day."[19] In general, our author seems to consider the prophet Habakkuk (see also sections 48 and 53) as the prototype of the Merkabah mystic. This notion must be very old, since the Tal-

16. As, above all, in sections 33, 46, 48, 60, 88, and 100. Moreover, the *realm* of the Merkabah is frequently described, notably in section 96, without the *concept* being named.

17. The work *mequbbal,* in section 46, signifies only, as in rabbinic usage, being favorably received before God. In section 134 a talmudic tradition is actually cited with *qibbalti,* "I received"; it has no mystical nuance there.

18. Cf. *Ḥagigah* 14a, *Shabbath* 120a, where the doctrine of the Merkabah is not expressly named but the context leaves no doubt about the reference. In the *Bahir* it is said in section 100: "R. Raḥmai said: what is the meaning of [Prov. 6:23]: 'and the way to life is the rebuke that disciplines'? That means that for him who occupies himself with the doctrine of the Merkabah and the doctrine of the creation, error is inevitable, as it is said [Isa. 3:6]: 'this error is in your hand,' [that is:] things which are only understood by him who has erred in them."

19. Habakkuk as a man of prayer who actually forces God to respond to his supplication is also known to aggadic literature; cf. *Midrash Tehillin,* ed. Buber, fols. 172a, 35b ff. and *B. Ta'anith* 23a, but more especially *Pereq Shirah* (see the wording in Ms. Parma 2785). Since *Pereq Shirah* is closely related to, if not an actual part of, the Hekhaloth texts, the notion of Habakkuk as a recipient of divine mysteries must have been current in certain strata of Merkabah literature.

mud already (*B. Megillah* 31a) prescribes the third chapter of Habakkuk as *haftarah* for the Feast of Weeks, alongside the Merkabah vision of Ezekiel 1. Our text also mentions the rapture of Habakkuk, who in his Merkabah prayer advanced to a "certain place" where he understood divine mysteries.[20] But apart from this, ecstasy plays hardly any role here. An ascetic tendency is occasionally noticeable, in keeping with the character of the old Merkabah.[21] He who withdraws from the world apprehends the name of God; he who wishes to possess "life" must reject the pleasures of the body (section 100)—but nowhere does the *Bahir* give specifically ascetic instructions of the kind that frequently appear in the Hekhaloth writings.

As we have already noted, there is a striking absence of unity in this book, in its literary form as well as its content. Yet, it is difficult to separate with complete certainty the different strata that are combined in the text. Nevertheless, it is possible to recognize certain passages as parts of the latest stratum or the last redaction. Thus, the interpretation of *tohu wa-bohu* in Genesis 1:2 at the beginning of the *Bahir* can definitely be said to be borrowed from the writings of the Jewish Neoplatonist Abraham bar Ḥiyya, who wrote during the third decade of the twelfth century. This scholar appears to have been the first to interpret *tohu* as matter and *bohu* as form, following an etymology that also reappears in the *Bahir*.[22] His writ-

20. The phrase employed here, *hith 'annagti li-maqom peloni,* in the sense of "I came, in rapture, as far as a certain place," is most unusual. Does it reflect a foreign usage? Inexplicable neologisms of this kind are also found elsewhere in the *Bahir*—for example, in section 37, the striking *'alpayim be-eḥad* for "two thousand times."

21. There is, however, a weighty objection against an early dating of the ascetic "Merkabah paragraphs" in the *Bahir.* The crucial words in section 46 (no earlier instances are known) correspond *literally* (as I noticed only in 1968) to the wording in Yehudah ibn Tibbon's Hebrew translation (made in 1161) of Baḥya ibn Paquda's *Book of the Duties of the Heart,* introduction to chapter 4, with the difference that the *Bahir* substitutes the vision of the Merkabah for Baḥya's *biṭṭaḥon*-inspired abandon to God. This would suggest that the *Bahir* passage was written in Provence after 1161.

22. Abraham bar Ḥiyya, *Hegyon ha-Nefesh* (Leipzig, 1860), fol. 2b commenting extensively on Genesis 1:2: "Everything that has been said about the hyle, you can also say about the [biblical] *tohu.* But they [the philosophers] said of the form that it is something that has the power to clothe the hyle with a figure and a form. And in this sense, the word *bohu* can be divided into two meanings, since, according to the sense of the language, it is composed of two words, each of which has two consonants. One is *bo* and the other *hu* . . . [and thus *bohu* means] that through which the *tohu* is endowed with existence. *Bohu* is thus the form in which *tohu* is clothed and given

ings came into the hands of the German Hasidim as early as the twelfth century, as I have shown elsewhere.[23] The author seems to have composed some of his works in Provence and hence this borrowing may just as well have taken place in Provence as in Germany. Apparently, the same author was the source of the idea (*Bahir,* section 10) that the verb *bara'* designates only that which is created from nothing, such as the hyle or darkness; by contrast, the primordial light, which possesses form, or, as the Book *Bahir* puts it, a reality *(mammash),* is connected with the verb *yaṣar.*[24] Here the *Bahir* evidently also makes use of the *Yeṣirah* 2:6.

The discussion of the vowels, as well as the statement that the "vowels of the Torah within the consonants are comparable to the soul of life in the body of man" are based upon the writings of the grammarians. It is interesting to note here that in Jewish literature outside the *Bahir* this simile appeared for the first time in Yehudah Halevi's *Kuzari* 4:3, though it ultimately goes back to the neo-

---

existence." Without explicitly referring to matter and form, this explanation reappears in section 2 of the *Bahir,* where the subject is—as in the following paragraphs —the beginning of the creation. The interpretation offered by Baeck, *Aus drei Jahrtausenden,* 273–275, who, in ignorance of the passage in Abraham bar Ḥiyya explained *tohu,* on the contrary, as form and *bohu* as matter and evil, is unacceptable. *Tohu* is explicitly defined in sections 9, 93, and 109 as the principle of evil, which is completely in accord with the Neoplatonic tendency of Abraham bar Ḥiyya's interpretation, although section 109 still (or already?) belongs to another line of thought.

23. G. Scholem, "Reste neuplatonischer Spekulation bei den deutschen Chassidim," *MGWJ* 75 (1931): 172–191.

24. The discussion concerning light and darkness that continues the reflections on *tohu* and *bohu* in sections 2 and 9 are taken almost literally from Abraham bar Ḥiyya *Megillath ha-Megalle* (Berlin, 1924), 16–17. This book was composed between 1120 and 1127 (cf. Julius Guttman's introduction, p. x). "We find," it is said there, "that Scripture employs the word 'create' for the being of things that have no form or that are of no use to the world, whereas 'form' and 'make' are used for the being of things that have a form and are of use to the inhabitants of the world. Hence it is written [Isa. 45:7]: 'I form the light and create darkness, I make weal and create woe.' For light, which has form and reality, the term employed is 'formation,' for darkness, which has neither form nor reality but which designates the absence of the form of light and its privation, it says 'creation.' " Abraham bar Ḥiyya speaks of "form and reality," *ṣurah we-ḥashashah,* whereas in his interpretation of the same verse from Isaiah, Rabbi Bun disputes the *mammash* of darkness, which is less clear since the term can signify substance as well as reality. Apart from that, there is complete agreement. Section 10 is naturally in contradiction with the passages concerning evil in the *Bahir,* as these clearly presuppose a substance or a positive being of the powers of evil. The philosophic and mystical interpretations evidently go back to different sources.

Pythagorean school and the grammarians dependent upon it. The vowels there stand for the psychic, in opposition to the hylic represented by the consonants.[25] The *Kuzari* was translated from the Arabic original only in 1167 at Lunel, in Provence. If the passage in the *Bahir* could be proved to derive from this source, it would be evidence that it belongs to the last stratum; but we cannot be certain about this. The passage occurs in connection with a statement of Rabbi Rahmai concerning the expression "twelve tribes of God" in Psalms 122:4. It follows rather abruptly on a relatively long magical text devoted to the names of God and is found in connection with the symbolism of the "source" that also appears in important passages elsewhere in the book. Starting from the conception of God as the origin of a source that irrigates everything else, the text interprets the twelve tribes in the upper world as the channels through which the water of the source is conducted. This source is perhaps the name of God, which, through the twelve channels, indicates the thirteen attributes of the divinity, deduced by Talmudic theology from Exodus 34:6. The discourse concerning the elements of language appears as the continuation of this section 82. The vowels have the form of points, therefore of circles; the consonants, on the other hand, are square, which is in the nature of the Hebrew script. And just as there is a chain of analogies: God—soul—vowel—circle, so also the corresponding members of each pair should be correlated, to wit, the primordial images of the twelve tribes—bodies—consonants—square. It is difficult to separate one series of symbolism from the other. If these symbols are themselves older, then the pair vowel-consonant which figures among them must also belong to an older tradition reaching back beyond the book *Kuzari.* In that case the continuation of the paragraph, at first sight enigmatic, can also be interpreted in a logical and consistent manner. The text says:

> And the vowel comes along the way of the "channels" to the consonants through the scent of the sacrifice, and it descends from there, as it is frequently said: the savor is a thing which descends toward God. For [the first] YHWH [of the two four-letter divine names mentioned one after another in Exod. 34:6] descends toward [the second]

25. Cf. W. von Baudissin, *Studien zur Semitischen Religionsgeschichte,* vol. 1 (Leipzig, 1876), 247–250; Franz Dornseiff, *Das Alphabet in Mystik und Magie* (Leipzig, 1925), p. 52, referring to Nicomachus of Gerasa, as well as my commentary on the *Bahir,* 87–89, 168.

> YHWH, and that is the meaning of Scripture [Deut. 6:4]: "Hear O Israel, YHWH our God, YHWH is one.'

Here, therefore, the symbolism is transferred to the magic of the sacrifice. Through the savor of the sacrifice the current of life enters from the soul, which is the source, into the attributes, which are the tribes, the consonants or the bodies. By means of a sacramental magic it is attracted toward them through the twelve channels introduced in section 82 in the form of a simile. And corresponding to this mysterious event at the hour of sacrifice, in the prayer, which mystically replaces the sacrifice, is the "unification" of the name of God in the formula of *Shema' Yisrael.*

This example should suffice to show how difficult it is to separate the various strata. Nevertheless, the attentive reader cannot avoid acknowledging the existence of such strata. Throughout, the order (or the disorder) in which the different texts are juxtaposed or connected by association shows that we are dealing with a composite work. In this regard, the first and last paragraphs of the book are typical; both serve as a frame, as it were, for the truly mystical material. Section 1, a kind of exordium, may perhaps have entered the pages from which the *Bahir* was edited via an old midrashic source; the last paragraph (141) is taken almost verbatim, with a few omissions, from *Pirqe Rabbi Eliezer,* a late, eighth-century midrash. What is missing in this passage is precisely the symbolic note that distinguishes everything that precedes it in our text. Literal borrowings of a similar length are found nowhere else in the *Bahir,* and the reasons for placing this particular passage at the end of the book remain unexplained. It tells the story of the temptation by the serpent and the Fall—without the mystical overtones we hear elsewhere—every time the subjects of paradise, evil, and the relations between the masculine and feminine element in man are mentioned.

The composite character of the book that obtrudes itself on the reader accords well with the existence of ever so many passages about which it would be absolutely impossible to explain how they could have been written as late as the twelfth century.[26] A more

---

26. On the whole, the book is organized in such a way that the texts of a cosmogonic character come at the beginning, sections 2–18; but from section 11 onward they are interwoven with language-mysticism. Considerations of this nature—consonants, vowels, accents, and divine voices—essentially predominate in sections 11–61. (Sec-

thorough and detailed analysis should, perhaps, enable us to cast some light upon the true nature of these texts. For it is the very existence of such fragments that introduces us to the real problem posed by this book. The *Bahir* cannot be compared either with any other midrashic work or with any of the kabbalistic writings that were subsequently composed. It stands, so to speak, at a crossroads. What kind of juncture is this? From where do the roads come and whither do they lead? What is the new and specific element that lends its importance to the *Bahir?*

The answer seems clear to me. This new element presents itself to analysis as two interconnected aspects of a single entity. We have here a new conception of the divinity exhibiting gnostic components that enter almost everywhere into the contexture of the work and determine its religious physiognomy. The God of the Book *Bahir* is not known to us from any other source of Jewish thought before the twelfth century. He is no longer the holy king of the Merkabah gno-

---

tions 12–23, 24–28, 29–32, 33–41, for example, constitute subdivisions that make reference to one another.) These passages display a growing interest in speculations that take up the motifs of the *Book of Creation* and develop them further. The mysticism of the *Yeṣirah* is particularly evident from sections 53 to 72 and also appears in passages that in large part treat of the magical names of God, only to return once again (up to section 83) to the mysticism of language. With section 84 there begins a series of scriptural interpretations concerning the mysteries of the sefiroth, remarkable for their strikingly symbolic character. Occasionally earlier paragraphs are specifically quoted, for example, section 78, which is referred to in section 87. Altogether, references back to earlier paragraphs are not lacking, though they do not necessarily appear as direct quotations. In section 96, this sequence leads to an explanation of the ten sefiroth as the ten logoi of God, an explanation that extends, though full of interruptions, up to section 115. In sections 107–113, a coherent text is inserted concerning Satan and the principle of evil, which, however, refers to types of symbolisms developed earlier, in sections 81–83. Perhaps the subsequent paragraphs, up to section 124, are also meant to be a continuation of what precedes them. Finally, the last paragraphs are intertwined with halakhah-mysticism, which is scattered throughout the different parts of the book and predominates from section 117 onward. In these texts the theme of the transmigration of souls is treated with particular emphasis and consistency, and correlated with various types of sefiroth-symbolism (sections 124–135). The concluding paragraphs of the book, sections 136–140, once again take up various earlier motifs; and in section 141, as we have already remarked, an artificial conclusion taken from the Midrash is tacked onto the text. From this sketch of the general outline of the work it is apparent that statements concerning the specific location of the sefiroth or attributes in the position and structure of the divine world, and especially their numerical fixation, are found mainly in the latter part of the book. The enumeration of the "list" in section 96ff. provided the redactor with some measure of support that enabled him to accommodate parallel versions, often of a contradictory character, within the firmly defined schema of the divine potencies.

sis and the writings of the Hekhaloth who sits upon his throne in the innermost rooms of the Temple of Silence and is conceived as utterly transcendent. Nor is he the distant and yet infinitely close God of the German Hasidim, the God who fills all being and penetrates everything. But neither is he the hidden One of the Neoplatonists, entirely separated from the world of multiplicity and connected with it only through the intermediary degrees of the emanations. Least of all is he the God of the Jewish rationalists of medieval philosophy. Here we are dealing with a theosophically conceived notion of God, a God who is the bearer of the cosmic potencies, the source of the internal movement in his attributes, hypostatized as aeons. This is the God who wove his powers into the cosmic tree of the worlds, from which all being proceeds and develops. Even though the language is that of the Aggadah and the forms of expression are Jewish, the God described is of the kind we know from gnostic mythology. Most of the expositions and the scriptural interpretations in the *Bahir* are, in this sense, gnostic. It is astonishing to see how far removed the ideas of this book are from the philosophic conceptions that prevailed in the Middle Ages, and particularly from Neoplatonism. The degrees of being that this school taught (from the One through the world of the nous and the soul down to nature and the lower material world), its anthropology and eschatology, in short all those doctrines that in their medieval monotheistic versions also produced such a powerful effect in the Jewish world—none of all this seems to be known by this book. There is nothing to indicate any influence of Ibn Gabirol and his metaphysic of the will. Occasional points of contact with Neoplatonic ideas merely reflect notions that were common to Gnostics and late Neoplatonists, such as the view of matter as the principle of evil, or the distinction between "a world of darkness" and "a world of light."[27] Certain Neoplatonist turns of expression such as, in section 96, "the One among all the Ones which is One in all of his names"[28] occur precisely in one of the main texts of gnostic

27. Cf. sections 109, 127.

28. *'Ahad ha-'ahadim,* which closely corresponds to an expression like the "Henade of all the Henades," in Proclus. In general, however, there is no trace of Proclean terminology in the *Bahir.* Weinstock's reference (*Be-Ma' agale,* [see ref. ch. 1, n. 66] 112) to a similar Neoplatonic usage in Joseph ibn Ṣaddiq's *'Olam Qatan,* ed. Horovitz (1903), 67—ibn Ṣaddiq's original text (twelfth century) probably had some Arabic equivalent for *'aḥad ha-'aḥadim*—is utterly misleading, as if ibn Ṣaddiq needed the *Bahir* for this phrase.

speculation on the aeons. As we have already emphasized, the spokesmen or redactors never even thought to argue their case or justify their views in the face of the ascendant Aristotelianism of the age, as one would quite naturally expect from a text of Jewish "theology" of the second half of the twelfth century. The mythical expression in many passages is so strong here that it is not at all surprising that pious readers like the aforementioned Meir ben Simon of Narbonne were horrified by the book and suspected it of heresy. We must therefore, above all, acquaint ourselves, through several examples, with the *Bahir*'s world of gnostic images.

2. Gnostic Elements in the Bahir: *Pleroma and Cosmic Tree*

The concept of the pleroma, the divine "fullness," occupies a central position in the thought of the ancient Gnostics. This concept has two shades of meaning: sometimes the "fullness" is the region of the true God himself, and sometimes it is the region to which he descends or in which the hidden God manifests himself in different figures. It is the place "where God dwells." The pleroma is a world of perfection and absolute harmony that develops out of a series of essences and divine emanations known in the history of Gnosticism by the name aeons, "eternities," supreme realities. According to the definition of Hans Jonas, gnostic knowledge of the divinity was concerned, at least at its point of departure, with the internal history of the creation of the universe as a history of the supernal world of the pleroma and as an inner-divine drama from which the lower world finally issued. The first half of this definition can certainly be applied to the range of ideas present in the *Bahir;* as regards the inner-divine drama as conceived by the Gnostics, though not absent from the book, it appears in a modified form that made it possible to safeguard the strictly monotheistic and Jewish character of the fundamental doctrines. We shall see how this could have happened when we analyze the conception of the Shekhinah in the *Bahir.* But first we must demonstrate the gnostic structure of the pleroma itself.

We saw in the previous chapter that the Merkabah mystics substituted the divine throne for the gnostic pleroma, and that the place of the aeons was taken by the apparatus of the Merkabah as described in very concrete symbols in the vision of Ezekiel or developed from it.[29] But precisely that which these mystics hoped to eliminate from their universe of discourse by means of translation or transformation into a purely Jewish terminology that would not expose itself, at that time, to "suspicion" of foreign origins now appears, to our surprise, in the fragments we have recognized as belonging to the oldest strata of the *Bahir.* The language and concepts are the same, and we look in vain for an answer to the question how this terminology could have originated or been re-created anew in the twelfth century, unless there was some filiation to hidden sources that were somehow related to the old gnostic tradition.

The curious fact should be noted here that the technical term pleroma appears, somewhat deformed but still clearly recognizable, in the exact Hebrew translation, *ha-male',* "the full" or "the fullness." Referring to Deuteronomy 33:23, section 4 very emphatically throws this "fullness" into relief as a technical term, or, if one prefers, as a symbol:

> What is the meaning of the verse [Deut. 33:23]: "And full of the Lord's blessing, take possession on the west and south." That means: In every place the letter *beth* [with which the Torah and also the word *berakhah* begin, as it was previously explained in section 3], is blessed, because it is the fullness. The verse may thus be understood: And the "fullness" is the blessing of God. And it is He who gives drink to the needy and with it counsel was taken at the very beginning.[30]

This passage is very strange. The word *ha-male'* certainly does not refer to the world of angels, for which the medieval Hebrew of the Spanish Jews used the same term, taken from an Arabic expression in the Koran.[31] Rather, it represents the highest reality, hinted

---

29. An early stage of such a development, between the book of Enoch and the Merkabah literature preserved in Hebrew, particularly the "Greater Hekhaloth," has now conclusively been demonstrated by an important discovery in the remains of the literature of the Qumran sect; cf. the two fragments published by J. Strugnell, "The Angelic Liturgy at Qumran," *Supplements to Vetus Testamentum, Congress Volume,* vol. 7 (Oxford, 1959; Leiden, 1960), 318–345.

30. An old reading, preserved by Todros Abulafia, Ms. Munich Heb. 344, has: "And out of the fullness, at the very beginning, arose the counsel." Other manuscripts read: "He took counsel [with God]." The same phrase, "With whom did he take counsel when he created the world?" is found, with reference to the Torah, in *Seder Eliyahu Rabba,* ed. Friedmann, 160.

31. Cf. David Kaufmann, *Studien über Salomon ibn Gabirol* (Budapest, 1899), 68, as well as his *Geschichte der Attributenlehre in der jüdischen Religionsphilosophie* (Gotha, 1877), 211 and 506. (There also exists a reading *ha-millo'.*)

at by the beginning of the Torah in which the fullness of God's blessing is contained. The author plays, in the same way as the oldest Kabbalists after him, upon the double meaning of the group of consonants *BRKH,* which can be read as *berakhah,* "blessing," as well as *berekhah,* "pool." From this pool, in which God's sources bubble and in which his fullness of blessing is dammed up, "he gives drink to the needy." This "fullness," which sounds like a literal translation of the Greek term, stands at the beginning of all things, and the author interprets Deuteronomy 33:23 as if it said: the blessing of God [or the pool of dammed-up waters] is the fullness, and you [Israel, to whom the blessing is promised] shall possess this aeon and the future aeon, which are compared to the south and to the sea. The imagery is further developed in sections 5 and 7. This fullness of the blessing of the *male'* at the beginning of all creation is compared to the primordial source: "A king wished to build his palace in the strong walls of a rock. He broke open the rocks and had the blocks hewn out. A great source of flowing water sprang up before him. Then the king said: since I have the water welling up,[32] I will plant a garden and take delight in it, me and the entire world." Here, as already in the interpretation of the same verse from Deuteronomy 33 in section 3, the symbolic use of *male'* for pleroma is connected with the symbolism of the Torah, which on the one hand is the infinite sea (according to Job 11:9), but on the other hand is also the highest wisdom and the source, a delight for all creatures—indeed, for God himself, as the continuation of section 4 proves with an expression taken from the ancient midrash on Proverbs 8:30. It appears as if an old gnostic terminology, transmitted through sources or contexts unknown to us had become unintelligible over the course of time and was subjected to a reinterpretation that applied it to the Torah.

This primordial fullness, in which all creatures and God himself take delight, is discussed again in section 14, where we find another image of a mythical character that likewise exhibits surprising relations with the pleroma. The fact that this image appears already thoroughly reinterpreted in the immediately following section 15 suggests that section 14 contains particularly old material, a myth

---

32. Thus according to the strange construction of the Hebrew text in section 4, "improved" in later manuscripts (as in many places where the syntax is abnormal).

that "was gently forced into a system to which it did not originally belong."[33]

At the beginning of section 14, we read in a quotation (from *Bereshith Rabba*) that the angels were not created before the second day, in order to ensure that no one could say that Michael spread out the universe in the south of the celestial vault, Gabriel in the north, and God himself measured it in the middle. To prevent such an error, God says of Himself (Isa. 44:24): "It is I, the Lord, Who made everything, Who alone stretched out the heavens and unaided [*me'itti*] spread out the earth"—who could have been with me, since the text says [who is with me] *mi'itti.*" After citing this ancient aggaddah the Book *Bahir* continues as if it were merely reproducing more fully the source of the midrash:

> It is I who have planted this "tree" that the whole world may delight in it and with it I have spanned the All, called it "All," for on it depends the All and from it emanates the All; all things need it and look upon it and yearn for it, and it is from it that all souls fly forth. I was alone when I made it and no angel can raise himelf above it and say: I was there before thee, for when I spanned my earth, when I planted and rooted this tree and caused them to take delight in each other [the tree and the earth] and myself delighted in them—who was there with me to whom I would have confided this secret?[34]

The cosmic image of this tree as the origin of the souls proves that it is impossible to interpret this passage as referring to the Torah as the tree of life. It is a cosmic tree that God planted before anything else in "his earth," this last word perhaps symbolizing, in this context, a sphere in which the tree of the worlds has its root. But in section 15 the parable of the tree is already transposed to the setting of an entire garden (in contradistinction to a single tree) in which the king wished to plant the tree, first digging for water and finding a source that could support it. "Only then did he plant the tree and it remained alive and bore fruit and its roots thrived for it

---

33. Cf. my commentary on the *Bahir,* 19, where, however, I did not yet emphasize the gnostic nature of the image.

34. Cf. following, the same phrase in the Slavonic Enoch. This passage and section 99 are the only ones where the word *sod,* "secret," which subsequently becomes ubiquitous in kabbalistic literature, occurs in the *Bahir.* This restraint in the use of the term is rather remarkable. The word is largely used in the old Merkabah literature where the term *raz* (Aramaic: *raza*), which appears nowhere in the *Bahir,* is relatively frequent. Cf. pp. 106ff. herein on the *Raza Rabba.*

was continually watered with what was drawn from the source." The source in this passage is apparently the same as in section 4, where the "fullness" of God's blessing is associated with the Torah. It may also be that here we already have a specific relation with one of the created potencies, namely the Sophia or *ḥokhmah.* However, in section 14 we are not dealing with an artificially narrowed parable in which the tree would be in need of a source, but with a gnostic image representing the pleroma. In fact, among the Valentinians, the "all, (Greek: *to pan, to holon*) is one of the most common designations for the pleroma and the realm of the aeons.[35] Indeed, a passage in the newly discovered gnostic *Gospel of Truth* reads like a parallel to our *Bahir* passage: "They found . . . the perfect Father who generated the All, in the midst of which is the All and of which the All has need," and, further on, "for what did the All need, if not the gnosis concerning the Father."[36] Similarly in the recently published *Gospel of Thomas,* Jesus says of himself: "I am the All and the All proceeds from me."[37] The idea, also to be found among the later Spanish kabbalists, that the souls proceed from this cosmic tree and actually are its fruits is already attested in the gnosis of the Simonians, which as researchers have repeatedly noted, is essentially an heretical form of Judeo-syncretist Gnosticism.[38]

A vestige of this idea of the tree of life as a cosmic tree that grows between the celestial Garden of Eden and the terrestrial paradise and on which the souls of the righteous ascend and descend as on a ladder has also been preserved in the *Midrash Konen,* which

---

35. Cf. Karl Müller, "Beiträge zum Verständnis der valentinianischen Gnosis," *Nachrichten der Gesellschaft der Wissenschaft zu Göttingen, philosophisch-historische Klasse* (1920): 179–180.

36. Cf. *Evangelium Veritatis,* ed. Malinine, Puech, Quispel, et al. (Zürich, 1956), 64–65.

37. *Evangelium nach Thomas,* ed. Guillamont, Puech, et al. (Leiden, 1959), 43 (section 77); Jean Doresse, *l'Évangile selon Thomas* (Paris, 1959), 189.

38. Hippolytos, *Elenchos* 6:9. The extensive fragment of the "Great Annunciation" that is preserved there also contains many other concepts and images that recur in the Book *Bahir,* although it is not possible for us to speak of a direct contact. Various authors have already remarked that this fragment has a fundamentally heretical Jewish character and that it ought to be seen as a gnostic midrash on the history of the creation in Genesis. The common exegetical framework explains many, though by no means all, parallels—such as, for example, the conception of the six days and the "seventh power."

reflects many ancient Merkabah and *bereshith* speculations. In the *Bahir,* this same motif is apparently utilized in later passages as well (sections 71 and 104); but the passage in section 14 goes much further, containing, as it does, the undisguised image of the tree of souls. It therefore seems clear that among the sources upon which the final redaction of the *Bahir* was based there were old fragments of a boldly mythical character.

Using the image of the planting of the cosmic tree, this text describes the creation of a primordial aeon. This aeon, it seems to me, not only contains something of the pleroma of the Gnostics but also suggests some relationship to the strange cosmogonic passages in the Slavonic *Book of Enoch* (from the first century of the Christian era) where mention is made of precisely such a primordial "great aeon." This aeon bears the inexplicable name Adoïl; the proposed etymology "aeon of God" would, in any case, be very poor Hebrew.[39] What does the Slavonic Enoch know of this great and enigmatic aeon in the two places that manifestly treat the same motif but partially contradict each other? God, enthroned alone in the primordial light[40] and passing through it, calls forth Adoïl from the depths (of nonbeing?). From his stomach is then (chap. 11) "born," as if it were different from Adoïl, "the great aeon of him who bears all creation," which should probably be read, "the great aeon that bears all creation." This aeon thus appears as a fairly close parallel to the primordial light, the *'or ganuz* of the ancient Aggadah, which preceded the rest of creation, and it is similarly associated here with the exegesis of Genesis 1:3 and the creation of the throne. The enigmatic stones that God firmly places in the abyss must also be somehow related to the equally obscure cosmogonic tra-

---

39. A. Vaillant, *Le Livre des Secrets d'Hénoch* (Paris, 1952), xi, derives it from a Hebrew term *'ado,* "his eternity, his aeon." But in Hebrew the word *'ad* has the peculiarity of not being able to carry a pronominal suffix. This does not prevent some writers from finding this kind of explanation "wholly convincing" (for example, A. Rubinstein in "Observations on the Slavonic Book of Enoch," *JJS* 16 (1962): 16. I am unable to accept Vaillant's assumption that the Slavonic Enoch was composed by a Christian author; cf. my observations in "Der Gerecht" in *Von der mystischen Gestalt der Gottheit* (Zurich, 1962) 93–94; cf. also below, n.162. It is just as difficult for me to accept the arguments of J. Daniélou, *Théologie du Judéo-Christianisme* (Paris, 1957), 25–28, 140–142, 175. Insofar as they are not based on dubious exegeses, Daniélou's proofs never refer to ideas of an unequivocally Christian character.

40. Thus in Vaillant, *Secrets d'Hénoch,* 29.

dition of an esoteric baraitha (a mishnah not universally and canonically accepted) in which the word *bohu* in *tohu wa-bohu* of Genesis 1:2 was interpreted as "muddy stones, sunk in the abyss."[41]

But in chapter 17, the same idea is expressed in a novel, more incisive formulation: prior to all creation God established an "aeon of creation," which, as indicated by what is said afterward about its division into elements of time, is the primordial time of all creation, subsequently broken up into hours and days, etc. At the redemption, this *Urzeit* ("primordial time"), the great aeon, will once again become the indivisible *Endzeit* time ("time of the end.") (In the *Bahir,* "everything yearns" for this tree, a decidedly eschatological expression.) The righteous unite themselves with this aeon and it unites itself with them—a reversible formula of the kind very much in vogue in the literature of the Merkabah but also in non-Jewish gnosis. Here we have more than the usual "bliss," in Hebrew literally "having a part in the future aeon or becoming worthy of it." It is rather a matter of an eschatological identity with the aeon of creation to which everything returns[42]—an idea that also reappears, in a different form, in the Kabbalah, where everything proceeds from the aeon *binah,* also called "the future aeon," and where everything, but above all the souls of the righteous, returns to it and reunites with it. The secret of how God formed being out of nothing and the visible out of the invisible[43]—that is, the mystery of the great aeon as a medium of all creation—was not revealed even to the angels, who did not obtain any "knowledge of this infinite and unknowable creation," exactly as in the conclusion of the passage in the *Bahir.* (The

---

41. Ibid., 31, and *Ḥagigah* 12a. The Targum, Job 28:8, also knows "the muddy stones from which darkness flows." The Hebrew word *mefullamoth* (from Greek *pēloma*) is given in its correct form also in *M. Shabbath* 22:6; see Albeck's commentary on the Mishnah *ad loc.*

42. If the aeon is related to the "tree" of the *Bahir* (and perhaps also of the Simonians), one could very well explain that the righteous "unite" with it—since their souls originally proceeded or "flew" from it. In "Der Gerechte" (ibid., p. 94), I suggested that perhaps the aeon itself was originally called *ṣaddiq,* "righteous," and that Adoïl might be a corrupt form of [S]ado[q]il, somewhat as the "righteous" is depicted in the *Bahir,* section 105, under the figure of a tree of this kind.

43. Here too we must remember the parallel between the Slavonic Enoch and the *Yeṣirah* 2:6, where it is said: "From *tohu,* he created the real and he made nonbeing into a being, and out of the invisible [or the immaterial] ether he hewed great columns." The image not only of the transition from nonbeing to being but also from the invisible to the visible recurs twice in the same sentence.

angel Gabriel is mentioned here as well as in *Bahir* section 15, though in a different context.)

This symbolism of the pleroma represented by a tree is taken up again in other texts of the *Bahir* that no doubt already constitute later developments and that refer to the world of the aeons in its entirety or to a specific aeon. Of particular importance is, in the first place, section 85, which again speaks in thoroughly mythical imagery of God's powers—not in the sense the term has in philosophic language, but in that of the gnostic (for example, the Valentinian) idiom, where the powers (Greek: *dynameis*) are the aeons that fill the pleroma. This passage is inserted into a later interpretation of *'ish,* "man," as a name of God, the letter *shin* being explained there (section 84), on account of the form it has in Hebrew (ש), as "root of the tree," which seems to be an allusion to a specific sefirah. The text continues as follows:

> And what is [this] "tree" of which you have spoken? He said to him: all powers of God are (disposed) in layers, and they are like a tree: just as the tree produces its fruit through water, so God through water increases the powers of the "tree." And what is God's water? It is the Sophia, *hokhmah,* and that [the fruit of the tree] is the soul of the righteous men who fly from the "source" to the "great canal" and it [the fruit] rises up and clings to the "tree." And by virtue of what does it flower? By virtue of Israel: when they are good and righteous, the Shekhinah dwells among them, and by their works they dwell in the bosom of God, and He lets them be fruitful and multiply."

The totality of the powers of God thus constitutes a cosmic tree that is not only the tree of souls from which the souls of the righteous fly out and to which, apparently, they return, but a tree that also depends upon the deeds of Israel—an idea taken up with still more vigor in other texts. It seems as if at this stage we already have a detailed and specific symbolism and localization of the aeons. If the source that waters the tree is the Sophia, which in all other passages is quite naturally explained as the second sefirah (and which is expressly designated as such, later, in section 96), then the root is the third sefirah, the "mother" in the language of the *Bahir,* and the tree itself obviously represents, in this case, the totality of the seven other powers that are active in the creative work of the seven days. Since they are ordered in layers, they evidently also possess a fixed structure. At first they are compared only with the tree, but in the sequel the image is employed in a more realistic manner.

The mythical cosmic tree has its roots above and grows downward, an image that is known to have numerous parallels in many different cultures.[44] It is interesting to note that some scholars claim to have found this idea among the Bogomilian heretics in the Balkans as well.[45] When Israel is good, God produces upon the tree new souls of righteous men. That is no doubt the meaning of the remark: "He makes them become fruitful and multiply." This idea accords perfectly with parallel passages. The trunk of the tree, which in section 85 grows out of the root, corresponds to the image of the spinal column in man, above all in sections 67 and 104. If Israel is good, God brings new souls out of the place of the seed, which corresponds to the great channel of section 85. The manner in which the myth of the tree is varied here (as well as in sections 104 and 121) corresponds to the interpretation given by section 15 to its oldest form, as we encounter it in section 14.

It is difficult to say when the oldest material was reinterpreted in this manner. The symbolism of the tree underwent a further development in the latest stratum of the *Bahir,* as is evident from sections 64–67, which, despite all their differences, are closely related.[46] The cosmic tree of section 14 is no longer the pleroma of the divine powers as in section 85; but it is implanted as in the beginning, in the center of the universe as its core. To the structure of this core correspond, in the regions of the cosmos that are here taken over from the *Book of Creation,* lower potencies, "overseers," and "archons" *(sarim).* Section 64 refers directly back to *Yeṣirah* 5:1 and its twelve directions of the world, which, however, the author of the *Bahir* arranges in his own mythical fashion: "God has a tree, and this tree has twelve radii:[47] northeast, southeast, upper east, lower

44. Cf. Ad. Jacoby, "Der Baum mit den Wurzeln nach oben und den Zweigen nach unten," *ZMRW* 43 (1928): 78–85.

45. I am indebted for this information to a private communication from Professor Otto Maenchen-Helfen, University of California, dated 1 July 1952.

46. Cf. my commentary on the *Bahir,* 67.

47. In Hebrew *gebhuley 'alakhson,* understood here as radii and branches of the cosmic tree, in their relationship with the root of the twelve tribes of Israel. The twelve radii may well be identical with the constellations of the zodiac. The astral-mysticism of late antiquity has many examples of the zodiac as a cosmic tree with twelve branches; see S. Agrell, *Spätantike Alphabetmystik* (Lund, 1932), 14, and *Die pergamenische Zauberscheibe* (Lund, 1936), 40. The "arms of the cosmos" are the branches of the cosmic tree, and the souls of the righteous are the thirty-six spirits of

east, northwest, southwest, upper west, lower west, upper north, lower north, upper south, lower south, and they extend outward into the immeasurable, and they are the arms of the world. And in their core is the tree." To these branches of the tree correspond, in the three regions of the world of the Book *Yeṣirah,* namely the "dragon" *teli,*[48] representing the world; the visible celestial sphere, representing time; and the "heart," representing the human organism—twelve "overseers" each and twelve archons each, thus totaling two times thirty-six potencies or powers that are active in the cosmos and always return to each other:

> The potency of one is [also] in the other, and although there are twelve in each of the three they all adhere to each other [this is taken literally from *Yeṣirah* 4:3] and all thirty-six potencies are already found in the first, which is the *teli* . . . and they all return cyclically one into the other, and the potency of each one is found in the other . . . and they are all perfected [or comprised] in the "heart."

Very possibly the thirty-six decans of astrology and their supervisors are lurking behind the thirty-six potencies of the *Bahir.*[49] In the *Bahir,* the two times thirty-six overseers and archons combine with the seventy-two names of God, which Jewish esoteric doctrine had already developed in the talmudic period and which the

---

the dekans or gods. The cosmic tree itself would then be the axis *mundi.* All this would suggest an ancient date for this *Bahir* paragraph.

48. *Teli,* considered in the early Middle Ages as the constellation of the dragon (Syriac: *'athalia*), "stella quae solem tegens eclipsim efficit," according to the dictionary of Payne-Smith 1:423. In this sense the term already occurs in the *Manichaean Book of Psalms,* ed. Allberry, fasc. 2, p. 196. This terminology corresponds exactly to that of the *Baraitha of Samuel,* an astronomical treatise of incontestable antiquity, and goes back to the Assyrian *atalû,* as has been shown by A. E. Harkavy in *Ben 'Ammi,* vol. 1 (1887), 27–35. The *teli,* "celestial serpent" or dragon, causes eclipses by moving its head and tail.

49. Zofia Ameisenowa was apparently the first to have seen this, cf. *Journal of the Warburg and Courtauld Institutes* 12 (London, 1949): 33. The thirty-six regents are the thirty-six dekans that Ameisenowa, following Gundel (*Dekane und Dekansternbilder,* [1936]), associates with the thirty-six righteous of rabbinic lore; cf. also the passage in *Pistis Sophia* (quoted by Gundel and thence by Ameisenowa), which declares that human spirits can be transformed into dekan-gods, namely, spirits. If the two sets of ideas are really related, then the amoraic teacher Abbaye (to whom *B. Sanhedrin* 97b attributes the statement concerning the thirty-six righteous) may well have been familiar with doctrines regarding the dekan spirits.

Bahir frequently discusses beginning with section 63 (above all in sections 76–79).

Section 64 leaves the impression of being a very old text that has as yet had no direct contact with the mystical symbolism developed in most parts of the *Bahir.* The "heart" is still mentioned in the old sense of ruler of the human organism (as in the Book *Yeṣirah*), and not as a mystical symbol. But in section 67, which takes up and continues the ideas and especially the terminology of section 64, we are suddenly confronted with mystical symbols, although no doubt we should assume a lacuna between these paragraphs. The heart is nourished by the seventy-two overseers and archons and nourishes them in return. At the same time, however, it is interpreted as a symbolic term, signifying a sphere named "heart" in which are contained "the thirty-two wondrous paths of the Sophia," corresponding to the numerical value of the Hebrew word *lebh,* heart. Here we are right in the middle of kabbalistic symbolism, to which we shall have to return.

The symbolism of the heart of the cosmos exhibits a close parallelism with the well-known idea developed quite independently by Yehudah Halevi in his *Kuzari* 2:36–44. According to Halevi, all nations constitute an organism of which Israel is the heart, and hence must fulfill special duties and functions throughout the course of history. It seems that at the time of the final redaction of the *Bahir* in Provence, the *Kuzari,* which had been translated there into Hebrew in 1167, was already available to the redactors; this image apparently so appealed to them that they combined it with their gnostic symbolism. The concept of the totality of the historical process becomes one of the theosophic interconnection of the cosmos. Israel is the trunk or the heart of the tree of which the individual souls are the fruits. However, the metaphor is somewhat blurred, since the heart and the fruit are confounded with one another. The heart is explained as the "precious fruit of the body," which is then associated with the ritual symbolism of the bouquet of the Feast of Tabernacles, when Israel "takes the product of goodly trees" (Lev. 23:40). The parallelism between the trunk of the tree[50] and the spi-

---

50. The original reading may have been *guf ha-'ilan,* although the version *nof ha-'ilan* is found in the oldest witnesses for our text. The latter reading renders meaningless the images of section 67 and the parallel between Israel and the trunk of the tree.

nal column of man, the most essential part of the body, is central to this symbolism. The aforementioned seventy-two powers now appear as the archons and "holy forms" placed over every people, while the "holy Israel"[51] occupies the place of the trunk of the tree and its heart. The peoples are clearly the secondary branches which issue from the twelve main branches, the latter being related in some way to the twelve tribes of Israel. This looks very much like the application of Yehudah Halevi's idea to an older representation of the cosmic tree and its trunk, now combined with the originally distinct and totally unrelated notion of the heart derived from the *Book of Creation.* Here the archons of the peoples are still "holy forms," that is, angels, in perfect conformity with Jewish tradition.[52] Such forms also reside as guardians of the road that leads to the tree of life upon the thirty-two wondrous paths of the Sophia, which are themselves situated above the world of the angels, but are protected and guarded by them. This relation between the holy forms and the symbolism of the tree recurs later in an important passage in section 78. Sacrifice, in Hebrew *qorban,* is interpreted as "bringing near" in accordance with the meaning of the Hebrew root,[53] "because it brings the holy forms so near to one another that they become [thus the author's understanding of Ezekiel 37:17] *a single tree.* The tree is thus regarded as the realm of God's potencies, a sphere that extends beneath God, who is conceived as definitely personal and independent of the potencies. It results from this analysis that the symbolism of the tree developed differently in the various strata of the *Bahir.*

This symbolism of the tree stresses an element that was to become essential in the kabbalistic doctrine of the mystical vocation of the Jew. The tree is not only kept alive and watered by the source; its flowering, growth, and prosperity, its vigor or, alternatively, its languor depend upon the deeds of Israel. The special emphasis

---

51. A talmudic expression, for example *Ḥullin* 7b; as well as in *Seder Eliyahu Rabba,* ed. Friedmann, 71.

52. This would provide a remarkable analogy to the seventy-two forms *(morphē)* at the Merkabah (a notion undoubtedly derived from *Jewish* tradition) mentioned in the gnostic (Coptic) text, "On the Origin of the World," generally known as the "Tract Without Title." See the German translation of that text by H-M Schenke in *Theolog. Literatur Zeitung* 84 (1959): esp. 33.

53. Thus Flavius Mithridates, the first translator of kabbalistic texts into Latin, correctly rendered *qorban* for Pico della Mirandola as *appropinquatio.*

placed upon this explanation of the cosmic relevance of the deeds of Israel as well as the dialectic that such a representation implies for the "purity" of the concept of God are thrown into relief already in these texts, only to be expressed with even greater intensity in the writings of the later kabbalists. Between the Creator God and man there is an intermediate zone that does not simply belong to the creaturely side, but its relationship to the God who, after all, "planted" this tree is not precisely defined. In symbols and images whose meaning remains imprecise, a thought is formulated here that is not completely absent from old aggadic literature, to wit the somewhat dubious theological notion that "the righteous increase the power of the Omnipotence [*geburah,* the divine dynamis]."[54] What is new in the kabbalistic sources is the mythical imagery with which this influence is presented: the influence of the "holy Israel" on the higher spheres is exercised by the performance of rituals, the elements of which stand in a mystical relation to the aeons or the sefiroth in the tree of divine potencies. This is plainly the reason for the different ritual symbolisms advanced in the *Bahir,* as well as for its explanations of specific precepts of the Torah.

The notion of an "influx from above, and an influx from below," as the Spanish Kabbalah, especially the *Zohar,* later expressed it, can thus be found already in the *Bahir.* The influx from above is always presented here, as far as I can see, in connection with the symbolism of the Sophia as the source of the cosmic tree. Many passages dealing with the symbolism of the source—characteristically, almost exclusively in parables—can without difficulty be associated with the Sophia.[55] Only in the last third of the book is the symbolism of the source, which is the Sophia, applied to the "channel" through which the water of this source is conducted toward other spheres. The channel clearly has to be understood as a later aeon in the structure of these potencies that stands in a particular relation with the Sophia.[56]

54. *Midrash 'Ekha Rabbathi,* ed. Buber, 70, and the parallels cited there.

55. Cf. sections 3, 4, where the relation between the Sophia of Psalms 111:10 and the source is explicitly established at the end of the second parable, as well as sections 84, 85.

56. Thus in sections 105, 121, 125.

3. Other Gnostic Elements: The Potencies of God— Middoth*—Gnostic Reinterpretations of Talmudic Sayings—The Double Sophia and the Symbolism of the Sophia as Daughter and Bride*

It is upon these powers, separately or in concert, that the Book *Bahir* principally concentrates. The greater part of the book is engaged in discovering references to these "powers of God"—which we have every reason to identify with the aeons in the pleroma—in biblical verses as well as other symbolic expressions, including the concepts of the Bible, the mysticism of language, and the ideas of the Aggadah, together constituting a virtually inexhaustible reservoir of symbols for that purpose. Here, too, the symbols and notions of the ancient Gnostics frequently reappear, either because of actual historical connections or as the result of analogous methods of exegesis, though, no doubt, such exegesis must have received some kind of impetus from the transmitted material, even if it subsequently went its own way. Moreover, a large part of the book consists of mystical variations on motifs from the Book *Yeṣirah.* In fact, the term sefiroth was taken by the *Bahir* from that work, though it is no longer understood in the sense of ideal numbers that contain within them all the powers of creation, as was the case with the author of the *Yeṣirah.* The sefiroth now signify the aeons, the powers of God, which are also his attributes. The term sefiroth, however, does not occupy an important place in the *Bahir.* It appears only in section 87, where the ten fingers raised in the benediction of the priests are found to be "an allusion to the ten sefiroth by means of which heaven and earth are sealed." In the Book *Yeṣirah* itself, only six of the sefiroth perform this function, and in this particular instance the term is evidently identified with a different conception. This is also indicated by the book's new explanation of the meaning of the term sefiroth. The word is not derived from *safar,* to count, but from *sappir,* sapphire. They are thus sapphirine reflections of the divinity, and Psalm 19:2: "The heavens declare the glory of God," is interpreted by the author in accordance with this etymology: "the heavens shine in the sapphirine splendor of the glory of God." This mystical etymology subsequently became classic in kabbalistic literature. In view of the fragmentary condition of the book, it may not be possible to infer very much from the fact that the term sefiroth is missing in other parts of the text. It nevertheless remains surprising that the notion of the sefiroth was, so to speak, eliminated from just those passages that are very clearly based upon the *Book of Creation,* but appears as something known and self-evident in precisely a passage that otherwise has no connection with the motifs of the Book *Yeṣirah.*

Instead, these aeons, if we may speak of them as such, are described in completely different terms. These names reflect the fullness of meaning and "multivalence" of the aeons in gnostic mythology. They are, as we have seen, the powers of God. But they are also the ten words of creation, *ma'amaroth* (henceforth rendered as logoi), by means of which, according to a celebrated passage of the Mishnah (*'Aboth* 5:1), everything was created. They are the different qualities and attributes (Hebrew: *middoth*) that belong to God. Each *middah* is a particular spiritual potency. This manner of speaking, which renders the *middoth* autonomous and hypostatizes them, is already found in the ancient Aggadah. We occasionally encounter words there that almost seem like Jewish prefigurations of, or parallels to, the gnostic terminology regarding the aeons. "Seven *middoth* serve [perform a definite function] before the throne of Glory; they are: Wisdom, Justice and the Law, Grace and Mercy, Truth and Peace."[57] The Babylonian amora Rab (around 230), an avowed adept of Jewish esotericism and the Merkabah gnosis, said: "By ten things was the world created: by wisdom and by understanding, and by reason and by strength [*geburah,* a synonym for power], by rebuke and by might, by righteousness and by judgment, by loving kindness and by compassion" (*Ḥagigah* 12a). These abstract names read like the enumerations, in some gnostic texts, of the aeons in the pleroma. However, in the *Bahir,* abstractions of this kind do not occur incidentally as in the above citations; they appear at the very center of its speculations as more or less definite designations of particular *middoth,* and as occupying, apparently, a fixed place in the structure of these aeons or *middoth.* Here and there, as we shall see, this place may still be uncertain, but it is beyond doubt

57. *'Aboth de Rabbi Nathan,* first recension, ed. Schechter, 110. The end of this passage is particularly curious. It is said there that "this teaches that every man who has these qualities as *middoth,* obtains the knowledge of God"; but it could also be literally translated: "He knows the gnosis of God [*da'atho shel maqom*]." The phrase phosphoresces in two colors, one purely moral and the other gnostic, depending on the aeons that are named after these qualities.

that the redactors of the book already had in mind a definite structure, as is also presupposed in the image of the tree of divine powers in section 85. These powers also appear as "beautiful vessels" or "treasures"—once again, well-known gnostic metaphors occurring frequently in the description of the upper worlds and the pleroma.[58] The later Coptic-gnostic texts of the *Pistis Sophia* type as well as Mandaean literature abound with references to such "treasures" or "treasure houses." The six days of the creation of the world, which the *Bahir* designates in section 92 as primordial days, *yeme qedem,* are aeons of this kind, of which the book says: "God made six beautiful vessels." This "precious vessel," *vas pretiosum* (also in section 52; see following) is well known to us from the Valentinian gnosis.[59]

It is not easy to specify when and where the word *middah* was utilized in the sense presupposed here. Its use is not restricted to the ancient Aggadah. The renowned commentator Rashi, who was certainly not a kabbalist, also employed the term in the sense of spiritual potency or hypostasis.[60] In the Book *Yeṣirah* itself, the sefiroth are not designated as *middoth,* although it is said of the totality of these ten numbers that "their measure, *middah,* is ten, but they have no end" (1:5), which there still simply refers to the decade by means of which all numbers can be expressed. In a text that already had circulated among the German Hasidim before the year 1200 and whose age has not yet been established, the so-called *Mishnah of Yosef ben Uziel,* the ten sefiroth are designated as ten *middoth* and ten principles, *shorashim.*[61] In other respects, however, this pseudepigraphic Merkabah text has hardly anything in common with the symbolism and the world of ideas peculiar to the *Bahir,* and precisely those gnostic elements to which we have called attention are entirely absent there. In other medieval texts, on the other hand, the "powers of God" are spoken of with much the same gnostic nuance that the term has in the *Bahir.* For example, Tobias ben Eliezer, writing in Byzantium around 1100, refers directly to the liter-

58. On the aeons as treasures or treasure houses in the *Bahir,* see sections 96, 97, 126, 129.

59. Cf. R. Reitzenstein, *Das mandäische Buch des Herrn der Grösse* (Heidelberg, 1919), 87.

60. For example in his commentary on *Sotah* 33a, in the sense of a created potency, conceived as personal.

61. The text was printed by Abraham Epstein in *Ha-Ḥoqer,* vol. 2 (Vienna, 1894), 43.

ature of the Merkabah and the *Shi'ur Qomah* and warns against characterizing the essence of God with anthropomorphisms that can only be predicated on the "powers and *dynameis* of the creator of the universe."[62] This conforms precisely to the usage adopted in the *Bahir,* where the formulations of Merkabah mysticism are understood in this manner.

To these notions and images, well known from gnostic tradition, the book adds new designations for these essences. These powers are also the ten "kings" (sections 19, 32, 49), the seven "voices" heard during the revelation at Sinai (sections 29–32), and the "crowns" (sections 23, 101) borne by the king. This image enables us to understand the designation of the highest of all aeons as the "supreme crown," *kether 'elyon* (sections 89, 96). This designation is particularly noteworthy and occurs with great frequency later, in early kabbalistic literature. It appears that this image of the crowns established some sort of connection between the new ideas and the conception of God in the Hekhaloth writings. Was not God there, above all, the holy king enthroned upon the Merkabah? The authors of the *Bahir* refer back to this motif when they speak of God's attributes and powers as the various crowns he bears. But we would commit a grave error were we to draw from these epithets alone theoretical conclusions with respect to the relationship between these powers and the divinity. Alongside sayings that appear to presuppose a clearly personalistic conception of this God and a distinction between him and those kings, treasures, voices, words, etc., we find others in which this relationship remains vague. In particular, the relationship between the divinity and the first of these powers is by no means unequivocally clear. One may wonder whether in certain parts of the book the first sefirah itself might not be the divinity, above which stands no other bearer, creator, or emanator. In these texts everything is still in flux, and the powerful imagery has not yet crystallized into clear concepts. Indeed, it must not be forgotten that at this stage the lord or bearer of the sefiroth is hardly spoken of except in metaphors. These metaphors appear to identify the bearer of these powers as their first source or origin, with one or another of the essences included in this interrelation of potencies; they do not, however, permit us to draw precise conclusions as re-

62. Tobias ben Eliezer, *Leqaḥ Tob* on Deuteronomy 4:12, ed. Buber, p. 14.

gards the "theology" of the metaphors. The main concern of the book lies with the aeons and the mystical symbolism related to them. In the numerous passages where the book speaks in a general way of "God," its language remains rather vague; it may just as well mean the lord of the aeons as the being represented in all or in one of them. Nevertheless, many sayings not only distinguish clearly between the Sophia and its origin in God or in the *ennoia,* the thought of God that is above it, but in section 53 the expression "God's thought" presupposes that a separation exists between them and that the "thought" itself is not the higher of the two. Nowhere, however, does the symbolism of the book lead us beyond this sphere of "thought," a subject to which we shall return in the sequel.

The decisive step beyond the other gnostic systems consists in the fixing of the number of these powers or aeons at ten, according to the ten sefiroth of the *Book of Creation* and the ten words of creation through which, according to the ancient Aggadah, God called the world into existence. Once the number of these "qualities" or *middoth* of God was fixed they came to be associated with a large number of symbolic names, since each of the epithets by which God could be presented or named was necessarily related to one or another of the *middoth.* In the *Bahir* we can still recognize quite clearly the efforts that were made to introduce a more or less consistent terminology in the use of these symbols in relation to specific sefiroth, though it took some time until this process of the definitive crystallization of the symbolism of the old Kabbalah came to its final conclusion. The different attempts often contradict one another. While the commentators of the Kabbalah strove to bring the symbols into accord or to unify them, the historian naturally has no interest in a harmonistic exegesis of this kind. We shall see several examples that suggest conflicting traditions that were simply juxtaposed in the *Bahir.* Here, too, the choice of symbols and appellations for this or that sefirah duplicates the process by which the Gnostics designated their aeons. They liked to adopt as names of aeons abstract terms such as thought, wisdom, penitence, truth, grace, greatness, silence, or images such as father, mother, abyss, etc. These designations, some of which are identical with those found in the ancient documents while others were newly created in accordance with the methods of gnostic exegesis, fill the pages of the *Bahir.* There, however, they are derived from biblical verses or even the aggadic dicta of the rabbis.

Once again the question is posed: should we admit, at least for one of the strata of the book, the existence of vestiges of an ancient Jewish gnosis, of fragments that antedate the Middle Ages and in which anonymous Jewish Gnostics sought to express their mystical conception of the divinity without impairing their Jewish monotheism? Or are we dealing with attempts by medieval men, who felt themselves newly stimulated for one reason or another, to view traditions that were intrinsically and purely Jewish from a gnostic perspective? Is our material essentially nothing but the well-known and straightforward Jewish tradition, the adaptation and transformation of which into symbols proves just how great was the psychological and temporal distance between these later authors and the period when the aggadic sayings originally crystallized? This is the fundamental question that imposes itself upon the reader of the *Bahir.* It is a question that cannot be answered on the basis of general considerations; only a careful examination of the details can help us here. I do not hesitate, for my part, to affirm that the literature of the Spanish Kabbalah, especially that imbedded in the *Zohar,* clearly reveals a psychological attitude that, in the Middle Ages, led men to recast ancient talmudic and midrashic material according to an entirely new spirit by means of an exegetical and homiletical method that in its structure was gnostic, but that reached its full development only under the influence of the *Bahir.*

But what about the oldest text, the Book *Bahir* itself? Here, too, many passages show that we are dealing with a later exegesis, which reinterprets, on the basis of a medieval mentality, older material that had already become authoritative and confers upon it a symbolic character. Assuredly, biblical verses could already be interpreted in the talmudic era as symbolic of events taking place on a higher plane of being. The psychological distance between the gnostic exegetes, Jewish or not, and the biblical canon is evident. The elaboration of pagan mythology in terms of gnostic exegesis, as, for example, in the "Naassene sermon" preserved by Hippolytus, indicates a similar psychological distance between ancient myth and its new interpretation.[63] The *Bahir* already presents this type of interpretation of the talmudic Aggadah. This can be seen not only in the many passages in which parables drawn from aggadic literature in

63. On the Naassene sermon, cf. R. Reitzenstein, *Poimandres* (Leipzig, 1904), 83–101, as well as *Studien zum antiken Synkretismus* (Leipzig, 1926), 104–111, 161–173; H. Leisengang, *Die Gnosis* (Leipzig, 1924), 112–139.

the Talmud and the Midrash, where they have a perfectly exoteric significance, are transposed to a mystical plane, the new parable often becoming, in the process, much more strange and problematic than the one upon which it is based;[64] we can observe it above all when talmudic quotations themselves are treated as old materials of this kind.

Only during a period when, for the pious consciousness of broad sections of the Jewish population, the Aggadah itself could already claim the authority of a sacred text, and at a time when for other circles its very extravagance became a problem—from the eighth century onward, after the emergence of Karaism—is a passage like section 52 of the *Bahir* possible. The Talmud, *Baba Bathra* 16b, transmits various opinions with regard to the value of the birth of daughters. In this connection, a discussion is reported between mishnaic teachers (second century) concerning Genesis 24:1: "And the Lord had blessed Abraham in all things." "What is meant by 'in all things?' R. Meir explained: it means that he had no daughter. R. Yehudah said: Abraham had a daughter whose name was *Bakol* [literally: with all things]." The *Bahir* made this last remark the object of a mystical exegesis, which elevated the strange statement concerning the daughter *Bakol* to an allegorical plane. *Bakol* thus becomes a designation for the Shekhinah, the last of the divine powers, which is mentioned at the end of section 51 and to the symbolism of which I shall return. Abraham is there designated as the father of this Shekhinah. Section 52 then continues:

> And whence did Abraham have a daughter? [we learn that] from the verse [Gen. 24:1] the Lord had blessed Abraham with "all things" and [Scripture also] says [Isa. 43:7] "every one" will be called by my Name, etc. Was this "blessing" his daughter or not? [another version: Or was it rather his mother?][65] Yes, she was his daughter. It is like a king who had a perfect servant . . . Then the king said: What should I

64. Parables of this kind, which are in fact kabbalistic revisions of midrashic parables, are found for example in section 4 (closely related to *Shemoth Rabba, parashah* 20); section 5 on Song of Songs 4:13; section 7 (from *Shemoth Rabba,* the end of *Parashah* 15); section 12 (from *Midrash Tehillim* on Psalms 27:1); section 23 (from *'Ekha Rabbathi* 2:1); section 25 (from another parable in the same text); section 36 (from *Shir ha-Shirim Rabba* 3:9); section 43 (from *Wayyiqra Rabba, parashah* 37, section 10); section 86 (from *Shabbath* 152b); section 89 (from *Sifre* on Deuteronomy, ed. Finkelstein, 83); section 101 (as in section 25).

65. This reading would be quite consistent with the quotation from the Midrash in section 43: "Sometimes, he calls her 'my sister' and sometimes he calls her 'my daughter,' and sometimes he calls her 'my mother.' "

> give to this servant or what should I do for him? There is nothing left for me to do but to recommend him to my brother, so that he may counsel, protect, and honor him. The servant went home with the king's great brother and learned his ways. The brother grew very fond of him and called him his friend, as it is said [Isa. 41:8]: Abraham, my friend. He said: What shall I give him or what shall I do for him? Lo, I have made a beautiful vessel, and inside it are beautiful gems to which none can be compared, and they are the jewels of kings. I shall give them to him, and he may partake of them instead of me. That is what is written: God blessed Abraham with "all things."

This passage not only presupposes a developed symbolism of the Shekhinah as a "beautiful vessel" in which all the powers of God or the "great brother" are contained, but it already interprets in an allegorical sense the talmudic Aggadah itself, which is its antecedent. This procedure with regard to the more bizarre passages of the Talmud is, however, thoroughly medieval, and indicative of a great distance from the sources of the aggadic production. There is no instance in early aggadic literature of the reinterpretation in terms of mysteries of entirely straightforward sayings of the aggadists. In the Middle Ages, on the other hand, this was customary procedure: the philosophers finding in such texts esoteric allusions to their own opinions, the mystics making use of them for their own purposes. We also have reinterpretations of this kind—influenced by mystical ideas—in aggadic collections of oriental origins from a later period. Thus, the talmudic sentence discussed here is mystically reinterpreted in a very late Yemenite collection of midrashim. This reinterpretation is not very far removed from the tendency of the *Bahir.* The pseudepigraphic disguise that lends it the appearance of an ancient teaching cannot deceive us concerning the true character of this dictum. "The rabbis have taught: *Kol,* Abraham's daughter, is not dead. She still exists, and whoever sees her has made a great find, as it is said [Prov. 8:17]: and those who seek me will find me."[66] By means of this verse from Proverbs, the daughter is clearly identified as the *ḥokhmah* or Sophia, which would be in accord with the symbolism of the Shekhinah in the *Bahir,* itself related to the mysticism of the Sophia (see following).

It is quite possible that the author of this dictum, preserved only in the Yemenite midrash, knew of an interpretation similar to the one that we read in the *Bahir,* and which must therefore already

66. Cf. the text in D. S. Sassoon, "Alte Aggadoth aus Jemen," *Jahrbuch der jüdisch-literarischen Gesellschaft,* vol. 16 (Frankfurt-am-Main, 1924), Heb. part, 9.

have been known in the Orient. But it is just as possible that he produced a similar interpretation quite independently stimulated by the desire to allegorize a strange phrase. The tradition of the German Hasidim, around 1250, also shows familiarity with older materials that dealt with the interpretation of the *Bakol* of Genesis 24:1, though in a direction somewhat different from that taken in the *Bahir.* In connection with this same verse, Ephraim ben Shimshon (ca. 1240) cited a dictum of the adepts of esotericism, *ba 'ale ha-sod,* according to which this blessing consisted in God's charge to the "Prince of the Divine Presence" to grant Abraham's every wish.[67] The role of the Shekhinah in the Book *Bahir* is here assumed by the angel Yahoel, the oldest name of Metatron, prince of the angels, whose relation to the patriarch is not only known from the Apocalypse of Abraham (early second century C.E.), but was also familiar to the German Hasidim of the twelfth century.[68] However, the particular exegesis relating the word *Bakol* to Yahoel probably originated in Germany, for it is based on the gematria method of interpretation practiced there at that time.[69] Whether there is a relation between the *Bahir*'s reference to the Shekhinah and the idea of the universal presence of the Shekhinah as current at the time particularly among the German Hasidim I would not venture to decide. Such a connection, if it exists, would rest upon a punning interpretation of the Talmud: "The Shekhinah is in every place" (*Baba Bathra* 25a). By abridging this phrase to *shekhinah bakol,* "the Shekhinah is in all things," an association is suggested with the *bakol* in Genesis 24:1: the Shekhinah is *Bakol.*

Another example of such a reinterpretation can be found in section 126. The Talmud relates a dictum of the Babylonian amora R. Assi: "The son of David will not come until all the souls in the 'body' are exhausted" (*Yebamoth* 62a, 63b). Here "body" means the storehouse of the preexistent, unborn souls. This traditional interpretation was evidently also known to the *Bahir.*[70] But there this dic-

---

67. Ms. Munich Heb. 15, on Genesis 24:1. The passage is also printed in the brief version of this commentary, of which a fairly large extract appeared, without title page, as *Commentary on the Torah by Rabbenu Ephraim* (Smyrna, ca. 1850), fol. 15a.

68. Cf. *Major Trends,* 69.

69. The word בכל has the same numerical value as the name of the angel יהואל.

70. The beginning of section 126 says: "In his power is the treasure house of the souls."

tum is further interpreted as a cue for the doctrine of the transmigration of souls: the "body" mentioned there would be the body of man, through which the souls must wander. The dictum itself is quoted according to the formula used by the medieval authors for introducing a citation from the Talmud without naming the author: "And this is what we say." The personal view of an individual talmudic master has already become authoritative to the point where it permits reinterpretation in terms of a notion of which talmudic tradition itself has no knowledge. To this corresponds, in section 86, the reinterpretation, or rather the revision, of a talmudic parable (*Shabbath* 152b), which is similarly interpreted in terms of the doctrine of the transmigration of souls with utter disregard of its original meaning.[71]

We may conclude from the preceding that a considerable portion of the material in the *Bahir* presupposes an attitude with regard to the sources that is not conceivable until the early Middle Ages. Nevertheless, the details do not permit us to exclude the possibility of the existence of a much older stratum. In fact, they occasionally seem to force this hypothesis upon us. In that case it is not too much to assume that the gnostic material of Oriental origin in the Book *Bahir,* once it was received and adopted by a circle of religiously agitated and productive men, amply suffices to explain the inner development of the Kabbalah up to, and including, the *Zohar.* But how are we to understand the development that led to that ferment, the evidence of which we have before us in the Book *Bahir* itself? On this point we are forced to assume the existence of some kind of connection, whether in literary or oral form, with older, premedieval materials.

Certain details, as far as I can see, can have no other explanation and above all cannot be attributed to fortuitous coincidences. They prove that the gnostic symbolisms that occupied a meaningful and comprehensible position within their own framework—as for example in the system of the Valentinian gnosis—found their way into Jewish sources, largely detaching themselves, of course, from their organic connection with gnostic mythology. Today we can no longer (or not yet?) say anything about the nature of these sources, or whether, perhaps, there once existed entire systems of a Jewish

---

71. An ancient critic of the Catalan kabbalist Shesheth des Mercadell (around 1270) already recognized the relation between these two passages; cf. *Tarbiz* 16 (1945): 148. Hence my remark in my commentary on the *Bahir,* 159, is to be corrected accordingly.

character parallel to the classic systems of Gnosticism or to the later gnostic ramifications of the kind that survived in the Aramaic-Syrian linguistic area, such as, for example, the Mandaean gnosis. Only obscure traces of these sources, not a system but merely fragments of symbols, seem to have come into the hands of the redactors of the *Bahir.* Nevertheless, their attraction was still strong enough to stimulate the combination of old material with new associations of ideas and, thus, to give it a new content.

A surprising detail of this kind is the doctrine of the double Sophia or *ḥokhmah* that among the first kabbalists and as early as the Book *Bahir,* served as a model for similar symbols occupying a double position within the framework of the divine world, the pleroma. Thus we have a double "Fear of God" (sections 97, 129, 131), a double "Justice" (*ṣedeq,* sections 50, 133), a double *he* in the Tetragrammaton *YHWH* (section 20), and also, without a doubt, a double Shekhinah (section 11). The region and position of these power symbols ("the lower *he;* the lower Justice") are always, in this case, close to the margin and termination of the world of the aeons, and are connected with the symbolism of the Shekhinah. But these expositions in the *Bahir* are most precise in just those instances where they are related to the double *ḥokhmah.* That should give us cause for thought. The Gnostics, especially those of the Valentinian school, developed the idea of two aeons that are both called Sophia. One, the "upper Sophia," is high above, in the world of the pleroma; the other, however, which is also related to the symbolism of the "virgin of light," is found at its lower end. The gnostic myth of the cosmic drama told of the fall of the lower Sophia, which succumbed to the temptation of the hyle and fell from the pleroma into the lower worlds, where it is either wholly, or at least in certain parts of its luminous being, "in exile." Even so, this lower, fallen Sophia remains related to the pneuma, the highest constitutive part of the human soul, the contact between these two entities being described by means of different symbols in different systems. This divine spark in man is connected with the drama of the exile of the "lower Sophia."[72] It is precisely in the corresponding levels of the

72. Cf. for example Ferdinand Christian Baur, *Die christliche Gnosis* (Tübingen, 1835), 124–158; the Valentinian symbols of the lower Sophia are enumerated there on page 145. They correspond rather closely to the symbols that the Kabbalah later attributed to the last sefirah; F. Sagnard, *La Gnose Valentinienne* (Paris, 1947), 148–176.

structure of the divine *middoth* that we find, in different passages of the *Bahir,* the two hypostases or aeons named *ḥokhmah,* as the second and the tenth sefirah. Wisdom simply is, in section 96 for example, the upper Wisdom, the "beginning of the paths of God" in the midst of creation. When God placed this Wisdom in the heart of Solomon he adapted the upper Wisdom to the form of the lower Wisdom, which he was able to grasp. In the form of the lower Wisdom, which is the "daughter" whom God, as it were, gave in marriage to Solomon, "the thirty-two paths of the Sophia," all the powers and ways of the pleroma are united (sections 43, 62, 67).

But while the Kabbalah, after the *Bahir,* always distinguished between the upper Sophia, "the wisdom of God," and the lower Sophia, "the wisdom of Solomon," in the *Bahir* itself, as sections 3 and 44 show us, the terminology is still different. The book does not yet know a fixed symbol called "Solomon's wisdom." The last sefirah here is named *ḥokhmath 'elohim.* She is herself the "daughter" in whom thirty-two paths of the upper *ḥokhmah* are united, and who is married or "given as a gift" to Solomon—here the Solomon of history and not a symbolic Solomon. This *ḥokhmah* is depicted in three passages by means of parables in which she is married and "offered as a gift," as a princess, to another prince, hence to one of the other aeons or powers.

Originally, as in section 3, this *ḥokhmah* is simply the Torah. With regard to the Torah, Yehudah ben Barzilai said (p. 268), citing old sources, "God said to the Torah: Come, my daughter, we are going to marry you to my friend, Abraham." But in section 3, Solomon is substituted for Abraham. He is the prince to whom, according to 1 Kings 5:26, the king marries his daughter and offers her as a gift. However, in section 36, the prince is one of the aeons themselves, without it being said which one. In section 44, it is he who bears the divine name of Elohim to whom the *ḥokhmah* was thus married and offered as a gift. The biblical expression *ḥokhmath 'elohim* here means something like "the *ḥokhmah* that was given to Elohim and that is with him in the same chamber," according to the very remarkable reading of the oldest *Bahir* manuscript, which was later (perhaps owing to theological samples?) corrected. Since she is already "married" in the upper spheres, she was only "offered as a gift" to the Solomon in the terrestrial world, according to section 44, and she governs in him, as *middath ha-din,* and aids him in exercising judgment. This is, according to section

44, the meaning of the two verses "YHWH gave wisdom to Solomon," and "they saw that the wisdom of Elohim was in him, to do judgment." The conception of the Torah as daughter and bride thus combines with the gnostic conception of the Sophia, which possesses the qualities of the last sefirah and helps not only Solomon, but all men: "As long as a man does what is just, this *ḥokhmah* of Elohim assists him and brings him close [to God], but if he does not do it, she removes him [from God] and punishes him." Also for Yehudah ben Barzilai, in his commentary on the *Yeṣirah* (p. 57), 1 Kings 3:28 and 5:26 refer to the Sophia as the beginning of all creatures which the king kept for his friends and people without, however, the symbolism of the daughter and of the marriage playing any role. This particular symbolism is evidently the element which, deriving from older sources and gnostic traditions, was added to the traditional material concerning *ḥokhmah* as presented by our author.

In important details, certain gnostic statements concerning "the daughter of light" and the divine soul that is related to her agree with passages in the *Bahir* that discuss in a variety of formulations the mystical significance of the Shekhinah. We shall soon have to analyze this symbolism more closely. Here it is important to note that the identification of the Shekhinah as a divine hypostasis, with the gnostic Sophia, could make use, as the most important *tertium comparationis,* of the idea of exile in the lower world. This was all the easier once a distinction was established, as we shall see, between God and the Shekhinah. "In every place," says the Talmud, "where they [Israel] were exiled, the Shekhinah is with them" (*Megillah* 29a). Originally the passage simply meant that even in Israel's exile, the presence of God (the Shekhinah) remained among them. Only in the course of later developments could this image be transformed into the notion of the Shekhinah as one of the aeons, to wit the aeon called the "daughter," being exiled in the lower world. But then the gnostic motif, preserved in one way or another in Jewish circles in the Orient, imposed itself with redoubled force. Just as the last aeon of the pleroma was of central interest to the Gnostics because the mystery of the cosmos and the mystery of our own existence were interwoven in it, the Book *Bahir* and in its footsteps the Spanish kabbalists directed their attention, to the tenth sefirah more than to all the others. In this powerful symbol, the understanding of which is of central importance for the religious world of the Kabbalah,[73] diverse ideas and sequences of motifs meet and join in a single conception that is, nevertheless, rich in aspects and nuances.

The most astonishing text in this ensemble of gnostic motifs is undoubtedly section 90. There we read:

> What is meant by [Isa. 6:3]: the whole earth is full of his glory? That is the "earth" which was created on the first day, and it corresponds in the higher spheres to the land of Israel, full of the glory of God. And what is it [this earth or glory]? His "wisdom," of which it is said [Prov. 3:35]: The wise shall obtain honor. And it also says [Ezek. 3:-12]: Blessed be the glory of God from His [here read by the *Bahir* as "its"] place. But what is the glory of God? A parable. It is like a king who had in his chamber the queen, who enraptured all of his legions; and they had sons. These sons came every day to see the king and to praise [literally, also: to greet] him. They said to him: Where is our mother? He replied: You cannot see her now. Then they said: Praised [greeted] may she be, wherever she is. And what is meant by "from its place?" From this it follows that there is no one who knows its place![74] A parable of a king's daughter who came from afar and nobody knew whence she came, until they saw that she was capable, beautiful, and excellent in all that she did. Then they said: Truly, this one for sure is taken from the form of light [another version: comes for sure from the side of the light], for through her deeds the world becomes luminous. They asked her: Where are you from? She said: From my place. Then they said: If that is so, the people in your place are great. May she be praised and celebrated in her place!

This passage, where the lower Sophia, which reaches the "wise," is identified with the "earth" of the pleroma and the Glory, the *kabhod* of God, but also, at the same time, with the daughter of the king, a veritable "maiden from afar," uses the undisguised imagery of Syrian gnosis. The king's daughter illuminates the world in which nobody knows whence she comes; but those who perceive her deduce from her person the greatness of the place of light where she has her origin. She corresponds in a surprising manner to the "daughter of light" in the gnostic bridal hymn in the *Acts of Thomas* and similar well-known gnostic texts, the exact meaning of which has been a subject of much discussion among modern scholars.[75] The

---

73. Cf. my study on the Shekhinah in *Von der mystischen* (ibid., ch. 4, 135–191).

74. This is a quotation from the interpretation of Ezekiel 3:12 in *Hagigah* 13b.

75. Cf. for example B. A. Bevan, *The Hymn of the Soul* (Cambridge, 1897); G. Hoffman, "Zwei Hymnen der Thomasakten," *Zeitschrift für die neutestamentliche Wissenschaft* 4 (1903): 273–309; Erwin Preuschen, *Zwei gnostische Hymnen* (Giessen,

lower Sophia, the gnostic redeemer, and the soul are among the interpretations proposed. The researcher who inquires into the origins of the kabbalistic symbolism has much to learn from this uncertainty on the part of modern scholarship with regard to the meaning of symbols occurring in the gnostic hymns. The original significance of these symbols matters less for our immediate purpose than the illustration provided by the different interpretations of how symbolism from the old sources can become the object—among the oldest kabbalists or their predecessors, as also among modern scholars—of corresponding transformations and metamorphoses of meaning. The kabbalists, of course, did not have access to the vast comparative material that now, since the discovery of the original Manichaean sources, renders the explanations of earlier scholars so dubious or makes them seem out of date. On the other hand, it is extremely instructive to see that as acute and sagacious a scholar as Ferdinand Christian Baur, who certainly had at his disposal more extensive fragments than those, for example, that came along tortuous paths to the redactors of the *Bahir,* nevertheless characterized the Manichaean "daughter of the light" in this hymn with exactly the same figures of speech employed by the kabbalists when they described the role in the world of the Shekhinah and daughter of the king: "She seems to me in general to be the overseer and the regent of the created and the visible world and to represent it, in its manifold relations, in herself."[76] The attitude of the older kabbalists to gnostic fragments that found their way to them was probably just such an attempt at interpretation, the only difference being that their interpretations remained within the Jewish conceptual framework. The king's daughter is hidden, yet she also is visible, depending on the phase of her appearance. Hence it is not surprising that to these two aspects of her being, emphasized here in the two parables, there corresponds in another passage a lunar symbolism that in due course acquired great importance in the Kabbalah. The moon alternates between visible and invisible phases. Thus, in very different

---

1904); Alfred Adam, *Die Psalmen des Thomas und das Perlenlied als Zeugnisse vorchristlicher Gnosis* (Berlin, 1959); Günther Bornkamm, *Mythos und Legende in den apokryphen Thomas-Akten* (Göttingen, 1933); A. F. Klijn, "The so-called Hymn of the Pearl," in *Vigiliae Christianae* 14 (1960): 154–164.

76. Ferdinand Christian Baur, *Das manichäische Religionssystem* (Tübingen, 1831), 225.

images, this lower Sophia is sometimes the queen *(maṭronitha)* who remains invisible yet is sought after by all the king's sons; and sometimes she is the daughter of the king himself, having taken up residence in the world, conceived as a world of darkness, even though she has her origin in the "form of the light."[77] Nothing is said about the circumstances under which this daughter of light came into the world. Is her residence in the world an exile for her, as suggested by the gnostic symbolism as well as by the interpretations that see her as the Glory of God or the Shekhinah? That is not stated here, although other parables (such as sections 45, 51, 74, and 104) seem to allude to it. In any case, it is important for the Jewish conception of the *Bahir* that it is the daughter's *destination* to rule and to reign in the lower world, and thereby to indicate the place where she really belongs in the realm of the aeons. Here is how section 97, taking in a literal sense the words *leqaḥ tob,* understands Proverbs 4:2: "For I gave you that which is taken from the good." But this daughter is also "the reflection which was taken from the primordial light" (section 98), just as in the beginning of the bridal hymn of the Sophia, where it is said that "the reflection of the king is in her." Moreover, parallel to the same passage of the *Bahir,* which says that the thirty-two paths of wisdom of the beginning of the *Book of Creation* are united within this *middah,* we also have in the Greek hymn the as yet unexplained praise addressed by the thirty-two to the daughter of the light.

The agreement among these three motifs gives us cause for reflection. It is evident that the gnostic material was radically Judaized. That which "was taken from the good" is no longer removed from that which is above in order to be sent into the world to bring about its redemption; henceforth, it is the light of the Torah and the action of the Shekhinah that form the "heart" of the lower world. Nevertheless, the Judaization of these concepts cannot obscure the very tangible link with the gnostic images and symbols. Our investigation therefore constrains us to admit the assumption that Oriental sources originating in the world of gnosticism influenced the elaboration of the symbolism of the Book *Bahir* or that fragments relat-

77. The reading "form of the light" could also be medieval Hebrew; cf. the quotation from Abraham bar Ḥiyya, n. 22 of this chapter. On the other hand this expression already occurs in the Manichaean *Kephalaia,* chap. 7 (ed. Polotzky, p. 36), where it represents the celestial "garment."

ing to the Shekhinah in that work themselves belong to such a stratum of sources.

4. Identification of Ancient Sources Preserved in the Tradition of the German Hasidim: Raza Rabba *and* Bahir

In the preceding pages, we analyzed a series of examples that seem to indicate that the Book *Bahir* contains elements for which the general attitude of medieval Jewish thought does not at all offer a satisfactory explanation. By contrast, an analysis of the incomparably simpler theosophy of the German Hasidim of the twelfth and thirteenth centuries may teach us what the evolution of things might have looked like if it had been determined by a purely immanent causality, and how the beginnings of a theosophic theology could have emerged even in the twelfth century. In order to understand the formation of these Hasidic ideas, little more is required than a knowledge of the old commentaries on the *Yeṣirah* and of the theology of Saadya as it penetrated into these circles in the form of an old Hebrew paraphrase—often poetically imprecise and written in an enthusiastic style—of his classic philosophical work, written in Arabic.[78] There, everything revolves around the notion of the *kabhod,* the Glory of God, and his Shekhinah, which the Hasidim, following Saadya, consider to be the first-created. In the Book *Bahir,* by way of contrast, our concerns take us beyond that to materials whose spiritual physiognomy is completely different and which closer analysis reveals to be vestiges of an older spiritual world that had already vanished.

The doctrine of the double *kabhod* and the prominent role attributed to the cherub upon the throne developed among the Hasidim independently of the problems posed by the Book *Yeṣirah* and its ten *sefiroth.* It has its origin in Saadya's thinking, which concerned the establishment of an unbridgeable gulf between God the creator and the created *kabhod.* The writings of the Hasidim clearly show how embarrassed they were by the task of explaining the ten sefiroth of the *Yeṣirah* in the light of this teaching. In general the

---

78. Cf. on this subject *Major Trends,* pp. 86, 111–114. The origin of the paraphrase is undoubtedly to be sought in the Orient.

sefiroth are located below the divine *kabhod,* but sometimes they are also interwoven with the idea of the *kabhod* itself. In the works of Eleazar of Worms, the German contemporary of Isaac the Blind, we discover here and there such linkages of motifs as, for example, the identification of the last sefirah with the Shekhinah, a conception that we otherwise find only in the old Kabbalah. Eleazar's writings contain no systematic exposition of a conception of this kind. In a small tract of his, *The Book of Wisdom,* we read in the course of an explanation of the seventy-three gates of the Torah—seventy-three is the numerical value of the word *ḥokhmah*—that "the Shekhinah is called the daughter of the creator . . . and she is also called the tenth sefirah and royalty [*malkhuth*], because the crown of the kingdom is on his [probably, therefore, God's] head."[79] Passages like this force us to conclude that around 1217, when this work was composed, Eleazar had knowledge of at least some kabbalistic symbols that are also characteristic of the Book *Bahir.* To be sure, he employs these symbols in an entirely different direction.[80] In his other books, notably in his commentary on the *Yeṣirah,* the *kabhod* is mentioned not as the tenth sefirah but as the first.

These isolated appearances of kabbalistic symbols naturally raise the question whether there may not be a relation between this "prehistoric" development of the Kabbalah and some subterranean current that made its way to the circles of the German Hasidim. After all, this singular life of the divine *middoth* and aeons could also be understood as a representation of the various stations within the divine *kabhod,* of phenomena that unfold before the latter becomes manifest in the created world. We can easily imagine mystics who would have sought to penetrate to the interior of the *kabhod,* which manifested itself to the outside from its throne, and who then fortuitously discovered fragmentary texts of Jewish Gnosticism and speculations concerning the aeons—texts that contained more than the talmudic dicta on the logoi of creation or the *middoth* before the throne and their abstract names, with which we are already familiar. These sources may have contained fragments of a much more pronounced mythical character, as sections 2 and 3 of this chapter sought to show or, in any event, to prove likely.

---

79. Ms. Oxford, Neubauer 1568, fol. 24b, in *Sefer ha-Ḥokhmah.* Cf. pp. 184–6, herein.

80. Cf. also our discussion on the subject of *kether 'elyon,* n. 129 and above all pp. 124–5, herein.

Many other passages of the *Bahir* permit us to draw a further general conclusion: once such a repristination of gnostic elements and attitudes takes place, it may also produce, on the basis of the same or similar presuppositions, new mythical materials in the spirit of the ancients. The process within the pleroma that brought forth the aeons or the sefiroth could have been developed anew, using purely Jewish forms and based on purely Jewish material, as soon as the preliminary historical and psychological conditions were present. In fact these preconditions existed at the time of the religious movement of Hasidism after the Crusades, in France and the Rhineland as well as in Provence—in areas, therefore, where the gnostic religion of the Cathars attained considerable influence if not complete dominion.[81] A similar attitude with regard to Old Testament material was held in common, at least in part, by the Gnostics and the first kabbalists and could produce similar results; there is nothing particularly enigmatic about this. The conjunction of these old and new gnostic materials with the religious and ascetic orientation of the German Hasidim may explain the formation of the gnostic theosophy of the very earliest Kabbalah as we find it in the Book *Bahir.*

The question of a possible link between the sources of the *Bahir* and the German Hasidim is by no means merely a matter of hypotheses and analytical deductions. Various passages in the book, as we possess it, distinctly indicate a connection with certain interests of the German Hasidim as well as with the traditions that, so far as we know, were known and cultivated only among them. The internal analysis of these parts of the work supports the testimony of Isaac Cohen, cited in the first chapter, with respect to the origin of the *Bahir,* that it came to Provence from Germany. In this regard, it is important to note the relationship that exists here between speculations on the Book *Yeṣirah* and magic, and in particular the mystical expositions and interpretations concerning the secret names of God, which occupy an important place in the *Bahir,* sections 63–81. This relationship and these interests are characteristic of the German Hasidim who, for their part, had already received much of this material from Italy and the Orient.

The material contained in three of these magical texts (sections

---

81. On the expansion of Catharism in Germany and northern France, cf. the studies of J. Giraud, *Histoire de l'Inquisition* 1:1–33.

79–81) is written almost wholly in the style of the old theurgic tracts without being subjected to a speculative or symbolizing interpretation, as is the case for most of the other texts. The rigid and stylized formulation bears the clear stamp of an unaltered borrowing from an older source. Section 79 presents the great seventy-two-letter name of God that is derived from the three verses, Exodus 14:19–21, where each verse numbers seventy-two letters. This great name was already known in the Hekhaloth literature, and it is also mentioned several times, albeit briefly, in the Midrash in such a manner as to leave no doubt that there too it derived from the same tradition.[82] Here, however, it is unexpectedly combined with the conclusion of the Book *Yeṣirah,* as if there were a link between the two traditions. The seventy-two magical names are also sealed with the name YHWH, much as the six directions of heaven in the Book *Yeṣirah* are sealed with the name of YHW. Section 80 speaks of the twelve-letter name of God known also in talmudic tradition (*Qiddushin* 71a), but the *Bahir* also transmits the vocalization. Only in the literature of the Hasidim does this vocalization have corresponding parallels.[83]

Section 81 deserves special notice. Mention is made there of another seventy-two-letter divine name, composed of twelve words that God "transmitted to the angel Masmariah, who stands before

82. On the construction of the seventy-two names of God, each of which numbers three consonants, cf. for example M. Schwab, *Vocabulaire de l'angélologie* (Paris, 1897), 30–32. The name already had appeared in this form in the theurgic texts of the Hekhaloth tradition. Midrashic literature only mentions the dictum of a fourth-century master to the effect that God redeemed Israel from the Egyptian yoke by means of his name, "for the name of God is composed of seventy-two letters;" cf. the references in Ludwig Blau, *Das altjüdische Zauberwesen* (Budapest, 1898), 139–140. Blau rightly concluded from the extant statements that this name was already known in the first half of the third century. In a responsum of Hai Gaon the name is already transmitted in the same form as in the *Bahir,* and thus it is also found, for example, in the magical book *Sefer ha-Yashar,* where Tobias ben Eliezer (ca. 1100) attests to having read it (Tobias ben Eliezer, *Leqaḥ Tob* on Exodus 14:21).

83. According to talmudic tradition, the twelve-letter divine name is related to the triple Tetragrammaton in the priestly blessing Numbers 24:24–26. According to the *Bahir,* its vocalization, *Yahāwā Yahōwē Yihwō,* is undoubtedly construed as an allusion to the existence of God in the past, the present, and the future. This looks more like a speculative rather than an old magical tradition. From the tradition of the German Hasidim, Elḥanan ben Yaqar of London, in his *Yesod ha-Yesodoth,* Ms. New York, Jewish Theological Seminary 838, cites the vocalization *Yahwāh Yahōweh* and *Yahweh,* which is remarkable precisely because it does not conform to any grammatical form.

the [celestial] curtain; and he transmitted them to Elijah, on Mount Carmel, and by means of them, he ascended [to heaven] and did not taste death, and these are the precious, explicit, and magnificent names, which are twelve, according to the number of the tribes of Israel."[84] The magical names that follow are attested in various contexts in the tradition of the German Hasidim only, and they plainly derive from analogous sources. Eleazar of Worms includes these names in a magical prayer of atonement[85] that certainly goes back to older models, as is always the case when he uses materials of this kind. A miscellany on these twelve names in a manuscript of the National Library in Vienna[86] contains precise instructions for their theurgic use. A certain Rabbi Todros, it is reported there, received permission from "Rabbenu Jacob of Ramerupt [that is, R. Jacob Tam, the grandson of Rashi] and from Rabbenu Eliyahu of Paris to bring down to earth, by means of these names, the soul of his son [who had been murdered]" in order to obtain information concerning the circumstances of the crime. This leads us to the milieu of the French Jews of the twelfth century. The sequence of twelve names is also transmitted in a magical collection coming from the same Hasidic circle in Germany, but undoubtedly copied from a much older source. In this list of magical names of God, *shemoth meforashim,* the angel Masmariah is designated as the "angel of rain."[87] In a New York Hekhaloth manuscript originating in the circles of the Hasidim and containing various magical formulas dating from the early

---

84. Twelve such divine names "corresponding to the tribes of Israel" are also mentioned (though the names are not quite the same) in the Hekhaloth text from the Genizah published by I. Gruenwald, *Tarbiz* 38 (1969): 364.

85. In his *Sode Razayya,* Ms. Munich Heb. 81, fol. 53a.

86. Ms. Vienna Heb. 47, fol. 1b–2a of the Wiener Nationalbibliothek (A. Z. Schwarz, no. 152). It is said there that the names serve to "abolish fatalities and to bring back the dead in the presence of the whole community."

87. Cod. British Museum, Margoliouth 752, fol. 95a. There are many reasons to suppose that this passage belongs to the *Sefer ha-Yashar,* of which at least parts must have been extant, and which is, perhaps, identical with the magical work of the same name mentioned from the ninth century onward. The *Bahir* says that this is the *shem ha-meforash,* which was written upon the forehead of Aaron. The first of the names that follow corresponds in fact to this introduction, since it can easily be explained as "Aaron's frontal diadem": *AHṢIṢIRON,* which looks like a composite of Ahron and *ṣiṣ.* But in the manuscript cited this sequence of names appeared as a magical means of inducing rain, whereas in the same collection, fol. 94b, a completely different name is given as "the divine name which was engraved upon the forehead of the high priest, Aaron." The tradition must therefore have split very early.

Middle Ages, a "dream question" has been preserved. It contains an appeal to the *shemoth meforashim,* which "are engraved in the throne of Glory and which the angel Malkiel, who always stands before God, transmitted to Elijah, on Mount Carmel, and by means of which he ascended."[88] But the names themselves are in this case long *voces mysticae,* entirely different from the twelve names of the *Bahir.* In any case, we are dealing here with a fixed formula from the store of tradition in which only the name of the angel fluctuates between Masmariah and Malkiel.

It therefore seems certain that the redactors of the *Bahir* drew on the same tradition as the sources mentioned, and that this tradition is precisely that of the German Hasidim. These paragraphs must have reached Germany from the Orient along with other old talmudic and gaonic magical texts; perhaps they were joined to the preceding paragraphs already before the final redaction of the *Bahir.* In fact, the end of section 81 refers directly back to section 75, which deals with the mystical significance of the *teli,* the celestial sphere, and the heart in *Yeṣirah* 4:1 (and here in section 64).

This combination of magic and the study of the *Yeṣirah* among the German Hasidim led to the development of the idea of the golem—that is, to the creation of a magical man, effected by the application of the procedures delineated in the Book *Yeṣirah.* I have discussed these ideas more fully elsewhere.[89] For our purpose it is important to note that precisely this idea, which in the Middle Ages

---

88. Ms. New York Jewish Theological Seminary 828, fol. 27b (this passage is lacking in the parallel Oxford manuscript, Neubauer 1531). Whereas the Book *Bahir* or its source knew of a "name of twelve *words*" that an angel transmitted to Elijah on Carmel, the tradition of the *Zohar* mentions, in two places, a "divine name of twelve *letters*" that was transmitted to Elijah, who made use of it to ascend to heaven. The author of the *Zohar* seems to have utilized variations on the passage of *Bahir,* at least if the two traditions do not go back to the same motif of a "name of twelve" that was then developed differently in various magical tracts. The twelve names of the *Bahir,* in part badly corrupted, often appear in later manuscripts of "practical Kabbalah," but that is no longer relevant to our analysis. In the course of his polemic against the theoretical and the practical Kabbalah, Yosef Solomon Delmedigo (ca. 1630), cites sarcastically the first two of these names: "Do not be a horse and an ass and do not believe everything they tell you about Henoch ben Yared and Metatron, and about Elijah and Ahaṣiṣharon;" cf. *'Iggereth 'Ahuz,* in Geiger's *Melo Chofnayim* (Breslau, 1840), 6. Delmedigo probably derived his information from Cordovero's *Pardes Rimmonim* (Cracow, 1592), fol. 123a, where this text is cited from the *Bahir.*

89. Cf. my book *On the Kabbalah,* chap. 5.

remained alive only in these circles, also in the *Bahir* (section 136) became the object of considerations that go far beyond the talmudic source cited but are very close to the ideas of Eleazar of Worms regarding the creation of a golem.[90] All this could be easily explained if one of the strata of the *Bahir* had had its origin in Germany. Also the pair of notions "world of shadows" and "world of light" (which admittedly conforms to the medieval conceptions regarding this world and the next) make their first appearance in Hebrew literature, as far as I can see, in Germany at the beginning of the twelfth century. That would also accord with the appearance of these concepts in section 127 of the *Bahir.*[91]

But we may go even further. One of these Hasidim, the aforementioned Ephraim ben Shimshon, (see p. 89 herein), quotes a passage from the *Bahir* around 1240.[92] His quotation is nothing other than an entirely different version of a passage found in the *Bahir* texts originating from Provence and Spain. In the ordinary text, Exodus 15:3, "God is a man [*'ish*] of war," is explained (section 18) by a parable to the effect that the three consonants of the word *'ish* indicate the three supreme powers of God. According to the text of Ephraim ben Shimshon, however, there is no reference to the sefiroth, but to the three divine names Elohim, YHWH, Shaddai, and their rank. The tenor of this text is completely in the spirit of the Hasidim, and it may be worthwhile to juxtapose the two versions:

Bahir, Section 18

R. Amora said: What is meant by the verse [Exod. 15:3] God is a man [*'ish*] of war? Mar Raḥmai bar Kibi [probably to be read as Babai?] said to him: A thing so simple should not pose any problem for you. Listen to me and I will give you counsel. It is

Bahir according to Ephraim ben Shimshon

R. Simlai asked R. Reḥumai:[93] What is meant by the verse: a man of war. He said him: I will relate to you a parable. It is like a king to whom a son was born. He went to a market and bought him a crown which he named *'alef.* When another

90. Cf. ibid., 246–247.

91. Cf. my commentary on the *Bahir,* 138. In an old version, in the margin of Cod. 209 of Munich, we read: "For in the world of darkness man lives by bread, but in the world of light he lives not by bread alone, but by everything that goes forth from the mouth of God," that is, the Torah. Cf. the appearance of this pair of notions in the text in Neubauer-Stern, *Hebräische Berichte über die Judenverfolgungen während der Kreuzzüge* (Berlin, 1892), 54.

92. Ms. Munich, Heb. 15, fol. 74b.

93. In Cod. Heb. Vat. 236, fol. 92a, the received text is cited as coming from the *Midrash Bahir,* but with the introduction: "They asked R. Simlai."

like a king who had beautiful apartments and he gave each of them a name and each of them was better than the other. Then he said: I wish to give to my son the apartment which is called *'alef,* but that which is called *shin* is also beautiful.[94] What did he do? He united all three and made a house out of them.[95] They said to him: For how long will you still cover your words? He said to them: My sons, *'alef* is the beginning, *yod* is the second after it, *shin* embraces the whole world. And why does *shin* embrace the whole world? Because with it the word *teshubah,* repentance, is written.

son was born to him, he went and bought him a crown which he named *yod.* When a third son was born to him, he went and bought him a crown and named it *shin.* When another son was born to him, he took all of their crowns and made them into one and put it on the head of the fourth, and that signified *'ish,* man. He said to him: How long will you still make of your words a mystery? He answered him: First, when Abraham came, He revealed himself to him on account of the great love with which He loved him, by the name of Elohim, and that is *'alef.* When Isaac came, He revealed Himself under the name of *shaddai,* and that is *shin.* But when God revealed Himself to Israel on the shores of the Red Sea, He took the initials of these three names and made a crown, and that is *'ish.*

The two versions of the quotation are instructive. The common version speaks of the three consonants mentioned, as other passages in the *Bahir* text suggest, as symbols of the three supreme sefiroth.[96] The second version, on the other hand, knows nothing of any such speculations and merely sees allusions to the names of God that were revealed to the Patriarchs and combined under the heading *'ish.* The text of the *Bahir* was therefore treated in various ways: either the first version reflected the spirit of the Hasidic speculations on the names of God and was subsequently elaborated in accordance with the new, developing symbolism, or the received text had reached the Hasidim already in this form and was then revised in keeping with

---

94. At the beginning of this paragraph Ms. Munich 290 also read: "That which is called *yod* is also beautiful." But these words are missing in old quotations. An old commentator even takes the trouble to explain why they do not figure in a text where they obviously belong.

95. In the Book *Yeṣirah* the consonants are called "stones," the words, "houses"; this may have influenced the wording of this parable.

96. *'Alef* is thus interpreted in sections 13, 48, 53, 95; *shin,* in sections 84 and 89. Elsewhere *yod* is no longer interpreted clearly. In section 84, a parallel interpretation of the word *'ish* in Exodus 15:3 connects it, in accordance with the numerical value of the letters, with the ten logoi by means of which the world was created. Cf. my commentary on the *Bahir,* 91.

their much simpler ways of thinking. The text was therefore still in flux, and, in fact, old kabbalistic miscellanies still exhibit a number of transitional stages between the two versions.[97] I have already indicated in my commentary on the *Bahir* that Ephraim ben Shimshon, or the author, whoever he may have been, of the anonymously transmitted commentary found in the Ms. Munich Heb. 15, evidently had not seen the *Bahir* itself, certainly not in the form in which it has come down to us. He cites from it only once, and then, indeed, at the very end; on the other hand, he does not mention it at all in places where, judging from the very pronounced character of his commentary, one would expect to find citations from the *Bahir,* if only he had seen our text.[98] This holds true not only of the passage related to Genesis 24:1, which I have already discussed (see p. 89) but also of the doctrine of metempsychosis, mentioned by him immediately after a parable on Isaiah 5:2. But he neither establishes a connection between this parable and the doctrine that follows, nor cites, on this subject, section 135 of the Book *Bahir,* where Isaiah 5:2 appears accompanied by a parable as a scriptural cue for the doctrine of metempsychosis. No mention is made of the *Bahir* in connection with divine names, the priestly blessing, etc., although the corresponding passages in the *Bahir* would have offered strong support for the author's ideas, largely based as they are on numerological mysticism. He was therefore familiar with a text of the *Bahir* entirely different from our own, or else he had only indirect knowledge of certain parts of it, without having actually seen the book.

To this appearance of a passage of the *Bahir* in two completely different versions we must now add an important discovery that may shed some light on the enigma of the *Bahir,* at least with regard to one of its aspects, but that at the same time complicates the problem of the book's redaction considerably. This is the discovery of a con-

---

97. Thus, in Cod. Vat. 236 the Vulgate text is cited, with the introductory formula "R. Simlai was asked," a name that appears only in the second version. The quotation is connected in a strange manner with a passage from the commentary of Menaḥem Ṣiyoni on the Torah, where the parable of the apartments is cited with reference to Exodus 15:3, but also connected, as it is here, with the three names of God.

98. Ms. Munich 15 and the other versions of the so-called Torah commentary of Rabbenu Ephraim deserve a special examination. The (very rare) partial Smyrna edition deviates significantly not only from the manuscripts, but also from the edition published by Ḥayyim Yosef Gad (Johannesburg, 1950) according to an unidentified manuscript, without knowledge of the first printed text; all of them together also deviate considerably from the numerous quotations found in the writings of H. Y. D. Azulai.

nection between a number of passages in the *Bahir* and a lost text of the Merkabah-mysticism, to which we must now turn. The situation is as follows.

Among the most important books of esoteric literature in the hands of the Merkabah mystics in the Orient, in Palestine and in Mesopotamia, as late as the ninth and tenth centuries, various authors mention a work bearing the title *Raza Rabba,* "The Great Mystery." The magical and angelological character of its contents are well attested. The oldest testimonies concerning the book were found by Jacob Mann. Daniel Al-Kumisi, a Karaite author living in the ninth century in Jerusalem, writes, polemically of course, against the "books of magic" circulating among the Rabbanites: "they [the Rabbanites] have various groups of books, such as that of Bartalia Qansarin [corrupt? They are probably the names of two authors or books] and the "Book of Bileam" and other books such as the "Book of Adam," and the Book *Yashar* and the "Book of Mysteries" [read *Sefer ha-Razim*][99] and the Great Mystery [*Raza Rabba*], and they say to Israel: "From these books, we will make known to you the hidden secret."[100] Elsewhere, the same author writes:

> Who practices magic today in Israel? The Rabbanites, surely, who speak of pure and impure divine names, who write amulets and perform clever tricks, and give their books such titles as *Sefer ha-Yashar, Sefer ha-Razim, Sefer Adam,* and *Raza Rabba,* and still other magic books [containing recipes] if you wish to make a man love a woman, or if you wish to excite hatred between them, and many other abominations of the same sort, may God keep us far from them.[101]

In Jerusalem, another Karaite author of the tenth century, writing in Arabic, reported on the contents of the *Raza Rabba* in greater detail:

> They [the Rabbanites] ascribe a book to Adam . . . and they also have the book *Raza Rabba* on the history of the seven heavens [*sab' sāmawāt*] and the angels and the *parurim* and *dewim* and *latabhin* and *jarorin* without numbers, and the amulets [against the classes of demons], as well as the book on *'Uza* and *'Uziel* [or *'Aziel*] which de-

---

99. This is none other than the magical work completely reconstructed on the basis of Genizah texts (until now we only possessed odd fragments preserved in the *Sefer Raziel*) by M. Margalioth. The book must undoubtedly be dated to the talmudic period. It is closely related to the magic papyri but has no relationship to Merkabah-mysticism.

100. Jacob Mann, *Texts and Studies in Jewish History and Literature,* vol. 2 (Philadelphia, 1935), 75–76.

101. Ibid., 80–81.

scended from heaven, according to their mendacious sayings, as well *Bartalya* and *Qansarin* [with recipes] for love and hate, seven-league boots and dream inquiries.[102]

We may thus obtain a clearer idea of the content of the book, which apparently corresponds in part to what we know of other texts of the Merkabah gnosis. There is here, as in the Hekhaloth and the "baraitha on the history of the Creation," a report concerning the seven heavens and the angels who minister in them. But to this are added elements of a theurgic, magical, and demonological character of the kind known to us from the magical papyri. This latter element has no analogies in the old Merkabah literature, but it does correspond to the magical inscriptions on the inside of clay bowls in Judeo-Aramaic,[103] of the type published above all by Montgomery and Cyrus Gordon, and to the parts of the *Sefer ha-Razim* (now completely reconstructed by M. Margalioth) preserved in the *Sefer Raziel.* The four Aramaic names for the classes of demons named by the author are familiar to us from this kind of literature.[104] The combination of the various elements would suggest that the *Raza Rabba* dates from roughly the same period as the aforementioned inscriptions, that is, between the fifth and the eighth centuries, and that it represents a later stage of esoteric literature than the most important Merkabah texts.[105] These and other texts of an entirely or partly magical character were still known in the Orient at the beginning of the eleventh century. The Babylonian head of the academy Ḥai ben Sherira voiced his opinion of this literature in a responsum

102. Ibid., 82.

103. James Montgomery, *Aramaic Incantation Texts from Nippur* (Philadelphia, 1913); William Rossell, *A Handbook of Aramaic Magical Texts* (Skylands, 1953); Cyrus Gordon, "Aramaic and Mandaic Magical Bowls," *Ar.Or.* 6 (1934): 319–334; 9 (1937): 84–106; as well as his study in *Orientalia* 20 (1951): 306–315; J. Naveh and S. Shaked, *Amulets and Magic Bowls: Aramaic Incantations of Late Antiquity,* (Jerusalem, 1985).

104. But instead of *parurim,* which Mann mistakenly associated with the Persian *fravashis,* one must read *parukhin,* from the Assyrian *parakku,* an expression that appears in the Mandaean catalogue of spirits in the *Ginza,* together with *dewin* and *latabhayya* (malevolent spirits; literally: not good) (cf. H. Petermann, *Rechtes Ginza,* 279, line 3ff.); the list of spirits is discussed by M. Lidzbarski, "Uthra und Malakha" in Carl Bezold (ed.), *Orientalische Studien* (Festschrift Theodor Nöldeke zum 70. Geburtstag), vol. 1 (Giessen, 1906), 541–545. Details on the *yarorin* are found in Montgomery, *Aramaic Incantation Texts,* 81.

105. On the age of the Merkabah texts cf. my book *Jewish Gnosticism* and chap. 1, pp. 19–20, herein.

on the subject of formulas for magical practices, "such as they are found among us in large numbers." In this connection he named three writings: "the *Sefer ha-Yashar* and the one called the *Ḥarba de-Moshe,* 'Sword of Moses'[106] as well as the book which is named *Raza Rabba.*"[107]

This *Raza Rabba* was considered until now to have been lost. To the extent that literature relating to the Merkabah theurgy and ordinary magic has survived—and there is no small quantity of it—we are largely indebted to the circles of the German Hasidim who, according to their own testimony, received this Oriental material by way of Italy. It would not be the least bit surprising, therefore, if fragments of this lost text had found their way to Germany along with other documents. I have, in fact, succeeded in discovering in a text emanating from these circles and dating from the latter part of the thirteenth century many quotations, some rather lengthy, from a book that bears the Hebrew title *Sod ha-Gadol,* which is nothing other than the exact translation of the Aramaic *Raza Rabba.* It is no longer possible to determine whether the metamorphosis of the title from Aramaic into Hebrew also corresponds to a partial revision of the old book. For the most part the language of the quotations is still Aramaic. The old authors who referred to the book in the Orient only mentioned such of its contents as they found, for one reason or another, particularly striking or which seemed to them of importance in connection with the subjects they were discussing. This by no means excludes the possibility that the book also dealt with other mysteries or occasionally touched upon matters such as the hierarchy of the world and heavens, the angels and the holy names.

These quotations can be found in a commentary on the *Shi'ur Qomah,* that old fragment on the mystical figure of the Godhead that we have already discussed in the previous chapter. The author of the commentary belongs to the family of the Kalonymids, known in the history of the German Hasidim as the principal representatives of the esoteric tradition of German Judaism, which they brought with

106. This text was published by M. Gaster (London, 1896). A much better manuscript has been preserved in the great magical Cod. 290 of the Sassoon collection.

107. Cf. the Hebrew text in *'Oṣar ha-Geonim* on the tractate *Ḥagigah* (Jerusalem, 1931), 21.

them from the land of their origin, Italy. He was probably R. Moses ben Eliezer ha-Darshan ben Moses ha-Darshan. His grandfather, Moses ha-Darshan, "the preacher," was the husband of Golde, a granddaughter in the direct line of the celebrated R. Yehudah Hasid, the central figure of German Hasidism.[108] The text was apparently torn apart at a very early date, and the two parts are found under different titles in completely different manuscripts. But they fit together perfectly, and both parts (unlike any other work from these circles known to me) contain quotations from the "Great Mystery."[109] The author clearly distinguishes this book from the Book *Bahir,* which he also had before him and from which he quotes, something that certainly should not come as a surprise around 1270–1300, even if it is a question of the reemigration of the *Bahir,* in its final redaction, from Provence back to Germany.

It is not always possible to demarcate unequivocally the beginning and the end of the quotations preserved in this newly discovered source. Sometimes a quotation ends with the note: "So far, the text of the Great Mystery," without any corresponding introductory formula. The beginning of the quotation can only be deduced from the structure of the quotation itself; and it is quite possible that passages that are not identified as coming from there but whose nature suggests they belong there have their origin in the same source. The quotations prove that the "Great Mystery" was a mixture composed of a mystical midrash in which many old masters appear and interpret biblical verses and a kind of Hekhaloth text, especially in the manner of the "Lesser Hekhaloth."[110] But while in the Hekhaloth writings exegesis plays no role and is found only occasionally, many heroes of the Merkabah tradition or their disciples converse here not only about the vision of the Merkabah, but also about various biblical verses that are associated with angelological and cosmogenic ideas. The pseudepigraphic character of the sayings attributed to Neḥunya ben Haqqanah, R. Akiba, R. Ishmael and R. Meir is evident. Some of the pieces have no literary relation with

---

108. I shall not summarize here the detailed evidence presented by me in *Reshith ha-Qabbala* (Jerusalem–Tel Aviv, 1948), 203–210, but shall restrict myself to stating the results insofar as they are relevant in the present context.

109. On the manuscripts of the two fragments, ibid., 196–199, 210–212. I published the full text, ibid., 212–237 insofar as it is of significance for an examination of the *Raza Rabba.*

110. On the "Lesser Hekhaloth" cf. *Jewish Gnosticism,* sec. 10, 75–83.

other sources known to us, although they present themselves as a kind of gnostic midrash and contain discussions among the Merkabah authorities that make the text look like a preliminary stage of the *Bahir.* While it is clear that we are dealing with quotations, it is less clear where these quotations end. Other passages, however, are evidently connected with paragraphs of the *Bahir,* which a careful comparison of the texts reveals to be revisions of questions and theses figuring in the "Great Mystery," some of which are taken up literally but developed in an entirely different direction, namely, that of kabbalistic symbolism.

In the extant quotations we find a strong magical element, just as the testimonies concerning the book *Raza Rabba* would lead us to expect. Secret names of the angels are discussed. Elsewhere it is said:

> Moreover, it is said in the book of the "Great Mystery" that everyone who knows this mystery, which proceeds from the Trishagion [Isa. 6:3] and [the verse Ezekiel 3:12, which follows it in the liturgy of the *qedushah*]: "Blessed is the Presence of the Lord in his place" may be assured of the life of the future world [bliss], and this is the name of the Holy One, blessed be He.

The final remark clearly shows that it is a magical mystery concerning the divine name whose importance is underscored here, even though the formulation: every man who knows this mystery can be assured of bliss, is exactly the same as that given in the beginning of our fragment of the *Shi'ur Qomah,* for the man who immerses himself in the study of God's Glory. Here, too, it is curious to note how in the *Bahir* mystical interpretations of the mysteries of these two verses of the *Qedushah,* sections 89–90, with whose frankly gnostic terminology we have already become acquainted, follow the magical texts of the *Bahir* concerning the sacred names as well as other paragraphs that, as we shall see, are likewise connected with the source in *Raza Rabba.* The secret, indicated or promised, on the subject of these verses in the "Great Mystery," seems to have been revised in the *Bahir* on the basis of another source that had absorbed the gnostic terminology in much greater measure and substituted it for the originally more magical content.

In the Book *Bahir,* the magical stratum begins mainly in section 63, where the interpretation of Exodus 28:11 and Joshua 4:9 states that each of the twelve stones set up by Joshua contained six names, which together correspond to the seventy-two names of God or directly contain them. The original version of this paragraph is given at the end of a lengthy angelological quotation from the "Great Mystery" where it is also stated that this text was found in several manuscripts of the book. We may conclude that the Hasidic author still had the book before him in its complete form and in different versions. The old source as yet knows nothing of the seventy-two divine names, although it is already familiar, evidently, with the interpretations of the names on the stones as being names of God that correspond to the names of the tribes. With that, an important sentence in the *Bahir* is taken verbatim from this source. In the *Raza Rabba,* the passage is perhaps still connected with the speculations concerning Metatron, which are of no interest to the *Bahir.* In fact, it is said in a fragment of the *Shi'ur Qomah* that the name of Metatron is "given on six of their names [as in Exod. 28:11] and engraved upon the twelve stones [of Josh. 4:9]."[111] Very possibly the magical stratum in question, especially the *Bahir* sections 63–84, was entirely or partially borrowed from this source, that is, adapted from sentences to be found there.

However, most curious of all is the fact that this passage, which corresponds to section 63, of the *Bahir,* is immediately followed by a piece that corresponds to section 86, that is, to the paragraph in the *Bahir* that comes almost directly after the magical part. I place the two passages side by side:

Bahir, section 86

R. Meir said: What is meant by [Ps. 146:10]: The Lord shall reign forever, your God, O Zion, for all generations? What is meant by: for all generations? R. Papias said: It is written [Eccles. 1:4]: One generation goes, another comes. And R. Akiba [too] said: What is meant by: One generation goes, another comes? A

Sod ha-Gadol

R. Meir said: What is meant by [Ps. 146:10]: The Lord shall reign forever, your God, O Zion for all generations? This teaches that those angels praise the Lord of the world. What are they? They are those who issue from the name of man, who praise him for twenty years until another generation.[112] And when an-

111. Cf. *Merkabah Shelemah* (Jerusalem, 1921), fol. 39b, the text of which I corrected on the basis of the manuscripts.

112. The view presupposed here that twenty years constitutes one generation is in fact quoted in *Midrash Tehillim* and Psalm 90 section 17 (ed. Buber. 393) in the name of the tannaitic teacher R. Jose. The reference there is to the talmudic passage *B. Quiddushin* 29b. The wording in the *Raza Rabba* proves that the author is elaborating on the talmudic source. Cf. also *Qoheleth Rabba* 3:1.

generation that has already come [once].

other generation comes, these [angels] go away and others come. And if there is no other generation, they continue to praise for twenty years and no longer. And on that point the Lord of the world said: May his bones dry up [it is time for him to die], he who abandons the praise of the Lord of the world. And these angels [who correspond to man's name] are transformed into a star, and that is a man's lucky star.[113]

The difference between the two versions strikes the reader's eye. The older (Aramaic) version is connected with the idea, also known elsewhere in the Merkabah literature, of man's lucky star.[114] As long as man praises God, the angels who issue from his name also praise him. He who interrupts God's praise below disturbs the celestial praise. The Book *Bahir,* on the other hand, lacks the answer that R. Meir gave, in the source, to his own questions. In place of that, the expression "from all generations" has the secret sense of an allusion to the doctrine of the transmigration of souls, which is then explained more precisely by means of a parable that is nothing other than a revision of an almost identical parable from the Babylonian Talmud, *Shabbath* 152b. The soul that God gave to man pure must be returned to him pure. The Talmud compares it with a king who gave his servants royal garments.

---

113. Cf. the original text, *Merkabah Shelemah,* p. 232. The citation concludes with the notice עכל"ה , i.e., an abbreviation for *'ad kan leshon ha-sefer* or *ha-sod.* Perhaps it should also be read עכלס"ה : "up to here, the citation of the *Sod ha-Gadol.*" Cf. my note to the Hebrew text.

114. A man's personal angel is equated with his lucky star, *kokhab mazzalo.* The Merkabah literature already speaks of a celestial curtain before the throne into which all beings are woven: cf., for example, in the third Book of Enoch, chap. 45. In the *Alphabet of Rabbi Akiba,* a work composed from the same Merkabah materials, Moses sees "the star [*mazzal*] of R. Akiba in the celestial curtain"; cf. ed. Wertheimer (Jerusalem, 1914), 50. The same idea also dominates the psychological theories of Eleazar of Worms, who treats it at length in his *Ḥokhmath ha-Nefesh* (Lemberg, 1876), fols. 18, 23, and 28. According to him, the archetype, *demuth,* of a man is his "angel" as well as his "star." This relationship between angel and star is already found in a familiar dictum of *Bereshith Rabba,* section 10: "There is no blade of grass that does not have its star in heaven which strikes it and says to it: grow." Similar ideas are also found frequently in *Sefer Ḥasidim;* for example, ed. Wistinezky, section 1514.

The wise kept them clean, but the fools dirtied them in their work. When the king demanded the garments back, he was pleased with the wise, but angry with the fools. Of the wise he said: "Let my robes be placed in my Treasury and they can go home in peace." Of the fools he said: "Let my robes be given to the fuller, and let them be confined in prison."

To this the Talmud relates the verse of Ecclesiastes 12:7: "And the dust returns to the ground as it was, And the lifebreath returns to God who bestowed it." The soul is therefore the splendid garment with which the servants are dressed. But in the *Bahir,* this splendid garment changes its owner, in a distinct allusion to the transmigration of souls:

A king had servants and he dressed them in garments of silk and embroidery. They went astray. Then he threw them out and pushed them away from him and removed their garments and they went away. He took the garments and washed them well, until there were no longer any stains on them, and arranged them in order and engaged other servants and dressed them in these garments, without knowing whether they would be good servants or not. Thus they partook of garments which had already been in the world, and others had worn them before them.

Here, too, the same verse of Ecclesiastes 12:7 is cited. It is clear therefore that the new idea of transmigration of souls, of which the earlier text knew nothing, was only introduced with the revision of the old source of the *Raza Rabba.*

In the Hasidic source, shortly after the preceding passage, another part of the "Great Mystery" is quoted; it further develops the first idea but then leads to another subject that, to our surprise, also turns out to be a source for a subsequent text of the *Bahir.*

And R. Meir therefore said: One generation goes, another comes, but the earth remains the same forever. But this is quite obvious. So what did Solomon wish to stress with this? Rather, he interprets it as follows: It is because a generation goes and another comes that the earth remains the same forever. For if it were not so, the world would not have any righteous for a foundation [who are necessary for its existence]. But where a generation goes and another comes, the [the celestial] singers sing and praise God, without their voices being heard. And R. Akiba said: What is meant by the verse [Hab. 3:2]: Though angry, may You remember compassion? This verse is uttered by the prince of the angels [archon] of the world every time he brings you as an offering the souls of the righteous. Remember the quality of mercy

> and accept my sacrifices . . . Some explain the verse: though angry remember compassion: even in the hour of your anger, remember.[115]

While the beginning of the citation pursues the earlier line of thought concerning the righteous who praise God in every generation, and thereby adopts the interpretation of a verse that is taken up again in section 86 of the *Bahir,* the continuation, though no longer given in the name of R. Akiba, is found at the end of section 51, with a new shift toward the symbolism of the sefiroth. In other words, in the revision of the older passages, the *Bahir* always added new elements that led far beyond its source. It is just the last lines of section 51—we are in this manner still able to trace the source—that then lead to those speculations on Abraham's daughter, whose gnostic symbolism we recognized earlier.

These quotations make it possible to prove that the "Great Mystery" already contained ideas that stood in some direct relationship with the speculations of the *Bahir* on the aeons. The *Bahir* gives a list of ten *ma'amaroth* or logoi of God that is by no means identical with the list of the ten sefiroth in the *Book of Creation* but that refers to it in part. They are already designated here by a series of symbolic synonyms that are very closely connected to the symbolism of the ten kabbalistic sefiroth, the same symbolism that will serve as the basis in other passages of the *Bahir* and in the oldest tradition of the Kabbalah for a variety of interpretations. We shall have to return later to the problems posed by this list. At the present stage it is important to note that such a table of logoi—it remains unclear whether the objects enumerated in it were designated as sefiroth, as in the Book *Yeṣirah,* or as *ma'amaroth*—is already found in the "Great Mystery." The Hasidic author was evidently aware of the relationship between the two tables or their identity; in one of the two instances where he refers to it, he expressly cites "that which is found in the 'Great Mystery' and the Book *Bahir.*" It would, of course, be of the greatest importance for an understanding of the transition from the ten sefiroth of the Book *Yeṣirah* to the sefiroth of the kabbalists if we possessed this table in its entirety. For the moment we must content ourselves with the knowledge that in regard to the seventh and ninth logoi (and the tenth,

115. Cf. the Hebrew text in my *Reshith ha-Qabbala,* 236.

which is connected to them), the old source already contained exactly or almost exactly the same as that which we now read in the *Bahir.* The *Bahir* preserves, in sections 102–104, three different versions, which are difficult to reconcile with one another, concerning the place and significance of the seventh logos. Of these paragraphs, section 104 refers anew to the transmigration of souls; it surely belongs, therefore, to another source. But section 103 is already found in the "Great Mystery," in such manner as to make it probable that section 102, too, preceded it there:

Bahir, section 103

The seventh? But, after all, there are only six? This teaches that here is the Temple of the [celestial] Sanctuary, and it bears all [the other six], and that is why it is the seventh. And what is it? The Thought that has neither end nor limit. Similarly this place, too, has neither end nor limit.

Sod ha-Gadol

And the Holy Temple is in the celestial city [the celestial Jerusalem] and the Prince of the Countenance is the high priest. And whence do we know that there is a Temple there? As it is said there [in the "Great Mystery"]: The seventh? But there are only six? That teaches that they see[116] the Holy Temple, and it bears all.[117]

The sentence stating that the celestial sanctuary is in the center of the world and bears all six directions, which at the same time correspond to the last six sefiroth, figures in the fourth chapter of the *Book of Creation;* however, that book knows nothing of a relation between the temple and the seventh sefirah. This correlation would fit a revision of the ten sefiroth of the *Yeṣirah* in the sense of the doctrine of the Merkabah and the cosmology that corresponds to it. The continuation of the sentence in the *Bahir,* on the other hand, introduces a new element of mystic-gnostic speculation. Neither the

116. The manuscripts all have שרואי , as I have translated, but which has hardly any meaning. The reading of the Bahir, שכאן, seems better, and the graphic corruption can be explained easily.

117. Directly after this passage, the source continues with the second citation of R. Meir, discussed above, which likewise ends with the words of R. Akiba on the sacrifice in the Temple of the celestial Jerusalem. This sacrificial service is described in *Ḥagigah* 12b, in the fragment of the *Shi'ur Qomah,* in the "Visions of Ezekiel," in the third Book of Enoch, and other Merkabah texts. On this idea in general cf. H. Bietenhard, *Die himmlische Welt im Urchristentum und Spätjudentum* (Tübingen, 1951), 123–137, and the excellent work (which Bietenhard did not take into consideration) of A. Aptowitzer, "Das himmlische Heiligtum nach der Aggada,"(Hebrew), *Tarbiz* 2 (1931): 137–153, 257–287.

Yeṣirah nor the *Raza Rabba* knows anything of the "thinking" or the "thought" of God conceived as an aeon or a sefirah. The *Bahir,* on the other hand, wavers between two conceptions: the one saw the *maḥshabah,* just like the speculations of the ancient Gnostics on the *ennoia,* as the highest of all the sefiroth or aeons; the other conflated it, as here, with the seventh, which remains rather enigmatic. In other passages of the *Bahir,* in sections 48 and 84, it is the Holy Temple of the celestial Jerusalem that is conceived as the symbol of the highest sefirah, represented by the letter *'alef* as the beginning of all letters. The logic of the *Yeṣirah* passage, which served as the point of departure, would suggest, in fact, the seventh place in its system of enumeration; the logic of the mystical symbolism of the *ennoia,* which was apprently introduced from another source, points to the first. One can clearly see that two motifs of different origin are contending with each other here and that the Book *Bahir* adopted both traditions.

A later quotation from this table in the "Great Mystery" also accords well with the hypothesis of a revision of the list of the ten sefiroth of the Book *Yeṣirah* in the direction of Merkabah speculations.

> In the "Great Mystery" and in the Book *Bahir* mention is made of the existence of two *'ofannim,* the wheels [of the Merkabah][118] which proceed from beneath God's feet, one going toward the north and the other toward the west, and these *'ofannim* go to every place [extend themselves everywhere?], and this is not the place for explanations. This is deduced there [in the sources mentioned] from Isaiah 66:1: "The heaven is My throne and the earth is My footstool," which is to say: these *'ofannim* are a throne for that which is above, and under the seven earths they are the footstool of my feet.[119]

Almost all of this, with the exception of the remark concerning the throne represented by the *'ofannim,* is found in section 115 of the *Bahir,* where these two powers are designated as the ninth and tenth logoi. Our commentator therefore evidently found the same enumeration, with slight variations, in his source, the "Great Mystery."

---

118. The *'ofannim* had already become angelic beings in the Hekhaloth writings; in our texts they are more than that; and have become cosmic potencies. The Hebrew of the text is, like that of the *Bahir,* section 115, particularly poor.

119. The Hebrew text is quoted in my *Reshith ha-Qabbala,* 218.

This passage also stands in manifest contradiction to the symbolism already adopted elsewhere in the *Bahir,* according to which the last sefirah can no longer be equated with the *'ofannim* of the Merkabah, but is the Shekhinah of God. The present text of the *Bahir* seeks, in a very artificial manner, to bring this symbolism into harmony with the preceding one. But apparently the enumeration of the "Great Mystery" still knew nothing of such a symbolism of the Shekhinah.

Two conclusions may be drawn from these comparisons of the corresponding texts in the two sources: 1. one stratum of the *Bahir* was certainly revised according to the source we possess in part in the quotations from the "Great Mystery"; 2. this revision proves that the *decisive* advances made in the conception of the *Bahir* beyond the Merkabah mystics were effected through recourse to other sources. In just those places where gnostic images appear with the greatest force, there is nothing to indicate their dependence on the *Raza Rabba.* Either they come from another stratum of sources that is no longer, or not yet, identifiable by literary methods, or else this revision is based upon novel and independent speculations on the part of the authors or of the circles where these authors found their inspiration. The examination of several passages of the *Bahir* that we undertook previously provides, in my opinion, unequivocal evidence for the thesis that here, too, we must take into account the use of older sources, at least in part. An independent origin for this symbolic language would be much more difficult to explain than a knowledge of, and contact with, ancient Hebrew or Aramaic fragments of gnostic language and ideas. The very circumstances in which the pieces still attributable to the *Raza Rabba* have been preserved permit us to suppose that in the flow of texts of this kind, other material that left no independent traces in the literature also came to the knowledge of those responsible for the redaction of the *Bahir* and for the development of the kabbalistic symbolism.

At any rate, the link between the *Book of Creation* and the rest of the Merkabah tradition, of such decisive importance for the development of the Kabbalah, was already established in what has now been shown to be the Oriental source of the table of the ten logoi. Since in the *Raza Rabba* we have only vestiges of the second part of this table, we cannot say for sure whether a distinction had already been made there between the qualities of God, conceived as autonomous aeons, and the entities of the Merkabah world.[120] One of the most striking differences between the *Bahir* and the later Kabbalah is the absence of this important distinction in parts of the *Bahir,* nota bene, in just those contexts that seem to be connected with the list of the ten logoi. We now have a perfectly satisfactory explanation of this fact, since we know that a corresponding table already figured in the source. It is entirely conceivable that from the outset this enumeration included aeons that were nothing but hypostases of divine qualities, such as Wisdom, Grace, or Severe Judgment, as well as names of aeons that were nothing other than figures of the Merkabah, such as, for example, the *ḥayyoth,* the *'ofannim,* and the sanctuary of the celestial Jerusalem (which also appears, as we know, as the name of an aeon in many gnostic systems). Only later did a process of separation begin, in the course of which the entities of the Merkabah came to be considered symbols of higher entities within the divine potencies. It is possible, I believe, to determine from the point of view of the system when exactly this process started, even though we cannot fix the date with precision: it began when the Shekhinah of God came to be identified with the last of these ten potencies. This identification—about which more will be said later—no longer permitted the correlation of the world of the Merkabah with that of the divine *middoth* other than by understanding the symbols of the former in a new sense. This process was essentially finished by the time the Book *Bahir* was edited, but traces of the older state of affairs have survived in many places. That is what renders so difficult the interpretation of such texts as sections 115 and 123, which still presuppose another conception.

This also explains the fact that some paragraphs obviously derive from a source that as yet knew nothing of a kabbalistic symbolism of the sefiroth. Instead, the divine names and their relation to the Merkabah are treated in such a way that one has the impression

---

120. A very brief and therefore rather obscure quotation from the "Great Mystery": "For God has a seat [*moshab*] of mercy," (*Reshith ha-Qabbala,* 237) might suggest a relationship between the mysticism of the throne and the hypostases of the *middoth.* But it is not clear in what context this sentence originally appeared in the source. The notion of a "throne of mercy" is also known in the ordinary Aggadah. In the table of the logoi, in section 96, and perhaps already in the text that served as its model, the "Great Mystery," the throne is the sixth logos. Perhaps this passage too stems from the same context as the enumeration of the ten logoi as powers of the Merkabah.

of reading an old Merkabah text. This would accord perfectly well with the character of the *Raza Rabba,* though passages of this type could equally well have been borrowed from a parallel source. Sections 76 and 88, which obviously belong together, are fragments of this kind. In section 76 a relationship is established between the divine *shem ha-meforash* of twelve consonants and that of seventy-two names (see pp. 76–78, herein). There it is said that the names of God "form three hosts [perhaps "hierarchies" would be a better rendering] and each host is similar to the other, and its name is like the name of the other," since, in fact, every host is "sealed" with the Tetragrammaton. Section 88, taking up the subject of these hosts once again, describes, at least in a fragmentary manner, the "domains" or "realms" (Hebrew: *memshaloth*)[121] that belong to each of these three hosts:

> The first is light, and light of the perfect life. The second are the holy *hayyoth,* the *'ofannim* and the wheels, *galgalim,* of the Merkabah. All the hosts of the Holy One, may He be praised, extol and glorify and praise and exalt and sanctify the king, who is enveloped in sanctity and glorified in the council of the saints, the powerful and awe-inspiring king, and they crown Him with the threefold holy [of Isa. 6:3].

Here one sees clearly how gnostic language ("light of the perfect life" —a mode of expression that brings us very close to the language of the Mandaean texts) irrupts into a Merkabah text, recognizable as such by its style and its characteristic emphasis on the Trishagion. Above the Merkabah, properly speaking, stands the supreme "realm," the "light of the perfect life," a concept that returns nowhere else in the *Bahir* or in old kabbalistic literature. Gnostic language has combined here with that of the traditional Merkabah texts. This combination undoubtedly took place in the Orient, in

121. These three *memshaloth* exhibit a remarkable analogy to a hymn by Yehudah Halevi (cf. Schirmann, *Ha-Shirah ha-yehudith bi-Sefard u-Provence,* vol. 1 [1954], 534–535). In Halevi's hymn, too, the first realm is that of the source of life and of the *kabhod,* the second that of the *hayyoth* and *'ofannim!* There is food for thought here, especially as further contaminations can be detected (cf. ibid., 532). Perhaps Halevi's hymn antedates the *Bahir?* Or did the poet use the same source as the *Bahir,* to wit a Merkabah text? The parallels have already been noted by Schirmann, 532. However, the same division is also mentioned in a strictly philosophical context by Abraham ibn Ezra (also quoted by Schirmann) in his commentary to Daniel 10:31. The antiquity of the symbolism is thus far from established.

texts that reached the redactors of the *Bahir* only in fragments (for example, the third "realm" is missing in ours). It is certainly no accident that section 88 is found in proximity in texts that we have shown to have a literary relationship with the "Great Mystery," but that, on the other hand, have also undergone a gnostic revision, such as sections 85, 86, 89, and 90.

Other citations of the "Great Mystery" no longer have their counterparts in the *Bahir.* Worthy of note, for example, is the remark ascribed there to R. Ishmael: "I saw the faithful envoy and the Prince of the Countenance, and they had the same face, and all of them sanctified and praised the Holy One, may He be praised, and said . . . "—but what follows is nothing other than the beginning of the second paragraph of the eulogy in the *Qaddish* prayer, which was therefore already known here in practically the standard received text.[122] That Moses, the "faithful envoy,"[123] has the same face as the angel Metatron, the "Prince of the Countenance" and together with him conducts the celestial liturgy is an idea that is not found in the Merkabah texts known to date. Circles must therefore have existed in which speculations concerning Metatron, whose relation with Moses is attested in the Talmud, *Sanhedrin* 38b, were pushed much further, even suggesting that when Moses ascended toward Metatron, the latter came to meet him, showing him his own face. Speculations of a much broader scope with respect to the nature of the relations between Moses and Metatron could very well stand behind this statement.

The language of the quotations from *Raza Rabba,* like that of the *Bahir,* is a mixture of Aramaic and Hebrew. In many dialogues one has the impression that the *Raza Rabba* as used was interspersed with additions edited in a later style.[124] Reference is made to the

---

122. Cf. the Hebrew text in *Reshith ha-Qabbala,* 226.

123. Hebrew: *ṣir ne'eman,* a designation that certainly corresponds to the old phraseology of the Aggadah and that also appears in the poems of Qalir (ca. fifth through sixth centuries), but is not devoid of gnostic overtones.

124. This can be assumed for the long passage that I have published in Hebrew, *Reshith ha-Qabbala,* 227–230; its continuation is clearly designated as coming from the *Sod ha-Gadol* (232). Certain words from a prayer of thanksgiving in the text of the *Shi'ur Qomah* are equated there by means of gematria with the names of angels —a procedure more in accordance with the later Italo-German tradition of the Hasidim than with the old Merkabah texts for which there is still no evidence of this manner of relating all words in the prayers to the names of angels. Moreover, the quotation, which incidentally is not in Aramaic but almost entirely in Hebrew, has

creation of a golem in a manner closely connected with section 136, without being clear whether the passage derives from the commentator or from his source. The text says: "If a man creates a creature

---

only the loosest connection with the name of the angel it purports to interpret: *Mi Yad'el* (in two words! literally: who is the hand of God?). Our text says:

> And this is the explanation. *Mi Yad'el?* That one sings: who announces the manifestations of the power of the name? And *El* [in the names of angels] is an expression for power, as it is said in many places. [At this point the quotation from the older source apparently begins]. And with that praise, God is praised [namely, the prayer from the *Shi'ur Qomah*], for no creature can praise him in a fitting manner and give expression to even a small part of his praise. These are the words of R. Akiba. [In the *Pirqe Rabbi Eliezer,* chap. 3, this same sentence is quoted, almost literally, in the name of R. Eliezer!] R. Ishmael said: *Mi Yad'el,* that is, who might be God's counselor? God has no need of any [counsel], unlike an earthly king, who shares his power with his counselors, so that they will give him good advice. But God is not like that. R. Akiba said to him: but it is said [Gen. 1:26]: Let us make man; does that not indicate that he took counsel with the heavenly academy? R. Ishmael said: He did so only in order to honor and to exalt them. And know that if He took counsel with them, He did not act according to their advice, for they said [Ps. 8:5]: What is man that you have been mindful of him, etc. R. Akiba said: but is it not said that in every place where the Torah employs the expression "and God" it means God and His academy? R. Ishmael answered him: Indeed, so it is; but in any case, the true counsel comes from God, and He has no need of counsel; the counsel [apparently His heavenly academy] has need of Him, in order to obtain influx [*shefa',* "overflow" or "influx"] from Him. He is unlike an earthly king, who has need of counsel. R. Neḥunya ben Haqqanah said to them: how long will you neglect the essentials and occupy yourselves with matters of secondary importance? *Miyad* [in the name of the angel *Miyad'el*] actually signifies hand, *yad,* and that angel, praising God, says: who is the hand of God? That means: who can say of himself: I am the hand of God? That is to say, God has no hand. And there is no greater praise than that, for everything that has a hand also has need of a hand, but God, who has no hand, has no need of a hand [that is, the aid and support of others]. They said to him: but is it not said [Job 12:10]: In His hand is every living soul? He answered them: [this is a metaphor] in order to explain it to the ear in such a way that it can be understood. And just as He has no hand, He also has no other limb, for everything that has a limb has need of a limb, and one cannot say of God that He has need of anything . . . . And at the hour when they say the praises, they [the angels] rise before the celestial curtain, but not completely in front of it. [Next, the text explains other names of angels associated with the words of the prayer in *Shi'ur Qomah:*] Raphael, who in his praises gives magnificence [*pe'er,* "magnificence," has the same consonants as *rfa'* in Raphael] to God, who made him the messenger for healing Israel, in such a way that no other angel interferes within his limits [that is, sphere of authority]. These are the words of R. Neḥunya. R. Akiba and R. Ishmael said to him: but have you not often said to us that he sings: who can say that he has obtained healing, and not from God? [He answered]: my children, these and those [both dicta] are the words of the living God. They

by means of the Book *Yeṣirah,* he has the power to create everything except one thing."[125] It is not said what this one thing is, but it may well be language, as is suggested by many parallel texts and

---

> said to him: but it is impossible to say at the same time two [contrary] things. He answered them: All of this is a single scheme of things. They said to him: permit us to say a word before you [a phrase that also occurs in the Merkabah texts in *Ḥagigah* 14b]. He said: speak. They said to him: He is so named because he heals the song of the king [that is, the song that is sung to the king]. He answered them: this is the work of another [angel], and no one has the power above [in heaven] to interfere in the domain of his companions. . . . Gabardael proclaims the praise of his creator, saying: who could come whose power, *geburah,* is such that he could abolish a single one of God's acts? These are the words of R. Neḥunya ben Haqqanah. R. Akiba and R. Ishmael said to him: but you have often told us that he is called *gibbor,* "full of power," because his power is greater than that of Sammael [Satan]. When, for example, Sammael comes and incites the king or the prince to do harm to the Jews, he [this angel] abolishes his plan, as it is said [1 Kings 8:50]: Grant them mercy in the sight of their captors that they may be merciful to them. For the numerical value of Gabardael [that is, 248] is the same as that of *raḥem,* which is an expression for mercy. He said to them: give me refreshments, for there was nothing to my words. At that hour, a laugh resounded in the Merkabah and it was said: the disciples have defeated their master. Then a heavenly voice was heard to say: a man is jealous of everyone except of his son and his pupils [*Sanhedrin* 105b]. They began to laugh. He said to them: go, eat your bread in the morning and drink your wine with good cheer, for we are all inscribed for life in the future world. Immediately, they descended to the Merkabah and all the inhabitants of the heights made way for them until they arrived before the Prince of the Countenance [Metatron], and they presented all their doubts and returned in peace and doubled on that day the good [the text perhaps ought to be corrected—קבעו instead of כפלו: and they fixed that day as a holiday]. And henceforth, R. Neḥunya ben Haqqanah no longer descended with them, but he by himself and they by themselves.

This curious angelology perhaps confirms the old testimony concerning the content of the *Raza Rabba,* which would then represent a later stage of angelology than that found in the other Merkabah texts.

125. Cf. my *Reshith ha-Qabbala,* 231. Psalms 8:6, cited in this connection, is also mentioned in the *Bahir,* section 136. The manner in which the passage is formulated in the commentary on the *Shi'ur Qomah* is characteristic of the milieu of the German Hasidim, who spoke of the creation of a "creature" by means of the Book *Yeṣirah,* instead of employing the technical term golem, which was otherwise in use among them. Cf. the quotation from Eleazar of Worms in the commentary on the prayer book by Naphthali Hirz Treves (Thiengen, 1560), sheet 28, fol. 2b:

> He placed together [in the hymn commented upon there] "speech" and "knowledge," for a man can well have the knowledge that would enable him to create a new creature according to the prescriptions of the Book *Yeṣirah,* but he cannot endow him with speech by means of the *shem ha-meforash,* as only God is able to do.

by the *Bahir.* This sentence may well be an interpolation by the commentator, especially since he appeals expressly to the Book *Yeṣirah.* The immediate continuation, however, which refers back to certain sources in the "Great Mystery," resumes the preceding angelological quotations with the remark: "there are manuscripts where it is said . . . ," as if that which had been quoted previously was found in all manuscripts, whereas that which followed figured in only a few of them. Nevertheless it is highly possible that precisely the sentence concerning the creation of the golem is an interpolation by the author. If this is not the case, the text would be even more significant.

The conclusion remains clear: the Book *Bahir* was not composed as a result of a completely new inspiration of a gnostic character. On the contrary, it took over sources, in part reconstructed and in part inferred by our analysis. These sources, which are not homogeneous, came from the Orient. It is easy to understand how they could have come into being there in regard to the Merkabah literature or to some other purely gnostic tradition; their birth in the Occident, on the other hand, would be inexplicable. There remains the question of whether the transmission of these fragments was accompanied by an oral tradition that already delineated the course to be followed by the groups that were to make them the object of their meditations. It would be completely appropriate, given everything we have said, to seek these circles somewhere in France, in connection with the esoteric tradition of the German Hasidim. Sometime between 1130 and 1170 the leaves of the original *Bahir* arrived in Provence, where they were subjected to a final revision and redaction into the form in which the book has come down to us. Its world of ideas seems to have been touched only lightly by the specific developments of German Hasidism.

5. The First Three Sefiroth

After our preceding analysis of the sources, we may now pose the question regarding the ideas about the ten powers of God as they had crystallized in the oldest form of the Kabbalah accessible to us. The schema of the sefiroth is still in flux, at least in regard to several of the powers and their position in the whole. It is precisely its unfinished state that enables us to distinguish more clearly certain stages in the development of this schema, which was to be appropriated by the Kabbalah, and to discern the greatly variegated motifs that led to its formation.

Whereas the ten sefiroth are often spoken of as a unity, particularly in the parables, one can nevertheless already clearly recognize in many places a fundamental division into two groups that was to become canonical in the Kabbalah. This division into three higher and seven lower sefiroth goes back to *Pirqe Rabbi Eliezer,* a late midrash that also contains much older material. In chapter 3 we read: "Some say: By means of ten sayings, *ma'amaroth,* the world was created, and they were united in three [attributes]." These three supreme *middoth,* deduced from Proverbs 3:19, 20, are Wisdom, Understanding, and Knowledge, which are mentioned together in several verses of the Bible.[126] Yet precisely these verses are not mentioned in the *Bahir;* and in fact only once, in passing as it were (section 129, does *da'ath,* "knowledge" or gnosis, appear as the name of an aeon. Instead, we find in sections 89 and 96, not as the third but as the highest of all the logoi, an entirely different image: that of the supreme crown, *kether 'elyon.* "Wisdom" and "Understanding" are named in section 32 as the second and third groups of logoi,[127] whereas the highest, the third, which is above the two others, is designated as the wondrous and the impenetrable. "Which is the third? On this subject that old man [here the reference is undoubtedly already to the prophet Elijah[128]] said to that child: that which seems too wondrous for you, do not explore it, and that which is hidden from you, do not dig for it: seek understanding in that which is permitted to you and do not meddle with secrets." The old quotation from Sirah 3:21, 22, used by the esoteric speculation and also,

---

126. Cf. Exodus 31:3, 1 Kings 7:14; Proverbs 24:3.

127. The Ten Commandments correspond to the "ten kings," which are divided into seven voices and three words, *'amarim.* Deuteronomy 26:18 alludes to these three as a supreme word:

> and of them it is said [Prov. 4:7]: The beginning of wisdom is—acquire wisdom; with all your acquisitions, acquire discernment. As it is also said [Job 32:8]: The breath of Shaddai, that gives them understanding; the soul that corresponds to Shaddai mediates to them "understanding."

Section 32 then continues as in the text above.

128. "That old man," mentioned in this general form in several talmudic passages, was taken by many commentators, already at an early date, to refer to the prophet Elijah; cf. the gaonic responsum in Harkavy, *Zikhron la-Rischonim,* pt. 4 (Berlin, 1887), 9–10, where, however, this interpretation is rejected.

many times, in the Talmud, here becomes a mysterious word designating the supreme rank, that which is situated even above "Wisdom."

In the writings of Eleazer of Worms, the epithet "supreme crown" is clearly employed several times as one of the names of God, but not as a synonym for the first sefirah.[129] In section 96, however, it attains an unmistakably divine rank, which raises the question of to what extent it is accessible to thought. "Which are the ten logoi? First: *kether 'elyon,* praised and greatly glorified be his name and his people. And who is his people? Israel, as it is written [Ps. 100:3]: 'Acknowledge that YHWH is God, He made us and not we'—to recognize and know the One among all the ones, who is One in all His names." The ambiguity of this phrase is striking. The supreme crown is, according to the sense of the image, a crown of the king himself, who manifests his kingship through it albeit while remaining ever so hidden. The formula of praise, although in reality intended for God who bears the crown, is transferred to the crown itself.[130] The formula proves that the author of this table in the *Bahir* clearly had in mind the sefiroth of the *Book of Creation* in which the first *sefirah* (1:9) is described as "the spirit of the living God, praised and glorified be the name of the eternally living." This eulogy, which in the *Yeṣirah* clearly refers to the living God and not to his sefirah, undergoes a slight alteration in the *Bahir* and is transferred, at least according to the grammatical construction, to the sefirah itself. On the other hand, the philosophical expression "the One among all the ones," which we have already characterized as Neoplatonic on page 67, indicates the bearer of the crown rather than the crown itself. In Yehudah ben Barzilai's commentary on the *Yeṣirah,* we also read that God "is one in all of His names";[131] but

---

129. Thus in Eleazar's commentary on the piyyut, *ha-'oḥez ba-yad,* (Ms. Munich 92, fol. 26b), which says of the attribute of "omnipotent" given to God: "similarly, his name is supreme crown." According to Eleazar's *Sefer ha-Ḥokhmah,* Ms. Oxford 1568, fol. 6b, God showed to Moses a clear mirror, "and that is the supreme crown, which is also called the tenth royal dominion." Here, therefore, the tenth sefirah, which is the "royal dominion" as such, is simply called "supreme crown," a symbolism that contradicts that of the *Bahir.* In the texts of the Merkabah known to date, I have not found the notion of a "supreme crown."

130. *Kether,* "crown," is masculine in Hebrew; the "praised be He" placed in apposition can therefore refer to *kether* as well as to the bearer of the crown.

131. Ed. 1885, 13, last line.

this is no doubt a figure of speech that can also be found in other writings. In fact, the source of this expression (as I realized only in 1970) is to be found in the second great prayer *(bakashah)* of Saadya Gaon (ed. Davidson [1941], 64), where the term *meyuḥad* is given a special nuance: "You the Lord are *eḥad, meyuḥad, be-khol shemothekha.*" The fact that the *Bahir* quotes from a prayer by Saadya is not without significance. In any case, it appears as if these speculative additions belong to the final redaction in Provence. In its oldest form, the table that figures in the *Raza Rabba* was edited in a milieu already saturated with formulas and concepts of a different provenance.

Having said that, we must pose the question of the origin of the other designations of the first sefirah, as we find them (in a singularly modified form) in the table in section 103 as well as in several other passages in sections 48, 53, 59, 60, 94, and 134. Mention is made there of the thinking or the thought of God, *maḥshabah,* as the most hidden sphere, but also as the center of the innermost of the first six logoi. Not the divine will of Solomon ibn Gabirol and his Neoplatonic sources, of which the *Bahir* is completely ignorant, but precisely the thought or the primordial idea is the innermost point that can be reached by all meditation and all comprehension of God. Does this terminology derive from a gnostic tradition in which, as indeed in several systems, the "thought," (*ennoia*), is likewise conceived as the supreme aeon of the pleroma?[132] Similarly, in section 134, the "thought" is directly opposed to the other "powers" in which God manifests himself. Or must we seek the origin of this terminology among the Jewish Neoplatonists, from whom it could have been borrowed and incorporated into the *Bahir* only in the twelfth century? It is Without doubt important to know this in order to be able to determine the character of the Oriental sources of the *Bahir.* Nevertheless, I cannot presume to answer this question and must leave it open. We may in any case affirm that in the usage of Abraham bar Ḥiyya, the Jewish Neoplatonist with whom we already became acquainted in section 1 of this chapter as a source of the final Provençal stratum of the *Bahir,* the "pure thought," *maḥ-*

---

132. On the *ennoia* in Gnosticism, cf. for example the references in F. Sagnard, *La Gnose Valentinienne,* 640, in the index under ἔννοια, and in W. Bousset, *Die Hauptprobleme der Gnosis* (Göttingen, 1907), 160–162 (on the Simonians and the Barbelognostics).

shabah ṭehorah designates this primordial divine idea that precedes everything and embraces everything within itself. Within it, there existed, in potentia and hidden, the two "highest principles" or "supreme roots," that is, original matter and original form, until the divine will combined them.[133] This pure *maḥshabah* is also elevated to the highest rank in the *Bahir,* even higher than the Sophia of God.

All these passages emphasize a single quality of this "thought," which, as conceived by the *Bahir,* connects human and divine thinking. This quality is its boundlessness. The two kinds of *maḥshabah* are placed parallel to one another, without it being clearly said whether one leads to the other, as was the case, for example, in the Kabbalah of the generations that followed the *Bahir.* But since it is only thus that the parallelism receives its full significance, we may, perhaps, assume that here, too, the pure thought of man, detached from any concrete content and meditating upon no definite object but itself, is conducted along a path of pure meditation to the divine thought and enters into communion with it. If I have correctly interpreted the allusions in section 60, we are witnessing here the sketchy beginnings of a method of mystical meditation that no longer has any need of the apparatus of the doctrine of the aeons but sets out directly for its mystical goal. If, nevertheless, speculation on the aeons is associated with it—as is the case with the Jewish form it assumes in the final redaction of the *Bahir*—this is not because it necessarily had to take this path; it is for historical reasons: these other ideas were already familiar to those who developed the mysticism of the *maḥshabah.* In order to understand this very ancient Kabbalah, it is necessary to analyze the most important relevant texts.

A certain transition from the human to the divine *maḥshabah* can be assumed in a passage concerning prayer, which says that he who prays—in this case the prophet Habakkuk in his psalm—attains a mystical "place" whence he understands the *maḥshabah* of God. This *maḥshabah* is represented in three important symbols: the consonant *'alef,* the beginning of all language and expression as well

---

133. Abraham bar Ḥiyya, *Hegyon ha-Nefesh,* fol. 2a. Many thirteenth-century kabbalists use this expression "the pure thought" as a fixed mystical technical term. Cf. herein, chap. 3, sec. 5. According to ibn Gabirol, *Fons Vitae* 5:10, matter and form are contained separately and potentially, in God's *sapientia.*

as the "root of the ten commandments" (which begin with an *'alef*); the ear of a man, *'ozen,* which is an image of the *'alef,* by means of which man perceives the word of God; the temple of the sanctuary. This last symbolism is particularly striking, for while in most passages where it appears it clearly refers to the highest potency of God, it is designated in section 103 as the seventh logos, the Holy Temple that bears all others, those others apparently being the preceding six. "And what is he [this logos]? The thought, which has no end and no conclusion *(takhlith).* Similarly, this place has neither end nor conclusion." However, in section 48 it is said:

> The ear is the image of the *'alef* and the *'alef* is the beginning of all the letters; and more than that, the *'alef* is the necessary condition for the existence of all the letters, and the *'alef* is an image of the brain [the seat of thought]: just as when one pronounces the *'alef* one opens only the mouth [and does not produce any audible sound, which would already be something definite], so the thought goes without an end and a conclusion.

Even the Tetragrammaton, as Micah 2:13 is interpreted here, "is contained in their beginning [that is, in the beginning of all things or all of the letters]," that beginning being the *maḥshabah* itself. The name of YHWH itself obtains his Holiness, as it is said there later, in the Temple of the Sanctuary, which has its place "in the *maḥshabah,* and this [the temple] is the *'alef.*"[134]

The temple in the celestial Jerusalem, the cosmological symbol that the author of the *Bahir,* as we have seen, had borrowed from the *Book of Creation* and the "Great Mystery," here becomes a mystical symbol. The infinite divine thought, which precedes everything and includes everything, is the mystical "Temple" where all spiritual beings have their place. In the "raptures" or "ecstasies" of his prayer, Habakkuk arrived at a certain place, from where he understood the *maḥshabah* of God and the *shema'* of God. The *shema'* in this context is equivalent to the highest sphere of hearing, designated by the ear, or that which God is heard to say, the "rumor" of God. He who understands this will be filled with the fear of God, and that is why Habakkuk said in his prayer (3:2): "Oh Lord! I have learned of your renown; I am awed." Since the verb *shema'* in

---

134. Similarly, in section 84, where the *'alef* and the Temple indeed appear, but not the *maḥshabah.*

Hebrew signifies not only "hearing" but also "thinking, understanding," the link between the spheres of thought and of hearing established in the *Bahir* is not at all surprising. This thought, as the highest and hidden potency, is evoked by the parable (section 48) "of a retired, wondrous, and hidden king, who went into his house and commanded that no one ask for him. Thus, whoever asks for [him] would be afraid that the king might learn that he had transgressed his order." The epithets that are used here for the king are identical with those employed in section 32 for the highest logos, concerning which it is forbidden to ask questions. In section 59, the thought from which "ear and eye draw" is designated as "the king of whom all creation is in need."

The symbolism of the Temple for the most profound divine thought can well be understood by analogy with the very similar symbolism of the "Temple" with which, as with so many other metaphors, Meister Eckhart, about 150 years later, described the most elevated domain of the soul, its "rational knowledge." The *Vernünftlichkeit* of the soul, as Eckhart named reason in its most elevated state, is its pure thought, in which it touches the *intelligere* of God, yea, is itself this reason of God.

> Where is God if not in His temple where He reveals Himself in His Holiness? Reason is the "temple of God." Nowhere does God reside more truly than in His temple, reason, as that other master [Aristotle] said: God is a reason which lives in the knowledge of itself . . . for only there is He in His repose.[135]

The symbolism is the same, although in the *Bahir* the point of departure is different from that of Meister Eckhart, who, for his part, proceeds from Aristotle's concept of God, a concept of which there is no trace in the *Bahir.*

This can be seen quite distinctly in section 60, an important passage that proves that its author had a clear notion of the differences between the old mystics' vision of the Merkabah and the new realm that, in his mysticism, opened up beyond it.

> Why do we employ [in Hebrew] the expression "it arose in the thought" [in the sense of: it came to mind], and we do not say: "it descends," while we do say [in the "Greater Hekhaloth"]: whoever

135. Meister Eckhart, *Die deutschen Werke,* vol. 1, (Stuttgart, 1957), 150, 464.

> plunges into the vision of the Merkabah descends and [only] afterwards ascends? There [it is written "descend"], because we say: whoever plunges into the vision of the Merkabah . . . but here, in the *maḥshabah,* the thought, there is no longer any vision or any end. And everything which has neither end nor conclusion suffers no descent, as people [indeed) say: someone descended [that is, penetrated] to the end of the opinion of his companion; but not: to the end of his thought.

The *maḥshabah* is therefore the object of a vision and a contemplative immersion, *histakluth;* indeed, it is the last and the most profound object of all such contemplation. The vision finds its limit in the object contemplated. It can therefore be said that these old mystics "descend toward the Merkabah."

The thought, however, is no longer the object of any vision or contemplation, but is related to a different domain. It no longer leads to an object determined by it. It has no end and no conclusion, and it is sufficient unto itself, for "man thinks and thereby arrives at the end of the world."[136] A thinking that is related to this or that thing or to this or that opinion as its specific content can be exhausted, and one can advance to its end. It is not the same with pure thought, which has no object other than itself and which is not determined by anything outside itself. That is precisely why, as is always emphasized, infinity is the principal property of the *maḥshabah.* On the other hand, our book still knows nothing of an expression *'en-sof* in the terminological sense of "infinity," designating that hidden reality of the Lord of all the logoi, of God who conceals himself in the depths of his own essentiality. To be sure, the compound *'en-sof* appears in an adverbial form in section 48: "the thought with which one can think up to infinity and the endless," *le-'en sof we-takhlith,* but there is not the slightest hint here of the "infinite" as a noun, concerning which or of which one thinks.[137]

Between this supreme *maḥshabah* and the powers and potencies

---

136. The text of this sentence in section 53 is in Aramaic; the author writes literally: *shafel le-sofeh de-'alma,* "descends to the end of the world," apparently in order to avoid the Hebrew word for descend, the use of which he specifically prohibits (section 60) in connection with "thinking."

137. According to Graetz there was not more than a faint whiff of *'en-sof* in the *Bahir,* cf. vol. 7(4th ed.), 402. But as I have shown above, this misses the point. Ehrenpreis, *Die Entwicklung der Emanationslehre in der Kabbala* (Berlin, 1895), 22, correctly denies the presence of the term in the *Bahir.* On the question of the term *'en-sof,* cf. herein, chap. 3, pp. 266–70.

of God in which it "extends itself" (which may or may not be a technical expression for emanation),[138] there exists a relation which, according to section 134, was the object of Moses' request (Exod. 33:18): "Let me behold your presence."

> Moses said: I know the paths of the powers, but I do not know how the *maḥshabah* extends itself in them. I know that the truth [another aeon, which according to section 94 "acts through the *maḥshabah*"] is in the *maḥshabah.* But I do not know its parts [the parts of the truth][139] and I would like to know them, but he was not allowed to know it.

This ignorance indicates an older state of kabbalistic speculation that, in the thirteenth century, believed it knew full well what Moses himself, according to our text, did not yet know. It even ascribed this knowledge to Moses.[140]

In sections 13, 18, 32, and 95 the second and the third sefiroth are conceived as forming a unity with the first, which is symbolized by the *'alef.* According to section 13, the mystical place of the *'alef* even preceded the origin of the Torah, which, accordingly, only begins with the *beth* (the first letter of the first word of the Pentateuch, *bereshith*). Certain designations employed in the milieu of Merkabah mysticism for the second and third sefiroth are missing in the table of logoi, section 96, as well as in other parts of the book, which to me does not appear accidental. The concepts by which they are known throughout the Kabbalah, *ḥokhmah* and *binah,* are already found here: *ḥokhmah* in numerous passages, *binah* only in sections 32 and 74.

That the second sefirah is designated as the "beginning" can certainly be understood on the basis of Proverbs 8:22, where Wisdom says: "The Lord created me at the beginning of His course." But this fact has a further implication, one that could not have been

---

138. *Hithpashet* has this technical meaning in the philosophical literature of the Jewish Neoplatonists.

139. The masculine suffix in *ḥalaqaw* must refer to *'emeth,* which is always employed in the masculine in medieval Hebrew, and not (as I had first supposed in my translation and in the accompanying commentary) to *maḥshabah,* which is feminine.

140. Cf. Moses de Leon, *Mishkan ha-'Eduth,* Ms. Berlin Or.Q. 833, fol. 41b. Already Philo, *De specialibus legibus,* 1, section 44ff., taught that Moses only grasped the powers of God, but not His essence.

far from the minds of the authors of the *Bahir.* The first sefirah is still not a "beginning," properly speaking. It is still completely hidden and perhaps even without a beginning, uncreated and inseparable from God himself, whose supreme crown it represents. This is never expressed explicitly, but the consistency with which the image of the source is applied to wisdom in passages (sections 3, 4, 15, 82, 85, 121) points in this direction.

In section 4, as we saw in an earlier analysis, the pleroma itself begins only with the mystical *beth,* which is not only the blessing of God but also the pool from which everything drinks, and especially the garden that contains the world of the logoi or the last of them. It is difficult to say how far we may press the mystical metaphors found in many passages in this context. Thus the image may be understood as saying that the source gushes forth from the strong rock, that is, from the primordial stone of the first sefirah, which the king had broken open. In any event, every action occurring inside the pleroma, in the parables as well as in more direct exegetical statements, always begins at this place. The cosmic tree itself, as we have seen, is watered from here (sections 15, and 85, whereas section 15, as we saw on pages 71–2, is a reinterpretation of the more ancient myth of the cosmic tree in section 14). This Sophia is naturally also the primordial Torah, which corresponds to the aggadic equation of the two concepts but also to the aggadic identification of the source of water, fresh water, and water in general with the Torah.[141] With a little courage, an interpreter could also view the cosmic tree, from which souls originate, as the Torah itself, (as happens, for example, section 8 and 15.) Section 8 is interesting in that there the Torah is the hidden beginning of the world. The Midrash[142] already had interpreted the order of the words in Genesis 1:1 as if they meant: "only after he had created that which his world needed [*ṣorkhe 'olamo*—the Torah, which is also called "beginning"] He mentioned [as the third word of the verse] His name [*'Elohim*]." Similarly, it is said in the *Bahir:* "In the beginning He created, and what did He create? That which the all needed, *ṣorkhe ha-kol,* and only then is it said: *'Elohim.*" That which the "all" requires is in the more mythical image of section 14 the cosmic tree; in the more in-

141. Examples of the equation of wisdom with Torah can be found in Strack-Billerbeck 2:353; that of water and the Torah, ibid. 2:435.

142. *Bereshith Rabba, parashah* 1, section 12; ed. Theodor, 11.

nocuous aggadic reinterpretation of sections 8 and 15, it is the Torah, which is also the Sophia of God. After having "excavated" this source, as in section 4, he plants the cosmic tree of worlds, whose root, the third sefirah, is watered from there. This must be the harmonizing exegesis that the redactors of the *Bahir* had in mind when they juxtaposed these originally so different texts.[143]

Judging from the context of the passages in question, this third logos must be the "root of the tree" referred to in sections 54, 84, and 118. The same seems to hold true for section 18, though the latter passage lacks enumeration. To this "root of the tree" corresponds section 74, which speaks unequivocally of *binah,* the symbol of the "mother of the world." With that, the oldest Kabbalah again took up a mythically charged image, for which it could even provide justification by referring to the Talmudic exegesis (*Berakhoth* 57a) of Proverbs 2:3, which read the verse (with a homiletic vocalization that is different from the Masoretic one): "You will call understanding (*binah*) mother."[144] Deuteronomy 22:7 is similarly associated with this mystical mother and her seven children who, although designated here as the seven days of the Sukkoth festival, undoubtedly correspond in this context to the group of seven lower logoi, the

---

143. It is also possible that the obscure passage in section 65, with its mystical interpretation of Ecclesiastes 5:8, refers to wisdom. The three words of the verse *yithron 'ereṣ ba-kol* are considered, each one separately, as symbols. *Yithron,* here without doubt in the sense of "superabundance," "superior existence," is opposed to the earth, *'ereṣ,* which was "hewn" from it, which here probably has much the same meaning as "emanated." This "earth" is the last sefirah. "And what is *yithron?* Everything in the world, if men in the world are worthy to take from its brightness, is *yithron."* Does this mean all things have something of the brightness, *ziw,* of the Sophia? Perhaps the verse should be read, in the spirit of the *Bahir,* roughly as follows: "The Sophia, from which emanated the last sefirah, named 'earth' [which, as we know, is the lower Sophia] is in everything." This brightness of the *yithron* or mystical being, which is referred to here but does not recur elsewhere in the *Bahir,* would accord very well with sections 97 and 116, where the primordial light of creation, which was later hidden and whence the Shekhinah or the lower Sophia emanated, could also have been, originally, the higher Sophia. This, in fact, is what is expressly affirmed, in section 116 of the oldest manuscript, Munich 209, and by other witnesses: The Shekhinah below "is the light emanated from the first light, which is the *ḥokhmah."* The sequel, however, with its parable of the king and his seven sons, suggests that *binah* is the primordial light by means of which the seven lower sefiroth are maintained. Evidently there were at first two different interpretations of the primordial light as one aeon among the aeons. The passages cited do not permit a definitive interpretation.

144. Similarly the Targum corresponding to this passage.

"primeval days" of Creation (section 92). The seven lower sefiroth are the children of the mother of the world. It is interesting to note that this symbolism, whose imagery confers on it a distinctly gnostic character, appears in a context of halakhic mysticism, namely, in an interpretation of the biblical precept concerning the bird's nest. A corresponding symbolism of the father for the Sophia, as it was consistently developed by the kabbalists of the thirteenth century, is not found in the *Bahir,* although at the end of the same section 74, in an obscure mystical explanation of the Sukkoth festival, this sefirah is expressly mentioned as the mystery of the Sukkoth booth. Furthermore, the maternal symbolism of the *binah* seems to underlie the interpretation, in section 13, of the consonant *gimmel* as the third sefirah. It is from her who draws from above, that is, from the source of the Sophia, and thus receives the emanation, that the "child" obtains his beneficent nourishment: (thus the interpretation of Genesis 21:8).

The statements in the table of logoi, in section 96, are of a different character. Only the Sophia, "the beginning of its paths" is named there as the second logos, whereas the third logos is given several very significant designations.

> The third: the quarry of the Torah, the treasure house of the Sophia[145] [*ḥokhmah*]; the quarry of the spirit, the spirit of God. This teaches that God there chiseled all of the letters of the Torah and engraved them in the spirit and there generated the forms [another version: his forms, that is, those of God] and of that it is said: [1 Samuel 2:2, utilizing the interpretation of the verse in *Berakhoth* 10a]: "There is none that shapes forms like our God."

How are these curious symbols to be explained? Should we assume a contradiction between this passage and those in which the Torah is identified with the Sophia, or should we seek an accord? The expression "treasure house of the Sophia" suggests that such an accord is not implausible, since it is a specification of the second logos, which is the Sophia itself. The Sophia is already lodged in a treasure house, where her treasures are available for the use or government

145. The "treasury of the Sophia" has an ancient (fourth-century?) parallel in the *memar* of the Samaritan *Marqah* 6:3: "The Torah is the treasury of all wisdom." Perhaps we are dealing here with an old expression preserved by the *Bahir* that is capable of shedding light on the relationship obtaining between such old fragments.

of the cosmos. This is a house into which Wisdom is received, a house that she built around herself (cf. Proverbs 9:1: "Sophia has built her house"). The expression "quarry of the Torah," *maḥṣeb ha-Torah,* should probably be understood in the same sense as "the hewing of the Torah," the place where this operation occurs, and not, as one would perhaps be tempted to explain, as the place where it was extracted from the rock. Just as the Sophia has a treasure house, so also the Torah, a primordial essence, has its place where it is hewn, that is, where it is more precisely specified. What exactly is hewn there is explained in the sequel, which however includes two contradictory statements. They are the consonants of the Torah that God "broke" or "hewed" into the solid rock of the primordial Torah. This could lead to the idea that the primordial Torah, which is none other than wisdom itself, contained these forms in an undifferentiated manner and an indistinct unity. This idea would be in perfect accord with what the first Provençal kabbalists expounded later and in clearer formulations, in their speculations on this sefirah. But at the same time this logos is also designated as the spirit of God, *ruaḥ 'elohim,* and as the place where this spirit is "hewn out." In the Book *Yeṣirah,* the "spirit of God" was still expressly designated as the first sefirah. The place of the pneuma is therefore consciously modified in this table. The *Yeṣirah* was still ignorant of the first two logoi, and the "Wisdom" of which it speaks in the image of its thirty-two paths, in manifest connection with the speculations of contemporary circles regarding the Sophia, is not yet one of the ten sefiroth. This development evidently occurred only in another circle. According to the Book *Yeṣirah* 1:10, it is precisely in the second sefirah, the air, which issues from the pneuma of God, that he "engraved and hewed" the twenty-two letters. The two statements therefore seem to have been merged in the *Bahir* and transferred to the third sefirah, which thus contains, in a sense, matter and form at the same time. But in this case it is not matter in the sense hyle as the place of evil, such as the *Bahir* knows it for the *tohu;* it is a "matter" of the pneuma, to be positively valued, in which God produces his "forms." That a certain contradiction is in this manner established between the pneuma and the primordial Torah, which both serve at the same time as media of this formation and "hewing," is unmistakable. The third logos, one could say, is overdetermined: the symbolism of the Sophia and its treasure house is not so much united as jumbled together with that of the pneuma of God, borrowed from the *Yeṣirah,* and with that of the letters engraved in the air that issues from it.

Whereas the symbols of the *binah* that we have discussed derive from historically identifiable speculations, others were developed without any connections of this kind, but simply from mystical exegesis of biblical verses. Such is the case, for example, for the interpretation of *binah* as "fear of God," *yir'ah,* (sections 72 and 139), or "superior justice" (sections 98, 129, 139), or of Habakkuk 3:4 as a description of this sefirah. In sections 98 and 131, this potency is associated with the primordial light of creation, the supreme bliss and the "hidden good"—a combination that also results from the other symbols that serve to designate the primordial light. At the same time it is also the light of the world to come, an expression to which section 106 gives the meaning of an eternal presence of this hidden primordial light:

> What does it signify that we speak every day of the "world to come" [*'olam ha-ba'*] and we do not know what we are saying? The Targum translates the "world to come" by the "world which comes [in the present tense]." What does that mean? That teaches that before the creation of the world, a plan was formed [literally: arose in the *maḥshabah*] to create a great light for illumination. Then a great light was created that no creature would be able to bear. God foresaw that no one would be able to bear it; then he took a seventh part of it and gave it to them in its place. As for the rest, he hid it for the world to come. He said: If they show themselves worthy of this seventh and guard it, I will give them the rest in the other world, which means "the world which comes"—which already comes since the six days of creation.

This mystical interpretation of the "world to come" as a symbol of the third sefirah plays a great role in the subsequent development of the Kabbalah, which on this point always invokes the *Bahir.* The aeon from which everything comes, as from its mother, is also the aeon to which everything will return. The bestowal on the world of precisely one seventh part of the primordial light derives from the exegesis of Isaiah 30:26, which prophesied that "the light of the sun shall become sevenfold, like the light of the seven days," that is, as the primordial light of the Creation (sections 37, 39). At the same time a reference may be implied to the seventh sefirah as well, which has its origin in this primordial light of the *binah* distributed and diffused throughout the seven primeval days of creation. This seventh part is, therefore, the last of the ten potencies of God. It is the light that shines in the "Oral Torah," that is, in the halakhah applicable in life, to which Israel must prove true. If it does so, then the "reflection received from the primordial light will one day be like the light itself" (section 98). While the light taken from the primordial light is here called "Oral Torah," it is designated in section 116 as the lower Shekhinah. This *tertium comparationis* established the relation that subsequently linked these two symbols—the Shekhinah and the Oral Torah—in the Kabbalah.

Section 34 seems to present a continuation of the initial, especially the first three, sefiroth. It has the appearance, like many other passages in this part, of older cosmogonic fragments that underwent a revision in a symbolic direction. The "beginning," the pneuma or "degree whence the souls come," "the stream of God," silver and gold seem to be enumerated here one after the other. The transition from cosmogonic to mystical exegesis is evident. The idea that God drew from the primordial waters of Creation in order to place one half in the firmament and the other half in the ocean is typical early Aggadah.[146] But here this "water" in the "stream of God" of Psalms 65:10 has already become something else: a pneumatic force "through which man arrives at the study of the Torah, as the Lord instructed [a quotation unknown to me that is ascribed here to Rabbi Beraḥya]—through the merit of good deeds a man arrives at the study of the Torah." Here we have two motifs that prima facie contradict each other. On the one hand, the water is that of the Torah; on the other, it is that of the good deeds; and the two exegeses are simply juxtaposed.

More probably this text does not relate to the first sefirah at all but to the second through the fourth sefiroth. In this case the waters would agree perfectly well with other passages concerning the symbolism of the fourth sefirah. The place whence the souls issue would then in fact be the *binah* as in the directly preceding section 32. In the second paragraph after section 34, in section 36, this symbolism no longer refers to *binah* but to the last sefirah; however, this passage on the "daughter" is of a purely gnostic character and evi-

146. Cf. for example the cosmology of the Book *Raziel* (Amsterdam, 1701), fol. 22b, which goes back to old sources on *Ma 'aseh Bereshith.*

dently originates in another source. The two paragraphs belong to different strata and are only linked to each other through an association of ideas, by means of the exegesis of the word "gold."

6. The Six Lower Sefiroth: The Limbs of the Primordial Man and Their Symbolism—The Place of Evil

The next seven logoi, with which the *Bahir* is chiefly concerned, are very emphatically treated as constituting a separate whole. Indeed, all ten "kings" (sections 19, 32) form a unity, just as the Ten Commandments were all "uttered in one word"[147] at the time of the revelation; but below the three supreme "words" in the hierarchy of the pleroma are seven other words identical with the seven voices with which the Torah was given and with the seven voices mentioned in Psalm 29 (sections 29, 32; the details are somewhat obscure). They are also the seven days of the week and, more specifically, of Creation, each possessing its own potency or power with which it "accomplishes the effect that is within its power" (sections 54, 55, 105, where the terms "logos" and "potency" are alternately used as synonyms for these aeons). Other similes speak of the seven sons to whom the king assigned their places according to an hierarchical order, but each of whom, even the last, wishes to be equally close to him (section 116), or of the seven "gardens" of the king. It is from these seven "primordial days" that the patriarchs received the potencies associated with them and characterizing them, and which they filled with power and manifested in this world through their personal conduct (sections 92, 131, 132). They are also the "seven" for which the Psalmist daily praises God, according to the interpretation given here (sections 41, 45) to Psalms 119:164. But above all, they are the seven "holy forms" of God in accordance with which God created man in his image. The book speaks of "holy forms" in various contexts. In section 67, the archons of the peoples bear this designation. In section 77 we are told of seventy-two such holy forms, which are evidently related to the seventy-two names of God

147. Thus, for example, already in the *Midrash Tanhuma, parashath Yithro,* section 11: "The ten words proceeded from the mouth of God . . . and the voice divided into seven voices."

and the seventy-two forms in the cosmic tree in section 64. Another enumeration of forms of this kind seems to be presupposed in section 67 (and in its continuation in section 69), which speaks of the forms that guard the thirty-two paths of the Sophia but also "the way to the Tree of Life." Whether these are the angelic powers or the preexistent forms of the *ḥokhmah* remains unclear. At first, it is said in section 69, a potency preexisted of the forms that are correlated with the mystical Garden of Eden (whose position is not specified) or that perhaps are inherent in it. Only then did the "holy forms" themselves receive existence. In this case the forms may be identical with those that, according to section 78, are brought together through the mystical power of sacrifice and become "one tree."

In connection with these seven forms, mention is always made—most clearly in section 116, but also, unmistakably, in sections 55 and 115—of the seven limbs that principally constitute man. Here the limbs of the terrestrial man undoubtedly correspond to those of the primordial man, which are these "holy forms." The concept of an *'adam qadmon* or *makroanthropos* (in the language of Philo), which contains in its totality the kabbalistic pleroma of all the aeons and potencies, is not yet clearly expressed in the *Bahir;* but the basic idea is certainly present. For even the three supreme logoi can, as we have seen, be characterized if not as anatomical limbs of the primordial man, then at least as the highest intellectual powers, Thought, Wisdom, and Understanding, that act in him. Thus a relation is without doubt established between the old *Shi'ur Qomah* speculations and their early kabbalistic reinterpretation in the *Bahir,* even though this is not clearly expressed in our fragmentary text. All later kabbalists correctly understood the statements of the *Bahir* concerning the sefiroth or the forms of God as a mystical interpretation of the old ideas. There, indeed, the limbs of primordial man were described as Ezekiel 1:26 saw him on the throne of the Merkabah, or as the Song of Songs portrayed him in the description of the beloved. At that stage, of course, no relationship existed as yet between this idea and the sefiroth of the *Book of Creation* or the logoi by means of which the world was created. To the redactors of the *Bahir,* however, such a connection must already have been self-evident. Already in the old *Shi'ur Qomah* itself, that which appeared upon the throne was not God himself but his Glory, which there is also named "the body of the Shekhinah," *guf ha-shekhinah*—that is, the representation of the divine presence with corporeal symbols—as the ecstatic visionary became conscious of them before the throne of God.

Corresponding to all we find in the terrestrial world, there exist in heaven archetypes, *demuyoth,* or powers, from which they draw sustenance. The number of these powers is limited to that of the sefiroth or logoi, while that of the archetypes does not appear to be fixed. Nevertheless, one cannot fail to recognize that there is a certain wavering here. The powers that correspond to the seven limbs of man (sections 55, 116) are, with slight variations, firmly circumscribed. But God possesses not only these seven forms; He also has "seventy figures," *qomoth,* which are probably archetypes of the kind mentioned in section 107 in an interpretation of the seventy palms that, according to Exodus 15:27, Israel found at Elim. They were "favored" there with the archetypes of these palms, which probably means that they attained a spiritual rank that permitted them to grasp these figures. It is in identification of these mystical figures with the palms of Song of Songs 7:8—"Your stately form is like the palm"—that the *Bahir* (section 112) comes closest to the terminology of the *Shi'ur Qomah.* Perhaps we should also see a relationship between these figures and the seventy names of God mentioned in many midrashim.[148] These figures themselves already draw upon the "twelve sources of water" mentioned in the same verse of Exodus, but are also (sections 111 and 112) coordinated with the "twelve simple consonants" of the theory of language expounded in the *Book of Creation.*

There are no precise indications regarding the place of these figures and sources within the *Bahir*'s schema of aeons. Nevertheless, it is natural to suppose that all of them are merely different manifestations of the last sefirah. The beginning of the verse—"They came to Elim" (*'elimah*—is explained in section 111 by a mystical play on words: *'elimah* is the same as *'eli mah,* which means either "to the what" or "my God is [the] what." In this sphere of "what" they found the twelve sources of water, which are probably the same as the twelve "sources of wisdom" mentioned together with twelve magical names and in relation with another symbol of the last sefirah at the end of section 81. In fact, this mystical "what" would

148. Cf. *'Agadath Shir ha-Shirim,* ed. S. Schechter (Cambridge, 1896), 9.

remain a major kabbalistic symbol of the lower Sophia, of the supreme object that is still within man's grasp, a "what" of his investigation or his contemplation. This symbolism, which was later to become very popular, does not reappear in the *Bahir.*

These seven powers or sefiroth are now represented by a combination or juxtaposition of anthropological, cosmological, and moral symbolism borrowed from the Merkabah. This union of elements is characteristic of the kabbalistic gnosis of the *Bahir* and is one of the most important legacies it left to the following generations of kabbalists. The combination of at least the first three of these elements is frequently found in ancient gnosis as well, and may already have had its roots in the oldest sources that form the basis of the *Bahir.* It is evident that such a combination could result from an association of the cosmological symbolism of the Book *Yeṣirah* with the speculations of the Merkabah and the *Shi'ur Qomah.* The gnostic passages in the Pseudo-Clementines, whose relation with Jewish ideas is still visible, exhibit the same combination of moral and cosmological symbolism.

In section 55, the six directions of space and their center, the holy temple, are correlated with the seven limbs of the terrestrial or celestial man.

> What are the seven of which it is said (Gen. 1:27): "He said to him: we count as one [the place of] the circumcision and the wife of man; his two hands—three; and his torso—five; his two legs—seven, and to them correspond their powers in heaven.

Section 114 has a variant enumeration: the place of the circumcision and man's wife are counted separately, which makes eight limbs,[149] reduced to seven, not through the mutual relationship between the masculine and the feminine (as in section 55) but by the observation that fundamentally, the torso and the place of the circumcision are one. Different again is the enumeration in section 116: the legs, the hands, the torso with the place of generation [as one] and the head, to which woman is added as the seventh element, since according to Genesis 2:24 she forms "one flesh" with man and she herself issued

149. The *Bahir* speaks of eight *qeṣawoth* in man, a notion that it borrowed from the *Book of Creation,* where the term signifies the "limitations" of space, that is, the directions of heaven.

from one of his limbs. Evidently the concept of the limbs underwent an important extension, one that is manifestly connected with the idea of syzygies in the *Bahir.* The two ways of writing the consonants *nun* and *mem* refer, as is explained in the continuation of section 55 in sections 56–58, to the conjunction of the masculine and feminine. Even redemption is related to this conjunction, in an obscure passage interpreting the name of the Messiah, Yinnon. Psalms 72:17: "His name springs up before the sun" is interpreted in *Sanhedrin* 98b in the following manner: Before the sun [before the creation of the world], his [the Messiah's] name is Yinnon. This name contains the two *nun*s, and the *Bahir,* section 58, adds: "This must happen through the masculine and the feminine," which no doubt relates less to the formation of the name of the Messiah through the union of the two principles than to redemption itself. This is Jewish gnosis, in pronounced contrast to antinomian and encratist tendencies. A well-known apocryphal remark of Jesus related by the gnostic Gospels speaks similarly of a triumph over the masculine and the feminine in the redemption that reestablishes their original unity,[150] but says nothing of redemption itself resulting from the union of the masculine and feminine. The conjunction of the two principles is certainly not the same as overcoming them in the reestablishment of an original androgynous state.

This syzygy of the masculine and feminine is a precondition of the existence of all the worlds. In conformity with the archetype of the feminine of which Song of Songs 6:10 says: "Who is she that shines through like the dawn, . . .?" Section 117 states that "the woman was taken from man, for it would be impossible for the upper and lower worlds to exist without the feminine." The two verbs *zakhor* and *shamor,* occurring in the two versions of the Decalogue respectively, at the opening of the commandment enjoining the sanctification of the Sabbath[151]—literally "mention" or remember, that is, actively, and "keep," that is, passively—are related in section 124 to the masculine and the feminine as principles of the celestial or divine world. The double meaning of *zakhor*—which in He-

---

150. Cf. the discussion of the pertinent passages in J. Doresse, *l'Evangile selon Thomas,* 155–161.

151. Exodus 20:8: "Remember the sabbath day"; Deuteronomy 5:12: "Keep the sabbath day." The idea that "keep" refers to the feminine is already found, in an entirely different context, in *Midrash Tanhuma,* ed. Buber 4:34.

brew can signify "remember" as well as "masculine"—naturally plays a role in the author's association of ideas. Section 36, to which I shall return in the discussion of the symbolism of the last sefirah, is similarly based upon the idea of a syzygy of the masculine and feminine through the medium of Wisdom or the Torah.

In the table of the ten logoi, this anthropological symbolism appears only in a variation of an account of the eighth logos (section 114). It does not seem to have been in the source—that is, in the corresponding table in the *Raza Rabba*—and must, therefore, have come from other Jewish-gnostic sources. In the original table, the symbolism of the Merkabah evidently played a decisive role as regards the fourth of the tenth aeons. We saw this in our analyses of the "Great Mystery" in the section before last, and the text of the *Bahir,* sections 96, 102, 105, 115, in its present shape also preserves this relationship quite distinctly. On this point, the *Bahir* differs radically from the later symbolism of these sefiroth, which deliberately ignores any possible identification of the sefiroth and the objects of the Merkabah and considers the latter, at best, as symbols to be distinguished from the real Merkabah that is situated beneath the world of the sefiroth. Besides the objects of the Merkabah, the *Bahir* enumerates other symbols of the kind mentioned above, which seem to derive from other series of images in the following sequence:

4 and 5. God's right and left, from whose powers the *ḥayyoth* and *serafim* issue, which "stand at the left." They are described in a long sentence whose solemn style manifestly indicates that it is taken from a Merkabah text.

6. the Throne of Glory.

7. the heaven of the *'araboth.* In Merkabah Gnosticism this is always the highest of the seven heavens.

8. The original correspondence to the Merkabah is apparently missing here; in its place, the passage introduces the "righteous" as an aeon, but the continuation, to judge from its formula-like style, suggests that it originated in a source that described some element of the world of the divine throne that was subsequently replaced by the mystical symbol of the "righteous." Cf. following.

9 and 10. the wheels of the Merkabah, *'ofannim.*

To these should be added, as has been pointed out before, symbols of a completely different character, some appearing in the aforementioned table and an even larger number in many other places in the *Bahir.* The symbolic associations for logoi 4–6 are relatively consistent, while with regard to the last sefiroth, the contradictions are so striking that they can be satisfactorily explained only by assuming a juxtaposition of fragments from different sources. Places 4–6 are occupied above all by the following groups of three:

The *middoth,* qualities or attributes, of Grace, Stern Judgment, *ḥesed* and *din* or *paḥad* (designated in part, as strength, *geburah*), among which Truth, *'emeth,* has the function of maintaining an equilibrium (sections 24, 77, 92, 94, 129, 131).

Left, Right, Middle (sections 35, 77, 96, 102).

Water, fire, the union of the two elements in "heaven" in conformity with the Talmudic cosmology, and the etymology, in the Talmud, of the word *shamayim* as a composite of *'esh* and *mayim* (sections 9, 29, 30, 40, 68, 96, 102).

The three Patriarchs: Abraham, representing Love or Grace, *ḥesed;* Isaac, representing Stern Judgment or Fear, *paḥad;* Jacob, representing Truth and Peace (sections 92, 94, 131, 132, which is related to the symbolism of "Truth and Peace" in section 50).

To this same series belong the "primordial images" of wine and milk in section 93, as well as the symbolism of silver and gold in sections 34 and 38, which correspond to the right and left of God—to his Grace and Stern Judgment. This symbolism, which in large measure makes use of aggadic motifs, and adds to them a gnostic character, no longer has any connection with the ideas of the Book *Yeṣirah* concerning the sefiroth. The talmudic Aggadah knows above all two principal qualities or *middoth* of God: *ḥesed* and *din,* Love and Stern Judgment. *Middath ha-ḥesed* and *middath ha-raḥamim* are synonymous, and there is no distinction between them. God's "love" and His "mercy" are regarded as one and the same for the Aggadah. This seems to remain true of the *Bahir* as well, where the "quality of mercy" is mentioned only once (section 24), and, according to the context, in the same sense as that of Grace or Love—the Hebrew word *ḥesed* signifying both. This is remarkable, for it indicates one of the oldest stages of kabbalistic symbolism. In all other kabbalistic texts mercy, *raḥamim,* is in fact considered as the principle of equilibrium between Love and Stern Judgment. In the *Bahir,* however, insofar as abstract notions are employed at all, this equilibrium is represented by the quality of truth, which Micah 7:20 associates with Jacob: "You will show truth to Jacob." In the same verse, *ḥesed* is also associated with Abraham.

In section 94 of the *Bahir,* truth is also associated with the idea of the Torah, the symbolic equation being taken from Malachi 2:6, "the Torah of Truth." According to our text:

> The *middah* which is named Israel contains the Torah of Truth. And what is this "Torah of Truth"? Something which indicates the true nature of the worlds and whose action takes place through the *mahshabah,* and it bestows existence upon the ten logoi, through which the world exists, and it is itself one of them.

Here, therefore, a new, intermediary aspect of the Torah, positioned in the center of the schema of the aeons, is interpolated between the Sophia, as the primordial Torah, and the Oral Torah, as the last sefirah, both of which are already familiar to us; this aspect completely corresponds to what was later designated by the kabbalists as the "Written Torah," as understood in traditional Talmudic terminology. It is explicitly mentioned in section 99 as the light that nourishes the lamp of the Oral Torah: "Such is the Oral Torah: although it is a lamp, it has need of the Written Torah in order to resolve its difficulties and to explain its mysteries." The relation between the exposition there and the idea of the hidden primordial light (sections 97 and 98) would suggest the possibility that the Written Torah was originally connected not with the sixth but with the third sefirah, where, as we have just seen, the Torah was "hewn" and received its specific forms. That would accord perfectly well with the identification established in several passages (sections 131, 133) between the third sefirah and the primordial light. On the other hand, the interpolations in the table of the logoi, which speak of the Torah (sections 97–100) just after the exposition on the sixth sefirah, would seem more in harmony with the later localization of this symbolism.

It is therefore difficult to come to a decision on this matter. The table of the logoi says nothing, in the sixth place, of the Torah, even as it betrays no knowledge of the symbolism of the three Patriarchs. The Throne of Glory is "the house of the world to come and its place is engraved in the *ḥokhmah.*"[152] Hence, much as the second sefirah, *ḥokhmah* has a "treasure house" in the third, so also the third sefirah (which, as we learned from section 106, is designated as the "world to come") has a house in the sixth. The remark concerning the place engraved into the *ḥokhmah* remains obscure. But in one of the interpolations that follow, a relation is in fact established (section 101) between the throne of God and the "crown of the Torah."

152. The reference to Genesis 1:3 as proof text for this statement is unintelligible. Perhaps it is only meant as a transition to the paragraphs on the primordial light in section 97ff.

This crown is compared there, in a paradoxical parable, with the tefillin of the head. For it is not only the Jew who puts on these tefillin every morning as a crown he offers to God; according to the talmudic aggadah in *Berakhoth* 6a, God himself wears such tefillin, which are compared in sections 25 and 101 to a throne that the king "sometimes took in his arms, at other times placed upon his head."

The idea, very emphatically maintained in the *Bahir,* of the three Patriarchs as the representatives on earth of the three divine *middoth* of Love, Fear, and Truth takes up a motif that already appeared in a mystical saying of the third-century Aggadah and carries it in a completely new direction: "the Patriarchs are themselves the Merkabah,"[153] an assertion repeated for each of the three Patriarchs. This audacious saying occurs in a context of biblical exegesis, but that is certainly not where it originated. This line of thought is taken further in the *Bahir,* where the epigram itself is not cited at all (just as it is not cited in the Hekhaloth). Each of the Patriarchs was given the "archetype" or the "celestial power" of the quality he realized in his life (section 92). Section 132 says plainly: "Thus spoke the quality of Love, *ḥesed:* As long as Abraham was in the world, I did not have to do my work, for Abraham stood there, in my place, and guarded my post [fulfilled my task]. For that is my work: to intercede for the world." All this was done by Abraham, who called upon the world to repent and also pleaded on behalf of the guilty. Thus the Patriarchs are practically the incarnations of the principles of divine governance that they chose as guidelines for their conduct.

The "heaven" that harmonizes and makes peace between the *middoth* of water and fire thus appears to be the symbol of a potency that no longer can simply be equated with the elementary powers of water, fire, and heaven. In section 102, developing a statement concerning *'araboth,* heaven is mentioned as the seventh logos; but everything said there fits the sixth rather than the seventh logos. The most likely resolution of the contradiction would seem to be this: the source of the saying about the ten logoi, in which the throne is followed by the heaven called *'araboth,* was a document belonging to the Merkabah literature of the kind of which we still possess remnants —for example, the list of the *Raza Rabba.* This source as yet knew nothing of a cosmological symbolism correlating water, fire, and

153. *Bereshith Rabba,* ed. Theodor, 475 (Abraham), 793 (Isaac), 983 (Jacob).

heaven with these logoi. Since in the Merkabah the throne was elevated above *'araboth,* it was natural to place them one above the other, in the same order. However, with the evolution of the kabbalistic schema the original logoi came to be correlated with other symbols, and the first three triads, mentioned above, were added to the schema; the immanent logic of their introduction then necessitated the placing of *shamayim,* heaven, in the sixth position. It was easy enough to invoke Isaiah 66:1: *"Shamayim* is My throne," as a proof text. In fact, in section 65 the throne is expressly equated with heaven. Of the verse of Isaiah, which one would expect here, only the continuation concerning the earth as a stool for his feet is cited in section 115. In section 40, too, heaven, in this definite sense, is identified with truth, by then already a fixed designation for the sixth logos. The same paragraph also mentions the relationship with the head, *rosh,* which also appears in section 102 in a somewhat obscure sentence. ("Why is it called heaven? Because it is round like a head.") I therefore incline to the view that the main part of section 102 is in reality an account of the sixth logos, but for the reason stated it was subsequently connected with the seventh, which was mentioned originally only in the first words of the corresponding enumeration in section 102.

Our thesis that the *Bahir* is a redaction of partly contradictory sources is confirmed no less convincingly by an analysis of the statements concerning God's left and the nature of evil. The list in section 96 still ignores any connection between the "great fire" of God and his left with the principle of evil. On the contrary, the "holy *serafim,"* among whom we undoubtedly should also count Gabriel, stand at God's left. A different explanation of God's left and right is given in section 77; there the seventy-two names of God derived from the magical tradition discussed in connection with sections 76 and 79 are placed in relation with the kabbalistic schema of the aeons.[154] The seventy-two names can be divided into three times twenty-four, and over every twenty-four is placed an archon, *sar.*

> And who are these archons? They are three. This teaches that the Power, *geburah,* is the archon of all the holy forms on the left side of God, and that is Gabriel, and on his right Michael is archon over all

---

154. Section 77 should undoubtedly come after section 79, which it continues or explains. At the final redaction, sections 77 and 78 were awkwardly interpolated in the text 76–79, which is all of one piece.

> the holy forms, and in the middle, which is the Truth, Uriel is the archon of all the holy forms. And every archon [rules over] twenty-four forms, but his hosts are innumerable, according to Job 25:3.

Here, the abstract names of the sefiroth, such as *geburah,* (dynamics or Power) and *'emeth* (Truth), are to a certain extent merged with the names of the archons, who are angelic beings. This confusion, which would be completely inconceivable in the later Kabbalah, also recurs, as we have seen, in section 96, where the right and left are in no way designated by the abstract names of aeons but in a more concrete form as expressions of divine Grace, as the great fire of God, as well as by the orders of angels that stand under their influence. But these orders of angels are different from those of section 77.

However, the doctrine of the "left of God" has a completely different character in the texts on Satan (sections 107–115),[155] which probably formed a unit that at a later stage of redaction was inserted into the list of the ten logoi. We learn that Satan is the "north wind" (section 107), a power that acts from the north, the proof text, quoted in sections 109 and 110, being provided by Jeremiah 1:14. The story of the sojourn in *Mara* (Exod. 15:23–25), "there He made for them a fixed rule, and there He put them to the test," is interpreted—perhaps on the basis of an old aggadic source that has been lost?—in the following manner: God passed judgment on Satan at this place for having tempted Israel.

This temptation is described at length in aggadic language. Near the water of *Mara* stood the Tree of Life—a very curious motif that occurs in the earliest Aggadah but does not reappear later.[156]

---

155. Points of contact between the origin of evil as expounded in these paragraphs and certain Cathar sources have been argued by Shulamit Shahar in *Tarbiz* 40 (1972): 488–490. But the analogies adduced by her relate to aggadic motifs in the *exoteric* literature. Her theses require further examination but will not withstand a thorough analysis. A further attempt by the same author to prove Cathar influences on Abraham Abulafia (cf. her article in *Cahiers de Franjeaux* 12 [1977]: 345–361) is equally futile; cf. the refutation of her arguments by M. Idel in the philosophical review *'Iyyun* 30 [in Hebrew] (1981): 133–140.

156. Cf. L. Ginzberg, *Legends of the Jews* 6:14, who points out the existence of this aggadah already in the pseudo-Philonic "Antiquities," one of the oldest midrashim in our possession. Rabbenu Ephraim's commentary on the Pentateuch (Smyrna, ca. 1847, fol. 35a), explains this verse much as does the *Bahir.* The link must have been constituted by a passage in the *Mekhilta* that is no longer preserved in our extant texts but that was still found there by a medieval author.

Satan had removed this Tree of Life in order to incite Israel to sin against their heavenly father. But when Moses saw Satan, "he cried out to the Lord, and the Lord showed him a tree [Exod. 15:25], that Tree of Life which Satan had taken away, and he threw it into the water." However, this act of throwing is interpreted here at the same time as a suppression of Satan and a diminution of his power. *Ruaḥ ṣefonith* is perhaps better rendered here as "spirit from the north" rather than north wind. The text already makes mention of the seventy "primordial images" that Israel grasped, at Elim, in the image of the seventy palms, but Satan does not belong to it and appears independent of them. In section 113 we learn that the contradiction between these seventy primordial images or figures, *qomoth,* and the seventy-two forms of sections 76 and 77 is resolved by interpreting the two surplus forms or archons as Israel and the "Prince Satan," these two probably completing the seventy archons of the nations to make up the number seventy-two. The forms Gabriel had under his direction in section 77 are figures over which Satan is placed as archon, insofar as they stand at the left of God. He is here, at the same time, the "archon of *tohu.*" Section 109 goes even further by designating him as a *middah* of God himself, situated at the "north of God." In its mythical formulation, the passage goes beyond the aggadic motif upon which it is based.

> And what is this [principle of the seduction to evil, mentioned in an immediately preceding parable]? It is Satan. This teaches us that God has a *middah* which is named "Evil," and it lies in the north of God, for it said [Jer. 1:14]: From the north shall evil break loose; that is: all the evil that comes upon all the inhabitants of the earth comes from the north. And what is this *middah?* It is the "form of the hand," and it has many messengers, and the name of all of them is "Evil, Evil." However, there are among them small and large. And it is they who plunge the world into guilt, for *tohu* belongs to the north side, and *tohu* is nothing other than the evil that throws men into confusion until they sin, and every evil urge in man comes from there.

In sections 114 and 116, however, the left hand is designated as one of the seven holy forms of God, which well fits the definition of evil as the "form of the hand" in our quotation. Since according to the conception of the Midrash, which is based upon the parallelism of "hand" and "right" found in many passages of the Bible, hand without further qualification signifies the left hand, the expression "form of the hand" is easily explained. The redactor of the *Bahir* apparently vacillated between two possible ideas that he found in his sources: in one, Satan is one of the seven forms and thereby one of the holy forms themselves; in the other, he is (section 113) the seventy-first figure, above the seventy figures mentioned there.

The sentence, "The Holy One, may He be praised, has a *middah* which is called evil," has a particularly bold ring to it. In fact, it is only an extreme version of an old aggadic conception. There, too, "the quality of Stern Judgment," *middath ha-din,* is personified and portrayed as speaking before God. In parallel versions we find in its place "Satan" or even the "ministering angels."[157] In the *Bahir,* evil is one of the powers or forces by means of which God acts and manifests himself. There is no trace here of a privative conception of evil as it was current among the philosophers. It is, however, remarkable that the etymology given in section 110 for the word Satan is the same as offered by Maimonides in the *Guide of the Perplexed* 3:22. This need not be a borrowing, for such an homiletical etymology readily suggests itself. The *nun* in Satan is not considered one of the consonants of the stem but a formative affix of the *nomina agentes.* Hence Satan (from the root סטה) means "He who inclines downwards, for it is he who seeks to incline the world toward the side of guilt."[158]

This identification of evil with a *middah* of God and with *tohu* may be one of those novel and audacious formulas of the *Bahir* that aroused the suspicion of heresy among pious readers like Meir ben Simon of Narbonne. In section 93, "the *tohu* whence evil comes" is in fact identified with the "fire of God," and, referring back to section 92, with "fear," *paḥad,* the quality of Isaac that, as we have seen, is identical with the *middath ha-din* and the *geburah* of God. This explanation of *tohu,* which associates it with the fifth logos of the table in section 96, may well be a kabbalistic variant of the conception of *tohu* as the principle of matter (section 2), the philosophic source of which we identified as Abraham bar Ḥiyya (see p. 62). In section 9, too, *tohu* and *bohu* are explained as evil and peace, respec-

---

157. The best example is offered by the aggadah on the temptation of Abraham in connection with Genesis 22:1. In *Sanhedrin* 89b it is Satan who speaks; in *Bereshith Rabba, parashah* 55, section 4, ed. Theodor, 587, it is the angels, who form the heavenly "tribunal"; in *Yalqut,* on Genesis, parashath *Vayera,* 1, section 96, it is the *middath ha-din,* conceived as one of the ministering angels, that speaks.

158. To this corresponds the striking combination of words *sar ha-satan* in section 113.

tively, and in the sequel it is not Satan who appears but, as in section 77, Gabriel as the archon of the left, which is fire. A purely harmonistic interpretation would logically lead us to conclude that the *Bahir* identifies Gabriel with Satan. The reality is different: there existed, on the subject of the left, two distinct traditions that were subsequently united or juxtaposed during the redaction in keeping with the midrashic character of the book and without aiming at any false consistency. The interpolations in sections 106–113 which, in keeping with the kabbalistic symbolism that the redactors had in mind, relate to the third and fifth logoi of this sequence, happen to be placed between two paragraphs dealing with the eighth logos, where they obviously do not belong. Moreover, sections 105 and 114 are peculiar enough in themselves, for according to their content they are not really concerned with the eighth but with the seventh logos. "He is called the eighth only with regard to the enumeration; according to his activity, he is the seventh" (section 114).

7. The Syzygy of the Masculine and the Feminine: The Seventh and the Tenth Sefirah in the Bahir*— The Symbolism of the Righteous*

We have emphasized that the enumeration of the ten logoi in the oldest list preserved in the *Bahir* deviates from the order generally adopted by the kabbalists. This is the case not only as regards the identification of these logoi with certain regions of the Merkabah but especially with a view to certain very definite statements concerning the seventh (respectively, the eighth) and the tenth of these powers. These two are of particular significance for an understanding of the developing doctrine of the sefiroth. They constitute, as their symbolism shows, the syzygy of the masculine and feminine, whose introduction into the world of the aeons places the Kabbalah, in a particularly emphatic manner, within the gnostic tradition. In the old table (sections 96 and 102) these new conceptions regarding the seventh sefirah were inserted merely as a variant of the older formulations (found in sections 104, 105, 114) into the old list in sections 96 and 102. By way of contrast, the corresponding statements relating to the tenth sefirah do not appear at all in this table, although they already possess a major significance in other parts of the *Bahir.* Here, again, it seems clear to me that at least two different gnostic traditions have merged in the *Bahir* or in its sources. One, the *Raza Rabba,* represents a later speculative development of the Merkabah gnosis; the other, though not yet identified from a literary point of view, evidently concerns symbolism of the last sefirah, of which we have seen several significant examples in our earlier analysis of gnostic elements in the *Bahir.* A closer investigation of the *Bahir* material on these two sefiroth will provide important information about the oldest forms of the Kabbalah at the time of its historical appearance in Provence.

The seventh logos of the *Bahir* corresponds exactly to the ninth sefirah in the later canonical sequence. Its symbolism is characterized by a combination of four motifs, which remained constant even after its location in the "sefirotic tree" was changed: that of the righteous, that of the foundation of the world and the soul, that of the Sabbath, and the symbolism of the phallus. The relation with the celestial temple which represents "Thought" or that which is within "Thought" as expounded in section 103 in one of three variations on the seventh logos of our table (sections 102–104), is completely outside this particular series of motifs, as we saw above in our discussion of the first sefirah. Only the notion of the six dimensions, by means of which the world—space—is sealed, is taken over from the Book *Yeṣirah.* The same notion also figures in section 21 in terms of the mysticism of letters. In the center of this terrestrial world is the Temple of Jerusalem; in the center of the corresponding world of the logoi, the celestial temple. What is novel and so pregnant with consequences for the Kabbalah is precisely the conjunction of the other motifs.

The symbol of the righteous goes back to the well-known agadah in *Ḥagigah* 12b: "The world rests on one pillar, and its name is righteous, for it is said [Prov. 10:25] that the righteous is the foundation of the world." The Talmud speaks of this single column in contrast to another opinion, according to which the world rests upon the seven columns hewn out of the rock by wisdom (cf. Prov. 9:11). By a combination of cosmological and ethical symbolism and its application to the doctrine of the aeons, the righteous could thus be made to appear as the union of these other columns, which are the seven logoi. With this new twist, the Righteous is obviously no longer the ideal moral type on earth but rather a cosmic potency that realizes above and below, for the entire cosmos, what the earthly righteous accomplish in this world. This gnostic transfiguration of the talmudic notion is clearly visible in section 71, where it is said:

> A column goes from the earth up to heaven, and its name is righteous, after the [earthly] righteous. When there are righteous upon earth, it is strong, but when there are not, it grows slack; and it bears the entire world, for it is said: "The righteous is the foundation of the world." But if it is slack, the world cannot exist. That is why [it is said in the Talmud, *Yoma* 38b]: Even if there were only a single righteous man upon earth, he would maintain the world.

Here is it quite clear that for the redactors of the *Bahir,* the *tertium comparationis* that commended both the celestial temple and the righteous equally as the seventh sefirah, was the fact that they both "bear" and "maintain" the world or the six directions of space.

The idea that this "column" reached from earth up to heaven can have two meanings. The column can represent the cosmic Tree of Life that grows from earth up to heaven and that had become in sections 14 and 64, as we saw in our discussion of the symbolism of the tree, the cosmic tree as such. The souls of the righteous ascend and descend on it. And just as the cosmic tree was also the tree of souls, from which the souls take flight or on which they appear as the fruits, so, too, once this motif is applied to the reinterpretation of a single sefirah, the latter becomes the foundation of the souls. But it may also be that "earth" and "heaven" are themselves already understood as mystical symbols: the "column" connects the last sefirah, named "earth," to the sixth, named "heaven." This would highlight even more clearly the image of the *hieros gamos* of heaven and earth, with its phallic symbolism implied by the image of the column that grows firm and slackens. Attention should be drawn to a parallel gnostic symbolism resulting from the same tendency to hypostatize the function of the "righteous" or "perfect man" in the world. I am thinking here of the Manichaean idea of a "column of splendor." This column is identical, for the Manichees, with the perfect man. At the same time, it is also the Tree of Life, on which (according to the report in the *Fihrist*) the souls of the righteous ascend after death from the lower world to the paradise of light whence they had come.[159] Similarly, in the Jewish *Midrash Konen*

---

159. Cf. the analysis in G. Widengren, *The Great Vohu Manah* (Uppsala, 1945), 13–16.

the souls of the righteous ascend and descend on this tree to the heavens and from there to the celestial paradise, named the Garden of Eden, "as a man ascends and descends upon a ladder."

The way in which motifs deriving from completely different traditions, the one gnostic-Iranian, the other aggadic-Jewish, coalesce can be followed here in instructive detail. The same image could arise in various ways. It is thus not at all certain whether, in this case, we have to assume an historical link. Nevertheless, if such a connection existed, as seems most likely to me, it would again point to the Orient. The Cathar tradition apparently did not preserve the image of the column for the description of the perfect man. Also, a relationship between the column and phallus is absent in the Mandaean texts, which otherwise place great emphasis on phallic symbolism.[160] However, it would not be surprising to find it in the well-developed Manichaean parallelism of microcosm and macrocosm. In any case, this symbolism of syzygy and phallus fits well into the same stratum of Oriental-gnostic sources as the fragments concerning the Shekhinah analyzed above.

In section 104, this seventh logos is designated as "the east of the world" whence the seed of Israel came, "for the spinal marrow extends from the brain of man to the phallus, and that is where the semen originates, as it is said [Isa. 43:5]: I will bring your seed from the East, will gather you out of the West." The idea that the semen has its origin in the brain was widespread in the Middle Ages and taken from Galenus. The phallus is therefore the mystical East that, as we shall see, corresponds to the Shekhinah in the west, of which the Talmud (*Baba Bathra* 25a) says "the Shekhinah is in the west." The east and the west, the righteous and the Shekhinah, form a syzygy. Just as the Shekhinah is the symbol of the feminine par excellence (as we shall see in due course), so the seventh logos corresponds to the masculine as such, represented by the phallus. It is therefore not surprising that in section 114 the phallus is counted as the seventh among the principal limbs of man, with the eighth "member," man's wife, being his counterpart and one with him. Though in the parallel enumerations of the limbs of "man" there is

160. Lady Drower, above all, has clearly and repeatedly demonstrated this in her study of the esoteric doctrine of the Mandaean priests, *The Secret Adam* (Oxford, 1960); cf. in particular her article on Adamas in *Theologische Literaturzeitung* (1961): cols. 173–180.

no direct correlation between the limbs and the actual sefiroth, the context leaves no doubt at all that our sefirah signified "the place of the circumcision," that is, the phallus.

In section 105, the question of the identity of the eighth logos is raised; the answer, however, seems to refer to the seventh. At this point the symbolism of the Sabbath, already present less distinctly in section 39, is described in direct relation with the other symbols.

> What is the eighth? God has one righteous in his world, and He loves him, because he maintains the entire world, and because he is its foundation. He maintains him and lets him grow and become great and he gives him joy . . . and he is the foundation of all the souls. You say [that he is] the foundation of all souls and the eighth [logos]. Yet it is said [Exod. 31:17]: "And on the seventh day *shabbath wa-yinnafash* [which can be literally understood as] "it was sabbath and animation"!? Yes, he is [in fact] the seventh [logos] for he harmonizes them. The other six, in fact [are divided into] three below and three above, and he harmonizes them. And why is he called the seventh? Was he, then, only on the seventh [day]? No, rather [he is thus counted] because God rested on the Sabbath, in that *middah,* of which it is said: "For in six days the Lord made heaven and earth, and on the seventh day he ceased from work and was refreshed [which can also be translated by:] was Sabbath and animation.

The Righteous is therefore one of the aeons in the divine world: he is a *middah* of God, and the epithets applied to God in the Talmud, *ṣaddiqo shel 'olam,* "the righteous of the world," and *ṣaddiq ḥay 'olamim,* "the righteous who lives forever," can be understood as names of this *middah.*[161] As the seventh of the primordial days, he creates harmony among the six other days or their logoi, which, as we have seen, are partly in conflict with one another. This motif of the element of equilibrium also returns in the symbolism of the phallus. Section 114 designates the seventh limb, literally, as being "the [place] of equilibrium of the sign of the Covenant." This conception of the phallus fulfilling a harmonizing function in the physical structure of man was taken by the *Bahir* from the Book *Yeṣirah* (1:3 combined with 2:1). Indeed, the righteous also makes peace in the world, according to the Talmud, and establishes harmony among the antagonistic powers. This relationship between the sexual sphere and the righteous is by no means due to some whim of the *Bahir* or

161. On these names cf. the texts cited in A. Marmorstein, *The Old Rabbinic Doctrine of God,* vol. 1 (London, 1927), 95–96.

the kabbalists, who in fact attached considerable value to it.[162] It rests upon the special preference of the Talmud for calling men who have mastered their sexual instinct and nature, "righteous." In the literature of the early Middle Ages "the righteous" came to be associated especially with Joseph as almost a fixed epithet. Although it associates divine *middoth* with the patriarchs who realized them, the *Bahir* still knows nothing of the role of Joseph as representative of the "righteous"; however, this attribution appeared immediately after the *Bahir* became known, and thus the mystical "level of Joseph" became a permanent element of kabbalistic terminology.

The symbolism of the Sabbath forms the link between the two motifs of equilibrium—through which "all the effects are realized" and come to rest (section 105)—and the home of the soul. From the region of the Sabbath "all the souls take their flight" (section 39), an image that goes back to the motif of the cosmic tree. The foundation of the world is at the same time the foundation of the souls. When the authors of the *Bahir* related these older mythical fragments concerning the cosmic tree which is the pleroma and the all, to the seventh sefirah, they also transferred to this entity the attribute of "all" (section 126). In this region is situated the "treasure house of the souls." Sections 123–126 thus connect with a different set of symbols. There evidently existed different traditions concerning the coordination between the last logoi and the cardinal points, and the passages on the subject, above all sections 119 and 123, are very obscure. While in sections 104 and 105 the righteous was the mystical east, he appears here, for reasons that for the present are inexplicable, as the southwest. He also is designated as the "foundation of the worlds," and as such stands in the middle, above the "powers" that are found below and that correspond to the two legs in man and to the northwest and the west in the world. Although he is himself in the southwest, he issues from the south of the world where apparently, in opposition to the evil north, the *middah* of God's goodness and grace, *ḥesed,* has its place.

162. I have examined the development of this idea more closely in my essay *Der Gerechte* (see n. 39 herein). This study of the kabbalistic concept of the Righteous appeared originally in *Eranos-Jahrbuch* vol. 27 (1958): 237–297. Part of this essay was also published in *The Synagogue Review* vol. 34 (1960): 189–195.

He [the righteous] also has in his hand the soul of all living things, for he is the "life of the worlds." Every act of creation spoken of [in Scripture] occurs through him. And it is of him that it is said: it was Sabbath and animation, for he is the *middah* of the Sabbath day, and of him it is said [Exod. 20:8]: *zakhor 'eth yom ha-shabbath* [which must be translated here according to the mystical etymology:] "correlate the masculine with the Sabbath day" . . . and all this is said of the seventh *middah* [the seventh logos].

The expression I translated here, in the spirit of the *Bahir,* as the "life of the worlds" is taken from Daniel 12:7 where it originally signified "the Ever-Living One." In this sense, *ḥay 'olamim* also occurs as a divine name in talmudic literature, and a celebrated hymn of the old Merkabah mystics invoked God under this name.[163] In the *Bahir,* the meaning shifted somewhat. The Righteous, corresponding to the phallus, is he who dispenses life; perhaps the idea of the anima mundi as an aeon also enters into this conception. The life of the worlds and the soul of the world that is its foundation can very easily be conceived together. The soul of the world as the origin of all the individual souls would likewise fit the image of a "treasure house of souls" situated in this region.[164] In any case, that which lives and that which is animated soul somehow appear here to be connected. The life of the worlds is the productive and preservative power that is directed from this place to the worlds. That is why it is called "the all" or "all." Just as the Righteous carries out the Torah on earth and represents, as it were, the incarnation of the commandments that he fulfills, so is the mystical place of all the commandments to be sought precisely in this sefirah of the Righteous who is the life of the worlds. We read in section 125:

Why do we say [in the benediction after a light meal of fruits, *B. Berakhoth* 37a, and especially in the parallel text of the Palestinian

163. Cf. *Major Trends,* pp. 58–59.

164. One could perhaps go further and refer to the image of Adam, in whose body all the souls of the righteous were originally contained, thus *Shemoth Rabba, parashah* 40, section 3, and *Tanhuma, parashath Ki Tissa,* section 12; cf. also Ginzberg, *Legends* 5:75, and Murmelstein, "Adam, ein Beitrag zur Messiaslehre," *Wiener Zeitschrift für die Kunde des Morgenlandes* 35 (1928):263. Some Judeo-Christians, followers of Symmachus, designated Adam as the *anima generalis;* cf. Söderberg, *La Religion des Cathares,* 188. To the terrestrial body of Adam corresponds the celestial body or *guf,* namely, the treasure house of the souls, situated in the aeon of the "righteous" or the perfect man.

> Talmud]: "For everything that He created, [praised be he, who is] the life of the worlds," and we do not say: "that which you have created"? Because we praise God, who lets His wisdom, *hokhmah,* flow into the "life of the worlds. . . . " For at the hour when, in this world, we are worthy of the world to come, it [the life of the worlds] increases.

This increase means the same as the growth of the Righteous in section 105 and the strengthening of the column by the acts of the Righteous in section 71.

Nevertheless there seems to be some uncertainty in the *Bahir,* with respect to the terminology and enumeration of the seven sefiroth as well as of the seventh and last sefirah. In the discussions of these oldest "prehistorical" kabbalists, of which these passages seem to be a kind of sediment, diverse possibilities of enumeration and different schemas appear to have been considered. This can be seen not only in section 124, where the seventh *middah* is designated as the goodness of God, in continuation of the symbolism of the Sabbath in which the interpretation of *zakhor* and *shamor* (see p. 142) causes the masculine and feminine principles to appear together. We already encountered this "good" in the exposition concerning the primordial light in sections 97 and 98. Here it is placed in relationship with a seventh sphere that, in the light of what was said in the aforementioned passages, no longer refers to the Righteous but to the symbolism of the mystical bride as the last of the lower seven *middoth.*

Leviticus 19:30: "You shall keep My sabbaths and venerate My sanctuary" is interpreted here as representing the feminine principle, which now is in competition with the masculine for the seventh place. The notion of the sanctuary as follows from section 118, is the symbol of the feminine; the sexual interpretation of "venerate My sanctuary" as "guard yourselves against lascivious thoughts, for my sanctuary is holy" thus becomes understandable. The syzygy of the masculine and the feminine in these two "sevenths" is clearly the same as that between the Sabbath and the ecclesia of Israel, already mentioned in the Midrash. In *Bereshith Rabba,* par. 11, section 8, the Sabbath complains to God: To all the days you gave a partner, only I have none. "Then God said to him: the community of Israel will be your partner." Here we have no mystical symbolism but simple aggadah, as also is shown by the inverted use of the genders: The Sabbath is feminine, and the community of Israel is promised to her as a male partner. In the *Bahir* and in kabbalistic symbolism, it is exactly the reverse. In section 124:

> And which is the seventh *middah?* Say: it is the *middah* of God's goodness [literally: the good]. And why is it said: keep my Sabbaths and not: my Sabbath? It is like a king who had a beautiful bride, and every Sabbath he let her come to him, in order to be near him for a day. The king had sons whom he loved. He said to them: Rejoice, you too, on the day of my joy, since it is for you that I exert myself. And why [is it said of the Sabbath] one time "remember" and the other time "keep"? Remember, *zakhor* for the male, *shamor,* keep, for the female.

A similar uncertainty appears with respect to the position of the seven primordial days. On the one hand they are considered (as in the aforementioned passages) as the first seven logoi, terminating with the Sabbath, which, for its part, still has three further logoi below it (section 123). On the other hand they are placed, in the groupings of sevens, as has already been pointed out, opposite the three highest sefiroth. But nowhere in the *Bahir* is there a specific interpretation of the Sabbath as the last of all the sefiroth. This mystical symbolism of the Sabbath appears only later. It also is easy to understand how the motif of the source, as soon as it was viewed as the phallic center of life, was transposed from *ḥokhmah* to the Righteous. God, as we have seen (section 125), let his *ḥokhmah* "flow into the life of the worlds, which then transmits all [that it has received]." Here the Righteous is a channel or a pipe, *ṣinnor,* that transmits the water from the source. This is probably the "great channel" in section 85; such is certainly the significance of the channel in section 121, where all the six brooks of God flow along "the equilibrium in the middle," which is the channel, into the sea of the last sefirah. This channel is called, following Song of Songs 4:15, a "garden spring, a well of fresh water, a rill of Lebanon." Lebanon is expressly defined, in this context, as the sphere of the *ḥokhmah.* The image is used in exactly the same way in section 105, in the symbolism of the Sabbath day and the Righteous. Every day

> has a logos, who is its ruler, not because it was created with it, but because it accomplishes with it the effect that is within its power. When all have accomplished their effect and finished their work, then the seventh day comes and accomplishes its effect, and all rejoice, even

> God [with them]; and not only that: it [the effect] makes their souls great, as it is said: on the seventh day there was rest and animation. . . . This is like a king who had seven gardens, and in the garden in the middle, from a well of living water, a bubbling source from a well waters the three to its right and the three to its left. As soon as it accomplishes this work, it fills itself; then all rejoice and say: it is for us that it fills itself. And it waters them and makes them grow, but they wait and rest. And it gives the seven drink. . . . Is it then [itself] one of those [seven] and does it give them drink? Say rather: he gives drink to the "heart" and the "heart" gives drink to them all.

The Righteous is therefore a channel through which all the brooks and streams of the superior powers flow into the sea of the Shekhinah or the mystical "heart." The metaphor of the Sabbath should certainly not be pressed to make any deductions regarding the localization of the sefiroth in three on the right and three on the left. The six other days have, as in the midrashic parable mentioned, partners, while the seventh, which forms their "rest" and their "equilibrium," has its partner in the feminine that receives all these powers, like the sea. To this syzygy also corresponds the symbolism of letters in section 42. Every letter has a "partner," if one counts the alphabet each time, forwards and backwards. *He* and *ṣade* then come in the fifth place. *Ṣade* is the Righteous, *ṣaddiq; he,* the last consonant of the Tetragrammaton, indicates the last sefirah (section 20).

The enumeration of the last sefiroth is rather confused. In section 114, the seventh logos is also designated as the eighth, "because with it the eight began, and with it the eight end with respect to the enumeration; but according to its function, it is the seventh." To this logos correspond the eight days of the circumcision and the eight "limitations," *qeṣawoth,* that is, the principal limbs of man that nevertheless are only seven, since "the torso and the phallus only count as one." The ninth and the tenth would then be the two *'ofannim* of the Merkabah, designated in the *Bahir* (sections 115 and 123) with an expression borrowed from Isaiah 34:10, as the *neṣaḥim. Neṣaḥ* in Hebrew means "duration," "permanence." The lowest of all these powers is also designated, in section 115, as *nishono shel 'olam,* the duration of the world, a power "that inclines toward the west." Concerning this power, we are told only that it is also "the end of the Shekhinah," still situated under the two wheels of the Merkabah. In any case it is obvious that the author of these paragraphs, including section 116, dismembered as it were, the unitary Merkabah source of *Seder Rabba de-Bereshith* (Wertheimer [2d ed.,

1930], 30) in the sense of "gnostic" sefiroth symbolism. In the Merkabah source the "holy *ḥayyoth, 'ofannim,* throne, glory, and end of the Shekhinah (namely, "feet of the Shekhinah") were connected with one another. It is hardly likely that section 116 depends on any other source than the preceding paragraphs, even though it combines in one circle or juxtaposes diverse tendencies. A certain confusion seems to reign here, for in the exegesis of Isaiah 34:10 three powers or aeons named *neṣaḥ* are mentioned. However, if the last power is "the end of the Shekhinah, beneath the feet of God," and "the last of the seven earths" of the old *Ma'aseh Bereshith* speculations,[165] as is said here, then this no longer agrees with counting the Righteous as the eighth logos, though it fits very well with placing it seventh (as probably was intended). Altogether, the few passages in the *Bahir* mentioning these two *neṣaḥim* and correlating them with the symbolism of the bouquet of the Feast of Tabernacles are obscure. Later, when 1 Chronicles 29:11 was interpreted as an enumeration of the name of the sefiroth and thus became a cornerstone of kabbalistic typology, these two *neṣaḥim* were called *neṣaḥ* and *hod.* These names are still unknown to our *Bahir* text; *hod* as the name of a sefirah appears only once in a quotation from the *Bahir* by Todros Abulafia, the authenticity of which is questionable.[166] Since these two powers are conceived here as being situated beneath the Righteous, namely, the "foundation of the world," the sexual symbolism that correlates them with the body's two testicles, where the seminal force is produced, is absent. This later symbolism, which then competes with the older one of the two legs, became possible only when in the course of the definitive organization of the kabbalistic schema of the sefiroth the seventh logos was put in the place of the ninth sefirah. Nevertheless, as we have seen, it is precisely its older position as the seventh that explains much better than the later reorganization some of the most important elements of this symbolism.

---

165. In the *Baraitha de-Ma'aseh Bereshith,* in the book *Raziel,* fol. 36a, the lowest earth is similarly understood as a region in the Merkabah related to the wheels of the Merkabah (the *'ofannim*) and to which Isaiah 66:1 is said to refer. A better text of this quotation can be found in Baḥya ben Asher's commentary on the Torah (on Lev. 1:1). This baraitha also contains a description of the seven earths, but these are understood there as regions of Gehenna.

166. Cf. my *Das Buch Bahir,* 159–160. Yehudah ben Barzilai makes frequent mention of *hod,* the "majesty" of the Shekhinah, whereas this term never occurs in the *Bahir.*

Aeons and archons could, at this stage, still be partly identified, as is apparent not only from the remarks on the fourth and the fifth logoi, where the aeon *geburah,* "strength" (section 77), is itself the archon, *sar,* over all the holy forms of the left, but also from those concerning the Righteous, which in section 123 is specifically designated as the archon standing above the two following "powers," represented by the legs of man. This terminology is comprehensible if we assume that the world of the Merkabah was equated with personified abstractions and hypostases in the oldest phases of the evolution leading to the Kabbalah. The more this process advanced the greater was the tendency to move the Merkabah itself down to a lower level, as indeed was later to be the case. That this tendency is present though not yet fully dominant in the *Bahir* is shown above all by the symbolism of the last of the powers, where hardly anything remains of the original Merkabah symbolism and the most salient characteristics originate in completely different spheres.

8. The Symbolism of the Shekhinah and the Feminine: The Jewel

Of primary importance for this conception of the last sefirah is its emphatic connection with the symbols of the feminine. While in the third sefirah, *binah,* an image such as that of the mother of the world appears only en passant, the last sefirah exhibits an abundance of images that are related, directly or indirectly, to the feminine. Similar images appear quite frequently in the Aggadah, above all in aggadic parables where, however, they are never related to God or to aspects of the Godhead conceived as feminine. The Aggadah knows nothing of such imagery, and one would look for it in vain in the literature of the Merkabah gnosis. The application of such images to a *middah* of God conceived as feminine and their consequent entry into the world of gnostic symbolism was one of the most far-reaching developments in the formation of the Kabbalah. It is difficult to say whether we should consider this process as the breakthrough of ancient, mythical images and "archetypes" into a world where they had been mere metaphors or as a renewed historic contact with a gnostic tradition that had never ceased to make use of these images. The condition of the oldest extant texts does not allow us to decide between these alternatives—if, indeed, they are genuine alternatives and not, as may well be the case, mutually reconcilable possibilities. A closer investigation of this symbolism will reveal how profound were the metamorphoses of the imagery of the Aggadah in the process of the formation of ideas concerning the last sefirah.

In particular, three or four concepts that go far beyond anything found in the older Aggadah are identified with each other in the *Bahir:* the bride, the king's daughter or quite simply the daughter as such, the Shekhinah, and the ecclesia of Israel. In addition, there is the symbolism of the earth (which conceives), the moon (which has no light of its own but receives its light from the sun), the ethrog, "the fruit of beautiful trees" in the festive bouquet (Lev. 23:40), which is considered to be feminine, and the date, considered as an image of the vagina. The first four concepts are employed interchangeably in the *Bahir;* and that is entirely new. In talmudic literature the Shekhinah is never a symbol of the feminine; still less is it identical with the ecclesia of Israel, no matter how frequently and readily the latter is personified. The Shekhinah, in talmudic literature, is always simply God himself, that is, God insofar as he is present in a particular place or at a particular event. This "presence" or "indwelling" of God is precisely rendered by the Hebrew term Shekhinah. The noun is used only to signify God's "dwelling," his presence, and never that of any created being. Nowhere is it separated from God himself, as are, for example, the *middoth* of mercy or stern judgment, which already in the Aggadah are represented as appearing before God and even arguing with him after the manner of the angels. In many passages, the term could be replaced by expressions such as God, Master of the world, the Holy One blessed be he, and so on, with no change in meaning. Contrary to what many scholars have assumed in their quest of hypostases and concepts that occupy an intermediary position between God and the world, the Shekhinah is not a quality of God, unless it is that of his undivided and undifferentiated presence.[167]

It is true that in the talmudic period this concept already had

167. I stress this point in opposition to assertions of the kind found in the monographs of J. Abelson, *The Immanence of God in Rabbinical Literature* (London, 1912), 77–149, or O. S. Rankin, *Israel's Wisdom Literature* (Edinburgh, 1936), 259. These authors and many of their predecessors have, without reason, read kabbalistic notions into the older texts.

the potential to undergo a gnostic hypostatization. Once, in fact, a multiplicity of shekhinoth is mentioned in the Talmud but in a deliberately negative and ironic manner. *Sanhedrin* 39b puts into the mouth of the Roman emperor a question with which he is said to have taunted Rabban Gamaliel (ca. 100 C.E.): "You maintain that upon every gathering of ten the Shekhinah rests? How many shekhinoth [Aramaic: *shekhinatha*] do you think there are?" This pluralistic generalization, which of course no longer permits the equation of the Shekhinah with the supreme God, appears to have been self-evident among the Mandaeans, whose literature overflows with references to myriads of worlds, *uthra*s (treasure houses of riches) and shekhinoth, though we never learn precisely what it is they represent. They are beings or places of light to which no specific function is attributed. In Manichaean usage, too, the five limbs of the king of the paradise of light are called his five shekhinoth.[168] This, however, is a usage that developed outside Judaism; the mystics of the Merkabah know nothing about it.

To the extent that the Shekhinah does not pertain to God's presence and manifestation in the terrestrial world but reveals itself in the celestial world of the Merkabah, it can naturally be identified with the *kabhod,* the Glory of God. Hence, the world of the Merkabah could be designated as the place "of his Shekhinah *hidden from men* in the highest heights,"[169] and the term "throne of the Shekhinah" substituted for "throne of glory."[170] It is the hidden Shekhinah that appears to the initiates in the vision of the *Shi'ur Qomah.* In the theophany, they gaze upon the "body of the Shekhinah."[171] A voice emanates from the Shekhinah sitting on the throne, and speaks to the lower orders.[172] A distinction between God and the Shekhinah may be adumbrated here to the extent that a gnostic differentiation between the hidden being of God and the figure that appears in the theophanies of his (similarly hidden) form perhaps already plays some part. Never, however, does it reach the point where it would be possible to speak of a relationship between the Shekhinah and God. The voice that emanates from it does not

168. H. C. Puech, *Le Manichéisme* (Paris, 1949), 75–78.

169. As in the Targum to Habakkuk 3:4.

170. Cf. 3 Enoch, ed. Odeberg, chap. 7.

171. *Alphabet of Rabbi Akiba* (Jerusalem, 1914), 29.

172. 3 Enoch, chap. 16.

speak to God on high, but as the voice of God himself is addressed to his creatures.

In a single passage found in the latest stratum of the Midrash we can detect the step that led to the establishment of the Shekinah as an autonomous entity. A comparison of the talmudic source, *Sanhedrin* 104b, with the late Midrash clearly shows this development:

Talmud

The men of the Great Assembly enumerated them [those who have no portion in the world to come]. R. Yehudah said: They wished to include another [King Solomon], but the image of his father came and prostrated itself [in supplication] before them. However, they disregarded it. . . . Whereupon a heavenly voice cried out to them, citing Proverbs 22:29 "See a man skilled at his work— He shall attend upon kings; he shall not attend upon obscure men."

Midrash Mishle

When the Sanhedrin wanted to put Solomon together with the three kings and four private persons [who have no portion in the world to come], *the Shekhinah stood up before God and spoke before Him:* Master of the World! "See a man skilled at his work" [Prov. 22:29]. But those men want to count him among the enemies of light [the damned]. Whereupon a heavenly voice went forth and said: "He shall attend upon kings," etc.

Thus the decisive phrase does not occur in the Talmud or in the early parallels to the same aggadah.[173] It became possible only after unknown aggadists of a later period hypostatized the Shekhinah into a divine quality distinct from God himself and capable of engaging in dialogue *with him.* A twelfth-century author seems to have had before him an even more extreme version of this passage: "Then the Shekhinah prostrated itself before God."[174] We find a similar distinction between God and the Shekhinah, long before the emergence of the Kabbalah, in the *Midrash Bereshith Rabbathi* of Moses [ha-Darshan of Narbonne (eleventh century)] or of his school.[175] Here, too, an older source belonging to the literature of Merkabah mysticism, *The Alphabet of Rabbi Akiba,* is paraphrased. "R. Akiba said: When God pondered over the deeds of the generation of Enoch

173. Cf. Buber's edition of *Midrash Mishle,* 47a. In his discussion of midrashic passages concerning the Shekhinah, Abelson overlooked this particular passage.

174. Moses Taku, *Kethab tamim,* (in the miscellany *'Osar Nehmad,* vol. 3 [Vienna, 1860], 63, 67), quoting Yehudah Hasid. This wording of the Midrash aroused the ire of Moses Taku, who declared it to be apocryphal.

175. *Bereshith Rabbathi,* ed. Albeck (Jerusalem, 1940), 27.

and saw that they were corrupt and bad, He withdrew *Himself and His Shekhinah* from their midst." The older source, however, in keeping with original usage, has only: "Then I withdrew My Shekhinah."[176] Our author, then, was already capable of separating God from his Shekhinah. It is, of course, possible that this separation is the result of an immanent development within the world of the Aggadah, especially as the Midrash on Proverbs evinces a strong inclination toward Merkabah mysticism and shows no trace of philosophical speculation. On the other hand, it is entirely conceivable that philosophical ideas may have made their way into the late Aggadah. I have summarized this process elsewhere in the following manner:[177]

> The Shekhinah as a manifestation of god was thoroughly familiar to the medieval philosophy of Judaism; it was seen as something distinct from God Himself. This hypostasis, however, in accordance with the dominant rational tendencies to safeguard pure monotheism, took on a character far removed from anything kabbalistic. All the philosophers, from Saadya through Yehudah Halevi to Maimonides, unanimously declare that the Shekhinah, identical with the *kabhod* mentioned in the Bible or the luminous splendor of God, was *God's free creation,* albeit the first one, the being which preceded all creation of a more grossly material nature. As a creature, it has no part in the divine being or in the unity of god. "The luminous manifestation which must validate for the prophet the authenticity of the revelation he has received is a created light; it is called *kabhod* in the Bible, and Shekhinah in the rabbinic tradition.[178] As a matter of fact, the term *'or ha-shekhinah* ("light of the Shekhinah") occurs several times in the writings of Saadya and Yehudah ben Barzilai.[179] This theory of Saadya's constitutes henceforth one of the main pillars of the philosophical exegesis of the Bible. Yehudah ben Barzilai, for example, writing one generation before the emergence of Kabbalah in southern France specifically defines this primordial light as the first of all created things. He says, "When God conceived the idea of creating a world, he created as the first of all His creations the holy spirit, which

---

176. Ed. Jerusalem, 10. But cf. ibid., 83, for a similar differentiation in (later?) additions: "God looked, and beheld his throne, and his *kabhod,* and his *shekhinah.*"

177. *"Schechinah:* das passiv-weibliche Moment in des Gottheit," *Der Gerechte* (ibid.), 149–150.

178. Saadya, *'Emunoth we-De'oth,* treatise 3, ed. Slucki (Leipzig, 1859), 63.

179. Cf. G. Vajda in *REJ* 134 (1975): 133–135, who refers to Saadya, *'Emunoth* 8:6 (Slucki, 156), the Saadya quotation in Abraham ibn Ezra's commentary on Exodus 25:7 (shorter recension, ed. Fleischer [1926], 232), as well as ben Barzilai's commentary on *Yeṣirah,* pages 16 and 18.

is also called the Glory of our God. This is a radiant splendor and a great light which shines upon all His other creatures. . . . And the sages call this great light Shekhinah. No creature, neither angel, nor seraph, nor prophet, can behold it in its original essence, and no prophet could survive such a vision, either. That is why God shows the angels and the prophets something of the end of this light.[180] Yehudah Halevi also holds the Shekhinah to be a subtle, corporeal substance—and as such, ipso facto, created—a body which adopts whatever form God wishes to show the prophet, in accordance with the divine will. Similarly, Maimonides speaks of the Shekhinah as a "created light that God causes to descend in a particular place in order to confer honor upon it in a miraculous way."[181] It could hardly have escaped the attention of these eminent authors that such a conception of the Shekhinah as a creature entirely separated from God, however elevated its rank, was completely foreign to the Talmud and that it would be necessary to do considerable violence to the texts in order to bring them into harmony with it. Evidently, however, they preferred to cut the Gordian knot in this manner rather than to incur the risk which was involved, from the standpoint of monotheism, in the recognition of an uncreated hypostasis. However, with the single exception of Yehudah ben Barzilai, they avoided, as far as possible, applying their new principles to the concrete exegesis of rabbinic passages concerning the Shekhinah. Nowhere do they make even the slightest reference to a feminine character of the Shekhinah.

The kabbalistic conception of the Shekhinah is very remote from philosophic conceptions of this kind. Its symbolism would have made these thinkers shudder or shake their heads in sad disapproval. We cannot say whether the Shekhinah was identified with the ecclesia of Israel only after it had been conceived as a feminine aeon, or conversely, whether this identification, once established, led to the resurgence of the feminine archetype. The fragments of the oldest stratum of the *Bahir,* whose gnostic character we analyzed earlier, seem to argue in favor of the first hypothesis. Essential for the kabbalistic symbolism was the manner in which the gnostic motif of the daughter of light and the aggadic motif of the ecclesia of Israel coalesced in the new conception of the Shekhinah as the last

---

180. Cf. his commentary on *Yeṣirah,* pp. 16–18. The expression "the end of the shekhinah" in *Bahir* section 115 may well have occurred already in a version of his source, the baraitha on Creation. It could, however, also be connected with the term employed several times by Yehudah ben Barzilai, "the end of the *hod ha-shekhinah.*" Indeed, on page 39 this author explicitly speaks of the *"hod,* which is the created end of the Shekhinah."

181. *Kuzari* 4:3; Maimonides, *Moreh* 1:64 and the end of 76.

sefirah. For *kenesseth yisrael* as the ecclesia elevated to the rank of a person, the hypostatized "synagogue," was always represented in the Aggadah by feminine images. It is she who, at the conclusion of the Covenant, is conceived as betrothed to God; from that point on she can be spoken of, without qualification, as a feminine figure. The Midrash, however, has no idea about a possible introduction of the "Community of Israel" into the sphere of the divine. Hence the images of daughter, bride, and matrona remain inoffensive. In the Book *Bahir* all this is transposed into a new sphere, and the old images are consciously recast in the spirit of Gnosticism.

This terminology of the daughter, the princess, and the wife or the matron occurs no fewer than ten times (sections 36, 43, 44, 52, 62, 90, 97, 104, 124, 137), always with the same intention. The old Midrash contains a parable expressing the importance of the Sabbath, which the Talmud was also fond of likening to a princess:

> A king passed through his land and had his herald proclaim: Let no guests that are here see my face until they have first seen the face of the matrona (queen). In the same way, the Holy One, blessed be He, said: You shall not bring an offering unto Me until a Sabbath day has passed over it.[182]

In section 43 of the *Bahir,* by means of a play on words, the bride of the Song of Songs is interpreted as a "field," *sadeh,* and, similarly, as a vessel, *shiddah,* into which the higher powers flow. Both images recur in other passages as well. In section 90, the *kabhod* of God is compared to a plot of ground that adjoins a beautiful garden and is separately irrigated from a mysterious "place," "although all is one." We are already acquainted with the image of the vessel from our analysis of section 52, concerning Abraham's daughter. In section 43, the bride is also the "heart" of God; the numerical value of לב, "heart," is thirty-two, indicating the thirty-two hidden paths of the Sophia, by means of which the world was created.

> And what are these thirty-two? It is like a king who was in the innermost chamber and the number of the chambers was thirty-two, and a path led to each chamber. Did it suit the king that every one could take his paths and enter into his chambers at will? No! Did it suit him

182. *Wayiqra Rabba, parashah* 27, section 10, and *Pesiqta de-Rab Kahana,* ed. Buber, fol. 78a.

> not to display openly his pearls and treasures, jewels and precious stones? No! What did he do? He took the "daughter"[183] and combined in her and in her garments [that is, manifestations] all the paths, and whoever wishes to enter the interior must look this way. And in his great love for her he sometimes called her "my sister," for they had come from the same place; sometimes he called her "my daughter," for she is his daughter, and sometimes he called her "my mother."

It should be noted in this connection that the application of this simile to the "lower Sophia" corresponds to the gnostic identification (attested for the second century)[184] of Mother, Daughter, and Bride (the Beloved) of the highest God. The final sentence of this text, which clearly describes the function of the mystical daughter, has its origin, however, in an older parable of the Midrash concerning the ecclesia of Israel.[185] In the Book *Bahir* itself, this ecclesia appears in section 45 as an extension of these metaphors. There she is the representative of a power that simultaneously exercises both punitive justice and mercy. If Israel does penance she will "return" together with them, a reference, no doubt, to the exile of the Shekhinah, now separated from her king. In reality, then, the daughter is only a pure vessel and has no identity of her own. She is the totality of all the paths converging in her, and it is only upon her garments that the jewels of the king first become visible. But that is precisely how she became the intermediary through which one must pass in order to gain access to the king himself.

This connection between the king and the daughter is developed in another passage (section 36) in a manner that is very instructive as regards the relationship to Gnosticism. We saw above that the seventh logos is the place of the souls of all living things and the place, also, of the masculine. Here, however, and here alone, the soul appears as the symbol of the feminine, who is the same daughter and princess with whom we became acquainted in section 90 as the "daughter of light" who had come from a foreign land—the *brath nuhra* of the Syrian gnostic texts. This corresponds to the statements of the Gnostics concerning the soul, but not to the symbolism that is predominant elsewhere in the *Bahir.* Section 36 sets

---

183. The Hebrew expression is very strange: *naga' ba-bath,* "he touched the daughter."

184. Cf. W. Bousset, *Hauptprobleme der Gnosis,* 337, and H. Drÿvers in *NUMEN* 14 (1967): 116.

185. *Shir ha-Shirim Rabba* 3:11.

forth a mystical etymology of the word *zahab,* gold, in whose consonants "three *middoth* are united," "the masculine, *zakhar,* and that is the *z,* the soul, and that is the *h* . . . which is a throne for the *z,* and *b* guarantees their existence," because the two principles of the masculine and the feminine are united by the *beth* at the beginning of the first word of the Torah. This union is evidently seen by the text as the primordial act of creation. The feminine, which is here presupposed, is designated as such, that is, as daughter, in the parable that follows, but not in the explanation itself.

> And what is the function [of the *beth*]? This is like a king who had a daughter, good and beautiful, gracious and perfect, and he married her to the son of a king and gave her garments, a crown and jewels, and he gave her to him with a great fortune. Can the king now live without his daughter [literally: outside his daughter]? No! Can he always be with her all day? No! What did he do? He made a window between himself and her, and whenever the daughter had need of the father and the father of the daughter they would come together through the window. That is what is written [Ps. 45:14]: "The royal princess, her dress embroidered with golden mountings" [the gold of the three *middoth* united in *zahab*].

Here, too, a midrashic parable about a king and his daughter, the ecclesia, found in the Midrash on Song of Songs 3:9, is mystically transposed.

In other parables of this kind, the king's daughter was the Torah from whom he did not wish to be separated even though he had given her, indeed "betrothed" her, to Israel. He therefore prepared a chamber (the sanctuary) in which he could live near them, as in the beginning of paragraph 33 of *Shemoth Rabba.* The midrashic parable of the king who built a palace for his daughter also speaks of the Torah. The king had her sit in the innermost of seven chambers and proclaimed: "Whoever enters my daughter's presence is as one who enters my presence."[186] In the *Bahir,* all these concepts are merged into one symbol. The daughter of the king is below, in this world whose mystical principle or *middah* she represents (as is explicitly stated in section 98), but she remains connected with her father through a "window." She is the fine plot of land outside the true garden that is at one with everything inside this mystical gar-

186. *Midrash Tanḥuma,* the ordinary recension, *Piqqude,* section 4.

den, even though it appears to be separated from it. Whatever she possesses, as the verse in Psalm 45 says, comes "from inside," from the world of logoi and of powers, and remains, in the last resort, within her. The position of the daughter indicates the passage of the Shekhinah from transcendence to immanence. As the active principle in this world, she is the Oral Torah by means of which the Written Torah is deciphered and rendered applicable. For this reason, it is also said of the Oral Torah in section 97 that God united in it the thirty-two paths of the Sophia and gave it to the world. Because these thirty-two paths are contained or appear in her, she is also the "heart" (sections 43, 67, 75, 105). "R. Raḥmai said: 'Glory' *(kabhod)* and 'heart' *(leb)* are [according to their numerical value] the same thing, only the one is named after its action above, and the other after its action below, and that is the meaning of the [biblical expressions, Deut. 4:11] 'Glory of God' and 'heart of heaven' " (section 91). Thus the term heart, employed in the Book *Yeṣirah* 6:1 for the sphere of man in general is used here in a completely different sense. In the ritual symbolism of section 62 the thirty-two fringes[187] are compared with the thirty-two guards who watch over the paths in the king's garden, which, according to section 67, are also the paths that lead to the Tree of Life. The guard who is placed in charge of them all is equated, in another parable in section 62, with the daughter of the king. This shows, incidentally, that the symbolism of the last sefirah as the Guardian of Israel, *shomer yisrael* (Ps. 121:4), was already known to the *Bahir.*

The king's daughter, who comes from the "form of light," is, as we have already seen, the lower Sophia (cf. p. 94f.). Like "wisdom" in the Bible and the Shekhinah in the Talmud, she descends upon the terrestrial beings. She is no longer merely the presence of God, but a specific moment in the unfolding of his powers. In section 44, the Talmudic saying to the effect that the name of Solomon in the Song of Songs was a name of God ("the king, with whom is peace")[188] is continued, in a mystical mode, in the following manner: "God said: Since your name sounds like the name of My Glory, I will marry you to my 'daughter.' But is she not already married? He said: she was given to him as a gift, as it is written (1 Kings

---

187. The number of fringes prescribed for garments by the Torah (Num. 15:37ff.) is, according to the talmudic regulation, thirty-two.

188. Tractate *Shebu'oth* 35b.

5:26), 'The Lord had given Solomon wisdom.' "[189] This wisdom has a double function: "If a man does good, she helps him and brings him close to God; if he does not, she removes him [from God] and punishes him," disposing of all the seven higher powers united within her for that purpose. To whom then is this daughter already married, if she can only be "given as a gift" to Solomon? Evidently, to the partner of her syzygy, the masculine principle, who is the beloved of the Song of Songs. Here, too, the symbols of bride and daughter are merging. The context, however, also permits another interpretation: she could be the bride of Solomon himself. In fact, 1 Kings 5:26 is explained in section 3 by means of a parable: "A king married his daughter to his son and gave her to him as a gift and said to him: 'Do with her as you will.' " One should beware of rash conclusions as regards the antiquity of this text on the basis of its apparent knowledge of marriage between brothers and sisters in royal houses as, for example, in ancient Egypt.[190] In fact our text presents a variation, albeit in a rather extravagant form, of a parable in *Midrash Qoheleth Rabba* 1, where, in imitation of Solomon's request for wisdom, the king's counselor asks for the hand of the king's daughter. In view of all the other similar passages it cannot be doubted that the symbolism of the bride in the *Bahir* is connected with the mystical syzygy discussed above. That is why, as we have already seen, she is mentioned among the seven sacred forms of the celestial man, as the feminine element correlated to the phallus (sections 55, 114, 116).

Particularly in the sections that follow section 115, this symbolism of the feminine plays a central role. In sections 117 and 139, reference is made to the bisexual character of the palm tree, which was apparently known to the authors from their own observation. This would bring us back again to the Orient, where the cultivation of the date palm occupies so prominent a place. A very pronounced

189. This is a play on words. At first it is said that "Solomon bore [*nassa'*] the name of God." The Hebrew word for "marry" is the *hiph'il* form of the same root. The pun is not, however, based upon an authentic usage of the expression *nassa 'eth ha-shem,* which in reality means "pronounced the name." The semantic modification suggests the influence of a Romance language.

190. In fact, many years ago Robert Eisler wrote to me that he had reached that conclusion. Concerning the "gift" to Solomon of the Sophia, already hypostatized, as the first of all created things, cf. also Yehudah ben Barzilai on *Yeṣirah,* p. 57.

symbol of the masculine, the palm tree also plays an important role in Mandaean gnosis.[191] As a counterpart to the palms, in section 117, we have the citron, ethrog, from the bouquet of the Feast of Tabernacles, but also the bride of the Song of Songs. Here is how the origin of the feminine principle in the world and in human beings is explained:

> It is like a king who planned to plant nine masculine trees in his garden and all of them would have to be palms. He said: If they are all of one species they will not be able to endure. What did he do? He planted an ethrog among them, and it was one of the nine which he had [originally] planned [*at first*] that they should be masculine.

When mention is made in Leviticus 23:40 of the "product of beautiful trees, branches of palm trees," in the description of the festive bouquet, the reference is to the feminine ethrog. The tree of beauty, *hadar,* refers to the beauty that is glorified in the Song of Songs, of which it is written, "Who is she that shines through like the dawn?" (6:10). "And on account of her, woman was taken from man, for the higher and the lower world could not endure without the feminine." While the Midrash knows only of a symbolism of the palm branch, lulab, that likens it to the spinal column[192]—an idea employed in section 118—the reference here to masculine and feminine is entirely new. A relation is established between the palm tree, *tamar,* and the syzygy of masculine and feminine in connection with the feminine name Tamar. The children of Tamar, Perez and Zarah (Gen. 38:-28–30), signify the moon and the sun, contained within the palm in the same way as the feminine and the masculine (sections 138, 193). But the more detailed exposition in section 139 again confuses the straightforward view of the masculine and feminine palm. The lulab, which stands upright, represents the masculine; the stone of the date, "cleft, the way females are," the feminine, "and it corresponds to the power of the moon above."

This sphere is at the same time the sea into which all streams flow (sections 120, 121), which is expressly identified with the ethrog. In section 65 it is called the "sea of the *ḥokhmah,*" undoubtedly because the powers of the *ḥokhmah* and its paths run into her

191. Cf. Drower, *The Secret Adam,* 7–8, 10–11.
192. E.g., in *Wayiqra Rabba,* the end of *parashah* 30.

and are contained in her. It is expressly emphasized in section 51 that she is the Shekhinah who dwells in Israel. There she is the *middah* that God gave to David and Solomon. In sections 50 and 85, the concept of the Shekhinah is also identified with *ṣedeq,* which we have already learned to recognize as a symbol of this sphere. She is a particular quality that was offered to the Patriarchs when they prayed for a *middah* of God by which they would be able to regulate their conduct, but which, when offered, they declined to accept. That is why she is called here (sections 61, 131, 132) "the stone which the builders rejected" that "has become the chief cornerstone" (Ps. 118:22). For when Abraham, Isaac, and Jacob rejected this *middah* and chose their own, it was given to David (sections 50, 85). But she is not merely the stone or cornerstone, but, above all, "the precious stone" and the valuable jewel. She is designated as such directly in sections 61, 65, 131 and indirectly in sections 16, 17, 49, and 61. The precious stone that adorns the daughter or the bride becomes a symbol of herself, in whose rays "all the commandments are contained" (section 131). The beautiful, preciously wrought gem of this passage becomes in section 137 the Torah, the adorned and crowned bride betrothed to God. This symbolism of the precious stone can be explained as reflecting aggadic symbolism, where the Torah (in the Talmud, *Zebaḥim* 116a) appears as a jewel in God's treasure and where the soul is compared to a pearl,[193] or—equally well—as a reversion to the language of Gnosticism, where the Sophia or soul is likewise described as a gem or pearl. This precious stone, in which the "gems of kings and provinces" (thus in section 61, referring to Eccles. 2:8) are united, is plainly distinguished from the kings, who are the active powers in the pleroma. They bring forth the years, that is, time. Here is how section 49 interprets Habakkuk 3:2:

> A king had a valuable jewel . . . and when he rejoiced, he hugged it and kissed it, set it upon his head and loved it. Habakkuk said to him: even though the kings are with you, that jewel is the ornament of your world; for that reason, he procured life for him "in these years" —in that jewel which brings forth the years.

---

193. *Bereshith Rabba, parashah* 7, section 5, ed. Theodor, 54. I. Scheftelowitz, "Die mandäische Religion and das Judentum," *MGWJ* 69 (1929):218, has already drawn attention to these passages and to similar ones in the Palestinian Talmud.

But this pearl, crown, or daughter is not limited to accomplishing a mission in this world in her capacity of "lower wisdom" and the "maiden from afar." She is also moved by an opposite dynamic of ascension, upwards to God. There is, then, not only an outward movement of the Shekhinah, but an inward movement as well, in the direction of those powers woven into her garments. This is particularly apparent in a mystical reinterpretation of a talmudic passage concerning prayer. In *Ḥagigah* 13b, it is said that the angel Sandalfon, who receives the prayers of Israel and wreathes them into a crown, pronounces the name of God over this crown. It then ascends (by itself) to the head of its Master and crowns Him. In section 61, this image is reinterpreted. The crown that "rises very high" is both "the crowned jewel in which everything is united, and the rejected cornerstone. And it rises until it reaches the place where it was hewn out." This place, whose name is "there," is clearly described in section 129 by the symbols of the third logos. That accords well with the relations between *binah,* as the place of the primordial light and the place where the Torah is hewn, and this last region, which is also called "the treasure house of the Oral Torah" (sections 97, 137). The same connection is established in sections 131 and 133. The primordial light and the light of this world are two powers that are both symbolized by the precious stone. A supreme jewel, which is here called *soḥereth*—in a punning use, signifying ṣummum bonum[194] is opposed to the other precious stone, which itself has but a thousandth part of the brightness of the supreme stone and, described by the epithets of the bride and the Torah, is named the "beautiful and preciously wrought gem" in which God unites all the commandments. The lower precious stone constitutes, so to speak, a small piece extracted from the higher precious stone. Its home, though, is forever there, and it returns thither, to its "there," in the hour of prayer and in the messianic times. This conception of a secret movement in the realm of the sefiroth, upward no less than downward and associated especially with the Shekhinah, subsequently acquired a central importance in the Kabbalah.

It is evident that the symbolism of the daughter receives greater emphasis in the *Bahir* than the specifically sexual symbolism

194. In section 131, *soḥereth* is placed together with *seḥorah,* "wares" or "goods."

of the feminine.[195] On the other hand, the syzygy of the masculine and feminine is frequently and explicitly stressed, as we have already seen in a number of examples. The closed *mem* is the masculine, the open *mem* the feminine (sections 57–58). To this corresponds the union of east and west, which provides the basis for a profoundly gnostic passage concerning the transmigration of souls. We have already seen that the seventh logos, where the seed of Israel has its origin, is also called the "east of the world." It is in this sense that section 104 interprets Isaiah 43:5:

> I will bring your seed from the east, will gather you out of the west. If Israel is good before God, then I bring your seed from this place and a new seed is born to you. But if Israel is bad, I take from the seed which was already in the world and of which it is said: "a generation goes and a generation comes"; that is, that it has already come once before. And what is meant by "I will gather you out of the west"? From that *middah* which is always inclined toward the west. Why is the west called *ma'arabh,* mixture? Because every seed is mixed there. This is like a king's son who had a beautiful and chaste bride in his chambers. And he was in the habit of taking riches from the house of his father and constantly bringing them to her, and she took everything and put it all aside and mixed everything together. After some days had passed, he wished to see what he had united and collected, and on this subject it is said: From the mixture I gather you. But the house of the father signifies the east, from which he brings the seed which he sows in the west, and in the end, he again gathers what he has sown.

This is a very remarkable text. There exist new souls that have not yet been in the world at all, but only descend if Israel is "good before God." In general, the souls circulate from generation to generation. The sowing is that of the souls in the world, that is, in the cosmos governed by the Shekhinah, the sphere of the west, where, according to the Talmud, the Shekhinah dwells. The bringing home from the west, or from the mixture and destruction, can only mean redemption. Until then, the punishment of sinful souls of Israel is their transmigration. The Shekhinah is at the same time the daughter of the king's son and the ecclesia of Israel. From her realm, which is both the terrestrial world and a mystical region, all the

195. The *Bahir* speaks of the queen or wife only in parables, sections 51 and 90. In section 51, the wife is the community of Israel as mother of the children of Israel. Indirectly she is also presented in section 45 as the wife of the king.

souls are gathered anew "when the days have passed"—that is, in the eschatological scheme of things, at the end of time—and return to the house of the father, the mystical east. The same eschatological meaning is attributed, at the end of section 50, to the prayer of Hezekiah: "If there is peace and truth in my days" (2 Kings 20:19). Hezekiah prayed that the *middah* of David—which is evening, evening and west having same root in Hebrew—and that of "peace and truth," which is morning, would make of his days "one day," so that "everything would become one." This one day is at the same time both the primordial time of Genesis 1:5 and the final time of the redemption, which consists precisely in the reunion of the masculine and the feminine, as we have already learned in section 58.

Nevertheless, as we have just noted, according to this symbolism, the sexual element remains in the background. The book speaks more of the ornaments offered to the bride or to the daughter than of her other attributes. This conception of the receptivity is particularly emphasized in the parables, with the two tendencies combined in the image of the vessel. The feminine is the beautiful vessel where all jewels are preserved, but it is at the same time also the receptacle for the power of the masculine. This last *middah,* to be sure, is not exclusively receptive. She is indeed the poorest of all, but she nevertheless possesses riches: she has within herself a positive force. This is said with a view to the letter *daleth,* understood here literally as "poverty": "Ten kings were once in the same place, and all rich. One of them was indeed rich, but nevertheless not as rich as any of the others.[196] Thus, though his riches were very great, he was called *dal,* poor, in comparison to the others" (section 19).

Whereas the texts hitherto discussed have stressed above all this relation between the Shekhinah and the masculine as the seventh logos, we also already saw in section 35 a symbolic description of the reciprocal interdependence of the last and the sixth logoi, which is "Truth" and "Heaven." Psalms 85:12 is interpreted in this sense: " 'Truth' springs out of the 'earth' [that is, the Shekhinah] and [conversely] 'justice' [as the name of the Shekhinah] [also] looks down from 'heaven' above." The two regions that are thus placed in reciprocal relation with each other are said to be the two phylacter-

196. I have intentionally avoided improving in the translation the particularly defective and awkward Hebrew.

ies of the tefillin that the king attaches to his elbow joint and his head. Here we can again see how ritual had already acquired a mystical significance. The commandments of the Torah indicate the process by means of which the divine powers act in their own world as well as in the lower world. The relation of the last sefirah to the "all" and its particular dynamic express themselves especially in those commandments to which the *Bahir* gives mystical interpretations. Thus the precept of the heave offering, *terumah,* indicates, according to sections 66 and 71, that the tenth sefirah is destined for such "elevation." It is she who, through asceticism and detachment from the world, must be "elevated" in prayer. Divine things are indicated by the process of setting aside the offering, that is, the detachment of the mystic from the world in order to seek God, as well as by the offering itself, the symbol of that which is to be elevated, that is, the Glory of God that is lifted up. The symbolism of the fringes and the tefillin has already been mentioned in this connection, as has that of the lulab and the ethrog of the Feast of Tabernacles (in sections 67, 117–120). The fulfillment of the Torah's commandments increases the plenitude of light in the world, as stated in section 98 in an eschatological interpretation of Habakkuk 3:4.[197]

A last symbolic development of importance for our analysis is that of the double Shekhinah. This fission of the concept of the Shekhinah is not identical with the division of the Sophia into an upper and a lower, but is parallel to it. The idea of the double Shekhinah originated in a reinterpretation of a quotation from the ancient "baraitha on the Creation." A sentence from this baraitha relating to the lowest earth is quoted in section 115, as we have already seen on page 160. The direct continuation of this sentence is used in section 116, albeit in a completely enigmatic context. Section

---

197. The interpretation of Habakkuk 3:4 in section 98 is related to that of Yehudah ben Barzilai (18–19), who reinterpreted the Targum of this verse in almost the same manner as the *Bahir* but transposed it to an eschatological plane. The motif of the primordial light is still absent from the talmudic interpretation of Habakkuk 3:4 in *Pesahim* 8a. Also the continuation of the interpretation in section 130 and of the following verse in section 121 (where *debher,* "plague," is understood as *dabhar* [holy] "word or logos") can already be found, in their essentials, in Yehudah ben Barzilai. Professor Flusser drew my attention to the fact that this interpretation is also found in the Septuagint version of the Bible. Does this indicate an old exegetical tradition or rather patristic influences mediated through Christian channels? This is the closest contact between Yehudah ben Barzilai and the *Bahir* that I have been able to discover.

115 included the enumeration of the ten logoi. In section 116, the disciples, to whom this list had been taught, question their master:

> Now we know [the order of the logoi] from the top downward, but we do not know it from the bottom upward. The master prudently replied: Is this not the same thing? To which the pupils responded: Our master! He who ascends is not like he who descends. For he who descends goes quickly, but not he who ascends. And besides, he who ascends can ascend by another path which he could not take for the descent.

Instead of giving a clear answer to this obscure question, the unnamed master embarks on an exposition that, as we have already noted in sections 116–123, is primarily concerned with the feminine and its symbolism, and thus appears, in any case, to deal with the ascent upward from below. The master introduces his response with a sentence that reads as follows in the source, the aforementioned baraitha on *ma'aseh bereshith:* "As His Shekhinah is above, so is His Shekhinah below."[198] The meaning there is that the same Shekhinah—God's presence that has not yet become a *middah*—is above and below. In the *Bahir,* on the other hand, the sentence is cited in a form that permits an interpretation to the effect that there is a Shekhinah below, just as there is a Shekhinah above. To the question what then is this (lower) Shekhinah? the reply is: "It is the light that emanated from the primordial light." We have already examined the question of whether this primordial light is *ḥokhmah* or *binah.* The lower Shekhinah, in any case, is designated here as the Glory of God, which fills the earth. The continuation then speaks of the seven sons of the king and the seven holy forms; it progresses, therefore, in fact, from the bottom upward.

It is difficult to decide whether this duplication of the Shekhinah should be understood as a fission of the feminine into mother and daughter or rather as analogous to the double Sophia. Section 116 (at least in the reading of the oldest manuscript) designates the Sophia precisely as this primordial light, whereas section 74 gives to *binah* not only the name of mother—as we already know—but also that of glory; this would give us an "upper glory" alongside "lower glory." Such an idea of the plurality of the glory is by no means a kabbalistic innovation; it had already appeared in the commentary

198. *Baraitha de-Ma'aseh Bereshith,* in *Raziel,* fol. 36a.

on the Talmud of R. Ḥananel of Kairouan (eleventh century), who had distinguished various degrees of *kabhod:* "There is a *kabhod* above the *kabhod.*"[199] This passage was also known to the ancient kabbalists and is cited by them. To be sure, Ḥananel's *kabhod,* just as that of Saadya and Yehudah ben Barzilai, is a created *kabhod,* while for the Book *Bahir* and the oldest Kabbalah the character of these logoi remains doubtful. Whenever the idea of the primordial light is applied to one of the aeons, as in sections 97 and 106, there is reference to the "creation" of this primordial light, whereas, in section 116 it is said of the lower Shekhinah that it has "emanated" from the primordial light. I am not certain to what extent verbs like "create" and "emanate" must be taken in a technical sense. We shall find other instances of such fluctuations in terminology among the Provençal Kabbalists and their disciples, despite their evident inclination toward the doctrine of emanation. Whether the aeons or logoi of the *Bahir* were created by God or rather emanated from him remains unclear, at least for the greater part of the *Bahir.* Perhaps the authors never asked themselves questions of this kind.

9. Elements of the Doctrine of the Aeons Among the German Hasidim

We have reached the end of our study of the ten logoi or sefiroth in the Book *Bahir.* Hebrew fragments of a gnostic character that we were able to identify in our analysis or that we found ourselves compelled to presuppose for the origin of our texts had had the effect of stimulating similar speculations among circles that we still cannot clearly define. Much in these sources clearly points toward the Ori-

---

199. Ḥananel's commentary on *Yebamoth* 49b. Eleazar of Worms, in his *Sode Razayya,* paraphrased the assertion of the aforementioned baraitha concerning the Shekhinah in the same sense: "There exist therefore a *kabhod* above and a *kabhod* below"; cf. the text taken from his book in *Raziel,* fol. 15b. It would be mistaken, however, to try to find the symbolic expression "place of the upper Shekhinah" already in the *Midrash Bemidbar Rabba, parashah* 4, section 14, as is done in Wünsche's translation of this midrash (Leipzig, 1885). For the midrash it is a matter of the Shekhinah dwelling in the terrestrial temple, "corresponding to the place of its Shekhinah [that is, corresponding to the Throne of Glory, which was mentioned there previously, *parashah* 4, section 13] above." The notions of *kisse ha-kabhod shel ma-'alah* and *meqom shekhinatho shel ma'alah* are synonymous.

ent; other elements may well have developed among the German Hasidim. The Book *Raza Rabba* was not the only Oriental source used for the composition or editing of the *Bahir.* Our detailed analysis demonstrated the existence of motifs and symbols deriving from a specific tradition that was perhaps not only literary, but that may also have been a living tradition. The academy of the very first kabbalists subjected its sources to an intensive revision. Certain things were allowed to remain as they were, but others were given entirely new Jewish forms. Others again were added to fit into the common framework they sought to create. We may therefore imagine a religious ferment proving its vitality by its receptivity to fragments of an ancient tradition. A ferment of this kind seems just as probable for northern France and the Rhineland during the period of the Crusades as for Provence, which was so deeply stirred at that time by the Catharist movement. In the *Bahir* certain details point to a connection with each of these lands, and perhaps there existed in each of them groups of the kind from which the *Bahir* finally issued in the form we know it. In both lands, the aggadic form of expression still existed with such vitality that the anonymous compilers were not inhibited from expressing their new ideas and the products of the new religious ferment in the style of the aggadic midrash, the style that suited them best and that was natural to them even if these new midrashim appeared rather provocative and paradoxical.

We possess religious documents emanating from the circle of the German Hasidim that show how close the doctrines of some of them came to gnostic speculations on the aeons. In this regard, one fact is of particular interest: certain texts that we know were finally edited about fifty years after the Book *Bahir* and that consequently are ruled out as possible sources of this work are notably lacking in precisely those strikingly gnostic elements that we discovered in our analysis of the *Bahir.* We are dealing with an internal Jewish process that had assimilated a subterranean tendency, which sought to describe the world of the Merkabah in a new way. Dating from the beginning of the thirteenth century we have the work of an anonymous author, the *Sefer ha-Ḥayyim,* the *Book of Life.* This book is remarkable not only for its parallels with the Kabbalah, but also because it clearly shows how many gnostic elements were still lacking in order to transform the doctrines of the book into something resembling the Kabbalah of the *Bahir*—and this in spite of the fact that the Book *Bahir* was already known at that time in southern France!

The *Sefer ha-Ḥayyim* says:

> All the heavens are like points under the heaven of the throne of Glory, and there all the wondrous [attributes] have their particular position: Knowledge for itself, Understanding for itself, Wisdom and the Fear of God for itself, Strength [*geburah*] for itself, all these wondrous attributes have their origin in the power of His *kabhod* for itself. And corresponding to these "glories" that are in the highest heaven which is called the "holy tenth," there are places in the ninth [heaven], and there the angels are created from these degrees, from the great light, each one according to the greatness of his degree from which he draws his holiness. According to the measure of what he receives from the supreme power, there is an angel who was created from the light of the knowledge, and he knows everything; there is one from the light of the discernment, from the light of the power, from the light of the wondrous, and so on without number and without end. These form the *"first kabhod,"* and they are contained in the universals.[200]

The universals, *kelalim,* thus constitute a world of ideas above the angels that forms the supreme or "first glory." The relationship with the sefiroth of the Kabbalah is readily apparent. The same view is formulated even more sharply in a passage at the end of the same book, which says of the divine *middoth,* considered as "places" in the world of the pleroma and as sources from which the angels and the lower powers are created or in which they have their origin:

> In the upper world there are innumerable places, of which one has a higher rank than the other, without number and without end. And for every thing there are other places: sources of Wisdom for itself, Understanding apart, Knowledge apart, Grace apart, Love *(ḥesed)* apart, Justice apart, Mercy apart, Vengeance apart, Anger apart. And the rank of the angels created by the word of God is determined according to the source. For it is from the source of Mercy that the angels of mercy were created. . . . And it is the same for every created group of angels. According to the light of the potency that it receives it is given its name, for that which is created from the light of the potency of Mercy is named merciful light . . . [and similarly for those angels that are created from the light of the source of Wisdom, Patience, from the light of Strength, from the place of *ḥesed,* from the light of Truth and the place of the remission of sins—a sequence partly reminiscent of several kabbalistic sefiroth]. And it is the same with all the *middoth,*

---

200. *Sefer ha-Ḥayyim,* Ms. Munich, Heb. 207, fol. 9a.

> and everything that comes to pass in the lower world takes place through them, and this is the secret of the whole Torah and the whole Scripture.[201]

These quotations show that the notion of *middoth* as aeons was also possible within German Hasidism. It would be difficult to say whether or not the oldest sources of the *Bahir* had influenced these views. The difference lies in the fact that everything in the *Bahir* that seems to us bizarre or specifically gnostic is missing here.

On the other hand it would be a mistake to overlook the possibility that such an esoteric conception of the symbols of the Merkabah in the spirit of the Book *Bahir* might be found in the writings of Eleazar of Worms, especially as he refers to an oral tradition concerning the mystical significance of such symbols.

> When it is said in the book of the Merkabah that the angels who are placed over the doors of the seven Hekhaloth ride fiery horses that eat fiery coals. . . .[202] It is well known that there is no eating and drinking in the supernal regions. But if I were to write down the interpretation, someone who is not worthy might see it and arrive at corrupt conceptions of it. . . . That is why [such an interpretation can be transmitted] only by way of tradition, *kabbalah,* that is to say, through oral transmission.[203]

The first kabbalists also interpreted the prophets' descriptions of the Merkabah and the revelations of the authors of the Hekhaloth literature as symbols of profoundly spiritual states. It is not without reason that the anonymous kabbalistic commentary on the Merkabah, whose true author can be identified as Jacob ben Cohen of Soria, is attributed in some manuscripts to "the Kabbalah of the Hasid R. Eliezer of Worms." In Narbonne around 1250, Jacob Cohen and his brother Isaac met a "Hasid and kabbalist," a pupil of Eleazar, who apparently knew how to combine the Hasidic tradition with the kabbalistic tradition of the Provençal group.[204] Perhaps

---

201. Ibid., fol. 28a–b. Also in excerpts from the book in Ms. Munich, Heb. 357, fol. 51b. The Hebrew text is printed in my *Reshith ha-Qabbala,* 48.

202. This quotation refers to chapter 16 of the "Greater Hekhaloth."

203. Quoted from Eleazar of Worms in *'Arugath ha-Bosem* of Abraham ben Azriel, ed. Urbach (Jerusalem, 1939), 204.

204. This mystic in Narbonne is mentioned three times by Isaac ben Jacob Cohen in his "Treatise on the Emanation" (sections 2, 10, 23); cf. *Madda'e ha-Yahaduth* 2:245, 254, 263. This historical personality was obviously one of the intermediaries between the German Hasidim and the circles of the Provençal kabbalists.

this anonymous disciple was more loyal to the oral transmission of his teacher's ideas than we are able to conclude from a simple comparison of his writings with those of the earliest kabbalists.

Elsewhere I have presented the ideas of the German Hasidim concerning the *kabhod.*[205] Among them, Saadya's doctrine of the first-created glory, "the great splendor which is called Shekhinah," is combined with a reinterpretation in the sense of a revival of the doctrine of the logos, which perhaps can be explained by a subterranean survival of Platonic ideas. In the twelfth century a distinction was still drawn between two forms or kinds of *kabhod,* an inner and an outer, the Shekhinah generally being identified with the inner glory or even with the divine will. Elsewhere, however, even Eleazar of Worms himself expresses a conception which makes of the Shekhinah a tenth "kingdom" or a tenth domain within the divine realm, quite in the sense of the speculations of the *Bahir* concerning the aeons. Most significant in this regard is a passage of his *Sefer ha-Ḥokhmah,* a commentary on the mystical forty-two-letter name of God. In a text on the tefillin of God, which are composed of the prayers *(tefilloth)* of Israel, it is said of the crown *('aṭarah),* which by these prayers ascends from below to rest upon God's head then to be called *Aktariel,* in thoroughly kabbalistic language:[206]

> For the *tefillah* sits at God's left like a bride by a bridegroom, and she is called the king's daughter, sometimes she is also called, according to her mission [to those here below] daughter of the voice [the talmudic expression for the celestial voice that mortals sometimes hear]. Of this Solomon said [reinterpreting Proverbs 8:30]: And I was Shekhinah by him, and the name of the Shekhinah is *'ehyeh* [I was] and the word next to it [in the verse] can also be explained, according to the Targum, as "she became great."[207] For she is called the king's daughter

---

205. Cf. *Major Trends,* 110–115.

206. For the complete text of this long piece cf. now Joseph Dan's work *Torath ha-sod shel Ḥaside Ashkenaz* (1968), 119–122. Dan argues (pp. 122–129) that these protokabbalistic passages were not authored by Eleazar, but were copied by him from a text attributed to Hai Gaon. Eleazar merely added comments (under the title *Sefer Yirkaḥ*) based on his number- and letter-mysticism without discussing or even taking note of the doctrine of the dynamics of the aeons, which was completely alien to him. This pseudo-Hai text, somehow related to the *Bahir* traditions though different from them, may have been composed by an earlier mystic of the Hasidic group—certainly earlier than Eleazar (1100–1150?). What remains puzzling is the corruption of the text of the commentary on the name of forty-two letters reproduced by Dan, which is far more corrupt than is usual for late manuscripts. A precise and thorough interpretation of the text seems well-nigh impossible.

207. Cf. following, n. 212.

> because the Shekhinah is with him in his house and it is to this that reference is made [in Ps. 91:1] to the dwelling in the shadow of *shaddai* [*ṣel,* "shadow," being taken here in the sense of *'eṣel,* "by"] which means: He has a shadow which is called "by him" and this is the tenth kingdom, *malkhuth,* and it is the mystery of all mysteries. And we know that the word *sod,* mystery, can be interpreted [by the method of letter-mysticism] as the word *malkhuth.* On every side of the Shekhinah are the crowns of royalty.[208] And she herself is 236,000 myriads of parasangs long [that is, she is the theophany of God upon his throne, as described in the *Shi'ur Qomah*]. . . . And she directs the world and is named angel of God by virtue [of this her] mission, but with her no separation [from God] takes place. And of this the verse [Exod. 23:20] said: I am sending an angel before you. This is the Shekhinah. And it is in this sense that the sages explain the verse [Num. 16:4]: Moses fell on his face, that is, because the Shekhinah was [there], he prostrated himself before God.[209] That is why the prophets saw the Shekhinah, which is emanated,[210] as it is said in *Sefer Hekhaloth* that the Shekhinah dwells beneath the cherub,[211] and [originally] angels and men saw it. But when the generation of Enoch sinned, the Shekhinah ascended heavenward. As for the Creator and Master of the Shekhinah, he is hidden from all and has neither measure [as in the *Shi'ur Qomah*] nor likeness, and no eye saw him. . . . And this is the mystery of the crown and the mystery of the Shekhinah, and whoever has this knowledge has a part in the world to come, inherits both worlds, and is saved from the judgment of Gehenna and he is beloved above and cherished below.[212]

Similarly, it is said in another passage of the same book (in a commentary on the name of forty-two letters, attributed to Hai Gaon):

> The Shekhinah of the Creator is named daughter, as it is said [Prov. 8:30]: And I was *shekhinah* with him, and this "with him" is translated in the Targum by מתרבית,[213] which has the same letters as

208. That is why it is itself named, as fol. 6b says here, the "supreme crown"; cf. above, n. 129.

209. The text is corrupt, and my translation is based upon a slight emendation. I have not found a rabbinic source for this interpretation. Abraham ibn Ezra's commentary on Numbers 16:4 conveys the same sense, though not in the same words.

210. The Hebrew word for emanated, נאצל , has the same root as the preposition "by" or "near," אצל .

211. The quotation is found in 3 Enoch, ed. Odeberg, chap. 5. There, however, the Shekhinah resides not above, but below the cherub.

212. Ms. Oxford, Neubauer 1568, fol. 5a. Cf. also the other quotations from the same text in nn. 79 and 129. The text is corrupt in two or three places, and the manuscript is generally rather poor.

213. The verb ואצלתי in Numbers 11:17 is, in fact, rendered in the Targum, by ואֵרבי . A Targum such as the one mentioned in the text is not known. Quotations from the Targum differing from the extant texts are very frequent in medieval literature.

> בת מריה, the daughter of his master, and she is named tenth sefirah and *malkhuth,* because the crown of royalty is upon her head.

The book that contains this curious quotation was composed in 1217, shortly after the death of Yehudah Hasid. It proves that the symbolism of the Shekhinah as daughter, as the *malkhuth* of God, and as the governance of the world and the tenth sefirah was already very well known in this milieu. The unity between her and her origin, from which she is not separated despite her mission to the lower world, is here emphasized much in the spirit of the *Bahir* section 90 [in the parable of the beautiful plot of land]. The biblical verses adduced here are different from those quoted in the *Bahir,* which, moreover, does not seem to know the conception of the Shekhinah as "God's angel," although it is entirely in the spirit of the German Hasidim. Since there is no evidence of Eleazar's acquaintance with the *Bahir,* we must attribute these correspondences, like others mentioned earlier, to at least partial knowledge of the same sources used in the *Bahir.* This is of considerable significance. The symbolism of the bride and the daughter of the king is here transposed from the ecclesia to the Shekhinah, much as in the oldest fragments of this symbolism in the *Bahir,* in which we caught an echo of gnostic language. The historical significance of this important step in the direction of kabbalistic symbolism consists precisely in the union between the national element of a mystically conceived ecclesia of Israel and a new religious conception of the Shekhinah. The mystical ecclesia is assigned a suprahistorical place in the internal evolution of the divine world, and in this new form it takes the place of the spiritual essences of the old gnostic symbols. She is the living bearer of the divine reflection in this world.

Where did this merging of two basic motifs into a new symbol take place? In the Orient or among one of the groups of German Hasidim? Our knowledge does not suffice for deciding this question. The distinct reversion to the language of gnosticism argues in favor of the first supposition; the second perhaps has in its favor the very vital significance that such a combination would have had in the context of the historical experience of a community as sorely oppressed as that of Western European Jewry in the period of the Crusades. The writings of the German Hasidim that are known to us emphasize the doctrine of the Shekhinah and the *kabhod* without suggesting any specifically historical factors. But when it was associated with the idea of the ecclesia of Israel, it received a new and very specific meaning. Each member of the mystical body of the community of Israel was also called upon to manifest in his own life the mystery of the Shekhinah as it expressed itself in the history of the community. This no doubt explains the special connection between most of the commandments and the particular interpretation of the mystery of the Shekhinah, already discussed at the end of section 8 (p. 178, herein). In fulfilling a commandment, man brings into view some of the hidden reflection that rests upon the entire world and upon each of its particulars as well as upon every action; in this manner he thus unites himself with the historical totality of the ecclesia of Israel and with the Shekhinah, which is its innermost part and its mystical reality. The sefiroth were thus conceived as the interior side of this Shekhinah, as powers that only manifest themselves outwardly in her and through her agency. But even if in this way we can shed some light on the relationship of the oldest kabbalists to the world of their symbols, the historical formation of these symbols themselves can only be adequately explained through their connection with the remnants of the gnostic doctrine of the aeons.

The quotation from Eleazar of Worms shows, moreover, that here the "daughter," whether gnostic or aggadic, can also be easily identified with the figure of Metatron, the angel or envoy whom God sends before Israel according to Exodus 23:20. This identification is frequently found in Hasidic writings as well as in old kabbalistic documents.[214] This is clearly a promotion of Metatron, who in the Merkabah gnosis also bears the name Yahoel. The angel himself becomes a figure of the *kabhod.* An analogous case is presented by the Manichees; according to Theodoret, the light virgin is named *Ioel,*[215] which is nothing other than the Hebrew Yahoel, though I would consider this as hardly more than a coincidence. The Book *Bahir* itself, as I have already stressed, has preserved no speculations concerning Metatron.

214. It is found for the first time in the traditions of Joseph ben Samuel of Catalonia, quoted in the old miscellanies of Ms. Christ Church College 198, fol. 7a. "He also says that according to their tradition, Metatron is the Shekhinah." I have given other references in *Tarbiz* 5 (1934):186–187.

215. Cf. F. Chr. Baur, *Das Manichäische Religionssystem,* 151. The doubts of E. Peterson, "Engel- und Dämonennamen," *Rheinisches Museum für Philologie* N.F., 75 (1926): 404–405, with regard to the identity of the names of Yoel and Yaoel are unfounded. Peterson was not acquainted with the esoteric Jewish tradition relating to Yahoël.

10. The Transmigration of Souls and the Mysticism of Prayer in the Bahir

If we wish to understand the possible relations between the *Bahir* and its sources as well as the tradition of the German Hasidim such as they must have taken shape already in the first half of the twelfth century, we must direct our attention to two further points that we have hitherto touched on only in passing: the doctrine of the transmigration of souls and the mysticism of prayer.

The problem of the transmigration of souls has already been mentioned in our analysis of section 86 and 104, and we have been able to establish that precisely the source of section 86, which is preserved in the *Raza Rabba,* contains nothing at all on this subject. It seems, therefore, to have entered the book from another source, at the time of its redaction. Perhaps the details contained in the *Bahir* may assist in reconstructing such a source. Remarkable in this respect is the fact that although the idea appears to be familiar to the *Bahir,* no term for it as yet exists. Still completely unknown to it, the expression *gilgul* became current only two or three generations after the *Bahir;* it corresponds exactly to the Latin *revolutio animarum* in Augustine's writings on the Manichees, from which, however, it seems completely independent.[216]

What matters here is the fact that this doctrine is taught as a mystery, accessible to initiates only, yet at the same time the author also takes it so much for granted that he does not consider it as requiring a special justification. The Cathars too taught it as a secret, which is not surprising since the Church had formally and dogmatically condemned this doctrine, and anyone adhering to it was automatically considered a heretic. The details of this doctrine as taught by the Cathars are very different.[217] Thus the *Bahir* does not know the idea of a migration into animal bodies or into any but human forms of existence. The doctrine of the transmigration of souls appeared as an answer to the question of theodicy:

---

216. As regards Augustine, cf. the references in Söderberg, *La Religion des Cathares,* 153. The Hebrew expression *gilgul* is one of the translations of the Arabic term *tanasuḥ,* and has the same significance of moving from place to place. I have discussed (in Hebrew) the history of this Hebrew term in *Tarbiz* 16 (1945):135–139.

217. On the Cathar doctrine of metempsychosis, cf. the works of Giraud, *Histoire de l'Inquisition* 1:59–60; Söderberg, *Religion des Cathares,* 152–154; Borst, *Die Katharer,* 168–171.

> Why do things go well for an evildoer and badly for a righteous man? Because the righteous man was already [once] in the past an evildoer and he is now being punished. But does one punish a person for [wrongs committed in] the days of his youth? . . . I do not speak of the [same] life; I speak of the fact that he was already there in the past. His companions said to him: How long will you still speak obscure words?

In response, R. Raḥmai expounds to them, Isaiah 5:2, the parable of the owner of the vineyard who repeatedly replanted and pruned because the grapes were not growing well.

> How often? He said: until the thousandth generations, for it is written [Ps. 105:8]: "The promise He gave for a thousand generations." And that is the meaning of the dictum [in *Ḥagigah* 13b]: 974 generations were wanting; then God arose and implanted them in every generation. (section 135)

The objections here show that the questioners were completely ignorant of the esoteric doctrine to which the apocryphal R. Raḥmai refers. His statements are incomprehensible to them. The notion is taught not in a coherent theoretical exposition but, as is also the case in other passages of the *Bahir* relating to this doctrine, in the form of parables. The parable makes express mention of only three unsuccessful attempts to improve the vineyard. It is not clear whether this is already an allusion to the later idea of a triple transmigration. The talmudic passage that is interpreted here in the sense of the transmigration of souls knows nothing of it either. According to the Aggadah, the Torah was given twenty-six generations after the creation of the world. But according to the rabbinic interpretation of Psalm 105, God gave His "word" (that is, the Torah) after 1,000 generations had passed. The contradiction is resolved by the talmudic Aggadah by saying that God had dispersed 974 generations of impious men among all the future generations where, in fact, they are the evildoers. In the *Bahir,* these evil ones are therefore the bad grapevines, which, however, are not denied the opportunity to submit to a new test and to emerge as righteous. Section 39 says the same thing when it speaks of all the souls flying "up to 1,000 generations" from the mystical region of the Sabbath. The idea that the generation that goes is, according to the number of existing souls, the same as that which returns (section 86), points in the same direction. Here, too, the justification, as we have seen, resulted from the revision of an aggadic parable in the Talmud. Only if Israel is worthy will it receive the new souls coming from the Sabbath or the east—from the seventh logos (section 104). The majority of the souls must wander until they are redeemed and can return from the world of mixture. The collection of the semen that is dispersed in the cosmos, the realm of mixture, is an old gnostic symbol that acquired great significance in the mystery rites of certain antinomian gnostic sects.[218] The same symbolism occurs in the *Bahir,* but without any antinomian overtones. The souls finally return home to the "house of the father," whence the king's son had taken them in order to bring them to his bride. This is reminiscent of the interpretation suggested by many earlier researchers for the gnostic "Hymn of the Soul," an interpretation that evinces a tendency similar to that with which kabbalists—whether they were historically correct or not—read the symbolism of their sources. In fact, the "house of the father" appears there in a similar context.

The further exposition of this theme in sections 126–127 is rather curious. Once again reinterpreting a talmudic dictum, this text explains that the Messiah can come only when all the souls "in the body of the man" are exhausted and have ended their migration. "Only then may the 'new [souls]' come out, and only then is the son of David allowed to be born. How is that? Because his soul comes forth new among the others." The soul of the Messiah is therefore not subject to migration. Here the kabbalistic doctrine evinces a characteristic note of its own. We are not dealing with a reminiscence from earlier doctrines of reincarnation such as are known to us in certain Judeo-Christian doctrines concerning the true prophet, as in the Pseudo-Clementines, which also exercised considerable influence upon corresponding idea among Shiite sects in Islam.[219] There the soul of Adam, the true prophet, traverses the aeon, this world, in many shapes until it finally finds repose in the appearance of the Messiah.[220] Later on, the kabbalists themselves developed this idea independently, in their assumed chain of reincarnations—Adam–David–Messiah; this doctrine, however, is not known before

---

218. Cf. L. Fendt, *Gnostische Mysterien* (Munich, 1922), 5–14. Fendt analyzed in detail the report of Epiphanius on the Phibionites.

219. Cf. Bousset, *Hauptprobleme der Gnosis,* 172–175, and above all H. J. Schoeps, *Theologie und Geschichte des Judenchristentums* (Tübingen, 1949), 98–116, 334–342.

220. Cf. above all the principal passages in the *Homilies,* 3, 20 and the *Recognitions* 2:22.

the end of the thirteenth century. Could this thesis of the *Bahir* have come into being in the Orient, perhaps even in conscious opposition to certain current ideas? Did it develop completely independent of them? It is difficult to answer these questions. The German Hasidim know nothing at all of the transmigration of souls and the ideas associated with it, as is shown by the detailed work of Eleazar of Worms on the soul, *Ḥokhmath ha-Nefesh.* According to the pessimistic view of the Cathars, all the souls in this world are nothing but fallen spirits. Here, too, there is a distinct contrast to the doctrine of the *Bahir,* which considers the descent of "new" souls, at any rate, as possible and determined by the good deeds of Israel.

The parable in section 127, long and almost garrulous but in itself very curious, does not render the question of the sources of this conception any easier. The totality of souls is compared to bread that the king sent to his soldiers, who through their negligence allowed it to go moldy. When this became known during the inspection, the angry king ordered that the bread be dried and restored, as far as possible, to its good condition. To these people, he swore, I will give no other bread until they have consumed this completely moldy bread.[221] Contrary to the conciseness that generally distinguishes the parables in the *Bahir,* this one is then very strangely distended and spun out, in the course of which the motif of the bread being the souls shifts unexpectedly to take on the sense of bread as the study of Torah. Here, too, there is new bread only when the old is eaten, that is, when the sinful souls are purified. The language of the parable is more appropriate to France or Germany than the Orient.[222]

As I emphasized above, the *Bahir* does not offer a justification of this doctrine, which is very curious since at the time the book was edited in Provence official Jewish theology completely rejected it.[223] Two explanations are possible: either the doctrine contained in the

---

221. One wonders whether there is not an intentional play on words here between *yikhlu,* "they will be exhausted [i.e. will have been terminated]" in the quotation from the Talmud in section 126 and *yo'khlu,* "they will consume" in section 127. The strange parable would then be based upon this pun.

222. The parable already employs the expression *ḥomer ha-guf* for "matter of the body," which suggests the twelfth century and would be impossible in ancient fragments. Section 127 may very well constitute a later development of the older text of section 126.

223. Cf. A. Schmiedl, *Studien über jüdische Religionsphilosophie* (Vienna, 1869), 157–166.

Bahir texts is older than the polemic that the Arabic-Jewish philosophers directed against it, or it was held in circles that were in no way touched by philosophic considerations of this kind and that paid no attention to them. Of course, such circles may also have existed in the Orient. We know that during the period of great religious ferment in the Orient, in the ninth and tenth centuries—when various forms of the doctrine of metempsychosis were propagated in Muslem circles, particularly among some Mutazilites and among Gnostics of an Ismailian tendency—this doctrine also had its adherents among Oriental Jews. Saadya polemicized at length against the Jewish adherents of these doctrines, which he rejected as fantastic.[224] An Arabic author tells us that there are Jews who support their belief in the transmigration of souls by citing the vision of the king Nebuchadnezzar in Daniel 3, which they related to the king's migration through different animal forms until he finally resumed human form again.[225] This exegesis is not found among the old kabbalists. The same is true for the reasons that Qirqisani, a tenth-century Karaite author, invokes in favor of the doctrine. We know from his *Book of Lights* that 'Anan, to whom the Karaite tradition traces the schism between the Rabbanites and Karaites in the eighth century, adopted the doctrine of metempsychosis and wrote a book on the subject. 'Anan came from Babylonia and must have been familiar with older currents and traditions, no longer accessible to us, of various Jewish sects. The Karaites themselves later separated from the adherents of 'Anan, who continued to maintain the doctrine of metempsychosis. Qirqisani knew the Arabic writings of this group, now lost—or at least the arguments these sectaries adduced from them orally—and he devoted two chapters of his work to their refutation.[226] His quotations show that these ancient sectaries based their view upon passages of the Bible completely different from those cited in the Book *Bahir* or among the old kabbalists. It is therefore difficult to admit a direct link between these Oriental Jewish groups of the eighth through tenth centuries and the oldest kabbalistic conventicles of southern France in the twelfth century. On

---

224. Saadya, *'Emunoth we-De'oth* 6:7.

225. Al-Baghdadi, *Moslem Schisms and Sects,* trans. A. Halkin (1935), pt. 2, 92.

226. These chapters were published in their entirety in the original Arabic version by S. Poznański, *Semitic Studies in Memory of Dr. Alexander Kohut* (Berlin, 1897), 435–453.

the other hand, it is possible that these ancient gnostic traditions, like others among the kabbalists, go back to different groups in the Orient, concerning whom we possess no written testimony. It is in the neighborhood of Mandaean and Manichaean communities in Mesopotamia, where gnostic materials were kept alive in such varied forms,[227] that we could most easily imagine the existence of such Jewish Gnostics; some fragments from their doctrines, mixed with other materials, may have made their way to Europe. Perhaps the symbolism of the date palm, occurring in some of these texts, points in the same direction. But we must not underestimate the difficulties raised by such an hypothesis. Whereas certain parts of these fragments may have been known to the German Hasidim, as we have frequently shown in this chapter, others may have remained unknown. Could such traditions have come directly from the Orient to Provence, evolving there in a manner parallel to that of Catharism? The difficulty with this lies in the completely untheoretical and unphilosophic form in which the idea of metempsychosis is presented in the *Bahir.* For the dualistic religion of the Cathars, which taught an essential difference in the nature and origin of the physical and the spiritual worlds, this idea did not present the same difficulties as it did for the philosophic theology and the psychology of monotheists. The hypothesis of a passage of the individual soul into another body must have appeared much more objectionable to the Aristotelian doctrine of the soul as the entelechy of the organism than for a dualist psychology such as that of the Platonists, where such a doctrine could more easily lodge itself. However, even a Jewish Neoplatonist like Abraham bar Ḥiyya had no patience for the doctrine of the transmigration of souls.[228] How, then, did it nevertheless enter Provence one or two generations after him? For now we must, I think, leave open the question of where the doctrine of metempsychosis such as it is presented in the *Bahir* originated historically, despite its proximity in time and place to the Catharist movement. On the whole I tend to accept the first hypothesis, to wit that we are dealing with fragments of an older Jewish-gnostic tradition that

227. The Manichaean teachings on the transmigration of souls, which adopted older gnostic doctrines, were specifically examined by A.W. Jackson in *JAOS* 45 (1925): 246–268.

228. He explicitly qualified this doctrine as "empty words and great absurdities"; cf. *Megillath ha-Megalleh,* 51 as well as his *Hegyon ha-Nefesh,* fol. 5b.

came from the Orient by paths no longer discernible to us and that reached the circles in which the Book *Bahir* originated.

On the other hand, the few passages in the *Bahir* relating to the mysticism of prayer suggest a more specific connection with the German Hasidim. According to their own tradition, these teachings came from the Orient. We saw previously, in analyzing the vestiges of the *Raza Rabba,* that developments in this direction could in fact already be observed in that book. But it is only among the Hasidim that the mysticism of prayer was fully developed. The words of the standard liturgical prayers are full of secret allusions and references to the names of angels and to the Godhead itself, which are meditated on (in ways not quite clear to us) by the person who prays, or which imply a magical effect of prayer. In the *Bahir,* prayer is already linked to the meditative concentration upon the sefiroth or powers of God. The mystical immersion in the Merkabah, in the new signification acquired here by the old concept, is like a prayer that evidently traverses the same spheres or directs itself toward them. It is in this spirit, probably, that in sections 46–49 the prayer of Habakkuk (beginning at 3:1) is interpreted as a mystical prayer. It traverses the mystical "places" and seeks to understand the unity of God in the diversity of his works, which are the effects of his action (the aeons?) (section 48). Corresponding to this in sections 77 and 83 is the "unification" of God's name in his powers, the symbols of which one finds in the prayer of the *Shema'* (Deut. 6:4). The prayer is considered here, in accordance with the old talmudic conception, as a substitute for the sacrificial service. Its meaning is the same: to proclaim the unity of the "powers" in God or to accomplish it through meditation.

It is in this sense, above all, that the raising of the hands in Aaron's blessing (Lev. 9:22) and during the battle against Amaleq (Exod. 17:11) is explained. The raising of the hands in the priestly blessing, at the end of the *'Amidah* prayer, corresponds to the raising of the hands after the sacrifice (section 87): it is a gesture marking the union of the sefiroth, which are specifically mentioned here as being contained in one another. The victory of Israel over Amaleq when Moses raised his hands is on the same level. Moses directed the "concentration of the heart," *kawwanath ha-leb,* to that *middah* that is named Israel and that contains the Torah of Truth. "He indicated with the ten fingers of his hands, that [this *middah*] gave permanence to the ten [logoi], so that if it [this *middah*] would not assist Israel, the ten logoi would no longer be sanctified every day—and then Israel was victorious." The expression *kawwanath ha-leb* is taken from the Targum and the Midrash[229] and means concentration of the spirit; from the Book *Bahir* on it was used by the kabbalists in the sense of "mystical meditation" on the sefiroth. It serves as the fundamental concept of their mysticism of prayer. The Midrash already states that Israel's prayer is not heard now, for it does not know the full, explicit name of God, *shem ha-meforash.*[230] If, therefore, someone knows this secret, his prayer will be heard. The same idea is very boldly developed in an interpretation of Habakkuk 3:10 in section 95:

> If there are in Israel enlightened men[231] and such as know the secret of the venerable name and raise their hands, they will be heard immediately, for it says [Isa. 58:9]: "Then, when you call, the Lord will answer." [This is to be understood as follows:] If you invoke [that which is indicated by the word] *'az,* God answers. And what does this *'az* [composed of *'alef* and *zayin*] signify? This teaches that it is not permitted to invoke the *'alef* alone or to pray to it, but only together with the two letters that are connected with it and that sit highest in the royal dominion.[232] And together with the *'alef,* they are three. Seven of the logoi [still] remain, and that is signified by [the letter] *zayin* [whose numerical value is seven] and of this it is also said [Exod. 15:1]: "Then sang," *'az yashir,* [that is, the *'az* praised] "Moses and the Israelites."

This reinterpretation of the Hebrew word *'az* utilizes an old nonmystical midrash in which this word in Exodus 15:1 is interpreted according to the numerical value of the two consonants א

229. Cf. Pseudo-Jonathan on Numbers 35:20; *Pesiqta Rabbahti,* ed. Friedmann, fol. 198b; *Midrash Tanḥuma, parashath Naso,* section 18, ed. Buber 4:34; *Bemidbar Rabba, parashah* 11, section 4. For the corresponding verb *kawwen libbo* during prayer, cf. *Midrash Tehillim* on Psalm 108, ed. Buber, 464.

230. *Midrash Tehillim,* the end of Psalm 91, 400.

231. *Maskilim* is a term utilized by Abraham ibn Ezra in the recension edited by Fleischer of his commentary on Exodus, chap. 24, for designating those who know the secret of the vocalization of the divine name. According to A. Parnes, *Kenesseth* 7 (Jerusalem, 1942): 286, *maskil* was employed in this sense in a poem of Solomon ibn Gabirol, cf. *Piyyutim,* ed. Bialik-Rawnitzki 2:56, line 8. This interpretation does not appear certain to me.

232. A phrase taken from Esther 1:14.

and ז , as if Moses had said: "Let us praise the *one* who thrones above the *seven* heavens."[233] The new idea is: if you invoke (in your *kawwanah*) the ten logoi that represent the secret of the true name of God, then God answers! It is understandable that this passage, which speaks so clearly of a prayer addressed to the logoi and sefiroth, would have been considered offensive. It evidently was one of the many heretical utterances that, according to Meir ben Simon of Narbonne, filled the *Bahir.* He specifically taxed the kabbalists with praying to the sefiroth as intermediaries instead of to God, thus making themselves guilty of polytheism. No wonder that many manuscripts and citations have omitted the words "or to pray"! The first sefirah, the *'alef,* cannot be invoked alone; it is too hidden, as section 48 interpreting Habakkuk 3:2 had already taught in connection with *'alef* as the hidden and withdrawn king. It has to be linked to the two following letters, though it is not clear whether *yod* and *he* are meant, which together with *'alef* form the divine name *'ehyeh,* or possibly the two letters *yod* and *shin,* which form, as we have seen in section 84 (in connection with Exodus 15:3), the mystical and symbolic word *'ish.* In both cases we are dealing with symbols of the second and the third sefiroth, which are therefore the only means of gaining access to the first: the prayer, in its entirety, embraces all ten sefiroth, which man, in the act of prayer, draws into his meditation.

Nothing of such a meditation or *kawwanah* on the sefiroth is found in the literature of the German Hasidim known to date. But the transition is easy to conceive. If the ten sefiroth of the Book *Yeṣirah* were considered as divine *middoth,* then the *kawwanah* directed toward God in prayer could similarly be transferred to them. Whether this occurred first in Germany or in southern France cannot be determined; either is possible.[234]

We may now summarize the results of our analysis of the old-

---

233. Thus in the Oxford manuscript of the *Midrash Tanḥuma,* ed. Buber 2:60, n. 52.

234. Attention should, however, be drawn to the fact that *kawwanoth* of the prayer texts combined with figures from the pantheon do occur in esoteric Mandaean texts, although they are not easily datable; E. S. Drower, *A Pair of Nasoraean Commentaries* (Leiden, 1963), 33, contains some characteristic parallels where, of course, instead of sefiroth we have the "names" of the figures peopling the Mandaean pantheon.

est kabbalistic text, having examined at least its principal ideas. The hypothesis that the oldest kabbalistic ideas were born in Provence and that the Book *Bahir* was composed there cannot be maintained. Materials coming from a number of much older Jewish sources arrived in this region, presumably by different paths, toward the middle of the twelfth century; they were edited sometime between 1160 and 1180 in a circle that had absorbed these materials, traditions, and concepts in creative ways and had developed them further. The intimate acquaintance of this circle with aggadic literature and with the corpus of the Merkabah writings shows that we are not dealing here with an illiterate group of men devoid of culture; this is all the more striking when contrasted to the careless language and the poor quality of their editorial work. Numerous traditional elements in the literature of the German Hasidim offer us direct proof or permit us to draw highly probable inferences with respect to the older sources of the *Bahir.* Others may have come directly from the Orient to Provence. The affinity with the language, terminology, and symbolism of Gnosticism suggests an Oriental origin for the most important among the ancient texts and sources of the *Bahir,* many of which had at least passed through certain circles of the German Hasidim. Apart from the traceable, that is to say identifiable, sources of the *Bahir* such as the *Raza Rabba* there also must have been other Hebrew or Aramaic fragments of a Jewish-gnostic character among its sources. A relationship between the speculations of the *Book of Creation* on the ten sefiroth and certain elements of the Merkabah gnosis and other Jewish-gnostic currents had already developed in the Orient and subsequently stimulated the elaboration of the oldest kabbalistic doctrines and symbolism in the Provençal circle that acquired knowledge of these materials.

Many details still remain hypothetical, and it is not impossible that further discoveries and analyses, particularly relating to the traditions of the German Hasidim, may provide new insights. However, the essentially gnostic character of this most ancient form of the Kabbalah can no longer be doubted. The question of a possible link between the crystallization of the Kabbalah, as we find it in the redaction of the *Bahir,* and the Cathar movement must also remain unresolved, at least for the present. This connection is not demonstrable, but the possibility cannot be excluded. In the history of ideas the *Bahir* represents a reversion, perhaps conscious but in any case perfectly corroborated by the facts, to an archaic symbolism that is utterly unique in medieval Judaism. With the publication of the Book *Bahir,* a Jewish form of mythical thought entered into unavoidable competition with the rabbinic and philosophic forms of this same medieval Judaism. It is to this process that we shall now turn our attention.

CHAPTER THREE

THE FIRST KABBALISTS IN PROVENCE

1. Abraham ben Isaac of Narbonne

We have hitherto been concerned with the analysis of the oldest literary document of the Kabbalah, which made its appearance in Provence. We must now turn to the other side of the problem and ask: What do we know about the first personalities whom the kabbalists regarded as their earliest masters? Here, too, the paths of research are intricate and at times even thorny. Complete writings and other documents that could take us with certainty to the period before 1200 have not been preserved. On the other hand, we are no longer facing the vacuum that prevailed until now in kabbalistic research with respect to the family of Rabbi Abraham ben David (designated henceforth with the acronym Rabad, in accordance with the traditional usage in Hebrew literature), his colleagues, and his disciples. Scattered fragments whose authenticity cannot reasonably be doubted have been preserved here and there. Thanks to these texts we are able to see more clearly into the world of mystics who did not come, as had the redactors of the *Bahir,* from anonymous and perhaps somewhat suspect circles of Jewish society; rather, they belonged "to the nobles of the land and the propagators of the study of the Torah in the community," according to the proud words of Isaac the Blind in an important letter that has been preserved.[1]

The first link in this chain of the Provençal Kabbalah was Abraham ben Isaac of Narbonne, who is known in Hebrew literature as "R. Abraham, President of the Rabbinic Court" and who was one of the most eminent talmudists of his time. His connection with the Kabbalah is not based solely on later legends, as many scholars have supposed, but also upon the explicit testimony of his grandson, Isaac the Blind. He reported that "his fathers" (in the plural, and thus not only his father, Abraham ben David) were among the masters of esoteric knowledge. But he stressed above all that "no word on this subject ever escaped their lips and that they conducted themselves with them [with those not initiated into the secret doctrine] as with men who were not versed in the [mystical] science, and I saw [this conduct] of theirs, and I learned a lesson from it." It goes without saying that according to this authentic testimony, we cannot expect to find any kabbalistic discourses in the *Sefer ha-'Eshkol,* the great halakhic work of Abraham ben Isaac, intended for talmudic scholars. The question remains: what is the source of the mystical influence that brought this eminent scholar to esotericism? What inclinations or research served as a backdrop for his receiving the "revelation of the prophet Elijah" that, as we have seen, the oldest kabbalistic tradition attributes to him?

Here we touch upon a paradoxical but essential state of affairs that throws some light upon the different sources from which the oldest kabbalists were able to draw. As has been shown, Abraham ben Isaac was himself a pupil of Yehudah ben Barzilai in Barcelona,[2] the author of the detailed commentary on the *Book of Creation* that has already been mentioned here several times. We may therefore assume that he was acquainted with this commentary, even though he never mentions it explicitly. It is, of course, quite possible that it was this work that inspired him to occupy himself further with the Book *Yeṣirah* and the Merkabah gnosis. In his *'Eshkol* he makes an obscure allusion to a mystical commentary on the aggadah according to which God showed Moses the knot of the tefillin: "He

1. I published and commented upon this letter (which I shall discuss in greater detail below, p. 393ff.) in *Sefer Bialik* (Tel Aviv, 1934). For the passage quoted above as well as the rest of the citation, cf. ibid., 143.

2. Cf. S. Assaf, *Sifran shel Rishonim* (Jerusalem, 1935), 2–3.

showed him something that resembled the forms of the [divine] majesty and splendor, in order to announce to him that this commandment was particularly dear to Him."[3] The text does not indicate the nature of the forms contained in the celestial light that Moses contemplated. In his teacher's commentary on the *Yeṣirah* we find the same expression of "forms of the majesty," which is the Shekhinah, and Moses' or the prophets' perception of it.[4] Here it is clear that Abraham ben Isaac followed in his teacher's footsteps—keeping to a tradition inaugurated by Saadya Gaon—concerning his conception of the Shekhinah and the doctrine of the kabhod. Historically, we thus have a uniform and unbroken chain of tradition from teacher to pupil, from the scholar in Barcelona, whose work does not yet betray the slightest hint of basic kabbalistic doctrines, to Isaac the Blind, who lived one hundred years later. Nevertheless, during this period the doctrine of the Book *Yeṣirah* on the sefiroth and that of Saadya on the Shekhinah were completely transformed, if not changed into their opposites. There is a profound difference between the created light of the Glory and the Shekhinah in Saadya and in Yehudah ben Barzilai, who never tires of emphasizing the created nature of this Glory and the notion of the Shekhinah in the *Bahir* as it later prevailed in the Kabbalah. We are presented here with two entirely distinct religious conceptions and ways of thinking. It is by no means an accident that the detailed work of Yehudah ben Barzilai lacks all those gnostic symbols of the Shekhinah that we analyzed in the previous chapter. Where, then, does the decisive turn in the direction of a gnostic conception take place? Would it not lie on the route that leads from the great scholar in Barcelona to the "president of the rabbinic court" in Narbonne? Is it not here that we should look for the eruption of the gnosis that we find, in fact, in full bloom only one generation after him? Could this great change have been the outcome of an encounter between the pupil of Yehudah ben Barzilai and another tradition that entered into conflict with his own and subsequently prevailed, that is, the tradition

3. *Sefer 'Eshkol* 1:33, ed. Albeck.

4. Ibid., 223. Yehudah ben Barzilai frequently uses the expressions "majesty and splendor" as fixed terms for the light of the *kabhod.* Thus he speaks of the forms appearing in this supreme light to the visionaries; cf. his commentary on *Yeṣirah,* 22, 32, 35 ("forms of the majesty," *ṣuroth ha-hod*), as well as his commentary on the talmudic aggadah of the knot of the tefillin, p. 33.

that found its expression in the Book *Bahir*? Concerning the interest manifested by the circle of Abraham ben Isaac in Narbonne in the *Book of Creation* as a fundamental document of the esoteric doctrine, we happen to possess a very reliable testimony. As late as the first half of the thirteenth century Moses Taku (from Tachau in Bohemia?) saw a commentary on the *Yeṣirah* composed by the "scholars of Narbonne," as we have already noted on page 34, n. 57. However, nothing regarding the general character of this book can be deduced from Taku's single, brief quotation. On the other hand, there is no reason to suppose that in a book known to the public as a collective work, the authors would have expounded explicitly kabbalistic ideas. We cannot expect, on the part of this circle, any such public disclosures.

In any case, the writings of Abraham of Narbonne that have become known to us conceal more than they reveal. Statements which might perhaps have gone further in the communication of his mystical views have not been preserved. This involves, to be sure, a problem of literary criticism. Shemtob ibn Gaon, a kabbalist from the beginning of the fourteenth century and a disciple of Solomon ibn Adreth, tells in one passage of the beginnings of kabbalistic literature in France. What he relates in this connection is reliable and in large measure subject to verification. But he also states that concerning kabbalistic matters R. Abraham, the "president of the rabbinic court" (unlike Abraham ben David) committed to writing only key words, *rashe peraqim.* He himself had seen these notes. "They make known a series of excellent words, in order to stimulate every kabbalist so that his attention will be aroused in every passage in the Bible or in the Talmud where he finds such a word."[5] It goes without saying that a notebook of this kind containing key words and nothing more, if it really came from the pen of this author, would be for the uninitiated a book with seven seals. The recording of such key words, precisely because the meaning remained unexplained, would not, in fact, have constituted a profanation of the esoteric tradition through public communication. Elsewhere Shemtob ibn Gaon has a literal quotation from these notes, which clearly shows that it could only have served as a kind of mnemotechnic aid

5. Cf. the Hebrew text of the passage in *Sefer Bialik,* 143, from Ms. Oxford, Neubauer 1630 of the book *Badde ha-'Aron* of Shemṭob ibn Gaon.

for those already familiar with the principal doctrines. Our judgment with regard to the authenticity of this document, which unfortunately does not appear to have survived, depends upon the extent to which we are prepared to ascribe to this mid-twelfth-century scholar familiarity with the developed symbolism of the sefiroth, whose presence in the single remaining quotation from this text strikes the reader's eye despite its enigmatic language.[6]

As we have seen, it was around this time that the Book *Bahir,* or the sources from which it was edited, reached Provence, where it underwent its final redaction. Among the few key words occurring in the quotation, we already find symbols that do not appear at all in the *Bahir* but that do, however, appear later in the writings of Abraham ben Isaac's grandson. Moreover, the text contains an allusion to which the Kabbalah of the first generations does not provide any key. If we can actually suppose that Abraham ben Isaac had already found himself stimulated to develop further the symbolism of the divine *middoth* along the lines of the *Bahir* tradition, nothing would prevent us from accepting the testimony of Shemtob ibn Gaon. But it is equally possible that this list was composed toward the end of the twelfth century by a pupil of the president of the rabbinic court in Provence. A definitive judgment with regard to the authenticity of this text is no longer possible today.

Elsewhere an esoteric fragment of Abraham ben Isaac on the subject of redemption has been preserved by a thirteenth-century

6. The original passage, which is based upon literary allusions and puns, by no means rare in texts of this kind, is untranslatable. R. Abraham evidently attached his mystical allusion to a comment on the variously interpreted word *teshi* in Deuteronomy 32:18. If the quotation is authentic, it would prove that the word *'ayin,* which can mean in Hebrew "where" as well as "nothing," was already known in Narbonne around 1160 as a mystical symbol of the supreme sefirah. The Hebrew quotation combines a mystical interpretation of Job 28:12 on the subject of the origin of the divine Sophia with another, from the talmudic aggadah, on Ben Zoma, in *Y. Ḥagigah* 2:1. The Book *Bahir* still does not know this mystical terminology, which no doubt comes from a different tradition. Besides, another observation of Shemtob ibn Gaon in his *Migdal 'Oz* on Maimonides, *Hilkhoth Teshubah* 6, probably goes back to the same source. "I know," it is said there, "that our master Rabad, may his memory be blessed, was a recipient of this esoteric science [*mequbbal be-nistaroth*], which is indicated in the *gam* and *'eth* [of the Torah], and it is from his waters that we drink." As regards the reference to Ben Zoma in the aforementioned Hebrew quotation, cf. also the full discussion of Saul Liebermann in *Tosefta ki-fshutah* 5:1292–1294 (on *Ḥagigah* 2), who is inclined to interpret the word *'ayin* in the sense of the gnostic terminology ("nothingness" in the mystical sense).

author. If it is authentic—and I see no reason to think it is not—R. Abraham already appears here as a link in a chain of mystical familial traditions. "This is what I received from my fathers: when *ṣedeq* [which in Hebrew can mean justice as well as the planet Jupiter] reaches half of the throne of Glory, redemption immediately comes to Israel, etc."[7] The image of *ṣedeq* at half the height of the throne is very strange. If *ṣedeq* here signifies the planet Jupiter, it is difficult to understand to which astrological constellation the author wished to allude in employing the term "throne of Glory," which, as far as I can see, has no place in such a framework.[8] Or should we suppose that "righteousness" as well as "throne of Glory" are here already mystical symbols, as they are, in fact, in the Book *Bahir?* In that case these two symbols would allude to the conjunction of two aeons entering into relation with one another. This would accord quite well with the symbolism of redemption in the *Bahir,* where (in section

---

7. The piece was published by Alexander Marx in *Ha-Ṣofeh me-'Ereṣ Hagar* 5:198. The continuation proves the author's acquaintance with the apocalypse of the *Sefer Zerubabel,* which dates from the early Middle Ages. Abraham ben Isaac was familiar with *Yeṣirah* and other Merkabah writings and therefore drew on the esoteric literature of prekabbalistic times; this emerges with certainty from the commentary on the tractate *Baba Bathra* that must be attributed to him (and not to his son-in-law), as Raphael Rabbinovicz has already shown, *Diqduqe Sofrim,* vol. 11 (1881), 9–10 of the preface (against H. Gross, *MGWJ* [1873]: 456). Gross considered the citation of *Hilkhoth Yeṣirah* on the twelve pairs of oppositions in the world to be a copyist's addition borrowed from a later commentary on *Yeṣirah* 1:2 by a pseudo-Rabad. In fact, however, the passage from the Book *Yeṣirah* itself is preserved in the authentic Arabic commentary on *Yeṣirah* by Saadya (chapter 8, according to his subdivision). Gross's suspicions are equally unfounded as regards the passage in which Abraham ben Isaac cites the various magical means of protection (*qibhla* has nothing to do with Kabbalah), taken from the *Books of the Merkabah.* These magical recipes provide means of finding favor with the authorities, overcoming enemies, winning wars, etc., through the evocation of the names of the mothers of biblical personages mentioned in the talmudic passage, *Baba Bathra* 91a, on which he comments. These traditions have been accurately preserved, in the name of Abraham ben Isaac, in very old collections of Jewish magic going back to the thirteenth century—as for example in Ms. Casanatense 179, fol. 119a. Many manuscripts also attribute to *Abraham 'ab beth-din* the well-known amulet of the seven seals, which H. A. Winkler dealt with in *Siegel und Charaktere in der Muhammedanischen Zauberei* (Berlin, 1930), 55–149; cf. the manuscript preserved in the Schocken Institute, Kabb. 101, fol. 3a.

8. There might possibly be a relationship between a mystical symbolism of this kind and ideas of the sort found in the Hasidic commentary on *Shi'ur Qomah,* to which we frequently referred in the preceding chapter. There it is said of the Shekhinah just as paradoxically that it has "a sphere [*galgal*] of its own and that there exist some other stars that have their abode near it; but it is itself still the essential principle." Cf. the Hebrew text in my *Reshith ha-Qabbala,* 238.

50) precisely these two notions are employed in the same sequence. We might still ask, however, what is the meaning of the singular expression "up to half of the throne of glory"? The question is not easy to resolve. In any event, this quotation, preserved by sheer accident, should arouse our interest. It implies that Abraham ben Isaac already based himself on traditions concerning mystical symbolism that he had received from his ancestors, in which case an even greater antiquity can be attributed to the kabbalistic traditions of Narbonne. Even though prudence denies us complete certainty as to what specific mystical traditions this scholar already possessed and propounded in the circle of his colleagues, it nevertheless seems beyond doubt that he was already in possession of at least some elements of the kabbalist tradition.

Perhaps at that stage things were still very different from the ideas we find developed later in the Kabbalah of Isaac the Blind. In this case, there is no reason to give less credence to statements concerning family tradition than is granted to similar statements on the subject of an esoteric tradition in the Kalonymos family in Germany, where no one seriously maintains that they were concocted by Yehudah Hasid or his father. In both cases there appear at the end of a chain of familial traditions great personalities who undoubtedly added to those traditions, gave things a new form, and combined ideas in a more or less organized manner.

2. Abraham ben David (Rabad)

A serious problem is posed regarding the multi-faceted mystical ideas current in this circle. This becomes particularly clear when we consider the information we possess concerning R. Jacob the "Nazirite" and R. Abraham ben David, the son-in-law of the president of the court of Narbonne. As we noted in the first chapter, the kabbalist tradition attributes to them a revelation of the prophet Elijah, which means that new sources of vision or contemplation inspired them to develop kabbalistic ideas that had not come to them by the usual channels of transmission. What exactly was this new element —particularly in relation to the tradition of the *Bahir,* which was undoubtedly known in their circles? We must attempt to clarify this point, basing ourselves on what little remains of their own words.

Rabad composed commentaries on many tractates of the Talmud. And Shemtob ibn Gaon, who had read them, attested that he "made allusion to something [kabbalistic], wherever he deemed it necessary, but no more," and "it was sufficient for him to rely [for the treatment of kabbalistic themes] on his learned son [Isaac the Blind], who is renowned in this science, which he received from his father."[9] Apart from these commentaries, Rabad is above all known for his objections and critical glosses on the great halakhic code of Maimonides. There too in certain passages connected with halakhic controversies, we find mystical expressions of an altogether unusual form. There is no great difference between his own words and the tradition reported by the disciples of his disciples, according to which the prophet Elijah appeared to him (this being no more than a metaphor for an illumination he received from above). Rabad wrote: "The Holy Spirit has already appeared in our school," and "it was revealed to me from the mysteries of God, which he communicates to those who fear Him," as well as other, similar phrases. These are talmudic expressions for direct inspiration and illumination.[10]

Rabad appears before us as a markedly independent personality, and even his halakhic utterances lay claim to higher inspiration. In this regard it is appropriate to note the proud assertion of his own self-worth in the preface to his commentary on the tractate *'Eduyoth,* written in a style not at all customary elsewhere in rabbinic literature. Here too we catch a glimpse of the soul of the mystic.

> Above all, I must inform every reader of this book, which I begin here, that regarding the matters treated here, I have no tradition from the lips of a teacher or master; but [I treat these things] with the help of God alone, who imparts knowledge to men. And if there is any error here in the handwriting or any error in the meaning, the

---

9. Cf. the original text in *Sefer Bialik,* 153.

10. Still, expressions of the kind mentioned here do not necessarily indicate a mystical inspiration. They also occur in the Talmud in purely halakhic contexts in order to designate the source of statements that do not emanate from oral tradition but that nevertheless claim authority. The "appearance of the holy spirit in the academy" is found in the Babylonian Talmud, *Makkoth* 23b. The other expression, which is based on Psalm 25:14, appears frequently in the Talmud. The evaluation of the significance of such expressions in the case of the Rabad is a matter of subjective judgment.

reader should know that the fault lies with me and not with my teachers. But he should also know that whatever there is here of the good and the true comes from the mystery, as the psalmist says [Ps. 25:14]: The secret of the Lord is for those who fear Him.

The Hebrew word *sod* can just as well mean the counsel of God as, in later usage, the secret of God; the manner in which the author stresses this formula indicates the latter nuance. In my opinion it is wrong to believe, as do many modern commentators, that with such turns of phrase, extremely uncommon in halakhic discussions, "he only wished to express the idea that he had hit upon the truth."[11] From here it is only a step away from the entirely mistaken notion that even the clearest and most important utterances can be dismissed as falsifications or later additions if they contradict preconceived opinions.

In fact, a great deal can be learned from the surviving statements of the Provençal scholars named here, many of which stand the test of literary criticism. In this connection it is particularly noteworthy that statements of a mystical tendency in the writings of these scholars either are rendered in an allusive style or else seek to veil their underlying mystery by means of exoteric forms of expression. Hence only the traditions preserved among the earliest Spanish kabbalists can reveal to us the esoteric, truly kabbalistic aspects of the statements made by the aforementioned Provençal teachers. We have no reason to question the authenticity of these kabbalistic traditions in which we find, in part, exactly the same figures of speech and the same extraordinarily peculiar expressions, whose precise meaning in those exoteric sentences is obscure. It should be added here that Jacob the Nazirite, too, is no longer a blank page in the history of literature. In fact, we know exactly with whom we are dealing. This mystic is none other than Jacob ben Saul of Lunel, the older brother of Asher ben Saul, who refers to him explicitly several

---

11. This, for example, is the opinion of Heinrich Gross, *MGWJ* 23 (1874): 169. What Gross says in his study "Die Mystik des Rabed" (ibid., 164–182) seems to me completely erroneous. The author tries to dispute the most manifest facts and to interpret away even the most patently mystical elements in the works of Rabad, by means of appropriate "explanations." His study is a model of misplaced hypercriticism. N. Weinstein demonstrated a deeper comprehension of these elements in his book *Zur Genesis der Aggada,* vol. 2 (1901), 261ff., notwithstanding the fantastic considerations that, in other respects, abound in this work.

times in his *Sefer ha-Minhagoth,* "Book of Customs."[12] This work emanates from the closest circle of the Rabad's pupils and already contains, in a number of passages, kabbalistic interpretations that use the doctrine of the sefiroth and the specific terminology of the kabbalists.[13] In the extant writings of Jacob the Nazirite, as for example his completion of Rashi's commentary on the book of Job, composed in 1163 or 1183,[14] there is nothing mystical. On the other hand, the remnants of his commentary on the prayers reveal the double aspect of esoteric and exoteric, and a closer examination shows that beneath the apparently simple meaning there lies a mystical one.

According to a tradition of the German Hasidim, Jacob the Nazirite interpreted the passage in the *qedushah* of the Sabbath morning prayer "knowledge and understanding (*da'ath* and *tebunah*) surround Him" as referring to two angels, *Da'ath* and *Tebunah,* who surround the Throne of Glory.[15] This interpretation calls to mind the quotation from the *Sefer ha-Ḥayyim,* mentioned at the end of the previous chapter, where among other things *da'ath* and *tebunah* were said to be mystical places situated beneath the Throne of Glory, from which emerged the angels of the same name.[16] But we have other statements by Jacob the Nazirite in which he goes fur-

---

12. This identity of Jacob the Nazirite was established for the first time by S. Schechter in *JQR* 5 (1983): 22–23; cf. my remarks in *Tarbiz* 6:4:96, as well as S. Assaf in the edition of the *Sefer ha-Minhagoth* in his collection *Sifran shel Rishonim,* 124. E. Urbach, in his notes to Abraham ben Azriel's *'Arugat ha-bosem* vol. 3 (1963), 462, 473, refers to commentaries on the prayer book by Jacob and also draws attention to direct personal contact between Jacob and Abraham ben Nathan (אב"ן), the author of the *Manhig,* who actually quotes Jacob in a passage preserved in *Maḥzor Vitry,* 368.

13. Cf. in Assaf's edition, p. 133, the passage relating to *Shema' Yisrael,* as well as p. 144 on the *Qedushah*—passages whose kabbalistic intent and terminology are unmistakable.

14. The date of composition varies in the manuscripts; cf. Neubauer's note in his catalogue of the Oxford Hebrew manuscripts, on no. 295.

15. Ms. Vatican, Heb. 274, fol. 205b, in mystical commentaries on the prayer book emanating from the circle of the German Hasidim. It is said that Jacob the Nazirite based this explanation on the fact that contrary to the feminine gender of *da'ath* and *tebunah,* the verb "surround him" is in the masculine gender, which must refer to the proper names of the angels so called. A more far-reaching commentary on this passage in the spirit of the kabbalistic doctrine of the sefiroth emanating from the tradition of the Provençal kabbalists can already be found in the commentary on the prayers by Yehudah ben Yaqar, one of the teachers of Naḥmanides; cf. Schechter, *JQR* 4:249.

16. Cf. chap. 2, pp. 181–2, herein.

ther. In several manuscripts traditions have been preserved concerning certain points of liturgical mysticism, regarding which Jacob the Nazirite and Rabbi Abraham, the Rabad, differed. These divergences concerned details of the mystical *kawwanah* in certain prayers, e.g., toward which sefirah or *middah* should the mystical intentions at prayer (*kawwanah*) be directed and to which sefirah the soul should relate itself during a particular prayer? It seems to me that there is no reason to doubt the genuineness of these statements transmitted in the name of Jacob the Nazirite. On the contrary, their authenticity follows from the simple fact that some of the kabbalistic symbols and terminology employed fell into desuetude after the time of the Rabad. Moreover, details relating to a number of points, some of which are quite important, contradict the kabbalistic doctrine of the mystical *kawwanah* in prayer as transmitted from the beginning of the thirteenth century. I shall return to these differences in the following pages. However, we see here that the *binah* or *tebunah,* which in the aforementioned quotation was merely an angel, appears in these traditions in all its splendor as a divine hypostasis, as one of the sefiroth with whose light the man who prays, ascending in his meditation, seeks to unite himself. I do not believe that in this instance Jacob the Nazirite still confused the world of angels with that of the sefiroth. Rather, we seem to have before us an excellent example of the use of an ambiguous terminology, one of its meanings intended for the true initiates and the other for outsiders. In many of these valuable traditions on the secret meaning of the prayers we hear clear echoes of the mystical terminology of the *Bahir.*[17]

Another circumstance lends particular importance to these traditions concerning the mysticism of prayer. The notion of the demiurge, *yoṣer bereshith,* often recurs here in the pregnant mystical sense it already had in the fragments of the *Shi'ur Qomah,* where it designated not merely the nature of the deity, but precisely its manifestation as a demiurge and creator God. On this point Rabad and Jacob the Nazirite differ. The one affirms that in the prayer of the

17. These traditions are preserved, for example, in the Mss. New York, Jewish Theological Seminary 838 (from the fourteenth century), fol.48a, and British Museum, Margoliouth 755, fol. 85b. They also are found in a third manuscript, Oxford 1646, where, however, the sequence of transmitters is given in a different order. I published the complete Hebrew text in *Reshith ha-Qabbala,* 73–74.

shemoneh 'esreh (that is, the *'Amidah,* the prayer of the eighteen benedictons) the *kawwanah* is divided between two of the ten sefiroth, namely between *binah* and *tif'ereth,* the third and the sixth sefiroth respectively. The other declares, on the contrary, that "the first three and last three benedictions are directed toward the Cause of Causes, but those in the middle are directed towards the *yoṣer bereshith.*" This pair of concepts, *causa causarum* and demiurge, is no longer familiar to the later Spanish kabbalists; that is precisely why it is so important for our present discussion. Here, at the beginning of the Provençal Kabbalah, we find the distinction between the First Cause, which is completely hidden, and the gnostic creator god, who in this Jewish conception naturally designates not a lower and inferior entity in the hierarchy of being, as among the Gnostics, but the manifestation of the hidden God, the First Cause itself. One could even find a Philonic element in this terminology of the demiurge, as it is not a little reminiscent of the logos of Philo. Whether this kabbalistic demiurge is to be identified with a specific sefirah is not certain. Still, in the commentary on the *Book of Creation* by Isaac the Blind the notion of *yoṣer,* creator, is explained as applying to the sixth sefirah, *tif'ereth,* which is also called the Throne.[18] Quite probably the same idea is also present here. What is certain, however, is that the term *yoṣer bereshith* does not refer, as it sometimes does among the Spanish kabbalists (for example, in the *Kether Shem Tob* of Abraham Axelrad), to the sefirah *binah,* for it is expressly said: "The *yoṣer bereshith* is named 'the great God,' and the sefirah *binah* is like a soul for him, but he himself is like a body for that soul. And he is also called 'throne of the Glory,' since he is a throne for the *binah.*"

Three things attract our attention in connection with these conceptions, so paradoxical in their appearance. First of all we have a continuation of the old idea, albeit raised to a new level, of the *Shi-'ur Qomah* and the Merkabah-mysticism, which speak of a "body of the Shekhinah" and of a "Creator of the Beginning," *yoṣer bereshith,* who sits upon the Throne and in this manifestation has, as it were, number and mass. In the kabbalistic fragment, this demiurge is a more external manifestation of an inner soul that dwells within him and which is itself in no way identical with the First Cause but

18. Cf. his manuscript commentary on *Yeṣirah* 1:4.

represents (as in the Book *Bahir*) the third sefirah, *binah.* In section 32 of the *Bahir* we read that *binah* in fact constitutes a kind of mystical soul, or is in any case associated with this concept. Perhaps Jacob the Nazirite came closer to the original intention of this difficult passage in the *Bahir* than the kabbalists of the following generation, who saw in it above all an indication of the view that the souls of men have their origin in the sefirah *binah.*

Second, we have an exact parallel to the doctrine of the "particular cherub" who sits upon the Throne, a doctrine widely held among the German and French Hasidim of the twelfth century. Apart from the notion, simultaneously old and new, of the *yoṣer bereshith,* which was at first identified with the form of the cherub—an identification attested among ancient Jewish sects in the Orient[19] —the revival of the gnostic tradition only adds the new idea that this cherub has an interior aspect, a "soul": It is precisely this soul that constitutes the realm of the sefiroth.

Third, the mystical intent behind the apology for anthropomorphism in the Rabad and the kabbalists reveals itself here. For although they, too, undoubtedly maintained the absolute spirituality of the First Cause, the aforementioned apologetic is unmistakable. This aspect of the matter is of special interest to the historian. On this point the mystics appear, precisely by virtue of their gnostic convictions, as the advocates of popular religion and of the faith of the common man. When Maimonides says that whoever believes the Creator has a body is a heretic, and Rabad, in a celebrated gloss objects that "many, and his betters" have believed just that,[20] it seems clear to me that behind this criticism stands the doctrine of the Jewish mystics in France concerning the cherub who is the demiurge.

---

19. The cherub as angel of creation and demiurge was taught, for example, by Benjamin Nahawandi (around 840), who no doubt made use of an older sectarian tradition; cf. L. Nemoy in *HUCA* 7 (1930): 386, and above all Harry A. Wolfson, "The preexistent angel of the Magharians and al-Nahawandi," *JQR* 51 (1960): 89–106. The term employed by the German Hasidim, "the particular [or excellent] cherub" also comes, evidently, from these Oriental sources; cf. the passage of Nahawandi cited by Wolfson, p. 91. The question whether creation took place through the medium of angels already preoccupied the oldest Jewish heretics during the period of the Second Temple; cf. G. Quispel, "Christliche Gnosis und jüdische Heterodoxie," *Evangelische Theologie* (1954): 4 of the offprint I have before me.

20. Cf. his remark in connection with Maimonides' *Hilkhoth Teshubah* 3:7.

The accuracy of this interpretation, and at the same time the authenticity of those traditions transmitted in the names of Jacob the Nazirite and the Rabad, to which I have referred, emerges with certainty from a surviving fragment of Rabad's commentary on the Talmud. It deals with the passage in *Berakhoth* 6a: "Whence do we know that the Holy One, blessed be He, puts on tefillin?" His grandson, Asher ben David, quotes in this connection:

> the exact wording [of the explanation] of my grandfather, the great Rabbi Abraham bar David: This refers to the Prince of the [divine] countenance [that is, to Metatron], whose name is like the name of his Master. But perhaps there is one above him who emanated from the highest cause, and in whom there is the power of the Supreme. And it is He who appeared to Moses and who appeared to Ezekiel in the vision of the man above [Ezek. 1:26] and to the other prophets. But the Cause of causes did not appear to any man and no left or right, front or back [can be predicated of it]. And this is the secret, of which it is said in the cosmogony, *ma'aseh bereshith,* "whoever knows the measure of the Creator of the beginning, *yoṣer bereshith,* can be assured, etc. [can be assured of his share in life eternal].[21] And it is of him that the verse [Gen. 1:26] 'Let us make man in our image' speaks."

Graetz, who questioned the authenticity of this quotation (about which, however, no reasonable doubt can be entertained[22]) discerned here quite rightly the doctrine of the logos. But since he had no knowledge of the analogous dicta emanating from this same circle, he erroneously supposed that these thoughts formed the initial point of departure of the Kabbalah. Graetz saw this point of departure in the need "to give to the anthropomorphistic aggadoth, wherever possible, an interpretation that is literal, and yet plausible."[23] He also interpreted it as an "uncertain groping" with regard

21. The sentence is not found in the *Baraitha de-Ma'aseh Bereshith* but is in the correct texts of the principal fragment of *Shi'ur Qomah.*

22. The entire passage is printed in *'Oṣar Neḥmad,* 4:37. Graetz *Geschichte der Juden,* vol. 7 (4th ed., 1908), 389 and H. Gross in the study mentioned previously raised doubts as to the authenticity of part of this text, but their objections are without foundation. Gross did not understand that the cardinal print of the text is made in the final passage, whose authenticity he too felt compelled to recognize. The analysis of this part of the quotation in connection with the aforementioned statements of Jacob the Nazirite also proves the authenticity of the other parts. There is therefore no reason to dismember the text. Besides, the same citation is also quoted in *'En Ya'akov* on the tractate *Ta'anith,* chap. 1, where it serves as an illustration for another aggadah on the "emissary," that is, Metatron.

23. Graetz, *Geschichte der Juden* 8:389–390.

to the question of the relation between the First Cause and the world, a relation for which the Kabbalah only later devised a definite solution. In this, Graetz proceeded from the undoubtedly false assumption that the Book *Bahir* was composed only at the beginning of the thirteenth century. He did not take into consideration that the cautious but nevertheless highly suggestive formulation of the passage in the commentary on the Talmud could have been the result of a conscious desire to veil an esoteric position and not of an uncertain groping.

For us, better placed to see things in their proper context, the quotation is by no means incomprehensible. It fits perfectly into the framework of the kabbalistic-gnostic reinterpretation of the Merkabah gnosis, with which we have already become familiar in our analysis of the *Bahir.* The pairing of concepts "Cause of causes" and "Creator of the beginning" is by no means accidental, as is shown by its presense in the aforementioned traditions concerning the mystical interpretation of the prayer texts. We are evidently dealing with a fixed terminology current in this circle. The idea of the demiurge does not contradict the doctrine of the sefiroth, as Graetz believed, but includes it, as we can deduce from the considerations of Jacob the Nazirite. It seems, moreover, that the two motifs could easily be linked to this earliest kabbalistic interpretation of the concept of the demiurge. The *yoṣer bereshith* or the cherub on the Throne could be combined with the *Bahir*'s conception of the Shekhinah as the last sefirah. The divine *kabhod,* which reveals itself to the prophet, is no longer conceived as created, as in Saadya and Yehudah ben Barzilai, but rather as emanated from the First Cause, even if this occurred perhaps only at the Creation, as the Book *Bahir* maintained with respect to the Shekhinah.[24] On the

---

24. That this was in fact the opinion of the Rabad could be asserted with certainty if we could convince ourselves of the authenticity of the long quotation printed by Joseph Solomon Delmedigo, *Nobeloth Ḥokhmah* (Basel, 1631), fol. 51 of the unpaginated preface, from a manuscript of the *Hassagoth,* the objections to Maimonides. Unfortunately, I am by no means persuaded that this text is genuine. We are dealing here with a comment on *Hilkhoth Yesode ha-Torah* 1:3, where the author engages in a rather prolix discussion of the notion of the sefiroth as divine "attributes of action," *to'are pe'ullah.* The extraordinary length of the quotation, which stands in marked contrast to the generally laconic style of the Rabad's glosses, militates against its authenticity; I therefore did not take it into account in my previous argument. It presupposes in fact an elaborate philosophical interpretation of the concept of sefiroth, which would be as significant in the mouth of the Rabad as it would be

other hand, a new mystical conception of the supreme prince of angels, Metatron, could be connected with this. Naturally, this Metatron is no longer the biblical Enoch, the son of Yared, transformed into an angelic being and taken up to heaven to minister at the head of the celestial court. This earlier figure can hardly be said to be an emanation of the First Cause. The author must, therefore, have had in mind a higher Metatron whose power was invested in Enoch, the son of Yared, after his ascension. It is not so surprising, then, that we later find among the kabbalists of the mid-thirteenth century, and perhaps already in their sources, the concept of a "Great Metatron," *metatron rabbah,* contrasted with the Metatron who exercises, as Prince of the Countenance, a function in the world of the Merkabah.[25] It is entirely possible that the cautious wording of the Rabad already contains an allusion to this double Metatron when he says that the talmudic passage refers to "the Prince of the Countenance . . . or perhaps to one who is above him." Underlying this formulation may be the view that this emanation of the supreme cause could also be named "Prince of the world,"[26] Great Metatron,

---

improbable. Unfortunately, we still do not have a critical edition of Rabad's *Hassagoth* or even one that comes close to being complete. Surprises are therefore by no means inconceivable. In another passage of his book, fol. 195b, Delmedigo refers to his possession of a manuscript of the "Kabbalah of Rabad of Posquières." Perhaps the aforementioned quotation, to which no one so far had paid attention, comes from this source. I have long endeavored, but in vain, to find Delmedigo's manuscript.

25. It seems to me by no means inconceivable that the source of the expression *Metatron Rabbah* is to be sought in the older texts of the Hekhaloth literature. Jacob Cohen of Soria already found it in the sources he used for his commentary on Ezekiel's Merkabah (Ms. Munich 408, fol. 107a). Traditions that denied any such difference between Enoch elevated to the rank of an angel and an angelic being, *Metatron Rabbah,* placed above him were circulating in the thirteenth century; cf. for example the text of Ms. British Museum, Margoliouth 746, fol. 108b, which I published in *Reshith ha-Qabbala,* 252–253 as well as the literature cited in chap. 2, n. 214.

26. I dealt more extensively in my book *Jewish Gnosticism,* 44–50, with the question of the date of this identification of the angel Metatron with the "Prince of the world." My statements there invalidate earlier opinions, according to which this identification is a medieval product and does not go back to an older tradition. Metatron is expressly designated as "the great archon of the entire universe" in a Jewish-Aramaic incantation of the sixth century (from Babylonia) that C. Gordon published in *Ar. Or.* 9 (1973):95, but which he did not interpret correctly regarding the point relevant to our inquiry. Moreover, this identification also lies at the foundation of the fragments of the Merkabah text *Raza Rabba,* which we discussed in the preceding chapter. The passages of the Talmud relating to the "Prince of the world" do not name Metatron directly but may already have had him in mind, at least occasionally as in, for example, the passage *Yebamoth* 16b. Rabad himself was surely thinking of

or "body of the Shekhinah"—symbols that all relate to the doctrine of the logos and to the idea of the last sefirah and its powers in the writings of the oldest kabbalists.

Here we seem to have a remarkable instance of reciprocal influence between the circles of the Provençal kabbalists and the German Hasidim. The doctrine of the Glory and the cherub upon the Throne came from Germany to Provence with the oldest fragments of the "prehistoric" Kabbalah. But after 1200 certain ideas pertaining to the doctrine of the sefiroth as found in the *Bahir,* as well as other notions of the Provençal kabbalists, made their way back to the circles of the Hasidim in Germany—unless we assume that these ideas had been known in one of their groups all along—and there merged with the doctrine of the cherub, which was native to that country. We possess from these circles some statements on the mystical meaning of the prayer texts that are couched in the language of Jacob the Nazirite and the Rabad, though the demiurge is replaced by the cherub. We have, for example, an amalgamation of this kind in the following text, cited "from the Kabbalah of R. Eliezer[!] of Worms" in a New York manuscript. The author could very well be one of his disciples who confused the doctrines of the two groups, such as that anonymous Hasid of Narbonne, of whom we have already heard. The text reads as follows:

> When someone enters the synagogue or any other place where he wishes to pray in the morning or evening, he should meditate in his heart that the Creator, praised be He, is called the Cause of causes, and that one cannot conceive any thought or any allusion with regard to what He is, since past, present, and future are contained in Him and indicated, for those who know, in the four letters of His name. Therefore man should intend in his heart to pray in such a manner that his prayer be accepted before the Creator, praised be He, by the power of the "particular cherub" who was emanated and created from his great fire which consumes the fire. Just as the Creator emanated ten sefiroth and the cherub is one of them, and everything is united in a unity that is complete and without distinctions, so does the Creator direct an influx toward the particular cherub and from the cherub the influx rises upward [it must, without doubt, be read: downward] and

---

Metatron when he explained, in the remark cited in *'En Ya'akob,* beginning of the tractate *Ta'anith,* that the messenger *(shaliaḥ)* of God is the prince of the world who appeared to the prophets and who reigns over the Merkabah. Maimonides, in *The Guide of the Perplexed* 2:6 and the tosafists (on *B. Yebamoth* 16b) presuppose the same conception.

> from there, to Israel. And no one should be surprised that one can say that the *kawwanah* of man can rise toward the cherub, through which intermediary his prayer can be accepted before the Cause of causes, and that he should not address himself [directly] to the Cause of causes. Did not the Creator make His voice audible to Moses, our master, and say [Exod. 23:21]: "Pay heed to him and obey him. Do not defy him, for he will not pardon your offenses, since My name is in him." That means: do not change anything in your *kawwanah,* but direct your heart toward Him in the hour of prayer. And yet He warned him not to yield to the erroneous idea that he [the cherub] had power and greatness of his own. For everything derives from His power as is proved by the conclusion of that verse: "since my name is in him," which means that he has no power of his own. . . . And if you wish to say: why should I direct the *kawwanah* toward him, since he does not have any power of his own, but only through you, God has already said [to Moses]: think of him in prayer, for my name is in him, for his name is the "Great Metatron" and he is also called the "lesser YHWH."[27]

We thus have a conclusion a fortiori: "If even Moses must direct all his *kawwanah* in prayer toward the cherub alone, in order to have his prayer accepted through his mediation, and not towards the Cause of causes—how much more so does this apply to us. And with that, enough has been said for him who fears the name of God."[28]

Having thus become more closely acquainted with one of the fundamental kabbalistic conceptions of the Rabad, we are now able to place greater faith in the authenticity of other fragments that the kabbalists quote from his writings and that contain indications of a more developed theosophic doctrine. Rabad's commentary on the Talmud, about which we learn from Shemtob ibn Gaon that here and there it also dealt with kabbalistic matters, may easily have also been known to his contemporary and fellow disciple in the school of Solomon ibn Adreth, Meir ibn abi-Sahula. It is probably there that he read Rabad's interpretation of the aggadah in *'Erubin* 18a, according to which man was originally created as an androgynous being. He refers to this passage in one of his writings, without however quoting the text.[29] Nevertheless, the text has been preserved in some kabbalistic miscellanies that used old materials. Here, too, a

---

27. On the notion of the "little YHWH," cf. my *Major Trends,* 68, as well as H. Odeberg, *3 Enoch or the Hebrew Book of Enoch* (1928), 188–192 of the introduction and 33–34 of the commentary.

28. Cf. the Hebrew text in *Reshith ha-Qabbala,* 78.

29. In his commentary on the kabbalistic passages found in Nahmanides' commentary on the Torah, *Be'ur le-Perush ha-Ramban* (Warsaw 1875) fol.4c, cited henceforth as Sahula.

careful analysis seems to confirm the authenticity of the citation. The author offers a kabbalistic interpretation of the concept *du-parṣufin,* central to this aggadah, which is very different from that given by all the Spanish kabbalists, up to and including the *Zohar.* Forgers of this period would obviously have attributed their own views to the Rabad, much as they did in the case of ever so many pseudepigraphic writings with regard to other authors. Here the two "faces" are not yet the sefiroth *tif'ereth* and *malkhuth,* as in the Spanish Kabbalah, but the two *middoth* of pure judgment and pure mercy of God. The passage reads as follows:

> The reason for the creation [of Adam and Eve] as "double faced," *du-parṣufin,* consists therein that the woman must obey her husband and that her life depends on his, and they should not each go his own way, but on the contrary an inseparable closeness and brotherhood should reign between them. Then there would be peace between them and harmony in their abode. And this is also true of the [divine *middoth* that are called] "agents of truth, whose action is truth."[30] The reason for the two faces indicates two things. First, it is known that two oppositions were emanated, one of pure sternness (judgment) and the other of pure mercy. If they had not been emanated as a "double face," each of them would act in accordance with its own principle. It would then appear as if there were two [independent] principles, and each would act without any link to the other and without its assistance. But now that they were created as a "double face," all their action takes place in an evenly balanced manner and in complete unity and without separation. Moreover, if they had not been created "double faced," no complete unity could emerge from them, and the quality of sternness would not be able to elevate itself to that of mercy, or [vice versa] that of mercy to that of sternness. But now, since they are created double faced, each of them is close to the other and unites itself with it and longs to be joined to it, in order that all may be one edifice. This is proved by the fact that the names of God refer to one another [in their significance], for you find that the Tetragrammaton [which refers to the divine mercy] sometimes also indicates the quality of sternness, and [the name of] Elohim [which indicates sternness], the quality of mercy, as in Genesis 19:24, and the [functions of the] qualities merge. That, briefly, is the reason [for the creation of man "two-faced."] Reflect upon this and you will find it.[31]

30. This is an expression one finds in the prayer for the sanctification of the new moon, where it means the sun and the moon. Here it is already reinterpreted in a mystical sense.

31. I published the text in *Reshith ha-Qabbala,* 79, from the Mss. British Museum 768, fol. 14a, and Oxford 1956, fol. 7a. Exactly the same explanation of the necessary mixture of Stern Judgement and Mercy recurs later in, for example, Gikatilla's *Sha'are 'Orah* (ed. 1715), 61a.

The two *middoth* of God do not, therefore, act as autonomous principles independent of one another, but must be regarded, despite all their opposition, as an inseparable unity in God. It is precisely because they are thus conjoined that the one can pass into the other, each having something of the other. The blurring of the distinction between the two notions employed here, "created" and "emanated" (with the latter merely defining more closely the content of the former), points to links with the tradition of the *Bahir.* There too, as we know, the light of the Shekhinah is said on one occasion to be created, but on another to be emanated. From the use of words such as "creation," we can deduce nothing a priori with regard to the precise theological or mystical sense in which such expressions are employed. The content of creation may consist precisely in emanation. In any case, this is the meaning of the creation of the divine *middoth,* which are the sefiroth.

But it is not only incidentally, in connection with this aggadah on the nature of man, that the Rabad refers to esoteric notions, which clearly point toward the doctrine of the sefiroth; he does the same in connection with other themes. In his objections to Maimonides, he remarks on the subject of the pair of notions "before" and "behind," used in Exodus 33:23 with reference to God, that we are dealing with "a great secret, which it is not appropriate to divulge to everybody," and that Maimonides apparently knew nothing of it.[32] He offers no more precise information about this secret; but it must somehow be related to his conceptions of the demiurge and to that which exists above or within him. (The Hebrew word for "before" is related to the word for "inside.") Several times—it is noteworthy that it happens only rarely—later kabbalists quote in the name of Rabad brief kabbalistic remarks or allusions, suggesting that they possessed either a short treatise composed by one of his disciples or isolated fragments transmitted in his name. They are written in the fixed terminology of the Kabbalah. There is, to be sure, no compelling proof that they are genuine, although precisely their very small number argues in favor of their authenticity. After all, nothing would have been easier than to produce false texts. On the other hand the possibility cannot be excluded that these "quota-

---

32. Rabad's remark on *Hilkhoth Yesode ha-Torah* 1:10, preserved in Karo's commentary *Kesef Mishneh.*

tions" were in fact written down shortly after Rabad's time and then mistakenly ascribed to him. I do not see, for the moment, any possibility of deciding this issue, although I am rather inclined to accept their authenticity. The quotations derive from the tradition of the school of Barcelona.

Thus, Isaac of Acre quotes "in the name of Rabad" "that the [sefirah] *binah* is the future world, but the [tenth sefirah, named] *'aṭarah* is this world and it is to this that the verse [Ps. 106:48] refers: 'from eon to eon.' "[33] The gist of this symbolism already figures, as we have seen, in the *Bahir.* Only the symbolic term *'aṭarah,* "crown," is not yet employed there though its use is foreshadowed in sections 12 and 60. But since it is frequently used by his son, Isaac the Blind, it is entirely plausible that the citation is genuine. It is more difficult to establish the authenticity of two quotations, perhaps from one source, that are contained in a work of Shemtob ben Shemtob on the sefiroth, composed around 1400. Mention is made there, likewise "in the name of Rabad," of the symbolism of the first sefirah, whose nature is said to be indicated by the word *bi* in the formula of the oath *"by Myself* I swear, the Lord declares" (Gen. 22:16). According to its numerical value, twelve, this word at the same time alludes to the twelve directions of space mentioned in the *Book of Creation,* chapter 5, which are emanated from the twelve "sources of wisdom" that, in their turn, are hidden in the supreme sefirah, *kether.* "Rabad also calls this sefirah 'the comprehension that has no end,' for it is impossible to speak of any comprehension of them."[34] Since later kabbalistic texts of the thirteenth century often speak of thirteen rather than twelve sources that burst forth from the first sefirah, this quotation attributed to the Rabad might well point to an older conception. The word בי in the oath was in fact also used as the symbol of the first sefirah by the disciples of Isaac the Blind.[35] Immediately afterward, another dictum regarding the first sefirah, *kether 'elyon,* is quoted "in the name of Rabad," according to which the designation of this sefirah

33. Isaac of Acre, *Me'irath 'Enayim,* Ms. Munich 17, fol. 42a.

34. I published the text in *Reshith ha-Qabbala,* 80–81, from Ms. British Museum 771, fol. 38a.

35. Cf. for example Ezra, *Perush ha-'Aggadoth,* Ms. Vatican. 441, fol. 69a (as well as *Zohar,* fol. 66a, 130a) Isaac himself uses Genesis 22:16 as a proof text for the doctrine of the sefiroth; see *Sefer Bialik,* 144.

as "the light which conceals itself" *('or ha-mith'allem)* would have been known to him: "And he explained [that this sefirah was so called] because it was withdrawn and hidden from everything."[36]

Insofar as they are not taken from his commentaries on the Talmud, these quotations are based upon the notes of disciples who cite them in his name. If they are genuine, they show that in his oral remarks to the adepts of mysticism Rabad expressed himself more clearly on the doctrine of the sefiroth than in his writings, which were designed for a larger circle of rabbinically educated readers. The terminology seems to me to be closely related to that of his son, and this argues for the authenticity of the tradition. Isaac the Blind, in his commentary on the *Yeṣirah,* also speaks of a "light which conceals itself." It is also noteworthy that he goes so far as to elevate the incomprehensibility of the first sefirah to the rank of a symbolic designation. His son Isaac does exactly the same, albeit in a somewhat different formulation. The sefirah, which in its unknowability is beyond all positive determination, is named precisely in accordance with this negative determination. The expression *'en sof* does not yet appear in these quotations, although the circumlocution *hassagah she-'en lah sof,* literally "the comprehension which has no end," approaches it.[37] If these figures of speech regarding the high-

---

36. Ms. British Museum 771, fol. 139b.

37. In 1932 I discovered another sample of the Rabad's mystical symbolism, (of whose authenticity I am however not fully convinced) in a manuscript of the Carmoly collection, in the municipal library in Frankfurt-am-Main, no. 218–221, fol. 21a. Whether the manuscript still exists is doubtful. The passage reads as follows:

> The Rabad, may his memory be blessed, was asked, "Why are there in the *'Emeth we-yaṣib* [the prayer that follows the *Shema'* in the morning service] fifteen words that begin with the consonant *waw?* He answered: Because God created His world with twenty-two letters that form the divine name *Yah* [how is not said here], which has the numerical value of fifteen, as it is said [Isa. 26:4]: because through *Yah* has YHWH created the world [this is how the Talmud interpreted this verse]. The prayer begins with *'alef* and ends with *he,* an allusion to the name *'ehyeh.* And why did He take the consonant *waw* before all the other letters? Because it represents the *middah* of Jacob, our father, which is the quality of truth, with which it begins [the prayer *'Emeth we-yaṣib*] begins. Thus, it is also said [Mic. 7:20]: 'You give truth to Jacob,' who represents the middle line, as it is said [Gen. 32:11]: 'With my staff alone I crossed this Jordan,' that is, with my staff, which is the *middah* of truth. And that is the *waw,* which is the middle line. The symbol of the middle line, which for Jacob corresponds to the form of the letter *waw,* does not yet appear in the book *Bahir,* but is already familiar to the Rabad's son. It would therefore not be impossible that this symbol, too, already formed part of the mystical sym-

est sefirah are authentic, a Neoplatonic note would already be detectable in them. In the case of Isaac's father-in-law the kabbalistic-gnostic tradition cuts across the older Saadyanic one; with Isaac we find an encounter between the gnostic tradition and a rising Neoplatonic one, an encounter that would subsequently become even more clearly marked in the spiritual world of his son.

All this would fit in rather well with other historical facts. During these very same years, when the Book *Bahir* underwent its final redaction and was published in Provence, and in the same city of Lunel where Jacob the Nazirite lived, there resided also Yehudah ibn Tibbon of Granada, who brought with him a literary and religious tradition formed, in part, by Arabic-Jewish Neoplatonism. This tradition was very influential in the Muslim regions of Spain. Between 1160 and 1170, on the initiative of a group that had ascetic tendencies and was interested in Jewish religious thought, this scholar translated, among other works, *The Duties of the Heart* by Baḥya ibn Paquda and the *Kuzari* of Yehudah Halevi.[38] According to his explicit testimony it was precisely at the instigation of Rabad that ibn Tibbon, the "father of translators," translated the major part of Baḥya's work.[39]

This testimony provides an interesting perspective. In the circle of Jacob the Nazirite and of Rabad, an esoteric tradition of gnostic character that had arrived in these regions about one or two generations earlier was cultivated, apparently with profound devotion. At the same time, however, this circle was also exposed to the influence of a thoroughly or partly Neoplatonic literature that was being translated, just then, from Arabic into Hebrew, and that had not been known to earlier scholars in the Provence. Recent research has shown that the Hebrew translation of Moses ibn Ezra's Neoplatonic

---

bolism and terminology of his father. The oppositions of Grace and Stern Judgment are united in the "middle line." We are already acquainted from the *Bahir* with the relationship between Jacob and the *middah* of truth. In contrast to these decidedly mystical fragments, the homilies of the Rabad, to the extent that they have been preserved (e.g., his sermon for the New Year's festival) contain nothing mystical; cf. *Derashah le-Rosh ha-Shanah,* ed. Abraham Shisha (London, 1955), and I. Twersky in *Kiryath Sefer* 32 (1956): 440–443.

38. However, according to Nathaniel Kaspi's commentary on the *Kuzari* (1424), preserved in Ms. Paris 677, the translation was made in 1175; see Catalogue Paris, 106.

39. Cf. the translator's postscript to the first chapter of *The Duties of the Heart* (which he already had translated in 1161 for Meshullam ben Jacob in Lunel).

philosophic *Book of Learning on the Meaning of Metaphor and of Reality* (Hebrew: *'Arugath ha-Bosem*) was made for that same circle of the "Sages of Lunel"—apparently in the same generation—and could thus have been known to the early kabbalists (for example, Azriel; see also p. 447, n. 195.[40] M. Idel rightly considers this translation as one of the main channels through which the ideas of ibn Gabirol reached the early Kabbalah. That *The Duties of the Heart,* the most widespread and important ethical treatise of medieval Jewish literature, had a fundamentally mystical tendency and moved in many cases on the fringes of mysticism is not disputed. In the eleventh century, under the strong and unmistakable influence of Muslim mystical literature, its author preached a thoroughly ascetic morality. His views can easily be linked to the tendencies of the new Kabbalah and the German Hasidim. Nor is it surprising that the novel views of Yehudah Halevi—on the nature of the Jewish people and the mystery of its fate, his doctrine of Israel as the heart of all peoples and of its specific prophetic gift transmitted by heredity from the first man to the nation—could easily establish links with the gnostic traditions and mysticism concerning the secret meaning of the ecclesia Israel. It is in Lunel and Posquières that a connection was formed between these two currents, which for all their differences converged in their ascetic inclinations as well as in their attempt to construct a mystical or semimystical doctrine expounding the special status of the Jewish people in the world. The anti-Aristotelian tendency of the new Gnostics could likewise find support in these two works, which are certainly not to be included in the Aristotelian branch of Jewish thought. We may therefore affirm that the fusion of those elements of Jewish philosophy that were best suited to lend support to the mystics on the one hand and the "prehistoric" Kabbalah on the other could very well have taken place in this circle in which the Kabbalah made its first appearance.

In fact, we find that when discussing the relation between Creator and creature in one of his halakhic works,[41] Rabad resorts both to Saadyanic ideas and, with slight variations, to formulations that

40. Cf. M. Idel, in *Kiryath Sefer* 51 (1976): 485, who published the text of the introduction by the otherwise unknown translator Yehudah (not ibn Tibbon) from Ms. Neofiti 11 in the Vatican.

41. In *Sefer Ba'ale ha-Nefesh,* ed. Berlin, fol. 32b.

bear the mark of Baḥya.[42] The Creator God, he says, is beyond transcendence and immanence—a conception characteristic of mystics and appropriate to a critic of Maimonides: "All that is created should know that it is not separated from the Creator," although the Creator, for his part "is not connected to it." The being and existence of things do not form a barrier before the Creator. "It is in this case as it is with the world, which is full of air, and everything enters into the air, and is affected by it, and it nevertheless remains invisible to them"—this is precisely the relation between the Creator and creation. The analogy between the air that penetrates everything and the Creator goes back, in the Jewish tradition, to Saadya (who no doubt derived it from older sources), and it gained great popularity among the first kabbalists, particularly in the generation that followed Rabad. The kabbalists, to be sure, took Saadya's words very literally: the subtle ether, created by God and representing the Holy Spirit becomes with them the "primordial ether," *'awir qadmon,* which is nothing other than the first sefirah, from which everything emanated. It should be noted in passing that in the pair of concepts "cause of causes" and "demiurge" that I analyzed above, Rabad used for "cause of causes" the same Hebrew term that appears in the translation of Yehudah ibn Tibbon.

More doubtful is the origin of the kabbalistic term for the tenth sefirah, which in the *Bahir* is never designated as *malkhuth,* "kingdom." The term is first found in Jacob the Nazirite of Lunel's *kawwanoth* for prayer. Henceforth it becomes among the kabbalists, next to the designation *'aṭarah,* the most common name for the tenth sefirah. It may have had its origin in Yehudah ben Barzilai,[43] who equated the *kabhod* and the *malkhuth* of God, or in Yehudah Halevi's *Kuzari,* where the three concepts of *kabhod,* shekhinah, and *malkhuth* are expressly identified.[44] But the same terminology is also found in the writings of Eleazar of Worms.[45] It is therefore entirely possible that the influence of the *Kuzari* was beginning to

---

42. He uses, in the passage mentioned, the syllogism developed by Baḥya in *The Duties of the Heart* 1:7. This was pointed out by my late colleague, Professor Julius Guttmann.

43. Cf. his commentary on the *Yeṣirah,* bottom of 16.

44. Cf. *Kuzari* 2:7 and above all 2:3, where other biblical notions are equated with these; all, with the exception of fire, appear in the kabbalistic literature after 1280 as symbols of the tenth sefirah.

45. Cf. the quotation in chap. 2, pp. 184–186.

make itself felt in mystical circles well before the kabbalists of Gerona at the beginning of the thirteenth century. In fact these kabbalists frequently referred to the *Kuzari* as a source, and many of them, such as Ezra ben Solomon, regarded its author as one of the *maskilim,* a term that in philosophical circles designated the adherents of philosophical culture, whereas among the mystics it denoted the esotericists and illuminati. Ezra approvingly cites the sentence in the *Kuzari* 1:109 concerning the rank of Moses: "As one of the *maskilim* said in his book: the material light settled upon his countenance, but the intelligible light was united with his heart."[46] It is not impossible, however, that right from the time of its appearance this classical work of Hebrew literature was accepted in the circles of the oldest kabbalists as congruent with their thoughts.

The great kabbalistic commentary on the Book *Yeṣirah,* attributed in its editions to Abraham ben David, has nothing to do with Rabad. It belongs in fact to a certain Joseph ben Shalom, who wrote around 1300, shortly after the publication of the *Zohar.*[47] The commentary came to be ascribed to Rabad only much later, and until the sixteenth century various manuscripts and authors still knew the real name of the writer.[48] On the other hand, the magical citations that appear in his name and that partly conform to the tradition of his father-in-law, Abraham ben Isaac, are no doubt genuine. Thus the kabbalist Isaac of Acre refers around 1320 to some of the apotropaic formulas mentioned previously (n. 7) as deriving from the tradition of the Rabad.[49]

Another valuable and authentic testimony concerning the Rabad and his father-in-law as well as other esoteric writers of their time is contained in a fragment of a letter that was probably written around 1230/1240 in Provence and is preserved in the lengthy epistle of (the otherwise unknown?[50]) Samuel ben Mordekhai to Yequtiel ha-Kohen[51] against the opponents of Maimonides in Ms.

---

46. Cf. Tishby's edition of Azriel, *Perush ha-'Aggadoth,* 34 n. 15.

47. Cf. my study on this question in *Kiryath Sefer* 4 (1927): 286–302.

48. The true author is still named in the parchment Ms. Or. 11791 in the British Museum, fol. 42a; cf. *British Museum Quarterly* 16 (January 1952).

49. Cited in Ms. Gaster 720, fol. 52b, now in the British Museum.

50. Professor Dinur informs me that a halakhic scholar by that name (from Narbonne?) is mentioned in the book *Orḥoth Ḥayyim* of R. Aaron Kohen of Lunel, that is one or two generations before Menaḥem Meiri.

51. Whether this Yequtiel is identical with the rabbi mentioned by Neubauer, *Rabbins Français,* 693, is difficult to determine. Dinur suggested Yequtiel of Anduze

Neofiti 11*34* (Sacerdote, p. 16). The German Hasidim and their Provençal contemporaries are clearly considered by the writer of this letter as members of one and the same spiritual group. He mentions the Kabbalah on the sefiroth of a certain R. Abraham his teacher and their doctrine concerning the composition of the angels of matter and form. The author of the letter lived in Marseilles and was in contact with Samuel ibn Tibbon, who died before 1230. Conclusive proof of the genuineness of the letter and the statements it contains is provided by the fact that the author considers precisely this doctrine concerning the angels, whose proponents he names, as an error resulting from an unsubstantiated esoteric tradition. He thus excuses these scholars while explicitly rejecting their doctrine in favor of that of Maimonides. We may therefore regard him as an unimpeachable witness for the esotericism of his time and consider his testimony as reliable even where it contains novel information uncorroborated by other texts. It is noteworthy that Isaac the Blind, apparently his contemporary and still alive at the time, is not named. The author of the letter seems to make mention only of deceased authorities as bearers of the Kabbalah. He writes:

> I meditated on the books of the *Guide* [of Maimonides] and I found that his words agree with the Kabbalah of the late R. Abraham and of the Nazir, and deviate from it only in minor matters. I make known the truth in brief. They received a tradition concerning ten sefiroth, the first sefirah being *ḥokhmah;* and it is also the first Intelligence, which is called "living God," and it is of this that it is said: "God created me at the beginning of his path." With the *ḥokhmah* everything was built, and from it emanated the separate intelligences. And with regard to the tenth sefirah they received a tradition that it was identical with what our teachers named in one place the Prince of the Divine Countenance and in other places Prince of the World, and it is he who appeared to the prophets and who transmitted the prophecies . . . and that is why, in many passages of Scripture, where this angel speaks, the speech is attributed to God, as in [Gen. 31:3]: "Then the Lord said to Jacob" . . . and this is the mystery that is signified in the Song of Songs, and it is in every respect a parable for this matter [the relation between man and the supreme Intelligence, the nous or the Sophia]. And thus, the learned R. Yehudah [in the Vatican Ms. R. J. Halevi][52] wrote on the subject of the Song of Songs: "a song that is the most exquisite of all songs, which is addressed to the angel of

(rather than the לונדרש of the manuscripts). The Neofiti manuscript enables us to correct the text significantly.

52. Mss. Neofiti 11 and Mortara 8 read: "Yehuda Halevi in his commentary on the Song of Songs."

glory and the holy spirit." And it is there said at the end: "Flee my beloved"—as a parable for the angel of glory who was revealed once at the burning bush and once in Sinai. And when it is said in the Book *Yeṣirah* that the beginning of the sefiroth is intertwined with their end, it thereby means to say that from the first sefirah emanated the second and thus all the others. And the master wrote in the *Guide* that the upper world consists entirely of immaterial forms that are separated from all matter and that are called angels. . . . [Here the author of the letter also quotes Maimonides' conception of the ten degrees of angels, the last of which is named *'ishim.*] And I learned, when I was in Marseilles, from the lips of the learned R. Samuel, the son of the learned R. Yehudah[53] [apparently ibn Tibbon], that each time the beloved is mentioned in the Song of Songs, it is this angel named *'ishim* that is meant. Know then and understand that they all go the same way. But the scholars of the land, such as R. Abraham the president of the rabbinic court and RABD [Abraham ben David],[54] may his memory be blessed, and the scholar R. Abraham,[55] the Hasid R. Yehudah the Pious of Germany and the Hasid R. Eliezer [often designated as such instead of Eleazar] of Garmiza [Worms] and the Hasid R. Yehudah ibn Ziza of Toledo, may all their memories be blessed, from whom [R. Abraham][56] the Nazirite received—they all received by way of tradition, Kabbalah, without any proof, as when someone transmits a secret to his friend without adducing any proof. And that is why some of them were of the opinion that the angels are made of matter and form and that man resembles them in that respect, as seemed probable to them on the basis of the verses of Scripture where it is said: "He made man in the image of God"; and there are among them angels made of fire and water. . . . And all this was due to the fact that they lacked insight into the [different] levels *(ma'aloth)* of non-material forms, and believed that reality is stronger in the forms containing matter. And that is why there are those among them who think that *Shi'ur Qomah* is to be understood literally. But they are all united in the opinion that no corporeality is to be attributed to the Creator Himself.[57]

It cannot be determined whether the unknown Abraham the Nazirite,[58] who must have lived in Provence, was personally ac-

---

53. Thus the reading of Neofiti 11, fol. 206.

54. Spelled out fully in Ms. Neofiti "Abraham ben David."

55. Ms. Neofiti adds מברידו, which may mean Bordeaux. The scholar named here is otherwise unknown. Strangely enough the name of Abraham ibn Ezra is not mentioned at all.

56. Missing in Ms. Neofiti.

57. I originally published the text of this important document to the extent that I could restore it (on the basis of Mss. Oxford 1816, fol. 63a, and Vatican 236, fol. 81a.) in my Hebrew study "The Traces of Gabirol in the Kabbalah," *Me'assef Sofre Ereṣ Israel* (1940), 175–176. We now possess a better version in Ms. Neofiti 11, fols. 205–206.

58. The more recently discovered manuscripts suggest that there was no Abraham Nazir but, rather, two persons: a R. Abraham *and* a Nazir (the latter perhaps

quainted with the leaders of the German Hasidim and the Hasid of Toledo or whether he only corresponded with them. However, it would not be at all unusual for a scholar and ascetic of Provence to travel personally to Toledo or Worms. In any case, he was among those who received the tradition of the family of the Rabad, and he apparently interpreted the *Shi'ur Qomah* in like manner. His tradition concerning the first sefirah as the highest intelligence is a variant of that found in Isaac the Blind. Of the *maḥshabah* or supreme crown situated above the Sophia he knows nothing—but then even kabbalists who did know of it often enough described *ḥokhmah* as the first sefirah. The author of the letter is not yet aware of any particular tension between the opinions of Maimonides and those of the kabbalists, although he does recognize the differences between them and sides with Maimonides. But there is no trace here of the harsh tone and the hostility discernible in controversies between the two camps after the battle concerning the position of the Maimonists flared up again, that is, after 1232. The author seems to be unaware that the opinion rejected by him concerning the angels and the intelligences is that of Solomon ibn Gabirol. There is no way of knowing whether "the scholar R. Abraham," is Abraham ibn Ezra who in fact borrowed his opinion from ibn Gabirol and propounded it in his commentaries. It may only be a case of an impersonal, literary influence exercised by Ibn Ezra on Abraham the Nazirite.

3. Jacob the Nazirite and the Groups of Ascetics in the Community, Perushim *and* Nezirim—*Catharism and Kabbalah—Revelations Granted to the Ascetics and the Forms of These Revelations—The Doctrine of* Kawwanah *in Prayer*

What can we learn from the evidence surveyed so far? It appears that various traditions met and mingled in the circle of Rabad, Jacob the Nazirite, their colleagues, and their disciples. We have no conclusive evidence that they developed a systematic, let alone complete, doctrinal system. But it is certainly permissible to say that this circle served as the intermediary and spokesman for different tendencies that crystallized in the course of their or the following

---

Jacob the Nazirite. We know that he was a wanderer. He may have received traditions from R. Abraham of Bordeaux (not from Abraham ibn Ezra).

generation. The few extant fragments bear witness to a profound ferment. We notice the influence of the doctrine of the *kabhod,* in vogue among the French and German Hasidim. At the same time, we also find this doctrine in its purely Saadyanic version as mediated by the old, pre-Tibbonite translations and by the commentary of Yehudah ben Barzilai on the *Book of Creation.* In addition, a new doctrine is undoubtedly gaining ground here, precisely that of the Book *Bahir* or of the various fragments that went into the making of this work.

This is above all the case for the doctrine of the aeons that are within the *kabhod,* and of which Saadya's *kabhod* by this time represents but the lowest manifestation. Unlike the version of the doctrine of *kabhod* generally accepted among the French scholars, the new teaching presents itself as a great mystery; evidently, the members of this circle were clearly aware of the difference between the new doctrine of the aeons and the exoteric Saadyanic doctrine, which could indeed be propounded in public. This is apparent, for example, when Asher ben Saul of Lunel speaks of the *kabhod* without secretiveness, but immediately afterward alludes to an interpretation based upon the doctrine of the sefiroth in the specific kabbalistic sense of a "great mystery."[59] The doctrines of the logos and the aeons are fused into one. To meditations and researches on the depths of the deity is now added a further mystical teaching on the *kawwanah* in prayer, to be transmitted to initiates only.

At the same time, still other forces and influences were at work in this Provençal circle, in the form of a flood of translations from Judeo-Arabic and, in particular Neoplatonic literature, both original texts and Jewish adaptations. The kabbalists thereby absorbed a spiritual heritage that enriched both their ideas and their language, and whose influence was to become very apparent in the following generation. In the three great monotheistic religions, Neoplatonism often appeared, at that time, in a popular garb; many of its works enjoyed greater popularity among wider circles of enthusiasts and religious minds than among the adepts of rigorous scientific thought. We need but recall the eschatology of the souls as presented in Pseudo-Empedocles' *Book of the Five Substances* or the pseudohermetic *Book of the Twenty-four Masters* with its audacious

---

59. *Sefer ha-Minhagoth,* p. 133.

and paradoxical definitions of the deity.[60] This region, moreover, witnessed the great religious ferment that had begun with the Cathar movement and also made itself felt in various Jewish groups.

In this generation in France and especially in its southern part we hear with increasing frequency of scholars called by the epithet *ha-parush,* the ascetic, or *ha-nazir,* the Nazirite. The exact definition of these terms is provided by a regulation that was undoubtedly composed in this region at the beginning of the thirteenth century, or at best a short time earlier. There it is said that

> one should appoint scholars whose vocation it is to occupy themselves incessantly with the Torah, so that the community might fulfill the duty of the study of the Torah, and in order that the reign of heaven sustain no loss. *Perushim* [literally: those who are separated, detached] is the name given to scholars who devote themselves exclusively to the study of the Torah; they are called in the language of the Mishnah *perushim* and in the language of the Bible *nezirim*—and this detachment [from worldly affairs] leads to purity.[61]

From this definition it is evident that this institution in France has nothing in common with the ascetic movement of the "Mourners of Zion," *'abele ṣiyon,* that several centuries earlier had been widespread in the Near East, and above all in Palestine. The traveler Benjamin of Tudela still found remnants of it in Jerusalem in the twelfth century. The origin of the *perushim* is, rather, connected with the religious enthusiasm that gripped France in the twelfth century, finding expression in the Jewish milieu as well as in the surrounding Christian world, including the reform movements and their religious heresies. Naturally, the very choice of words already reflects the spirit of asceticism that characterized the period. These *perushim* took upon themselves the "yoke of the Torah" and completely detached their thoughts from the affairs of this world. They did not engage in commerce and sought to attain purity. The

60. Cf. Clemens Baeumker, *Studien und Charakteristiken zur Geschichte der Philosophie des Mittelalters* (Münster, 1927), 194–214.

61. The quotation is taken from the important statutes *Ḥuqqe Torah,* published by M. Güdemann in *Geschichte des Erziehungswesen und der Kultur der Juden in Deutschland und Frankreich* (Vienna, 1880), 268. The discussion of the literary or fictitious character of this statute from Provence by S. Baron, *A Social and Religious History of the Jews,* vol. 6 (1958), 395, has been superseded by the evidence presented here concerning the actual use of terms such as *parush* and *nazir.*

similarities between this phenomenon and Christian monasticism on the one hand and the condition of the *perfecti* or *bonshommes* among the Cathars on the other, are especially striking, despite the clear divergences resulting from the different attitudes of Judaism and Christianity toward celibacy. The Nazirites are not simply hasidim in the well-defined sense of the *Book of the Pious* and German Hasidism.[62] But it is evident that we are dealing with a parallel stratum in the Jewish communities, many of whose members undoubtedly also inclined toward the more radical demands of German Hasidism. At the end of his halakhic work Rabad himself picked out of his talmudic material precisely that definition of *ḥasiduth* that most closely approximated the mentality of the German Hasidim.[63] R. Ezra of Gerona, in his commentary on the aggadoth, also calls Jacob the Nazirite by the name Jacob the Hasid.[64] What is important for us is the existence of a stratum with society that by its very definition and vocation had the leisure for a contemplative life. It goes without saying that such a stratum could give rise to men with mystical tendencies.

Members of this group are also mentioned in the earliest kabbalistic sources after Jacob the Nazirite as representatives of a mystical tradition; the names may as well be those of historical personalities as of fictitious figures appearing in pseudepigraphic documents.[65] Indeed, it is precisely the fictitious character of these

---

62. On the notion of the Hasid in this group, cf. *Major Trends,* 91–95.

63. Cf. his *Ba'ale ha-Nefesh,* fol.32d: "He who acts *within* [and not merely in accordance with] the strict line of the law is called hasid." Besides, Rabad himself is often designated in kabbalistic writings as hasid.

64. Cf. my remarks in *Tarbiz* 6:3 (1935): 96.

65. For example, the (probably conflated) Abraham Nazir in some of the versions of the letter mentioned above, around 1240; a certain Yehudah Nazir ben R. Eli ha-Kohen is mentioned around 1230 in Abraham ben Azriel's *'Arugath ha-Bosem* (see J. Perles, *MGWJ* 27 (1877): 365). However, according to E. Urbach in the introduction to his edition of *'Arugath ha-Bosem,* vol. 4 (1963), 141–142, this Yehudah Nazir did not belong to the circle discussed here. At the beginning of Ms. Merzbach 81 (earlier in Frankfurt-am-Main), the brother of Isaac the Blind is designated as R. David *ha-parush wehe-ḥasid.* The father of a certain Moses who signed a document in Marseilles in 1225, is named Menaḥem *ha-parush;* cf. *REJ* 15:88. A certain Isaac, the son of the *parush* R. Menaḥem signed a document in Barcelona in 1268; cf. J. Millas, *Documents Hebraics de Jueus Catalans* (Barcelona, 1927), 89. A kabbalistic commentary on the *'Alenu* prayer that was attributed to Hai Gaon but that actually must have been composed at the beginning of the thirteenth century in the south of France mentions many of these *perushim,* cf. *Ma'or wa-Shemesh* (Livorno, 1839), fol. 9a. Güdemann, *Erziehungswesen,* 267, has compiled many more such references to *perushim* taken from halakhic writings of the thirteenth century.

names of *perushim* and *nezirim* that seems so characteristic of the mood prevailing in these kabbalistic circles. The authors of these fictions evidently knew very well which stratum was linked to the revived gnostic impulses of the Kabbalah. These men studied the Torah but kept aloof from the new philosophic and rationalistic enlightenment. They were as deeply rooted in popular beliefs as the German Hasidim, and it is probably they who introduced religious impulses and popular religiosity into the new forms of the kabbalistic movement. It seems dubious to attribute to these circles an active part in the battle against the new rationalist currents, or the role of any kind of opposition for that matter. Rather it appears that they played a natural, organic, and nonopposing role in a society pervaded with religious ferment, which also sought an outlet in this institution of "communal ascetics."

Jacob the Nazirite of Lunel was a man of this type. And we happen to know that he was not the only one in his community to have adopted this kind of life. In 1165 Benjamin of Tudela saw in Lunel R. Asher ha-Parush, "who has withdrawn from the affairs of the world and who devotes day and night to study, practices asceticism, and does not eat meat."[66] It was for this ascetic that Yehudah ibn Tibbon translated into Hebrew ibn Gabirol's moral tract "On the Improvement of the Qualities of the Soul." Graetz, basing himself upon Benjamin's description, conferred on him his favorite label of "obscurantist"; he seems to have smelled the mystic in him, which immediately aroused his animus. Asher ben Meshullam, a son of the most eminent scholar in a community as well endowed with scholars as Lunel, was therefore a *parush* not only in the sense defined previously, but a representative of more radical tendencies: a genuine ascetic. It is unnecessary to remind ourselves that in the Middle Ages ascetic ideals could manifest themselves at any time and in any place, in Islam just as well as in Christianity and Judaism. Nevertheless, we should bear in mind that analogous ideas emerged in the same Provençal environment where the moral decadence observed among the Catholic clergy moved men to the glorification of ideals apparently embodied by the Cathar *perfecti.* Just as

66. Benjamin of Tudela, ed. Adler, 4. Fragments of a commentary to the aggadic parts of *B. Berakhoth,* which also include speculative passages, by this same R. Asher (who seems to have died between 1285 and 1290) have been preserved in quotations by Baḥya ben Asher and Samuel ben Mordekhai. See M. Idel in *Kiryath Sefer* 50 (1975): 149–53.

the Jewish Nazirites of France took upon their shoulders the full weight of the yoke of the Torah, to which a further ascetic emphasis could be added, so did the "perfect ones" take upon themselves the full burden of the world-denying morality of the "neo-Manichaeism," which the Bogomils had transplanted to Italy and France and which was, in their eyes, identical with primitive Christianity. Abstinence from meat was one of the most conspicuous elements in the conduct of the Cathar "perfect ones."

It is in this milieu that we must place Jacob the Nazirite. Among the few fragments that have come down to us from him, there is a distinctly ascetic text preserved by Ezra of Gerona; it also figures in the *Book of Customs* of his younger brother Asher ben Saul. The additional soul that, according to talmudic Aggadah, man receives on the Sabbath is, he asserts, identical with the highest faculty of the human soul, the *anima rationalis,* which stirs man to seek knowledge of God.

> But at the same time it stimulates him to celebrate the Sabbath with pleasure. His desire thereby increases. But at the end of the Sabbath, it says to him: Restrict your nourishment; and because his desire is thus diminished it causes weakness in him. This is why the sages prescribed the smelling of spices at the end of the Sabbath [in order to confine this weakness as well as the desire].[67]

Although he received his kabbalistic education from Isaac the Blind in Posquières, in the vicinity of Lunel, Ezra may not have known Jacob the Nazirite personally; however, he must have been in a position to obtain reliable traditions concerning him. His assertion that Jacob had been in Jerusalem and had there received mystical and angelological traditions cannot, therefore, be dismissed as unreliable.[68] Ezra ben Solomon is unusually sparing with quotations

---

67. *Sefer ha-Minhagoth,* 176, as well as the citation of Ezra in his *Perush 'Aggadoth,* Ms. Vatican 294, fol. 36a. Cf. also the ascetic interpretation of this quotation in Moses de Leon, *Ha-Nefesh ha-Ḥakhamah* (Basel, 1608), quire H, fol. 1d. Possibly the additional expositions found there are likewise taken from Jacob the Nazirite. The three souls in man are defined by Jacob entirely in the manner of Platonizing psychology, a distinction being established between *nefesh ḥayyah,* the vital soul that has its foundation in the heart, and *nefesh behemith,* the animal soul, which resides in the liver.

68. Another scholar of the Rabad circle, R. Joseph ben Pelath, made (at about the same time?) a pilgrimage to the Holy Land; see S. Assaf, *Sifran shel Rishonim,* 123. I. Ta-Shma sounds a warning note concerning reports of pilgrimages; see *Tarbiz* (1969): 398–399.

from kabbalistic authorities, but the ones he adduces are, as far as I can see, reliable. The relatively simple content of that tradition also corresponds to Jacob's other angelological statements, with which we have already become acquainted on page 208. Jacob is said to have received from a certain R. Nehorai in Jerusalem the tradition that the ritual of libations of water and wine on the Feast of Tabernacles was practiced in the Temple of Jerusalem because "at this ritual two angels were present, whose function it was to bring the fruits to ripeness and to lend them flavor." One of these angels is certainly Gabriel, whose function (according to *B. Sanhedrin* 95b) is to cause the fruit to ripen. The other is probably Michael. Water and wine seem to symbolize the qualities of Grace (water) and Sternness (wine), much as in the Book *Bahir.* Whether this symbolism came from the Orient—together with the angelological tradition—or whether it belongs exclusively to the Provençal stratum of the *Bahir* cannot be established with certainty. We know nothing else about this R. Nehorai, and the doctrine of the sefiroth is implied in no other twelfth-century text that can definitely be said to have been composed in the Orient. This pilgrimage of "Rabbenu Jacob Hasid," which I see no reason to doubt, must have taken place at the earliest not long after the conquest of Jerusalem by Saladin, after 1187; before that, under the rule of the Crusaders, access to the city was generally forbidden to Jews. It cannot be fixed at a date prior to the time Jacob the Nazirite commenced his esoteric studies; it was on the contrary, occasioned by those studies. According to the preceding argument, we have in fact every reason to suppose that such studies were already in vogue before 1187 in the circle of Posquières and of Lunel. Later legends of the Spanish kabbalists related the visit of the old kabbalist of Lunel to the Orient to the interest in the Kabbalah allegedly displayed by Maimonides toward the end of his life. Our R. Jacob is supposed to have gone to Egypt, where he initiated Maimonides in the esoteric science. This legend, whose origin around 1300 I have examined elsewhere, has no historical value.[69] Even the writings of Abraham, the son of Maimonides, whose penchant for mystical religiosity is quite obvious, draw their inspiration from Sufi sources and do not evince the slightest familiarity with kabbalistic ideas,[70] as has already been mentioned on page 12.

69. Cf. my analysis in *Tarbiz* 6:3 (1935): 90–98.

70. The alleged acquaintance of R. Abraham's son David with the *Zohar,* argued by A. I. Katsh (1964), editor of the Arabic homilies on the Torah attributed to

Our discussion of the groups of Jewish ascetics in France devoting themselves to a contemplative life gives added urgency to the question of a possible relationship between the emergence of the Kabbalah and Catharism in the middle of the twelfth century.[71] The only scholar who, to my knowledge, has raised the problem—albeit in a rather aphoristic style—was Moses Gaster in his programmatic *The Origin of the Kabbalah* (Ramsgate, 1894). It is doubtful, however, whether such a relationship can be deduced with certainty from an analysis of the oldest kabbalistic traditions.[72] The information regarding the beliefs of Cathar groups or individuals contained in Cathar sources or in the acts of the Inquisition reveal few if any elements parallel to kabbalistic doctrine. There is, no doubt, a general similarity in the fundamental assumption common to both groups regarding the reality of a separate higher world belonging entirely to God himself and in which there occur certain dramatic events that have their counterpart in the lower world. This supreme world may correspond, in the case of the kabbalists, to the gnostic pleroma. We saw in the previous chapter that different details of a gnostic character entered into the Book *Bahir* through an internal Jewish tradition, just as a number of gnostic details turn up here and there in Cathar doctrine.[73] Thus the Cathars recognize four elements as composing that supreme world, in a manner reminiscent of the circle of Isaac the Blind. The Creator God or demiurge, who for the Cathars is identical with Satan, has a form and a figure in which

---

David, is a product of sheer imagination, unsupported by even a single shred of evidence.

71. Cf. our earlier references to this problem, pp. 13–16, herein.

72. Cf. the discussion by Ernst Werner, "Die Entstehung der Kabbalah und die südfranzösischen Katharer," *Forschungen und Fortschritte* 37 (1963): 86–89, whose argument culminates in the assertion: "Jewish mysticism finds its organic place in the great spiritualist movement; it was no foreign body but part and parcel of the cultural metamorphosis in southern France." This seems to me a premature Marxist conclusion unsupported by the evidence presented in this work. Another attempt to connect Catharism with the mystical tradition of the *Bahir* has been made in Shulamit Shaḥar's Hebrew article "Catharism and the Beginnings of the Kabbalah in Languedoc," *Tarbiz* 40 (1971): 483–450.

73. Cf. the presentation and discussion of the Cathar doctrines in C. Schmidt, *Histoire et Doctrine de la Secte des Cathares ou Albigeois,* vol. 2 (Paris, 1849), 1–78; Jean Giraud, *Histoire de l'inquisition au moyen âge* (Paris, 1935), 1:35–77; Ignaz von Döllinger, *Geschichte der gnostisch-manichäischen Sekten im früheren Mittelalter* (Munich, 1890), 132–200; Hans Söderberg, *La Religion des Cathars, Étude sur le Gnosticisme de la Basse Antiquité et du Moyen Age* (Uppsala, 1949); Arno Borst, *Die Katharer* (Stuttgart, 1953), 143–222.

he appears to his prophets; the good and true God, on the other hand, is imperceptible to the eye. We may also detect a certain resemblance between the doctrine in the *Bahir* of Satan as the seducer of souls, as the prince of *tohu* and the material world fashioned from it, and the conceptions of the Cathars with regard to the role of Satan. To be sure, the texts of the *Bahir* are formulated in a thoroughly Jewish manner, and from the standpoint of the history of religions might also be rooted in other traditions of an earlier period.

One detail found in the older scholarly literature on the Cathars would certainly seem to provide an unexpected parallel to certain sources of kabbalistic demonology. This is the idea of the two wives of Satan, which is preserved in various statements on the diabolical hierarchy collected by the brothers Jacob and Isaac Cohen of Soria, who brought them back from their travels in Provence around the middle of the thirteenth century. It would conform to a surprising extent with the same idea, inferred by C. Schmidt from a remark of the generally exceedingly well informed Cistercian Peter de Vaux-Cernay, to the effect that the two biblical figures Ahalah and Ahalibah (Ezek. 23:4) were regarded by certain Cathars as the two wives of Satan. In reality, however, the source in question refers to the two wives of the supreme deity, of whom one was the mother of Christ while the other was that of Satan.[74] The analogy with the demonological speculations of the Kabbalah is therefore spurious; besides, these speculations have no direct relation to the doctrine of the aeons and the sefiroth, with which they must have become linked at a later date. Most probably the sources of the demonological systems that emerged in Provence, go back to the Orient, although the statements on this subject in the texts available to Isaac Cohen were pseudepigraphic in character.[75] Incidentally, the idea of Lilith as one of the wives, or even as the true wife, of Satan originated in these sources and subsequently passed into the *Zohar.* Earlier Oriental sources of Jewish magic mention no such marriage and seem to know nothing about a bride or wife of Satan.[76]

74. Cf. Schmidt, *Cathars ou Albigeois,* 13, and the correction in Borst, *Die Katharer,* 153.

75. Cf. pp. 293–296 in the text and notes herein.

76. In general, Arabic demonological sources appear to know nothing of a wife of Satan. But in Hebrew texts of the fourteenth century, which certainly go back in part to Arabic sources, I found mention of a "wife of the Iblis," *'esheth 'Iblis,* who is said to have slept with Pharaoh every night. Lilith plays the role of the devil's grand-

The coupling of masculine and feminine potencies in the upper world, which subsequently came to play such a significant role in the doctrines of the Spanish kabbalists, seems also to have been known in Cathar circles.[77] Here too we should assume a common source in the ancient gnosis rather than immediate influences. However, it is plausible that some details were taken over by the Cathars from Jewish mystics as, for example, the idea, well known to us from the Hekhaloth texts, that Israel was the name of a celestial angel.[78] Such ideas may also have been introduced into the movement by Jews who attached themselves to the Cathars. Thus, we learn for example that at the end of the twelfth century, a weaver named Johannes Judaeus stood at the head of the Italian Cathars as their bishop. The name would suggest, though it by no means proves, Jewish origin. The surname Judaeus does not always signify Jewish lineage in the Middle Ages.[79] Another angelological doctrine to be found only among the Cathars and in the kabbalistic traditions of Moses de Leon and the *Zohar* asserts that the prophet Elijah was an angel descended from heaven.[80] The ideas of the two groups resembled one another, here and there, on the subject of the soul's fate in the terrestrial paradise and its entry into the celestial paradise after the last judgment, and regarding the garments worn by the souls before their birth that are then preserved in heaven during their earthly existence.[81] But all of these are disparate, and unconnected details, and they concern points of secondary interest only.

As regards the fundamental conceptions, there could of course be no real agreement between the two movements, since in their rejection of the world as the creation of Satan and of the Torah as the law of Satan, the Cathars go much further in their metaphysical anti-Semitism than does the Catholic Church. Besides, the Jewish scholars of Provence were thoroughly conscious of the gulf separat-

---

mother in the secular German play on the "Pope Ioanna," written in 1480; cf. Maximilian Rudwin, *The Devil in Legend and Literature* (London, 1931), 98. (The chapter on Lilith in this book is otherwise worthless.)

77. Döllinger, *Geschichte* 1:168.

78. Ibid., 140.

79. Cf. Borst, *Die Katharer,* 99.

80. Cf. *Zohar* 2:197a, as well as *Midrash Ruth* in the *Zohar Ḥadash* (Warsaw, 1885), fol. 84c; Moses de Leon in his kabbalistic responsa, ed. Tishby, in *Qobeṣ 'al Yad,* vol. 5 (1951), 38. On the Cathar statements, see Döllinger, *Geschichte* 1:154, 169.

81. Döllinger, *Geschichte* 1:138, 156, 178.

ing the Jewish conception of the world from that of the Cathars.[82] From the circle of the Rabad himself, in other words as early as the twelfth century, we have a statement with an unmistakably anti-Cathar polemical slant from the highly esteemed R. Joseph ibn Plat, who belonged to the group of aforementioned *perushim* and Hasidim. According to him, the *Qedushah* in the morning prayer is inserted in the text of the prayer *yoṣer 'or,* which speaks of the creation of the sun and the stars, precisely "in order to oppose the opinion of those people, that the sun and the other stars do not exist by the order of their creator, blessed be He [but of Satan as the demiurge], for all of the hosts on high sanctify Him [in this prayer] and proclaim Him the one who created all and governs all."[83]

The only major doctrine in which kabbalists and Cathars seem to concur is that of the transmigration of souls. But here, too, the details are very different. The Cathars regarded the higher souls as those of fallen angels that must continue to wander until they reach the body of a Cathar *perfectus.* This connection between psychology and the myth of the angels who fell away from the good God, of major import for the Cathars, is totally absent in the Kabbalah. The earliest Kabbalah knows just as little of a migration of souls through the bodies of animals; the idea appears for the first time

---

82. On the knowledge of Cathar ideas and arguments among Jewish anti-Christian polemicists cf. the (partly dubious) material quoted by David Berger, "Christian Heresy and Jewish Polemics in the Twelfth and Thirteenth Centuries," *HTR* 68 (1975):3–4 (actually published in 1977). Ibid., p. 297 quotes a view of the "Albigenses" taken from a work allegedly written by Mordekhai ben Joseph of Avignon in the thirteenth century; but cf. also the Berger article in HTR, 303.

83. Cf. *Sefer ha-Minhagoth,* 133. On Joseph ibn Plat, cf. H. Gross, *Gallia Judaica,* 284–285, and the more recent literature cited by I. Twersky, *Rabad of Posquières* (1962), 17 n. 88. The kabbalist Azriel of Gerona also refers, in his commentary on the prayers (Ms. Oxford 1938, fol. 202a) to "men who say that the world is evil and defective and has no blessing in it"; similar remarks are found in his "Chapter on Heresies," which I published in the memorial volume for A. Gulak and S. Klein (Jerusalem, 1942), 209. It seems clear to me that these remarks refer to the Cathars. This opinion "of groups that you [Catholics] call heretics" is also quoted explicitly by Meir ben Simon of Narbonne in his anti-Christian work, which thus appears to be directed also at the Cathar heresy in his Provençal environment; cf. on this passage my study in *Sefer Bialik,* p. 152. The "heretics" referred to by Jacob Anatoli, *Malmad ha-Talmidim* (Luck, 1866), fol. 118b, are probably Cathars since they are accused of considering matter as the work (creation) of Satan. Fol. 6b speaks of them as if they were contemporaries and reference is made to "troubles in the land" (the Crusades against the Albigensians). It is therefore possible that Jacob ben Abbamari wrote in Provence and not in Italy.

around the middle of the thirteenth century, at a time when kabbalistic doctrines were already fully developed.[84] Whether we are dealing here with an echo of Cathar ideas is anyone's guess.

The revival of mythical elements in the faith of the Cathars has been noted by many scholars. In this regard, one can perhaps speak of a common mood. In the early phases of the Kabbalah, one also sees a religious movement that transcends the boundaries separating Judaism from Christianity and breathes new life into such elements. This tendency gained strength in certain circles of Provençal and, later, Spanish kabbalists, up until the *Zohar.* There is no uniform and simple answer to the question of the origin of these elements. We have examined several ideas of this kind as they reappeared in the Book *Bahir* and found that their roots went back to an internal written and perhaps also oral Jewish tradition, though with respect to the likelihood of an oral tradition, I have expressed doubts. On the other hand, we must take into consideration the possibility of one-way (Cathar-Jewish) influence, or a reciprocal influence of Cathar and Jewish ascetics upon one another. As soon as a first impulse toward the elaboration of a new gnostic system emerged, as was the case with the sources of the *Bahir,* its effect would be determined by the laws of immanent evolution. But we run again into the same problem: what exactly was specifically new? The analysis of the oldest kabbalistic sources and of the testimonies relating to their first appearance as well as of psychological considerations do not admit any doubt that something really new occurred in Provence among groups of mystics and in the related stratum of *perushim* who sat in the great talmudic academies or the schools of smaller communities, scattered across Provence and the center of France.

We must thus return to the question of the character and content of the revelation of the prophet Elijah, already briefly discussed in the first chapter. Taking into consideration the information gathered to date, two observations impose themselves. In the first place it is not difficult to see how the type of contemplative life

84. On the Cathar doctrine of the transmigration of souls cf. Söderberg, *La Religion des Cathars,* 152–154; Borst, *Die Katharer,* 168–171; Schmitz-Valckenberg, *Grundlehren katharischer Sekten des 13. Jahrhunderts* (Paderborn, 1971), 190–196. Cf. also pp. 458 and 468, herein.

led by men like the *perushim* and Hasidim could engender a psychological disposition enabling them to immerse themselves in the inner aspects of their faith. To the extent that they also had mystical inclinations—something that we can by no means presume with respect to *all* those belonging to this stratum—it is easily conceivable that many of them received illuminations and revelations from above. Such revelations can adopt two forms, both of which are attested in this group. We learn of the existence, in France and Germany of the twelfth and thirteenth centuries, of scholars who bear the surname "the prophet." This designation, by no means a mere honorific without specific connotation, indicates either that the persons thus named practiced Merkabah mysticism and experienced visionary journeys through the heavens like the celebrated tosafists Isaac of Dampierre[85] and Ezra of Montcontour or Rabbi Tröstlin the prophet in Erfurt; or that they actually appeared as prophets. Of Ezra the prophet of Montcontour it is reported that

> he showed signs and wonders. A voice was heard speaking to him out of a cloud, as God spoke to Moses. Great scholars, among them also [the illustrious mystic] Eleazar of Worms, after having fasted and prayed for days, obtained assurance that all his words were truth and that there was no falsehood in his mouth. He also produced talmudic explanations the like of which had not been heard before and he disclosed mysteries of the Torah and the prophets.[86]

This took place between 1226 and 1240, at a time when messianic predictions also emanating from him gave rise to great agitation. Here we have a case of an eminent talmudist who is at the same time a pneumatic and a prophet. From a somewhat earlier period, around

---

85. Cf. the testimony concerning him in *Ha-Ṣofeh* 5 (1921): 195, in a text dating from the thirteenth century; see also p. 251, herein.

86. On R. Ezra the prophet cf. the evidence I collected in *Tarbiz* 2 (1931): 244, 514, as well as S. Assaf in *Zion* 5 (1940): 117, 124, who rightly relates the document he there discusses to the appearance of R. Ezra. With regard to Tröstlin the prophet, cf. *Major Trends,* 88. Tröstlin is equivalent to Hebrew Menaḥem; could he be identical with Nehemiah? Around 1200 a certain R. Nehemiah the prophet is named among the German Hasidim; cf. the text composed by him, quoted in *Merkabah Shelemah* (Jerusalem, 1921), fol. 31a–32a. He is probably identical with Nehemiah ben Solomon quoted in Abraham ben Azriel's *'Arugath ha-Bosem,* ed. Urbach, 1:33. As regards a still earlier period a certain R. Jacob the prophet is mentioned by chroniclers as one of the oldest scholars of Narbonne; cf. Neubauer, *Mediaeval Jewish Chronicles,* 1:83.

1200, comes the Hebrew protocol, recorded in Rouen, of the appearance of a prophet of the same type, R. Shemuel ha-Nabi,[87] who conversed, in the presence of witnesses, with Moses and the angel Metatron as well as with the tosafist masters Rabbenu Tam and R. Elias of Paris, and who communicated mystical revelations dealing with talmudic matters. Similar revelations concerning talmudic and halakhic questions likewise occurred in the Languedoc, in the neighborhood of the Rabad and the same generation. Even if we regard as metaphorical rather than strictly mystical the expressions employed by Rabad (see pp. 205–6) with regard to the manifestation of the Holy Spirit in his school, the occurrence of such revelations is conclusively proven by the curious case of Jacob of Marvège (today in the Department of Lozère), who flourished around 1200. He sought the answers to halakhic problems through "dream questions," *she-'eloth ḥalom,* that is, through a visionary procedure.[88] Alongside figures of this kind there also appeared pure mystics whose illuminations were of an inward kind that resulted, when the occasion warranted it, in esoteric doctrines.

How did these revelations come about? Did they appear spontaneously, without preparation, to mystically inclined souls, or were they the result of specific acts and rituals that required a certain preparation? Is it possible that a theurgic element also played a role? There is no unequivocal answer to these questions. We do, however, possess certain testimonies suggesting that in this Provençal circle such revelations were linked, at least in part, to a specific ritual and that they were even tied to a particular day.[89] In the

87. Cf. the study by Nahum Golb, *History and Culture of the Jews of Rouen in the Middle Ages* (in Hebrew) (Tel Aviv, 1976), 98–99, which corrects earlier views on the subject of the prophet. Mr. Isaac S. Lange (in a letter of 6 April 1980) informs me that Ms. Oxford 271, in a text dating from the thirteenth century, quotes a "Prophet from Cologne": The reference may be, perhaps, to Abraham Achselrod (active 1260–1270) or to some other unknown person.

88. Cf. the text concerning the prophet in Paris in D. Kaufmann, *REJ* 5: 274–275. On Jacob of Marvège cf. Gross, *Gallia Judaica,* 364, and R. Margulies in the preface to his edition of Jacob's "Responsa from Heaven" (Lwow, 1929). One wonders whether the celebrated halakhist and preacher Moses of Coucy, who was led around 1236 by dreams and visions to engage in reformist activity, should not be counted among this type.

89. What follows is based upon texts I published and analyzed in *Tarbiz* 16 (1945): 196–209. The most important of these texts was published for the first time in a very corrupt form by Jellinek, *Beth he-Midrash* vol. 6 (1877), 109–111. Jellinek held it to be a piece of eleventh-century Oriental theurgy, which indeed is what it purports

middle of the thirteenth century there lived in Narbonne an old kabbalist, also a disciple of Eleazar of Worms, "of whose teacher it was attested [that is, by the people of Narbonne, and not only by the former student himself] that Elijah, may his memory be blessed, revealed himself to him every Day of Atonement."[90] Whether this teacher was the Eleazar just named or some other Provençal kabbalist is not clear. But the identity of the teacher is of less importance for us than the information concerning the date when the prophet Elijah regularly appeared to him. In the Talmud such an appearance of Elijah on the Day of Atonement is mentioned, to my knowledge, only once in passing (*Yoma* 19b) and not as something that is repeated periodically. This revelation, whose supreme value is thrown into sharp relief by the fact of its occurrence on the most sacred day of the year, was certainly attained only after spiritual preparation and special concentration.

We possess two texts that give an exact description of the magic rituals for conjuring up the archon who is in charge of the mysteries of the Torah. These rituals take place precisely during the night of the Day of Atonement. The first of these texts is a responsum attributed to two fictitious Babylonian geonim of the eleventh century that appears to have been composed in Provence around 1200 in an artificial Aramaic. We are given here, among other things, an utterly fantastic report concerning a very peculiar procedure that the scholars of earlier times supposedly followed on that night in order to conjure up "Shaddiel, the great king of the demons *(shedim)* who rule in the air," thereby to acquire possession and knowledge of "all the mysteries of heaven."[91] This mixture of angelology and demonology is very strange. It seems to me impossible that this ritual, transferred in this instance to Babylonia, was ever really practiced. But it does indicate the mood of the group from

---

to be; in reality, however, it is a product of the fantasy of the early Provençal kabbalists transposed into an Oriental setting, but reflecting conceptions and practices that were in vogue in their own circle.

90. Cf. my article in *Tarbiz* referred to in the preceding note, p. 240. Later authors, such as Abraham Herrera interpreted these statements emanating from the writings of Isaac Cohen as referring to Isaac the Blind himself. An appearance of the astral body of the deceased every Day of Atonement, which might implicitly also evoke Elijah, is mentioned by Baḥya ben Asher (1291) in connection with Genesis 49:33.

91. Cf. *Tarbiz* 16: 197–200.

which it stems. The second part likewise contains theurgic instructions, but these, we may assume, describe a ritual that was actually performed. These directions constitute only one link in a long chain of incantations given since very early times for conjuring up the "archons of the Torah." At the end of the "Greater Hekhaloth" there is a text, *Sar Torah,* that is also found independently and has the same aim. We possess several other conjurations of this kind that originated in the Orient and passed, in part, into the manuscripts of the German Hasidim. This text too, which similarly prescribes the eve and the night of the Day of Atonement as the time for the performance of these rituals, certainly originated in materials that came from Babylonia through Italy to France. But the content, half conjuration and half prayer, leaves no doubt that in its extant form it was edited in France. The text contains a long list of things that one of these *perushim* wished to learn from the archon of the Torah. He desires that his heart be opened to the study of the Torah, with special emphasis on the various types of gematria and number-mysticism and on the comprehension of various talmudic disciplines—such as cosmogony, the Merkabah, the divine glory, the *kabhod*—as well as many other specific subjects of the talmudic tradition that the author considered worth knowing.[92] There is nothing to indicate the author's acquaintance with the Kabbalah; his area of interest coincides, regarding theosophical matters as well, with that of the German and French Hasidim. At the same time, we learn that in those circles too one hoped for revelations concerning the exoteric and esoteric Torah during the night of the Day of Atonement. We have before us, therefore, the sort of prayer that Jacob the Nazirite might have recited had he wished to prepare himself for a revelation of this kind.

This brings us back to the question of the actual content of the "revelations of Elijah" as they were disclosed to these mystics of Narbonne, Posquières, and Lunel. Are we to suppose that it merely concerned religious exaltation or revelations of mysteries of diverse kinds, explanations of one thing or another, visions connected with the Merkabah, such as could be deduced, for example, from the description contained in the document under discussion? In that case there would be nothing really new; the experience would merely add

---

92. Cf. ibid., 208–209.

more information to a framework whose basic outline was already known beforehand to the praying ascetic. Or should we perhaps see in these revelations a genuinely new phenomenon that was added to the kabbalistic tradition of the *Bahir* and lent it a specific character? Since we possess no reliable documents on this subject, it is difficult to answer this question with any certainty. Nevertheless, I would be inclined to interpret our reports in the sense of the second possibility. What was really new in the Kabbalah of the circle of the Provençal scholars and *perushim,* I would venture to guess, was their doctrine of the mystical meditations at prayer.

It was indeed apparent at the end of the last chapter that here and there texts concerning the mystical meaning of prayer or of specific prayers are already found in the *Bahir* and that, for example, a verse that plays as important a role in the liturgy as the *Qedushah* (Isa. 6:3) was there correlated with the aeons or sefiroth. But in the *Bahir* we are dealing with commentaries, not with instructions for meditations intended to accompany recitation of the verse at the very moment of prayer. What is a new step and what surpasses this position is the linking of the individual words of the main prayers with specific sefiroth. This development gave rise, among the kabbalists, to the doctrine of *kawwanah,* which occupies such a major position in the history of the Kabbalah. In his recitation—for according to talmudic prescription the prayers must be uttered aloud not only thought—he who prays must concentrate his soul upon one or several divine *middoth.* In this sense the *kawwanah* represents only a practical application of the doctrine of the existence of the sefiroth or aeons in the world of the Godhead. The prayer is a symbolic reiteration of processes that occur in the pleroma of the deity. Hence it no longer resembles the old magical prayers that also, as we have seen, filtered through into the circles of the Hasidim and the first kabbalists. There too the person who prays pronounces magical words or holy names, largely incomprehensible *nomina barbara* that make up part of the text of the prayer itself. The *kawwanah,* on the other hand, represents a process that takes place exclusively within the domain of thought. It is most remarkable indeed that kabbalistic usage is, in this respect, very similar to that of the scholastics for whom *intentio* does not mean "intention" in our usual sense but rather the energy or tension of the act of cognition. (The etymology would be derived from the tension of the bow when directing the arrow.) The *kawwanah* of meditation is the tension with which the consciousness (of a person performing a prayer or another ritual act) is directed to the world or object before him.[93] Nothing is pronounced but the words of the statutory prayers, as they had been fixed of old, but the mystical meditation mentally accompanies the current of words and links them to the inner intention of the person who is praying. Among the German Hasidim the beginnings of such a process seem to be inherent in the prayer itself; among the kabbalists of Provence these initial stages led to a comprehensive discipline of contemplation concerned with man's communication with God.

It is difficult to determine to what extent this *kawwanah* also contained, from the outset, a magical element of action whose goal was to force the divine *middoth,* toward which the intention of the mediation was directed, to emanate something of their power upon the person who prays. The oldest of these *kawwanoth* to have been preserved, those of Jacob the Nazirite and the Rabad, are undoubtedly instructions relating to mystical mediations in the sense explained here, and nothing in them indicates the pursuit of another, magical aim. But let us not be deceived on this point: the differences between these domains are sometimes extremely subtle and the transition from the realm of pure contemplation to that of magic can take place in a completely unexpected manner. Sometimes it simply depends upon the forms of expression employed in the prayer. In the abstract, we can easily imagine that, by the manner in which he expressed the sense of his prayer, the person who prayed hoped to draw to himself a power from above or, in other words, to attain a position in which his prayer would be heard. This kind of prayer may well be called magical. We might contrast it with another, pure form of prayer in which the person who prays rises spiritually from degree to degree and strives to become contemplatively absorbed in the domain of the highest *middoth* or of the divine Thought itself; such a prayer may be said to contain a mystical *kawwanah.* In terms of abstract definitions of this kind, the *kawwanoth* of the oldest kabbalists certainly incline toward mysticism. But I strongly doubt whether in the concrete act of prayer performed with *kawwanah,* the distinction can be maintained. The living prayer is indeed, as Yehu-

---

93. Cf. Fritz Mauthner, *Wörterbuch der Philosophie,* vol. 1 (Munich, 1910), 584–585.

dah Halevi formulated it in one of his poems, an encounter: "As I went towards you, I found you on the road towards me."[94]

It is entirely possible that here, too, the two elements come together. Only in extreme cases does the encounter of the human and the divine will assume an unequivocally clear form that is entirely magical or altogether free of magical elements. The history of the doctrine of the *kawwanah* among the kabbalists may serve as a typical example of the various possibilities latent in every mystical doctrine of prayer. Already in the case of the first Spanish kabbalists, among the disciples of Isaac the Blind, the magical elements in their doctrine of the *kawwanah* occasionally come to the fore, as we have seen. Similar elements are discernible in the "mysteries of the prayer" of the German Hasidim, in that he who prays must think of the various names of angels as they relate—in respect to the mysticism of words and numbers—to the words of the traditional prayer. But in the earliest kabbalist circles, as far as our information extends, this magical element is missing; at least it does not manifest itself openly.

The teaching of the mystical *kawwanah* in prayer corresponds perfectly, it seems to me, to the objective and psychological conditions surrounding a doctrine born into an exclusive circle of men who possess the gift of meditation. With it, a new layer is added to the old gnostic elements that were contained in the tradition of the *Bahir,* elements that these men continued to develop in greater detail. The creation of this doctrine bears the seal of the *vita contemplativa.* No element of the old Kabbalah better corresponds to the tradition of a revelation of Elijah, and we may regard this tradition as testimony that in this circle something really new had burst forth from the depths. An indication, if not an absolute proof, of this connection may be found in the fact that the remarks concerning the revelation Elijah is supposed to have vouchsafed to Isaac the Blind or his teachers are found precisely in texts in which the *kawwanoth* of prayer were collected by the Spanish kabbalists at the end of the thirteenth century.[95] No other specific doctrine among the kabbalists

---

94. *Beṣethi liqrathekha, liqrathi meṣathikha;* cf. *Diwan des Jehuda Halewi,* vol. 3, ed. Brody (1910), 151.

95. *Gilluy 'Eliyahu* is discussed in connection with the mysticism of prayer by Shemtob ibn Gaon, *Kether Shem Tob,* printed in *Ma'or wa-Shemesh* (1839), fol. 35b;

expressly relates to this revelation and this, perhaps, provides us with a key to our problem. A notion analogous to that of *gilluy 'Eliyahu* can be found in Sufi mysticism in the accounts of revelations of Khidr (the Muslim metamorphosis of Elijah). Reports or testimonies concerning such revelations exist with regard to Muḥi al-din ibn Arabi (1165–1240) of Andalusia, who shortly before 1200 —the time of Rabad and Isaac the Blind—was still wandering about in Spain (cf. G. Husaini, *The Pantheism of Ibn Arabi,* 28.).

In its initial stage of development in the circle of the Rabad, the doctrine of *kawwanah* differed in at least on one important and instructive point from the form in which it was to become familiar to his successors. As soon as the kabbalists grasped the fundamental difference between the Emanator and the emanated, between the hidden God, subsequently to be called by them *'en-sof,* and the attributes or sefiroth by which he manifested himself and through which he acts, they immediately emphasized the thesis that there can be no *kawwanoth* addressed directly to *'en-sof.* The nature of the hidden God excludes any such possibility. If we could meet him in *kawwanah* he would no longer be that hidden God, whose concealment and transcendence cannot be sufficiently emphasized. It would therefore only be logical for the kabbalists to argue that *kawwanah* could be related only to his *middoth,* the being and reality of which affect us, whereas *kawwanah* directed toward *'en-sof* is impossible. When the kabbalists' propaganda in favor of mystical prayer reached wider circles, this thesis, with its far from innocent implications, must have incensed a good number of people. In the circle of the Rabad, however, we still find *kawwanoth* directed without the least scruple toward the "Cause of causes," which is but a philosophical expression for the Lord of the attributes and of the other causes that depend upon him. We find here certain prayers directed to the Creator of the world, *yoṣer bereshith,* but also others in which the *kawwanah* is addressed directly to the Cause of causes. The difference between the latter and the Creator of the world has already been discussed previously. *Kawwanoth* of this kind had already dis-

---

Menaḥem Recanati, commentary on the Torah (Venice, 1545), fol. 173d; Isaac of Acre, *Me'irath 'Enayim,* Ms. Munich 17, fol. 48b. Similarly, a tradition on the revelation of Elijah to the oldest kabbalists is found just before a text from Azriel's commentary on the prayers in Ms. Halberstam 388, fol. 19b; cf. his *Katalog Hebräischer Handschriften* (Vienna, 1890), 109.

appeared by the time of Rabad's son. It is precisely this difference in the conception of the *kawwanah* that proves the genuineness of these traditions, which at least partially contradict the *communis opinio* of later generations. One may suppose that the doctrine of the *kawwanah* initially represented a sort of compromise between different tendencies. Some of the oldest kabbalists still considered the direct orientation toward the Cause of causes to be possible, although the pleroma of *middoth,* potencies or forms whose nature was not yet speculatively defined, already absorbed their interest. Their gnostic way of seeing things likewise penetrated their prayer mysticism, without being able to overcome it entirely.

In sum, we can in fact say that this oldest Kabbalah was nourished by two sources: the elaboration of ancient traditional literary sources that served as a kind of raw material and the illuminations experienced by certain individuals for whom "at the beginning a door was opened to the science of the Kabbalah."[96] These illuminations no longer occur, as in the time of the Merkabah mystics, by way of an ecstatic ascent to the divine Throne. The transmission of celestial mysteries concerning cosmogony and the Merkabah no longer takes place, either, in the ways indicated in the Hekhaloth literature. The difference is considerable. Instead of rapture and ecstasy we now have meditation, absorption in oneself, and the pious, inward communion, *debhequth,* with the divine. The doctrine of the mystical *kawwanah* in prayer is about to supplant the doctrine of the ascent of the soul. The objective elements, so to speak, of the Hekhaloth literature (that is, the descriptions of the world of the Merkabah) serve as the foundation for a reinterpretation that conceives of everything that had existed there in terms of mystical symbols. I have already shown in the preceeding chapter how much the kabbalists stressed the need to support or develop their assumptions on the basis of ancient sources. But it is precisely that subjective element—the description of the ascent of the soul and its methods, the personal aspect and everything that relates to the technique of the "vision of the Merkabah"—that no longer plays a role in the circle of these earliest kabbalists and their disciples.[97] To be sure, a problem

---

96. Thus, Ms. Halberstam, just mentioned.

97. I. Tishby has drawn attention to this point as regards the circle of the kabbalists of Gerona in the introduction to his edition of Azriel's *Perush ha-'Aggadoth,* 24. But the same also applies to the earliest kabbalists of Provence.

remains unresolved in this regard. For many of the prophets named previously—such as Ezra of Moncontour and Tröstlin of Erfurt, but also for Samuel of Speyer, the father of Yehudah the Hasid—these old rules and descriptions still had a demonstrable and eminently practical significance. They continued to accomplish the ascension to heaven of the Merkabah mystics and noted what they perceived there.[98] The same is true, as we have seen, of the texts of Merkabah-mysticism in the *Bahir,* where among others the prophet Habakkuk also figures as a prototype for this kind of mysticism and the raptures corresponding to it.

This difference between the character of the Kabbalah in the Book *Bahir* and that in the circle of Rabad is noteworthy in another respect as well. The doctrine of the *kawwanah* is the product of the contemplative mood and ideals of the Middle Ages, just as the doctrine of the Merkabah betrays its ancient character. Both reflect rather faithfully the mystical possibilities of different epochs. Nevertheless, vestiges of antiquity also survive in various forms and to different degrees into the world of the Middle Ages. This continuity, however, in no way obliterated the profound differences among the different periods. In fact, as it underwent its renaissance, the ancient material was profoundly modified, as the *Bahir* shows us, and adopted new forms.

4. *Isaac the Blind and His Writings*

While the historical character of the traditions concerning the Rabad's circle in southern France has been established with considerable certainty, the situation is by no means so favorable with respect to the other French centers of mystical activity reported in kabbalistic sources of the thirteenth century. In large measure, the reports in question are found in texts whose pseudepigraphic character is indisputable. If, however, the specific content of the kabbal-

98. Cf. the reports on the heavenly journey of Ezra of Moncontour, n. 86, herein, and those concerning Samuel of Speyer, the father of Yehudah Hasid, also designated elsewhere as R. Samuel the prophet in many old sources. In the Ms. Jerusalem 8⁰ 1070, fol. 58b, one reads, in a collection containing old materials of the German Hasidim, "the verses which R. Samuel of Speyer heard when he ascended to heaven through the powerful name of God."

istic doctrine they attribute to the schools of France and the Rhineland cannot be regarded as authentic, the ascription of a "local habitation" nonetheless gives us cause for reflection and may very well provide an indication of the actual situation. We have no reason to suppose that the letters allegedly exchanged between the schools in Apulia and Worms regarding details about the kabbalistic doctrine of the sefiroth originated outside the circle in southern France that was the source of many other documents of the same style and character. The real authors of this kind of pseudepigrapha undoubtedly knew that in Worms, Speyer, and other places theosophical studies were indeed pursued and that the new Kabbalah identified these with its own interests. In fact, the latter did not recognize any difference between the mysticism of the German Hasidim and its own.

Of particular interest in this regard is the reference, recurring in several reports, to the city of Corbeil on the Seine as a center of esoteric studies. In kabbalistic pseudepigrapha it is mentioned as the residence of many so-called kabbalists between 1160 and 1220. Chronicles mention a "holy martyr," Jacob of Corbeil "the kabbalist," who is said to have died in 1203 or 1233.[99] Gross claims to have noted a "mystical tendency" in some of the quotations attributed to this Jacob, but there is nothing in them but the usual mysticism of numbers (gematria) of the kind characteristic of the German Hasidim. A lengthy epistle on the symbolism of the sefiroth preserved by Shemtob ibn Gaon is replete with fanciful accounts (see pp. 355f.) and mentions no fewer than three such kabbalists in Corbeil: a certain R. Akha; his son R. Yehudah, who is said to have studied the Kabbalah of the Babylonian geonim of the academy of Sura with a certain R. Qeshishah;[100] and a somewhat older contemporary, R. Elḥanan. An historical figure of the same name, the son of the famous tosafist Isaac of Dampierre, died a martyr's death in 1184. Traditions of a purely kabbalistic nature deriving from the mystic Elḥanan are cited in writings of the thirteenth century. One of them

---

99. This "Jacob the Saint" is mentioned in the literature of the tosafists. Cf. Gross, *Gallia Judaica,* 562. According to Gross, the year of his death should be corrected to 1193. Professor N. Golb of Chicago, in a letter of 18 June 1976, suggests that this personage is identical with "Jacob of Marvège and Corbeil." (This is the form in which the name of the aforementioned [p. 240, n. 88] author of the "Responsa from Heaven" appears in David ibn Simra's first edition). According to Golb, Gross was mistaken in assuming two different persons.

100. See p. 355, n. 309.

mentions "the heads of the talmudic academy of Lunel in the days of Rabbi Elḥanan, a colleague of Rabbi Eleazar of Worms."[101] Another kabbalist, Solomon of Corbeil, is named in a fictitious responsum by a certain Yeḥushiel bearing the entirely imaginary honorific title *gaon ashkenazi,* German gaon. He is said to have been in contact with a certain Yedidyah of Marseilles concerning kabbalistic matters.[102] The text of this responsum suggests a Provençal origin; there is no evidence that the views concerning the "emanations of the left" expounded in it were developed elsewhere than Provence. Though it is hardly possible to regard the specific traditions traced by the kabbalists to Corbeil as authentic, we cannot dismiss the possibility that they were influenced to some extent by the recollection of an actual center of esoteric studies similar to those of the German Hasidim. If we are right in assuming that Elḥanan of Corbeil is indeed the son of the famous tosafist Isaac of Dampierre then this theory would gain plausibility, for Isaac is, in fact, known as a commentator on the *Book of Creation,* on which he also delivered lectures to his disciples.[103] Early traditions concerning Isaac's nocturnal ascensions and the revelations he received from the angels are mentioned in a treatise on the year of redemption dating from the thirteenth century; however, we are unable to reach any conclusion regarding their authenticity.[104]

---

101. Concerning the historical Elḥanan, cf. Gross, *Gallia Judaica,* 165–168. His sojourn in Corbeil is not mentioned, however, in any nonkabbalistic source. In his writings on the emanations of the left, namely, the "demonic" sefiroth, Moses of Burgos quotes the "tradition of the old gaon, Rabbenu Elḥanan, the martyr," cf. *Tarbiz* 4 (1933):224. In an old apologia for the Kabbalah, Ms. Berlin Or. Qu. 833, fol.90a, he is similarly referred to as a contemporary of Eleazar of Worms. The same passage, which derives from the epistle mentioned above, is also quoted by Todros Abulafia in *Sha'ar ha-Razim,* Ms. Munich 209, fol.56b.

102. Concerning Yeḥushiel or Yeḥushiel Ashkenazi, cf. my remarks in *Tarbiz* 3: 278 and 4:68–70. According to the text of Ms. Casanatense 180, fol. 59b, Yehushiel's missive was received not only in Corbeil and by R. Yedidyah in Marseilles, but also in Worms "and from there to the grand academy in Lunel," which, however, is not dated here, as one would have expected, in the twelfth century but in the "days of the old scholars," *yeme ha-zeqenim ha-qadmonim;* cf. *Tarbiz* 4:70.

103. Cf. my book *Major Trends,* 85, 370. Elḥanan ben Yaqar of London, a disciple of Isaac's disciple from whom we also have a second commentary on the *Yeṣirah* and other mystical treatises in the spirit of the theosophy of the German Hasidim, does not seem to have been identified with the above-mentioned Elḥanan of Corbeil. On Elḥanan, cf. also G. Vajda in *Archives d'histoire doctrinale et littéraire du moyen âge* (1961) 28:17–19.

104. Cf. Alexander Marx, *Ma'amar 'al Shenath ha-Ge'ullah,* in *Ha-Ṣofeh* 5 (1921): 195.

Evidence from other sources also points to the same circle of Isaac of Dampierre, who died about 1195. After his death, his academy in Dampierre was headed by his disciple Isaac ben Abraham, the older brother of the important tosafist Samson of Sens.[105] This Isaac, who may be counted among the adepts of esotericism, is referred to as Isaac ben Abraham *Ṣarfathi* (Frenchman) by Yehudah ben Yaqar and in the old kabbalist anthologies whenever they report mystical statements in his name.[106] A remark attributed to him concerns the symbolism of unleavened bread, the taste of which is neither sweet nor bitter but in between, here symbolizing the sefirah *tif'ereth,* which mediates between opposites (sweet and bitter, mercy and justice).[107] The same Isaac figures among the addressees of Meir Abulafia of Toledo's first letter against Maimonides (around 1203–1204).[108] Since he had already died by 1210, we have early proof of relations between the first kabbalists and the northern Franch adepts of esotericism around the turn of the twelfth century. Around 1240 a kabbalistic author of the next generation mentions the *maskile ṣarfath,* the "adepts of esotericism in France" as a group, which could just as well refer to northern France as to Provence though the former is more likely.[109] In addition to Isaac, the son of Rabad, this author mentions the name of Isaac Ṣarfathi, from whom he heard semikabbalistic or entirely kabbalistic comments on the *Sefer Yeṣirah.* It appears that this is not a reference to Isaac ben Abraham but to an otherwise unknown Isaac ben Menaḥem Ṣarfathi, who must have lived in Provence.[110]

---

105. Concerning his activity as a talmudist, cf. E. Urbach, *Ba'ale ha-Tosafoth* (Jerusalem, 1955), 219–226. Naḥmanides mentioned him in his *Toledoth 'Adam* (Venice, 1598), fol .32c, and in his sermon for New Years Day, 22.

106. Cf. *JQR* 4 (1892): 250, and chap. 4, n. 6, herein. Schechter could not come to a decision concerning Isaac's origin: northern France or Provence.

107. Ms. Christ Church College 198, fol. 129. It is possible, however, that the second part of the sentence is an addition by the kabbalistic compiler and only the first part, which does not use the sefiroth symbolism of *tif'ereth,* originates from Isaac ben Abraham.

108. Cf. *Kitab al-Rasa 'il* (Paris, 1871), 4.

109. Cf. *Sefer ha-'Emunah veha-Biṭṭaḥon,* chap. 18, as well as Jacob ben Shesheth, *Meshibh Debharim,* Ms. Oxford 1585, fol. 71b, where "the rabbis of France and their *maskilim*" are also mentioned. Jacob ben Shesheth's *Meshibh Debharim Nekhoḥim* has since been published in an annotated critical edition (ed. G. Vajda [Jerusalem, 1969]), but the references to this text remain, as in the original German version of the present work, to Ms. Oxford.

110. Cf. *Sefer ha-'Emunah veha-Biṭṭaḥon,* chaps. 9 and 18. According to chapter 9, the author had been a personal disciple of Isaac Ṣarfathi. According to

Accounts of this nature, which can stray so easily into the realms of legend and pseudepigraphy, show that the Provençal kabbalists of the generation after the Rabad were concerned with establishing the historical legitimacy of their mystical tradition, the "Kabbalah." As to the identity of the actual representatives and intermediaries of the oldest traditions that arrived in Provence during the twelfth century we cannot go beyond the evidence already discussed. In Provence itself in any case, the transmission of traditions from master to disciple was complemented by direct mystical illumination, which contributed its part to the rise of kabbalistic ideas.

Among the most important representatives of this type of illumination, and as the central figure in the oldest Kabbalah, we must no doubt consider the son of the Rabad, Isaac the Blind, surnamed with the customary Hebrew euphemism *sagi nahor,* "rich in light." He is by no means the only kabbalist in the family or among his father's disciples. We learn that his older brother David also belonged to a group of mystics. The latter's son, Asher ben David, carried on the traditions of his father and uncle during the first half of the thirteenth century in Provence and at the same time served as one of the most important links with the mystical centers newly forming in northern Spain, above all in Gerona.[111] From an unknown work of his uncle[112] Asher quotes a long mystical passage relating to the continuation of the souls' development after the resurrection. I have already quoted above (page 230, preceding) an old source in which Jacob Nazir is called *parush* and Hasid. Other scholars from Narbonne and Lunel are known to have been kabbalists—for example Asher ben Saul, the author of the *Sefer ha-Minhagoth,* or Yehudah ben Yaqar, the teacher of Nahmanides, who certainly studied there though he may originally have come from northern

Steinschneider in the Munich catalogue of Hebrew manuscripts, Ms. Munich 357 of *'Emunah u-Biṭṭaḥon* gives the full name of Isaac ben Menahem Ṣarfathi both times. In chapter 18 he is quoted immediately after a passage from the *Yeṣirah* commentary of Isaac the Blind, who is there designated simply as *Ben ha-Rab,* the son of the Rabad (but never as Isaac Ṣarfathi). Furthermore, this Isaac is introduced both times as *he-ḥakham,* whereas Isaac the Blind is always called *he-ḥasid.*

111. In his *Sefer ha-Yiḥud* Asher cited his "parents and teachers," by which he meant not only his father and uncle but also his grandfather. Cf. Ḥasida's edition of Asher's writings in *Ha-Segullah,* fasc. 24, p. 14 of the special edition of his commentary on the thirteen *middoth.*

112. Cf. below, p. 307ff.

France. His commentary on the prayers[113] contains several passages of a distinctly kabbalistic character.[114] In the writings of Asher ben David, additional Provençal kabbalists are named, concerning whom we are otherwise uninformed.[115] Asher ben David displayed no pseudepigraphic tendencies. (The practitioners of this method of writing have remained anonymous and are not to be sought in the immediate circle of the Rabad and his family.) His factual assertions are trustworthy.

Isaac the Blind surpasses all his contemporaries in authority and in the lasting influence he exercised upon the earliest kabbalists. To the nineteenth-century scholars of the Kabbalah he was little more than a name. His personality and his world of mystical conceptions were so completely shrouded in obscurity that it was even possible to advance the erroneous and totally unfounded hypothesis that he was the author of the Book *Bahir.*[116] In fact, a thorough investigation of the kabbalistic sources (in particular manuscripts) proves that his pupils and their disciples had preserved many of his sayings as well as reports about him. We possess treatises that were certainly dictated by him, fragments of other such treatises, and descriptions of his personal characteristics and of the practices in which he engaged, the authenticity of which there is no reason to doubt. His *ipissima verba,* to the extent they have been preserved, are mysteriously formulated and exceedingly difficult to understand. I myself cannot pretend to have understood more than half the material transmitted in his name. He has a peculiar way of expressing himself, the syntax of his sentences is in part impenetrable, particularly in the longest of the extant texts, and he often expounds opaque ideas without explaining them. Much of what he says, therefore, remains enigmatic. Only by carefully analyzing and weighing every sentence can we obtain reliable results concerning those sections not clarified in the writings of his disciples. Fortunately, much can be learned from the literature of his disciples even when they do

113. Ed. S. Yerushalmi, 2d ed. (Jerusalem, 1979).

114. Cf. *JQR* 4 (1892): 248–250.

115. Asher ben David mentions a certain Jacob bar Samuel of Anduze (cf. Gross, *Gallia Judaica,* 64) as well as an Abraham bar Isaac of Carcassonne; cf. M. Soave, *'Oṣar Neḥmad* 4 (1863): 37.

116. Thus M. H. Landauer, *Literaturblatt des Orients* 6 (1845): col. 215. Landauer promised to furnish proof for his theory, but although no such proof was produced, far too many authors have simply copied his views.

not quote him directly, for we may suppose that whatever kabbalistic conceptions they have in common can be traced back to him.

Isaac the Blind is a kabbalist through and through. We possess no exoteric writings by him—halakhic, homiletical, moral, or otherwise.[117] An epistle that seems to be a sort of responsum dealing with the text of a benediction in the *'Amidah* prayer, of which only a single manuscript exists, is in fact full of kabbalistic allusions. It is clear that his reputation and authority did not rest upon his distinction in any other branch of Torah study. According to a statement of Shemtob ibn Gaon, Isaac's father, the Rabad, contented himself with allusions to kabbalistic teachings in many passages of his commentary on the Talmud, since he relied completely upon the mystical knowledge of his son. This assertion appears to confuse cause with effects. The Rabad's restraint may well be explained otherwise. It is also doubtful whether the writings of Isaac, in which according to Shemtob ibn Gaon every single word constitutes an allusion to great mysteries, had already been compiled before the death of his father as repositories of kabbalistic knowledge. We have no precise information concerning his biography and the composition of his writings. We must assume, however, that he lived to an old age, for his letter to Gerona, which I shall discuss in the next chapter, must have been written around 1235. On the other hand, quotations from his works are already found in works composed earlier, such as Ezra ben Solomon's commentary on the talmudic aggadoth. Therefore he must have lived from about 1165 to 1235.

He, too, undoubtedly belonged to the group of *perushim* that we have already discussed, although he is never characterized as *parush* or *nazir,* but always as the Hasid. In the writings of the Spanish kabbalists it is he who is meant whenever reference is made simply to "the Hasid" without further qualification or name, just as in the writings of the German Hasidim this honorific title by itself always refers to Yehudah the Hasid. His disciples rarely use his actual name, and usually refer to him simply as "our master, the Hasid" or "the Hasid." His nephew, Asher ben David, speaks of

117. Only one completely exoteric prayer of a general character has been published by Gabrielle Sed (*REJ* 126 [1967]: 265–267. The name of the author of this prayer is given as "the learned Hasid R. Isaac of blessed memory, the son of the Master R. Abraham ben R. David of blessed memory." The prayer is published from a Spanish prayer book of 1484 and may well be authentic.

him as "my master, my uncle, the holy Hasid R. Isaac the son of the Rabh." For them Rabh simply meant Rabad. Judging by the superscription that appears over many of the manuscripts of his commentary on the *Book of Creation,* Isaac seems to have lived at least temporarily in Posquières.

The kabbalistic tradition of the end of the thirteenth century uniformly reports that he was blind. However, the solitary statement of Isaac of Acre to the effect that "this Hasid, in his whole life, never saw anything with his terrestrial eyes"[118] is, in my opinion, questionable. His immediate disciples never speak of blindness. The assumption that he was blind from birth seems to be contradicted by the elaborate discussion of light mysticism in a large number of the extant fragments of his work and in his commentary of the *Sefer Yeṣirah.* The discussion contained in his responsum on the formula "God of David and builder of Jerusalem," appearing in one of the benedictions of the daily *'Amidah,*[119] also militates against that assumption. It betrays the efforts of a scholar who was in the habit of thoroughly examining old manuscripts. He makes reference to out-of-the-way mystical texts of the Gaonic period (a magical adaptation of the *'Amidah* entitled "the prayer of Elijah," *ṣelothah de-'Eliyahu,* preserved in a few manuscripts),[120] as well as to writings that have not survived. On one occasion he writes "I found in an old manuscript of the maḥzor" as if he himself had made the discovery, not one of the pupils working for him. This leads us to assume that it was only during the course of his life that he lost his sight. On the other hand, his contemplative mysticism is not essen-

118. Isaac of Acre, *Me'irath 'Enayim,* Ms. Munich 17, fol.140b, who adds that he heard this from a pupil of Isaac the Blind who had accompanied his teacher as an acolyte. This is chronologically impossible, for Isaac of Acre did not arrive in Spain until approximately 1305, some seventy years after the death of Isaac the Blind. Perhaps in place of "I have it from the mouth of a scholar who saw . . . the Hasid, who served before him," we should read, "who saw a pupil of the Hasid," etc.

119. So far only one fragment of this epistle exists in Ms. British Museum, Margoliouth 755, fol. 118a. The kabbalists repeatedly attested that Isaac employed precisely this formula in the *'Amidah;* cf. *Sefer ha-'Emunah weha-Biṭṭaḥon,* chap. 15; Baḥya ben Asher, commentary on the Torah, Venice 1544, fol. 45d. The author of the letter refers to himself in the first person: "I, Isaac, the son of the Hasid [Rabad], may the memory of the just be for a blessing."

120. The magical prayer of Elijah, for example, is preserved in Ms. Cambridge, Add. 502[2]. Perhaps the prayer is identical with the one mentioned by Isaac's grandfather in *Sefer ha-'Eshkol,* ed. Ḥanokh Albeck (Berlin, 1910) as has been suggested by Sch. Abramson.

tially visual. Whatever the case may be, the anecdotes told about him prove only that he was blind during his adult life. It was also said of him that he could sense the aura surrounding a man and that this perception enabled him to predict who would live and who would die. He also knew whether the soul of a man had passed through previous transmigrations or whether it was one of the "new" souls.[121] As far as his charismatic gifts are concerned, tradition has it that his prayers for the sick were as effective as those of the renowned talmudic charismatic Ḥanina ben Dosa.[122] His nephew undoubtedly had him in mind, too, when he wrote about the mystics of his surroundings, calling special attention to the efficacy of their prayers:

> The mystics of Israel [*maskile Yisra'el*], those who seek God, who call out to Him and are answered, who share in all the misery of their fellowmen, who supplicate before the face of God on their behalf and mortify themselves, whose prayers are accepted [by God] and through

---

121. Shemtob ibn Gaon, *Kether Shem Tob,* Ms. Munich 341, fol. 50a (the printed text in *Ma'or wa-Shemesh,* fol. 52a is corrupt): The master, R. Isaac, the son of Rabh, possessed this knowledge, and felt the aura [*shehayah margish be-hargashath ha-'awir*], even though he was blind, and could say, "this one will live and that one will die" (rather like the thaumaturge R. Ḥanina ben Dosa in the first century, according to the account given the Mishnah in *Berakhoth,* v. 5). Recanati, obviously borrowing from Shemtob, tells the same story in his commentary on the Torah (Venice, 1545), fol. 209a. Recanati, fol. 70a, also mentions the tradition concerning the "new souls": "I have heard that the Hasid, our master Isaac, the son of R. Abraham ben David, could tell by a man's face whether he was from the 'new' or the 'old' souls." The literal sense of this quotation suggests Isaac's knowledge of physiognomy, which would also imply that he lost his sight only later in life. The author of the *Tiqqune Zohar,* writing at the same time as Recanati, indicates criteria for determining from the lines of the forehead whether a man had already passed through transmigrations and at which stage he was at present. Shemtob ibn Gaon's teacher, Isaac ben Todros, told his disciple that in his time a scholar was still alive who was able to distinguish between old and new souls, Ms. Munich 341, fol. 18b (missing in the printed text). Chronologically this can hardly refer to Isaac the Blind, but rather to an unknown kabbalist of the next generation, around 1260. Shemtob ibn Gaon wrote the first draft of his *Kether Shem Tob* at the age of twenty-eight, around 1300; cf. *Zion (Collected Papers of the Historical and Ethnographical Society)* 6 (Jerusalem, 1934): 50.

122. Cf. Recanati, fol. 209a, and *Kether Shem Tob,* Ms. Munich 341, fol. 50a. Isaac of Acre reports in the above-mentioned passage, fol. 140b, that Isaac instructed the disciple who was accompanying him to accelerate his steps as much as possible when passing near a church. "He did this on his own initiative for the glory of God, with whom his thought was in communion, and because the presence of the 'spirit of impurity' over the place of the foreign cult compelled him to interrupt his thoughts."

whom many miracles have been performed, both for the benefit of the individual and of the community.[123]

Isaac is thus by no means the only "master of prayer" in this group, in the specific sense of the term, although he is the most outstanding. In this circle, a life of intense prayer is linked to the doctrine of *kawwanah.* Detailed instructions by Isaac concerning the meditations to be performed during the recitation of certain prayers have been preserved.[124] In those instructions, the mysticism of prayer is already related to the fully developed doctrine of the aeons into which the kabbalistic gnosis had crystallized, forming a close relationship with the contemplative mysticism of the divine and human *maḥshabah,* "thought." The extant remains of his teaching are all based on a fully articulated symbolism and theory of the sefiroth as the divine *middoth* flowing out of the primordial thought, the "pure thought." In addition to these *kawwanoth,* we also possess notes of an entirely speculative character that were probably written down by his disciples. Perhaps he also wrote some of these notes himself before he lost his sight. Above all, there can be no doubt as to the authenticity of the commentary on the Book *Yeṣirah* that appears under his name, and of which some fifteen manuscripts are known to exist.[125] His immediate disciples quote this commentary and copy parts of it without mentioning their source by name. One passage in chapter 3 clearly shows that a disciple is transcribing Isaac's lecture or writing from his dictation. He introduces a line of

---

123. Cf. the text of the passage in *Sefer Bialik* (1934), 151 and p. 401, herein.

124. Cf. the sources named, n. 95, herein, as well as the *kawwanoth,* communicated in my *Reshith ha-Qabbala,* 245–248, of his disciple Abraham Ḥazan, the cantor of the community of Gerona. These *kawwanoth* are even simpler than those developed by another pupil of Isaac, R. Azriel, also in Gerona, in his commentary on the prayers; cf. herein, pp. 372–373, and n. 24, ibid.

125. Manuscripts of Isaac's commentary are found, for example, in Jerusalem 8° 2646; Cincinnati, Hebrew Union College; British Museum Or. 11791; Oxford, Christ Church College 198; Leiden, Warner 24; Vatican Ebr. 202; Angelica 27, as well as another manuscript in the library of the Jewish community of Rome; Berlin, Staatsbibliothek Qu. 942; Amsterdam, Library of the Portuguese Congregation B. 49; London, Jews' College, Hirshfield 174; Harvard College, Ms. Friedmann 1; New York, Jewish Theological Seminary, Ms. Mortimer Schiff, no. 76326, as well as Halberstam 444; Milan, Ambrosiana, Bernheimer 57 (unrecognized until now). As an appendix to my Hebrew University lecture course on the Kabbalah in Provence (mimeographed ed., 1963) I gave the full text of the commentary, based on the manuscripts of the Angelica and Hebrew Union College.

thought with the words "our teacher says," which in the general context certainly means Isaac himself and not one of his teachers. The text plainly bears Isaac's personal stamp. The same holds true of many of his other notes. His quotations are simply introduced by his disciples with *leshon he-ḥasid.* That is in accord with their often enigmatic brevity and intensity of expression. The commentary barely exceeds five thousand words, of which three quarters make up the first three chapters. Unfortunately, none of his disciples or their pupils composed a commentary upon these notes, a work that would have been of great use to us. Only Isaac of Acre, in the first third of the fourteenth century, prepared a paraphrase of his explanations of a few of the *mishnayoth* of the first chapter.[126]

Furthermore, until the fourteenth century a work of Isaac containing "mysteries" regarding various passages in the Torah was known; they treated, among other subjects, the account of Creation and the mystical reasons for several of the commandments. A substantial number of fragments from this work, occasionally also fairly long ones, have been preserved by the kabbalists of Gerona and the disciples of Solomon ibn Adreth as *leshon he-ḥasid.* The latter's school in Barcelona apparently inherited a great deal of written material from Naḥmanides of Gerona. In any case, the tradition of the schools seems to be continuous. Above all, Meir ibn Sahula included many quotations in his supercommentary on the kabbalistic passages of Naḥmanides' commentary of the Torah. The relatively homogeneous character of these texts leads me to suppose, as I have already said, that they derive from a single collection or work.[127] To these should be added some smaller fragments that his pupils received orally, as well as some anonymous material that can be attributed to him. Thus all his disciples present an almost identical interpretation of the Sophia in Job 28, in terms of the doctrine of the sefiroth.[128] Job 28:12: "But where can wisdom be found?" is al-

126. I have published Isaac of Acre's commentary in *Kiryath Sefer* 31 (1956): 376–396.

127. Sahula's commentary, *Bi'ur Sodoth ha-Ramban,* was edited in Warsaw in 1875. In the old Ms. Munich 344 of Todros Abulafia's *'Oṣar ha-Kabhod,* the quotation is introduced by the words: "I have seen it written in the *book* of the Hasid, our master Isaac." Other manuscripts and the printed edition (Warsaw, 1879), 46, only say: "in the *name* of the Hasid," etc.

128. In fact, Isaac also alludes to the doctrine of the sefiroth in his commentary on *Sefer Yeṣirah,* with reference to Job 28:23. In a letter I have published in

ways interpreted here as if it read: "But wisdom comes out of nought," that is, "the nought of thought," the place where all thought ceases, or rather, where it becomes the divine thought itself, which, as the highest sefirah, now is designated as Nought or the mystical Nothing. It seems clear to me that this interpretation of Job 28 originated in Provence. It represents, in effect, a reinterpretation in kabbalistic terms of views attested by Saadya Gaon, though opposed by him as "sheer imagination," but held by ninth-century Jewish Platonists or atomists, who related these same verses to the doctrine of "spiritual points," by which they meant the ideas or possibly also the atoms. In the old paraphrastic translation of Saadya dating from the pre-Tibbonite period, which was used by the earliest kabbalists before the adoption of the Tibbonite translation, the Hebrew term, modeled after the Arabic *ruḥaniyyim* is employed for atoms. In Provence this expression was no longer understood, and next to nothing was known about the doctrine of the atomists; thus it became possible to identify Saadya's "spiritual elements" and "subtle points" with the sefiroth.[129] They are now the "mystical atoms," and Job 28 is regarded as a locus classicus for the support of this theory.

Apart from the *Yeṣirah* commentary, we have about seventy different fragments stemming from Isaac as well as statements re-

---

Sefer Bialik, 156, Ezra ben Solomon says that the Hasid interpreted Job 28:1ff. as referring to "the ten sefiroth." But the fully elaborated interpretation was preserved only by his disciples, Ezra and Naḥmanides.

129. Cf. Saadya's *'Emunoth we-De'oth* (Leipzig, 1864)1:3, 22, concerning this interpretation. The use of the old paraphrase of Saadya's work at the beginning of the thirteenth century by a kabbalistic group whose writings we still possess can be proven through an examination of the literature of this circle, which I designate further on as the *'Iyyun* circle or the group of the *Sefer ha-'Iyyun.* In a "Prayer of R. Neḥunya ben Haqqanah" that should be attributed to this circle the sefiroth are explicitly designated, in accordance with the definition borrowed from Saadya, as atoms, "indivisible parts," *ḥalaqim she-'enam mithḥalqim,* which is a literal reproduction of the paraphrase, Ms. Munich 42, fol.323a, b. There is some difference of opinion with regard to which Greek conception—atomist, Platonic, or Pythagorean—Saadya had in mind; cf. Jacob Guttman, *Die Religionsphilosophie des Saadia* (Göttingen, 1882), 47–48; Israel Efros, *Louis Ginzberg Jubilee Volume,* vol. 1 (New York, 1945), 132–142. For our analysis this question is not relevant, though I would be inclined to believe that the express mention of Jewish adepts of this idea at the beginning of the tenth century rather indicates that Saadya is in fact speaking of a particular group of Jewish atomists. The text of the old paraphrase, which Guttman did not take into account, was far more suggestive of a reinterpretation in the spirit of the doctrine of the sefiroth than the text of ibn Tibbon's translation.

garding him and his traditions that can be regarded as genuine. On only two occasions does he refer to his father.[130] Although most of the texts are very short, they nonetheless constitute a considerable fund of resource materials, even if we disregard, as we should, later erroneous attributions, or pseudepigraphic texts.[131] I include among these authentic pieces a commentary preserved in a New York manuscript on the beginning of *Midrash Konen,* a cosmogonic-cosmological compilation consisting of Merkabah and *bereshith* texts. The commentary is attributed to a certain R. Isaac *ha-zaqen,* the elder; but the terminology and the basic ideas are so close to those of Isaac the Blind in his commentary on the *Yeṣirah* that I am inclined to consider both Isaacs as one and the same person.[132] It is not surprising either, that Isaac wrote mystical commentaries on texts relating to the creation of the world, such as he found them in Genesis 1, the Book *Yeṣirah* and the *Midrash Konen.* The mysticism of light is formulated in a particularly incisive manner in the last named of these texts, but this is clearly due to the wording of this midrash itself.

The opinion of some scholars that the epithet "father of the Kabbalah," conferred on Isaac the Blind in 1291 by the kabbalist Baḥya ben Asher,[133] should be considered evidence that the kabbalists themselves looked upon Isaac as the creator of the Kabbalah is entirely without foundation.[134] *'Abi ha-kabbalah* means nothing other than "particularly eminent in the Kabbalah." It is an imitation of the honorific title *'abi ha-ḥokhmah,* conferred upon Yoḥanan ben Zaqqai in the Palestinian Talmud *(Nedarim).* Moses too is designated in this way at the beginning of *Wayyiqra Rabba.* Eleazar of

---

130. Thus in *'Emunah u-Biṭṭaḥon,* the end of chap. 1, and in Ezra, *Perush 'Aggadoth,* Ms. Vatican 185, fol. 11a.

131. Among these are certain statements of Moses of Burgos in his tract on the left emanation, where he occasionally refers explanations of the first, the fourth, and the sixth demoniacal emanations to alleged traditions of Isaac, cf. my study of this question in *Tarbiz* 3 (1932): 276–279. Samson of Ostropol (d. 1648) asserts in the preface to his *Dan Yadin,* that the later demonological book *Qarnayyim,* upon which Samson wrote a commentary (and which he had probably composed himself) was attributed by many authorities to Isaac.

132. The text appears in a collection whose materials date back to the fourteenth century and which is found in Ms. Enelow Memorial Collection 699 of the Jewish Theological Seminary in New York. We are dealing with the notes of a disciple that were based upon a lecture or dictation of Isaac.

133. Cf. Baḥya's commentary on the Torah, Genesis 32:10.

134. Cf. M. H. Landauer in *Literaturblatt des Orients* (1845): col. 215. M. Ehrenpreis, *Emanationslehre,* 20.

Worms, in his commentary on the prayer book (Ms. Paris 772, Fol. 73) calls Yehudah Hasid "father of wisdom." Phrases of this kind teach us nothing about the origins of the Kabbalah.

5. Isaac's Doctrine of the 'En-sof *and the Sefiroth*

In Isaac's writings, the esoteric tradition, which was still fluid in the *Bahir,* crystallized in fixed conceptions and continued its development in a manner peculiar to the author. He quotes the *Bahir,* though only infrequently, but also implicitly assumes his reader's acquaintance with it.[135] It is obvious that an intense spiritual activity had taken place during the interval that separates this book from his own thought. Much of that activity may be considered as Isaac's personal contribution and reflective of his mystical conceptions. A great deal may have reached him from the traditions of the circle of Lunel. To judge by the uniform terminology of his disciples, the use of the expression Kabbalah in the sense of esoteric tradition, that is, secret doctrine, seems to go back to him, even if the word does not appear in any of the extant texts written by him.[136] The transition from the usual meaning of the word Kabbalah to the esoteric nuance

135. In the fragments of Isaac quoted by Sahula we find three explicit citations of the *Bahir:* fol 23b (section 83); 25c (section 104); 32d (section 96). In a quotation of the "opinion of the Hasid" with regard to the origin of the souls from the sefirah of the Righteous, that is, the foundation of the universe, in Ezra's commentary on the aggadoth (Ms. Vatican 441, fol. 33a), the *Bahir* statement regarding the souls that fly out from there is mentioned without any indication of its source. A word should be said here about the probable relations of the Provençal Kabbalah to the ideas of Abraham ibn Ezra. N. Krochmal *(Moreh Nebhukhe ha-Zeman)* has repeatedly drawn attention to this subject, which, however, still requires futher research. Ibn Ezra's writings were current in the Provence, having been partly composed there and in France before the rise of the Kabbalah. It should be noted (as H. Greive, *Studium zum jüdischen Neuplatonismus* [Berlin, 1973], 22, has correctly pointed out) that Krochmal's interpretations seem to be closer to the Kabbalah than to the system of ibn Ezra.

136. His nephew in particular already used such formulas as "in conformity with the Kabbalah," or "in the language of the Kabbalah" with great precision, and not in the older sense of tradition in general. The same is true for all the kabbalists of Gerona. There the mystics are already called *ba'ale ha-kabbalah* and *ḥakhme ha-kabbalah.* However it is curious that Asher ben Saul and Meir ben Simon, who wrote in Provence at the beginning of the thirteenth century, did not employ the term "kabbalists" for this group, although this designation was nevertheless current in the writings of Ezra, which were surely known to Meir ben Simon.

was easily made. We find the first sign of it in Yehudah ben Barzilai. Speaking of the creation of the Holy Spirit, which is the Shekhinah, he says: "The sages did not deal with it at length, in order that men would not come to form ideas concerning 'what is above,'[137] etc. and that is why they were accustomed to transmitting this thing in whispers and in secret, as a tradition to their pupils and to the sages."[138] The ordinary expression "to transmit something as Kabbalah [orally]" here acquires through the addition of the adverbs "in whispers and in secret" the quality of an esoteric tradition. Somewhat similar is the use of the term in an Arabic text of 1223 that counters Maimonides in its assertion that where the Kabbalah of the sages of Israel is mentioned the reference is to the baraithoth of the Hekhaloth literature as the true interpretation of *Ma'aseh Merkabah* (A. Harkavy, in his appendix *Ḥadashim gam Yeshanim* to the Hebrew translation of Graetz's *Geschichte* 5:47). But contrary to Harkavy's view, this passage in no way proves that the term Kabbalah in its novel, technical sense was known in the Orient in 1223. That, precisely, is Kabbalah, in the sense of the Provençal school. But Eleazar of Worms also cites traditions of this kind—for example, with respect to the names of the angels—as "Kabbalah."[139] Besides, still other expressions were used in Isaac's circle. In a letter sent to Gerona, Isaac himself speaks in this sense of *ḥokhmah,* wisdom or science, without adding the adjective *penimith,* "esoteric," although this often occurs in other places.[140] In the twelfth century, the expression of *sefarim penimiyyim* appears in France for writings considered there as esoteric literature, such as *Seder 'Eliyahu Zuṭṭa.*[141] In the liturgical manual *Sefer ha-Manhig,* composed in

137. A quotation from the Mishnah *Ḥagigah* 2:1 prohibiting this.

138. Yehudah ben Barzilai, commentary on *Yeṣirah,* 189. The end of the citation reads as follows in the original: *hayu mosserim ha-dabhar le-talmidehem ule-ḥakhamim be-laḥash ube-ṣin'a be-kabbalah.*

139. Thus, for example, in his *Hilkhoth ha-Kisse',* printed in *Merkabah Shelemah* (1921), fol. 28a. Similarly also Eleazar's *Sefer ha-Shem,* Ms. Munich 81, fol. 233b, quotes "Commentaries of the Gaon R. Hai in his Kabbalah" (that is, as esoteric tradition), which deal with the magic names of God.

140. Cf. the text of the letter in *Sefer Bialik,* 143. The use of *penimi* in the sense of esoteric corresponds to the Arabic *baṭin,* and is also current in philosophical literature. The kabbalists of the thirteenth century often call their gnosis *ḥokhmah penimith.*

141. Cf. *Maḥzor Vitry,* 112. Friedmann already drew attention to this fact in connection with pseudo-*'Eliyahu Zuṭṭa,* 23–24.

1204 by Abraham ben Nathan ha-Yarḥi of Lunel, who in his youth had studied with the Rabad, the "Greater Hekhaloth" are twice designated by this term.[142]

The *Bahir*'s idea of the sefiroth appears in Isaac's writings in a fully crystallized form. In his commentary on the *Yeṣirah* 4:3, the verse 1 Chronicles 29:11 is used for the first time as a biblical reference for the names and the sequence of the seven lower sefiroth, especially the first five among them: "Yours, Lord, are the greatness *(gedullah),* might *(geburah),* splendor *(tif'ereth),* triumph *(neṣaḥ),* and majesty *(hod)*—yes all *(kol)* that is in heaven and on earth; to You, Lord, belong kingship *(mamlakhah)* and preeminence above all." From here come the designations not yet used in the *Bahir*, of *gedullah* for *ḥesed, tif'ereth* for *'emeth,* and *hod.* Isaac himself for the most part uses the names *ḥesed* and *paḥad* (as in the *Bahir*) instead of *gedullah* and *geburah.* The name *tif'ereth,* however, is already familiar to him. Whereas the word *kol,* occurring in the aforementioned verse, already served in the *Bahir* as an epithet designating the "Righteous," Isaac uses for this sefirah the noun "Righteous" and the epithet "Foundation of the world." For the last sefirah, on the other hand, he employs almost exclusively an epithet still not familiar to the *Bahir,* although it is undoubtedly alluded to there. This epithet is *'aṭarah,* a synonym for *kether,* which designates the lowest of the ten "crowns." Like the *Bahir,* he names the first three sefiroth *kether* or *maḥshabah, ḥokhmah* and *binah.*

In his commentary on *Yeṣirah,* Isaac mentions many of these sefiroth in the framework of fixed schemata, but this does not always enable us to comprehend the sequence of the sefiroth within them.[143] What is strange is that in point of fact the structure of the sefiroth beyond the supreme three only interests him in detail when it is a question of prayer mysticism, or the interpretation of certain ritual commandments. They have their importance as stages of the contemplative ascent or of the eschatological elevation of the soul,

---

142. Cf. *Manhig* (Berlin, 1855), fol. 15b, 16b. A diametrically opposed terminology is found around the same time in Germany, in Eliezer ben Joel Halevi, *Rabi'ah,* ed. Aptowitzer, 2:196. He calls the books of the Merkabah *Sifre ha-Ḥiṣonim,* probably in order to underline their noncanonical character.

143. In the enumeration of the six directions of space, *qeṣawoth,* it is not *ḥesed,* but the first sefirah, which is mentioned as that of Height, *rom.* The manner in which the two *shins* in the tefillin are coordinated with the sefiroth is completely enigmatic, and so are many other details.

after death, to even higher spheres. But never are any coherent thoughts presented concerning their function and structure. This is particularly the case for the potencies of *tif'ereth, yesod* and *'aṭarah,* which play an especially important role in the evolution of the doctrine of the sefiroth. In contrast to this lack of interest in detail, one discerns in Isaac a more pronounced interest in the totality of the spiritual potencies expressed in language and, in a more general manner, in spiritual entities. Having said that, the terminological differences between concepts like sefiroth, *middoth,* letters (of the alphabet) and *hawwayoth* (literally: essences) are by no means always clear, and their interpretation is often fraught with difficulties.

However, these difficulties are closely related to what is truly new in Isaac's Kabbalah. Indeed, from the historical point of view their interest lies in the combination of the world of ideas of the *Bahir* and the entirely new elements that erupt, inspired by gnostic ideas, into the oldest form of the Kabbalah as represented by the *Bahir.* This combination reflects speculative interests whose origin is no longer essentially determined by Gnosticism but rather by Neoplatonism and a language mysticism generated by the latter. Isaac is visibly struggling with new thoughts for which he is as yet unable to find clear and definitive expression. The awkwardness of his new terminology militates against the supposition that this lack of clarity, which often makes it so difficult to penetrate his meaning, is intentional. His new terminology seems to be derived from philosophy, although we cannot identify its philosophical sources in the Hebrew tradition. The special importance of Isaac's commentary on the *Yeṣirah* lies in the attempt to read into the old texts the new, speculative thoughts of a contemplative mystic. But we are no less surprised by the boldness with which he presents far-reaching ideas in his other cosmological fragments and in his remarks concerning the mystical theory of sacrifice. The particular manner in which Isaac applies his ideas to the task of man, to the connection between the terrestrial and the celestial worlds, and to eschatological matters merits closer consideration.

The path of the mystic, described by Isaac at the beginning of his commentary on the *Yeṣirah,* is (as Isaac of Acre already recognized in his paraphrase of several of these passages in his own commentary) that of systematically uncovering the divine—by means of reflective contemplation and within the innermost depths of such contemplation. Isaac postulates three stages in the mystery of the deity and its unfolding in creation and revelation. They are called in his works the Infinite *('en-sof),* Thought, and Speech. The principle of Speech, *dibbur,* is divided into the plurality of speeches and words, by which he often means the seven lower sefiroth, called not only *dibburim* but also *debharim.* In Hebrew *dabhar* means "word" as well as "thing," and this coincidence was obviously decisive for the formation of Isaac's thought. The sefiroth, above all the seven lower ones, are the words or things "which shape reality."[144] They take the place of the *ma'amaroth,* the logoi of the *Bahir.* The "Thought," too, already comes from this text, as we saw in the previous chapter. But what is entirely new is the emphasis laid on a domain of the divine that is above all reflective contemplation, indeed above the divine Thought itself, a domain called by Isaac "the cause of Thought" and designated by a new term: *'en-sof.*

The birth of this concept is of great interest for the history of the Kabbalah. This designation is usually explained as a borrowing from Neoplatonism. Christian Ginsburg, whose essay on the Kabbalah has been appropriated by many authors (who do not always bother to acknowledge their source), says:

> Any doubt upon this subject must be relinquished when the two systems are compared. The very expression *En Sof* which the Kabbalah uses to designate the Incomprehensible One, is foreign, and is evidently an imitation of the Greek *Apeiros.* The speculations about the *En Sof,* that he is superior to actual being, thinking and knowing, are thoroughly Neo-Platonic."[145]

Ginsburg, however, proceeded on the completely erroneous assumption that the oldest document of the authentic Kabbalah was the Neoplatonic catechism on the sefiroth composed by Azriel, Isaac's disciple. There the notion is in fact explained in a manner that comes particularly close to Neoplatonic thought. But this says nothing about the origin of the concept. Indeed, the expression is strange, by virtue of its very grammatical formation. It certainly is not a rendering of a fixed philosophical idiom, whether it be from

---

144. The expression *debharim ha-methaqqenim ha-meṣi 'uth* appears frequently in his writings—for example, in Ms. Halberstam 444 New York, fol. 29b on Genesis 1:26: "Let us make man: he took counsel with the words that shape reality and by means of which everything was realized [Hebrew: *yaṣa bahem le-ma 'aseh*]."

145. Christian David Ginsburg, *The Kabbalah* (London, 1865), 105.

the Greek or from the corresponding Arabic *(lā-nihāya)*—in spite of the readiness with which some scholars have adopted this view.[146] The form *'en-sof* corresponds in no way to the translations of privative notions in medieval Hebrew literature: in these the conjunction *bilti* always precedes the negated notion; the negation *ayin* is never employed for this purpose. Thus "inconceivable" is rendered by *bilti-mussag* and not by *'en hassagah,* and "infinite" is *bilti ba'al-takhlith* and not *'en-sof.* The form *'en-sof* is altogether unusual, and Graetz had good reason to see it in a proof of the late origin of the term. However, he should have added that in the Hebrew literature of the Middle ages, too, it represents a completely isolated phenomenon. It is only in biblical literature that we find forms such as *'en 'onim* or *'en 'eyyal,* for powerless. Subsequently, locutions of this kind disappear completely.

How, then, are we to understand the origin of the term *'en-sof?* It did not result from a deliberate translation, but from a mystical interpretation of texts that contain the composite term *'en-sof* in a perfectly correct adverbial sense, and not as a specific concept. The doctrine of Saadya Gaon, in particular, abounds with affirmations of the infinity of God—in fact, it is asserted at the very beginning of his well-known "Supplication" (*Siddur R. Saadia* [1941], 47), and in the old Hebrew paraphrase, known among the Provençal Kabbalists as well as the German Hasidim, it is reiterated incessantly. Tobias ben Eliezer, who wrote around 1097, also stressed precisely this quality of God, in the context of a reference to the mystical Hekhaloth writings. For him God is "the first up to the unfathomable, the primordial beginning up to the infinite *('ad 'en-takhlith),* among the last up to infinity *('ad 'en-sof).*" The adverbial construction is perfectly correct. "Up to infinity" results from a combination of "up to there, where there is no end." Expressions of this kind, in which *'en-sof* has the function of an adverbial complement, are found with particular frequency in the writings of Eleazar of Worms. We find the same usage in the *Bahir* (cf. p. 130 preceding). Thus, Eleazar writes, for example: "When he thinks of that which is above, he should not set any limit to this thought, but thus [should

146. Cf. on this subject A. Harkavy, in his appendix to the Hebrew translation of Graetz's *Geschichte der Juden* 5:43–46. Utterly fantastic speculations concerning the ancient origin of the expression *'en-sof* can be found in Robert Eisler, *Weltenmantel und Himmelszelt* (Munich, 1909), 470–474.

he think of God]: high, higher up to the Boundless [*'ad 'en-qeṣ*]; down deep, who can find him; and the same above in the expanse of all the heavens . . . and outside the heavens up to the infinite [*le'en-sof*]." Or: "in the Throne of Glory are engraved holy names, which are not transmitted to any mortal, and which sing hymns unto infinity [*meshorerim shiroth le'en-sof*]."[147] The transition here from the innumerable hymns sung by holy names and angels[148] to a hypostasis that, as a mystical reader might perhaps conceive it, "sings hymns to *'en-sof*" seems easy enough. The term *'en-sof* came into being when one of the Provençal kabbalists read this combination of words that actually represents a phrase as a noun, possibly influenced by the aforementioned kind of adverbial composites and perhaps also by some expressions in the *Bahir.* The sentence now referred to an elevation or orientation of the thought toward a supreme degree of being for which the appellation is *'en-sof.* It is, after all, one of the principles of mystical exegesis to interpret all words, if possible, as nouns. This emphasis on the noun character, on the name, may be taken as an indication of a more primitive attitude in the mystics' conception of language. In their view language is ultimately founded on a sequence of nouns that are nothing other than the names of the deity itself. In other words, language is itself a texture of mystical names.

We cannot determine with certainty the combination of words or specify the contexts from which *'en-sof* was elevated to the rank of a concept, a technical term designating the absolute essence of God itself. In the writings of the German Hasidim, the emphasis placed upon the infinite nature of God serves as a complement to the doctrine of the *kabhod,* which, in its manifestation, assumes finite forms. A similar relationship likewise could be assumed to exist between the *middoth* and sefiroth (each one of which renders effective or makes manifest a particular aspect of the deity) and their infinite source. One could therefore assume that the notion was formed under the influence of Saadyanic theology, the kabbalists conferring a specific meaning on the new word. It does not present itself so

147. Eleazar, *Hilkhoth ha-Kabhod,* printed under the title *Sode Razayya* (Bilgoraja 1936), 40, as well as Ms. Munich 43, fol. 217a.

148. Nathan Spira, in *Megalle 'Amuqoth,* section 194, cites a passage from Eleazar's *Sode Razayya,* according to which the seraphim *'omrim shiroth le-'en-sof* (sing hymns to the *'en-sof*).

much as a negative attribute of the deity within the framework of an intellectual knowledge of God, but rather as a symbol of the absolute impossibility of such knowledge. This motif can be detected quite clearly at the time of the earliest appearance of *'en-sof* in the writings of the kabbalists. The transformation of rational concepts into mystical symbols in the transition from philosophy to the Kabbalah is a normal phenomenon. On the other hand, we should not overlook the fact that despite the threads connecting the German Hasidim with the kabbalists in Provence, no major influence on Isaac the Blind can be ascribed to Saadyanic ideas, even if they played some role in Provençal circles close to him. We should also remember in this connection that the commentary of Yehudah ben Barzilai on the *Yeṣirah* stands precisely in this Saadyanic tradition. Isaac's father and grandfather, as we have seen, express at least in part ideas that belong to the Saadyanic universe of discourse. With Isaac, however, these elements disappear completely. Isaac is a contemplative mystic who combines Gnosticism and Neoplatonism. I would therefore avoid making any definitive statements as to whether the concept *'en-sof* was derived from certain phrases in the *Bahir* or from Saadyanic sentences. We can delineate with certainty only the process by which this new concept came into existence.

This process left its mark on a state of affairs that merits special attention: in many kabbalistic writings, up to and including the *Zohar,* we still frequently encounter sentences containing the composite word *'en-sof* in adverbial usages of the kind indicated. Often it is difficult to decide whether a given sentence speaks of *'en-sof* in the new sense of the term or whether it refers to the ascension of a divine *middah* "up to infinity" and the like. It is particularly interesting to note in this regard that Isaac the Blind himself as well as the majority of his disciples were not at all prone to speak of a supreme and hidden reality whose name would be simply *'en-sof.* They do so only rarely and under special circumstances in which adverbial determinations are completely renounced and, as in Azriel, *'en-sof* appears as an actual proper name (without an article) of the supreme essence. However, most of the allusions to *'en-sof* here are still couched in a veiled and obscure language. It seems evident to me that this silence and obscurity of expression are not unintentional. Azriel's catechism is in no way characteristic of the phraseology current among the oldest kabbalists. Nevertheless, with him as well as others, the absence of the article together with the word *'en-sof* indicates the origin of the notion. In the case of an artificial philosophical coinage, nothing need have prevented a construction combining the new noun with the definite article. In fact, such a usage is attested only in a much later period, when the sense of the original meaning ("without end, infinite") had already become blunted, and nobody was conscious any longer of its origins. Isaac himself uses the "infinite cause," the "infinite being" [*ḥawwayah be-'en-sof*], and similar phrases, especially in his commentary on the *Yeṣirah.*[149] But certain passages unmistakably betray the new, hypostatizing terminology. Thus, for example: "The creature has not the strength to grasp the inwardness of that to which the Thought, the *maḥshabah,* alludes, to grasp *'en-sof.*"[150] The opening sentence of his commentary should be understood in the same sense. Here it is said of the letter *beth,* which begins the *Book of Creation* as well as the Torah and which has the numerical value two: "The *beth* contains an allusion to the *ḥokhmah* and to the *haskel,*[151] and it thereby indicates all that the Thought [of God] grasps at the *'en-sof,*[152] and how much more so, that which is contained in itself [in the Thought]." This conception of *'en-sof* as a fixed term finds support in his explanation of the notion of *'omeq,* depth, in *Yeṣirah* 1:5, which describes the ten depths of the primordial numbers, "whose measure is ten, but which have no end." Isaac's commentary not only says that "depth is the *intelligere* [*haskel*] up to the *'en-sof"* (which could also signify, simply, "unto infinity"), but we also read there of the "depth from *'en-sof,"* that is, the depth of each sefirah that comes from *'en-sof.* Isaac nowhere mentions any positive function of this *'en-sof* envisaged as the

---

149. Thus, for example, *hithbonenuth sibbatham* [that is, of the cause of the essences] *be-'en-sof* (on 1:4); *'aṣiluth hawwayah be-'en-sof* (1:5); the notion of *'omeq,* depth, is explained as *ha-haskel 'ad 'en-sof* and as *sof hassagath maḥshabah le-'en-sof.* In connection with 1:6 he mentions the power of the soul *lehithpasheṭ bi-praṭim be-'en sof.* Other passages of the commentary and the use they make of the term *'en-sof* are examined in the text above. Also the quotations in ibn Sahula 4c mention the chain of causes up to "the infinite cause." In the *kawwanoth* of Isaac for the prayers it is said of the word *barukh,* with which all benedictions begin, that "it draws forth [the benediction] from *'en-sof* [*mamshikh me-'en-sof*]", Ms. Christ Church College 198, fol. 4a.

150. Cf. the context of the passage in the long citation translated pp. 274–275, herein.

151. Cf. on this concept p. 272.

152. Hebrew: *we-ramaz bah kol mah she-hassagath ha-maḥshabah massegeth 'ad 'en-sof.*

cause of the creative *maḥshabah,* nor does he ever posit its personal character, which would permit us to say that this is simply the Creator God of whom all the other degrees are but *middoth* or qualities. Not "the infinite one" but "the infinite" is apparently intended here. Even when in reference to 1:7 he explains the expression "sole Lord," which in the *Yeṣirah* implies a personalistic concept of the Lord of the sefiroth, he only says, in a strangely attenuated fashion: "Now he makes allusion to an infinite *middah* [or: to a *middah* in *'en-sof*] which has no end on any side." This curious attenuation, precisely on a point in which the emphasis upon the personal element of the deity would impose itself most forcefully, seems to indicate that Isaac inclined toward Neoplatonic concepts of the deity, and more particularly toward the original forms of this thought, which ignore the personal character of the "One," the absolute being.

The point of departure for Isaac's considerations lies in the mysticism of the *maḥshabah.* However, at the very source of his thought we are confronted by a paradox. The notion of Supreme Being exhibits two determinations: one is the "pure thought," a notion employed for the divine thought in Neoplatonic texts, also found in Hebrew;[153] and another, no less Neoplatonic, "that which thought cannot attain," *ma she-'en ha-maḥshabah massegeth.* This clumsy phrase looks like an exact rendering of the Greek *akataleptom,* or its Latin equivalent such as, for example, the *incomprehensibilis* of Scotus Erigena.[154] It would be logical to assume that the latter definition tends toward a higher degree of being than that of pure thought. To this correspond two statements of Isaac that refer to

153. Thus in Abraham bar Ḥiyya, *Hegyon ha-Nefesh,* fol. 2a, and in the Neoplatonic quotation that Azriel used, *Perush ha- 'Aggadoth,* 82. The existence of matter and form in the "pure thought" of God corresponds to their existence in the divine *sapientia* in ibn Gabirol, *Fons Vitae* 5:10, but the analogous statement in 3:57 says that *all* things exist in God's *knowledge* (that is, *scientia* and not *sapientia;* Falaqera's Hebrew rendering reads *biyedi'atho*). It is, however, by no means certain that—as Neumark supposed in his *Geschichte der jüdischen Philosophie,* 1:507—ibn Gabirol must for this reason be the source of the idea, which could very well have come from older Neoplatonic sources.

154. Cf. *De divisione naturae* 3:19. In the usage of Scotus Erigena (as well as of Philo, for whom God is *akataleptos*), the term is not neutral—as in the case of Isaac the Blind, but personal. The same holds true of the Gnostics, as, for example, in the *Excerpta ex Theodoto,* section 29 and of the Ismailiyya (for examples see Strothmann, *Ismailitische Gnosistexte,* [Göttingen, 1943]).

the hidden subject of the third person, past tense, which Hebrew does not mark by a specific termination. In his comment on Genesis 1, he says: "In every place [in the Scriptures] where you find simply *bara', 'asa,* 'he created, he made,' know that it [the subject] is above the pure thought."[155] But in his commentary on *Yeṣirah* 1:1 he explains the hidden subject of the verb *ḥaqaq,* as "that which thought cannot attain." Since for Isaac (who knows nothing of a definition of the Will as the first emanated being) the *maḥshabah* itself is the first sefirah, then that which it cannot attain would therefore be nothing other than *'en-sof,* which is itself transcendent and hidden in relation to thinking. The pure thought would be the supreme creative sphere of being, while *'en-sof,* as the Unknowable, already existed before all thought. Quite possibly this was in fact Isaac's opinion, and I find nothing in his own statements to contradict this supposition. The difficulty, however, lies in the fact that all his disciples, Ezra ben Solomon, Azriel, Jacob ben Shesheth, and above all his own nephew, Asher ben David, who was closest to him, identify the Unknowable, at times explicitly, at times implicitly, with the first sefirah.[156] The rules of simple logic would lead to the conclusion

155. Ms. Halberstam 444, fol. 29b; Paris 353, fol. 31a.

156. Ezra says in his commentary on the aggadoth, Ms. Vatican 185, fol. 8a, that God is elevated above all praise, *yother mimah she-'en ha-maḥshabah massegeth.* Asher ben David, in Ms. Paris 823, fol. 180a, speaks of *kether 'elyon,* "of which [human] thought can grasp nothing." The terminology is particularly noteworthy in Jacob ben Shesheth, *Meshibh Debharim Nekhoḥim,* Ms. Oxford 1585, fol. 28b. It is there said of the first-emanated: "and we name it the Unknowable up to the infinite." The Nothing of the first sefirah is, according to fol. 52b, "a subtle being that the thought cannot grasp." The *intellectus agens* is, according to this conception (f. 20b) the Sophia, one of the highest degrees, "above which there is only one degree, which unifies itself and rises up to *'en-sof* [and it is this] that the thought cannot grasp." The origin of all the benedictions (thus fol. 57a), according to their intention, is "the height until the infinite [Hebrew: *ha-rom 'ad 'en-sof*], which in the language of the philosophers is that 'which is neither a body nor inherent in a body,' but in the language of the masters of the true faith [the kabbalists] is the 'Unknowable.' " This identification is particularly remarkable. It shows very clearly that for this group it is not so much the quality of the impersonal that is defined in speaking of the unknowable, but that of transcendence. God is everything contained in the heights up to infinity, that is he is both the unknowable as the first sefirah and the *'en-sof* above, with which, according to this conception, it is united. The author of the book *Ha-'Emunah weha-Biṭṭaḥon,* chap. 3, also sees the *'alef* of the word *'eḥad* in the profession of faith as a symbol of the unknowable. Baḥya ben Asher, who usually copies the sources of Gerona, still uses the term "unknowable" as a designation for the highest sefirah, ed. 1544, fol. 211d.

that Isaac is the common source of this identification. The divine Thought would then be that which cannot be attained by human thought, and Isaac would therefore employ the word *maḥshabah* in different senses: in one context it would designate the Thought of God, but in the expression "that which cannot be attained by thought," the reference would be to human thought. However, in the fragment of his commentary on Genesis, he even speaks, as we saw, of that which is above the "pure Thought," that is, above the divine Thought. I cannot resolve this difficulty without doing violence to the texts. The unknowable in God is identified by the Christian Neo-platonist, Scotus Erigena, with the Nothing from which all creation proceeds. But with Isaac himself and his disciples, this Nothing is rather the first sefirah, out of which proceeds the divine Sophia. This would accord perfectly with the second interpretation of the notion. Isaac's disciples seem to have been aware of this problem, since some of them, as may be seen most clearly in the case of Jacob ben Shesheth, understood by "unknowable" the first sefirah in its ascension up to *'en-sof* and in its union with it.[157]

The further evolution from the Thought, the *maḥshabah* as the first sefirah, to the *ḥokhmah* or Sophia as second sefirah is also problematic. Between the Sophia, which already represents the beginning of being out of the *superesse,* which is the Nothing, and the *maḥshabah* Isaac knows another symbol, taken from the intellectual sphere, which he names *haskel* or perhaps to be read *heskel.* This word, iridescent with a variety of meanings, is used by Isaac in his *Yeṣirah* commentary as well as by his disciples. *Haskel* is an infinitive form denoting the activity of *sekhel,* or nous. It is therefore an hypostatized rational comprehension that the Sophia exercises; a degree of being of the *intelligere* as distinct from *intellectus.* We also find a similar distinction with Meister Eckhart (would there be a common source? and if so, which?); cf. his Latin works, 5:40, where *intellectus* as the power or faculty of thought coincides with *intelligere* as the thinking *within God alone.* Should we think, perhaps, of Scotus Erigena? Anyway, in Isaac, it appears as a higher degree within the *ḥokhmah* itself, and as such, is sometimes difficult to distinguish from the *maḥshabah.* The testimony of later kabbalists to the effect that Isaac divided the sefirah of *ḥokhmah* in two no doubt

157. Cf. the two passages from fols. 20b and 57a cited in the preceding note.

refers to this differentiation.[158] The concept of *haskel* is taken from Jeremiah 9:23, where it is found (as elsewhere in the Bible) together with *da'ath* and *yedi'ah,* knowing and knowledge. Isaac vacillates in his use of the word, which has the sense of an act directed upward from below in human thought, but downward from above in divine Thought. In this latter sense the term is often employed by his disciples. The *maḥshabah* itself stands above both these intellectual degrees of *haskel* and *ḥokhmah;* it is identical with the sefirah *kether* and with the dimension of "height," *rom,* in the Book *Yeṣirah.* It is from here and from a similar exegesis of Habakkuk 3:10 in the *Bahir,* section 95 that there arose among Isaac's disciples the designation, common in the thirteenth century, *rom ma'alah,* in the sense of "supreme degree," for the first sefirah.

An important passage in Isaac's commentary on *Yeṣirah* 1:4 shows how difficult it is to interpret his doctrine of the *maḥshabah,* for his statements about human and divine thought merge to the point of deliberate obscurity and raise the question of how Isaac really counted the decade of the sefiroth. Did he posit, beyond the sefiroth that contain the divine speech or the divine words, the existence of a secret decade of the *maḥshabah* itself, which is then continued in that of the word *(dibbur)?* Isaac's statements are so opaque that they can often be construed and hence translated in completely different ways. In any event, the *maḥshabah* here seems to be opposed to the other sefiroth in the context of a problem posed for the author by the formulation of the sentence of the *Yeṣirah,* which is the object of his commentary: "Ten sefiroth of closure, ten and not nine, ten and not eleven, understand with wisdom and know with understanding, etc." I translate here as well as I can the entire paragraph, which leaves no doubt about a supreme transcendent principle set above the *maḥshabah* and at the same time emphasizes the importance attributed by the author to the meditative process, by means of which the human *maḥshabah* strives to grasp something

---

158. According to a passage from Shemtob ibn Gaon in his tract on the sefiroth, which I published in *Kiryath Sefer* 8 (1932): 405. His nephew, Asher ben David, also says: "There are masters of the Kabbalah who count the *ḥokhmah* as two, because she surrounds everything"; cf. *Hebräische Bibliographie* 12 (1872): 82–83. He also explains there that the *yod* in the divine name YHWH, even though it is only one letter, contains an allusion to two spheres, the *ḥokhmah* and the "thread of the emanation drawn towards it from the first sefirah." This thread or effluence, *meshekh,* is perhaps identical with the *haskel,* that turns toward *ḥokhmah* and flows into it.

of the divine. Whereas other kabbalistic exegetes after Isaac understood the wording of the *Yeṣirah* as a warning not to exclude the highest sefirah (ten and not nine!) from, and not to include *'en-sof* (ten and not eleven!) in, the sefirotic decade, Isaac understands the warning as referring both to *ḥokhmah* and to the *maḥshabah* set above it. It is possible that we have before us, as the resumption of the sentence of *Yeṣirah* in the course of his commentary might suggest, two different explanations of the warning, juxtaposed by Isaac or the disciple responsible for the redaction, and thus producing the present form of this problematic paragraph.

> Ten and not nine: Although it [the *ḥokhmah,* named previously] is counted with all [the other sefiroth], do not say: how can I say that it is one [particular] sefirah? Ten and not eleven. And if you wish to say: since the *ḥokhmah* is the beginning of the Thought of the word [*dibbur*],[159] how should I not say eleven?[160] Thus you should not make this assertion and you should not separate *ḥokhmah* from *kether,* which is the thought of the beginning of the word, although you cannot grasp the *maḥshabah* of him who counts and unites [the sefiroth, that is, the Supreme Emanator, and although you are not in a position to] meditate on that or to immerse yourself[161] in the cause of the thought of the beginning of the word, which [in their totality as sefiroth] are nothing but ten. And do not say nine: since the cause of the Thought of the beginning of the word is infinite [or in the infinite, *be-'en-sof*], how could I include it in an enumeration [or how can I make it into a sefirah]?[162] Do not say therefore either that they are eleven or that they are nine. Although the speech [the divine language that is expressed in the *debharim*—words or things] is infinite, there nevertheless exists, in any case, a subtle cause or a subtle being, of which the

---

159. Thus the text reads in all manuscripts; but perhaps *maḥshebeth* is to be deleted here, since *ḥokhmah* is elsewhere designated by him as *teḥillath ha-dibbur.*

160. Immediately preceding this passage, commenting on *Yeṣirah* 1:3, the ten sefiroth are enumerated in two corresponding series of five, each containing the *ḥokhmah,* which is said to be *makhra'ath ba-kol,* decisive in everything. These two series are rather strange: *Neṣah, Hod, Tif'ereth, Ḥesed, Ḥokhmah* constitute the one, and *'Aṭarah, Ṣadiq, Paḥad, Binah, Ḥokhmah* constitute the other. The highest sefirah therefore does not appear at all.

161. The verb *le-hithpasheṭ,* "to extend," employed here, is already used in the *Bahir* in connection with the extension of the *maḥshabah,* but in a different sense. There it concerns the manner in which the divine *maḥshabah* spreads out, that is, emanates in the potencies; here, on the other hand, it relates to the inaccessibility of the cause of the *maḥshabah* to meditation.

162. The sentence is difficult: logically, we should expect the questioner to want to exclude the *maḥshabah* from the decade of the sefiroth, but not the cause of the *maḥshabah,* which is above it.

> thought attains a hint in meditation [*hithbonenuth*]. That is why it[163] is a sefirah in the *maḥshabah,* which is a subtle being containing the decade [i.e. in which the decade is already hidden]. And the *debharim* have *middoth,* dimensions, and a *shi'ur,* measure, but the *maḥshabah* has no measure and therefore they [the words?][164] go in decades, from the subtle to the formed [essences] for [they are developed] ten from ten, the subtle from that which is in the interiority of the subtle [essences]. And from the power of allusion of the *maḥshabah* [from that at which the *maḥshabah* can hint] we recognize what we are able to grasp and what we should leave [as unknowable], because, from that point on, there is no more apprehension of the allusive *maḥshabah.* For the created being does not have the power, [even] where it seeks to grasp the interior which the *maḥshabah* indicates [being contained within it], of grasping [at the same time] *'en-sof.*[165] For every meditation of the *ḥokhmah* out of the *intelligere* [or: from the degree named *haskel*] relates to the subtlety of its infinite thought [or: its *maḥshabah* (founded) in the *'en-sof*].[166] And thus he says "ten and not nine," since [human] thought can set a measure over the *ḥokhmah* and in the *ḥokhmah* [itself] by means of meditation [and not through discursive thought], as it is said [in the text of the *Yeṣirah*]: Understand with wisdom [conceived by Isaac as: grasp the *ḥokhmah* in the meditation that has its place in *binah*].

This quotation gives us an idea of the difficulties besetting the interpretation of Isaac's texts. It clearly shows, in any case, that here *'en-sof* is eliminated as an object of the mystic's speculation. The highest degree of interest to the mystic is the *maḥshabah;* he seeks to advance to it, or, as Isaac says, to "suck" from it. In it is manifested the hidden cause that stands above it. His contemplative mysticism turns on this pivot of the "pure *maḥshabah.*" But as we have already seen, this first sefirah, derived from another strand of symbolism, is also the Nothing. As far as I know, Isaac did not expound on the subject of the relation between these two symbols for

---

163. Judging by the construction of the sentence, should not the subject be the cause that, in activating itself in the *maḥshabah,* becomes a sefirah?

164. The word *holkhoth,* the feminine plural of the participle as found in the manuscripts, has no subject in this sentence. *Debharim* should be accompanied by a masculine form. Perhaps we should read *holekheth,* which would then be related to the *maḥshabah* itself, which contains the decades.

165. The phrase "even when it . . . seeks to grasp" is missing in all manuscripts, with the exception of the best among them, Ms. Fondo Antico Orientale 46 in the Angelica in Rome.

166. This difficult sentence is missing precisely in the Ms. Angelica. Hebrew: *she-kol hithbonenuth be-ḥokhmah min ha-haskel hi' daqquth remez maḥshabto be-'en-sof.*

the highest sefirah. We may assume, however, especially on the basis of the above quotation, that the pure Thought of God can also be called Nothing. This is not only because it is not determined by any definite content, but because in it the human thought that strives to advance toward it in meditation ceases to be, or as Isaac's disciples put it, "comes to nothing." Isaac did not, however, include any of these considerations on the divine Nothing in his commentary on the *Yeṣirah*.

The *Yeṣirah* commentary does not pronounce itself clearly on the question whether the highest sefirah, that which is unattainable by thought, is linked from eternity by a beginningless process of emanation to its cause, the *'en-sof,* which is set above it, and whether it is therefore coexistent with it. On the other hand, an important theorem relevant to the subject is contained in Isaac's interpretation of Genesis 1:1, quoted by Sahula. In fact, Isaac is the first kabbalist who refers to the rendering of the Palestinian Targum: "God created by means of *ḥokhmah"* in order to discover the second sefirah, *ḥokhmah,* in the first word of the Torah. The consonant *beth* in *bereshith* "indicates and contains the *ḥokhmah* and its crown [which is above it, the sefirah *kether*] in this one word [*bereshith*], in order to intimate that both [sefiroth] were emanated in conjunction with one another, without any interval between them, so that the one cannot exist without the other."[167] This is a very striking thesis that, as far as I can see, no longer reappears among Isaac's disciples. *Kether* is clearly conceived as emanated by a single act together with Sophia and hence, we may conclude, it is not without beginning like *'en-sof* itself. Isaac nowhere says, as does his disciple Azriel, that the first sefirah was potentially in *'en-sof* before it was actualized in the emanation. If ibn Sahula's quotation is exact, we would have a clear theistic concept of a God elevated above all the sefiroth. This would accord well with Isaac's statement in his commentary on the *Midrash Konen* that *binah* was emanated from "the two innermost degrees, the *ḥokhmah* and the *maḥshabah,"* both of which therefore are conceived together. However, there is a situation in which these two did not yet exist. One must ask in this connection whether the "infinite cause" mentioned by Isaac in his *Yeṣirah* commentary is perhaps to

167. Sahula 3d. The decisive words are utterly corrupted in the printed text and must be reestablished according to the old Ms. Parma, de Rossi 68, fol. 4a: *ne'eṣlu be-samukh bli shehuth klal benathayim.*

be distinguished from the infinite *middah* of the "sole lord" whom he mentions in commenting on 1:5, in which case this *middah* would have to be regarded as created.

Whatever the precise nature of the supreme sefirah, *ḥokhmah* is in any case the "beginning of being" as it is also the "beginning of the *dibbur.*" From *ḥokhmah,* all the sefiroth proceed in a clear chain of emanations. In terms of Isaac's language-mysticism, the divine things are at the same time the divine words. The ideas are names. This motif, already prefigured in the *Bahir* where the sefiroth coincided with the ten logoi, now appears in a much profounder form. For the kabbalist, evidently, language-mysticism is at the same time a mysticism of script and of letters. The relation between script and language is a constitutive principle for the Kabbalah. In the spiritual world, every act of speaking is concurrently an act of writing, and conversely every writing is potential speech, destined to become audible. The speaker engraves, as it were, the three-dimensional space of the word on the plane of the ether. The script, which for the philologist is only a secondary and otherwise rather useless image of real speech, is for the kabbalist the true repository of its secrets. The phonographic principle of a natural transposition of speech into script and vice versa manifests itself in the Kabbalah in the idea that the sacred letters themselves are the lineaments and signs that the modern phoneticist would want upon his disc. The creative word of God is legitimately stamped upon just these sacred lines. Beyond language lies the unarticulated reflection, the pure thought, the mute profundity, one could say, in which the nameless reposes. From *ḥokhmah* on there opens up, identical with the world of the sefiroth, the world of the pure name as a primordial element of language. This is the sense in which Isaac understood the saying of *Yeṣirah* 2:5, according to which all language proceeds from a name. The tree of divine powers, which formed the sefiroth in the *Bahir,* is here transposed to the ramifications of the letters in this great name.

But more than that of the tree, Isaac liked the simile of the coal and the flames *(shalhabiyoth)* that are fed by it, inspired by another passage of *Yeṣirah* (1:7) to which he often has recourse:

> Their root [that is, that of language and things] is in a name, for the letters are like branches, which appear in the manner of flickering flames, which are mobile, and nevertheless linked to the coal, and in

> the manner of the leaves of the tree, its boughs and branches, whose root is always in the tree . . . and all the *debharim* become form and all the forms proceed only from the one name, just as the branch comes from the root. It follows therefore that everything is in the root, which is the one name (on 2:5).

The world of language is therefore actually the "spiritual world." Only that which lives in any particular thing as language is its essential life. Raising the above to the level of kabbalistic discourse, the words, *dibburim,* constitute the world of the sefiroth,[168] which are united in their configurations in order to form letters, just as, conversely, the words themselves are the configurations of letters. Isaac uses both images though their kaleidoscopic relations are not entirely transparent. In any case, letters are for him the elements of the universal script. According to him, the Hebrew word for letters, *'othiyoth,* derives from the verb *'atha,* to come; the letters are "things which come from their cause," thus, that which "proceeds" from the root. But each of these elements comprises in ever new configurations all the sefiroth: "In every letter there are the ten sefiroth." Thus we are told, in connection with *Yeṣirah* 4:1 that the ten sefiroth are "inner [or: hidden] essences" whose inner [hidden] being is contained in the *ḥokhmah,* and that they are at the same time the roots of principles in which good and evil are still united. "They [the sefiroth] begin to grow forth like a tree whose beginnings are unrecognizable, until a plant issues from them." The verbs employed by the Book *Yeṣirah* to describe the formation of the letters that God "hewed" in the pneuma suggest to Isaac the image of a mountain from which raw stones are extracted, then hewed and chiseled, and from which well-ordered edifices come into being. This "edifice" is the world, but the world of the sefiroth as such also represents a building of this type that issues from its elements, and, in the last analysis, from the *ḥokhmah.* The sphere in which this hewing of the innermost elements takes place is not the hidden Sophia, where everything is still conceived as united without form, but the sefirah that follows it, *binah* or *teshubah* ("that to which all

168. The same terminology can be found later with Ezra ben Solomon (in his commentary to the Song of Songs, ed. Vajda, 264). The expression *ha-debharim ha-ruḥaniyyim ha-penimiyyim* is also used by Moses de Leon toward the end of his commentary on the sefiroth, the text of which I have edited from the manuscript at the Escorial.

returns"), which is itself a mystical hyle from which the forms are chiseled.[169]

In all these statements Isaac repeatedly uses the notion of *hawwayoth,* the essences of all things, a notion which in his view replaces the sefiroth as well as the letters, yet extends beyond them. He nowhere suggests that these essences were formed or created. On the contrary, they have an original being within God and, above all, in the *maḥshabah;* and as we have already observed, the commentary on the *Yeṣirah* nowhere mentions any coming-into-being of this realm. Hence, it is to Isaac that we should trace back at least the meaning of the formula found among his disciples in Gerona, which is in complete accord with the position taken in the commentary: "The essences were, but the emanation came into being."[170] These essences are simply assumed, and it is only the manner and the degrees of their manifestation in the emanations, as well as the manner in which they can be grasped in meditation, that are the subject of Isaac's considerations in his commentary. One might even conclude from his comments on *Yeṣirah* 1:1 that there are essences that no longer belong to the Sophia and to the process of thinking; therefore, they represent modes of being with God but cannot become objects of thought.

This could be implicit in Isaac's remark on the subject of the words *peli'oth ḥokhmah* in 1:1 where he explains that they are "the beginning of the essences which are given to thought." The "marvelous paths of the *ḥokhmah*" are, according to him, "inward and subtle essences" that exist in the *ḥokhmah* as the root in the tree, and that proceed from it like sap passing through the trunk. The secret arteries, by way of which the sap circulates throughout the tree, are themselves these paths. "No creature can know them by meditating [Hebrew: *lehithbonen*], apart from he who sucks from it [from the *ḥokhmah* itself], on the path of meditation through his sucking

---

169. The *tohu* (primordial matter) of *Yeṣirah* 2:6 is explained by Isaac as "a formless being, which is emanated from the power of *binah, me-hazmanath ha-teshubah,"* and whence darkness proceeds as a real principle. One would be inclined here to consider *tohu* not as *binah* itself, but as an emanation from it; but Isaac, in his brief commentary on Genesis 1, explicitly designates it as "the depth of the *teshubah."* This is what the Talmud (*Ḥagigah* 12b) meant by its definition of the *tohu* as "a green line that surrounds everything," Ms. Halberstam 444, fol. 29a.

170. Frequently in Ezra, cf. *Sefer Bialik,* 158, as well as in the name of Naḥmanides; cf. the references in *Kiryath Sefer* 9 (1932): 126.

[sic!] and not through knowledge." These enigmatic words seem to suggest that Isaac knew of a way to connect with these hidden essences, obtained not through knowledge but by means of another process, a contemplation without language, which he names "sucking," *yeniqah.* This is how he was understood by Isaac of Acre, who distinguished between the "acquisition" of knowledge by "learning" and the direct "meditation of the intellect."[171] To be sure, another idea could also be intended here, namely that no creature is capable of such meditation; this power is given only to the sefiroth emanating from the *ḥokhmah,* which are not creatures in the strict sense of the term. This would accord with the fact that in another passage of his commentary (on 1:3), Isaac speaks of the essences hidden in the *ḥokhmah,* in which nothing is yet formed, and of which he says that "only the thing emanated from them has the power to know them through meditation." But here, too, Isaac adds: it is significant that "either the mystic [has this power] which meditates it [within the context of the construction of the sentence it is not clear to what this "it" refers], for in leaving the formed essences [he arrives at] a meditation of their cause in the *'en-sof* [or: their infinite cause]." The answer to the question whether the mystic of whom Isaac speaks (arriving at a meditation on the infinite cause in the contemplative progression of his meditation from degree to degree) is also capable of this "sucking" relationship with the origins of all being would very much depend on how far one is willing to go in the interpretation of the relevant passage quoted previously.

In any case, it is evident that these essences are in fact "visible to the heart"; they can, therefore, become the object of a contemplative apprehension. Toward the end of chapter 2, Isaac has this to say regarding the emanation of the corporeal essences from the spiritual ones: "From the inner spiritual essences which are not apprehensible [by the senses], but visible to the heart, he has chiseled, and there emanated from them, material [essences] which are apprehensible." No doubt the expression "visible to the heart" is still a long way from the terminology of sucking, which perhaps applies only to the mode of knowledge of the sefiroth among themselves. There seems little doubt that this definition of the sefiroth and of the elements of language as inner essences within the Sophia of God but at the same time apprehensible to the mystic in meditation presup-

171. Cf. *Kiryath Sefer* 31 (1956): 383.

poses a philosophical terminology and tradition. The Hebrew word appears to be a translation-adaptation of the Latin *essentiae,* much as the infinitive *haskel* is perhaps patterned on the Latin term *intelligere.* This terminology is very different (contra the views I expressed in my Hebrew book *Reshith ha-Qabbala,* 118) from that of Eleazer or Worms and the German Hasidim. There they are the manifestations of God's presence (*hawwayoth,* from *howweh,* "present"). God is present in the ten "depths" of the Book *Yeṣirah,* which are none other but his ten "immanences" in creation, modalities of the divine presence in the world. God is infinite within all of them.

These subtle essences, which are the spiritual origins of the formed letters, constitute the primordial Torah in their undifferentiated and still unformed unity within the divine Sophia. Here Isaac mystically reinterprets the well-known Platonizing statement of the *Midrash Bereshith Rabba,* according to which God created the world by looking at the Torah much as the creator in Plato's *Timaeus* looked at the ideas: "God beheld in Himself these essences, which would manifest themselves at the creation of the world, such as they had their being in the *ḥokhmah.*"[172] This primordial Torah, the *torah qedumah,* is different from its manifestations as the Written and the Oral Torah in the sefiroth *tif'ereth* and *'aṭarah.* In his commentary on the *Midrash Konen,* Isaac offers some profound thoughts on this mysticism of the Torah in its three degrees of manifestation, to which I shall return in the following text (p. 287).

Such essences also exist for external and perceptible things. In the world of the sefiroth beneath *ḥokhmah,* they are, despite their spiritual nature, determined, fixed, and limited *(qebu'oth* and *ḥaquqoth)* in their mode of existence. Through them the mystic can arrive "at the meditation upon the defined, subtle, but unlimited [*she-'en lahem gebhul*] essences." This progress in the understanding of the interior by means of the exterior is emphasized over and over again. Already at the very beginning it is stated:

> The paths [of the Sophia] are like the threads of the flames which are the paths for the coals, and through the flames man can see the coal [which is at their base] in the manner of a skein, for by following the

172. Quoted in *Sefer ha-'Emunah weha-Biṭṭaḥon,* chap. 18, and in a somewhat better text, in the old miscellanies preserved in Ms. Christ Church College 198, fol. 25b.

> thread, he arrives at the place of the skein. Similarly, man finds through the leaves, boughs and branches, and the numerous trunks, the conduits (literally: the cavities, namely of the sap] which lead to the essential [*'iqqar*] and to the subtle reality of the root, invisible on account of its subtlety and its inwardness.

From the *ḥokhmah* on, an unbroken stream of emanation also leads beyond the sefiroth to all existence below. All things are linked to one another and intertwined like a chain: "one from another, the inner from the still more inward" and "all things are essences issuing from essences, face issuing from face [or interior issuing from interior]"[173] (3:1). But that which was a unity in the "higher world" of God's sefiroth and *middoth,* even if it progresses from cause to cause, became, on leaving this realm, the world of multiplicity, which is called by Isaac the "world of separated [things," *'olam ha-nifradim.*[174] This terminology apparently rests upon a transformation of the philosophic concept of separate intelligences, thus called by the philosophers because they are forms separated from matter, that is pure forms. The mystics reverse the expression and relate it to the separation between this domain and that of the divine unity. It is to this conception that they later applied, already in Isaac's circle, it seems, the verse Genesis 2:10. The stream that goes forth from Eden is that of the emanation of the sefiroth; but at the point of departure from the garden, at the lowest sefirah, it divides and becomes the multiplicity of the creaturely world, the world of separation.

In this world, too, however, there occurs a union that makes of the separated powers an organic and efficacious whole, "in the manner of the flames linked to the coal." In the verbs used by the *Book of Creation* for the action exercised by God with the aid of the letters representing the cosmic elements—"He weighed them, substituted them, and combined them"—Isaac saw the different acts occurring

---

173. The reading *panim* ("face," "countenance") is, however, probably the correct one, since the author speaks (at the end of chapter 1) of the "faces above," which the Creator made and which man finds in every direction as he immerses himself in higher things. The opposite is here clearly *'aḥor,* and not, as it would otherwise have to be, *ḥiṣon.*

174. The term is already found in the *Yeṣirah* commentary and recurs later among his pupils, as, for example, in his nephew Asher ben David on Genesis 1, Ms. Paris 823, fol. 180a, and in Ezra, in the letter published in *Sefer Bialik,* 156. Cf. also, on this subject, *Tarbiz* 2 (1931): 419.

within the promordial hyle. The weighing still takes place within the world of the sefiroth; it establishes a harmony between the powers such that one emanates from the other, "for without equilibrium [literally: weighing out] between the potencies, none can emanate from the other" (on 2:1). The same idea was already expressed by Isaac's father: the oppositions only act by virtue of the fact that a certain harmony exists between them and that each already contains something of the other. According to him, the "substitution" refers to modifications in the order of time: when one *middah* has fulfilled its function, another begins to act; their powers do not enter into action together (2:1 and 3:1). According to Isaac, in relation to the world of *nifradim* the combination, *ṣeruf,* represents the same process of association and fruitful action that the weighing designates in the world of the sefiroth. He saw in the action of the *ṣeruf* a renewed connection with the uniform root of the separated things. Without this reference back to the single coal, the flames cannot take effect; without their cooperation in the entire tree, the branches, too, cannot preserve their strength. In the course of this process all things are in constant movement from cause to cause,

> until they come to the separated things which are found beneath the ten sefiroth, from which the separated sucks in the juice like the fruit of the tree, until they reach their full maturity, and upon the completion of their maturation they fall from their place at which they sucked their power, and others are newly born in their place. (on 2:1)

This process is the same for all the things of the creaturely world, "of each thing according to the rank of the place where it sucked in its power," and also for the souls, "which are subtle essences bound together [*ṣeruroth*] in one place, and which all exist from the beginning, but whose vitality stems from an inner power, from something that the heart is incapable of contemplating" (on 2:2).

Everything is therefore linked together and everything is in everything, as is frequently stressed in formula-like expressions. It is not easy to judge the extent to which a pantheistic element, which the imagery employed here naturally evokes, is actually involved. In any case, the continuity of this cosmic chain is evident to the author; one can speak only relatively of a separate and isolated existence: "In all things and *middoth* which appear to be separated, no [real] separation takes place, for all is one, as the primordial beginning [another version: in the primordial beginning or principle] which unites all [in itself]."[175] Of this One, Isaac says: "He is united in everything and everything is united in Him," which seems to be a clear formulation of the principle of divine immanence. The world of separated existences that represents, so to speak, an extradivine world, is of course also included in this chain; to this, precisely, corresponds the possibility of a knowledge through *hithbonenuth,* contemplation or meditation, in gradual ascension and through the perception of all things in one another. From the contemplation and meditation of the formed, the mystic advances toward the contemplation of the formless and the inward, and from there to that of the *maḥshabah* and the "infinite cause" of all the essences or, as it can also be translated, to the cause of all the essences in *'en-sof.*

In this transition from the unity of the divine emanation to the multiplicity of the separated, the notion of *middah* seems to play a considerable role for Isaac, taking on a new sense. The word is no longer employed by him in the older sense of the *Bahir;* it acquires a speculative, although by no means transparent, significance of a particular kind. Nor are the *middoth* attributes that describe the action of God. They are the principles, *hathḥaloth,* of all that is found outside the divine unity. In order to avoid the pantheistic consequences to which their presuppositions could lead, the kabbalists had to try to establish a distinction between the action of the divine *middoth* in the world of the sefiroth and the action of the *middoth* that already had emanated from them and were operative in the creaturely world. This is, in fact, what Isaac's nephew attempted to do, in conformity no doubt with his uncle's doctrine. According to him, all discourse on the *middoth* in relation to God has to be understood in a hyperbolic sense. For

> it is inconceivable that a limited and decided [absolute] measure could be found in Him, since He is one, united with all [the *middoth*] and He acts in all at once, or else in one of them, embracing all of them in it; and also in a single one he produces at the same time a thing and its opposite, for the power of one is in the other, since each *middah* is contained in the other."[176]

---

175. Hebrew: *shehakol eḥad kemo ha-hathḥalah shehu meyaḥed hakol.*
176. In Asher's *Sefer ha-Yiḥud,* ed. Ḥasida, 18.

The sefiroth are therefore called *middoth* (measures) only by us, since they are visible and apprehensible to us in terms of their effects. The kabbalists could thus identify the sefiroth with the attributes of action, which according to the doctrine of Maimonides may be attributed only to the deity. But this applies, above all, to the seven lower sefiroth, which erect the "edifice" of the Creation. In this respect, these *middoth* may also be regarded as instruments through which the Creator or Master of the emanations acts "like the instruments of the artisan, with which he performs his work, and these instruments, which the sages name sefiroth, are radiated from the light of God." The *middoth* below the sefiroth are distinguished from the upper *middoth,* in that each one can only accomplish a single function by virtue of the fact that they are endowed with a limited measure only. Here the oppositions cannot unite in their root, as in the upper *middoth.* However, they also act, as we have seen, only in conjunction with these upper *middoth.* A relationship between this concept of the *middah* and the language-mysticism of the logoi is indeed attested by Isaac, but in such obscure manner that his definitions remain incomprehensible. Thus in reference to *Yeṣirah* 1:4, *middathan 'eser,* "their measure is ten" is "explained" as follows: Each logos [and there is little doubt that here this and not simply "thing" is the meaning of *dabhar*] is a *middah,* and that which is above it is its "fulfillment" [*millu'ah,* completion], for *middah* is the potency of that which is emanated from the *middah* of Him who measures, and the essences [are] themselves *middah,* and the emanation an infinite essence [or: an essence in *'en-sof*]. I am unable to make any clear sense of this this obscure sentence.

In another way, however, Isaac's mysticism of language is easier to understand. From the Sophia, which we have come to know as the primordial Torah as yet undifferentiated by language, the voice is formed in the next sefirah, *binah.* This voice is not yet audible and is still hidden; it becomes audible only at the later stages of emanation and at the end of this process becomes articulated speech. But already the hidden voice becomes differentiated, by prolonging itself, into many letters. "Hewn in the pneuma," which is *binah,* they acquire, according to Isaac, an exterior and an interior, body and soul. This power of the letters flows into the world beneath the sefiroth, forming on the celestial sphere the secret but nonetheless primordial images of all things in the figure of the 231 gates of this sphere; the gates represent the combinations, two by two, of the elements of the Hebrew alphabet. There are 462 such combinations, but the other half of this power remains above the sphere. Hence the letters, no matter how they are combined, are only the visible ramifications of the one promordial name. It remains unsaid, however, whether this primordial name is the Tetragrammaton, the name *'ehyeh,* or some other mystical name underlying both of these. The entire process of emanation remains condensed in all the letters, and "in each individual letter are contained all ten sefiroth" (3:2). The letter becomes, therefore, a world in itself encapsulating the whole future as something already preformed in it. "In each individual letter there are subtle, inward, and hidden essences 'without what' [that have not become anything definite]. Whatever could be chiseled out of them was already in them, just as all a man's descendants are already in him." These secret essences in the letters, which exert their influence in the midst of creation, are conceived "in the manner of the essences given in the Sophia." It is quite possible that the "whatless" being, being without quiddity, to which this passage refers and which is hidden in the letters, had something to do with the punning definition of the Sophia, given by Isaac's disciples as being the "potency of the what."[177] This conception is in perfect accord with the quotation from the *Yeṣirah* commentary.

Similar ideas on the development of the world of the sefiroth and what lies below it are found, albeit expressed with enigmatic brevity, in Isaac's commentary on Genesis 1 (which already ibn Sahula admitted was partly incomprehensible). Mention is made there of a progression from the "splendor to the Sophia" toward the "light of the Intellect" as the content of the creation of the first day, which, as the mystical primordial day, contained within itself "in spirit, though not yet in their form" all the essences. It is only with the diffusion of the light of the intellect that the light of all other things radiated therefrom; and it seems that for Isaac, the primordial creation of the first day embraces all ten sefiroth. He interprets the events of the second day of creation as constituting a transition representing the "extension of the spirit in the form." The souls, too, only "extend in the form" on the second day. We do not learn what constitutes this specifically formative power of the spirit, which is the *ruaḥ 'elohim* of Genesis 1:2. It is a pneuma that comes from the sefiroth of *ḥokhmah* and *binah,* "and it is called among the

177. Thus in Azriel, *Perush 'Aggadoth,* 84, and Tishby's note there.

sages the power that shapes the form." The "sages" named here must be the philosophers, judging by the terminology employed; in the Midrash one finds no such expression. From this supreme pneuma, apparently, come all the souls, which are stamped with the letters engraved in the spirit. The details of this exposition are impenetrable. Having established a distinction between spirit and form, Isaac goes on to declare that "the spirit, in the words of the philosophers, is called form," and that there exists an infinite chain in the course of which "spirit is formed in spirit until *'en-sof.*" Isaac leaps straight from the explanation of the second day to the sixth, and the creation of man. We do not learn how he imagined the functions of the other primordial days.

The aforementioned fragment of Isaac's commentary on the beginning of *Midrash Konen* contains a very curious cosmogonic exposition. Of particular importance here is his explanation of the aggadic dictum according to which the Torah was written before the creation of the world with black fire on white fire. Isaac combines this passage with his speculations on the three degrees of manifestation of the Torah—the Primordial Torah, the Written Torah and the Oral Toah. The Primordial Torah was, according to the Midrash, in the right hand of God. Isaac says in this connection:

> In the right hand of God were all the engravings [i.e. the innermost marks, which are, as yet, not real forms] that were destined one day to proceed from potentiality to actuality. From the emanation of all the crowns [sefiroth] they are engraved, incised, and informed in the degree of Grace [the sefirah *ḥesed,* which is also called the right of God], in an inward, inconceivably subtle formation. And that is called, since the very beginning of the *maḥshabah,* the "folded," or not-yet-unfolded Torah, or Torah of Grace. Together with the other engravings, two [principal] engravings were made in it. One has the form of the Written Torah and the other the form of the Oral Torah. The form of the Written Torah is that of the colors of the white fire, while the form of the Oral Torah is that of figures of color as of a black fire. All these engravings, and the not-unfolded Torah itself, exist potentially [in the idea or in the Sophia?], and could be perceived by neither a spiritual nor a material eye, until the will [of God] stimulates the thought to bring them to actuality by means of primordial wisdom [*ḥokhmah qedumah*], and the hidden knowledge [*da'ath genuzah*]. Thus, there was at the beginning of the entire work [of creation], in a preexistent state, the not-yet-unfolded Torah, which is God's right, with all the incisions of the engravings hidden there. This is what the Midrash has in mind, when it wants to say that God took the primordial Torah [*torah qedumah*] which comes from the quarry of the *binah* [designated here as *teshubah,* Return] and from the source of the pri-

> mordial *ḥokhmah;* and it emanated, in a spiritual act, the not-unfolded Torah, in order to grant through it permanence to the foundations of the world.

Reveling in light-mysticism, the author then depicts, again in a highly opaque manner, the progress of the emanation from the luminous drop of *ḥesed* of which his source speaks. First, God took two names. The first became the great fire or the sefirah *geburah,* while the other unfolded to become the "form of the Written Torah, which is the color of white fire." It corresponds to the sefirah of the divine Mercy, or *tif'ereth.* The lowest sefirah, on the other hand, contains, by virtue of its correspondence to the action of divine judgment in the world, the Oral Torah, which is black fire burning upon an underlayer of white fire. "But the form of the letters is without vowels and is only potentially engraved in this black fire, which is like ink [on white parchment]." In the white fire itself the forms of the letter still do not actually appear, and where they do so we are already (in the symbolism of the black fire) in the domain of the Oral Torah.

> And thus the Written Torah cannot adopt corporeal form, except through the power of the Oral Torah; that is, that the former cannot be truly understood without the latter, just as the mode of divine Mercy can only be grasped and perceived through the mode of Judgment. And the figures of color, *gawwanim,* of black, which are those of Judgment, rise up and spread out over the configurations of white, which are those of Mercy, like the light of the coal. For the power of the colored configuration of the flames prevails until the light of the coal can no longer be perceived at all because of the excess of flames covering it.

The simile of the coal and its flames is the same as that employed by Isaac so often in his commentary on *Yeṣirah.* The mystical Written Torah is still hidden, as it were, under the invisible form of the white light represented by the parchment of the Torah scroll and is in no way perceptible to the ordinary eye. It is only when the mystical lights, in the play of flames, sometimes veer away from one another that they offer a momentary glimpse of the white light or the sphere of divine Mercy. At such moments, "many a prophet" can "snatch, by means of the 'crown of royalty,' [the last sefirah, accessible to their contemplation] something of this mystical splendor, each according to the spiritual degree of which he is worthy." But this can be no more than a momentary intuition. A truly lasting contemplation of this hidden form of the white light is as inconceivable as that of the sun by a terrestrial eye. Only Moses, the master of all the prophets, could attain a continuous contemplation of this "luminous mirror" and by virtue of his prophetic rank enter into spiritual communication with it.

The language of this symbolism is identical to that found in other of Isaac's fragments. Hidden behind mystical symbols, we find a conception according to which there simply is no Written Torah within reach of the ordinary mortal. Everything we call by that name has already passed through the mediation of the Oral Torah. The Torah apprehensible to man is not the hidden form in the white light but precisely the obscure light that already had adopted definite forms and determinations and that thereby designates the quality of divine Sternness, the quality of Judgment. The Torah scroll itself symbolizes that. The ink and the parchment form a unity. But the element rendered visible by the ink is the blackness, the "obscure mirror" of the Oral Torah; the true secret of the Written Torah, which embraces everything, is contained in the signs, still not visible, of the white parchment. In a word, there is only an Oral Torah, and the concept of a Written Torah has its place, in the final analysis, in the mystical domain, the sphere accessible only to the prophets. Therefore, here, at the very beginning of the historical appearance of the Kabbalah in the West, we have a thesis whose mystical radicalism can hardly be surpassed and was in fact not surpassed in the entire history of the Kabbalah.[178] It proves, more than anything else we know of him, that Isaac was a genuine esotericist. Isaac's fragment fell into oblivion, but his thesis was taken up and elaborated more than once in the history of the Kabbalah, at times in much less veiled language.[179]

6. Good and Evil in Isaac and Other Sources

The divine power spreading from the sefiroth into Creation, from the world of the Throne and the angels outward, also descends below the human domain to living beings of a lower order, even to plants.

---

178. I have discussed this subject in the chapter on the meaning of the Torah in *On the Kabbalah,* 50.

179. Cf. ibid., 74–77.

Trees, too, have a mystical root in those of Paradise, which represent the primordial images of all future trees. Everything below is linked to that which is above, to which it owes its existence, until it is linked by a chain of this kind to the Infinite. "All creatures on earth depend on the higher powers, and these on still higher, up to the infinite cause."[180] This cosmic chain is, at least in the realm of the sefiroth, a magnetic one. The sefiroth and logoi "rise above themselves like something rising under the influence of a magnet and thus their end [in the words of the Book *Yeṣirah*] is [enclosed] in its beginning" (on 1:7).

But in addition to the connection through emanation there is also one through vision, *ṣefiyah.* In connection with *Yeṣirah* 1:6, we learn that this vision itself is the magnetic act of communication in which everything ascends to its origins. The *Book of Creation* says that the vision of the sefiroth is like lightning, and Isaac explains: "The vision is the meditation of one thing out of the other. . . . Every cause is taken up and rises and then looks down from a cause that is higher than itself. . . . Everything is in the other and in communication with the other." Thus, not only does God contemplate the depths of his own wisdom when he produces the world, but a contemplative communication of the same kind also takes place among the sefiroth. The contemplation of the mystic in a state of *kawwanah* is thus not unlike that which occurs among the spiritual essences themselves. In creation, it is not the divine *middoth,* the "fathers," that act directly but rather the derivative *middoth, toladoth,* which issue from them. In isolation, without communicating with "fathers" or "mothers," they are unable to produce anything.

Man too is inserted into this process. He is "built out of combinations of the letters" (chap. 3). "And this higher edifice of spirit [*ruaḥ*] that directs him [also] directs the All, and thus the All is connected to the upper and the lower ones and is composed of the world, the year and the soul. . . . And the soul is the determining factor in the All" (ibid.). Man, our text continues, is "the quintessence of all creatures, a great seal, in which the beginning and the

---

180. Quoted by Sahula, fol. 4c. In the epistle of Samuel ben Mordekhai against the detractors of Maimonides (Ms. Neofiti, fol. 208b; cf. pp. 224–5, herein) a very similar idea is quoted from the writings of the Sage (R. Ezra?). The same manuscript contains in the sequel (fol. 209) other traditions from that same sage ("I have heard") with a markedly kabbalistic character.

end" of all creatures are enclosed. The soul of man is therefore the most precious factor acting in the world. The human body is of no lesser rank:

> The righteous is a sacred body woven by the angels, and that is the meaning of "Let us make man in our image," and over every single member there is posted an angel who thereby helps it perform a commandment [of the Torah]. The sinner has a body woven by the angels of destruction, and over each member is posted an archon, so that he commits a sin with it [the member]. The sinner has an intellect light as straw, but the righteous [has one] heavy as gold.[181]

The strict determinism between righteous and sinners is striking. The soul is of an immediately divine nature.

> Man draws upon himself a higher power, more intimate than all others, and his reasonable soul is particularly pure, since it does not originate in a meditation in the concatenation of other things, but is emanated from something nobler than itself. (ibn Sahula 4c)

The Hebrew expression employed here, *'inyan me'ulleh,* might lead one to believe that Isaac was influenced by Yehudah Halevi's doctrine of the *'inyan 'elohi* in the *Kuzari* 1:95.[182] According to the latter, the spirit of Adam in fact contained such a "divine something," though Halevi conceived of it, of course, in a manner very different from that of the kabbalists. Isaac comments on Genesis 2:7, "He blew into his nostrils the breath of life," with the following words: "Whoever blows into a goatskin puts his own breath in it."[183] We may therefore assume that he regarded the human pneuma as coming directly from the world of the emanations; it was the divine in man, which had only to be actualized. This corresponds to Isaac's statements on the soul, in connection with chapters 2 and 3 of the *Yeṣirah,* quoted previously. No doubt the tradition from Isaac is also the source for Naḥmanides' commentary on Genesis 2:7, regarding the divine origin and character of the soul, though he uses a

---

181. A fragment of Isaac in the Ms. Vatican 202, fol. 116b, a very old collection of materials from the school of Gerona.

182. Cf. on this doctrine, behind which there lies, albeit in a modified form, the notion if the logos, I. Goldziher, "Le Amr ilahi *(ha-'inyan ha-'elohi)* chez Juda Halévi," *REJ* 50 (1905): 32–41; Isidore Epstein, *JQR* 25 (1935): 215–219; Israel Efros, *PAAJR* 11 (1941): 31–33.

183. Quoted in Sahula 5b.

slightly different metaphor: "Whoever blows into another's nose imparts to him from his own soul."[184]

It is not quite clear how Isaac distinguished between the different degrees or powers of the soul. He speaks of *nefesh,* as representing sense perception in its general signification, and of the more inward levels of *ruḥoth* and *neshamoth,* without clearly explaining himself on their relations to one another. The character of emanation seems to be attributed specifically to *neshamah.* In one passage, he also mentions "souls that are internal and united [to their origin]," and that apparently originate with *binah.* They act by means of organs, *kelim,* which constitute the transition leading to the "perceptible forms," which in turn stem from the power of these intermediary causes (on 2:2). This concept of the "innermost souls" for certain essences in the world of emanation also recurs later in other sources.[185] Also belonging to the world of the supreme emanations is, by virtue of its very nature, the good. Isaac laid much stress on the particular, "light" nature of the good. The good is that which "was illuminated at its origin," as candles are lit from one another, and it is in this sense that he interprets Genesis 1:4: "He saw the light that was lit." He derives this mystical etymology of the good from an Aramaic translation, no longer extant, of Exodus 30:7.[186]

---

184. This is also the origin of a very similar idiomatic expression occurring in kabbalistic and Hasidic literature; cf. M. Halamish, "On the origins of a proverb in kabbalistic literature," (in Hebrew), *Yearbook of the Bar-Ilan University* 13 (1976):-211–223.

185. Cf. for example the piece designated as the "secret of the inner souls, spirits and *nefashoth,"* which I published in *Madda'e ha-Yahaduth* 2:285. Its author, probably Isaac Cohen, bases himself on traditions he received from the "Hasid and perfect kabbalist," who may be identical with the anonymous kabbalist of Narbonne whom he generally introduced with the same formula, and to whom he often refers. The text is also closely related to that quoted at the end of this chapter, pp. 360–1

186. Cf. this quotation from the Targum in Ezra's commentary of the Song of Songs where, perhaps, originally Isaac was also named: *we-ken perash* [*he-ḥasid*]; cf. Azriel, *Perush 'Aggadoth,* 89; Joseph ben Samuel on Genesis 1, in chapter 31 in the name of Jacob ben Shesheth, *Meshibh debharim Nekhoḥim,* as well as Jacob ben Shesheth himself, in the same work, Ms. Oxford, f.61a. The substance of the interpretation has also been adopted by the *Zohar;* cf. 1:230a. Here, too, the line of transmission is clear: Moses de Leon cites the passage from Ezra (who is not named) together with the quotation from the Targum, in *Sefer ha-Rimmon,* Ms. British Museum, Margoliouth 759, fol. 51a. G. Vajda, *Recherches,* 303 n. 2, has pointed out the interpretation of the biblical expression *behetibho* as "lighting" (the candles) occurs for the first time in Maimonides' *Code* (*Hilkhoth Temidin u-Musafim* 3:12), which, however, does not appeal to any source from the Targum.

But it is not only the good that has its origin in the irradiation of lights of the emanation; there also exists a positive evil, which is related to the root of death. In this way Isaac adopts a modified form of the corresponding idea of the *Bahir* concerning the nature of evil. The oppositions discussed in chapter 4 of the Book *Yeṣirah,* in connection with the seven consonants of the Hebrew alphabet that can be pronounced in two different ways, also include that of life and death; and Isaac explains that "after the cause of life, the cause of death was emanated." Also at the beginning of chapter 2 he emphasizes that in each case the poles of oppositions come "from an autonomous principle." Death is therefore something more and something other than the mere cessation of life. It has a positive root. Certainly Isaac stresses at the same time that in the world of the sefiroth and of the "inner essences," good and bad are not yet dissociated from one another but are harmoniously united, *be- 'aḥduth ube-shalom.* Only when the "roots" continue to develop into a tree—and in the emanation that later derives from it and to which the double letters correspond—does evil also exist in isolation. Otherwise, Isaac's thinking remains determined by the image of the organic body (on chap. 4). The letters are like the branches of the tree and in them the intertwined pattern of good and evil is unfolded, so that each good *middah* also has its corresponding evil and vice versa. The question of the nature of evil also plays a part in other fragments from Isaac. Thus we are told in one fragment (quoted by Sahula 24b), that "all things that come from the left are dominated by impurity as it is said [Jer. 1:14]: 'From the north shall evil break loose.' " There exists therefore an emanation of things that come from the power of the left, which is the sefirah *paḥad* or *geburah.* This special emanation of the left is not conceived in a dualistic perspective as an autonomous hierarchy parallel to that of the sefiroth; it belongs to the world of the sefiroth itself and originates in *paḥad* in order to act in the lower regions.

To these and similar ideas, which trace the origin of these unholy or destructive powers back even to *binah,* Provençal kabbalists of the early thirteenth century added a more elaborate theory of the emanation of the left and its powers, including an entire metaphysic of demonology. The treatise in which Isaac Cohen of Soria expounded this doctrine around 1270 is based on, among other things, old papers that he claims to have found in Arles among the local kabbalists and that were purported to have come from the

Orient.[187] But the texts in question seem rather to follow the intellectual tradition of Provence and in any case have nothing in common with the Oriental sources of the Kabbalah that can still be identified in the *Bahir.* On the other hand, what might very well be of Oriental origin are purely mythical statements regarding the realm of demons, in which kabbalistic ideas like the doctrine of the sefiroth or the idea of emanation in general play no role. These doctrines are mentioned by Isaac Cohen as coming from theurgic texts, which he connects with the "Lesser Hekhaloth" and a *Sefer Malbush* which, however, bear no relation to the old theurgic texts known by these names.[188] In these sources, Sammael and Lilith appear for the first time as the demonic couple placed at the head of the hierarchy of darkness. The connection between this strange mythic construction and the properly kabbalistic theories was only established later by the editors, the brothers Isaac and Jacob Cohen or their teachers. The great antiquity of these ideas, the details of which I do not wish to discuss here,[189] is also attested by the fact that the very old etymology, borrowed by the Gnostics of the second century from Jewish circles, of the name of the devil Sammael—a name that arose

---

187. *Madda 'e ha-Yahaduth* 2:248. The old leaves shown him by the kabbalists of Arles supposedly came from a great scholar named Masliaḥ ben Palatia, from Jerusalem. They were brought by a certain "R. Gershom of Damascus," who is said to have lived in Arles for two years, and about whose learning and wealth miraculous things were related there. Judging by the context, there can be little doubt about the legendary character of this account.

188. Cf. on the subject of the "Lesser Hekhaloth" my book *Jewish Gnosticism,* 75–83; on the *Sefer ha-Malbush,* the "Book of the putting on of the divine name," cf. my book *On the Kabbalah,* 136–137.

189. The relationships between the different sources and systems employed or expounded in Isaac Cohen's writings are complicated. I dealt with this question in *Tarbiz* 2 (1931): 436–442; 3:33–36; 4:285–286. Isaac and his brother, who searched around 1250–1260 for remnants of old traditions preserved by the local kabbalists in Provence, managed to lay their hands on all sorts of things. Alongside his own system, which had a Neoplatonic and speculative character, we have that of the alleged treatise of Damascus (which, for its part, already represents an adaptation of the spirit of the doctrine of the sefiroth of older, quasi-gnostic sources of a rather pronounced dramatic character) and the still older system that he expounds on the basis of the two aforementioned sources. In this system there is absolutely no reference to the doctrine of the sefiroth. We are dealing with demonological myths of a concrete type that make no use of abstract notions. A close connection exists throughout with magic and with the doctrine of the efficacious "names" and their operations. The so-called practical Kabbalah came into being in circles that were especially concerned with the cultivation and development of the traditions that Isaac Cohen himself expressly distinguished—as the Kabbalah of the masters of theurgy—from the speculative Kabbalah, that is, mystical theology.

concurrently with that of Beliar—is still preserved here: the "blind archon," *sar summa.*[190] In Provence, Aramaic texts appeared that could in fact have arrived there, at least in part, directly from the Orient in the twelfth century, even if they did not necessarily reach the circle of Rabad and his family. It seems, however, that in some of the earliest circles of kabbalists further variations were composed in an obviously artificial Aramaic on these same themes of the demonological hierarchies. Remnants of these compositions still exist, for example, the pseudo-gaonic responsum on the conjuration of the prince of the demons, which incidentally also speaks of the revelation of the prophet Elijah during the night of the Day of Atonement. Already the earliest stratum of these texts distinguished between an old and a young Lilith and is familiar with strange names for the demonic rulers of the three realms of the ether and

---

190. The (sethian?) gnostic texts of Nag Hammadi know this etymology of Sammael as the blind God; cf. the tract "On the Nature of the Archons," trans. H. M. Schenke, *Koptisch-gnostische Schriften aus Nag Hamadi* (1960), 77, and the reference there to the "God of the blind." On the subject of the blind god Yaldabaoth-Sammael, cf. also H. Jonas, *Gnosis und spätantiker Geist,* pt. 1: *Die mythologische Gnosis,* suppl. 3 to the 1st and 2d eds. (1964), 384 (for example, the designation of the demiurge as "the blind" in a Peratite sect mentioned by Hyppolytus); cf. also Jean Doresse, *Les Livres secrets des Gnostiques d'Egypte* (1958), 188, 195, and the evidence (that he obtained from me) pertaining to this point added in the English edition, *The Secret Books of the Egyptian Gnostics* (1960), 175 n. 49. As late as about 900 C.E., Theodor bar Konai still knew that the Ophites regarded Samiel (Sammael) as a "blind angel" in the first heaven who is evil and satanic; cf. H. Pognon, *Inscriptions Mandaites* (Paris, 1898), 145, and the translation of the Syriac text, ibid., 213. (According to the *Ascensio Jesajae* 7:9 too, Sammael is below the first heaven). Isaac Cohen even had knowledge of traditions that spoke of Leviathan—identified by the Ophites with Sammael—as the "blind dragon" (Hebrew: *tannin 'iwwer* or also Tanninsam, which corresponds to *tannin summa*), cf. *Madda'e ha-Yahaduth* 2:262, 264. In Mandaean literature Samyael is known as a demon of blindness, cf. E. S. Drower, *The Canonical Prayerbook of the Mandaeans* (Leiden, 1959), 248. Among the Sabians of Harran, Mars was called "the blind master," cf. the Arabic text in *Picatrix,* ed. Ritter (Berlin, 1933), 226, where the Aramaic term *mara samya* is preserved, as well as Chwolson, *Die Ssabier,* vol. 2 (1858), 188. Chwolson could not explain this epithet, the simple explanation of which lies in the fact that in the very old Jewish list of angels the angel of the planet Mars was precisely Sammael. In the known Sabian texts the name Sammael itself had fallen into oblivion, but not its Aramaic and Arabic translations. On Sammael as the angel of Mars, cf., for example, Yehudah ben Barzilai on *Yeṣirah,* 247; *Raziel,* fol. 17b and 34b (in the old *Sefer ha-Razim*); Gaster, *Studies and Texts* (1925), 1:350. Magical prayers of the late Byzantine period still know the "blind serpent"; cf. A Barb, "Der Heilige und die Schlangen," separate reprint from *Mitteilungen der Anthropologischen Gesellschaft* (Vienna, 1952), 6, which obviously belongs in the same context. This detail, therefore, shows that Isaac's sources effectively preserved within Judaism old ideas that had originated there and whose ramifications had spread to the Oriental gnosis.

for their spouses, the Jewish names being combined with those of an obviously foreign provenance.

> The old Lilith is the wife of Sammael; both of them were born at the same hour in the image of Adam and Eve, and they embrace one another. Ashmedai, the great king of the demons, took as his wife the young Lilith, daughter of the king; his name is Qafṣafuni and the name of his wife is Meheṭabel, daughter of Maṭred [from Gen. 36:39], and her daughter Lilitha.[191]

The fact that the spouse of the last king of Edom (in the list given in Genesis 36) figures as a demon suggests a reinterpretation of the list of these kings that turned them into the archons of darkness. Sammael too appears in these sources as the ruler of Edom—a Jewish code word, since the early Middle Ages, for Christianity, which was regarded as originating from the realm of darkness. It is only in Provence that these and similar purely demonological traditions

---

191. Cf. *Madda'e ha-Yahaduth* 2:260. A "Lilitha, granddaughter of Lilitha" occurs in Montgomery, *Aramaic Incantation Texts,* 168. According to another tradition (ibid., 256), Sammael, the archon of Edom, has three subordinates: the three kings Ashmedai, Qafqafuni, and Qafṣafuni. Each of the four archons has two brides or wives whose names are the subject of various traditions; cf. my compilation in *Tarbiz* 4 (1933): 72. The doubling of the wives suggests that the origin of this system lies in the Orient. Ashmedai and Lilith have a son who bears, as the great prince of the demons, page 261, the surname of "Sword of Ashmedai"; since Ashmedai appears here as the archon of Ishmael, that is, of Islam, one wonders whether this epithet may not be a parody of the kunya *Saif al-Islam,* then in vogue among Arab princes. But his proper name, according to the same source, is אלפפוניאש , undoubtedly a distortion of Greek, possibly even of a demonized [Antiochus] Epiphanes. He is also called Guryahud (reading corrected according to the manuscripts) because he attacks the archons of Judah. The kabbalistic revision of this source added a corresponding archon of the holy side, born "from the root of the [tenth sefirah] *malkhuth,*" and appropriately called "Sword of the Messiah." That such ancient names and traditions referring to the great events of the distant past could have been preserved in mythic forms is not surprising. Also the name of Ahriman, Agro-Mainju, lord of the demons in Parsiism, has been preserved, in the slightly distorted form of Agrimus [from Agro-Mainus] in Jewish demonological tradition. He appears in many aggadoth, preserved in the Cairo Genizah, concerning the demonic descendants of Adam and his first wife Lilith, and is called "the first born of Adam and Lilith." An old aggadah on Methushelaḥ (literally: man of the sword) tells how the descendants of this demon Agrimus were put to death by the sword of the patriarch; cf. the references in L. Ginzberg, *Legends* 5:165–166. Ginzberg already recognized the connection with the Persian Ahriman. L. Ginzberg, in *Ha-Goren* 10 (1923): 66–68, and A. Marmorstein, in *Debhir* 1 (1923): 137–138, have published, independently of one another, the most important text. An abbreviated form of this aggadah also reached Eleazar of Worms from a *Book of Secrets.*

led to the elaboration of a doctrine of the "left emanation" that attempted to combine them with the kabbalistic doctrine of the emanation of the ten sefiroth. These ideas then passed from Provence to Castile, where they could readily be attributed to older pseudepigraphic authorities, among whom Isaac the Blind also figured; in fact, however, it is extremely doubtful whether ideas of this kind should be ascribed to him.[192]

Nevertheless, many extant fragments prove that Isaac had a certain interest in questions relating to the nature of Sammael, whose name had become for the Jews of the Middle Ages, the principal one associated with the devil and his dominion. The following dictum of Isaac makes good sense when viewed against the background of the large number of shepherds populating the western Languedoc:

> He who lives with herds of sheep, even if it is in the high mountains and in the desert wastes, which are uninhabited, has no need to fear Satan and the evil powers, for no evil spirit rules among them. But he who lives among goats [of him it can be said] that even when he is surrounded by ten houses and a hundred men, an evil spirit rules over them.[193]

In another fragment, we learn that Sammael's origins lie in the power of the sefirah *paḥad,* channeled to him through the last sefirah "without any other intermediary." He has, therefore, a legitimate position in the sacred totality of Creation. It was only when he pitted himself in the war of Amaleq against Israel and the sacred order it represents—a war that has always been interpreted in Jewish tradition as a metaphysical event of enormous significance—that he lost this legitimate place. Since then he receives his power only indirectly, from planetary spirits, and "no longer by the path of the primordial order of Creation." Only in the messianic era will the

---

192. According to the testimony of the most important transmitters of these traditions, and above all of Isaac of Acre, these doctrines were known only to the Castilian kabbalists (in Burgos and Toledo), but not to those of Catalonia (in Gerona and Barcelona). If the latter group had no knowledge of them, then these traditions cannot go back to Isaac the Blind. However, it is precisely Moses of Burgos who refers to the authority of Naḥmanides, Yehudah ben Yaqar, Isaac the Blind, and Shelemiah of Arles (from the circle of the Rabad) in these matters; but the alleged quotations are obviously fictitious. Cf. my study of this question in *Tarbiz* 3 (1932): 276–279.

193. Quoted in Isaac Cohen, *Madda'e ha-Yahaduth* 2: 280.

position of Sammael be restored; the Throne of God, which for the present is damaged, will then be repaired.[194] It thus appears that Isaac the Blind was a follower of the doctrine of the ultimate "restoration of Satan," the apocatastasis. Since, as is well known, Judaism recognized no official dogmatic authority that was entitled to determine the content of the faith, this question too, which played such an important role in the history of the Christian churches, remained open and a subject of dispassionate discussion. Opinions were divided, and many mystics adhered to the "restoration" doctrine. Later kabbalistic theories exhibiting the same tendency, such as Joseph ibn Gikatilla's *Mystery of the Serpent,*[195] probably owe their inspiration to Isaac the Blind. What is curious in the case of Isaac is that Sammael did not fall from his exalted rank, as one would expect, at the time of Adam's sin—for which the Aggadah holds him responsible—but only at the time of the battle against Amaleq. In this detail he was not followed by later kabbalists; even when they defended the doctrine of apocatastasis they placed it in relation to the reestablishment of the harmony of all things, which had been disturbed by Adam's original sin. However, also for ibn Gikatilla (as for Isaac), the serpent drew his original power directly from the sacred domain of the emanations, standing outside its "walls" and acting as the genius of the entire sublunar world. There, too, the rebellion of the serpent introduces disorder into the harmonious union of the worlds and isolates Sammael as genius of evil.

Isaac's view that the supreme angelic powers draw their influx directly from the tenth sefirah is also found in Ezra, who attests to having received "from the lips of the son of the master," that is, from Isaac the Blind, the doctrine "that Metatron is only a messenger, and not a specific thing bearing that name. Rather, every messenger is called in Greek *metator,* and perhaps the messengers received the influx of the [tenth sefirah] named *'aṭarah* to fulfill their mission."[196] Metatron is therefore not a proper name at all but a

---

194. Thus in the miscellanies in Ms. British Museum Margoliouth 768, fol. 115a, which is essentially identical with the less clearly formulated quotation of the Hasid in Sahula, fol. 17a.

195. Part of the text is quoted in my *Major Trends,* 405–406.

196. In Ezra's *Perush 'Aggadoth,* Ms. Vatican 294, fol. 48b. The abbreviation מהע' [for מהעטרה] was falsely written as מהעי' and interpreted as מהעילה . The same mistake appears immediately preceding this passage, in another quotation:

> I heard in the name of our master [probably also Isaac the Blind, with whose opinion this is in accord] that the place of the souls, *neshamoth,* is in the sefirah

designation for the whole category of celestial powers performing a mission. This conception is far more prosaic than that taught by his father, the Rabad (cf. the passage quoted, p. 212), in his commentary on the Talmud. Is this the whole truth about Isaac's view, or merely an occasional remark? No other kabbalist ever denied the existence of a specific angelic being called Metatron, even if he adopted Isaac's etymology.[197] The etymology itself is apparently taken from the old talmudic dictionary *'Arukh* of Nathan ben Yeḥiel of Rome, which was well known in Provence (as *metator*). Isaac obviously did not think of identifying Metatron with the last sefirah, the Shekhinah, although the identification is found later, among the first generation of Catalan kabbalists.[198]

7. Isaac's Contemplative Mysticism: Kawwanah *and* Debhequth

Isaac's picture of the universe rests, therefore, on the idea that the different realms of Creation, each according to its rank in the hierarchy of things, are in communication with the roots of all being as given in the world of the sefiroth. The limited powers proceed from the unlimited powers, and the secret signature of the letters acts in everything, but nowhere more clearly than in man. But to the current that flows downward there corresponds another, upward movement. When Isaac says in his commentary on *Yeṣirah* (end of chapter 3) that "all things return to the root of their true being,"[199] he

---

binah, named *teshubah.* They proceed from there and continue from degree to degree until *'aṭarah* [to be read thus instead of מהעי׳] and proceed from there and become attached to the human body. And after its separation from the body, it returns, if it is worthy [to the worlds of the sefiroth] and is bound in *tif'ereth,* which is "bundle of life."

197. Cf., for example, Naḥmanides who, in his commentary on the Pentateuch, (Exod. 12:12) says that he "heard" of this etymology.

198. Cf. chap. 2, p. 187, note 214, herein. For Isaac, however, the "guardian of Israel" mentioned in the psalms and prayers is not Metatron but the tenth sefirah, the Shekhinah in her quality of *Maṭrona.* He derives the word *Maṭrona* from the Aramaic *maṭara,* which means "guard"; cf. the quotations in Sahula, fols. 23d and 29b. Ezra and Azriel declare in their commentary on the Aggadah, which is almost identical in the part devoted to the tractate *Berakhoth* (ed. Tishby, 10, the section beginning with the words "we have received"), that this is the guardian of Israel who bears (in *B. Berakhoth* 7a) the mystical name Aktariel, which is nothing other than the Shekhinah and the cherub and is called "angel of glory." Cf. also p. 171, herein, as well as *Ma'arekheth ha-'Elohuth* (Mantua, 1558), fol. 72b.

199. Hebrew: *Kol ha-debharim ḥozrim le-shoresh 'iqqaram.*

means, in this context, that a thing can act only in that which is related to its principle. But his disciples already understood expressions of this kind in the sense of a return of all things to God. "Everything issues from the first Cause, and everything returns to the first Cause."[200] Such a return can have both an ontological and an eschatological aspect. Even before the end of all things all being seeks to return, in accordance with its nature, to its origin, in the spirit of the ancient philosophical thesis of the *appetitus naturalis,* which the Neoplatonists above all rendered popular in the Middle Ages. But also, the eschatological nuance of a "restoration of all things to their original being," *hashabath kol ha-debharim le-hawwayatham,* is not absent among Isaac's pupils, who probably derived it from him.[201] But beyond these eschatological perspectives, the return of man (whose special rank is due to the divine element in his soul) to communication with his root is furthered or facilitated by the path of contemplative mysticism that underlies Isaac's ideas concerning the values of the Torah and its commandments as well as the religious life of the Jew in general.

The notions of *kawwanah* and *debhequth* are of fundamental importance for this view. They are, to all appearances, closely bound up with one another. The theoretical basis of Isaac's doctrine of the *kawwanah,* which cannot be directly inferred from the concrete indications given for the *kawwanoth* to be performed during certain prayers, is found in his *Yeṣirah* commentary (1:8). From the knowable a road opens toward the Unknowable, "and it is to that end that the *middoth* are made," namely, in order to serve as an intermediary between the bounded and the unbounded. From the contemplation of the lower *middoth* the mystic ascends to the higher ones,

> for every *middah* is filled with that which is above it, and they are given to Israel [perhaps to be understood also in the sense of: their

---

200. Ezra quotes this sentence in an eschatological context in his commentary on the Song of Songs, Altona 1764, fol. 16a, attributing it to a "sage," who is probably none other than the "philosopher" at the beginning of the *Kuzari* 1:1. In the literature of the *'Iyyun* group (cf. pp. 320–1, herein) we find the well-known Neoplatonic saying "everything comes from the One and everything returns to the One" explicitly mentioned as a quotation; for example, in the *Book of the True Unity,* Ms. Jerusalem 8⁰ 488, fol. 16a.

201. Cf. Naḥmanides on *Yeṣirah,* in *Kiryath Sefer* 6 (1930): 401, and n. 201 on p. 449 herein. The Hebrew expression gives the impression of being an exact rendering of the Latin *restitutio omnium rerum ad integrum.*

> sequence has been transmitted to Israel], in order to meditate from the *middah* that is visible in the heart, to meditate up to the Infinite. For there is no other path to the [true] prayer than this one: by means of the limited words, man is made to enter [into their interior] and rises in thought to the Infinite.[202]

After what we have learned here concerning Isaac's conception of the *maḥshabah* and of words, this last sentence not only signifies that in prayer the limited human words and human thought elevate man to the Infinite, the *'en-sof;* it also shows the internal route the prayer must follow in the *kawwanah.* This route leads through the sefiroth, the relatively limited "words," to the unlimited, pure thought, and from there into the depth of the *'en-sof* itself. The divine *middoth* are therefore the object of meditation. He who prays orients himself toward the specific *middoth* signified and intended in the various parts of the liturgical texts, in accordance with the esoteric "transmission" to the mystics. In his concentrated reflection on the word he finds the "primordial word" and through it the contact with the infinite movement of the divine *maḥshabah* itself, in which he raises himself to *'en-sof.* Therefore, in the word, the mystical *kawwanah* reveals a spiritual inner space where the word soars up to the divine.

The ambiguous conclusion of Isaac's sentence is no doubt deliberate. *Maḥshabah* can be taken to mean, on the one hand, the divine Thought, but on the other hand, also human thought. Perhaps one could correlate this elevation of the pure thought toward the Infinite in the *kawwanah,* with the Catholic formula *elevatio mentis ad deum,* in which, according to Friedrich Heiler, "the specificity of mystical prayer is aptly defined."[203] The kabbalist, to be sure, adds a new element here: he seeks from the depth of his own thought to enter into contact with, or to insert himself into, the infinite movement of the divine Thought. This precisely is his real goal. The *kawwanah,* in prayer as well as in the performance of religious commandments, serves to actualize the contact with God, which is the final goal along the road that leads man toward Him.

It is this contact, connection, or *communio* with God that is designated by the Hebrew term *debhequth.* This kabbalistic concept

202. Cf. the text of the passage in *MGWJ* 78 (1934): 32.

203. Cf. Friedrich Heiler, *Das Gebet,* 2d ed., 291.

has its origins in the terminology of the medieval Jewish theologians, especially Baḥya ibn Paquda and Abraham ibn Ezra, who employed the biblical verb *dabhaq* ("adhere, cleave to,") to express the contact of the soul with God or the divine light. The biblical injunction Deuteronomy 13:5 is cited by Isaac's pupils as their master's cue for this doctrine:

> Our master the Hasid said: The essential thing in the divine service of the mystics [*maskilim*] and those who meditate on His name, lies in this [verse]: "and cleave to Him." And this is a cardinal principle of Torah and of prayer, that one make one's thought conform[204] with one's faith, as though it were cleaving to what is above, in order to conjoin the name [of God] in its letters and to link the ten sefiroth to Him as a flame is joined to the coal. With his mouth he must express it according to its paraphrase, but in his heart, he must conjoin it in its true structure.[205]

Debhequth is therefore not *unio* but *communio.* In the sense the term acquired in kabbalistic usage it always contains an element of distance despite its character of intimacy. *Debhequth* is not becoming one with God but entering into an infinitely close liaison with him, roughly corresponding to that called *adhaeresis* by medieval Christian mystics. In Hebrew, *debhequth* can denote the process as well as the state attained through it. The instrument of this process is the *kawwanah.* Isaac and his disciples do not speak of ecstasy, of a unique act of stepping outside oneself in which human consciousness abolishes itself. *Debhequth* does not consist in tempestuously rushing toward God and becoming absorbed in him; it is a constant state, nurtured and renewed through meditation. In contrast to some later schools, the old kabbalists did not go any further, and in this remained true to their Jewish-theistic character. For them, *debhequth* or the mystical *communio* is not, as for many non-Jewish mystics, a transitional stage leading to still higher regions. Any pantheistic

---

204. An ambiguous phrase that perhaps stands for more than conformity of thought and faith. *'Emunah,* faith, is frequently employed by Isaac as a symbolic term for the second and the tenth sefiroth, while *maḥshabah* represents the first. Perhaps this "cardinal principle" signifies therefore that in the meditation on the name of God the mystic brings the ten sefiroth—from the first to the last—into harmony.

205. Quoted by Ezra on the Song of Songs, fol. 8d, and again, though without indication of his source, in *Perush 'Aggadoth,* 16.

overstepping of the limits they fixed for themselves in their interpretation of the mystical path is far from their thoughts.[206]

The detailed expositions of the meaning of *debhequth,* as we find them above all with Isaac's disciples Ezra and Azriel (see chap. 4 following) employ an imagery close to that of Isaac and go back, we may suppose, to the master's teaching of their master; very probably were written down during his lifetime. Isaac's nephew, Asher, likewise speaks in a very similar manner of this path as the authentic return to God in which

> man conforms his deeds, purifies his soul, purges his thoughts . . . and holds fast to his Creator with his spirit and his soul *(neshamah)* and, for His sake, avoids transgressions. It is of him that the sages said: In the place where those who return [to God] stand, [even] the perfectly righteous cannot stand.[207]

It is therefore not to the penitents, in the usual sense of the term, that this famous talmudic dictum (*B. Berakhoth* 34b) is said to refer here, but to the mystics who are in a state of *debhequth* and thereby occupy a place above that of the righteous who have not traveled this path. Of particular importance are statements of essentially the same tenor found in Ezra and Azriel on the significance of this process and the state that is attained through it:

> He who prays must regard himself as if God spoke to him and taught him and instructed him, and he received his words in fear and trembling. And he should consider that all the words He teaches man are infinite, but that [human] thought spreads and rises to the place of its origin, and when it arrives there, it breaks off and cannot rise further. It is like a source of water flowing from a mountain. If you dig a pond beneath it, in order that the waters should not spread in every direction, they rise, but only up to the place of the source, and no higher.[208] Similarly, the thought can rise no higher than its point of

---

206. Tishby attempted to give the passages on *debhequth* in Ezra and Naḥmanides an interpretation that goes much further, in the sense of a complete ecstatic union with the deity, but his thesis seems to me unacceptable. Insofar as *debhequth* really contains moments of ecstasy, the individuality of the mystic nonetheless remains preserved in it, contra Tishby; cf. his comments in *Molad* 19: 151–152 (1961): 49–55.

207. Asher ben David, *Perush Shem ha-Meforash,* ed. Ḥasida, 7.

208. I translate according to Ezra's text, which is more logical. The simile is already found in another context, in connection with the origin of the souls, in Isaac's discussion of sacrifice, Sahula, fol. 23c.

> origin. And whoever dares to direct his thinking whither thought cannot extend and elevate itself [would this perhaps be the Unknowable in Isaac's system: the first sefirah?] cannot escape one of two things: either, as a result of the excessive compulsion of the thought, by which he constrains to grasp that which is unknowable and to communicate with it, his soul rises and detaches itself [from its link with the body] and returns to its root, or, his mind and intellect fall into confusion and his body is destroyed. . . . Therefore the old Hasidim[209] elevated their thought to its place of origin and they mentioned [in their meditation] the commandments and the words [of the prayer]. From the mention of the words and the thinking adhering to them,[210] the words acquired plenitude and blessing from the sphere of the "nought of thought," as when someone opens the sluice of a pond of water and it flows out in every direction. For the thought adhering [to God] is the source and the inexhaustible current of blessing. . . . Of the same kind was also the power by which prophecy was drawn down, for the prophet retired into solitude and directed his mind and attached his thought upward, and according to the degree of intensity of the prophetic *debhequth,* the prophet beheld and knew the future.[211]

Meditative prayer and prophetic ascension are therefore fundamentally the same spiritual act. On the subject of *debhequth,* Isaac's contemplative mysticism comes very close to the teaching of Maimonides, at the end of *The Guide of the Perplexed* (3:51) concerning the rank of Moses and the Patriarchs as the highest level accessible to terrestrial beings. The connection with Maimonides becomes clearer still in the generation following Isaac—for example, in Naḥmanides. In the case of Isaac, it is not necessarily a matter of direct dependence upon Maimonides but rather of a common ideal: the supreme value of the *vita contemplativa.* In certain of Ezra's statements this connection between *debhequth* and the theory of prophecy is elucidated even more clearly.[212] His utterances on the subject,

---

209. This refers to the *Hasidim* mentioned in *B. Berakhoth* 30b, where their liturgical practices are discussed.

210. Hebrew: *ha-maḥshabah ha-debheqah.* The same expression also occurs in Isaac of Acre's account of Isaac the Blind, published by Jellinek, *Geschichte der Kabbala* 2:xvii. It appears that Isaac used to instruct the pupil leading him to go as quickly as possible when they had to pass by a church. "He did this for the honor of God, to whom his thinking adhered [*haythah maḥshabto debheqah bo*], since on account of the impure spirit which resided there, he was obliged to interrupt his meditation."

211. Azriel, *Perush 'Aggadoth,* 39–40; Ezra, whose text is printed anonymously in the kabbalistic collection *Liqquṭe Shikhḥah u-Fe'a* (Ferrara, 1556), fols. 7b–8a.

212. Cf. Azriel's letter to Burgos, *Madda'e ha-Yahaduth* 2:239.

which perhaps go back to Isaac, link the doctrine of *debhequth* to his account of the ecstasy of Moses.[213] The adhesion of human thinking to the divine wisdom in *debhequth* actually results, according to Ezra, in two becoming one.[214] It is interesting to note that even Isaac's simile of following the thread until one reaches the actual skein is related by many kabbalists not only to conditions within the world of the sefiroth but also to the paths of mystical ascension in general. According to them, the paths of the Sophia of which the Book *Yeṣirah* speaks are those of the mystical ascent. In his contemplative thinking, man can follow the light that shines upon these paths until he arrives at its source, as if he were following the thread to the skein.[215]

Isaac the Blind connects prophecy with this apprehension of the *middoth,* to be attained by the upsurge of the human *maḥshabah.* "The prophets saw the *middoth,* each according to his rank." The essence of prophecy, he says in a rather obscure and difficult sentence, lies in the fact that in their assimilation of the divine Sophia, the prophets were more capable than others of "expanding" their thought[216] and thereby "obtaining a breadth of soul [that permitted them] to extend themselves in an infinite manner in individual things" (on 1:6). What exactly is meant by this extension of the soul or the thought in individual things is difficult to say. Isaac also speaks of such an extension and expansion in his explanation in the same passage of the mystical meaning of the commandments of the Torah, by means of which man "grasps at least the beginning of the *middoth.*" On Psalms 119:96: "I have seen that all things have their limit, but your commandment is broad beyond measure," Isaac comments:

> Although at first it appears to have a purpose, your commandment extends itself further and further to infinity. And if everything tran-

213. Cf. in Recanati, on Exodus 24:10.

214. Ezra, in *Liqquṭe Shikhḥah,* fol. 5b. This conception most probably has its source in Maimonides' commentary on the Mishnah, as has been suggested by Tishby in his notes on Azriel's *Perush ha-'Aggadoth,* 20.

215. This is how Isaac of Acre understood the beginning of Isaac's commentary of *Yeṣirah;* cf. *Kiryath Sefer* 31:381.

216. The relationship between *ḥokhmah* and *maḥshabah* in this passage is identical to that in the quotation referred to in n. 214 herein, and probably reflects Isaac's ideas.

> sitory has an end, nevertheless no man can penetrate [the interior] of your commandment, which is at the end of all comprehension, for man understands only the beginning of the *middoth.*

Man is therefore unable to plumb the depths of the commandments of the Torah, which appear to have a fixed dimension and end—this is probably the meaning of the Hebrew word *tikhlah*—for the more he turns his mind to its contemplation the further the commandment expands, like the contemplative thinking of man himself. It seems that Isaac is saying that in fulfilling the commandments man advances from the limited to the unlimited and the infinite. The activity of man in the accomplishment of the Torah converges, therefore, in the experience of the mystic, with the ascension and the expansion of his contemplative thinking. The two spheres are not separated, and here too it is apparently the concept of *kawwanah* that constitutes the link between commandment and prayer.

In contrast to the divine service in the Temple, which is essentially sacrificial, the Talmud designates prayer as "divine service of the heart" (*Ta'anith* 2a). Both forms of divine service, that of external action and that of internal concentration, are therefore two aspects of the same phenomenon. It is thus only logical that Isaac, in a relatively lengthy text on "the mystery of the sacrifice," should interpret the various stages of the ritual of the burnt offering (literally: "the offering of elevation"), *'olah,* in terms of his contemplative mysticism.[217] In sacrifice, man offers himself; everything else is merely a symbolic disguise. In the same spirit we read in an old text on prayer as a sacrificial service:

> Since the destruction of the Temple, there remained in Israel only the great name [of God]. And the righteous and the Hasidim and the men of [pious] action withdraw into solitude and rake the fire in the depths of the hearth of the altar in their own hearts: and then, from out of the pure thinking [of their meditation], all the sefiroth unite and attach themselves to one another, until they are drawn to the source of the infinitely sublime flame.[218]

---

217. Cf. Sahula, fols. 23b, c. Several manuscripts contain speculative and very interesting elaborations of this text by Azriel and Ezra; cf. Ms. Vatican 211, fols. 8b–12a.

218. Cf. the text of the passage in *MGWJ* 78 (1934): 506, which was also used by Meir ben Gabbai in his discussion of *debhequth* in *'Abodath ha-Qodesh* 2:6.

This last image suggests the writings of the *'Iyyun* circle, which repeatedly speak of the infinitely sublime flame, and the entire passage could very well come from a Provençal source. Isaac's commentary on *Yeṣirah* 1:6 clearly shows that for him this contemplative attitude is linked to an ascetic approach to life. He speaks approvingly of the one "who renounces [literally: leaves] his [other] qualities and devotes himself exclusively to thought, combining everything in thought, elevating thought and lowering the body, in order thereby to give predominance to his soul." In the same spirit, his disciple Ezra says that "when the power of the soul, which adheres to its creator [in *debhequth*], increases, the senses, thirsting after the pleasures of the lower world, become redundant."[219] In this passage the ascetic moment is associated with the ecstatic, for the quotation figures in an explanation of the elders of Israel who eat and drink before God (Exod. 24:11); the Midrash says of them: "their eyes were nourished by the splendor of the Shekhinah." This eating was therefore a spiritual event of the highest order, in which they could, indeed, had to, renounce all bodily things.

The rank achieved by man in his adherence to the divine *middoth* in the course of his bodily existence also determines his rank in the eschatological hierarchy after the resurrection, the bodily character of which Isaac maintains. His nephew explains, on Isaac's authority, the expression "bundle of life" in which the righteous are bound up, in a similar sense. "Those who have so conducted their lives that they sought to observe the commandments and to walk in the paths of Israel" are called the seed of Israel (cf. Isa. 45:25),

> even if they did not, in their lifetime, attain sufficient perfection to rise to this high rank. For no one can ascend to this rank if he has not become worthy of all seven *middoth* which are called "the bundle of life." And this is only possible if he had attained a *middah* to which he has adhered and in the plenitude of which he has stood [another version: in order to adhere to it and do the will of his Creator (by imitating it), and there his soul is bound up when it leaves the body, until its release also comes and it returns to its cause. . . . And even he who has undergone the purification of all the seven *middoth,* whether it be some of them or the majority of them, if he has not stood the test of all or almost all of them, he turns their *middah* [?][220] Of him it is said

219. Cf. the passage in Recanati mentioned in n. 213, as well as *Liqquṭe Shikḥah,* fol. 4a.

220. The text here is obviously corrupt. I cite according to the passage in Isaac of Acre, Ms. Munich 17, fols. 148b–149a. The text can also be understood as an allu-

> (Prov. 24:16) "seven times the righteous man falls and gets up,"[221] and if God permits him to rise, he completely traverses their paths. Then he rises in this rank [of the bundle of life] from degree to degree, up to the Infinite.

After the resurrection, the righteous and the average realize a new progress in their spiritual and moral perfection, one that takes them beyond everything they attained in their lives. By this adherence to the seven divine *middoth,* all will share perpetually in the gift of prophecy. From a brief allusion of ibn Sahula (f. 34a), we can infer that on several occasions Isaac expressed his views on eschatological matters, in the context of which he may also have discussed the preparation for redemption by means of the purification of souls during their transmigrations. In the extant texts, however, there is no clear statement on this subject, though on one occasion Isaac quotes a relevant passage from the *Bahir,* section 105. Isaac of Acre[222] states that in his commentary on *Yeṣirah* Isaac the Blind made a hidden allusion to the distinction between the migration of souls *(gilgul)* and the impregnation of souls *(ibbur)* as being two different things, but I have not been able to locate this allusion.

It should be clear from the foregoing that Isaac the Blind already had at his disposal a complete system of kabbalistic symbolism, partly inherited from tradition and partly elaborated by himself which he applied to a great variety of biblical and rabbinic subjects.[223] His epistle to Gerona, which has survived, offers a brief

---

sion to the transmigration of souls: after the ascension, man's soul must return to life one more time and enter into purification, *maṣref,* through all seven *middoth,* just in case he had not used them as his moral guideposts during his terrestrial life. This is how the somewhat different text, in Ms. Enelow Memorial Collection, Jewish Theological Seminary, New York, fol. 15a, seems to have understood the passage.

221. This is a pun, for the Hebrew verb "he stood up again" is the same as "he stood the test." He must in any case pass through all seven *middoth,* both as his own and as divine virtues, in this life or after the resurrection.

222. Cf. Isaac's *Me'irath 'Enayim,* Ms. Munich 17, fol. 100a.

223. Some of these have been briefly touched upon in the text. Isaac's interpretation of certain biblical prohibitions, for example, those of the fruit of the tree during the first three years, *'orlah* (ibn Sahula 26a) and of incestuous marriages, *'arayoth* (see Ezra, *Perush 'Aggadoth,* Ms. Vatican 441, fols. 30a, b, as a quotation from the Hasid; cf. also *Kiryath Sefer* 6:398, 417) show that many of the ideas current in the school of Gerona were already familiar to him. The quotation of Sahula 24b in the name of Isaac, on the subject of *niddah* and menstrual blood, is cited verbatim, though without any indication of the source in Ezra's commentary on the Song of Songs, 13c.

explanation of the last psalm, apparently in response to a question. The psalmist's tenfold invitation to praise God is interpreted as an allusion to the ten sefiroth, though the first sefirah is passed over in silence, and Isaac counts downward beginning with *ḥokhmah.* His mystical allusions in this epistle[224] scarcely differ from the instructions he gives for the mystical *kawwanoth* at prayer; there too, he briefly describes the process by which the mystic first traverses the world of the sefiroth from below upward during the profession of the divine unity, the *Shema' Yisrael,* and then, in his meditation on the word *'eḥad,* "one!" completes and closes the circle of his *kawwanah,* from above downward.[225] In this epistle Isaac already uses the expression "to damage (or cut down) the plants," which the Talmud had applied to the heresy of Elisha ben Abuya, in the kabbalistic sense of not preserving the unity of the ten sefiroth in God, and thus compromising the pure faith. This usage subsequently passed into the heritage of all kabbalists. Also, other elements of kabbalistic technical terminology, notably in the writings of the Gerona school, may well go back to him, although this cannot be proved. For our analysis it suffices to have demonstrated that in the fragments from Isaac a specific and completely independent form of the Kabbalah, very different from the world of the *Bahir* as we have learned to know it, can be localized and identified in Provence. The seed of the *Bahir,* landing in Provence, germinated in a singular manner.

8. The Writings of the 'Iyyun *Circle*

We do not know into whose hands in the various Provençal groups the Book *Bahir* first fell. Nor do we know exactly where it underwent its final redaction. It is equally difficult for us to ascertain exactly where firsthand Oriental traditions concerning the archons and the aeons of the celestial world first found their way into these regions and where they were elaborated further in conjunction with the new doctrine of the sefiroth. Communities like Narbonne and Marseilles had direct relations with the Levant, and we have already seen that the scholars of Arles too boasted of such connections. The

224. Cf. the text in *Sefer Bialik,* 143.

225. Cf. the relevant quotation in his name given by Sahula, fol. 32d; Recanati on Deuteronomy 6:4, ed. 1545, fol. 194d; Ms. Christ Church College 198, fol. 16a.

doctrines that may have arrived there in this manner, perhaps in the twelfth century, are very far removed from the specific spiritual universe of the *Bahir,* and the ostensible revisions of such materials in Isaac Cohen's sources likewise betray nothing of the spirit animating Isaac the Blind. The tendency of these writings to enumerate celestial beings and their names is sometimes reminiscent of the catalogues to be found in the *Pistis Sophia* and other gnostic (Mandaean) texts of a later period. Isaac Cohen, who preserved for us many such lists and enumerations, attributed them to a particular group of kabbalists who had not walked the "royal road" followed by the others. The source of these lists (as distinct from the demonological speculations discussed previously) is said to be a source he called the *Book of Rab Ḥammai,* which he claims to have found in Provence in three copies: one in Narbonne, in the possession of the aforementioned anonymous Hasid, and two in Arles.[226]

Here we find ourselves in a very curious situation. The *Book of Ḥammai* is lost; Moses of Burgos, Isaac's disciple, still quoted further catalogues of archons of a gnostic character;[227] the name appears in several other writings that in all probability also originated in Provence. But no historical personage by this name is known. Whether the Amora Ḥamma ben Ḥanina has been transformed into a pseudepigraphic author, or the name Raḥmai, רחמאי , known to us from the *Bahir* has perhaps become a Rab Ḥammai, ר' חמאי , or whether we are simply dealing with a new fiction, can no longer be determined.[228] In the most important of the extant texts, Ḥammai

---

226. *Madda'e ha-Yahaduth* 2:245. Already Steinschneider had drawn attention to this source, *Hebäische Bibliographie,* vol. 18 (1877), 20.

227. From several quotations in Moses of Burgos and Isaac of Acre one might possibly conclude that this *Book of Rab Ḥammai* was an expanded recension of the *Sefer ha-'Iyyun,* to be discussed below, or that it contained, at least in part, the same material. The quotation I published in *Tarbiz* 5:181 is in fact found in the latter book. Another quotation in Moses of Burgos, *Tarbiz* 5:54, is also mentioned by Isaac of Acre, Ms. Munich 17, fol. 25a; everything quoted there, except one line, is also found in the *Sefer ha-'Iyyun.* But it is clear from the context that this line too must originally have been there, since without it the text is deficient. My observation, *Tarbiz* 4:59, must therefore be corrected accordingly. Moses of Burgos quotes a saying from Ḥammai's book about the thirty-two paths, only thirty of which can be grasped. Nothing of the sort is found in our texts of the Book *'Iyyun.*

228. Reuchlin indeed names the author, Ḥammai ben Ḥanina; cf. *De arte cabalistica* (Hagenau, 1517), fol. 14a. He must have found it in his source. Later sources also quote a "Great Book *'Iyyun"* of R. Ḥamma bar Ḥanina; thus David Halevi (ca. 1500) in the *Sefer ha-Malkhuth,* printed in *Ma'or wa-Shemesh* (Livorno, 1839). There

appears as a speculative author of the eleventh or twelfth century who already relied upon pseudepigraphic kabbalistic writings circulating in the name of Hai Gaon (d.1040).[229] In addition to a "Book of the Unity," *Sefer ha-Yiḥud,* from which only some quotations remain,[230] we have a small tract entitled *Sefer ha-'Iyyun,*

---

are old quotations from the *Bahir* that read R. Hamai instead of Raḥmai as, for example, in the quotation from section 74 in Todros Abulafia, *'Oṣar ha-Kabhod,* Ms. Munich 103. Already Zunz, *Die Gottesdienstlichen Vorträge der Juden,* 2d ed., 420, drew attention to a similar passage by this author. The name of R. Ḥamma is also found in the Vilna edition of the *Bahir* (section 29 in the Vilna division of the text) and in the edition of R. Margalioth (based on the Vilna text) (Jerusalem, 1951). In his commentary *Qeseth ha-Sofer,* published anonymously, on the "Responsa from Heaven" of Jacob of Marvège (Cracow, 1895), 19, Ahron Marcus asserts that Ḥammai is not a name but signifies "my father-in-law" and identifies Abraham ben Isaac of Narbonne, the father-in-law of the Rabad, as the author. This explanation cannot be taken seriously. In revised texts of the Book *'Iyyun* as extant in several manuscripts (for example, a Florence manuscript dating from as early as 1328), this Ḥammai is distinguished from a "Rab Ḥammai the Great," his master. Later works even mention a "Book on the interior" (of reality), *Sefer ha-Penimiyuth;* cf. *Kiryath Sefer* 4 (1930): 275.

229. Writings falsely attributed to Hai Gaon seem also to have circulated outside kabbilistic circles, as appears from a quotation found in the anti-kabbalistic Meir ben Simon of Narbonne. In his *Milḥemeth Miṣwah* (Ms. Parma, de Rossi 155, fol. 243a), he quotes Hai to the effect that during the Shema' prayer one should move the head in all four cardinal directions "in order thereby to proclaim that He is in everything and rules over everything and exercises providence." The sequel (perhaps not Hai himself but Meir ben Simon) has a thoroughly kabbalistic flavor: "And I received from my father that one should direct his heart to each of the six directions, *qeṣawoth,* of space [according to the terminology of the book *Yeṣirah*] up to the Endless and the Boundless." My late colleague S. Assaf, a specialist on the writings of Hai Gaon, assured me that as regards style and the manner of thinking both parts of this statement were inconceivable in the mouth of Hai, and therefore spurious. At any rate a man like Meir ben Simon could take them to be authentic. If Meir used, without suspecting it, an unrecognized early kabbalistic forgery in the name of Hai, it is also perfectly conceivable that the second part also, with its entirely kabbalistic notion of *kawwanah*—which one would hardly attribute to the father of Meir ben Simon—already figured in a Pseudo-Hai of this kind, probably in a responsum. It should be noted that Pseudo-Hai is already mentioned by the German Hasidim as the author of explanations of the mystical names of God, both that "of forty-two letters" (in *Sefer ha-Ḥokhmah,* Ms. Oxford, 1568) and that "of seventy-two letters" (in *Sefer ha-Shem,* Ms. Munich, 81). These mystical interpretations probably reached the German Hasidim via Italy.

230. Cf. Jellinek, *Auswahl kabbalistischer Mystik,* 9 of the German part. Jellinek could not know that the kabbalists mentioned by him took their quotations from David Messer Leon, who testified around 1500 in his *Magen David,* Ms. Halberstam 465 (today in Jews' College, London) fol. 7b, that he had "seen this book a short time ago." On fol. 9a he says it was one of the most curious books of this discipline, but that only a relatively small part of it had been preserved.

"Book of the Speculation" (or "Contemplation"), preserved in numerous manuscripts.[231] What is surprising in this text is that it constitutes an irruption of Neoplatonic language and concepts into older cosmological and Merkabah teachings, as far removed from the language of the *Bahir* as it is from that of Isaac the Blind. The few extant pages appear to have been carelessly thrown together without any sense of structure, and the exposition is in part erratic and opaque. The book is written in a pure Hebrew and in a curiously enthusiastic style. The long superscription says:

> The "Book of the Speculation" of the great master Rab Ḥammai, chief of those who speak of the subject of the inner [hidden] sefiroth, and he unveiled in it the essence of the whole reality of the hidden glory, whose reality and nature no creature can comprehend, [and of all that] in a truthful manner, such as it [the hidden *kabhod?*] is in the indistinct unity, in the perfection of which the higher and the lower are united, and it [this *kabhod*] is the foundation of all that is hidden and manifest, and from it goes forth all that is emanated from the wondrous unity. And Rab Ḥammai has interpreted these subjects according to the method of the doctrine of the Merkabah—*'al derekh ma-'aseh merkabah*—and commented upon the prophecy of Ezekiel.

The language used in this superscription, as well as in the beginning of the work, is purely speculative. The notion of indistinct unity *('aḥduth shawah)* is unknown in prekabbalistic Hebrew texts. The term, as becomes quite clear in the writings of Azriel of Gerona, refers to that unity in which all oppositions become "equal," that is, identical. This concept, and the idea of a *coincidentia oppositorum* in God and the highest sefiroth—which subsequently plays such an important role, particularly in Azriel—seems to appear here for the first time. According to Azriel, God is

> the One who is united in all of His powers, as the fire's flame is united in its colors, and His powers emanate from His unity as the light of the eyes proceeds from the black of the eye,[232] and they are all ema-

231. Jellinek's edition, *Auswahl kabbalistischer Mystik,* 9–10, contains merely the beginning. The continuation (ibid., pp. 11–12) belongs to another text of the same group. A more complete text, but one marred by bad readings, was published in mimeograph by Ḥasida in *Ha-Segula,* nos. 27–28. A relatively good text can be established with the aid of the extant manuscripts; I have used above all Ms. Munich 408. The assertions of earlier scholars, such as Ehrenpreis, *Emanationslehre* 44, hardly require discussion after the analysis of the texts that follows.

232. This conforms to Galen's conception, according to which the light penetrates from the brain outward through the eye. In the poem entitled "The Royal

nated from one another like perfume from perfume and light from light, for one emanates from the other, and the power of the emanator is in the emanated, without the emanator suffering any loss.

Before all Creation he rested, transcendent, in himself, hidden in the power of his own reality. But at the beginning of Creation, "His *kabhod* became manifest, and the explication of his knowledge consisted in five things." The author in fact names, but does not explain, these five things, which lead to gnosis. They obviously belong to the sphere of language mysticism and are called *tiqqun, ma' amar, ṣeruf, mikhlal, ḥeshbon.* It appears that they constitute the processes by which the letters are placed in harmony *(tiqqun),* assembled into words *(ma' amar),* permutated *(ṣeruf),* collected together in all their combinations *(mikhlal),* and calculated according to their numerical value *(ḥeshbon).* Here, too, the process of emanation coincides with the process of language, but the details do not become clear. These five events are, as the author says in a curious image, "united in the ramifications of the root of movement [probably meaning the root of the movement of language], which is strengthened in the root of the thirteen pairs of opposites" and unfolds from a thin breath, the sound of the *'alef,* into the name of God (if I understand this difficult text correctly). These thirteen pairs of opposites are, at the same time, the thirteen *middoth* derived from Exodus 34:6, which play such a great role in Jewish theology as the modes of God's action. God acts in the *middoth* positively as well as negatively, which enables us to perceive a connection with the kabbalistic notion of *middah* that we found in Isaac. Here, however, not the sefiroth are meant but the powers or modes of action that are enclosed in the first sefirah and erupt from it. It is in these five modes of the movement of language that everything is realized "like a source for the flame and a flame for the source" prolonged "up to the unfathomable and infinite light, which is concealed in the excess[233] of the hid-

---

Crown," Solomon ibn Gabirol compares the act of Creation with this process: "He drew the effluence of Being from Nought, as a ray of light breaks forth from the eye." Jellinek already remarked upon this analogy; cf. *Auswahl kabbalistischer Mystik,* 9, as well as *Geschichte der Kabbala* 1:36–37; 2:29. The term *meshekh* in the sense of "emanation" was also adopted by Isaac the Blind and Asher ben David. David Kaufman, *Geschichte der Attributenlehre* (1877), 113, explained this word correctly (contrary to his own hypothesis, p.1).

233. But perhaps the term *tosefeth* is a rendering of the Neoplatonic *hyperesse* (as used by Scotus Erigena) and as such equivalent to *yithron* as used in this sense by Azriel. In that case "the light that is hidden in the inaccessible (concealed?) *superesse* of darkness" would be a more correct translation.

den darkness. And the knowledge of the unity and of its principle refers to this darkness."

The divine unity acts therefore out of the effusive darkness from which come all the lights, which are connected to it as the flame to its source. This world of images does not appear to me far removed from that of John Scotus Erigena and Pseudo-Denys the Areopagite; it is more closely related to them than to the world of the *Bahir.* Among the Hebrew Neoplatonists such language is not used to express the divine unity, and we touch here upon a possible connection that will emerge more often in the course of this investigation. It seems that the kabbalists of Provence combined the doctrine of the aeons, as found among the gnostics and in the *Bahir,* with Erigena's doctrine of the *causae primordiales,* which in all their multiplicity are nevertheless the unity of the divine *sapientia.* Such a relationship is historically plausible.[234] It is not difficult to suppose that the first kabbalists of Provence and Aragon, around 1180–1220, had direct or indirect knowledge of Scotus Erigena, whose influence reached its high point[235] at that time, just before the condemnation of 1210. Many Cathars too seem to have made use of Erigena's work as is suggested by two extant testimonies.[236] Writings of Erigena were no rarity in the cities where the first kabbalists lived, before Honorius III ordained the destruction of all copies found in France.

But from this speculative and novel introduction, the Book *'Iyyun* proceeds to an explanation of the primordial darkness and the potencies issuing from it. This explanation claims to be a kind of commentary on a Hekhaloth text by Neḥunya ben Haqqanah that however, is not identical with any of the Hekhaloth writings known to us. It is apparently against this commentary and, by the same token, against the Book *'Iyyun* in general (along with the *Bahir* and other writings) that the antikabbalistic attack in Meir ben Simon's

---

234. To my knowledge Jacob Brucker, *Historia critica philosophiae,* (vol. 3 [Leipzig, 1743], 621) was the first to notice this connection and to recognize it as a problem. I owe this reference to F. Vernet's article "Erigène" in *Dictionnaire de Theologie catholique* (1913).

235. Cf. Marie-Thérèse d'Alverny, *Archives d'histoire doctrinale et littéraire du moyen âge* (1953) 32–81, whose important study has proved the profound influence of Scotus Erigena on French authors of the twelfth century.

236. Cf. Frances Yates, *Journal of the Warburg and Courtauld Institute* 23 (1960): 36.

epistle is directed. Around 1245, therefore, the existence of such a commentary on the Hekhaloth, "where one finds things in the spirit of their [namely, the kabbalists'] heresy" was known in Provence.[237] This text names the signet rings sealing heaven and earth much as we also find them in the Wertheimer version of the "Greater Hekhaloth" (chap. 23). But here the magical name by means of which heaven is sealed is Araritha, and the corresponding name for the earth is 'EHWY. The latter name, which in the writings of this group frequently serves as an object of mystical speculation, is obviously not a secret name belonging to the theurgic tradition but an artificial product composed of the four consonants employed in Hebrew as matres lectionis. Abraham ibn Ezra and Yehudah Halevi were the first to propose interpretations of these four letters as the most spiritual elements among the consonants, and hence best suited to form the symbols of the divine spirit in the body of the world and the elements of the two most important divine names in the Torah: 'Ehyeh and YHWH.[238] In due course a magical primordial Tetragrammaton was formed, designating the unity of these two names and said to precede them.[239] However, the name Araritha can be found in very old magical texts of the German Hasidim as the secret name of the *ḥashmal* in the vision of Ezekiel 1:4.[240] The same name also appears in a magical piece from the Gaonic period, the "Prayer

---

237. Cf. *JQR* 4 (1892): 358.

238. Cf. Abraham ibn Ezra, *Yesod Mora,* chap. 11 (in M. Creiznach's German translation, [Frankfurt, 1840], 111ff.), and Halevi, *Kuzari* 4:3, as well as D. Rosin, *MGWJ* (1898): 55–58. Ibn Ezra and Halevi were preceded in the tenth century by Dunash ben Tamim in his commentary on the *Yeṣirah,* as has been shown by G. Vajda, *REJ* 110 (1949): 75ff. Abulafia describes these four letters as אותיות הנוח ונקראות אותיות ההעלמה (in grammatical terminology); cf. his *'Or ha-Sekhel* (Ms. Munich 92, fol. 54b): The view rejected by Cordovero (see below, n. 239) is precisely Abulafia's, ibid. fol. 44a, and Cordovero's "quotation" is a condensed summary of the ideas presented there at length and in detail.

239. Moses Cordovero, *Pardes Rimmonim,* chap. 21, section 3, quotes from such a text: "God conceals His name for the initiates in the name 'Ehyeh and in the name YHWH, and this is the true name אהוי. Names in which consonants appear doubled are given only for the crowd." Cordovero indignantly rejects this audacious opinion. Mystical reasons for this divine name are given in Ms. Munich 408, fols. 124b–125b, in a text emanating from the same circle.

240. Cf. Ms. British Museum, Margoliouth 752, fol. 93b (directly after a note on astrological magic, which refers to the year 988). Here the name is written אררית א, whereas in the Book *'Iyyun* and in the other writings of this group it is always written ארארית א. (In this spelling it also occurs as the name of the "for ever and ever real" in a quotation from the Book *Biṭṭaḥon,* in *Kiryath Sefer* 1:167.)

of Rab Hamnunah the Elder."[241] In the Book *'Iyyun,* these names are interpreted in the spirit of a Neoplatonic concept of God: they indicate his static as well as his dynamic unity, which also maintains its identity in its oppositions. Whereas one of these names thus illustrates the way from magic to Neoplatonic mysticism, the other marks the way from the theory of language of the grammarians to the magic of names, that is, in the opposite direction. Both currents meet in an impressive manner in the Book *'Iyyun* and related writings.

The sequel no longer makes any direct reference to the primordial darkness. First, an "order of the master of the world" is expounded, then an "order of Metatron," the second part obviously being conceived as some sort of explanation of the *Shi'ur Qomah.* The two parts describe, in their own fashion and constantly confusing Merkabah gnosis with Neoplatonic images, the potencies by means of which God acts at Creation as well as the supreme hierarchies of essences emanating from him, the *hawwayoth.* The exposition quotes other, presumably also fictitious, writings.[242] At the end of the text it suddenly seems as if R. Ishmael had read all the foregoing aloud to Neḥunya ben Haqqanah, as if everything had come from the aforementioned book of Hekhaloth. The framework of the old Merkabah literature clearly serves here as a receptacle for contents that are alien to it. There is scarcely any relationship between these ideas (in which the doctrine of the sefiroth is mentioned only very incidentally) and the world of the Book *Bahir.*

The thirteen potencies manifested from the supreme mystery, *sether 'elyon ha-ne 'elam*—no doubt the aforementioned primordial darkness—are enumerated by name. They are 1. the primordial *ḥokhmah;* 2. the wondrous or hidden light, *'or mufla;* 3. *ḥashmal;* 4. the cloud, *'arafel;* 5. the throne of splendor; 6. the *'ofan* of greatness; 7. the cherub; 8. the wheels of the Merkabah; 9. the surround-

241. This prayer is preserved, for example, in Ms. British Museum 737, fol. 298bff., in the *Sefer ha-Shem* of Eleazar of Worms.

242. Among others, a book entitled *Libhnath ha-Sappir* and another by the name of *Mikhlal Yofi.* Other writings of this group also quote dicta that cannot be traced but that are ascribed to the "sages of the Merkabah" and "the scholars," *ḥakhme ha-meḥqar,* which generally means Neoplatonic sources.

ing ether; 10. the curtain; 11. the Throne of Glory; 12. the place of the souls, also called "chambers of greatness";[243] 13. the outer Holy Temple.

We thus encounter pell-mell the names of sefiroth, a new light-mysticism, notions of the Merkabah, and cosmological powers. Moses of Burgos had before him a later redaction of this list, which exhibited significant variants and which apparently strove to identify the first ten potencies with the ten sefiroth of the tradition that had meanwhile become canonical.[244] In these potencies the unknowable God gives the appearance of assuming a body, and his *kabhod* is, just as in the old *Shi'ur Qomah,* the "body of the Shekhinah." God Himself is, in a Neoplatonic image (which likewise must have come from ibn Gabirol's poem "The Royal Crown") "the soul of souls." Below the *kabhod* there extend, in the form of the primordial man, the four "camps of the Shekhinah," which are also the four primordial elements and the four realms of the archangels. Here the "body of the Shekhinah" is inexplicably separated from the primordial man. In an equally inexplicable manner the elements are correlated with four of the aforementioned thirteen potencies, which apparently also correspond to the four principal sefiroth. These are the *ḥashmal* (corresponding to *ḥesed*), the cloud (corresponding to Stern Judgment), the Throne of Splendor (corresponding to *tif-*

243. This expression is taken from the ancient Merkabah text that I published in *Jewish Gnosticism* (section 107a), which is also the source of the phrase "the mighty one who dwells in the chambers of greatness," with which the alleged Hekhaloth text quoted at the opening of the *Sefer 'Iyyun* is said to begin.

244. Cf. the text in *Madda 'e ha-Yahaduth* 2:209. In his enumeration, the "wondrous light" appears as a designation of the first sefirah preceding the *ḥokhmah.* His text betrays a clear tendency to harmonize the very different sequence of the Book *'Iyyun* with the doctrine of the sefiroth. The term *ḥokhmah qedumah* for the primordial wisdom, used by Isaac (cf. p. 287, herein) and the writings of the *'Iyyun* group, had its origin in the rhymed preface of the Provençal scholar Moses Qimḥi (mid-twelfth century) to his commentary on Proverbs printed in the editions of the Bible under the name of Abraham ibn Ezra. This preface was published in its entirety in *'Oṣar Tob,* the Hebrew supplement to the *Magazin für die Wissenschaft des Judentums* 9 (1882):36. It is from there that N. Krochmal, in his *More Neboche ha-seman sive Director errantium nostrae aetatis* (ed. Ravidowitz [1924], 297 and 316) quoted this passage as belonging to ibn Ezra. (The indication of the source actually given by Ravidowitz is wrong. I am indebted to Mr. Naphtali Ben-Menaḥem of Jerusalem for pointing out to me the correct source, for which I long searched in vain.) Ibn Ezra's influence is also discernible in the expression *mathkoneth ha-guf,* which occurs at the end of the Book *'Iyyun.*

'ereth), as well as the *'ofan* of greatness (corresponding to *malkhuth*). This is not directly stated but implicitly understood. In this connection, verses are quoted from mystical poems that speak the same language.[245] One such quotation cites, in the name of Hai Gaon, a pseudepigraphic dictum on the creation of the hyle, from which, after the emanation of the "hidden degrees," the sefiroth, all creatures were emanated. The dictum leaves it unclear whether this "creation of primordial matter" that arose in the thought of God was a genuinely new act of creation or whether it was a continuation of the emanation of the sefiroth in a lower sphere. What seems clearer to me, on the other hand, is that this scheme, according to which the hyle and the world of the four elements are situated directly below the divine potencies of the *kabhod* or below the sefiroth, corresponds almost exactly to the order of being in Scotus Erigena: the hyle and the four elements appear not in their corporeality but as incorporeal *elementa universalia,* and as the direct effects of the *causae primordiales.* This would also explain the strange deviation of the kabbalistic schema from the classical Plotinian hierarchy of being; it seems that the hierarchy of the *Timaeus* had somehow been transmitted to the author in a mystical transformation such as can be found in Erigena's book. The biggest surprise, however, in this respect, is the brief remark that follows the quotation from Pseudo-Hai and reads like a paraphrase of the title and the metaphysical content of Erigena's work: "And this is what the mighty sages of nature [a reference to *De divisione naturae?*], the philosophers versed in metaphysics [*ḥokhmath ha-meḥqar*] have written [on the subject of the hyle]." It is only after setting forth this hierarchy of the supreme beings that the Book *'Iyyun,* in its final part, discusses Metatron, who is, however, described in the spirit of the *Shi'ur Qomah* doctrine as a manifestation of the "body of the Shekhinah" and in terms of the verses of the Song of Songs 5:11 and following. The exposition is strongly pervaded with both number- and language-

245. The verse quoted here from *Ma'yan Ḥokhmah* (a different book from the one named below) is quoted, in the text mentioned in n. 257, from a *Sefer ha-Shi'ur. 'Iyyun* also quotes a verse of a certain R. Pinḥas Ḥisma written in the same style. ("One is intertwined with the other in the wings of the secret of the movement.") Nothing at all is known so far concerning a *payṭan* by this name. The name would suggest a very ancient teacher in the Orient, but the language is very definitely that of the *'Iyyun* circle. Perhaps we are dealing here, once again, with a pseudepigraph.

mysticism. The angels are, in the view of our author, the cosmic potencies created on the first day.

Alongside this strange concoction there now also appears a large number of smaller writings and fragments, some pseudepigraphic and others anonymous, that are unmistakable witnesses to a similar spiritual tendency and that speak the same language. They frequently use identical or similar symbols, arranging them, however, in very different ways and explaining them differently. It is evident that the authors did not yet clearly distinguish between the Merkabah and the sefiroth; on this important point there is, therefore, continuity with the Book *Bahir.* The two are confused throughout, and Merkabah-beings such as the Throne, the *'ofan,* the wheel, the *ḥashmal,* the curtain, *pargod,*[246] and even the cherub and the seraph are regarded as belonging to the mystical world of potencies, as manifestations, of God, just like the sefiroth. As has been noted, they are in part regarded as identical with these latter, and in part juxtaposed with them without any essential distinction. Clearly a vigorous process of Platonization had set in, transforming this stratum of the old Merkabah world. In this reinterpretation, the world of the Merkabah consists of intelligible potencies that are, in part, still designated by the old names, although these no longer suit them. Alongside these names appear new notions of very diverse origin.

The enumerations of these potencies present a strange and confused picture and exhibit influences from the most diverse sources: Saadya, the first chapter of Maimonides' *Mishneh Torah,* indirectly perhaps ibn Gabirol's metaphysics of the will, and diverse unidentifiable Neoplatonists. The divine will, which played no role for Isaac the Blind, now appears alongside and above the "pure thought" of God. The texts give the impression of taking the first tentative steps into a speculative mysticism. Their language is replete with strange combinations of words and images that have only very few equivalents in the old paraphrase of Saadya. The prayers

246. This curtain before the throne is often mentioned in the old Merkabah-gnosticism; cf. the references in my *Jewish Gnosticism,* 35. Curtains before the celestial regions of the world of aeons play a great role—apparently a Jewish influence—in the enumerations found in the gnostic *Pistis Sophia.* Similar curtains between the emanations appear in personified form in the sources of Isaac Cohen.

composed in this circle as well as the many accounts of the intelligible lights evoke the most abstract ontological concepts in a solemn style reminiscent of the Pseudo-Areopagitic writings of Christian mysticism. The enthusiastic style and drapery of the language link this Neoplatonic pseudepigraphy with the hymns and prayers of the old Merkabah mystics, which otherwise breathe such a completely different spirit. The authors replaced the original world of the Merkabah—which evidently was no longer alive for them and of which they possessed little more than traditional knowledge—with the new world of divine lights, powers, and intelligible potencies. But with their manifestly weak philosophical orientation these authors did not know, or did not yet know exactly, how to systematize these notions. In their desire to maintain exegetical continuity they sought to project, as best they could, the new world onto the old, but apart from sonorous words and concepts, no definite tradition had as yet taken root among them. This is what gives their interpretations an often peculiar and abstruse character. The uncertain character of their thought is apparent, for example, in the treatment of fundamental philosophical questions such as that of matter and form that had somehow found their way to them. We are thus in a position to observe in these writings the irruption, in full force, of new ideas into an older tradition, at a stage when the former had not yet assumed a systematic form and a fixed direction. This lends considerable interest to what in large measure are particularly difficult texts.

But the adherence to the tradition and the formal language of Jewish Gnosticism in dissolution and transformation lead to an even more profound substantive problem. In the course of this evolution, the developing Kabbalah not only absorbed incomparably stronger Neoplatonic elements; at the same time, the gnostic tendencies also asserted themselves with new vigor, albeit on a new level. Platonism and the gnosticizing tendency thus went hand in hand. The same circles into which Platonism penetrated with so much energy coupled it with tendencies of a gnostic and mythologizing character resistant to any transformation of the mystical tradition into a mystical philosophy. These tendencies found their expression in a repristination of the gnostic elements preserved in an older stock of traditions, ones that were now developing their own life in a new context.

For lack of a better name, I shall designate these writings as those of the *'Iyyun* group or *'Iyyun* circle.[247] Its authors continue the pseudepigraphic tradition of the Hekhaloth and the Book *Bahir,* but not in the form of midrashim. They compose tracts on the name of God, on the thirty-two paths of wisdom, and on the knowledge of the highest reality, as well as kabbalistic prayers in which they expound their particular views. While Isaac the Blind and his disciples wrote and presented themselves under their own names, no pseudepigraphic tendencies being noticeable among them, things are completely different with the authors of this group. It is no longer possible to identify them; all we can say is that some of their writings reached Castile, where they found kindred spirits. In fact, it is quite possible that some of these writings were not composed in Provence at all but in Castile, in Burgos or Toledo. In particular, Jacob ben Jacob Cohen of Soria seems to have been in direct and personal contact with members of this circle, as it is in his writings that the spiritual inclinations of this group are most directly continued. He is concerned with interpreting, although he did not cite them by name. His teacher, an anonymous hasid of Narbonne, probably belonged to the *'Iyyun* circle.

The writings of these alleged authors are quite diverse. The *Ma'yan ha-Ḥokhmah* ("The Source of Wisdom") is, after the *'Iyyun,* of special importance; it purports to be the communication of an anonymous angel to Moses.[248] A detailed cosmogonic theory, propounded in the framework of an interpretation of the Tetragrammaton, is said to be derived from a "Midrash of Simon the Righ-

---

247. As early as 1853, Jellinek had already recognized the kinship of diverse writings of this tendency, although only three out of the colorful collection of these texts were known to him; cf. *Auswahl kabbalistischer Mystik,* 11–12 of the German part.

248. "Michael delivered this book to the nameless and the nameless to Moses, our master, and he revealed it, in order that the generations should become wise through it," as it is said in the superscription. The treatise was printed many times—for the first time in 1651 in Amsterdam—in a very corrupt text, but it can be restored in large measure on the basis of good manuscripts, such as Munich 341, Mussajof 210. For my quotations I rely upon a corrected text of this kind. Certain paragraphs seem to have been deliberately formulated in order to stymie comprehension. Moses of Burgos reports having read in another text of the same title statements on the personified emanations below the tenth sefirah *malkhuth,* which he likewise connected with the Kabbalah of the alleged Ḥammai; cf. *Madda'e ha-Yahaduth* 2:289. M. H. Landauer's interpretation of the book, in *Literaturblatt des Orients* 6 (1845): col. 228, as a "satire on the doctrines of the kabbalists," cannot be taken seriously.

teous."[249] The "Prayers of Unity," that is, prayers addressed to God in his unity in the different sefiroth, are attributed to the tannaitic teachers Neḥunya ben Haqqanah and Rabban Gamaliel.[250] A book entitled *Moreh Ṣedeq* is attributed to Ḥananiah ben Teradion.[251] A polemic against the idea, widespread among the German Hasidim, of the creation of the golem is quoted from a work entitled Book *Biṭṭaḥon,* ("On Trust in God") attributed to Yehudah ben Bathyrah, a Tannaite of the first century.[252] Responsa on the names of God and other questions are falsely attributed, with a leap in time from the Tannaites to the last of the geonim, to Hai Gaon.[253] These mystical writings were attributed to the aforementioned authors in part because the persons named had actually expressed themselves on the names of God and similar subjects, as had Hai, for example, in a genuine responsum on the forty-two-letter divine name, the tradition of which "is known in the academy." No less than four different texts give the names of the thirty-two paths, mentioned at the

---

249. This midrash, however, has nothing to do with the literary genre generally referred to as midrashic. A corrupt text of the treatise was printed in the commentary of Moses Botarel on *Yeṣirah* 2:3, Mantua 1562, fols. 62a–63b. Some manuscripts, such as Munich 215, have an excellent text.

250. The best printed text of the prayer of R. Neḥunya is found at the beginning of Mordekhai Eljaschow, *Haqdamoth u-She'arim* (Pjotrkow, 1909). This is one of the most widespread documents of the Kabbalah. The prayer praises God from every sefirah, each one being characterized in an enthusiastic style. The prayer of Rabban Gamaliel is preserved in Ms. Vatican 185, fols. 185–188, as well as in Ms. Jellinek 60 of Vienna (now in the Institute of Jewish History in Warsaw). The text printed by Jellinek as a continuation of the Book *'Iyyun* (*Auswahl kabbalistischer Mystik,* 10–12) is part of this prayer.

251. A fragment of this text is printed in my (Hebrew) catalogue of the kabbalistic manuscripts of the University Library (Jerusalem, 1930), 16–17, and links up with what is told of R. Ḥananya in *Abodah Zarah* 17b and in the "Greater Hekhaloth," chap. 6. The manuscript described in the catalogue (14 ff.) contains many important texts of the *'Iyyun* circle.

252. Cf. my book *On the Kabbalah,* 120–121, where I translated this piece. Steinschneider, *Hebraische Bibliographie* 16:66–67 did not make it clear that the book should be ascribed to this group. In the passage mentioned in note 240, herein, the quotation is attributed to the "students" of reality, which must mean the metaphysicians. Around 1300 the Spanish kabbalist Ḥananel ben Abraham names Ḥananya ben Teradion as the author; cf. Günzburg in *Hakedem* 1 (1907):117.

253. Hai's interpretation of the forty-two letter divine name is printed in my aforementioned catalogue, 213–217. On the subject of another responsum on the ten sefiroth and the thirteen modes of divine mercy, see pp. 349–50, herein. For another exposition of Hai on the spelling of the divine name in mystical script (astral letters), see Kobak's *Jeschurun* (1859), 3:55–57 of the Hebrew part. Cf. also n. 229 as well as pp. 327–328 in this chapter.

beginning of the *Yeṣirah,* by way of enumerating the intellectual lights or angelic powers that are the fundamental forces of creation.[254] Two of these texts are anonymous; the other two are attributed to the "sages of the Mishnah" and to R. Ishmael, the hero of the Hekhaloth. Other treatises of this group are anonymous. Such is the case for a commentary on the Tetragrammaton;[255] an exposition of the name of seventy-two letters that plays a major role in magical tradition and that appears in juxtaposition to the forty-two-letter name;[256] a "Book of the True Unity," later attributed to Eleazar of Worms; and another "Book of Unity, which it befits all the sages to confirm and corroborate," whose title already exem-

---

254. One of these lists is printed at the end of the preface to the commentary on *Yeṣirah* by Pseudo-Rabad. It figures as a separate treatise in many manuscripts. Another list, one that is particularly close to the "Book of Unity" mentioned below, is preserved in Ms. Vatican 291, fols. 11b–13b, among others. A list of the thirty-two paths that enumerates them, not as intelligible potencies but as secret magical names, is found in a manuscript of the Laurentiana in Florence, Plut. 2, Cod. 18, fol. 102b. Another short list figures in a manuscript of the Casanatense in Rome, Sacerdoti 180, fol. 60; cf. my catalogue of the Jerusalem manuscripts, 110. Since its translation into Latin by J. St. Rittangel in his *Liber Jezirah* (Amsterdam, 1642), the first list has been translated frequently into European languages; in English, for example, by Wynn Westcott, *Sepher Yetzirah* (London, 1893), 28–31; in German, by Johann Friedrich v. Meyer, *Das Buch Jezira, die älteste kabbalistische Urkunde der Hebräer* (Leipzig, 1830), 1–6. The utterly opaque character of the intelligences *(sekhalim)* enumerated in these lists is not clarified in the least by these translations.

255. *Perush shem ben 'arba' 'othiyoth,* Ms. Florence, Laurentiana Plut. 2, Cod. 41, fols. 198a–201a, in an excellent manuscript of 1328, as well as Munich 24[6], Paris 765[2]. The extant fragment from the Book *Biṭṭaḥon* criticizing the golem-magic comes from this text. This commentary already quotes the book *Ma'yan ha-Ḥokhmah,* as well as ibn Gabirol's poem on the Book *Yeṣirah,* ed. Bialik and Rawnizki, 2:58.

256. *Sod Shem ben 'ayin beth,* Ms. Florence, Plut. 14, Cod. 44, fols. 1–11. This curious text doubtless belongs to the later stratum of these writings, but it had already been excerpted extensively by Jacob Cohen in the introduction to his *Sefer ha-'Orah,* Ms. Milan, Bernheimer 62, fols. 85b–93b. Here the mystics are not only called (as is still often the case in the *'Iyyun* circle) "sages of the Merkabah" and gnostics—literally: "masters of knowledge," Hebrew: *ba'ale yedi'ah* (occasionally sayings attributed to them are simply lines taken from the *Shi'ur Qomah*)—but also "language-mystics" or "masters of language," in whose name angelological statements are quoted. At the end of the book there is an appendix written in the same style but containing a lengthy and surprisingly sharp polemic against the practical application of the names of God for magical purposes. The author (if he is the same) who had previously presented a speculative interpretation of the magical names, now takes up the cudgels against the liars and forgers who have invented magical books by the thousands in order to delude the simple folk. Similar polemics against applied magic were repeated after 1250 by the majority of kabbalists. Whether they were dictated by conviction or by discretion is not easy to decide.

plifies the literal use of the phraseology of the old paraphrase of Saadya.[257] This text, as well as another entitled *Sod wi-Yesod ha-Qadmoni* ("Mystery and Primordial Foundation [of the Creation]"), are interpretations of the ten sefiroth in the spirit of this circle; the latter of the two may already belong to a later stratum than the other, but it is still completely imbued with their concepts and their ways of thinking.[258] Finally, the two responsa of the fictitious gaon R. Yeḥushiel of Germany also belong to this group; they are evidently related to the sources from which Isaac Cohen, the brother of Jacob Cohen, drew his theories on demonology and the hierarchies of dark spirits. In these texts the esotericists of Worms, Corbeil, Lunel, and Marseilles seem to come together.[259] The "Mystery of the Knowledge of Reality" (*Sod Yedi'ath ha-Meṣi'uth),* a commentary on Ezekiel 1 preceded by a long preface, should be counted among the last products of this group.[260]

---

257. *Sefer ha-Yiḥud ha-'amitti,* Ms. Jerusalem 8⁰488 (cf. p. 14 of my catalogue, as well as additional evidence in *Kiryath Sefer* 6:275). The second, completely different *Sefer ha-Yiḥud,* a particularly difficult text, exists in numerous manuscripts, for example Vat. 211, fols. 3b–5b; Oxford Christ Church College 198, fols. 80a–82b; New York, Halberstam 444, fols. 23b–25b. The opening sentence: "This is the book of Unity, etc." derives literally from the preface to the old paraphrase of Saadya, even though the content is worlds apart from it. On this paraphrase, cf. the complete literature in H. Malter, *Saadia Gaon, His Life and Works* (Philadelphia, 1921), 361–369.

258. The treatise was incorporated in a corrupt form into the *Sefer Peli'ah,* compiled in the fourteenth century, cf. ed. Koretz (1783), fols. 109a–110b. As a separate treatise and with a better text it can be found, for example, in Ms. Munich 215, fols. 200b–204b. Here too we find rather long lists of the names of the intelligible lights; the author is visibly striving, however, to bring them into harmony with the doctrine of the ten sefiroth.

259. Cf. in this connection note 102, herein. The two responses of Yeḥushiel, outstanding for their interest in gnostic demonology and the secret names of the powers of this sphere, are juxtaposed in, for example, Ms. Casanatense, Sacerdoti 180, fols. 59b–60a; Vienna, Israelit. Kultusgemeinde, Schwarz 240, fols. 114–115. It seems as if the two fictitious names of Yeḥushiel and Yequthiel are related, and it is surely no accident that in the fragments containing them a Yedidyah also appears, located once in Toulouse and another time in Marseilles; cf. M. Steinschneider, *Katalog der Münchener Handschriften* (Munich 1895), 54.

260. The text is, in part, preserved in manuscripts such as Munich 83, fols. 165a–169b; Paris 843, fols. 20a–22a, and Schocken, Kabbalah 6. The latter manuscript has a long and important but otherwise unknown introduction. The Midrash of Simon the Righteous is named as a source; other writings are used without being named. Here too it is striking to see how the doctrine of the sefiroth is neglected in favor of the speculative interest aroused by other potencies. The predilection of this circle for solemn and sonorous terms finds its expression in this text when the supreme emanation, for example, is designated as "supreme inwardness," *penimiyuth*

In this strange and confused hodgepodge, experiences and contemplation based on light-mysticism are apparently associated with literary adaptations of materials deriving from cosmogonic theories and speculations. No relationship to a clearly delineated historical background can be discerned, unless by means of an analysis of the origin of the diverse concepts. Here and there, especially in several passages in the "Source of Wisdom," one discerns a clear link with ideas and images found in Isaac the Blind's commentary on the *Yeṣirah.* But the speculations on the world of the divine lights lack any reference to the doctrine of man and its culmination in the ideal of *debhequth.* In some of these writings, nevertheless, some connection with the prayer-mysticism of the *kawwanah* is discernible,[261] but in most of them this too is missing. The central theme everywhere is the description of the upper world. The elaborate light-mysticism occupies a preponderant place; next to it one finds, as in Isaac, language-mysticism and above all an interest in theoretical speculations

---

'elyonah, or as "the primordial inwardness," *penimiyuth qadmonith. Penimi* has in all the writings of this circle the connotation of mystical or hidden. The title of the tractate may indicate a certain dependence upon the pseudo-Maimonidean *Ma'amar ha-Yiḥud,* "Treatise on the Unity," where it is said (ed. Steinschneider [Berlin, 1847], 16) that the sages name the secret knowledge, insofar as it refers to the spiritual world, the "science of the sacred reality." I have not found this terminology anywhere else. It is this ontological science that Pseudo-Maimonides also designates (following *Ḥagigah* 14b) by the term *pardes,* no doubt inspired by *The Guide of the Perplexed* itself (1:32).

261. Thus, for example, at the end of the text (fol. 200b) named in note 255, herein. A similar type of text may have been one of the sources of interpretation for Moses of Burgos regarding the forty-two letter divine name to which the German Hasidim too had already devoted many interpretations, reflective of their own cast of mind. These Hasidic sources seem to have been revised subsequently by the Provençal kabbalists, and many such interpretations are quoted at length by Moses of Burgos, whose treatise was anonymously printed in the collection *Liqquṭim me-Rab Hai Ga'on* (Warsaw, 1798), fols. 1a–12b. I have analyzed this text in *Tarbiz* 4 (1933): 54–61, and have also edited the introduction and the conclusion, which are missing in the printed text in *Tarbiz* 5:51–58. One of these sources contained an interpretation of this magical name, "from the side of the *kawwanah* in the prayer." Its author depicts the ascension of the prayer through the thirteen gates in the seven heavens, the keys that open these gates, the angels who stand next to them, and the *kawwanah* of the one who prays as he should. This passage has already completely assumed the coloring of the doctrine of *kawwanah* in Isaac the Blind, even though little use is made of the doctrine of the sefiroth in the extant quotations. I consider it very probable that this source likewise had its origin in Provence, where the elements of Hasidic number-mysticism were first amalgamated with the new kabbalistic teachings. The author could have been a mystic who maintained contact with both circles, like the anonymous Hasid of Narbonne, already mentioned many times.

on the divine names. The mystical names, which in Merkabah gnosticism served as technical aids to concentration and to securing the path of the soul in its ascension, here become the repositories of speculative mysteries, which the authors seek to uncover. Here too the mystical lights and potencies are themselves names. In this spirit Jacob Cohen, who must have been familiar with many of these writings, said that "the names in the upper world are themselves substances and divine potencies, and their substance is that of the light of life, but even the names of terrestrial men, if one regards them closely, prove to be identical with the substances."[262] Already in a Merkabah text such as *The Alphabet of Rabbi Akiba* the mystical names are considered to be columns of fire that blaze before the throne of God. This conception, which identifies the lights with the names, was inherited above all from the *'Iyyun* group and in due course became the common property of the Spanish Kabbalah.

Are these writings older than those of the school of Gerona—which will be dealt with in the next chapter—or do they date from the same period? In order to decide this question it is necessary to analyze the relationship between the *'Iyyun* writings and those of Azriel, the latter being the only ones of this school that display clear connections with the *'Iyyun* group. He alone shared their predilection for solemn phrases, so common in this circle, and used the same Neoplatonic terminology. In favor of the priority of the Provençal *'Iyyun* writings one could argue precisely their authors' uncertainty, emphasized earlier, in interpreting the concepts and the names they used, as well as their vacillation with regard to the relationships between the sefiroth on the one hand and the potencies of the new Merkabah on the other. These hesitations no longer exist for Azriel. The reverse process of a dissolution in the *'Iyyun* writings of an already fixed schema would be much more difficult to fit into the chronological framework of this evolution and, in essence, much more difficult to explain. A line of development that led from Provence to Spain, as we were able to show so clearly in the case of Isaac's Kabbalah, is much more plausible than one leading in the

262. Cf. the long disquisition regarding the nature of the names printed in my catalogue of the kabbalistic manuscripts in Jerusalem, 209–210. At that time I still did not know that (as I have since been able to prove with the aid of quotations in Moses of Burgos) the author of this anonymous and very widespread commentary on Ezekiel's Merkabah was precisely Jacob Cohen.

opposite direction, from Spain to Provence, for which I see no historical basis. The most probable hypothesis is, in my opinion, that the most important of the *'Iyyun* writings originated between 1200 and 1225 parallel to the activity of Isaac the Blind and at a time only slightly prior to the crystallization of the center in Gerona. Some texts appear to have been composed as late as the period between 1125 and 1240.[263]

However, the Neoplatonic language used by kabbalistic speculation is combined with a conception that, in contrast to the negative theology of the Platonists, could be characterized rather as positive-theosophic. This is no doubt connected with the general character of medieval Platonism. A text like the "Book of the Five Substances," which was attributed to Empedocles, exhibits in its extant parts the same penchant for a theosophic description of the upper world as do the *'Iyyun* writings.[264] In the writings of the *'Iyyun* circle, the sefi-

---

263. Certain passages found in Azriel's writings that betray his peculiar style already occur very early as the independent dicta of a certain R. Yequthiel of London, who was supposed to have sent them to his disciple, "our master Yedidyah of Toulouse." There is, as far as I can see, no evidence of the existence of this Yedidyah, whom Jellinek mistakenly regarded as the father-in-law of Hai Gaon (*Geschichte der Kabbala* 2:24–26), but the fact that the epistle was addressed to Toulouse in the Languedoc is worthy of note. Cf. my remarks in *Tarbiz* 2:422 (p. 28 of the separate reprint). B. Dinaburg suggested that לונדריש in the manuscripts might be a corruption of אנדושא, that is, Anduze (in the Department Alais in Provence), where kabbalists were living, as is shown, for example, by the fact that Asher ben David quotes a certain Job ben Samuel of Anduze (cf. p. 253 n. 115). But the phrase "of the *city* of Londres" does not suggest a village or small town like Anduze. On the other hand, a Yequthiel of Anduze would be a more likely historical kabbalistic figure than a Yequthiel of London. The enumeration of the seven spiritually interpreted baldachins above the heads of the righteous in paradise, in Azriel and Yequthiel, breathes the same spirit as that of the seven Hekhaloth of paradise in the eschatological part of the responsum of Pseudo-Hai to R. Paltoy. Their Provençal origin appears certain; cf. p. 241f., herein, on the subject of the revelation of Elijah on the Day of Atonement, the ritual of which constitutes precisely the subject of the first half of this responsum. The relations between the writings of Azriel and those of this group are complex; this is also evident from the beginning of the text mentioned at the beginning of note 260 herein, which, in its altogether unusual phraseology, agrees in a striking manner with certain expressions from a letter of Azriel to Burgos. The introductory sentence of the anonymous commentary on the Merkabah seems to be patched together from three sentences taken from Azriel's letter, unless one prefers to suppose that, on the contrary, Azriel borrowed these expressions from the commentary in order to insert them in various places in his letter.

264. Cf. the texts in D. Kaufmann, *Studien über Salomon ibn Gabirol* (Budapest, 1899), 15–51. According to M. Asin Palacios, *Obras Escogidas,* vol. 1 (Madrid, 1946), 57, these fragments already represent an attenuated, late, and indirect form of

roth undergo a transformation: each one, indeed even each of the thirty-two paths of the Sophia, becomes an autonomous world in which the theosophist immerses himself.[265] In fact, even the mystical spelling of the divine name with twenty-four points, which Pseudo-Hai transmits here and which no doubt goes back to Oriental sources of Jewish magic,[266] is interpreted in this manner. The spelling obviously imitates the magical alphabet and characters as they are frequently found in amulets and that, in Jewish magic, are encountered, for example, in the old "alphabets of the angels."[267] They appear on the opposite page:

---

the original Pseudo-Empedoclean system of ibn Masarra, which he analyzed there in detail. In this case we should have to ascribe this text to the twelfth rather than the tenth century, thus coming close to the beginnings of the Kabbalah, where the eschatological views of the *'Iyyun* group on the beatitude of the souls in the supernal world coincide in a striking manner with those of the Pseudo-Empedoclean system.

265. Thus the alleged Qeshishah, writing to his disciple Yehudah from Corbeil on the ten emanations (without however employing the word sefiroth), concluded: "This is the quintessence of the ten 'crowns' that the heads of the academies received as a tradition, but the details of the paths are more than can ever be counted, and every one of the paths is a particular world in itself." The aforementioned Pseudo-Yequthiel teaches his supposed pupil that each individual sefirah represents a world in itself, even if the sefiroth are intertwined and interconnected. Moses of Burgos, *Liqquṭim,* fol. 7a; Todros Abulafia, *'Oṣar ha-Kabhod* (1879), fol. 5c; and the author of the *Tiqqune Zohar* later drew from these sources; the latter, in a text interpolated in the main part of the *Zohar* 1:24b, propounded the same conception, according to which each *middah* is called a particular world. Cf. also *Ma'arekheth ha-'Elohuth* (Mantua, 1558), fol. 89a, which presents this thesis in the same formulation as the *Tiqqune Zohar.*

266. This spelling is supposed to have come from a certain Ḥaninah or Ḥanunyah (the manuscripts vary), who is said to have lived long before Hai Gaon in Jerusalem and to have received the secrets of the Torah, *mequbbal be-sithre Torah.* Reference is also made to this spelling in the other responsum of Hai on the ten sefiroth; cf. Jellinek, *Geschichte der Kabbala* 3:13, who, however, misinterpreted the passage. The two responsa have their origin in the same kabbalistic circle.

267. The oldest, the "Alphabet of Metatron, the celestial scribe," is preserved in many manuscripts and came to the German Hasidim with the Babylonian Merkabah material. We possess a rather long commentary on it, perhaps from the pen of Eleazar of Worms; cf. for example, Ms. British Museum 752, f.81b–84a. Many manuscripts of Jewish magic contain such "alphabets of the angels" that very possibly preserve, in stylized form, survivals from the ancient Hebrew script. I have collected abundant material from manuscripts relating to this subject. Among the Arabs, alphabets of this kind were preserved in part through the tradition of the Sabaeans; cf. *Ancient Alphabets and Hieroglyphic Characters,* ed. Joseph Hammer (London, 1806) based on the alleged "Books of the Nabateans" of ibn Waḥshiyya. Cf. in addition Steinschneider's remark, *Zur Pseudepigraphischen Literatur* (Berlin, 1862), 30; it was this spelling, in Pseudo-Hai, that Steinschneider had in mind.

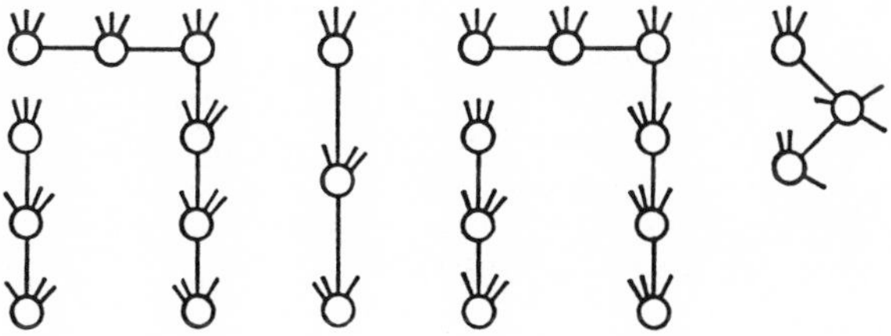

The twenty-four points or stars of this script correspond, according to the author, to the twenty-four books of the biblical canon, which are perhaps woven from this "hidden name."[268] The author instructs the initiate that each of these points in and of itself represents an entire world. This use of the term "worlds" for different levels of being is undoubtedly Neoplatonic. It first penetrated into kabbalistic literature in the *'Iyyun* circle. As we have seen, Isaac the Blind speaks of the "world of separation" below the sefiroth, but it seems he still did not take the step of considering the sefiroth themselves as just so many worlds. The upper world is henceforth no longer that of the separate intelligences, as it was for the philosophers and in Isaac's fragments on cosmogony, but the world of the divine emanations itself. In the "Book of the Unity" of Pseudo-Ḥammai it is said that before Creation all the powers were intertwined and hidden in God,

> until there came the time of the will of the first Acting One,[269] and they emerged from potentiality to spiritual reality, and the emanation

268. Although this conclusion is explicitly attested only sixty years later, in Joseph ibn Gikatilla, cf. my *On the Kabbalah,* 42–43.

269. Better reading (for example, Ms. Jerusalem 8° 404, fol. 34b): "until the will came, etc." The phrase corresponds to the *voluntas factoris primi* in ibn Gabirol's *Fons Vitae* 3:32. The designation of God as *factor primus (po'el qadmon)* has its origin among the Mutazilites and is still frequently found in the *'Iyyun* circle, where, however, the metaphysic of the will does not play any major role. Many of these writings, as for example the "Source of Wisdom," do not mention the will at all, and merely speak, like Isaac the Blind, of the *maḥshabah.* The terminology was therefore not necessarily mediated through ibn Gabirol, though the possibility should not be excluded that the early kabbalists did have some indirect knowledge of him. Cf. my Hebrew article "Traces of Gabirol in the Kabbalah" (1940). To this should be added new evidence to the effect that Cathars in Italy at the same period seem to have used the *Fons Vitae,* as F. Dondaine, *Liber de duobus principiis* (1939), 141, has demonstrated with regard to a statement attributed to Aristotle in that text.

> of the upper world emanated to that of the tenth fundamental stone which is called, in the language of the sages of the mysteries, the "condensed light," *'or 'abh*. On account of its condensation they also name it "mixed darkness," for all the powers of the flames[270] are mixed in it, but are also differentiated in it, and it is the foundation of all the spiritual and corporeal worlds . . . and the last seal of all the [other] seals [emanated in the higher sefiroth].

Thus the sefiroth are here conceived as worlds but also as seals, as minting stamps of all reality—just as the Platonists speak of the ideas as seals—but they are also the "luminous mirrors" of the deity through which its light is reflected in all reality.[271] Some texts specify, much as does the "Book of the Five Substances," a distinct "world of life," which is distinguished from the world of the intellect and from that of the soul in the hierarchy of being.[272] *'En-sof* as a name of the hidden God in his transcendence is still unknown in these texts, suggesting that they preceded the writings of the Gerona circle. But they also readily make use of adverbial phrases of the kind we have already discussed with regard to the Infinite and often speak of the "light whose sublimity has no end." The fact that the name Araritha was used for the primordial and transcendent being, as we have mentioned, proves that the writers felt the need to find some name for the absolute unity, which is above all these "worlds," the "One where everything originates, where everything has its existence and to which everything returns." The absence of the name *'en-sof* can therefore be no accident.

---

270. Isaac the Blind frequently speaks in a similar manner of the *shalhabhioth* in his commentary on *Yeṣirah* and the *Midrash Konen.*

271. Thus, for example, in the text referred to in note 255, herein. The conception of the sefiroth as mirrors presupposes that they collect the light of God coming from above but reflect it down below. The image was later very widespread among kabbalists, who received it through the intermediary of old lists of the ten sefiroth, as for example in the *Sod ha-Sefiroth,* Ms. Vatican 171, fol. 133a.

272. Cf. this notion in the eschatology of Pseudo-Empedocles in Kaufmann, *Salomon ibn Gabirol,* 19, 29, and above all 35. In the prayer of Rabban Gamaliel, this world is located above that of the souls and of nature. The "Book of the True Unity" mentions entities that are situated between the world of life and the world of intellect. These two worlds are also named, side by side, in the treatise *Sod we-yesod ha-qadmoni* in the commentary on the fifth sefirah; cf. *Tarbiz* 2:423–424.

9. Fundamental Conceptions of This Circle: The Primordial Ether—Light- and Language-Mysticism

In almost all the more important writings of this group, the notion of the primordial ether, *'awir qadmon,* occupies a prominent position, although its role in the different systems is not clearly determined. The notion was undoubtedly developed from Saadya's commentary on *Yeṣirah,* where a distinction is made between the perceptible, material ether, the air, and the imperceptible, subtle ether. Within the latter, says Saadya, the will of the Creator unfolds itself, moving it as life moves the body. This subtle ether, *'awir daq,* is for him identical with the *kabhod,* which fills everything: "and the nation calls it Shekhinah, and the author of the *Book of Creation* names it the pneuma of the living God."[273] But among the kabbalists these notions did not remain synonymous and in the *'Iyyun* writings we can observe various possibilities of differentiating between them. Sometimes the primordial ether is regarded as the first sefirah and identified with the "highest crown" of the *Bahir,* or the primordial *pneuma* that emanated from it is even identified with the *nihil.* The Shekhinah is considered, as in the *Bahir,* as the last sefirah. Where the doctrine of the sefiroth is not mentioned at all, as in the fragment of the book *Moreh Ṣedeq,* the primordial pneuma is described as an infinite potency inherent in the First Cause, but at the same time an autonomous potency and an autonomous light, "and precisely that is the Shekhinah," which is represented as the primordial foundation of all the active and formative powers. The Book *'Iyyun* itself makes no mention at all of primordial ether, unless the latter is concealed in the concept of the primordial darkness.

It does, however, play an important role in the "Source of Wisdom." This small book was always regarded by the kabbalists as one of the most enigmatic works of their literature. Baer of Mezritsch still boasted to his disciple Solomon of Luzk of having studied this book with the founder of Hasidism, Israel Baal-shem who, Baer said, explained it to him word by word. It consists of two parts. The first is concerned largely with the divine name YHWH, the manner in which it was engendered by the processes of language-mysticism,

---

273. Cf. Saadya, *Commentaire sur le Sefer Yeṣira,* ed. Lambert (Paris, 1891), 70–72 of the Arabic text, as well as the text of the old Hebrew translation in David Kaufmann, in his addenda to Yehudah ben Barzilai's commentary on *Yeṣirah,* 340.

its wondrous power, and the role of the primordial ether at the origin of all movement of language. Here it seems that the idea of the spoken word becoming "inscribed" in the air, issuing from the mouth of the person uttering it, was applied to the primordial processes of the creative divine speech. In the second part successive attempts are made to develop a cosmogony.

The name of God—so the book begins—is the unity of the movement of language branching out from the primordial root. This movement grows out of the primordial ether, in the form of the thirteen pairs of opposites that are at the same time the thirteen *middoth* of divine government. The author seeks to show how the name of God proceeds from the movement of the *'alef,* the pure breath. The details of this explanation are very obscure. In all the names, and hence in all elements of language, the *'alef* remains the innermost principle that, as the "balancing index of the scales" (according to *Yeṣirah* 2:1), is at bottom a point of indifference.

From the "primordial principle" that, unoriginated, persists in its movement, there proceed the lights of the flames that then become separated from their origin and, in their differentiation, increasingly removed from it. These are basically the thirten *middoth* that act by way of oppositions. In an audacious symbol derived from the figure of the Hebrew letter *yod,* י, the world of language is born from the wings of the *yod,* which unfold from its origin—that is, from the movement of the primordial *yod.* (One cannot help wondering whether the letter *'alef* is thought to contain within itself the *yod* as its wings.) This *yod* is represented as the "bubbling source" of the movement of language, which after differentiation and ramification in the Infinite returns again to its center and origin. The principle of cyclical movement in all cosmogonic processes reappears again and again in the most diverse forms in our text and seems to have held a peculiar fascination for the author. Whenever these processes have fully unfolded they turn about in a volte-face and, in a cyclical movement, return to their origin. Whoever is capable of placing himself at the root of this movement of language does in fact embrace all language and all expressions of the essential essence and hence becomes a master of all wondrous effects, described here in the best magical style. But at the same time, at the end of his road man stands "in perfect clarity, with a settled mind [*yishubh ha-da'ath*]" and "dwells in the supreme thought, which [in its turn] resides in the primordial ether, above which there is no higher degree." Here we thus have the idea that the dissolution of mystical thought in the *maḥshabah* of God, where divine knowledge is obtained, becomes by an inverse movement the perseverance of the master of the names who, "with a settled mind" and without losing himself, leads his thinking to its root and implants it there.

In all these symbols the primordial ether is described as the "indifferent identity" within which all things are transformed and become oppositions. Apparently it is regarded as the substratum of the world where all the powers are "rounded."[274] As among the ancient natural philosophers, this primordial ether is conceived as a spiritual fire in which everything is fused—the author uses the image of the smelting of metal to illustrate the unifying function of the primordial ether. The powers of the ether are warmed and in these heated circles they are fused into a single unity. From the primordial ether there spreads forth, like flames from coals, the chain of the paths, of which the Book *Yeṣirah* speaks. It gives rise to figurations that return cyclically to their primordial foundation and are described in symbols that seem to be connected with the beginning of Isaac the Blind's commentary on *Yeṣirah.*[275] But above all two sources gush forth one after the other, or, as in other writings of this circle, side by side. First there is a source of infinite light that disperses very quickly, like the sparks of a forge; then another follows, a source of darkness, that is nevertheless supposed to contain three kinds of light and "morning twilights." The ether itself is that which cannot be apprehended through questioning, and in this determination it is identical with the primordial darkness in the Book *'Iyyun.* Elsewhere, and in a slightly different manner, it is suggested that the two sources of light and darkness both well forth from the primordial darkness. The contemplative penetration into the mysteries of this primordial ether having been refused to him, Moses contents himself with the contemplation of these two sources, from which everything below now flows forth and comes into being.

This cosmogony of the second part, in which language-mysticism appears only incidentally and where everything is based upon

---

274. This is the source of the image of the primordial ether as a ring at the beginning of the *Zohar* 1:15a.

275. The image of the skein and its threads is common to Isaac and to the "Source of Wisdom," as is the explanation of the difference between *nathib* and *derekh* at the beginning of the commentary on *Yeṣirah,* though with different nuances.

the mystical lights, considers the primordial darkness of the ether from which everything has come as the unexplorable "Before" of the deity, as that aspect of it which is "before" Creation. From there on, that is, from the "back" that also contains God's glory and plenitude of power, everything is knowable. Moses found that from the process of the two sources (which are not expressly identified here with the potencies of the Merkabah although such an identification may well be implied) there proceeds a power that here and in other writings is called *liḥluaḥ,* the primordial moisture. At first, the jet of water issuing from the sources becomes, in fact, thinner and thinner, as thin as a hair, until nothing but little droplets seep out; but these expand with immense strength, and from their combination arises this humidity, which becomes increasingly clear and purified. Like foam upon the water there emerges from it, as in Genesis 1:2, the Holy Spirit, which in its turn is differentiated into many potencies. This primordial foam glitters in a play of colors in which red and white alternate but are nevertheless closely linked to one another. The Holy Spirit is then depicted in the same way the nature of the *ḥokhmah* is described by Isaac the Blind, without, however, any mention whatsoever being made of this concept.

> It is something which comes from the primordial darkness and that indicates form and creation and alteration of form and creation. This form undergoes permanent transformation, like something upright which is bent,[276] and it is at one and the same time both center and periphery and it stands at the beginning and sucks in [from its origin] the power of all and is counted with all, and all flows from it and proceeds from it without similarity or differentiation taking place within it.[277]

---

276. This image is used by Isaac in his commentary on *Yeṣirah* in connection with the letter *yod,* and thus, no doubt, for the *ḥokhmah,* which is symbolized by this letter. But in the context of the "Source of Wisdom," it refers to the transformation of the straight vertical line into the curved form of the circle in which all things also return to their origin.

277. These determinations are found word for word in connection with the *ḥokhmah,* compared with the letter *yod* and as the first consonant of the Tetragrammaton, in Isaac's commentary on *Yeṣirah* 1:2. It is compared there with the brain, which is in the center of the head and at the same time also acts in all the members, which receive their power from there. In Isaac's commentary the idea is organically developed and not taken out of context as in the "Source of Wisdom," where it is related to an idea alien to the basic imagery used, such as that of the primordial form.

From these and the following expositions regarding the ten lights, it is clear that the author knew the doctrine of the sefiroth and that without naming it he combined this doctrine with the independently conceived cosmogonic system of the four primordial elements. He associated the conceptions of Isaac, known to him either from his commentary on *Yeṣirah* or through oral sources, with his own meditations on color- and light-mysticism. The opposite supposition, that the "Source of Wisdom" might be older than Isaac's theory, seems to me to be ruled out by a consideration of the texts. Unless we assume a connection with Isaac's doctrine of the *ḥokhmah,* the passage does not make any sense; with such a connection it is perfectly understandable. But it seems to me equally clear that this entire theory of the ether and the primordial sources and their lights derive from a tradition other than that of the accepted theory of the sefiroth, to which it was only artificially attached.

The colors issuing from the primordial sources, which originally were only red and white (most probably symbols of Stern Judgment and Grace), are differentiated in the course of further developments first into five and subsequently into an infinity of plays of color. The source of darkness is regarded not, as one would have expected, as a uniform "dark," but as deriving from a mixture of green, blue, and white. These plays of color are "like the flame that issues from the ether"—an image that later passed into the *Zohar* 1:5a, in the description at the beginning of the book of the primordial beginning of Creation. In the transformation of this supreme form-principle that breaks forth from the darkness and the ether, there come into being ten forms and plays of color that are reflected in one another. From ten they become one hundred, and having reached their highest potency they finally return to their original unity.

The author then enumerates the names of the ten lights, which probably form a parallel to the ten sefiroth. They bear names that often reappear in these writings but are partly identified in an entirely different manner, such as *'or mufla,* wondrous light; *'or nistar,* hidden light; *'or mithnoṣeṣ,* sparkling light; *'or ṣaḥ,* clear light; *'or bahir,* bright light; *'or mazhir,* radiant light, etc. The ten lights are situated below the primordial darkness (of the *superesse?* See note 233 herein), which is not included in their number. The author promises to explain every single one of these lights, but our extant text does not keep this promise. Instead he returns to the explanation of the primordial source, which for him evidently represents the unity of the two aforementioned sources and is called "light of the source," *'or ha-mabbua'*. This source is also called "the light that is too dark to shine"—once again an image that served as the Hebrew model for one of the expressions used in the opening passages of the *Zohar,*[278] which we have already mentioned. This light is indeed called darkness, not because it is actually dark but because no creature, neither angel nor prophet, can bear or grasp it. It is the plenitude of light that blinds the eye. Evidently these definitions of the "dark light" agree with those of the Nothing that we have already encountered among the kabbalists. In any event, the idea remains in patent contradiction to the doctrine of the sefiroth, for what is said there of the supreme sefirah, *kether,* as being the "Nothing," is related here to the source that comes from the primordial darkness, which is the ether. This would agree well with the beginning of the *Zohar* 1:15a, apparently influenced by this text, but does not correspond to the usual explanation of the sefiroth. In our text the author then proceeds to an explanation of the wondrous light, which he separates, rather surprisingly, from the light that "withdraws itself," *'or mith'allem,* the "blinding darkness." In other texts emanating from this circle the two are identical with one another. This light is described as the mirror that receives all the forms or colors but has none of its own—a metaphor for the "hyle" that is subsequently mentioned in texts applying the images of this circle to the doctrine of the sefiroth, and more particularly for characterizing as "primordial hyle" a first sefirah conceived completely in the spirit of ibn Gabirol's doctrine.[279] It thus appears that the speculations found in this text are based on the dissolution of the philosophic conception upon which they originally rested. In this view, the hyle itself was naturally regarded as the substratum of all differentiation and the recipient of all the forms, and it is in this sense that it is presented, for example, in an interpretation of the first sefirah in an old commentary on the ten sefiroth belonging to the *'Iyyun* circle, or

---

278. The *buṣina de-qardinutha,* explained by many kabbalists as "dark light" in the sense of *buṣina de-qadrinutha.*

279. Thus in *Sod ha-Sefiroth,* where these determinations of the hyle serve to characterize the first sefirah, designated as *'or mith'allem.* Cf. also my discussion of the relationships of the symbolism of the first three sefiroth in this text and ibn Gabirol's definition of hyle and form in my Hebrew article "Traces of Gabirol" (in *Me'assef Sofre 'Ereṣ-Yisrael,* Tel Aviv, 1940), 173.

at least directly influenced by it. In the "Source of Wisdom," on the other hand, these determinations are torn apart. The mirror that receives all the forms is none other than the *'or mufla,* but it receives the differences of the "blinding light" that is above it instead of itself being located above these differentiations, as would correspond to the original sense of the idea. The determinations that actually belong to a single sphere, namely the hyle, are now distributed over two spheres. The author apparently lacked any clear conception of the philosophic formulas he used for his meditations on the celestial lights.

At the end of the text the author presents other variations of the same primordial process, as if he felt that he had to continue to clarify an original intuition by means of repeated attempts at explanation even though they contradicted each other in matters of detail. It is in the course of these considerations that the first source of darkness is directly identified with the primordial ether itself. It was a pure fire, "a fire that consumes fire"—reminiscent of Jacob Böhme's description of God as the "central fire"—and consisted of sixteen eyes, which were in motion and passed into one another. It is only in the course of further processes that, with the primordial ether splitting in two, two other sources burst forth from it. We then learn that the second of these sources corresponds to the *ḥashmal* of the Merkabah. The lights of this source inundate the world, and from their movement there emerges a sound. This motif reappears in all the writings of this circle. They all mention the clash of these lights that produces, as it were, a "cry of lights." This establishes a link, otherwise rather difficult to recognize, with the theory of creation founded on the four primordial elements as it is clearly expounded in other writings of the *'Iyyun* circle and which we shall discuss presently. The book closes with a surprising point taken from the sphere of the mystical names of God: the first of the two sources is identified with the primordial name אהוי, the second with the three-letter name הוי , formed from the consonants of the Tetragrammaton.

So far I have summarized the principal ideas of this tract, basing myself upon the texts of the manuscripts and without entering into the often utterly obscure details of particular points, especially where these are interwoven with letter-mysticism. The contradictions encountered within one and the same text may mitigate our sense of surprise at the contradictions between one text and other writings emanating, to all appearances, from a closely related spiritual environment but developing the same initial impulses in different directions. Since there is no direct reference to the sefiroth as such, there is also no direct contradiction between the ten lights and the thirteen *middoth* of divine rule, which here are apparently situated above them. The doctrine of the two sources is expounded more clearly and in less contradictory manner in other texts. Thus, for example, "Mystery of the Knowledge of Reality" presents a clearly recognizable system of four primordial potencies, which admittedly accords poorly with the classical sequence of the sefiroth, as sefiroth; the four fundamental cosmogonic powers. All have their primordial basis in a *maḥshabah* that takes the place of *'en-sof* itself. It, and no longer something above it, is the very reality of God. The first sefirah of the Book of Creation is said in this text to be the very last thing that can be known of the existence of God, which is "bound to the roots of the *maḥshabah.*"[280] From this *maḥshabah* emanates the primordial ether that is itself the primordial pneuma. This ether is split and there proceed from it two lights, which are called here and in other texts *'arafel* and *ḥashmal. 'Arafel* represents the twilight of darkness in the first source of the "Source of Wisdom,"[281] but also the divine omnipotence and force; while the *ḥashmal* is, in its overflowing plenitude of light, the second of these sources but also the divine Grace. This first triad became, however, a tetrad, for a second pneuma emanated from the primordial pneuma, the former being identified by the author with the second sefirah. Obviously this system contradicts the doctrine of the sefiroth in its received forms. The two *pneumata* are here the first two sefiroth of the Book of Creation, the "pneuma of God" and the "pneuma of the pneuma" or the "air from the air." Between them *'arafel* and *ḥashmal* have no place at all; nevertheless they are somehow related to the sefiroth *ḥesed* and *din* in the schema of the *Bahir.* In any case we have here the four supreme potencies, the primordial ether being defined as the "active potency" and the second pneuma as the "pas-

280. Hebrew: *'aḥuzah be-shorshe ha-maḥshabah.*

281. The names of these two lights appear juxtaposed so consistently in the majority of these writings that they must form part of the fundamental conceptions of this circle. Their origin still remains to be clarified. In the Merkabah literature, *'arafel* does not play any role. As the notion is connected with light-mysticism, reference should be made here to Baḥya ben Asher's explanation of *'arafel* as a particularly clear and pure light; Baḥya sought to justify his interpretation by means of an etymological pun; cf. his commentary on Exodus 20:21.

sive potency." It is only the tetrad in its entirety that constitutes the "reality of the intellect," *mammashuth ha-sekhel,* which, according to our author, is the true primordial man, *'adam qadmon.* The expression *'adam qadmon* appears here for the first time in kabbalistic literature, and it is from this circle that it came to the Gnostics of Castile and the Book *Zohar.*

This purely mystical theory of the intellect as a composite potency, which apparently has its origin in older Neoplatonic theories (not necessarily in ibn Gabirol himself), continued to be voiced in this circle. In this view, primordial man is not the totality of all the potencies of the pleroma or of the world of the sefiroth, but only a configuration of the supreme potencies. They also form, at least in the first part of this text, the *ḥayyoth,* the "living beings" of the Merkabah, also defined at the same time by way of a pun as the *ḥiyyuth,* the vitality or, strictly speaking, life. Following in these, we again find in very hazy detail the potencies of the Merkabah—such as the throne, the cherub, etc. But the roots of all things remain anchored in this primordial tetrad. In a somewhat different version of the same doctrine, the text also expounds the thesis according to which the *ḥayyoth* only represent potencies emanating from the *ḥashmal* itself. In this case the Merkabah proper appears in all its components—as indeed seems more logical—below the domain of the primordial man who sits on the throne above it. The author interprets the word Merkabah, which can also be taken literally to mean "composition," as the place where the synthesis of all those other lights takes place. The four columns of the throne of the Merkabah are identical with the four camps of the Shekhinah, which are described in great detail, though in an altogether different way than in the Book *'Iyyun.* The account of the first of these camps interpolates a complete exposition of the list of the sefiroth as given in chapter 1 of the *Yeṣirah,* but developed in the spirit of Merkabah-mysticism rather than that of the received doctrine of the sefiroth. The only link between the two is provided by the identification of the primordial ether with the divine thought. From the union of the active and passive potency there arises, according to this text, the hyle, identified here with the primordial moisture, *liḥluaḥ.* Why does the author reject the opinion (which in fact he shares) of the "scholar" whom he quotes and according to whom hyle is emanated from the Creator? This point remains obscure. The relevance of the author's enigmatic utterances on the subject of our problem remains incomprehensible.

Different again is the cosmogonic system presented by Pseudo-Hai in his interpretation of the forty-two letter divine name, in which the same notions appear, albeit in a different order. Here the primordial pneuma is placed at the beginning. Two potencies flow from it, and between them it rests: the moisture, the primordial water or *bohu,* and the primordial ether or *tohu.* This manner of subordinating the *tohu* to the *bohu* and the ether to the water is very striking. To these potencies is added the *ḥashmal,* which comes directly (as earlier, the second pneuma) from the primordial pneuma and produces, in its turn, the seven archangels or supreme archons as well as the intelligent soul. The *ḥashmal* thereby performs the double function of *ḥayyoth* and *ḥiyyuth.* The *'arafel* and the *pargod* (the "curtain") only appear below the *ḥashmal.* From the curtain flow the powers of the Merkabah, of which the highest is called the "stream of fire" (according to Daniel 7:10), from which the souls of the righteous emerge as sparks. The Neoplatonic realm of nature was transformed thereby into the paradisiacal place of the souls "implanted in the ether of nature." The Tetragrammaton symbolizes the concentration of all these powers. The doctrine of the sefiroth does not appear at all, not even in symbolic allusions.

In the two different texts entitled "Book of the Unity," the two possible tendencies of this group are clearly discernible. One of the texts, "The Book of the True Unity," pays only very superficial attention to the sefiroth but is interested, on the other hand, in the enumeration of the powers of the Merkabah; here Neoplatonic speculations appear in a decidedly retrograde form, crude and obscure in every respect. The other text, however, seeks to establish a close relationship between the concepts and images of these writings and the kabbalistic system of the sefiroth, the symbolism of the sefiroth, as we have come to know it, being combined with these novel symbols. However, the formulas and terminology of the two circles tend to converge. Thus it is said here of the first sefirah that

> it is named "Supreme Crown," because it is the power of the truth and of the essence and is something secret and hidden. And in it there are secret and hidden and precious things, and they are the 620 columns of light, according to the numerical value of *kether.*[282] And all

---

282. The letter *kaf* has the numerical value of 20, *taw* of 400 and *resh* of 200. These pillars of light reappear in the majority of these writings. In a verse quoted

are united in a bond,[283] without there being anything defective in it. And they [these columns] are the foundation of God's unity; each one has a proper name, which indicates divine things, that is, each one is designated by His name. They embrace one another and are joined to one another in the emanation of the intellect. And this is why the masters of this science name this sefirah the unknown primordial ether, and others name it the "source of probity," because it has the form of a crown which rests upon the head. It is also called "clear light," because something like a fissure appears in it, which changes its aspect, until [the ether] is split, and in this fission the power of all the sefiroth comes into being out of the effluence that flows from it. And in the impulsion of movement the unity is perfected.

The text, continuing in the same vein, deals with all the sefiroth. The sefirah *yesod 'olam,* the foundation of the world, is moved from seventh to ninth place. It is clear that such statements are as foreign to the *Bahir* as to the fragments of Isaac the Blind that are known to us.

In the foregoing we encountered the image of the fission of the primordial ether several times. This image probably owes its origin to a similar one in the "Royal Crown" of Solomon ibn Gabirol. In a poetic metaphor ibn Gabirol speaks of the fission of the Nothing from which God calls forth Being. This image was later transposed by the *'Iyyun* circle, which was very familiar with the "Royal Crown," to the primordial ether; in turn, the "Midrash of Simon the Righteous" equated it metaphorically with the Nothing so that the connection becomes perfectly clear. It may be useful to juxtapose the two passages where this small tract speaks of the primordial creation, not least of all because it can serve as an example of a phenomenon that occurs frequently: the same ideas are presented in parallel versions within a single text. (I have corrected the readings according to the Ms. Munich.)

Yeṣirah 1562, fol. 63a:

Before anything at all was created, God was unfathomable and limitless, alone and unique [*Yaḥid u-meyu-*

ibid. fol. 62b:

. . . And it is said on this subject, that before the world and any creature in it were created, the primor-

---

here whose source is unknown: *shesh me'oth we-'esrim hem rosh millulakh,* this number is apparently connected with the 620 letters of the text of the Ten Commandments, which is probably what is meant by the "beginning of your word."

283. The author frequently uses the term *'adiquth* in the specific sense of "emanation." Thus he speaks of the emanation of the intellect as *'adiquth ha-sekhel.*

ḥad],[284] capable of subsisting by Himself in the potency of existence [*qiyyum*] . . . And His power was not discernible. Then, it entered His mind to produce all His works, and He created a first potency and named it primordial *Ḥokhmah,* from which came the twelve other potencies [corresponding to the thirteen *Middoth*]. This potency corresponds to the ten [*sefiroth*] in the undifferentiated unity which are the ten sefiroth of withdrawnness [in the Book *Yeṣirah*], and it is to this that [Eccl. 7:19] refers: The *Ḥokhmah* gives power to the sage more than ten rulers in the city. The sage is God and the reality of this potency, which is the primordial *Ḥokhmah,* is a pure and completely unalloyed light of life, inscribed and sealed in the splendor of the supreme vault [*Shafrir*], which is called the Nought devoid of any notion. And this is the mystery of [Job 28:12] "The *Ḥokhmah* comes from the Nought." It is this supreme power [here, literally: side] that is called unlimited will. And why is it called will? Since by its word and its will, being was produced from nought. It is also called the radiant light or the glory of God, of which it is said [Ps. 104:2]: "He covers himself with light as with a garment," since it is one in all of its light and splendor, like the flame which is one in all its colors and which rises to the infinite. It is also called One because it precedes all the primordial beings which emanate from its wondrous unity. And this *Ḥokhmah* is the highest of the ten sefiroth.

dial ether was unique and, in its sublimity, did not lean toward any side. And God's power was hidden in it, and His *Kabhod* was entirely unrecognizable, until this ether split and His splendor appeared and His *Kabhod* was revealed. At that hour, He produced a potency and named it primordial *Ḥokhmah.* The knowledge of the primordial ether and the emergence of His creation was not revealed even to our master Moses.

284. The formula, whose origin is not clear to me, to the effect that God is *'eḥad yaḥid u-meyuḥad,* reappears in many of the *'Iyyun* writings, as well as in Azriel. In the fourteenth century we find a very similar though undoubtedly much older Arabic formula in a Sufi mystic; cf. R. Nicholson, *Studies in Islamic Mysticism* (Cambridge, 1921), 104. I found this formula also in piyyutim of the period after Saadya (for the first time?) as well as in the spurious gaonic responsum *Sefer Sha'are Teshubah,* Section 26, and in good mauscripts of the mystical commentary of Naḥmanides on Genesis 1:1 (see *Kiryath Sefer* 6:3 [1929]: 415–416. Cf. also chap. 2, n. 27, herein.)

While in ibn Gabirol's *Fons Vitae* the term *sapientia* is generally synonymous with the divine will,[285] here it is evidently situated below that primordial ether that is at once the divine and the Nothing. Here the will clearly appears as a supreme potency in God, a potency that even stands, so to speak, above the sefiroth, which only begin with the primordial *ḥokhmah.* The identity of these two symbols—for it is as such that the kabbalists conceive them—originating from such entirely different sources was generally accepted in the Spanish Kabbalah after 1250, above all through the meditation of Azriel. What still remains unclear is the contradiction in ibn Gabirol himself, who, in the "Royal Crown," placed the *sapientia* above the will, a conception the kabbalists never adopted.[286] Otherwise, however, the parallel between ibn Gabirol's poetry and the passages we have just quoted is striking. The primordial *ḥokhmah* is the first being, as already conceived by Isaac the Blind. The images of the "Source of Wisdom" and of the "Midrash of Simon the Righteous" explain, as we have already noted several times, the solemn beginning of the *Zohar.* The source of the light that breaks out of the dark flame "splits the primordial ether that surrounds it, and as a result of the force of this fission, a hidden supreme point is illuminated"—the first logos, which is nothing other than the primordial *ḥokhmah.*[287] Only the already established usage of the expression *'en-sof* does not derive from the *'Iyyun* circle; everything else is a paraphrase of its most vivid ideas.[288]

The predilection for the arrangement of primordial powers, of autonomous potencies of all being—that emanate from the deity—pervades all the writings of this circle. The "Midrash of Simon the

---

285. As appears from Bäumker's detailed index in the edition of the *Fons Vitae,* 511.

286. In order to explain the relevant verse of the "Royal Crown," S. Munk, *Mélanges de Philosophie juive et arabe,* 164, and his successors noted that it referred to a *ḥefeṣ mezumman,* a determined, limited will. If this were correct, one could explain the "unlimited will" of Pseudo-Simon as a deliberate contrast. But in reality *mezumman* never has this restrictive meaning; the word belongs to the second verse that follows: *mezumman . . . limshokh* etc.; one must therefore translate: "A will destined to produce the effluence of being out of the nought."

287. Cf. the exact translation of the beginning of the Zohar in my book *Zohar, The Book of Splendor* (New York, 1949), 27.

288. I have examined other developments of the doctrine of the will in the *'Iyyun* group in my study on the traces of ibn Gabirol in the Kabbalah, in *Me 'assef Sofre 'Ereṣ Yisrael* (Tel Aviv, 1940), 168–170.

Righteous" enumerates eight such potencies, whose origin must be sought in some Neoplatonic text or its reinterpretation. The usual hierarchy of being among the Neoplatonists is completed here by additional hypostases. The author speaks of the potency of unity, the potency of existence, the potency of the deity, the potency of testing (which fits least appropriately into this framework), the potency of the intelligible, the potency of the sensible (a term that here, as in Azriel, always stands for the world of the souls), the potency of the natural, and the potency of the perpetual renewal, *koaḥ ḥiddush.* The explanations he gives of these potencies are even more difficult to understand than the terms themselves and seem to be related to the most impenetrable paragraphs of the "Source of Wisdom." These potencies still recur here fairly frequently; elsewhere they are found almost exclusively in Azriel, who often refers to them in his writings. Perhaps the source should be sought in Latin texts, as yet unidentified, of the school of Scotus Erigena.

Pseudo-Simon does not establish any direct relationship between these eight potencies and the ten sefiroth. Besides, of the latter ones, he only mentions *ḥokhmah* and *kether,* which he discusses at length. The 620 lights in *kether,* mentioned in many *'Iyyun* writings, are the "roots of the primordial *ḥokhmah.*" The word *kether* is derived from the verb *kathar,* "to wait" (an etymology indebted to Job 36:2); it is therefore the possibility whose infinite development in the production of all things is to be awaited. This seems to be an indirect reference to *ḥesed* and *din.* Here, as in various fragments of Isaac the Blind, some wordplay seems to be made with the derivatives of the Hebrew root *'aman,* whose different modifications apparently were considered by the oldest kabbalists of Provence as symbols of the most diverse sefiroth, from the highest *'omen* in Isaiah 25:1 to *'amon, 'amen, 'emun* and *'emunah.*[289] What is striking is the absence of symbolism of the feminine and the daughter in connection with the tenth sefirah. It is missing entirely in the most important texts and only briefly indicated in the sefirotic commentary of the second "Book of the Unity," where it is not elaborated at all. This old gnostic motif, so very prominent in the tradition of the *Bahir,* and subsequently to undergo such a powerful development among the Spanish kabbalists, lacked any vital force in precisely

289. Thus in the Book *'Iyyun* and in the two "Books of Unity."

this circle. The *'Iyyun* mystics of Provence seem to have had no use for the idea of syzygies. The transformation of Neoplatonic concepts and metaphors into mystical images, in which they took such a decisive interest, was accomplished by them outside the world of sexual imagery. The profound difference between the oldest sources of the Kabbalah and the breakthrough that occurs here could hardly be accentuated with greater force. On the other hand, the conception of the divine potencies as a cosmic tree remains very much alive, and in many *'Iyyun* writings some of these potencies reappear as "root, branch, and fruit."[290]

A curious relation with the older Merkabah-mysticism is found in the speculative interpretation of the supreme angel 'Anafiel, preserved in a very old quotation from the book *'Iyyun* that does not appear in our text.[291] In older parts of the genuine Hekhaloth literature the rank reserved for this angel is even higher than that of Metatron.[292] His position is now combined with speculations concerning the first sefirah, not in the strict kabbalistic conception but in the spirit of the Book *Yeṣirah*'s definition of the first sefirah as the pneuma of the living God, which could be understood metaphorically as a "branch of God"—in fact the literal meaning of 'Anafiel. In the fragment under consideration, various determinations intersect. The first sefirah is unexplorable because it is without limits. But it is, at the same time, also the consonant *taw,* an intelligible potency that becomes an angel even higher than the *ḥashmal,* higher, therefore, than the potency of the Merkabah, to which such great importance was attributed by the *'Iyyun* circle. The supreme angel of the Merkabah, 'Anafiel is therefore at the same time the first sefirah, and he stands in the place usually occupied in the writings of this group by the primordial ether. But this sefirah is also a secret primordial image, *temunah,* in the figure of Man; in other words, it is the *'adam qadmon* whom we met in a very different context in other writings of this circle. This conforms perfectly with the cherub-mys-

---

290. Thus Pseudo-Simon the Righteous, in his commentary on the Tetragrammaton as well as in the "Mystery of the Knowledge of Reality."

291. This piece is quoted in an anonymous kabbalistic commentary on the prayers that can hardly have been composed later than 1260, Ms. Parma, Perreau 2:105, fol. 37a. In another rather lengthy quotation from *'Iyyun,* in the important Ms. Enelow Memorial Coll. 712, fol. 49a, a similar view is presented, only the subject there is not 'Anafiel but the *Ḥashmal* itself.

292. Cf. *Hekhaloth Rabbathi,* chap. 22, and Odeberg on 3 Enoch, p. 59.

ticism of the German Hasidim. Ezekiel 1:26 is related to 'Anafiel. Indeed, he is at the same time the indivisible, indifferent will, *raṣon shaweh,* which produces all the creatures; as such he also is the pneuma that directs, in the spirit of Ezekiel's vision of the Merkabah, the inner movement of the spiritual beings emerging from him in the process of differentiation. This movement is born when the will turns toward its origin in the "marvelous and nameless light" above it.

In accordance with this idea, the "Book of the True Unity" explains 'Anafiel as the seraph and the angel posted over the unity, whose power is ramified in seven lights that "stand before the place of the unity as a burning fire" and that are identical with the seven seraphim enumerated in chapter 7 of the "Tractate of the Hekhaloth."[293] Perhaps this decomposition of the supreme luminous power into seven seraphim or lights ought to be approximated to certain notions of the Cathars, for whom the Paraclete was sevenfold and who spoke of the seven *animae principales.*[294]

I mentioned above the rather striking hyle speculations of these writings. Despite all differences, the writings of the *'Iyyun* group without exception count the hyle as a positive principle that has its place as a hypostasis among the cosmic potencies. It is never conceived here as the root of evil. We thus have the same two elements that we also find in ibn Gabirol. The Neoplatonic depreciation of the hyle has disappeared; its rank, on the contrary, is raised higher and higher. In the Book *'Iyyun* itself the emanation was considered as being free of hyle. It was only after the emanation of the sefiroth, which shine above it, that the hyle was created. In the list

293. Cf. *Beth ha-Midrash* 2:47. Only the name of the first of these seven seraphim has a clear signification. Orpaniel (Orfaniel) obviously means: "the angel who receives the light from the face of God." This idea of the seven archangels is also found in *Pirqe Rabbi Eliezer,* chap. 4, where, however, no names are mentioned. They officiate there before the curtain and are considered to be the first-created among the angels. This tradition doubtless continues that of the seven angels stationed before the throne of God in the book of *Tobit,* chap. 12 and *Enoch,* chap. 20. Cf. on this subject W. Lueken, *Michael* (Göttingen, 1898), 36–37. The *'Iyyun* gives the same names as the Hekhaloth. For Jacob Cohen, these seven angels form the mystical menorah that was shown to him in heaven and whose design is preserved in his *Sefer ha-'Orah;* Ms. Milan, Bernheimer 62, fol. 107a; cf. Bernheimer's catalogue (1933), 78.

294. Döllinger, *Beiträge zur Sektengeschichte* 1:155; cf. R. Reitzenstein, *Die Vorgeschichte der christlichen Taufe* (Berlin, 1929), 136–140.

of the thirty-two paths, however, the hyle—designated not as *hiyuli* but as golem—is one of the thirty-two potencies or paths, but neither the highest nor the lowest of them. In the "Midrash of Pseudo-Simon" the conception is different. Here the hyle is found at the limit of the emanation and, facing outward, forms its reverse side. This potency of the back, behind which the conception of the hyle is concealed, is the *principium individuationis,* which first differentiates all the forms. Toward everything that is nature, and therefore is composed of matter and form, flows the force of this potency. A very different explanation is found in the "Book of the True Unity," where the Skekhinah itself in the *principium individuationis.* The throne—which is the *hyle* in ibn Gabirol's *Fons Vitae!*—is identical with the potency of the Shekhinah, into which all things enter without form in order to be formed and shaped and to leave individuated through matter and form. The Shekhinah is the origin of all separability; it is the "mother of all living things." (This idea may be based upon a conception of the hyle as feminine.) Pseudo-Simon's determinations with regard to the "back," the side of the emanation turned outward, are repeated here, but they are now related to a potency in the world of emanations itself. The "Mystery of the Knowledge of Reality" rejects the theory of certain sages or commentators according to which the hyle was emanated directly from God as the first potency. This is in fact the theory presented by ibn Gabirol in *Fons Vitae.* Did our author have ibn Gabirol in mind or possibly older sources for this idea, mediated by texts of Isaac Israeli? This vacillation is characteristic of the manner in which the *'Iyyun* circle absorbed philosophic conceptions into its kabbalistic universe.

10. The Thirteen Middoth, *Ten Sefiroth and Three Lights Above Them in Pseudo-Hai*

A final point, one that was to be of no small importance for the later Kabbalah, remains to be discussed. As we have seen, these writings in general are not excessively concerned with the relationship between the traditional ideas of the thirteen *middoth* of divine rule and the recently crystallizing doctrine of the ten sefiroth. This is not at all surprising, for, on the whole, the authors of this circle preserved a perfectly pure theistic conception of God. The intelligible lights and potencies discussed here, as well as the sefiroth themselves—insofar as they are mentioned—can hardly be considered aspects of the inner divine world. This is still less the case, naturally, for the descriptions of the cosmogonic processes taking place in and below the primordial ether. Here is how one author depicts the primordial ether:

> Why is it called primordial ether? Because it is a light in the height of the *'araboth,* heaven, and it is like a garment of rays which come from the light of the Magnificence of God, the creator of the worlds, and which is extended over the whole *kabhod,* all around. Its clarity is excessive and it radiates, and for this reason it is named inapprehensible ether, and not because there would be any other potencies there, which preceded it.[295]

For someone who writes in this manner, neither the primoridal ether nor anything else is an element or aspect of the world of the deity itself, which is clearly situated above all other things. What is described here are not events within the world of the deity, but events outside it, events that took place at the beginning of the creation of the world of the Merkabah, no matter how transformed this Merkabah-world might present itself here to a Platonizing thought.

But there must already have been in Provence kabbalists who clearly conceived of the sefiroth, in continuation of the *Bahir* and the tradition of Rabad's circle, as aspects of the deity. They consequently must have asked themselves how the assumption of ten divine *middoth* in the doctrine of the sefiroth, could be reconciled with the older talmudic idea of the thirteen *middoth* of divine mercy and government. We possess a quotation where such an explanation, no doubt old despite its late attestation, is attributed to Isaac the Blind.[296] It is, of course, most unlikely that it actually stems from Isaac, since his nephew Asher wrote a detailed treatise on these thirteen *middoth* without referring in any way to the tradition at-

295. Thus in the preface to the "Mystery of the Knowledge of Reality" in Ms. Schocken Kabbalah 6. The Hebrew text of the passage is in *Reshith ha-Qabbala,* 169.

296. I found this explanation, "in the name of the holy R. Isaac the Blind" in two authors who wrote shortly after 1500: Abraham Adrutiel, *'Abne Zikkaron,* Ms. Jerusalem 8⁰ 404, fol. 108b, and Joseph Alashqar, *Ṣofnath Pa'neaḥ,* Ms. Jerusalem 4⁰ 154, fol. 125b. The terminology of the first quotation in particular argues in favor of great antiquity. It mentions side by side, the degrees of *haskel* and *ḥokhmah.* This terminology is, in fact, characteristic of the school of Isaac the Blind.

tributed to his uncle in his later quotation. According to this tradition the thirteen *middoth* correspond to the members of the human body, from the brain to the shoulders and the arms without going any lower. The division establishes only partial equivalences to the sefiroth, of which not all ten are presented but only the first seven, in order of the *Bahir.* The thirteen *middoth* are therefore modifications of these seven sefirotic powers themselves in terms of a *Shi'ur Qomah* symbolism.

The problem appears in a completely different light in a responsum falsely attributed to Hai Gaon by an anonymous personage of Provence, probably around 1230. Whereas the aforementioned tradition played no significant role in subsequent kabbalistic literature, the responsum of Pseudo-Hai occupied an important place from the end of the thirteenth century on, and influenced the development of many subsequent kabbalistic speculations as late as the sixteenth century.[297] The text has also been preserved in many other old kabbalistic manuscripts. The phraseology is definitely that of the *'Iyyun* group. The mystics are not yet called kabbalists but *ba'ale reshumoth,* as in other texts of the same provenance.[298] The word *mequbbalim* occurs only in adjectival combination: "Our teachers, who received from the lips of the old scholars," even though the tradition referred to is obviously an esoteric one. In the text of this circle that Moses of Burgos still had before him, the contradiction between the numbers ten and thirteen is resolved by assuming the existence, below the tenth sefirah, of three potencies in which it manifests its powers.[299] The conception of Pseudo-Hai is entirely different. According to him there exist, above the first sefirah, in the

---

297. The responsum was first printed in Moses Cordovero's *Pardes Rimmonim* (Cracow, 1592), chap. 11, sec. 1, fol. 74a. Yael Nadav, *An Epistle of the Qabbalist Isaac Mar Hayyim concerning the Doctrine of "Supernal Lights,"* צחצחות has published the text as well as a treatise on it written by a Spanish kabbalist in Naples around 1491; cf. *Tarbiz* 26 (1957):440–458. The responsum is quoted in the thirteenth century by Todros Abulafia, *'Oṣar ha-Kabhod* (1879), fol. 16c, and by Baḥya ben Asher on Exodus 34:6. The first of these two authors observed that this responsum had escaped the notice of Asher ben David. David Messer Leon likewise commented on this text in detail around 1500 in his *Magen David,* Ms. Jews' College, Hirschfeld 290. Cordovero's text was reprinted in Jellinek, *Geschichte der Kabbala* 2:11–14.

298. On this expression, cf. chap. 1, p. 41, n. 70, herein. In other texts of this group, the mystics are also called *ba'ale yedi'ah* and *ba'ale mezimmah,* expressions which are synonymous with "gnostics." *Ba'ale kabbalah* are not yet mentioned.

299. See note 248 to this chapter.

"root of roots," three hidden lights that are called, following an old tradition: the inner primordial light, *'or penimi qadmon;* the transparent (or: ultraclear) light, *'or meṣuḥṣaḥ;* and the clear light, *'or ṣaḥ.* (The three adjectives are, however, characteristic of the phraseology employed in the *'Iyyun* circle.)

The translation of the principal part of Pseudo-Hai's responsum reads as follows:[300]

> The answer to your question [concerning this relationship] demands deep penetration. In fact, long before us and before you, this question had already been raised in the days of our old sages. The explanation is long, not for one day and not for two days, for it is profoundly linked to the esoteric science that was hidden in the chambers of the prophets and in the tradition of the mystics. It is for this reason that the paths of this answer are deep, even if it only reaches you in brief. The thirteen *middoth* of which the Torah speaks are branches and derivations that proceed from the ten degrees which are called sefiroth, some of them corresponding to others, with three other hidden [degrees], supreme principles [literally: chiefs of the chiefs], and even if they are not found among you, they are nevertheless transmitted to the holy scholars of earlier times. The "derivations" are the modes of action which are called *middoth,* qualities. But the roots, which are the fathers, are called sefiroth—not because they must have a number, or because they themselves are numbers, but according to the secret of the ten worlds, which are newly born from them. Since for them, there is no numerical determination, and no path for grasping them, except for Him who created them. And Solomon indicated this, when he said in the Song of Songs [6:8]: And worlds without number.[301] Out of respect for your learning, we shall transmit to you the names of the sefiroth, such as we received them from our elders, although we are by no means authorized to reveal to you more about the hidden glory. The ten sefiroth are divided at their formation into three former and seven latter. The three first are: the wondrous light, a light that cannot be grasped, but which corresponds to the "pure thought." To it coresond the [two other] lights of knowledge and intellect,[302] for the thought rules over both of them. The seven latter are seven lights. Three of them are the shell of merit and the shell of culpability, and the balance between opposites is [merciful] pardon which harmonizes them. The fourth light gave rise anew to the world of the souls, which

300. On this responsum see also G. Vajda, *Recherches sur la philosophie et la Kabbale dans la pensée juive du Moyen-Age* (Paris, 1962), 179–181.

301. The author reads, in a punning way *'olamoth,* "worlds," instead of *'alamoth,* "young women."

302. In connection with this terminology, in which *madda'* and *sekhel* are artificially separated, see p. 357, herein.

the mystics call the foundation of the world, but the sages of the Talmud call the righteous of the world. There exists, besides, an external light, which is called devouring fire and whose arms are the north and the right, and it represents the end of all the lights and beginning of all the acts. Now I will indicate to you the three supreme lights above the ten sefiroth, which have no beginning, for they are the name and substance of the root of roots, and thought cannot grasp them, for the comprehension and the knowledge of all that is created are too short for that. In the name of our holy elders, we received their names: the inner primordial light, the transparent light, and the clear light, and everything is one light and one substance, and an infinitely hidden root. . . . And when the mystics say that the sefiroth are like lights, they do not mean that they are anything like the light of the sun, the moon, and the stars, but spiritual, subtle, clear, and internal, a splendor that irradiates the souls. We have undertaken all sorts of inquiries with our masters and received from the lips of the old scholars, in order to learn whether the three supreme [lights] have particular names for themselves, like those which are below them. And we found that they all share the opinion that on account of the greatness of their hiddenness, their names cannot be known, apart from those names which are attributed to them as [those three] lights, and hence the root without beginning also has no known name. And the four-letter name and, still more, all of the other epithets [of God] are related specifically to the created Glory, even though the Tetragrammaton, which is the foundation of all the degrees [of the sefiroh] is written in the form, known among the mystics, of subtle points.[303] This indicates the marvelous secret that they [the degrees of the sefiroth, symbolized by the Tetragrammaton] took spiritual matter and form from the power of the three degrees which are name and substance and root. The first letter [*yod*] ascended from the hidden root and was diffused as a light of the Thought, and they [?] expand in the substance of the root, in it and not outside of it. From them [the three lights], matter and form took the power of knowledge [*ḥokhmah*] and the power of intellect [*binah*] and they are the beginning of the hidden, spiritual creation. And this first point received [from its origin in the primordial light] a strong and marvelous power of formation, so that ten degrees are formed in it in the subtlest manner. Thus their number increases to ten. And from the power of this point ten degrees are also materialized in the form of the letter *he,* which follows it, and they are indicated by the points of the correct spelling that we received from our ancient masters. And all the powers were hidden in it [the *he*] as in a spiritual treasure house. From the power of this second form, matter and form took the six "directions of the world" [which correspond to the six sefiroth and to *binah*]. In this letter *waw* [whose numerical value is six], the powers that were hidden in the second letter appeared in a more manifest fashion, and through them the hidden words began to become known. That is why the sages of the

303. Cf. herein the figure, p. 329, as well as note 253.

> sefiroth name this sefirah the Aspect [*mar'eh,* literally: the becoming visible] of the hidden world. The last *he* [of the divine name] is the preparation [*tiqqun*] of the effect, and it brings all the hidden powers to their complete effect and it is the perfection of all the powers.

In response to a further question alleged to have been posed with respect to the meaning of these three lights, Pseudo-Hai quotes the same tradition from the *Text of R. Ḥammai.* This "text" is identical with the aforementioned fragment of the "Book of Unity" of Ḥammai.[304] It is said here that the three lights[305] are one thing and one substance that "are found without separation and without union, in the most intimate relation with the root of roots." As a concrete illustration of such a connection, the author mentions the relation between the heart, the lungs, and the spleen, which have a common root with all the other parts of the organism. Similarly, from these primordial lights flow the three supreme sefiroth of "Pure Thought," "Knowledge," and "Intellect," through which all the "spiritual flames" take on substance even though they remain bound to the coal that nourishes them. The continuation of the text is that quoted above on pages 329–30. The three responsa of Pseudo-Hai, therefore, clearly refer to one another. In two of them the doctrine of the three primordial lights is propounded; two of them transmit the old magical spelling of the divine name, positing a speculative relationship between it and the development of the ten sefiroth indicated in its four consonants. The presentations of the doctrine of the primordial lights differ insofar as in the first, more detailed exposition, the "root of all roots" is not placed above them as in the second, but the lights themselves (as the correct version reads) are "name and substance of the root of all roots." All three are themselves a light, a substance, and an infinitely hidden root. The sefiroth flow from them as supreme potencies that somehow possess intelligible matter and form. This last idea is found nowhere else in the oldest documents dealing with the doctrine of the sefiroth and seems to me to have some relation to ibn Gabirol's doctrine of the composition of all the intelligible essences of matter and form. The emphasis placed here on the repetition of the two aspects of mat-

304. The responsum is printed in Kobak's *Jeschurun* 3:55. Cf. also Shemtob, *'Emunoth* (Ferrara, 1556) fols. 35a and 47a.

305. The printed version erroneously reads seven (ז) instead of three (ג) lights.

ter and form at every new level of the sefirotic process proves that it was, for the author, more than a mere fortuitous figure of speech.

What is truly remarkable about this entire idea is of course the trinity of the three hidden lights that flow without distinction and without beginning into the substance of the deity, intermingle their radiation in its midst, and emanate from it in the three supreme sefiroth. Above the "pure thought" that we found in the Book *Bahir* and even more clearly in Isaac the Blind as the highest sefirah, we now see appearing in the midst of the deity itself the "root of roots," that enigmatic triad, which is, however, distinguished from the Christian Trinity by a completely impersonal character and the absence of any specific relationships among its elements. The author of these responsa obviously was not content with the doctrine propounded in the Book *'Iyyun* and the "Source of Wisdom" of the thirteen pairs of oppositions that proceed from the ether as primordial potencies; he replaced them with a conception that is, on the one hand, simpler but on the other hand, much more paradoxical. The door was thereby opened for new mystical speculations that permitted one to assume even more profound levels of the deity above the world of the sefiroth. It is no wonder that this idea later acquired great importance in the doctrine of the kabbalists of the fourteenth but above all of the sixteenth century concerning the so-called *ṣaḥṣaḥoth,* the ultraclear or transparent lights that form the roots of the world of the sefiroth.

The various solutions offered in this circle for the determination of the relation between the ten sefiroth and the thirteen *middoth* show that there was no specific interest in a doctrine of the Trinity. The second responsum of Hai or Ḥammai further complicates the solution of the problem when it supposes the existence of an inner link between the "root of roots" and the three lights but does not identify them in any way. The sole function of these three lights is to serve as a source and origin for the supreme sefiroth that later unfold everything out of themselves. They are neither persons nor "hypostases" in God. Therefore, if on the one hand they can be regarded as the provisional last stage of a process that started from the Merkabah world, and by which the mystics seek to penetrate into ever higher spheres, then on the other hand the possibility cannot be dismissed that this specific solution to the question of the character of the thirteen *middoth* was developed in full awareness of the Christian doctrine of the Trinity, albeit with the elimination of everything that constituted its properly Christian character. What remains is a supreme intelligible triad more reminiscent of triads to be found in the spiritual universe of Proclus than in Christian dogmatics. It could, perhaps, be described as a reversion of the Christian notion to a more purely Neoplatonic light-mysticism. The sefiroth themselves, in this order of ideas, are clearly created, while the triad of the lights illuminate one another, uncreated, without beginning, in the hidden root.

That the kabbalists were not unaware of a possible connection between these ideas and the Christian Trinity is proved by the testimony of the Spanish scholar Profiat Duran. In his anti-Christian work "Ignominy of the Christians," composed in 1397, he relates having heard in his youth many adepts of the Kabbalah voicing the opinion that the Christian dogmas of the Trinity and the Incarnation grew out of an erroneous interpretation of kabbalistic theses that were true in themselves. Jesus and his disciples were not only great magicians—an opinion that was widespread in medieval Judaism—but real kabbalists, "only their Kabbalah was full of mistakes." "The doctrine of the trinity, which they erroneously attributed to the deity, arose among them as a result of their missteps in this science [the Kabbalah] which established the primordial light, the radiant light and the transparent light."[306] There was as well, already in the second half of the thirteenth century, no lack of philosophical opponents of the Kabbalah who, knowing nothing of this thesis of the three lights, nonetheless affirmed that the doctrine of the ten sefiroth was of Christian origin.[307] This thesis is, as our account of the true history of the idea of the sefiroth has shown, just as false as the historically unfounded suppositions of the kabbalists concerning the origins of the Christian dogmas. It is, incidentally, striking that the doctrine of Pseudo-Hai remained initially unknown to the first so-called "Christian kabbalists," who only took it up after the middle of the sixteenth century and reinterpreted it in Christian terms for their own purposes.[308]

---

306. *Kelimmath ha-Goyim,* in *Ha-Ṣofe le-Ḥokhmath Yisrael* 3:143; cf. on this subject my remarks in *Tribute to Leo Baeck* (London, 1954), 177–178.

307. Cf. *Tribute to Leo Baeck,* 176, as well as the testimonies in Abraham Abulafia (Jellinek, *Auswahl kabbalistischer. Mystik,* 19) and in the responsa of Isaac ben Shesheth, no. 156.

308. At first I thought that the Christian use of Pseudo-Hai began in the seventeenth century only (with the little tract *In Cabalam introductio* of Count Carolus Montecuccoli [Modena, 1612], 26 and above all with Joseph Ciantes, *De Sanctis-*

11. The Sefirotic Doctrines of a Pseudepigraphic Epistle

The responsa of Pseudo-Hai indicate that in Provence, and in connection with the light-symbolism developed by the *'Iyyun* circle, certain tendencies were at work that focused directly upon the doctrine of the ten sefiroth in its new form, and thereby entered into the mainstream of the tradition that we examined earlier. In this circle there must have existed very diverse personalities. What distinguished them from the circle of Isaac the Blind, with which they otherwise had much in common, was their penchant for pseudepigraphy. Thus we find, in the framework of a rather long epistle whose main part has been preserved, a number of brief passages doubtless composed in this circle a short time after the death of Eleazar of Worms. The author of the letter gives an account of his travels in Provence and speaks of allegedly ancient fragments that had there fallen into his hands; it appears certain to me that he is none other than Isaac Cohen. The text of the epistle is already partly transmitted in the writings of one of his relatives, Shemtob ibn Gaon.[309] The style of the narration that ties the pieces together, and the manner in which diverse sources are juxtaposed, conform in every respect to his style and procedure in similar epistles on the doctrine of the emanation of the "left," preserved in his name. The author of the letter

---

sima Trinitate ex antiquorum Hebraeorum testimoniis evidenter comprobata [Rome, 1657]), but meanwhile evidence of earlier use has come to light. François Secret, *Les Kabbalistes chrétiens de la Renaissance* (Paris, 1963), 130, 140, has shown that the notion of the three lights is quoted from Baḥya ben Asher's commentary on the Pentateuch (1544), fol. 121d, by Guy Le Fèvre de la Boderie in 1578 in the preface to his French translation of Fr. Giorgi's didactic poem *L'harmonie du monde.* An even earlier instance is Ludovicus Carretus, *Mar'oth 'Elohim* (Paris, 1553), (Secret, ibid., 242). Postel, at about the same time, in his marginalia to his translation of the *Zohar,* correlated the three lights with the Trinity (Secret, ibid., 253).

309. The first part of the epistle, whose author I had not yet identified in my earlier publications, is preserved in Shemtob ibn Gaon, *Badde ha-'Aron* 4:3, Ms. Oxford, Neubauer 1630, fols. 45a–47b. Steinschneider, who was unaware of this particular source, nevertheless knew the more complete text from an old, widely preserved apology for the Kabbalah, Ms. Berlin Qu. 833, fols. 88b–91b (as well as Kaufmann 240 and Ghirondi 117). He alluded to it in *Hebräische Bibliographie,* vol. 18 (1878), 20–21, in his essay on Isaac Cohen, without noting that Isaac himself was the author. The name Rab Qeshishah; literally "the old master," is apparently fictitious, like that of R. Amora in the Book *Bahir,* and formed as an artificial singular from the talmudic expression *Rabbanan qeshisha'e,* "our old masters," perhaps also in imitation of the name Mar Qeshishah, the "son of old age" of the talmudic sage R. Ḥisda.

travels about Provence, attracted by everything esoteric; however, he is not himself Provençal. His eschatology is the same as that found in other pieces that Isaac uses elsewhere. We learn that the author of the letter passed through Arles around the middle of the thirteenth century and that the writings he mentions came to light during the lifetime of the father of one of the scholars of that city. This brings us to approximately the fourth decade of the thirteenth century.

This epistle of Isaac Cohen consists of many loosely connected pieces; in each a fictitious authority speaks of the tradition he received concerning the ten sefiroth. This tradition is traced back to the school of the Babylonian geonim in Matha Meḥassya, near Sura—by which Sura itself is apparently meant. One of them, R. Qeshisha, is said to have come to Apulia and there to have passed on the tradition to his disciple Yehudah of Corbeil. This scholar is supposed to have been the master of Eleazar of Worms in mysticism—a pure fiction in which Yehudah of Corbeil and Yehudah the Pious of Regensburg are merged into one person. The tradition of these authorities concerning the ten sefiroth follows that of the *Bahir,* inasmuch as the Righteous, the "foundation of the world," is still the seventh sefirah here, whereas among the Spanish kabbalists it has already become the ninth. The names, as well as the symbols, are taken partly from the *Bahir;* but to some extent they also have their origin in the terminology of the *'Iyyun* writings, or are in any case very closely related to it.

The old gaon or his pupil speaks of the first sefirah, *kether,* as a power that "is hidden and guarded in the essence [one could also translate: substance] of the root"; this comes very close to the phraseology of Pseudo-Hai. The idea of the ether is also found here. Sometimes it is the second sefirah, *ḥokhmah,* that is called ether; on another occasion it is the tenth sefirah that appears in the enumeration as "the all-embracing ether," the ether that is "the treasure house of the mysteries and the light of life." The name of the sefirah *kether* is speculatively interpreted by Pseudo-Eleazar in exactly the same manner as in the "Book of Unity," by making use of the various etymological nuances of the Hebrew root. In fact, however, this passage is far removed from the terminology of Eleazar, where we have indeed found (see above, p. 125) the expression "supreme crown." In general, the text tends to call the sefiroth "crowns."

> All the crowns form a world of triads which share a relationship with one another; but the supreme crown is a world for itself, which is hidden and of whose emanation all the others are recipients. It alone is hidden and connected with the root of all roots, which no thought can grasp, and it always receives without interruption and in silence [*bi-demamah daqah*] from the root and empties its plenitude of benediction upon the other crowns, yet not without respite, but each time according to the will, which is the root of all the roots.[310] And the sefiroth receive together, three at a time, overflowing and exhausting the flux [of the emanation] up to the "treasure house of the mysteries," which is the crown of the reign of the creator of the worlds. All the triads surround one another and are interrelated; each one surrounds the other, but is at the same time surrounded by it; each one is above the other, and yet the other is at the same time above it; each is at the same time beginning, middle, and end; all in accordance with the manifestation, in them, of the supreme will, from which they are created.

Kether is therefore by no means identical with the deity, which is rather "revealed" in it as the "hidden power and the essence removed from all." Instead of *'en-sof,* which never appeared here or in Pseudo-Hai, these pseudepigraphers prefer the image of the "root of all roots," which in medieval Hebrew often has the meaning of supreme principle. No distinction is made between the creation of the sefiroth and their emanation. The realm of *kether,* still above the world of the intellect, is designated here as *'olam ha-mithboded,* a world that exists for itself alone, detached in "solitude." The term is probably translated from Arabic *'ālam mustabidd;* in Neoplatonic sources that still remain to be identified it must have signified the transcendent world that precedes the intellect. It is in old translations of Neoplatonic sources into Hebrew that this terminology seems to have made its way from Spain to Provence, where its meaning was modified—just as the two usual ways of rendering the Arabic word *'aql,* intellect, by *madda'* and *sekhel* in Hebrew produced among the oldest kabbalists two different notions, which were then correlated with the sefiroth *ḥokhmah* and *binah.* Similar reinterpretations of Neoplatonic schemata for the worlds came via Abraham bar Ḥiyya, who cites them in the name of the "sages of speculation" to the German Hasidim.[311]

---

310. This identification is striking. It contradicts the conception found elsewhere that separates the primordial will from the primordial root.

311. Cf. my study "Reste neuplatonischer Spekulation bei den deutschen Chassidim," *MGWJ* 75 (1932): 172–191.

After these utterances of Pseudo-Eleazar, the epistle continues with the communication of another revelation that is said to have been received in distant times by one of the scholars and ascetics of the academy in Matha Meḥassya. The recipient of the revelation is not named, despite the fondness usually displayed in these documents for identifying scholars by name. But the epistle communicates the revelation that was granted to him and the contents of which he is said to have uttered, after a long preparation, before ten scholars. Here the "sublime crowns" are connected, albeit in a very general manner, with the origin of the pneumata of the prophets. The revelation is concerned with the "paths" (the same, no doubt, as those that are evoked at the beginning of the Book *Yeṣirah*), but here they coincide with the sefiroth and each one represents a separate world. They are described by means of concepts that derive from the light-symbolism of the *'Iyyun* circle, but only the first three are defined with any precision. Here too the theistic character of the separation between God himself and these "paths" is clearly thrown into relief:

> The master of All is above all attributes and figures. In His omnipotence He created the paths of the world, path after path; he allowed world after world to be newly born. The first path, the first light, the "path which the eagle does not know" [Job 28:7], is the root of the thoughts [ideas?], and it rises on the "path of splendor," which is the primordial intellect [*madda' qadmon*], which is connected with the "pure thought." From it is emanated the path which irradiates the intellect [*sekhel*]. . . . It is the splendor of the firmly based throne, which is raised on the three primordial columns . . . and all created things exist in it, and from there all the souls of the prophets and of the holy Israel fly forth. And there is, besides, a path that is the jewel of all the paths [in which all the paths together form a jewel, cf. *Bahir,* section 43] and also the last throne.

The first three paths are apparently the first three sefiroth; the throne, with its three columns, forms the next triad of sefiroth, with the "righteous" as the seventh sefirah and the last throne as the last sefirah. Both thrones are described as the places of veneration and adoration for the hosts of angels.

Through an emissary, Beraḥya of Damascus, this revelation is said to have also reached Eleazar of Worms. The author of the letter then turns rather abruptly to his own travels in Provence. He recounts what he heard in Arles from a certain R. Solomon ben Maṣliaḥ. The letter relates in the name of his father:

> In the days of the holy Rabbi Elhanan, there was in Provence a distinguished old scholar of the Torah, a head of the academy of Lunel, who received from Eleazar of Worms a small pamphlet entitled "Book of the Mysteries," which he had undertaken to show only to those who were worthy of it.

Exactly what was contained in this book is not said, but one may suppose that it consisted of a summary of the revelations previously quoted, and which arrived in this way in Provence. We hear further on that sometime afterward the author of the letter met in his own country (Spain) a great scholar, Nathaniel of Montpellier, with whom he became very friendly.

> I copied from the notes of his uncle, Zechariah of Montpellier, who spent many years in the Byzantine lands and there received from an old man, who was nearly 120 years old [notes on the degrees of the emanations]. This Hasid, equally well-versed in philosophy and astrology, but who later scorned all the sciences and repented of his pursuit of them, turned to the search for God until he was finally initiated into the secret science over a period of three years by a descendant of King David named R. Ḥisdai ha-Nasi.

The pseudepigraphic character of all these statements need hardly be pointed out, and since the analysis of the writings of Isaac Cohen shows that he in fact collected and reworked older traditions, we must conclude that these literary inventions should be attributed to the circle of the Provençal group, given the general kabbalistic attitudes with which they accord so well.

Jellinek assumed that this Ḥisdai was none other than the famous scholar and court minister of this name, and that the text should therefore be dated to the tenth century.[312] However, both the language and the ideas expressed are those of the Provençal group under discussion. Perhaps the author had in mind an old poet of this name mentioned as the composer of a well-known piyyut.[313] In its conclusion, the long letter attributes to this Ḥisdai, an account of the beatitude of the souls in the higher world of the sefiroth.

---

312. Jellinek, *Geschichte der Kabbala* 2:iii, whose text (iii–vi) is taken from Shemtob's *'Emunoth.* I translate what follows according to a text corrected on the basis of the manuscripts; cf. *Tarbiz* 2:425.

313. Thus in a list of the old synagogal poets that I found in a copy of the first edition of the responsa of Solomon Luria, in the Jewish Theological Seminary in New York.

The description does not deny its proximity to Neoplatonic eschatology:

> The cause of causes has neither beginning nor place nor limit. When it arose in His will to create the worlds anew, they were not apprehensible and visible. Then came the will,[314] and from its great light there emanated ten inner points which are like a light that outshines the sun. The light of the innermost point is not separated from its substance, and it is an intelligible point, *nequdah maḥshabith,* from the light of which there radiates a second intelligible point.[315] And it represents the beginning of the paths of the first cause. From its light there radiates a third point, which is the mother of the inner souls, and our sages name this point the *'araboth*-heaven. . . . And from its light there radiates a great brilliance, a spiritual point that is the beginning of the world of holy spirits and that is called by the sages of the Mishnah [in *Ḥagigah* 12a] *zebul*-heaven. And this point is the foundation of the worlds, and when Solomon, at the construction of the Temple, built the Holy of Holies, it was this at which he aimed, as it follows from his words in 1 Kings 8:13. And in the beginning of the world, which is designated as the world of Mercy, two other points were still radiated together with it: the worlds of Grace and Judgment. Here is the beginning of the creation of the lower souls, *nefashoth,* which are born anew when the bodies are founded, and that is why [this world] is called by the sages the *makhon*-heaven, for it is the foundation, *makhon,* for the seat of all the worlds that emanate from there, and in it there exists and maintains itself the reign of the world of the last judgment. . . . And this is the figure of the throne, of which it is said: And with grace His throne is founded. And after all these emanations there radiates a light of the world [in Hebrew, this can also mean: an eternal light], out of which is built a column that in the language of the sages [in the *Bahir,* section 105] is called the Righteous of the World, from which the souls fly out. These came from the light of the world, which is called "world of the souls," and these are in-formed in the bodies of the prophets. And this column is the formative principle of the subtle pneumatic bodies, from which are also formed the bodies of the prophets, which are the forms of bodies but are nevertheless not bodies. For even if the seal is one, the most diverse forms are nonetheless engraved in it. After this emanation two lights radiate: a pneumatic point and a psychic point. From the pneumatic point fly forth the souls that were radiated from the light of Mercy, and they are in-formed in the bodies of the possessors of the holy spirit or pneuma, and this is the formation of the pneumatic bodies, which are similar to bodies and are nevertheless not [material]

314. Cf. note 269, herein.

315. It is here called *nequdah madda 'ith.* This is also the origin of Isaac's terminology in his commentary on the Merkabah, *Tarbiz* 2:195; cf. also my remarks, ibid., 206–207. Moses de Leon used *nequdah maḥshabith* as a symbol for the sefirah *ḥokhmah;* cf. his *Sefer Rimmon,* Ms. British Museum 759, fol. 26a.

> bodies. . . . From the psychic point fly forth the lower spirits, which radiate from the brilliance of the world of judgment and which are in-formed in the bodies of perfect and superior scholars, in whom there shine forth the sparks of the holy spirit that radiate over the world of the lower souls. And this is the in-forming of the pure bodies that have the attributes of bodies, but are nevertheless not [bodies], even if they are not as pure as the first and second [kinds of higher bodies]. And after this emanation there radiates from every single part of these light-points a light that is the emanation of the last point, toward which each one of the points emanates its light, in accordance with the divine will. Sometimes [this last point] receives from all, sometimes from only a few, always according to the command of the Supreme King. All yearn for it [the last point], and it yearns for them, and in it is the beatitude of all the seven worlds that are comprised in the seven days of creation. . . . From this point radiates the world of the separate [intelligences].

The systematic intent of this statement is clear. The ten sefiroth are presented as ten primordial points of an intelligible kind; their relationships to psychology, eschatology, and prophetology are simultaneously developed. What is striking is that it is expressly said of the first sefirah, the innermost point, that it is "not separated from the substance," the latter being, according to the context, the great light that already existed before the will began to be active —either primordially related to the first cause or identical with it. The three pneumatic degrees of the soul correspond at the same time to the degrees of the prophets, of the men animated by the Holy Spirit, and of the sages and scholars of the Scriptures, above whom the sparks of the Holy Spirit are nevertheless shining forth. The sefiroth are somehow related to the seven heavens; each is a world in itself, but also the initial starting place and the object of desire for the souls that issue from it. There is a very close link between Pseudo-Ḥisdai and the text of the Hasid (of Narbonne) concerning the inner souls, which was probably also preserved by Isaac Cohen (see p. 292, n. 185, herein) but differs from him in the correlation, unknown to Ḥisdai, of the secret names of these different degrees of the souls. The theory of the intelligible points is connected with the reinterpretation discussed previously (p. 259) of the ideas as spiritual atoms and their application to the sefiroth. From these and similar Provençal sources, this theory then made its way to the kabbalists in Castile, above all to Isaac Cohen and Todros Abulafia, and from there to the author of the *Zohar.*

The same hierarchical structure is expounded regarding the origin and still more the place of the supreme beatitude of the prophets, the hagiographers, and the mystical scholars in the description of the seven palaces of the lowest heaven, which comes immediately after the aforementioned account of the ritual for the conjuration of the Prince of the Torah. The sefirotic symbolism is here presupposed as self-evident. The palaces begin with the lowest and ascend in rank, just as do the archons in charge of them. The highest rank is held not by Metatron, who rules over the sixth palace, but by Sandalfon, whose name is associated with the secret of the conquest of matter by form.[316] This is the oldest source of this mystical etymology of Sandalfon, and it was in use later among many Spanish kabbalists.

We have so far analyzed the main elements of the genuine contribution made by the kabbalists of Provence to the development of conceptions that came to them chiefly from the Book *Bahir,* but in part also from other sources.[317] We have restricted ourselves to an

316. Cf. *Tarbiz* 16 (1945): 202–203. Moses of Burgos, who knew this source, later explained the name of Sandalfon in the same sense; cf. the text in *Tarbiz* 6 (1934): 184–185. Simon ben Ṣemaḥ Duran, *Magen 'Aboth* (Livorno 1785), fol. 14b, clearly using works of the *'Iyyun* group, similarly interprets Sandalfon, as the *intellectus agens,* that is, the power that unites matter and form. He based himself on a talmudic etymology according to which *sandal* signified an embryo still without form; The component *fon* is explained as derived from *panim,* face, that is, the inner form.

317. This implies the exclusion of writings that sailed under a Provençal flag as a result of either erroneous attribution or pseudepigraphic disguise. To the first of these categories belongs the voluminous commentary on the *Yeṣirah,* which in the printed editions appears under the name of Abraham ben David but whose real author, as I was able to prove (cf. *Kiryath Sefer* 4:286–302), is the Spanish kabbalist Joseph ben Shalom, also named Joseph the Long, who wrote shortly after 1300. To the second category belongs the curious book *Sod Darkhe ha-'Othiyoth,* "Mystery of the paths of the consonants," preserved under varying titles and in a generally fragmentary form in different manuscripts—for example, in Vatican 441, fols. 183a–209a; Paris 770, fols. 209–214; Mussajof (Jerusalem) 92, fols. 14b–27a; New York 844, formerly catalogue Schwager and Fränkel 35, No. 96, fols. 169a–173a; New York Enelow Memorial Collection 704, fols. 1–7. In its introduction, this book pretends to be an epistle of Abraham ben David, who is supposed to have collected the mysteries of the consonants, the vowels, and the effects produced by the holy names from old traditions (all of a pseudepigraphic nature) with the consent of an entire assembly of kabbalists united "in the manner of the great Sanhedrin." A Jacob ben Meshullam of Damascus, an Ezra ben Solomon Cohen of Germany, and a Jacob of Spain are mentioned among the members of this circle. In Ms. Enelow, the entire treatise is attributed to the "scholars of Lunel," and the name of the great master Isaac ha-Parush is added to those already mentioned. But the Kabbalah expounded here is late-thirteenth-century Castilian, and its goal is to offer a theoretical foundation of magic. Its style is at times strangely reminiscent of Moses de Leon. The text merits thorough consideration in other connections as well.

examination of the most important elements of this original development, without entering into the numerous details that must still be studied in the light of the new sources, in Isaac the Blind as well as in the *'Iyyun* circle. However, the decisive testimonies for a proper understanding of the breakthrough that occurred here have been adequately discussed. Until now research into the beginnings of the Kabbalah has proceeded in a total vacuum. At best it had assumed the Provençal origin of the Book *Bahir* itself, an hypothesis that, as we established in the preceding chapter, is undoubtedly false. It is characteristic of the traditional addiction to false hypotheses concerning all the main issues that the material relating to the Rabad, his son, and the *'Iyyun* circle surveyed in the present chapter were completely neglected by Neumark in the detailed discussion of these questions in his *Geschichte der Jüdischen Philosophie des Mittelalters,* as well as in the expanded Hebrew version (1921) of this work. The genuine sources of the kabbalistic literature of Provence remained unknown to him. When, at about the same time, I began my research in this field, the discovery or the correct arrangement of these sources was of decisive importance for the evolution of my views. In fact, unlike the case of the *Bahir,* these sources enabled the researcher to lay his finger on precisely those elements of the Kabbalah that had really grown in Provençal soil.

In conclusion, we may therefore see that the Provençal Kabbalah functioned historically to unite old gnostic traditions, which originated in the Orient and maintained a kind of underground existence, with medieval Neoplatonism. These gnostic traditions maintained themselves, even grew stronger in certain circles, but were pervaded by elements of another, namely the Neoplatonic, world, which proved to be particularly fruitful here. In the form in which the Kabbalah stepped into the light of history it included both traditions, the emphasis being placed sometimes on the one, sometimes on the other. It was in this shape—or rather dual shape—that the Kabbalah was then transplanted to Spain. Indeed, outside the period dealt with in this book both tendencies found particularly clear crystallization. This, for example, holds true for the kabbalists of Castile, and especially the author of the *Zohar,* who exhibited an almost purely gnostic orientation. On the other hand, the Neoplatonic tendency and the heritage of the *'Iyyun* circle are represented in several (largely unpublished) works from the beginning of the fourteenth century. Prominent among these latter are *Yesod 'Olam* ("Foundation of the World") by Ḥananel ben Abraham ibn Asqera,[318] the commentary on *Yeṣirah* of Meir ben Solomon ibn Sahula,[319] and the small published treatise *Massoreth ha-Brith* ("Tradition of the Covenant"), of David ben Abraham ha-Laban, the grandson of a French rabbi, of whom it is not clear whether he himself wrote in southern France or in Spain.[320] But in the beginnings of the Spanish Kabbalah—our sole concern here—the two traditions and their elements interpenetrated and amalgamated. They differ from the other type of literature discussed previously by the absence of appeals to revelations, both among the true historical representatives of this tradition and in pseudepigraphic disguises.

---

318. This book is preserved in its entirety (to date) in only one manuscript, Ms. Günzburg 607, now in Moscow. David de Günzburg spoke of it in his study "La Cabale à la veille de l'apparition du Zohar"; cf. *Hakedem* 1 (1907): 28–36, 111–121. The text breaks off in the middle.

319. The sole complete manuscript is preserved in the Angelica in Rome, Capua no. 53, fols. 1–210.

320. I edited this treatise in the *Kobeṣ 'al Yad* of the *Mekiṣe Nirdamim* society, n.s., 1 (Jerusalem, 1936): 25–42, and discussed it in the *Gaster Anniversary Volume* (London, 1936), 503–508. In the original (German) edition of the present work (p. 322) I also listed *Ginnath ha-Bithan* among the unprinted fourteenth-century kabbalistic compositions. The text is found under the title *Ginnath Bithan ha-Melekh* in Codex Gaster 1398, where it is attributed (by another hand) to a certain Meir, son of Eleazar of Worms. It was already commented upon by Jacob ben Todros and Shemtob ibn Gaon; cf. also Ms. Oxford, Neubauer 1577. Both commentators attest, in their prefaces, that the book appeared anonymously. Since then E. Gottlieb has incontrovertibly proved this text to be a late forgery (last third of the sixteenth century). The author used the printed edition of Yehudah Ḥayyat's commentary *Minḥath Yehudah* on the *Ma 'arekheth ha- 'Elohuth.* Cf. E. Gottlieb in *Studies in Mysticism and Religion: Essays in honour of G. Scholem* (Jerusalem, 1968), Hebrew part, 63–86.

CHAPTER FOUR

THE KABBALISTIC CENTER IN GERONA

1. The Kabbalists of Gerona and Their Writings

The first recognizable group of kabbalists crystallizing in Spain had its center during the first half of the thirteenth century in Gerona, a small Catalan city situated between Barcelona and the Pyrenees. At that time Gerona harbored a sizable Jewish community, the second largest in the land after Barcelona. Its importance emerges quite clearly from the documents relating to the history of the Aragonese Jews in the thirteenth century to be found in the well-known publications of Régné and Baer. The political conditions of the time were such that the region situated on both sides of the Pyrenees, up to Perpignan and beyond, was a part of Aragon. Only in 1258, that is, toward the end of the period under consideration in the present study, did Aragon renounce its Provençal possessions. Favored by the close relationship of the Romance dialects spoken below and above the Pyrenees, extremely close relations prevailed between Catalonia and the Languedoc, where the Aragonese counties of Gerona and Roussillon bordered on the domains of the Count of Toulouse and other feudal rulers of the Languedoc. The Jewish communities of Aragon maintained close ties with those of Provence, and the talmudic schools of the latter attracted Catalonian youths eager to study the Torah. These links had already existed for a long time; they were particularly strong in the twelfth century, when the academies of Narbonne, Lunel, and other centers were in full flower. It is therefore only natural that scholars who received their training and absorbed decisive impulses there would also come into contact with the esoteric traditions cultivated in those places and with their representatives, and that they would transplant to their own land, from around 1220 onward, their newly acquired kabbalistic knowledge. Among the significant Jewish communities of Spain, Gerona was the closest to these centers, and it was from there that the influence of the new Kabbalah emanated. One must of course also take into account the fact that other large Jewish communities of Spain, above all Burgos and Toledo, were likewise acquainted through direct relations with Provence with the new ideas, which at first were transmitted only in whispers. But the influence of the group of kabbalists in Gerona upon the evolution of the Spanish Kabbalah was particularly profound. The reason for this must be sought as much in the personal character and stature of the members of this circle as, above all, in their intensive and extensive literary activity. Therein lies the main difference between this group and that of Rabad. As much as possible the latter still attempted to keep kabbalistic ideas secret, and did not encourage the formation of a specifically kabbalistic literature. Where such a literature began to form, as in the *'Iyyun* circle, it did so above all in pseudepigraphic disguise and at first only in certain directions. Things were different in Gerona. There, for the first time, in a clear renunciation of pseudepigraphy—even if in at least one case anonymity was maintained—the doctrine of the Kabbalah was elaborated in the most diverse directions, and representatives of this doctrine were already explicitly designated as "masters of the Kabbalah." It goes without saying that there were considerable differences among the individual members of this group. Some wrote briefly and allusively, whereas others were more explicit. Some, in a conservative spirit, expounded the tradition as they had received it; others made entirely original contributions to its further development. Nevertheless, all these particular activities fit into a general picture that transcends these differences.

In the history of the old Kabbalah, therefore, this was a group of epochal moment. It stepped into the light of the history of religions undisguised and in full force. The group was composed largely of direct and indirect disciples of Isaac the Blind. Certain of his disciples undoubtedly also formed mystical conventicles in other places, but we are unable to identify them. In Gerona, however, that which remained difficult to discern in Isaac became clearly perceptible; that which had been narrowly conceived underwent a multifaceted elaboration. Nevertheless, it is by no means the case that these kabbalists unfold all their doctrines before us unreservedly and openly in clear expositions and in beautiful harmony as a mystical theology of Judaism. Unfortunately, the opposite is true: their writings are difficult, and the best known among them (those of Naḥmanides) abound with half- and quarter-hints, or are couched wholly in the language of allusion. A very close analysis is necessary in order to penetrate to an understanding of these texts. However, the fact that we have at our disposal a rich literature that has been largely preserved permits such penetration, even if not every passage in these writings can be unequivocally explained. In any case, we can recognize Gerona as a genuine center of the new religious forces in Judaism—one that could compare favorably in many respects with the kabbalistic center that flourished in Safed 300 years later. It is the center of the contemplative Kabbalah in its most complete development prior to the *Zohar.* The circle of kabbalists who lived there and, as their writings prove, were in close spiritual contact with one another can be regarded as forming a genuine unity. In spite of all the differences in detail, their conception of the world and their basic attitudes exhibit an overwhelming unanimity. Letters and emissaries went back and forth between Gerona and Provence. Scholars like Asher ben David, who did not themselves reside in Gerona or who only made brief sojourns there, maintained close relations with this center and can be regarded as the bearers of the message of the new trend to other parts of Spain.

The existence in Gerona of such a group of kabbalists is already attested by a document that dates from the beginning of the 1230s. An epistle by Solomon ben Abraham of Montpellier, the adversary of Maimonides, is addressed, according to the superscription, to Naḥmanides; but according to the contents the addressee is an otherwise unknown Samuel ben Isaac.[1] However, the tenor of the

---

1. Cf. S. Halberstam, *Qebuṣath Mikhtabim,* reprint from Kobak's *Jeschurun* (Bamberg, 1875), 50–53. Halberstam's suggestion that the recipient of the letter was R. Samuel ha-Sardi of Barcelona, the author of the halakhic work *Sefer ha-Terumoth,*

letter as well as that of its recipient's response accord perfectly with the personality of Naḥmanides. At the end of his letter the learned scholar of Montpellier turns to the group of scholars who live in his addressee's city and speaks of "my lord and his holy company."[2] The expression is characteristic; the group of mystics of Gerona is designated as a sacred society. The tone of the response is the same: "I have made the letter known to the notables of our city, our scholars and our elders; they all read it together, saw it, and praised it." In my opinion this sacred society is in fact none other than the kabbalistic group of Gerona. Similarly, Naḥmanides on one occasion calls Ezra ben Solomon "one of our companions."[3] In the following generation, Todros Abulafia is also familiar with this group. He speaks of the tenth sefirah, also named "Guardian of Israel," which walks in front of the camp of Israel: "And thus writes R. Moses ben Naḥman, and the scholars of his locality, the kabbalists, agree with him."[4] The oldest references to the earliest kabbalists similarly attest that "the principal source of this science [the Kabbalah] was in the city of Gerona," and they mention the names of many members of this circle.[5]

We cannot say exactly when this group was formed. Nor do we know for sure whether Yehudah ben Yaqar, whom Naḥmanides called his master in Talmud and who in 1215 signed a document of the rabbinical court in Barcelona, may have lived for some time in Gerona. We have from this scholar a commentary on the prayers in which he frequently offers unmistakably kabbalistic interpretations in the spirit of Isaac the Blind. Other members of the circle were apparently considerably older than Moses ben Naḥman (Naḥmanides), the most eminent figure of this group. We may in any case

---

has been rendered highly probable by A. Shohat in the quarterly of the Israel Historical Society *Zion* 36 (1971): 38–39. Shohat also considers the possibility of two more or less identical letters addressed to Naḥmanides and to Samuel ben Isaac respectively; if he is right, then Barcelona would seem to have joined in the ban against Maimonides, whereas Naḥmanides exercised greater prudence.

2. Read *qedoshah* instead of the adjective *qedumah,* which does not make any sense in this context.

3. Nahmanides on Leviticus 19:19: "One of our companions adds to the reason for the prohibition of mixing seeds that its purpose is not to throw into disorder the powers that bring about the growth of plants"; this is found verbatim in Ezra's commentary on the Song of Songs, fol. 18a (erroneously paginated 14).

4. *Sha 'ar ha-Razim,* Ms. Munich 209, fol. 96a.

5. Ms. Halberstam 388 (now in Jews' College, London), fol. 19b.

suppose that this center in Gerona functioned approximately between 1210 and 1260. Among its members we must also count many kabbalistic disciples of Naḥmanides explicitly designated as Catalans, such as, for example, Shesheth of Mercadell, although his activities already belonged to a later generation.[6]

We know no fewer than twelve kabbalists of this group by their real or assumed names—not counting the anonymous author of the Book *Temunah,* which will be discussed at the end of this chapter.[7] We find Abraham ben Isaac Ḥazan, the cantor of the community and a well-known liturgical poet. The kabbalists knew him as the transmitter of mystical meditations in prayer that he received from his master, Isaac the Blind.[8] In a group of mystics for whom the life of prayer was particularly significant, the cantor or *ḥazan* naturally occupied an especially important place. For it was he more than anyone else who had to know and accomplish the mysteries of the *kawwanah.* He watched, so to speak, over the elevation of the *word* to its primordial ground, much as in their day the Merkabah mystics cultivated the ascension of the *soul.* From the German Hasidim until the latest groups of kabbalists in the twentieth century, the mystics frequently cultivated mystical prayer with its secret meditations in their own conventicles and synagogues. We know the prayer for the dead composed in the style of kabbalistic poetry that Naḥmanides recited before the tomb of Abraham; in it he described in kabbalistic terms the ascent of the soul to its home in the higher sphere.[9]

---

6. Yehudah ben Yaqar in the document published by J. Millas, *Documents Hebraics de Jueus Catalans* (Barcelona, 1927), No. X, p. 19. Cf. also chap. 3, n. 106, herein. More details on his commentary on the prayers in S. Schechter, *JQR* 4 (1892):245–255. On Shesheth des Mercadell, whose family still lived in Gerona in 1415, cf. my article in *Tarbiz* 16 (1945): 135–150.

7. I can find no evidence in support of D.T. Silver's contention that Judah and Solomon ben Ḥisdai, relatives of the nasi Abraham ben Ḥisdai, "belonged to the Gerona circle of kabbalists." The society *(ḥevrah)* to which they belonged should be interpreted (in the light of the poem printed in Brody, *Otsar ha-shirah ha-ivrith,* 107, 1.55) simply as "circle of friends." See D. T. Silver, *Maimonidean Criticism and the Maimonidean Controversy 1180–1240* (1965), 174 n. 5. There is nothing in the poem that suggests kabbalistic interests or connections.

8. Cf. chap. 3, n. 124, herein and the text in *Reshith ha-Qabbala,* 245–248.

9. I published this prayer, ibid., 243–245. Naḥmanides composed another exposition on the ascension of the soul through the worlds upon the death of an otherwise unknown R. Pinhas of the same circle. This exposition is referred to in a partially preserved letter to Naḥmanides that I have edited, ibid., 249–251.

Next to Naḥmanides we find above all the two kabbalists Ezra ben Solomon and his younger colleague Azriel, who according to certain indications was his son-in-law. Shemtob ibn Gaon attests that both were from Gerona, and his testimony is corroborated by all the other known circumstances.[10] These two men were often confounded in the older literature as early as the fourteenth century. The writings of the one were attributed to the other, and many scholars ultimately maintained that Ezra and Azriel were one and the same person. The resemblance of the names appeared to support this conclusion. Graetz believed that even if two different persons were involved, "they nevertheless were to be counted as one in the history of the Kabbalah."[11] But these older hypotheses are all superseded by the examination of the texts, as is also the supposition (to which I myself inclined for some time)[12] that we are dealing here with two brothers. The research of I. Tishby in particular has definitely clarified the literary aspects of the work of these two kabbalists. This clarification was rendered possible by my acquisition (in 1928 for the Hebrew University Library) of a large part of Azriel's commentary on the talmudic aggadoth and by the proofs I was able to provide for the existence of the commentary of Ezra, which bears the same title and is extant in many manuscripts, above all in an undoubtedly complete form in the Hebrew Codex 441 of the Vatican Library. Tishby demonstrated that far from constituting a single person in terms of the history of the Kabbalah, these two scholars represent, on the contrary, two completely different tendencies.[13] Unfortunately, we must eliminate entirely from our analysis the beautiful biographical details that Senior Sachs found in the preface to a kabbalistic work entitled *'Ezrath ha-Shem,* and that he misunderstood as referring to Azriel. In this mistake he was followed

---

10. Cf. Shemtob ibn Gaon, *Badde ha-'Aron* 1, chap. 5, as well as the evidence I adduced concerning the familial connections of the two in *Kiryath Sefer* 6 (1928/29): 263. The report may be genuine.

11. Graetz, *Geschichte der Juden,* 4th ed., 7:60, which is taken from Jellinek's preface to *Beth ha-Midrash* vol. 3 (1855), xxxix. Following Landauer and Jellinek, M. Ehrenpreis also still assumed the identity of the two persons, *Emanationslehre,* 24.

12. Cf. in (the Hebrew) memorial volume for A. Gulak and S. Klein (Jerusalem, 1942), 201–202.

13. Cf. the studies of Y. Tishby in *Zion* (9) (1944):178–185, and his analysis of their writings and their relationship to each other in *Sinai* 8 (1945): 159–178.

by Graetz and others.[14] This preface, with its accounts of the author's debates with philosophic opponents of the Kabbalah and of his wanderings, belongs to an author of a much later generation. It was written by someone who picked up and plagiarized a small tract of Azriel but who must nevertheless be clearly distinguished from him.[15]

From Ezra ben Solomon, who died around 1235, we have the commentary on the Song of Songs printed under the name of Naḥmanides in Altona in 1734 in a very defective text, but preserved in many excellent manuscripts.[16] We also have his commentary on the talmudic aggadoth. Both books, or excerpts from them, were widely disseminated. I was able to publish two of his kabbalistic letters from a manuscript in the Vatican Library.[17] Abraham Abulafia saw a commentary of his, no longer extant, on the Book *Yeṣirah,* and characterized the commentary's traditions as "brief and correct."[18] Various other samples of his Kabbalah, including an important text on the Tree of Knowledge, are preserved in manuscript.[19]

---

14. S. Sachs, *Ha-Paliṭ* (Berlin, 1850), 45–49; cf. also Graetz *Geschichte der Juden* 7:392, who did not recognize that he was dealing with an untenable contrivance of Sachs and not an authentic preface by Azriel. A mere glance at Ms. Oxford, Neubauer 1940 revealed the error immediately.

15. I established this in *Kiryath Sefer* 5 (1928):274. The book *'Ezrath ha-Shem* already uses the *Zohar.*

16. A new edition of this important work, a longtime desideratum, has now been supplied by G. Vajda, *Le commentaire d' 'Ezra de Gérone sur le cantique des cantiques* (Paris, 1969). The confusion in the attribution to Azriel began with Baḥya ben Asher and continued with Menaḥem Recanati and Isaac of Acre. It has still not been explained why, in his commentary on the Torah, Recanati correctly identified the author as the ḥakham R. Ezra, while in his later work on the reasons for the commandments he constantly referred to the Ḥasid R. Azriel. In Ms. Parma, de Rossi 1072, the book is erroneously attributed, already in 1387, to Naḥmanides.

17. Cf. *Sefer Bialik* (1934), 155–162. These letters, whose contents are particularly rich, are addressed to a certain R. Abraham; they likewise mention (159) the "group of companions." In a defective and often abridged version (the first letter is preceded there by a different introduction) they are found under the name of Azriel (Ms. Enelow, Mem. Coll. 2271, fols. 5b–6b.). Did Azriel perhaps actually revise Ezra's letters?

18. Cf. *Beth ha-Midrash* 3:xiiii, Jellinek's introduction.

19. In most manuscripts, this text is anonymously preserved under the title *Sod 'Eṣ ha-Da 'ath.* In Christ Church College 198, fol. 8b, it is explicitly attributed to Ezra, with whom, in fact, it accords perfectly in style as well as content. I have translated and discussed the text in *Eranos-Jahrbuch* 30 (1962): 39–47; the study has been reprinted in my collection of essays, *Von der mystischen Gestalt der Gottheit* (Zurich, 1962), 58–65.

We do not know the name of Azriel's father. Moses Botarel, who mentions in his commentary on *Yeṣirah* 3:1 a certain Azriel ben Menaḥem, displays in his quotations such a spirit of invention that his testimonies, in the absence of further corroboration, merit no confidence. We possess a number of writings from Azriel, all kabbalistic in character. In his *Sha 'ar ha-Sho' el,* called by later authors "Explanation concerning the ten sefiroth," we have a catechism expounding the doctrines of the sefiroth in the form of questions and answers, and in the style of Neoplatonic logic. This treatise, on which the author himself apparently wrote a sort of commentary, was printed for the first time in 1850.[20] I published a rather long piece of a related text by Azriel called "The path of faith and the path of heresy," from Ms. Halberstam 444.[21] These pages are particularly valuable. The commentary on *Yeṣirah* printed in the editions under the name of Naḥmanides certainly belongs to Azriel, as Jellinek had already recognized. The erroneous attribution to Naḥmanides occurred at an early date.[22] The commentary on the talmudic aggadoth edited by Tishby represents a revision and in part a considerable enlargement of Ezra's commentary that is particularly instructive, precisely because of the differences that distinguish it from the first version of his older contemporary.[23] Unfortunately, the book seems to have been only partly preserved. Some lengthier excerpts are still found in many manuscripts. Tishby has convincingly shown that the "commentary" on the prayers (actually a collection of instructions relating to mystical meditation), though generally attributed to Ezra ben Solomon in the manuscripts, in fact

20. As an introduction to the edition of Meir ben Gabbai, *Derekh 'Emunah* (Berlin, 1850) from a Milan manuscript of 1285, Bernheimer 53, fols. 113–117b. Cf. the summary of the contents in Jellinek, *Geschichte der Kabbala* 1:61–66.

21. Cf. Gulak and Klein memorial volume, 207–213.

22. Jellinek, *Moses ben Shem-Tob de Leon* (Leipzig, 1851), 46. Abulafia distinguishes the commentary from that of Ezra in the enumeration, referred to in n. 18 herein, p. 371, of the commentaries on *Yeṣirah* that he had studied. The oldest manuscripts are, as far as I know, anonymous; the attribution to Naḥmanides is found for the first time in M. Recanati, *Ta 'ame ha-Miṣwoth,* Ms. British Museum, Margoliouth 743, fol. 130a. The passage is missing in the printed edition of 1580 but is quoted by Yehudah Ḥayyat in his commentary *Minḥath Yehudah* on the *Ma 'arekheth ha-'Elohuth* (Mantua, 1558), fol. 48a. Tishby proved in a detailed analysis (*Sinai* 8:-165–169) that Azriel was the author.

23. A detailed analysis of the relationship between the two commentaries is provided by Tishby in the introduction to his edition of Azriel's text according to the Jerusalem manuscript (1943).

belongs to Azriel. It appears to have been preserved, not in its entirety but in large parts, in many manuscripts, and is still unedited.[24] Tishby demonstrated that in all the characteristic traits of its language and specific terminology the book always agrees with Azriel, but never with the authentic writings of Ezra. In 1927, when I published a long letter sent by Azriel from Gerona to Burgos, I still hesitated between attributing it to Azriel or Jacob Cohen of Soria, under whose name it also appears in certain manuscripts. Since then I have found numerous remnants of Jacob Cohen's authentic writings, and there can no longer be any doubt concerning Azriel's authorship of the epistle from the point of view of both style and content.[25] From Azriel we also possess a detailed exposition concerning the mysteries of the sacrifice, *Sod ha-Qorban,* as yet unpublished; many shorter texts on prayer-mysticism; and above all a brief but extremely valuable list of kabbalistic theses on prayer, which I have edited.[26] There also exist the remains of kabbalistic verses coming perhaps from a didactic poem on the Kabbalah that has been lost.[27]

Both commentaries on the aggadoth represent a juxtaposition of all the aggadic material, insofar as it was considered in the kabbalistic circles of Provence to be particularly significant and filled

24. Although the manuscripts bear the name of Ezra or are anonymous, certain quotations taken from them, for example in the prayer book of Naphtali Hirz Treves (Thiengen, 1560), and certain excerpts that figure in old collections of texts, are often correctly attributed to Azriel. The fact that no manuscript of this kind was preserved among the seven manuscripts known to me seems therefore to be accidental. Aaron Cohen of Lunel (ca. 1330) knew Azriel as the author; cf. *'Orḥoth Ḥayyim,* section 38 (Florence, 1750), fol. 6b. Although Azriel's *Commentary on the Prayers* is still unedited, a complete French translation is contained in Gabrielle Sed-Rajna's monograph *Azrïel de Gérone, Commentaire sur la liturgie quotidienne* (Leiden, 1974). Cf. also the article by the same author, "Sur quelques commentaries kabbalistiques sur le rituel," *REJ* 124 (1965): 307–351.

25. Cf. *Madda 'e ha-Yahaduth* 2:233–240. The fragment on the divine name that there precedes it, 231–232, also belongs to Azriel.

26. Azriel's *Sod ha-Qorban* in Ms. Vatican 211, fols. 8b–11a; Christ Church College 198, fols. 12b–15a; Halberstam 444 (New York), fols. 24a–25a. I edited the texts on prayer-mysticism in the memorial volume for Gulak and Klein, 214–221. A French translation is available in G. Sed-Rajna's monograph (above, n. 24), 142–145. On the text *Sha'ar ha-Kawwanah,* which should likewise be attributed to Azriel, cf. pp. 416–9, herein.

27. The anonymous verses on the doctrine of the sefiroth, which Deinard published in the catalogue of the Sulzberger manuscripts, *'Or ha-Me'ir* (Philadelphia, 1896), 36, are preserved in part under Azriel's name; cf. A. Marx in *PAAJR* 4 (1933):159.

with esoteric meaning. Often these quotations contain no real explanation of their precise mystical sense, even if the latter is referred to as being "evident." Ezra, in particular, was very conservative in this respect and only rarely permitted himself detailed digressions. That he received his commentaries orally from others is beyond doubt. His commentary on the Song of Songs gives an equally traditional explanation of the kabbalistic meaning of Genesis 1[28] as well as an enumeration of the commandments of the Torah accompanied by many, often enigmatic indications of their mystical reasons. Ezra himself edited a fuller version of his commentary on the aggadoth of the tractate *Ḥagigah,* the principal talmudic storehouse of speculations on cosmogony and the Merkabah; it is preserved in Ms. Hebrew 294 of the Vatican. It seems that Ezra's books were composed in the 1220s, if not in part still earlier. They too aroused a lively indignation among certain "orthodox" scholars when they became known in non-kabbalistic circles. In the 1240s, Meir of Narbonne poured out his vials of wrath on these and other kabbalistic writings.[29] According to him, the commentary on the Song of Songs deserved to be destroyed in order to prevent simple souls from being ensnared by it. He charged that the commentary on the Talmud was nothing but a collection of apocryphal aggadoth attributed to the sages of the Talmud in order to strengthen the "evil faith" of the kabbalists. Therefore, the literature of Gerona already exercised its influence in Provence at this time. The author was also familiar with one of the two commentaries on *Yeṣirah,* as well as with a commentary on Qoheleth otherwise unknown to us and never mentioned by the kabbalists themselves; perhaps it fell victim, as a result of the objections to the extreme audacity of its theses, to kabbalistic self-censorship—unless the manuscript itself fell into the hands of the zealots and was destroyed.

Azriel's revision transformed Ezra's commentary on the aggadoth into an entirely new book. Azriel undoubtedly had the most speculative, productive, and penetrating mind in the group, and this gives his books their special personal character. Together with other pupils of Isaac he continued the process I designated in the preced-

---

28. Translated into French by Vajda, *Recherches,* 299–320: *"Le récit de la création commenté par 'Ezra de Gérone."*

29. Cf. the passage quoted in *Sefer Bialik,* 147, as well as *JQR* 4 (1892): 357–360.

ing chapter as the Platonization of the gnostic Kabbalah of the *Bahir.* With Azriel this process in fact reached its apogee. Other early kabbalists also read widely in the writings of "the sages of philosophic speculation," as they were accustomed to calling the philosophers. Azriel went further. His way of thinking is closely related to that of Asher ben David, the nephew of Isaac the Blind, as well as to the Kabbalah of the *'Iyyun* writings. To be sure, as far as I can judge, he seems to have taken over from them less of their conceptual framework than of their particular language. However, beyond these similarities he obviously still had access to sources of Neoplatonic thought that were available to him not only in Hebrew but also in other languages. We have no proof that the scholars in Gerona knew Arabic, since their province was one of the first to be wrested from Arab rule. On the other hand, there is good reason to believe that some of them read Latin. I would suppose that above all Azriel had contact, direct or indirect, with the mystical tradition of Christian Neoplatonism stemming from the great work *De divisione naturae* of John Scotus Erigena (cf. p. 314). There is much in his Hebrew terminology that cannot be explained on the basis of Arabic but that seems to me to be analogy formations of Latin terms that in turn go back to the Greek of the Areopagite. I shall return to this point later. It was, after all, precisely during the years in which Azriel's thought must have taken shape that the dispute broke out, starting in 1209, over the orthodoxy of Erigena's teachings, a dispute that ended in 1225 with the condemnation of his principal work by Pope Honorius III and its removal from the monastic libraries. The agitation produced by these controversies concerning the audacious Christian Neoplatonist could have penetrated deeply into the Jewish camp, whether in the form of oral dialogues between Jewish and Christian scholars or through direct acquaintance with his writings. It is even possible that the attack on the author may have provided many Jews with easier access to his ideas. In any case it can be said that the role played by this thinker and his influence on the speculative Kabbalah remain an unresolved problem.

The catechism in the form of question and answers by which Azriel expounded the doctrine of the sefiroth for novices in the Kabbalah was surely not composed for the use of kabbalistic initiates; its goal was to familiarize others with their opinions. Since the "biographical" data concerning Azriel on which some authors have relied are not authentic, as has been shown on pages 370–1, and since no other information is available, we have no way of knowing under what circumstances he came to adopt this form of writing. The fact that he felt it necessary to elaborate his ideas in a quasi-philosophic language, without simply referring back to the tradition of the kabbalists indicates one of two things: either the intention to defend himself against attacks or the desire to propagandize. Perhaps both motives are combined here. As long as we were ignorant of his other writings, it could be argued that his accommodation to Neoplatonism, so noticeable in this catechism, was motivated solely by external and didactic considerations. Now this can no longer be maintained. In works of great insight that certainly were not designed for novices but for the adepts of the Kabbalah, the same type of thinking and the same terminology, which are otherwise not found among his friends in Gerona, recur. Behind his ideas stands, apparently, a complete system, even if he did not present it as such in any of his writings. He developed the ideas of Isaac the Blind but gave them, in part, an entirely new formulation and direction. It is particularly unfortunate that of the tractate on faith and heresy, which comes closest to being a systematic exposition, we only possess the first part. The author enumerates the heretical deviations from "the path of the (true) faith," as he saw it, but in the extant manuscripts the positive exposition breaks off at the very beginning. The audacity of Azriel's thought is astonishing; his works are at the opposite pole from the obscure gnostic stammerings of the Book *Bahir,* even though here, too, many things remain unclarified.

Alongside these men appears Jacob ben Shesheth, from whom we possess two, if not three, writings. He too is an original spirit who presumes to produce anew mysteries and reasons of his own invention for the commandments, without relying solely on the tradition of his teachers, among whom he names Isaac the Blind. He openly boasts that "if I had not said this anew, from my own mind, I would maintain that it was a tradition given to Moses at Sinai."[30] Herein lies the main difference between him and Ezra, whose views he often and directly contradicts. By way of contrast, the speculative profundity of Azriel is foreign to him. His work is marked, however, by a quality that is new in this circle and that merits our

30. Cf. *'Emunah u-Biṭṭaḥon,* chap. 5.

special attention. None of the kabbalists mentioned so far, since Isaac the Blind, ever took on the role of combatant in his own writings. At best these authors sought to expound their opinions, perhaps veiled and softened, but certainly without a polemical tone. With Jacob ben Shesheth, the kabbalists appear on the battlefield for the first time, undisguised. The enemy is unmistakable: the radical philosophic enlightenment of the adherents of Maimonides.

Jacob's polemical work, *Meshibh Debharim Nekhoḥim,* "The Book which Returns the Proper Answer,"[31] is a detailed attack on a philosophic work on the creation by Samuel ibn Tibbon, the Hebrew translator of Maimonides' *Guide of the Perplexed.*[32] But there is more here than mere polemics; several chapters are devoted to an exposition of the authentic Jewish tradition, identified here quite openly with that of the kabbalists. The author's kabbalistic expositions on the creation of the world and other major themes, on the one hand, and his polemical effusions, on the other, are related only insofar as the latter are nourished by his fundamental kabbalistic convictions. Unlike Azriel, however, he never advances reasons for his kabbalistic views but is content simply to present them. In his polemic, however, he goes far. What is curious in this connection is that the same Samuel ibn Tibbon whom Jacob attacks with so much animosity is quoted with respect by Ezra ben Solomon. I am inclined to think that it was Samuel's commentary on the Song of Songs that Ezra had in mind when he declared in his own commentary on 1:1:

> [The author of the Song of Songs] compared the *debhequth* of the soul with a kiss, and since the kiss takes place through the mouth, he was compelled to say in the continuation of his parable [although in real-

31. Ms. Oxford, Neubauer 1585 and 1586. A critical edition of this work, a longtime desideratum, has been supplied by G. Vajda in the series *Publications of the Israel Academy of Sciences and Humanities* (Jerusalem, 1968).

32. Samuel ibn Tibbon's *Ma'amar Yiqqawu ha-Mayim* (Pressburg, 1837); cf. also Vajda in *Recherches,* 13–113. Naḥmanides quoted this work without ill feeling in his sermon on *Qoheleth,* and Abraham Abulafia, in the second version (?) of his commentary on the *Guide (Ḥayye ha-Nefesh?)* Ms. Munich 408, fol. 81a explicitly agrees with ibn Tibbon's version of the doctrine of Providence. The work that Abulafia quotes without mentioning its title is undoubtedly the *Ma'amar Yiqqawu ha-Mayim.* On the other hand Solomon of Montpellier's attacks on ibn Tibbon are much sharper than those on the author of the *Guide;* cf. his epistle to Naḥmanides in *Kebuzath Mikhtabhim,* ed. Halberstam, 52.

> ity, he meant the union of the soul with the Active Intellect]: he kisses me with the kisses of his mouth, as one of the contemporary scholars already explained it before me, in his book.

The same idea is expressed in the commentary on the Song of Songs of Simon's son, Moses ibn Tibbon.[33] It is unlikely, however, because of its date of composition, that the latter commentary was used by Ezra. We may therefore assume that in all likelihood Moses took this explanation, like so many other elements, from the unpublished commentary of his father, which Ezra quotes with respect.

The situation regarding Jacob ben Shesheth is very different. Jacob does indeed strain to draw a distinction between Samuel and his master and model, Maimonides. The latter stood much too high in his esteem, as in that of many other kabbalists, for Jacob to dare to attack him directly. Rather, he seeks to prove that it was ibn Tibbon who introduced the problematic heretical opinions into the system of Maimonides. This system, known to him, after all, only through the Hebrew translation of ibn Tibbon himself and not in the original Arabic, is in Jacob's opinion very close to the true theology and therefore to the Kabbalah, as he frequently and almost triumphantly notes whenever he believes that he can demonstrate that his adversary misunderstood the views of Maimonides. For him Aristotle and ibn Tibbon, not Aristotle and Maimonides, are the two heresiarchs. Indeed, in order "to dupe the vulgar" *(le-rammoth he-hamon),* ibn Tibbon made hypocritical use of pious words, avoiding any expression of his true opinion, which he concealed behind ambiguous phrases or through the prudently measured use of certain turns of phrase. In this manner he hoped to poison the crowd indirectly and gradually and to seduce it, by means of the orthodox appearance of his doctrines, into accepting and absorbing unwittingly what in the author's opinion were frightful heresies. The polemical part of Jacob's book is therefore largely devoted to exposing ibn Tibbon. The mask of the hypocrite and transgressor must be ripped off, and the dangerous implications of his (Averroist?) heresies must be clearly exposed and refuted on the basis of religious and philosophic considerations, in which kabbalistic ideas play scarcely any role. To the unbiased reader of ibn Tibbon's work it is clear that this polemic abounds in misinterpretations, exaggerations,

33. Cf. the edition published in Lyk (1874), 14.

and heresy hunting, though one may doubt whether ibn Tibbon was at heart really as orthodox as he pretended. Here we have a surprising phenomenon: at the same time that Meir of Narbonne in his epistle denounced the kabbalists as heretics, Jacob ben Shesheth and his friends attempted to play the role of defenders of orthodoxy. In this respect Jacob's position is even more explicit than that of Naḥmanides, since he devotes several chapters to a frank exposition of his kabbalistic point of view, unlike Naḥmanides in his utterances concerning the Maimonidean controversy. Considered from this angle, Jacob's polemic is of special interest. It proves that in Gerona the Kabbalah had already assumed the role of the true representative of religious Judaism, inheriting as it were the mission of Yehudah Halevi. In fact, Jacob explicitly states in his *Sha'ar ha-Shamayim* that he and the kabbalists of his circle "built the protective wall [around rabbinic Judaism]."

In this book as well as in the anonymously preserved work entitled *Sefer ha-'Emunah weha-Biṭṭaḥon,* "The Book of Faith and Hope," the author constantly refers to his personal opinions and original hypotheses. This book has hitherto been shrouded in darkness. Already at an early date it was attributed to the much more famous Naḥmanides,[34] to whose views it is, in actual fact, directly opposed on many points, as is shown by a comparison with his commentary on the Torah. Baḥya ben Asher, who was the first to quote it at length, names neither title nor author.[35] However, the very old collection of texts in Ms. Paris 843, contains (fol. 84a) a mystical interpretation of the benediction to be pronounced at a circumcision ceremony, which in fact appears in chapter 21 of this book. The manuscript states: "I saw from the learned R. Jacob ben Shesheth of Gerona [the following]." We may therefore conclude that there were circles in which his authorship was still known. Comparing the

---

34. Isaac of Acre gives the title, but does not know the author; cf. Ms. Munich 17, fol. 136a. From about 1350 on, the work generally was attributed to Naḥmanides both in the manuscripts and in the numerous printed editions, beginning with the collection *'Arze Lebanon* (Venice, 1601), fols. 7a–32b. In many manuscripts the book is simply called *Book of the Twenty-six Chapters.* The oldest known manuscript to date, Adler 1223, from the fourteenth century, is anonymous.

35. The book was erroneously attributed to Baḥya himself as a result of his extensive use of it, thus by Jakob Reifmann (cf. in *Ha-Maggid* 5 [1861]: 222 and at greater length in *'Alumma* 1 [Jerusalem, 1936]: 72, 96. The attribution had already been refuted by A. Tauber, *Kiryath Sefer* 2 (1925):67–68.

book with the two other writings transmitted under his name, we are in fact led to consider Jacob's authorship as at least highly probable, if not assured. There are particularly close links with the aforementioned polemical book. The same authorities are invoked, and the same critical reservations are voiced in both books with regard to his evidently older colleague, Ezra, whom he often quotes, though usually in order to contradict him. The style, the phraseology, the terminology, and the formulas employed are the same, and even specific problems (though these are, on the whole, rarely identical) are treated in a similar manner. Nevertheless, there are certain striking differences that have yet to be explained. Thus in his polemical work he disapproves of one of Ezra's explanations that he himself then offers in a similar context in this work.[36] In the twenty-six chapters of this work he deals with various questions of detail and comments upon biblical verses and commandments of the Torah, talmudic dicta, texts of prayers, and so on, interspersing kabbalistic statements with other, simpler explanations.

It is striking to note that in these two works the author almost entirely avoids the word *sod,* "secret," while the other authors of this circle use it frequently and readily.[37] His avoidance of this word is understandable inasmuch as his books were among the first in which the kabbalistic doctrines were expounded in a relatively undisguised and open manner. Jacob ben Shesheth goes far beyond the reserved style of Naḥmanides and discusses very frankly things that the latter takes great pains to circumvent or disguise. Thus Naḥmanides expressly forbids, in the preface to his commentary on the Torah, the exposition of anything whatsoever "in this science" (the Kabbalah) that one has not received and heard from a master. Of a more fiery temperament, Jacob ben Shesheth lacked all such reserve. "Everything that a man on the path of faith can devise anew in the Torah [that is, by studying the Torah] serves to propa-

---

36. In chapter 19 the author gives the same derivation of *berakhah,* blessing or benediction, from the similarly sounding *berekhah,* "pool," which is cited in Ms. Oxford 1585, fol. 66b in the name of Ezra and rejected. Perhaps the rejection is directed not at the etymology as such but at its specific application in a particular context. The etymology itself is the common property of the kabbalists, from the *Bahir* and Isaac the Blind on, and it is difficult to imagine that Jacob, who knew these two authorities, would actually have rejected it in principle.

37. The expression "secrets of prophecy" (Ms. Oxford, fols. 26a, 71a,b) is taken by him from Maimonides.

gate and glorify the Torah."[38] The "path of faith" is, of course, the Kabbalah. Adopting the same attitude in his polemical book, he defends the right to devise his own reasons for the commandments, in which he sides with Maimonides.

> I know very well that there may be some among the pious and learned of Israel who will accuse me of having put in writing a reason for two or three of the commandments of the Torah, in such a way that a door is opened to other explanations for numerous commandments by the path of science. However, I can prove that each scholar has the right to devise a reason for each of the commandments for which no reason is explicitly indicated in the Torah, and in this way to be of benefit.[39]

Therefore, each in his own way, Azriel and Jacob ben Shesheth clear the way for the free, personal creativity of the kabbalists. In this manner they found more successors than their more timorous and conservative comrades-in-arms.

A no less significant document is Jacob's treatise in rhymed prose, *Sha'ar ha-Shamayim,* "The Gate of Heaven," the first kabbalistic work written in this style.[40] A precise reference regarding the delay in the arrival of the Messiah allows us to date the book to 1243 or 1246—the versions vary on this point. The treatise is essentially an enumeration of the ten sefiroth. Its brevity and allusive style render the text intelligible only to those familiar with the kabbalistic symbolism used in this circle, who would recognize in it a summary of all the principal motifs of the individual sefiroth, their significance, and their symbols as well as their close relationship to commandments and prohibitions of the Torah.[41] Of particular interest are his rather extensive discussions of the first sefirah, which is designated as the First Cause, the Will, and the innermost essence—definitions also repeated in the two other books.[42] In place of the

---

38. *'Emunah u-Biṭṭaḥon,* chap. 19.

39. Ms. Oxford, fol. 9b. The same opinion is more briefly formulated in *'Emunah u-Biṭṭaḥon,* chap. 8.

40. Published by M. Mortara in *'Oṣar Neḥmad* 3 (1860): 153–165; he was unaware of an earlier edition based on another manuscript in *Liqquṭim me-Rab Hai Gaon* (Warsaw, 1798), fols. 15a–25a.

41. While later kabbalists strove to associate all the commandments of the Torah with the seven lower sefiroth, the older kabbalists still correlate groups of commandments with the three supreme sefiroth.

42. Cf. *Sha 'ar ha-Shamayim,* p. 155, with *'Emunah u-Biṭṭaḥon,* chaps. 5 and 12, and *Meshibh,* Ms. Oxford, fol. 66a. The consistent avoidance in his writings of the term *kether 'elyon* is remarkable.

mahshabah, or rather above it, Jacob too names the Will, regarding which he expresses himself in a manner similar to that of Azriel, who, however, is not mentioned. The exposition on the sefiroth is followed by relatively clear hints concerning the doctrine of the transmigration of souls and reward and punishment; it concludes with a fulminating invective against the rationalists and their theses. Their arguments, as quoted in his text, are those of the pure Aristotelians in *The Guide of the Perplexed* 2:14, whence our author apparently took them. Of special interest are his objections to their spiritualizing conception of prayer, which provides a case of the kabbalist speaking up in support of orthodoxy. He accuses the Aristotelians of holding that it was unnecessary to pronounce the prayers and that thinking them was sufficient. In fact, being united with the Active Intellect absolves one of the duty to recite the obligatory prayers. The true meaning of prayer was not being "heard" by God by the purification of one's thoughts and spirit.[43] Here we have, remarkably enough, a form of *debhequth* rejected by the kabbalists and standing in contrast to the kind of prayer-mysticism cultivated by them. In fact, the kabbalistic doctrine of *kawwanah* opposes a pure spiritualization of the symbolism in prayer. One wonders whether the theory attacked here was perhaps developed in the commentary on the Song of Songs by the same Samuel ibn Tibbon against whom Jacob had earlier taken up the cudgels.[44]

Jacob ben Shesheth was older than the most illustrious personality of this circle, Moses ben Naḥman, who, according to traditions preserved by his disciples, invoked the authority of the former in

---

43. The view attacked by Jacob is in fact propounded in the still-unlocated source of the pseudo-Maimonidean "Chapters on the Unity" *(Peraqim mi-Yiḥud),* chap. 6; cf. G. Vajda's edition of this treatise, a strange mixture of Kabbalah and philosophy, in *Qobeṣ 'al Yad* 5 (1951): 123–125; see also Scholem in *Tarbiz* 28 (1959): 214. The text from a *Sefer ha-Yiḥud* that I published there is precisely the one edited by Vajda and also translated by him into French in *Recherches,* 357–371. It is interesting to note that in the sixteenth century Joseph Ashkenazi of Safed, whose denunciations of unbelief I discussed in *Tarbiz,* ibid., is just as incensed by this theory as the kabbalist of Gerona more than three hundred years before him.

44. The description given previously shows how mistaken Steinschneider was in his judgment: "Jacob ben Shesheth is less a mystic than an orthodox theologian; but the polemical attitude that he maintains with regard to the philosophers sufficed for the kabbalistic school that soon followed him to invoke his authority"; cf. *Gesammelte Schriften,* vol. 1 (Berlin, 1925), 35. Jacob's epistle, quoted by Isaac of Acre and mentioned by Steinschneider is none other than the aforementioned invective at the end of the *Sha 'ar ha-Shamayim.*

oral statements on kabbalistic matters.[45] Naḥmanides (ca. 1194–1270) occupied the central position in this circle by virtue of his outstanding authority as a talmudic scholar. We shall not concern ourselves here with this aspect of his activity, which rapidly made him the greatest halakhic authority of his generation in Spain. He began to write at a very young age, around 1211, so that when in 1232 the great conflict broke out in France and Spain over the writings of Maimonides he already enjoyed a widespread reputation, and all parties addressed themselves to him. In the following generation he was the undisputed spokesman of the Jews of Aragon and also vis à vis the civil authorities, who knew him under the Spanish name Bonastruc de Porta (or, in Catalan, Saporta, as this widely dispersed family is often called in the documents).[46] When in 1263 a former Jew from Provence, Paulus Christiani, who was supported by the Dominican order, forced the Jewish communities to engage in religious disputations, Naḥmanides was designated by the king as the spokesman for the Jews of Aragon,[47] a role in which he demonstrated much strength of character and courage. We also possess a large and partly kabbalistic treatise, a discourse on the glory of the Torah that—according to later legend—he had been invited to deliver in Barcelona before the king and the nobility.[48] The exasperation felt by ecclesiastical circles with regard to his performance at the disputation of Barcelona finally led to papal intervention and to

45. I found such statements of Naḥmanides, for example, in the name of his disciple Isaac ben Todros in *Kether Shem Tob* of Shemtob ibn Gaon, Ms. Parma, de Rossi 1221, fol. 236a, as well as in a statement of Shesheth noted on a fragment of a parchment that I found in the binding of Ms. Vatican 202.

46. Naḥmanides' seal (on a ring found near Acre in 1972) gives the name as "Moshe ben R. Naḥman Girondi"; cf. I. Shaḥar in "The Seal of Naḥmanides," The Israel Museum Special Exhibition, (1972), no. 3.

47. Cf. the literature on the disputation of Barcelona in Graetz, *Geschichte* 7:120–126; Cecil Roth, *HTR* 43 (1950): 117–144. With regard to the propagation of the Kabbalah in Aragon, it is important to note that in 1263, when the Jews were obliged by royal decree to submit their books to examination by a commission of censors, not a single book of kabbalistic content was handed over. The fact that Raimundus Martini's *Pugio Fidei* was compiled on the basis of the materials submitted explains why this author knew nothing of the entire kabbalistic literature, even though it had its center in the school of Gerona—these writings had been withheld. Paulus Christiani, too, never referred to the role of Naḥmanides as a kabbalist, apparently knowing nothing of it.

48. The best edition, based on a complete manuscript, is Jellinek's second edition, entitled *Torah 'Adonai Temimah* (Vienna, 1873).

protests to King James I of Aragon. Naḥmanides went into forced or voluntary exile. He emigrated to Palestine in 1267, where it seems he died in Acre shortly after 1269.

During the 1250s, Naḥmanides probably began his famous commentary on the Torah, into which he admitted a considerable number of kabbalistic explanations "according to the way of truth," as these passages are always introduced. Its final redaction took place in Acre. According to the tradition of his school, he had originally intended to expound the kabbalistic doctrine much more openly and fully, but was diverted from this purpose by a premonitory dream. Consequently, we have his detailed commentary on the first chapter of Genesis only, which his disciples had succeeded in disseminating in the meantime.[49] The kabbalistic passages in the commentary, written in laconic and highly symbolic language, were soon being studied with extreme care and became the subject of special supercommentaries in which his disciples, such as Solomon ibn Adreth, Isaac ben Todros, David Cohen, Shesheth, and Abner, not only preserved the authentic explanations of the master but also attached their own speculations to Naḥmanides' authoritative utterances.[50] "I saw a disciple," reports Isaac of Acre,

> who received from the direct disciples of Nahmanides, who followed this path [of radical interpretation] to its extreme end, taking the words of the master, including those where he interpreted in a literal sense, and explaining them in a kabbalistic mode. He thereby erred in many matters in which the master never had the slightest intention of making any [kabbalistic] allusions, but where he stayed with the literal meaning.[51]

---

49. Edited by me in *Kiryath Sefer* 6:415–417. I also published there, 410–414, a small treatise on the esoteric meaning of the Torah attributed to Naḥmanides that, if it is not in fact authentic, in any case originates in the Gerona circle. It is of considerable interest.

50. Between 1290 and 1330 these supercommentaries formed a distinct genre of kabbalistic literature that is of great value for the investigation of the Kabbalah, especially for the period after 1250. Apart from Baḥya ben Asher, whose commentary on the Torah often has, in its kabbalistic passages, the character of a supercommentary of this kind, we must mention among others as belonging to this group the writings of Shemtob ibn Gaon, *Kether Shem Tob;* of Isaac of Acre, *Me'irath 'Enayim;* of Joshua ibn Shu 'eib, and their revision by Meir ibn Sahula, as well as the anonymous commentary *Kabbalath Saporta* (probably so named after the family name of Naḥmanides?).

51. *Me'irath 'Enayim,* Ms. Munich 17, fol. 162b.

This is very valuable testimony to the tendency, which had arisen already at an early date, toward the progressive complication of kabbalistic ideas. It is, however, certain that Naḥmanides disposed of a wide range of kabbalistic traditions that must have come to him by different channels during his youth; he arranged and combined them in his own fashion. In many of his writings, even ostensibly halakhic ones,[52] he hinted, in greater or lesser detail, at kabbalistic doctrines calculated to whet the reader's appetite for further initiation rather than to veil the mysteries. In this sense, the propagandistic impact of Naḥmanides' writings cannot possibly be overestimated.

The author's uncontested authority as a champion and representative of traditional Judaism must have taken the edge off any possible objections that might have been lodged with regard to the orthodoxy of the thoughts propounded by him as the true mystery of Judaism. The process that we were able to observe for the first time in the family of the Rabad—the acceptance of old kabbalistic material by, so to speak, the official rabbinic circles, reached its apogee in Naḥmanides. Apart from his commentary on the Torah and the book of Job (whose true meaning is unlocked, according to him, by the kabbalistic doctrine of metempsychosis), his sermons, many of which have been preserved, shed much light on his kabbalistic tendencies; even on these occasions he misses no opportunity to make lengthy allusions couched in the terminology of kabbalistic symbolism.[53] It is difficult to surmise what the lay audience must have thought of these orations, unless we assume that most of them are literary elaborations of what were simpler discourses, and that the rest were in fact only delivered in a small circle of adepts where Naḥmanides could be sure of being understood. Among the latter we should include, for example, a sermon, highly mystical in many pas-

---

52. He opens his tract on the halakhic rules relating to vows, *Hilkhoth Nedarim,* with a rather long kabbalistic poem in Aramaic, published with a commentary by J. Reifmann in the monthly journal *Ha-Karmel* (Vilna, 1874): 375–384. This poem is one of his early works. In his novella on the tractate *Shabu'oth* 29a, Naḥmanides has a piece written in rhymed prose that uses strictly kabbalistic symbolism on the difference between vows and sermons. [On the latter subject see Micheline Chaze, "Le sens ésotérique du voeu et du serment," *R.E.J.*] (1979) 138: 249ff.

53. His sermon on *Qoheleth,* written in his old age, was edited by A. Z. Schwarz (Frankfurt-am-Main, 1913); a sermon on the occasion of the New Year (composed in Acre) edited by the same (Frankfurt, 1912).

sages, that was probably delivered on the occasion of the marriage of one of the members of this circle.[54] At the end of his halakhic work *Toledoth 'Adam,* which deals with the laws and customs relating to death and burial among the Jews, Naḥmanides devoted a long chapter, *Sha 'ar ha-Gemul,* to the problem of reward and punishment after death as well as to eschatological questions in general. In this he not only distinguished his own position most decisively from the almost purely spiritual opinions of Maimonides; he also took into account, to a large extent, the kabbalistic views to which he often reverts in his writings.[55] Kabbalistic motifs are also developed in his religious poems.[56] In fact, he was the first to employ mystical symbols in religious lyric poetry—not in didactic poetry, in which he had predecessors—and thus stands at the beginning of a long line of kabbalistic poets.

In the aforementioned writings, the Kabbalah appears as one element among others—an element that takes one beyond the literal sense of Scripture and the talmudic interpretation of the Midrash to a new mystical or symbolical level that in large measure first became known to the Jewish public through Naḥmanides' opus. What is striking in these texts is the complete absence of allegory, a trait entirely peculiar to Naḥmanides. The kabbalistic mysteries of the Torah are altogether different qualitatively from those of which the philosophers speak. In philosophical usage, especially in the works of Maimonides and his disciples, "secret" means that which can be deduced speculatively by the application of rational principles to the literal text of Scripture or the Aggadah. *Sod,* for the philosophers,

---

54. This sermon was edited by O. H. Schorr, *He-Chaluz* 12 (1887): 111–114.

55. This chapter was often printed independently under the title *Sha'ar ha-Gemul.* On the other hand Naḥmanides' book on the messianic redemption contains only the most fleeting allusions to kabbalistic matters; cf. the edition by J. Lipschitz, *Sefer ha-Ge'ullah* (London, 1909), and the supplements of A. Z. Schwarz in *Zeitschrift für Hebräische Bibliographie* 15 (1911): 35–36.

56. The most important is his hymn on the fate of the soul, in Chaim Schirman's *Ha-shirah ha-'ivrith be-Sefarad ubi-Provence* (Anthology of the Hebrew Poetry in Spain and Provence), vol. 2 (1957), 322–325, which I translated into German in the *Almanach des Schocken Verlags auf das Jahr 5696* (Berlin, 1935), 86–89. Also the verses contained in the letter from Jerusalem to his son Naḥman, printed in the first edition of his commentary on the Torah (Lisbon, 1489), are couched in the language of kabbalistic symbolism. It has not been established that the poem of a certain Ezra (published by Jellinek, *Geschichte der Kabbala,* Hebrew part, 2:vi–vii, from the *Maḥzor Vitry*) is by the kabbalist Ezra.

is the achievement of thought in disclosing a level of meaning that unveils a rational truth contained in the word of Scripture. It does not necessarily belong to the sphere of illumination or tradition. In brief, *sod* is a rational concept determined by allegory. Authors like Ezra or Naḥmanides use the word in an entirely different sense: they understood by *sod* only that which, in their circle, had already become the subject of a kabbalistic tradition. Thus, for Naḥmanides, the "secrets" so often evoked for example in the commentaries of ibn Ezra are not secrets in the sense of his technical kabbalistic language, and consequently he can cast doubt on them. Incidentally, Naḥmanides believed—without any historical justification—that ibn Ezra possessed some knowledge of certain kabbalistic doctrines; hence he approved of some of his allusions to them, at least to what he thought them to be. It seems that kabbalistic forgeries attributing their mysteries to Abraham ibn Ezra were still being produced as late as the thirteenth century. R. Joshua ibn Shu'eib quotes such a passage, whose evidently kabbalistic character is clearly borne out by its terminology, in his *Homilies* (*Derashoth* [Cracow, 1573], fol. 26b).

Since it was not Naḥmanides who first designated these *sodoth* as such, and ibn Ezra had already done so before him—his *sodoth* being quoted by Naḥmanides himself—no conclusions can be drawn regarding his own terminology. Many kabbalists, like Jacob ben Shesheth, were indeed not at all disinclined to adopt such allegories when it suited them and to juxtapose philosophic and kabbalistic "secrets" of this kind or even to combine them. Naḥmanides was different: he polemicized against many of Maimonides' positions—against his views on the question of miracles, the transitoriness of the world, angelology, and eschatology, as well as his interpretation of the significance of sacrifice, the nature of the Shekhinah, etc. But he never entered into a polemic with him regarding the allegorical method by means of which philosophical ideas stemming from the realms of metaphysics, psychology, and ethics are clothed in religious concepts. He simply ignored this kind of allegory. Around 1240, when Naḥmanides was at the height of his activity, this was absolutely unique, given the cultural climate of Spanish Jewry. Fifty years later Solomon ibn Adreth and Baḥya ben Asher treated allegory as a category possessing the same legitimacy as the strictly kabbalistic interpretation of Scripture. The same Solomon ibn Adreth, who later (1305) anathematized the abuses of the radical allegorists, followed very similar paths in his own commentary on the aggadoth, which undoubtedly must have been composed much earlier. Naḥmanides—if this particular tradition refers to him—expressed himself against the spiritualizing consequences of a mystical interpretation of Scripture that might tend to devalue the observance of the commandments. He is said to have commented on Deuteronomy 29:28 to the effect that knowledge of the secrets of the Torah and the reasons for the commandments, did not give a dispensation from the duty of their corporeal and material fulfillment, for, in the words of the biblical text: "with overt acts, it is for us and our children ever to apply all the provisions of this Teaching."[57]

The only work of Naḥmanides that is exclusively kabbalist is his commentary on the first chapter of *Yeṣirah,* in which he expatiates at length on the ten sefiroth; its authenticity, as I pointed out elsewhere, is beyond doubt.[58] Naḥmanides expresses himself on some fundamental doctrines of the Kabbalah, thereby disposing of several false though oft-repeated opinions regarding him, that he was not in any real way deeply concerned with the Kabbalah and "can hardly be taken seriously as a kabbalist."[59] This view is evidently influenced by the prejudice that a man like Naḥmanides, well versed in

57. Baḥya ben Asher declared, on Deuteronomy 29:28 as well as in *Qad ha-Qemaḥ* s.v. "Sukka," that he had heard that this injunction was to be found in a commentary on the Torah by Maimonides (in the second text: by Naḥmanides) that was not widespread in Spain. What commentary Baḥya had in mind is not clear. It is also possible that he actually heard a quotation from an apocryphal writing of Maimonides.

58. Cf. my study and edition of the text in *Kiryath Sefer* 6 (1930): 385–410. I completely disregard here the treatise relating to marriage and its mystical significance, which is in its essential parts kabbalistic and very much along the line of Ezra's thinking. The treatise had been in circulation since about 1350 under the name of Naḥmanides. Reprinted often since 1546 under the title *'Iggereth ha-Qodesh,* it has until now been considered authentic. Cf. also the interesting text in Enelow's edition of *Menorath ha-Ma'or* 4 (1932): 87–112. The "analysis" by Monford Harris, "Marriage as Metaphysics," in *HUCA* 33 (1962): 197–220, with its alleged parallels with Philo, misses the point completely. A French translation can be found in Michel Weill, *La Morale du Judaisme,* vol. 2 (Paris, 1877). The spuriousness of the work and the late date of its composition (in the generation after Naḥmanides)—perhaps by Joseph ibn Gikatilla—have been demonstrated by me in *Kiryath Sefer* 21 (1944/45): 179–186.

59. M. Ehrenpreis, *Emanationslehre,* 32. Most of the assertions in this work on the development of the early Kabbalah are completely erroneous from the point of view of history as well as the history of ideas. The author's reference to Isaac of Acre for his judgment of Naḥmanides is based on a misunderstanding of the Hebrew text.

the higher learning of his time—halakhic, philosophical, and medical—could hardly have been guilty of kabbalistic inclinations, that is, of "obscurantism." Insofar as such inclinations could not be denied, they should at least be minimized. The authors in question failed to appreciate that for Naḥmanides, the great spokesman of traditional authority, the Kabbalah represented a conservative force in which tradition and contemplation of the mysteries merged. In the history of Jewish literature, Naḥmanides is often considered to exemplify the "most Jewish" spirit; he was the one among Spanish Jews who expressed the deepest convictions regarding the Judaism of his time and embodied what was best and highest in it. From the point of view of a "refined" Judaism or the pure halakhah, it must indeed appear as an aberration that so clear a mind, one that easily penetrated the most complicated halakhic problems, should have become involved with the Kabbalah. But it is precisely this dimension of his personality that must be grasped if we wish to understand the phenomenon. Without the Kabbalah and its contemplative mysticism Naḥmanides, would be as little understood in his Jewish context as would, in the Christian context, a man like Ramon Lull[60] (who was active in Catalonia a generation later and whose teaching exhibited structurally many analogies with the doctrine of the sefiroth) if one ignored his *Ars contemplativa,* in which his Christianity reached its culmination, and judged him solely on the basis of his wide-ranging activities in all other possible domains. From this point of view, Naḥmanides' commentary on *Yeṣirah,* which develops his conception of God, is of particular importance. The gnostic doctrine of the aeons and the Neoplatonic doctrine of the emanation are combined, and we see how well they harmonize with a Jewish consciousness. The monotheism of Naḥmanides, the Jewish coloration of which is certainly beyond question, is unaware of any contradiction between

60. I could not convince myself of any historical influences of the Kabbalah on Ramon Lull's doctrine of the *dignitates* of the deity, as José M. Millás Vallicrosa, "Algunas relaciones entre la doctrina luliana y la cabala," *Sefarad* 18 (1958): 241–253, has tried to suggest. The analogies in question are sufficiently accounted for by the structural relationship with the doctrine of Scotus Erigena; cf. Frances Yates, "Ramon Lull and John Scotus Erigena," *Journal of the Warburg and Courtauld Institute* 23 (1960): 1–44. As regards the names and the structure of the sefiroth and the *dignitates,* the correspondence is only superficial and slight, and in part the almost necessary consequence of the enumeration of the divine attributes. Precisely the number ten plays no role at all with Lull.

the unity of God and its manifestation in the different sefiroth, each of which represents one of the aspects by which the *kabhod* of God reveals itself to the Shekhinah. In his commentary on the Torah, in which he had to deal only with God's activity in His creation, making use of the symbols of theosophy, Naḥmanides could avoid touching upon this crucial point; he only discussed it in this document intended for kabbalists.

From whom Naḥmanides actually received the esoteric tradition is an open question. He does mention, in his commentary on *Yeṣirah,* the Hasid Isaac the Blind, but not as his master. Nor does the letter that Isaac sent to him and to his cousin Jonah Gerondi, of whom we shall have occasion to speak later, indicate any direct discipleship. Naḥmanides refers to Yehudah ben Yaqar as his master, especially in the halakhic writings. Contrariwise, in a series of undoubtedly genuine traditions going back to Naḥmanides' most important disciple, Solomon ibn Adreth, there emerges the thoroughly enigmatic figure of a kabbalist by the name of ben Belimah—the personal first name is never mentioned—who is said to have been the connecting link between him and Isaac the Blind.[61] Meir ibn Sahula, in his commentaries on the traditions of Naḥmanides (fol. 29a), contrasts those he had received from ben Belimah with those deriving from Isaac. In very old marginal notes emanating from the circle of Gerona and preserved in Ms. Parma, de Rossi 68, mention is made of a debate between Naḥmanides and ben Belimah over the fate of Naboth's spirit (1 Kings 22); the debate suggests that ben Belimah posited some kind of transmigration of souls or metamorphosis also for the higher spirits, even within the world of the sefiroth up to *binah.*[62] The existence of such a kabbalist therefore seems established beyond doubt, no matter how enigmatic his name. It is neither a family name nor a patronymic. Belimah is not known to me as a woman's name, and it is extremely unlikely that Solomon ibn Adreth would have transmitted the name in a corrupted form to his disci-

---

61. Thus as the end of Sahula's anonymously printed commentary on the *Bahir* (Vilna, 1883), fol. 20a. He is also designated as Naḥmanides' master in the Kabbalah in Sahula's supercommentary on Naḥmanides (Warsaw, 1875), fol. 32d, and in Shemtob ibn Gaon's *Kether Shem tob,* fol. 47b; cf. the passage in *Kiryath Sefer* 6:390.

62. Ms. De Rossi 68, fol. 6b: "I heard that the master and ben Belimah had a discussion on this subject and that ben Belimah proved the matter to him on the basis of Scripture." Cf. the text of these and other traditions concerning ben Belimah in *Reshith ha-Qabbala* 241–243.

ples. There remains the hypothesis of a pseudonym deliberately substituted for another name that was kept secret for reasons unknown to us and in a manner completely contrary to the habit of this circle. The pseudonym seems to be derived from *B. Hullin* 89a, where Job 26:7 is applied to Moses and Aaron who, when assailed by the Israelites, changed themselves into nothing! The kabbalist in question thus may possibly have been a [. . .] ben Moses (rather than [. . .] ben Aaron). B. Dinur's suggestion that the pseudonym refers to R. Jonah ben Abraham Gerondi (because of his attitude in the Maimonidean controversy) seems improbable. Perhaps new manuscript discoveries will one day clarify matters. In any case, this name, whose literal translation would be "son of the Nought" or "son of seclusion," provokes the historian's curiosity. It remains uncertain whether ben Belimah should be located in Gerona, which is quite possible, or in Provence, where Naḥmanides could have met with him during his youth.

In the writings of Ezra and Naḥmanides no reference is made to the kabbalistic conceptions of the *'Iyyun* circle. That these conceptions had, however, established themselves in Spain in the meantime follows from a letter to Naḥmanides in which the author expounds the doctrine of the sefiroth "in accordance with our Kabbalah," which he had received from his master Joseph ibn Mazaḥ.[63] The Mazaḥ family was among the most distinguished in Toledo; a judge by the name of Samuel ben Joseph ibn Mazaḥ, probably the great grandson of the Joseph named here, died there in 1349.[64] However, around 1240/1250 this kabbalist of Toledo transmitted doctrines that certainly derive from materials of the *'Iyyun* group. The epistle names the twenty-two paths of the ten sefiroth from the "wondrous light" up to the "curtain"—all these names are familiar from other contexts and similar to, though not identical with, enumerations in the *'Iyyun* circle. In a letter quoted in a previous chapter, (p. 226) mention was likewise made of a Toledan mystic from the ibn Ziza family. This would indicate the existence in Toledo of a kabbalistic circle that had connections with the Abulafia family of kabbalists in Toledo and Burgos, of which I shall speak in the following text.

---

63. I edited the text from a manuscript in the Mussajof collection (Jerusalem) in *Kiryath Sefer* 6:418–420. In other manuscripts where I later found the same letter, all the names were omitted. The text of Ms. Mussajof seems to be based on a copy of the letter that Shemtob ibn Gaon, in any case, must have had before him.

64. Cf. L. Zunz, *Zur Geschichte und Literatur* (Berlin, 1845), 425.

Naḥmanides' cousin, Jonah Gerondi, renowned not only as a Talmudist, ascetic moralist, and hasid but also as an opponent of Maimonides, did not play a public role as a mystic. He lived a long time in France but in the 1230s surely belonged to the circle in Gerona, as is demonstrated by a letter of Isaac the Blind to these two scholars in which he explicitly addresses them as adepts of the Kabbalah. Jonah moved to Barcelona only later, and from there to Toledo,[65] where he died in 1263. Although the extant inscription on his tombstone describes him as one who had spoken of "the secrets [or profundities] of Wisdom" and taught their laws, it is doubtful whether this metaphor alludes to the Kabbalah; the continuation of the epitaph militates against this assumption. In a letter to Jonah on the subject of the creation of souls, Naḥmanides avoids direct discussion of kabbalistic theories.[66] The incidental information gathered here shows that many important pieces of this group's correspondence that have been preserved are of considerable significance for us. These epistolary exchanges must surely have played an important role among the mystics, and it is very much to be regretted that for the origins of the Kabbalah we lack collections of letters similar to those assembled in W. Oehl's *Deutsche Mystikerbriefe* (1931). Nevertheless, the disciples of Naḥmanides copied numerous documents preserved in the academies of Gerona and Burgos without concern for their literary form (or rather, quite often, their lack of form), and thus have left us, along with many letters, a good number of shorter notes and precious explanations. These miscellanies, found in many manuscripts, are of great value for the detailed study of the Kabbalah in Gerona, which would in fact require a separate volume.[67] They also contain two lengthy texts of a kabbalist named Barzilai that include a brief treatise on the ten

---

65. Sometimes he also is referred to as R. Jonah of Toledo, for example, in the commentary *Migdal 'Oz* on *Mishneh Torah* (*Hilkhoth Tefillah* 8:5); cf. also *Dvir* 2 (1924): 223. For the text of the epitaph see S. D. Luzzatto, *Abhne Zikkaron* (Prague, 1841), 171 and M. Schwab, *Rapport sur les inscriptions hébräiques de l' Espagne* (1907), 73.

66. The letter is printed among the responsa of Solomon ibn Adreth, 1883, no. 284. The attribution made there to Naḥmanides is confirmed by the testimony in old kabbalistic collections; cf., for example, Ms. Vatican 185, fol. 191a.

67. Such collections are found, for example, in Mss. de Rossi 1221, Halberstam 174, Ghirondi 62, Casanatense 181, Oxford 1945, Christ Church College 198, Vatican Ebr. 202.

sefiroth[68] Jacob names still another kabbalist, Joseph ben Samuel of Catalonia, whose commentary on Genesis 1 he quotes in extenso at the end of his polemic against ibn Tibbon (chap. 31). This commentary appears to be a slightly revised version of the almost identical one of Asher ben David, whose writings—above all his interpretation of the divine name—must be regarded as a kind of connective linking the Kabbalah of Provence to that of Gerona.[69] Asher himself lived with his uncle, Isaac the Blind, for a long time, but he also came to Gerona and seems to have resided in Béziers for some time after his uncle's death.[70]

2. Debates and Disturbances Resulting from the Propaganda of the Kabbalists: Their Role in the Controversy Over the Writings of Maimonides

Asher's activity is bound up with historical events whose echo still resounds in various documents. The enthusiasm of certain adepts of the Kabbalah was apparently so great that they broke through the

---

68. Cf. Barzilai's treatise, Ms. Christ Church College 198, fols. 73b–74a, as well as Günzburg 131, no. 9. The second text found there is a verbatim extract from Jacob ben Shesheth's polemic against ibn Tibbon, with the omission of all digressions that do not bear directly on the exegesis of Psalm 144 quoted here. Jacob (Ms. Oxford fol. 38a) makes mention of Barzilai's interpretation of Genesis 1:3. Whether he really inserted and expanded Barzilai's treatise on the psalm in his own book appears to me uncertain; the opposite appears more probable.

69. Asher's *Perush Shem ha-meforash* was edited by Ḥasida in *Ha-Segullah,* nos. 2–10. In Ms. Paris 680 Naḥmanides' authentic commentary on *Yeṣirah* is followed by Asher's treatise, likewise given under Naḥmanides name as a "summary of the Book *Yeṣirah* by the great master Moses ben Naḥman." This explains why Abraham ibn Migash, *Kebhod 'Elohim* (Constantinople, 1585), fol. 110a–b, cited a long quotation from this work as if it came from the commentary on *Yeṣirah* of the Rambam (read: Ramban). Asher's writings are the source of many images that appear throughout the literature of the old Kabbalah in endless variation—such as the conception of the seven lower sefiroth as a menorah and as a bunch of grapes, and that of all ten sefiroth as garments that veil the splendor of the deity, even though at the same time it acts in them and is represented in them.

70. Some manuscripts of a text by Asher, which however do not name him as the author, refer to him in the colophon as "a learned kabbalist, from the city of Béziers, who received from our holy masters"; cf. Enelow Mem. Coll. 655, fol. 15a, and Gaster 199, end of no. 2.

barriers that should have kept esoteric communication confined to the academy and to personal contacts within their narrow circle and launched upon a campaign of public dissemination of their ideas. In doing so they were not content, as was Naḥmanides, to make obscure allusions that aroused curiosity but did not, however, reveal anything with regard to their actual teachings. They went much further, and in this way the Kabbalah became the subject of public debate for the first time. The dissemination of the writings of Ezra and especially those of Azriel also seems to have contributed to this development. Unrest must have spread to many communities. Isaac the Blind found himself obliged, on the basis of information reported by Naḥmanides and Jonah Gerondi (whom he called his friends), to protest against this propaganda. Until then he had kept silent.

> For I was filled with great concern when I saw scholars, men of understanding and Hasidim, engaging in long discourses and presuming in their books and letters to write about great and sublime matters [of the Kabbalah]. But what is written cannot be kept in the closet; often, these things are lost or the owners die and the writings fall into the hands of fools or scoffers, and the name of heaven is thus profaned. And this is in fact what happened to them. As long as I was still with them, in this life, I often warned them against this tendency, but since I separated myself from them [since their death?], they have been the cause of much harm. I am of an entirely different habit [that is, not to speak or to write openly of kabbalistic matters], since my fathers were indeed the most distinguished in the land and public masters of the Torah but never did a word [relating to mystical lore] escape their lips, and they conducted themselves with them [the uninitiated] as with people who were not versed in the [higher] Wisdom, and I beheld their practice and learned my lesson. Furthermore [apart from the aforementioned letter of Nahmanides], I have also heard from the regions where you dwell and concerning the men of Burgos that they openly hold forth on these matters, in the marketplaces and in the streets, in confused and hasty discourses, and from their words it is clearly perceptible that their heart has been turned from the All-highest[71] and they cause devastations of the plants,[72] whereas these things[73] are united as the flame is bound to the coal, for the Lord is unique and has no second [by his side], and what can you count before

71. The Hebrew expression used here, *min ha-'elyonah,* is very strange. My translation is conjectural.

72. This is the expression used by all kabbalists since Isaac for errors concerning the relationship between the sefiroth and God; it is not simply a general metaphor for heresy; cf. *Ḥagigah* 14b.

73. On this terminology, cf. p. 265, herein.

the One[74]—"before the One," that is the Great Name, which is united in all of the ten [sefiroth]: but I cannot enter at any greater length, in writing, into what you have asked.[75]

The addressees of this epistle had evidently requested that Isaac come in person to calm the unrest. However, at the end of his letter he refused:

I cannot perceive any decree of heaven according to which I would now have to leave my place of residence and come to you. But when R. Asher, the son of my esteemed brother, the learned R. David, may his memory be blessed, comes to you, follow every counsel that he gives you, for I will let you know my will through him. He also knows my position and he saw throughout my life how I conducted myself with regard to my companions.

We have here a clear authorization given to his nephew, who was close to him all his life and knew exactly the relations between Isaac and the other adepts of the Kabbalah. It was he who was commissioned to intervene in this delicate situation and to carry out, with the help of the addressees, the instructions of his uncle. According to the tenor of the epistle, there must have been serious incidents that apparently were not restricted to one place only. Two distinct elements in Isaac's letter require consideration. On the one hand he warns against highly respected scholars and Hasidim of his own group who, if we correctly interpret his flowery style, were no longer alive and whose writings had fallen into the wrong hands. On the other hand he complains about the pseudo-kabbalistic discourses of half-baked adepts in Aragon—this indeed seems to be the meaning of the reference to "the regions where you dwell"—and in the Castilian city of Burgos. Their discourses, which profane the Kabbalah "in the marketplaces," were apparently reported to him not only by the authors of the letter, to whom he certainly would not have needed to repeat this information in his reply. With these public manifestations they offended against the doctrine of the unity of God in speaking of the sefiroth as if they were autonomous essences, and not "things" or rather "logoi" enclosed in the unity of God.

As we know from an epistle of Azriel, there were in Burgos

---

74. The terminology of this passage is derived from chapter 1 of the Book *Yeṣirah.*

75. I published the Hebrew text in *Sefer Bialik,* 143–144.

adepts of the Kabbalah who received instruction from him. This fact, as well as the whole tenor of Isaac's protest against the circulation of kabbalistic writings contrary to his warnings, suggest that none other than Ezra and Azriel were the targets of this criticism. Their writings and letters, especially Azriel's, are the only texts corresponding to Isaac's description. The authors were personally known to him; they had met and studied with him in Provence. But after returning to Spain, they had engaged, despite his warning, in the literary propagation of their mystical ideas, thereby opening the door to all kinds of misunderstandings.

However, the great respect with which he speaks of the authors suggests that it is not just anybody to whom he is referring but to the foremost and most eminent exponents of the new tendency. From ancient notices on the beginnings of the Kabbalah that no doubt go back to the school of Solomon ibn Adreth, we learn that "from these two—that is, the previously named Ezra and Azriel—this science spread out, for they taught it to a great number."[76] This old testimony accords perfectly with the protestations of Isaac, which, if I interpret them correctly, are opposed to the excessively zealous and dangerous propaganda of these two mystics belonging to his own group. In formulating his criticisms, Isaac cannot have had in mind the Book *Bahir,* which was not composed in his time and certainly not by "scholars and men of understanding" known to him, or the literature of the *'Iyyun* group, whose authors did not appear under their own names but, on the contrary, disguised their identities. Certainly Isaac's complaints concerning the detail with which the mysteries were treated does not apply to the *'Iyyun* writings. Moreover, this literature was not yet widespread in Gerona at the time Isaac wrote his epistle with its explicit reference to "books and letters" that obviously must have been known to his correspondents. This, it seems to me, inevitably leads us back to Azriel and Ezra. The only possible difficulty is of a chronological nature. The authors whom Isaac criticizes were no longer alive—the Hebrew expression cannot be explained otherwise—at the time he wrote the letter. According to the indications of later chroniclers, Ezra died in 1238 or 1244, which would be contradicted by this letter, since it was

76. The last words were omitted, through homoeoteleuton, in the copy of the passage in the *Catalog hebräischer Handschriften von S. J. Halberstam* (Vienna, 1890), 109.

no doubt written earlier. Azriel was younger—according to some manuscripts he was Ezra's son-in-law.[77] Perhaps they died, one shortly after the other, even before 1235. Although their books are shorter and more condensed than we would wish, the fact remains that for Isaac's period they were the first to treat kabbalistic themes in public and in a relatively explicit fashion. (Isaac's own notes seem to have been kept secret with greater care.)

These works contained plenty of material that was apt to give offense to the pious men of the old school. This is evident from the texts themselves and is further confirmed by the antagonistic testimony of Meir ben Simon, who has already been mentioned several times. Referring to their books, Meir ben Simon, in his profound aversion to the novel doctrines, lumped together (unlike Isaac) all kabbalistic texts. His epistle was probably written between 1235 and 1245. It deals with similar phenomena in Provence that brought about the hostile intervention of the eminent talmudist Meshullam ben Moses, the author of the *Sefer ha-Hashlamah.* This intervention therefore took place at approximately the same time as the events in Spain that gave rise to Isaac's letter. In fact, this letter apparently was written at a time when Jonah Gerondi was back in Gerona, where he had met with Naḥmanides. We know that Jonah returned to Spain following a long sojourn in France only after the controversy over Maimonides (which had begun in 1232) had come to an end. We can thus date Isaac's letter to approximately the years around 1235. It was therefore written in his old age. Whereas Jacob ben Shesheth counts Isaac among the deceased around 1240, Ezra names him among the living in his commentary on the aggadoth. The fact that in the commentary on the Song of Songs he is twice named with the eulogy for the dead can be explained by the subsequent alterations of copyists; Tishby has provided good reasons for believing that Ezra wrote this commentary when he was over fifty years old, but before he composed his commentary on the aggadoth.[78]

Opposition to the rising Kabbalah may also be implied in Jacob

---

77. Cf. note 10, herein. Another statement, to the effect that Ezra was the father-in-law of Naḥmanides, probably resulted from this one. The indications relating to the year of Ezra's death are found in A. Neubauer, *Mediaeval Jewish Chronicles* 1:95, 103.

78. Tishby in *Sinai* 8 (1945): 160–163. Jacob ben Shesheth, Ms. Oxford 1585, fol. 60a speaks of Isaac as already deceased.

Anatoli's[79] preface to his *Malmad ha-Talmidim.* Anatoli, who wrote precisely during this period in Provence, mentions at the end of his preface that the despisers of science [philosophy?] who present their "vain talk concerning [magical?] names, invented by foolish people, as Merkabah-teaching." Whether the polemic is directed at magic or at speculations concerning the names as practiced in the *'Iyyun* circle remains a moot question.

On the other hand, the attitude of the kabbalists toward rabbinic tradition leaves no doubt that in the struggles with the Karaites that erupted again and again in the years 1170–1230, they were unequivocally on the side of rabbinism.[80] References to *minim* in the oldest kabbalistic writings should therefore be interpreted according to the context, as they may also be aimed at the Karaites.

The epistle to the Provençal communities reproduced in Meir ben Simon's tract (which I would date immediately after Isaac's death) is more explicit than Isaac's letter concerning the nature of the offense given by the kabbalists in the eyes of their antagonists, although we do not know the exact historical circumstances surrounding the incident that produced this scandal. The author of the letter restricts himself to the significant allusion that "some of the scholars of the land [of Provence] were informed secretly of the precise circumstances of the incident which caused us to write this letter."[81] We learn that what incensed the opponents was above all prayer-mysticism and the theology implied by it as well as its propagation and vulgarization. Meir of Narbonne writes, among other things:

> For some time now, fools and simpletons have advanced false opinions with respect to the belief in God and on the subject of the prayers and benedictions as they have been set down for us by our ancestors, things which have no basis either in the Bible or in the Talmud, nor in the Torah or in the tradition, or in the proper dialectical treatment [*sebarah*], not even in the apocryphal aggadoth, which they possess and which are [moreover] possibly corrupt and unreliable and from which one cannot draw any proof. These fools say that thanksgiving,

79. On Anatoli see also chap. 3 n. 83, herein.

80. On the controversies with Karaism in Burgos and Zaragozza at this period, cf. Judith Dishon in the Hebrew historical quarterly *Zion* 26 (1971): 194–195; she also quotes from Kobak's *Jeschurun* 8 (1872): 41 and the sources mentioned there.

81. Cf. *JQR* 4:358. Does this cautious formulation perhaps refer to a case of apostasy in the circles of the earliest kabbalists?

prayer, and benediction are not addressed to God, He who is from all primeval beginnings, and who is without beginning or end. Woe unto their souls for having uttered such blasphemies against the Holy One of Israel and for having turned away from He-who-is-for-all-eternity, from the refuge of old, the first-without-beginning and the last-without-end. . . . He has no one beside Him. He is One in complete unity, without it being possible for sefiroth to be associated and conjoined with Him. He is the Cause of all the causes, who called forth, alone, by His will, Being from Nought, and it behooves us to thank, praise, and exalt Him. It is He who, in the expressions of thanksgiving and in the blessings is called the Master of the Universe and the Creator of the Universe, and not His creatures, which have a beginning and an end. It is He who providentially oversees and directs the Universe, in general and in particular, and nothing must be associated with Him, for the creature must not be associated with its creator, nor matter with its molder, nor the emanated with the emanator, saying, for example, that His unity is perfect only when it is together with them. And he who puts together the name of God and some other thing, ought to be uprooted from the world.[82] This is the religion which all Israel must believe, and whoever deviates from it is a sectarian and a heretic. And why should we enter at length into the words of the fools for whom all the prayers and benedictions are addressed to gods, of whom they say that they are created and emanated, that they have a beginning and an end? For they say in their foolish imaginings that whoever is called first and last has a beginning and an end, for which they base themselves on Isaiah 44:6. We found this in one of the books of errors, a book which they call *Bahir,* and some of the scholars heard this from their lips. And they say that one must pray, at daytime, to one created god, and at night to another, who is above him, but who is created like him, and on holidays, to yet another. In the prayers for the ten days of repentance they caused utter confusion, praying to one created and to another who is below him. On the other days of the year they made numerous subdivisions [of the *kawwanah*] according to their imperfect temperament. They are an abomination to all flesh; the worm of their folly will not perish, and the fire of their nonsense will not be extinguished. For they have chosen many gods,[83] and they say in their unreason that they are all connected with one another and all is one. . . . If they say that He is one, why do they then divide their prayer between one of the day and one of the night, and why do they draw a distinction between workdays and holidays, between days of repentance and the days of the year, and what sense do all these distinctions make concerning Him? For they should know in truth that God is one, without beginning and end, and without change. For He is One, even before the sefiroth were created and emanated, those which really do have a beginning, as they too admit. And nevertheless they direct the intention [*kawwanah*] of their heart, in

82. A talmudic expression; cf. *Sukkah* 45b.

83. The text is corrupt. But also my reconstruction, *('iwwu l'Elohuth harbeh)* is unsatisfactory Hebrew.

> their prayers, toward them [the sefiroth]. They must therefore recognize that they speak falsely, but their eye is blinded, and their heart is hardened. In short, all their words are like chaff before the wind, empty words, devoid of sense, destruction of the Torah and heresy. How therefore could anyone with a little understanding share their view that it is not fitting to address prayers to the Name, the first without beginning or end, the Cause of all the causes, which in their language they call *'en-sof,* and he who does this is in their eyes one who destroys the plants and who does not deserve to contemplate the eternal beatitude assured to those who know God. How could all this not be explained in the Torah, the Mishnah, and the Talmud, and how could these books leave all Israel in error, so that they would be banished from the future world, since they destroyed the plants? Woe to the eyes that see this, woe to the ears that hear it, woe to the generation in whose days this has come to pass. . . . Do there exist in our time, even among the religions of the gentiles, books on the unity of God more worthless than these? And even if they admit that one who addresses his prayers to God as the Cause of all causes and to the Creator of the Universe is [not] banished from the [future] world and attains eternal beatitude and is not called destroyer of the plants, it is only because they think in their folly that this is the belief of the rabble, while they on the contrary belong to those who know the secret of God and who fear Him and hope to rise through this faith to a higher degree than the others.[84]

The conception attacked here with such anger and indignation is undoubtedly that of Isaac the Blind himself, as we find it in the traditions concerning his mystical meditations on the prayers and in his commentary on *Yeṣirah.* Even the radical opinion to the effect that whoever contemplates in his prayers, the "infinite cause" instead of the *middoth* stands in danger of "being banished," that is to say of losing beatitude, is cautiously hinted at in his commentary on *Yeṣirah* 1:7. The author of our epistle, of course, exaggerates when he describes the kabbalists as praying to many and created gods, and it goes without saying that the kabbalists of Isaac's school would have repudiated this account of their views in the strongest possible terms. Our polemicist blurs their basic distinction between that which is properly speaking "creaturely," that is to say outside the divine, and that which is emanated, which remains in God and only represents one of the stations of the inner-divine life process or, if we want to avoid this image as well, one of the aspects of his manifestation.

It is nevertheless certain that in medieval Judaism a strong

84. Cf. the text in *Sefer Bialik,* 148–149.

tension existed between the mystical conception of God that finds expression in this doctrine of the *kawwanah* and a static type of monotheism such as was taught outside the Kabbalah. This was no doubt the main reason for dealing with these ideas in an esoteric manner. The letter in which Isaac complains about the "destruction of the plants," that is the damage wrought to the unity of God in his sefiroth by immature spirits, proves in any case that the polemic of Meir of Narbonne had a real target and was not based upon a misunderstanding. The two documents complement one another and confirm that the emergence of the Kabbalah and its propagation in the communities did not take place without a certain amount of friction. The lasting influence of personalities like Naḥmanides, whose authority was so great in the eyes of the public that it could silence objections of the kind documented here, must be appreciated all the more. Isaac the Blind, on the other hand, however high the esteem he enjoyed among the kabbalists themselves, did not possess the status in the eyes of the Jewish public to enable him to counter such attacks effectively.

Asher ben David himself, who strove to lessen these tensions, has likewise described for us in very conciliatory language the same state of affairs and difficulties. Apparently, as he himself testifies, he wrote his rather lengthy expositions of the doctrine of the sefiroth only when these conflicts and scandals made it necessary to combat the misunderstandings. This explains why he abandoned the reserve shown by his uncle—a reserve that, under the circumstances, was impossible to maintain. Asher writes:

> I therefore developed my thought at length in many passages where I should have expressed myself more briefly—were it not for the words of the defamers and detractors, who were seized with audacity and raised long and unjustified accusations against the beloved disciples who received from the mystics of Israel [*maskile yisrael*], seekers of God, the faithful of the Highest, who cry to God and are heard, who suffer all the afflictions of their fellowmen and who in their prayer intercede for them with their Creator, . . . through whom many miracles have been wrought both to individuals and to the community. And with regard to the disciples who have studied with them and received from their lips, they [the opponents] have circulated many vile calumnies that are without foundation, and they would fain have raised their hands also against their teachers. But perhaps the disciples contributed to this themselves, by not choosing their words carefully, whether in their written expressions or in their discourses in the presence of whomever. Although their intention was praiseworthy, their

> language was nonetheless deficient and their science was thereby rendered untenable, as a result of which they did not know how to take in their discourses and writings the correct path between proper communication sufficient to the man of understanding [*maskil*] and the reserve [to be maintained] in the presence of the fool, which would have protected one as well as the other from error. Thus, they erred through obscurity, not having rendered their words intelligible in the appropriate place, and through excessively detailed exposition, where they should have kept their mysteries secret. Their readers or listeners did not comprehend their opinion and misunderstood their way of thinking. Thus they arrived at the idea that they [the disciples] believed in two supreme principles and hence appeared as deniers of the true religion, and that they lowered the Cause of All causes to the level of the corporeal, as if it were subject to change. And everything that they [the critics] thought of them [the disciples], they expressed, claiming that they posited an intermediary between themselves and their Creator. And although these disciples were fully instructed, it is due to their pride that they did not restrain their words, and even went so far as to lecture in public. And there were among them also some who were only half-baked and immature and had not sufficiently penetrated [this teaching]. They set out to storm the highest rungs of the ladder, even though they had not even ascended to the lowest, and they thereby gave occasion for polemic and ridicule.[85]

These words of Asher read like a response to the aforementioned epistle of Meir of Narbonne and were, perhaps, penned as such. Here too we find the same distinction—one that Isaac the Blind also had made in his letter—between true adepts, who merely did not know how to show the proper restraint, and the discourses of immature minds. Asher's criticism, too, doubtless refers above all to the writings of Ezra and Azriel: here, perhaps, lies the reason he never names them in his treatises, despite the unmistakable affinity, especially to the ideas of Azriel. Besides, Asher is by no means a mere kabbalistic litterateur and apologist. On occasion, above all in the epilogue to his *Sefer ha-Yiḥud* (20), he reveals himself as an authentic mystic. Even if it were permitted, he says, to write down these divine things, one could not do so; it would not even be possible to utter them orally since one would be reduced to helpless stammering. But even if these things are unutterable, there is nevertheless in these stammerings an authentic indication that can point the way for the disciple. The true mystics "who meditate upon the names of God" (one could also translate: "who engage in speculations of num-

85. Cf. ibid., 151.

bers-mysticism on the names of God") seek to show that "the emanated is not to be separated from the emanator," in other words, that the process of the Divine Life in the midst of the sefiroth must not be rendered autonomous in relation to God, but must be conceived—contrary to the deviations of immature disciples—in unity with its source as the totality of the active deity.

The position that the kabbalists occupied in the eye of the Jewish public was therefore by no means firmly established in the generation of Isaac the Blind and the first Spanish kabbalists. From the beginning, their appearance provoked objections and criticism. This opposition was never entirely stilled in the course of Jewish history, even at the times when the Kabbalah reached the peak of its historical and social influence. The kabbalists regarded themselves as the legitimate heirs of an authentic Jewish tradition that they sought to confirm and secure within the rabbinic framework. But while their attitude toward the halakhah was essentially positive, their relationship to the other powerful contemporary intellectual trend, rationalist Jewish philosophy, was still uncertain, at least in Gerona. Two tendencies can be recognized here. On the one hand, the kabbalists regarded themselves as the continuators of the philosophers; therefore, as far as possible they sought to avoid quarreling with them. They appropriated the foundations of philosophical thought as it had been developed by the Platonizing Aristotelians who preceded them. They claimed to have knowledge of spheres concerning which the philosophers had nothing to say, but they did not adopt a hostile attitude toward them. On the other hand, many of them felt themselves compelled to take just such a critical and directly antagonistic position, viewing the "traditional" science that they possessed as illuminati in contrast to the enlightenment type of rationalism that had struck root in influential Jewish circles. Ezra does not hesitate to oppose the Kabbalah to the opinions of the philosophers as well as to those of the ignorant rabble.[86] Naḥmanides himself is very circumspect in his utterances, but on the whole his judgment of the philosophers "who negate the Torah" is rather negative.[87] Neverthe-

86. Cf. in the *Perush 'Aggadoth,* Vat. 294, fols. 36a and 40b.

87. In his *Sha'ar ha-Gemul,* he speaks without ado of the *mithpalssefim mebaṭṭele ha-Torah;* cf. on Naḥmanides' attitude toward philosophy, the Hebrew study of Samuel Krauss, *Die wissenschaftliche Beziehung zwischen Nachmanides und Maimonides* (Cracow, 1906), 6–11 (offprint from *Ha-Goren* 5).

less, in the most stirring conflict of his time, the quarrel with the adherents of Maimonides that erupted once again around 1232, he adopted a conciliatory and rather positive attitude toward the study of philosophy.

The position taken by the kabbalists in this quarrel, which deeply agitated spirits in Spain and France, is in fact a question of considerable interest. A careful analysis shows that it is not so much the *Stocktalmudisten* ["arch-talmudists"] (as Graetz put it) but the esotericists who were the decisive spiritual force behind this controversy. This was not made clear in the earlier presentations of this conflict between faith and reason.[88] It is extremely instructive to see how, at a time when the kabbalists had not yet completely overcome or shaken off the suspicion of heterodoxy, they nevertheless turn up as the protagonists of orthodoxy in this struggle. The new gnosis that claimed to have discovered unsuspected depths in the Torah and prayer, in the aggadoth and the midrashim, stepped forward only a short time after its appearance on the stage of history as a defender of the rabbinic tradition and as its ally against the dangers of an allegoric blurring of borders—dangers that the increasingly powerful trend toward rational enlightenment rendered only too real.

In this conflict, however, the lines were by no means clearly and unequivocally drawn. Many of the most radical adherents of Maimonides took positions close to a spiritualizing mysticism. The position, for example, represented by the highly reputed Shesheth of Saragossa in his epistle (around 1200) to the scholars of Lunel on the resurrection of the dead comes much closer, in its resolute denial of corporeal resurrection, to a spiritualizing eschatology than that of the kabbalists.[89] One could suppose that already at this time, shortly before the death of Maimonides, certain scholars of Toledo and perhaps also of Lunel, involved in the first conflict over the doc-

---

88. Cf. Joseph Sarachek, *Faith and Reason: The Conflict over the Rationalism of Maimonides* (New York, 1935), 128f., whose discussion of the role of the Kabbalah in this conflict is misleading and devoid of any value; also E.E. Urbach, *Zion* 12 (1948): 149–159. On the whole subject, cf. also the (rather disappointing) study by D.J. Silver, *Maimonidean Criticism and the Maimonidean Controversy* (1965).

89. This is quite clear from the publication of the complete text by Marx in *JQR* 25 (1935): 414–428. The epistle is of particular value for an understanding of the religious atmosphere that facilitated the emergence of the Kabbalah in Spain; it has so far not been sufficiently taken into account.

trines of Maimonides on the resurrection of the dead, leaned toward the Kabbalah. Of Meir ben Todros Abulafia of Toledo (the family came from Burgos), who issued the call to arms in this combat, his nephew, himself one of the most eminent Castilian kabbalists after 1260, writes that he had "attained a hidden inner wisdom"—a phrase that for the writer certainly signified an initiation in the Kabbalah.[90] It is true that this tradition, in itself reliable, is not confirmed by the extant commentary of this author on the tractate *Sanhedrin.* At any rate he does not indulge in kabbalistic speculations, even in passages that were later interpreted mystically by all kabbalists.[91] But his brother, Joseph Abulafia, the father of the kabbalist, who lived in Burgos, refers in one of his letters written during the controversy of 1232 in a rather ambiguous manner to the "scholars of the Kabbalah." The expression could refer to the talmudic traditionalists, but also to the kabbalists as their commentators, upon whom we must rely when we are no longer able to understand the former. The precise meaning of the phrase is not clear, but it seems to have been deliberately formulated in such a manner that it could also be applied to the kabbalists in the new sense of the term. Since we know that it was just around this time that Burgos became an important kabbalistic center, it is not difficult to understand the passage in accordance with the following passage:

> You are not meant to weigh the foundations of religion on the scales of reason. . . . You should rather follow the traces of the visions of the prophets and their mysteries, and believe in the words and the riddles

---

90. Cf. Todros Abulafia, *'Oṣar ha-Kabhod* (1879), fol. 16d.

91. He would have had here, especially in connection with fol. 38 and in the entire tenth chapter of the tractate, abundant opportunity for alluding at least to his familiarity with mystical terminology. His use of the word Kabbalah is diametrically opposed to the esoteric usage. He often says that he wished to explain all questions of eschatology solely "according to the Kabbalah, which is widespread in all of Israel," that is, in conformity with the exoteric rabbinic tradition—the very opposite of the Kabbalah with which the mystics were concerned. His remark on the subject of the celestial Jerusalem (fol. 98b) would be difficult to understand coming from the mouth of one who possessed esoteric wisdom. He knows nothing, he says, of the location of this Jersualem and whether it is really the name of a degree in the celestial world, "and perhaps God will enlighten our eyes in order to explain the meaning of this doctrine." On the other hand he speaks of the incorporeality of God, determined by his infinity, in formulations that might also have been used by kabbalists (fol. 99b–c). The commentary on *Sanhedrin* was printed under the title *Yad Ramah* (Salonika, 1798).

> (allegories) of the scholars. And even where their words are closed and sealed, they are nevertheless inscribed in the writing of the truth [that is, perhaps: to be understood kabbalistically]. . . . For all their paths are paths of beauty and their discourses have a profound meaning, and what else can we do but rely upon the scholars of the Kabbalah whenever we do not understand the interpretation of their words, just as a blind man leans upon his guide, who leads him along the correct path. For all the plants of the scholars of the Kabbalah are a sowing of the truth and not empty words.[92]

We have already seen that Jonah Gerondi, the sharpest opponent of Maimonides, belonged to the kabbalistic circle although he (like the two Abulafias) left no kabbalistic writings.

The same applies to the other leader of the anti-Maimonidean party, Solomon ben Abraham of Montpellier. In the letters exchanged with him, Naḥmanides made use of an expression that in other places he reserves specifically for mystical knowledge: he therefore expected his correspondent to understand such phrases.[93] The most important evidence, however, is preserved, at least in fragments, in the polemical rejoinder by Abraham, the son of Maimonides, who still had before him two theological writings of Solomon of Montpellier and of the latter's disciple David ben Saul, probably of Narbonne.[94] The polemic directed by Abraham against these documents, which unfortunately he only quotes in incomplete and fragmentary extracts, nevertheless shows quite clearly, in all its bitterness, that both these writings represent esoteric and mystical doctrines similar to those found in the circle of the Rabad and, above all, reminiscent of the style and presentation current among the French and German Hasidim. The critical remarks concerning their alleged anthropomorphism apply equally to Eleazer of Worms and to the kabbalists. To characterize these anti-Maimonideans as inflexible and narrow-minded talmudists is therefore to fail to assess them correctly. That "the majority of the *ḥakhme ṣarfath,* with the excep-

---

92. *Qebuṣath Mikhtabhim,* 16.

93. Ibid., 54, where the wording suggests that Naḥmanides, who must indeed have known, counted Solomon of Montpellier among the *yod'e ḥen,* a term often used by him to designate the mystics. The anthropomorphic aggadoth are comprehensible, as he declares in his principal epistle in the course of the controversy, only to the *yod'e ḥen;* cf. *Qobeṣ Teshuboth ha-Ramban* (Leipzig, 1859), fol. 9d; similarly also on Genesis 46:1, and in his remarks on the soul in his halakhic work *Milḥamoth 'Adonai.*

94. Cf. I. Lévi in *REJ* 39 (1899): 241; [he is referred to also by D. J. Silver, *Maimonidean Criticism and the Maimonidean Controversy,* 160].

tion of Rashi, were addicted to anthropomorophism" is considered to have been a generally known fact during the Maimonidean controversy in 1232–1235.[95] The specific doctrines of these two Provençal scholars, at least as quoted by Abraham ben Maimonides, point clearly in this direction. It seems that they too had already combined the mysticism of the *kabhod* with the older form of Provençal Kabbalah. The passages are absolutely unambiguous in this regard, and one is only astonished to see how persistently they have been overlooked. Far from defending the literal sense of the anthropomorphist aggadoth, they rather point at their "true" esoteric sense.[96]

The esotericists and gnostics fought—and this is the paradox of the matter—against a spiritualization that they regarded as a danger to the living faith. Gnostic theosophy fulfilled the function of uniting a mystical conception of God with an unbroken faith in the values and ways of tradition, and in its concrete configurations. The aforementioned polemic of Jacob ben Shesheth against the spiritualization of prayer belongs to this same order of ideas. To the question what then was the dispute really all about we can answer that the philosophers wanted concepts whereas the mystics wanted symbols. The Maimonideans projected a contemplative picture of the world whose basic nature was allegorical and rational. Everything has meaning, but a meaning that is basically expressible. The kabbalists of Provence and Gerona, for their part, also developed a contemplative picture of the world, but one whose nature was symbolic and irrational. Allegory, the radical means of thought among the philosophers, is relegated to a secondary place. The first place is occupied by the great symbols of the divine life. Everything has meaning, but that meaning is inexpressible. A life without words and without concepts, a life that is in fact closed to them, finds its expression in the new symbolism. The struggle waged in a variety of

95. Cf. the epistle of Samuel ben Mordekhai, Ms. Neofiti 11, fol. 210b, also quoted by B. Dinur, *Yisra'el ba-Golah.*

96. Cf. the quotations in Abraham ben Maimonides, *Milḥamoth 'Adonai* (Hannover, 1867), 16, 20–21, above all 29–35. He reproaches them for speaking of esoteric matters without comprehending them. The conceptions relating to the *kabhod,* to its appearance in the west, over the throne, and before the curtain, exactly correspond to those in the esoteric writings of Eleazar of Worms. That his writings were known in Provence and Gerona cannot be doubted. Naḥmanides explicitly refers to them in his great epistle.

accents by the kabbalists of Gerona against the Maimonideans aimed at the destruction of an image of the world based upon allegorical immanence. The prayers and rituals of the Torah had to be preserved as symbols of the transcendence that erupts into our world, not as allegories of ideas inherent in the world, let alone as "methods of education" within the world. Gerona was thus no center of "enthusiasm" of the kind that, in Abraham Abulafia's teaching concerning the "prophetic Kabbalah," later invoked—paradoxically enough—the authority of Maimonides himself.[97] The voices speaking to us here are those of introvert contemplatives rather than of flaming ecstatics.

Symbols are born, in the last resort, of the memory of ecstatic moments of an inexpressible content. There is something wrenching and shattering about it. The kabbalists of Gerona attempted to contain the symbol within contemplation without permitting it to become pure allegory. This developing interest in the symbolic character of religious life led to the first great literary wave of mystical commentaries. The Bible, the aggadoth of the Talmud, the prescriptions of the Torah, and the prayers become mystical symbols of deeply hidden divine realities, whose expression in itself is inaccessible and denied to us. Seen in this way, Maimonides' *Guide* can at best only lead to the threshold of mysticism, but no further.

What has been said so far concerning the role of the kabbalists in the struggle over the philosophy of Maimonides is fully confirmed by the poems of Meshullam ben Solomon Dapiera. In medieval Hebrew, a high level of polemical writing was often composed in verse; its poetic merits may have been slight, but it rendered possible the pointed and vigorous formulation of controversial positions. Meshullam was one of the most gifted writers in this genre, and his poems (of which we now possess the entire collection) show him to have been an unusually skillful spokesman of the anti-Maimonidean party.[98] The author lived in Gerona and he also served for some time as head of the community. He maintained very close personal and spiritual contact with the circle of such kabbalists as Azriel, Ezra, and Naḥmanides, whom he considered his masters and spiritual

---

97. Cf. chap. 4 of my *Major Trends.*

98. Cf. the detailed discussion of this polemical poetry in D. T. Silver, *Maimonidean Criticism* (1965), 182–197, which is one of the few merits of this book.

guides. He made no secret of the fact that the Kabbalah was the positive ground on which he stood in his struggle against rationalist enlightenment. He derided the Maimonideans in witty verses in which he sought to expose the weaknesses of their position. But the kabbalistic doctrines themselves, which he manifestly opposes to them, are only for initiates who weigh their words and know how to keep silent. He had studied the secret science with Ezra and Azriel:

> Yes, my supports are Ezra and Azriel, who pour *kabbaloth* onto my hands.[99]

In a panegyric to the members of his circle he bemoans the death of the two "whose shields hang upon my walls." He stands on solid ground:

> The *'ephod* is in our midst; and why should we conjure the dead; in our hands the tablets are intact. The son of Naḥman is a firm refuge, his discourses are measured and do not gallop away recklessly. Ezra and Azriel and my other friends, who taught me knowledge without lying—they are my priests, the luminous stars of my night. They know number and measure for their Creator, but they guard themselves from speaking publicly of God's glory and they mind their words with a view to the heretics.[100]

His masters in mysticism taught him to keep silent; nevertheless, he mentions the mystical *kawwanah* of the prayers, the meditation in the profession of unity, the mystical reasons for precisely those commandments that were emphasized by the kabbalists of Gerona, and he alludes to the doctrine of the sefiroth.[101] Like Jacob ben Shesheth, he reproaches the rationalists for no longer knowing how to pray, and he defends the mystical character of those aggadoth that embarrassed them the most:

> Softly—you who find fault with the aggadoth! Perhaps they are mysteries, not to be discussed.[102]

---

99. In the editions of the poems by H. Brody in *Yedi'oth ha-Makhon le-Ḥeqer ha-Shirah* 4 (1938): 92.
100. Ibid., 104.
101. Ibid., 55, 56, 81, 109.
102. Ibid., 109 verse 17.

He defends the mystical anthropomorphism of the kabbalists, in whom he sees the true interpreters of eschatology and in particular of the concept of the "world of souls,"[103] as expounded in Naḥmanides' *Sha'ar ha-Gemul,* which became an authoritative rabbinic treatise on life after death and the first kabbalistic work to appear in print. (The printing was finished in Naples in January 1490.) These poems were written approximately in the thirties and forties and form a curious contrast, in their emphatically conservative attitude, to the contemporaneous attacks of Meir ben Simon. But the rationalists, thus attacked, later paid the kabbalists back in the same poetic coin, ridiculing the mysteries that Naḥmanides had introduced into his commentary on the Torah and accusing him of lacking a scientific education and of clerical arrogance.[104] He had covered his nakedness by escaping into the Kabbalah, where he could easily surround everything with an esoteric veil.[105] These and similar statements were, however, made mainly after Naḥmanides' death, though even in his lifetime the heat of the Maimonidean battle did not fail to produce attacks. This is proved by Naḥmanides' defense of himself (prior to 1244) against the criticisms of R. Meshullam ben Moses.[106] As a general rule, however, the towering authority of Naḥmanides was much too great for critics to dare to venture forth during his lifetime.

We have sketched in broad strokes the climate in which the Kabbalah in Gerona developed into an important factor in Judaism. Naturally enough, one also looked for allies and, if possible, for authorities whom the esoteric tradition could invoke without having to resort to pseudepigraphy. Thus, Yehudah Halevi, whose *Kuzari* was

103. Ibid., 18, 34, 41, 91.

104. Cf. the poem in *He-Ḥalutz* 2 (1853): 162, and in my *Reshith ha-Qabbala,* 154.

105. Schiller-Szinessy, *Catalogue of the Hebrew Manuscripts in Cambridge* (1876), 182. The two passages are taken from the polemic of Zachariah ben Moses Cohen. Around 1290, Zeraḥyah ben Isaac of Barcelona uttered more criticisms of Naḥmanides; cf. *'Oṣar Neḥmad* 2 (1857): 124–125. He accused him of having mixed up the opinions of the philosophers with those of the talmudists, thereby causing much confusion, whereas in reality not even a beginner in philosophy would have had any difficulty resolving the problems that so vexed Naḥmanides.

106. Meshullam was undoubtedly an opponent of the Kabbalah; see above, p. 397. Cf. also A. Shohat in *Zion* 36 (1971): 54, and Halbertstam's collection of letters, 71 (in Kobak's *Jeschurun* 8 [1875]: 119). As regards 1244 as the terminus ante quem, I have followed Shohat, 54.

often quoted in this circle,[107] rose to the rank of an adept; and Naḥmanides believed he had discovered here and there in the allusions to certain "secrets" made by Abraham ibn Ezra in his commentary on the Torah signs of his familiarity with the "proper Kabbalah."[108] The Neoplatonic mentality of these authors facilitated their adoption by the kabbalists, even though the freethinking tendencies of ibn Ezra aroused lively objections. It is not unlikely that other, possibly unknown texts of an earlier period of which the oldest kabbalists had no knowledge somehow reached Gerona. There is at least one piece of evidence for this. Naḥmanides quotes (in writings dating from his later period, the 1250s and 1260s) the apocryphal Wisdom of Solomon, which he had before him in "an Aramaic difficult to understand"; but his text, as is clear, was none other than the Syriac version of the Peshitta transcribed into Hebrew characters.[109] Naḥmanides knew that the book existed in a Latin translation; he expressly declared that it was not inspired, although he did not doubt its authenticity. This "literary and historical fact" misled Neumark to far-reaching conclusions.[110] He considers the influence

---

107. Naḥmanides in his commentary on Job (preface and on 32:2), as well as Azriel in *Sha'ar ha-Sho'el,* uses a formula taken from *Kuzari* 1:77. Ezra, in his commentary on the Song of Songs, fol. 4a, and in the *Perush 'Aggadoth* quotes *Kuzari* 1:109 and 4:25 without naming the source; in his letter to R. Abraham on the other hand he makes explicit mention of the book and quotes its explanation of the sacrifices (2:26), which he then proceeds to reinterpret mystically. Jacob ben Shesheth quotes *Kuzari* 1:103 in his *Meshibh,* Ms. Oxford, fol. 17b. Joseph Perl, "Über den Geist des Commentars des R. Moses ben Nachman zum Pentateuch," *MGWJ* 7 (1858): 153, already demonstrated its frequent use in Naḥmanides' commentary on the Torah.

108. Thus he finds fault with the "secrets" of ibn Ezra presented for Genesis 24:1, but praises those given for Exodus 29:46, (*Sha'ar ha-Gemul* [Ferrara, 1556], fol. 18a); cf. above all his sermon on the Torah, 28, where he comments as follows on ibn Ezra's remark on Leviticus 25:2: "In all his books, nothing better indicates his good Kabbalah than this passage." Since he speaks here of a decidedly kabbalistic doctrine, namely that relating to the cosmic *yobel,* of which he finds an indication in ibn Ezra, the term Kabbalah is doubtless used here in its new technical sense and not simply in that of tradition.

109. In the preface to the commentary on the Torah he quotes two texts from the *Sapientia Salomonis,* chap. 7. He also mentions the book in his sermon on the Torah, 22, and in that on *Qoheleth,* 9. The last passage is especially interesting, for it seems to prove that he had the complete book before him. N. H. Wessely was aware of the nature of this quotation by Naḥmanides when he appealed to the authority of the latter on the title page of his retranslation of the book into Hebrew (*Sefer Ḥokhmath Shelomo* [Berlin, 1780]).

110. D. Neumark, *Geschichte der Jüdischen Philosophie* 2, first half: 372.

of this text upon the Kabbalah to be self-evident and even speaks of an "intimate relationship between the conception of the world, or rather the philosophy of history, of this text, and the aforementioned [kabbalistic] systems." And "if Naḥmanides saw it, it stands to reason that also all the other Jewish philosophers and kabbalists had likewise seen it." But this is precisely what would have to be proved first. A manuscript that contained this text and perhaps others as well, transcribed from Syriac into Hebrew characters, apparently arrived in Gerona around 1250 from Palestine, probably from Acre—but only decades after the death of Ezra and Azriel and other kabbalists of this circle. There is not the slightest evidence that the speculations of this book concerning wisdom in any way influenced the subsequent evolution of the kabbalistic doctrine of the Sophia. There is no reason to assume that the book was already known in Provence, or that Azriel's ideas, insofar as they are new, can be traced back to it. The author of the *Zohar* did indeed know, through Naḥmanides, of the title of this work, but he no longer had any knowledge of its contents and, like Jean Paul's schoolmaster Wutz, invents quotations that he thought might have figured in it.[111] The appearance of this manuscript is thus a curiosity in the history of literature rather than of any significance for the real history of the Kabbalah.

The Kabbalah appeared in Gerona in the fully elaborated form of a contemplative mysticism that sought to draw all domains of Jewish existence into its sphere of influence and to embue them with its spirit. With its doctrines of *debhequth* as the highest value of the contemplative life and of *kawwanah,* the inner concentration and meditation that accompanies prayer and the performance of the commandments, this mysticism is very different from the free-ranging type of spiritualist tendencies that seek to establish a direct communication, without intermediary stages, between man and the infinite. In the form it now assumed, the Kabbalah tied this roaming spirituality to the world of human action by means of mystical symbols that light up in all areas and that refer everything terrestrial back to the world of the deity as manifested in the sefiroth. It sets

111. Cf. A. Marx in *JBL* 40 (1921): 57–69. The assertions to the contrary of Joshua Finkel (in *Leo Jung Jubilee Volume* [1962], 77–103) are based on utterly fantastic "interpretations" of *Zoharic* passages and cannot be taken seriously. Cf. herein, p. 6, n. 1.

up a ladder for the elevation of meditative spirits, avoiding the perilous leaps of those who plunge unprepared and undisciplined into the sea of contemplation.

It is precisely in this respect that the efficacy of the Kabbalah as a conservative force becomes particularly clear, notwithstanding its profound links with those forces that aimed at a spiritualization of concrete Judaism. If not perhaps in its historical consciousness then at least by virtue of its function it stood at a crossroads. It could, to a certain extent, attract many Maimonideans by means of one element common to the two camps, namely the doctrine of mystical *debhequth,* which is not absent from *The Guide of the Perplexed.* On the other hand, it could attract more conservative forces through its indefatigable struggle on behalf of the authority of tradition and its gnostic defense of the faith of the simple Jew—notwithstanding the dialectics implicit in such a defense. This explains why some kabbalists seized on the mystical possibilities they found in certain points of Maimonides' doctrine. Others, for their part, preferred to separate the world of esotericism completely from that of philosophic speculation and to link the former to the old symbols of the Aggadah.

This demarcation, vis-à-vis both sides, is well expressed in a pseudepigraphic statement attributed to Maimonides by an author writing around 1230.

> "He cannot trust his own servants" [Job 4:18]—these are the philosophers to whom he did not confide the secret of his reality. "And the heavens are not guiltless in his sight" [Job 15:15]—these are the ascetics *(perushim)* who seek solitude in the deserts; they too are not pure enough in his eyes to have the mysteries of his divinity and the secret of his cycle revealed to them.[112]

As far as we are able to judge, there were no connections between the kabbalists and the desert ascetics of Asia or Africa, but they definitely had links with the groups of *perushim* and Hasidim in the smaller and larger cities of France (see p. 229ff). It is precisely in these links that the Kabbalah, embarking on its journey through history, found the strength to combat the philosophic rationalism anchored in another social stratum represented and supported by

112. For this Pseudo-Maimonides see Moses Taku, *Ketab Tamim,* in *'Oṣar Neḥmad* 3:66. The verse quoted is, in fact, a conflation of two verses.

the courts of the powerful, the tax farmers, and other wealthy groups connected with them, as the research of Yitzhak F. Baer in *A History of the Jews in Christian Spain* (1961) has so convincingly shown. This social stratum, in which the inclination toward adopting of foreign ways of life and toward indifference with regard to the traditional law gained strength, also included a considerable number of physicians and astronomers. Above all Gerona, but also Burgos and Toledo, in spite of their being strongholds of rationalism, harbored concentrations of the conservative forces in this controversy that soon manifested themselves in other centers as well, such as Saragossa and Barcelona.

3. *Elevation Through* Kawwanah: *The Nothing and the* Ḥokhmah

Turning now to the conceptions of the kabbalists of Gerona, we can emphasize in the present context only a few particularly important points that illustrate the contribution made by this group to the crystallization of the Kabbalah. It will not be possible for us to discuss in detail the intensive elaboration of mystical symbolism that united the world of the sefiroth and the terrestrial and created order with increasing insistence. It was most probably in Gerona that there began to develop the literary genre that consisted of small and extremely brief tracts in which the symbols representing the ten sefiroth were systematized for every single sefirah. Most of these tracts, stemming from the earliest period and preserved in numerous manuscripts, are anonymous.[113] They show that the framework of this symbolism could be filled in very different ways and that many symbols were still in a state of flux. This is true not only of the three supreme sefiroth, though there it is particularly evident, but for all of them. On this subject there must have been considerable differences even among the kabbalists of Gerona—as is evident from a comparison, for example, of Azriel's symbolism of the sefiroth with that of Jacob ben Shesheth or Naḥmanides.

The most important contribution made in this circle to the

113. I published a bibliography of these treatises on the ten sefiroth in *Kiryath Sefer* 10 (1934): 498–515.

deepening of the essentials of the kabbalistic speculation came from Azriel. His decisive contribution relates to what might be called the ontology rather than the anthropology of the Kabbalah. On the latter subject the kabbalists were substantially in accord, since they saw in man the sum of all the powers of Creation, which, for their part, were also the powers of the deity. It was the reflected radiance of these powers that they sought to uncover by an active life lived in accordance with the Torah. Man, in whom all sefirotic being is mirrored, is at the same time the transformer by means of which these powers are led back to their source.[114] All things egress from the One and return to the One, according to the formula borrowed from the Neoplatonists; but this movement has its goal and turning point in man when, turning inward, he begins to recognize his own being and from the multiplicity of his nature strives to return to the unity of his origin. No matter how the coming forth of the creature from God is conceived, there is no doubt here concerning the manner of its return. It is accomplished in the elevation of the *kawwanah,* in the introversion of the will that, instead of spending itself in multiplicity, "collects" and concentrates itself and, purifying itself of all selfishness, attaches itself to the will of God, that is, joins the "lower will" to the "higher will." The commandments and their fulfillment are the vehicles of this movement of return to God. Inherent in them is a spiritual element of which man can and must take hold and through which he is joined to the sphere of the divine. For the commandments, in their spiritual element, are themselves part of the divine *kabhod.*[115]

We have seen in the previous chapter how the Provençal kabbalists already posited a precise parallelism between the mysticism of sacrifice and that of prayer. The divine "hearing" or "answering" of prayer, like the "acceptance" of sacrifice, indicates that the divine irrupts into the sphere of the human will, where the latter attaches itself to the divine. The two motifs of the abolition of personal will and its invigoration precisely by virtue of this abolition

114. "Man comprises all spiritual things (or words)" is a frequently recurring formula; for example, Ezra's *Commentary on the Song of Songs,* fol. 11b; Azriel, ed. Tishby, 5; Ezra in *Sod ha-Da'ath,* Ms. Christ Church College 198, fol. 7b. Moses de Leon *(Perush ha-Sefiroth)* still repeats this formula. Cf. also pp. 277–278, herein.

115. Azriel on the *'Aggadoth,* 38. Ezra says (*Commentary on the Song of Songs,* fol. 11a): "The accomplishment of the commandment is itself light of life," that is, a manifestation of the *kabhod* that inhabits it.

and self-abandonment, which appear to contradict one another, are juxtaposed and interpenetrate each other in the idea of *debhequth.* Azriel gave the clearest expression of this thought: "He who prays must cast off everything that obstructs him and disturbs him, and must lead the world back to its origin—literally to its Nought."[116] But if he brings the words to the limit of the Nought, their being does not thereby suffer any absolute interruption. Rather it renews itself and draws from this contact with its origin "the power for its own existence." The *debhequth* of man to God does not, therefore, erase the boundaries between Creator and creature but preserves them in this particular form of communion.

How far removed this conception was from the pantheistic identification of the human and the divine is shown most impressively in a text entitled "Chapter on the *kawwanah,* by the ancient kabbalists" that is found anonymously in many manuscripts but whose author is to be sought in Azriel's closest circle. It is my conviction that Azriel himself is the author, to judge by the style as well as the thought. This brief text gives a very precise and valuable description of what takes place in the *kawwanah.* The completeness and precision of expression are unrivaled in the literature of the Kabbalah; we doubtless owe these qualities to the fact that the author wished to describe the magic of the *kawwanah*—but at the same time also described, to a great extent, its mystical nature. The relationship between these two attitudes of prayer emerges here, in fact, with a rare clarity and penetration. The mystical conformity of the will is visibly transformed into a magical one, the roots of which, it must not be forgotten, reach back further than the Kabbalah. The magical nuance in the conformity of the will is already adumbrated in the famous dictum in the Mishnah tractate known as *The Sayings of the Fathers.* Rabban Gamaliel, the son of Yehudah ha-Nasi, used to say: "Make His will as your will in order that He make your will as His will. Abolish your will before His will, in order that He abolish the will of others before your will."[117] Here is a complete translation of the aforementioned kabbalistic tract, remarkable for its combination of the theory of *kawwanah* with the symbolism of light and the meditation on the degrees of different lights:

---

116. In Azriel's theses on prayer, section 9, Gulak and Klein memorial volume, 215.

117. *M. 'Aboth* 2:4.

He who resolves upon something in his mind with a perfect firmness, for him it becomes the essential thing. Therefore if you pray and pronounce the benedictions or otherwise truly wish to direct the *kawwanah* to something, imagine that you are light and that everything around you is light, light from every direction and every side; and in the light a throne of light, and, on it, a "brilliant light,"[118] and opposite it a throne and, on it, a "good light."[119] And if you stand between them and desire vengeance, turn to the "brilliance"; and if you desire love, turn to the "good," and what comes from your lips should be turned towards its face. And turn toward the right, and you will find "shining light,"[120] toward the left and you will find an aura, which is the "radiant light."[121] And between them and above them the light of the *kabhod,* and around it the light of life. And above it the crown of light that crowns the desires of the thoughts, that lights up the path of the representations and illuminates the brilliance of the visions. And this illumination is unfathomable and infinite, and from its perfect glory proceed grace and benediction, peace and life for those who observe the path of its unification. But to those who deviate from its path comes the light that is hidden and transformed from one thing into its opposite, [and it sometimes appears to him] as a chastisement and [sometimes] as right guidance,[122] everything according to the *kawwanah* of him who knows how to accomplish it in the right manner: through cleaving, *debhequth,* to the thought and the will that emanates in its full force from the unfathomable. For according to the intensity of the *kawwanah,* with which it draws strength to itself through its will, and will through its knowledge, and representation through its thought, and power through its reaching [to the primordial source of the will] and firmness through its contemplation, if no other reflection or desire is mixed in it, and if it grows in intensity through the power that guides it, in order to draw to itself the current that proceeds from *'en-sof*—[according to the measure of such an intensity of the *kawwanah*] every thing and every act is accomplished according to its spirit and its will, if only it knows to embrace the limits of the finite things and of the will that inhabits their thought from the principle

118. *'Or nogah,* according to Proverbs 4:18. Later passages in Azriel's text suggest that the reference is to the "brilliance of light" mentioned in the vision of the Merkabah, Ezekiel 1:4, possibly already with the nuance it has in the kabbalistic commentaries on this verse. In *nogah,* grace and judgment are combined. The *'Iyyun* writings know a "throne of the *nogah*" as one of the potencies of the Merkabah-world.

119. The absolutely good light, of which Genesis 1:4 speaks.

120. *'Or bahir,* according to Job 37:21. The differences of degree that the author had in mind are no longer known to us. In the old literature, above all in Saadya Gaon, the primordial light of Genesis 1:4 is itself the *'or bahir.*

121. *'Or mazhir* is, in the literature of the *'Iyyun* circle, a sort of astral light in which the prophetic visions appear; cf. here two sentences further on the light that "illuminates the splendor of the visions." Cf. also the text on this light in the commentary on the Merkabah by Jacob ben Jacob Cohen.

122. I understand *yosher* here in the sense of *haysharah,* the path to beatitude, as opposed to *tokhaḥoth mussar,* the trials of one who departs from the right way.

from which they derive. Then, it must elevate itself above them through the power of its *kawwanah* and go into the depths in order to destroy the [ordinary] path from its very principle and to pave a new way according to his own will: through the power of his *kawwanah,* which stems from the perfect glory of the withdrawing light,[123] which has neither figure nor image, neither measure nor size, neither evaluation nor limit, neither end nor foundation nor number, and which is in no respect finite. And he who elevates himself in such a manner, from word to word, through the power of his intention, until he arrives at *'en-sof,* must direct his *kawwanah* in a manner corresponding to his perfection, so that the higher will is clothed in his will, and not only so that his will is clothed in the higher will. For the effluence [of the emanation proceeding from the divine will] is like the inexhaustible source that is never interrupted only if, in approaching the higher will, it carefully watches that the higher will is clothed in the will of its aspiration. Then, when the higher will and the lower will, in their indistinctness and in their *debhequth* to the [divine] unity, become one, the effluence pours forth according to the measure of its perfection. But the perfection of the lower will cannot take place if it approaches [the higher will] for its own need, but only if it approaches it [the higher will] and if it clothes itself in the will through which enough of the nondistinctness[124] is manifested, which is [otherwise] concealed in the most hidden mystery. And if it approaches it in this manner, the higher will also approaches it and grants to its power firmness and to its will the impulse to perfect and execute everything, even if it be according to the will of its soul,[125] in which the higher will has no part. And this is what the verse [Prov. 11:27] says: "He who earnestly seeks what is good pursues what is pleasing [literally: the will]." For as far as the will clings to an object that corresponds to the higher will, the impulse [of the divine will] is clothed in it and is attracted, following its own [human] will, toward every object for which it exerts itself with the power of its *kawwanah.* And it draws down the effluence, which crowns the secrets of the things [126] and essences through the path of the *ḥokhmah* and with the spirit of the *binah* and with the firmness of *da'ath.*[127] And in the measure that it is clothed with the spirit and explains its *kawwanah* through its words and fixes a visible sign through its actions, it draws the effluence from power to power and from cause to cause, until its actions are con-

---

123. Here, therefore, the "perfect glory" and the "withdrawing light" that appeared above in a certain contrast to one another are united in a single notion.

124. On this notion of *hashwa'ah* cf. p. 439, herein.

125. The expression "will of the soul" occurs elsewhere in Azriel, for example, *Perush ha-'Aggadoth,* 104, and the *Commentary on the Sefiroth* (though in the latter text the modi, such as good and evil, are still undifferentiated and dwell together).

126. The Hebrew term *ḥefeṣ* is used here, indifferently, in its three acceptations: aspiration, impulse of the will, and object.

127. These three sefiroth designate the stages of the emergence of the essences of all things from the mystical Nought even prior to "Wisdom." Concealed in the Wisdom of God, they are manifested in his thought, and take shape in his knowledge.

> cluded in the sense of its will. In this manner the ancients used to spend some time in meditation,[128] before prayer, and to divert all other thoughts and to determine the paths of their *kawwanah* [during the subsequent prayer] and the power that was to be applied to its direction. And similarly [also] some time during prayer, in order to realize the *kawwanah* in the articulated speech. And similarly some time after prayer, in order to meditate on how they could also direct the power of the *kawwanah,* which came to its conclusion in the speech, in the paths of visible action. And since they were truly pious men, Hasidim, their Torah became action and their work was blessed.[129] And this is the path among the paths of prophecy, upon which he who makes himself familiar with it will be capable of rising to the rank of prophecy.[130]

The true *kawwanah* described in this text is therefore identical with the path of prophecy, which passes through the realization of the perfect *debhequth* with God, that is, the cleaving of human thought and will to the thought and will of God. To this corresponds Azriel's analysis of prayer in his commentary on the aggadoth, where the dictim of the Mishnah on the subject of the old Hasidim and their habits of prayer is interpreted in a similar manner, and a parallel is established with prophecy.[131] The illumination, which is to be obtained through *debhequth,* can therefore be distinguished from prophecy only by its degree and not by its nature. The prophet is here, as so often in medieval thought, none other than the perfect mystic.

Azriel's views on mystical prayer, remarkable for their conciseness, are then applied to the statutory prayers, the prayer of the eighteen benedictions (the *'Amidah*), and the profession of unity (the *Shema'*).[132] According to him the *'Amidah* contains three kinds of petitions: those that concern the well-being and needs of the body, those relating to the well-being and needs of the soul, and those dealing with the needs of the life of the soul, which is nothing other than the spiritual life of the future world itself. It is, of course, in this

---

128. Thus in *M. Berakhoth* 5:1 on the "early Hasidim."

129. Thus, in the same connection, the talmudic passage *Berakhoth* 32b.

130. I first published the Hebrew text in *MGWJ* 78 (1934): 511–512, but at the time I did not yet recognize the authorship of Azriel (whose characteristic terminology is evident in almost every line) and therefore dated the piece much too late. The bombastic Hebrew style suggests a close relationship with the language of the *'Iyyun* writings.

131. Cf. *Perush 'Aggadoth,* ed. Tishby, 40.

132. See n. 24, herein, the reference to G. Sed-Rajna's monograph.

last stratum that the mystical meaning of the prayers is disclosed. But there are various attitudes with regard to prayer itself corresponding to the three principles of all reality, which Azriel borrowed from the metaphysics of Aristotle while giving them a mystical twist. These three principles are matter, form, and *steresis;* this last notion is, however, influenced by the Hebrew translation and replaced by the principle of Nought.[133] The change of matter into ever-new forms takes place by means of this Nought, which can be made to refer on the one hand—and entirely in the sense of the genuine Aristotelian doctrine—to the privation of that which, in the transformations, is new each time, and, on the other hand—in the sense of the kabbalists—to the influence of the sefirotic principle of Stern Judgment. In either case this notion can link up with that of the mystical Nought, from which everything creative proceeds.

For Azriel, these principles present themselves essentially as follows: the Nought is that which is present in everything that arises as the medium of its transformation. The sefirah of Stern Judgment and delimitation is at the same time the power of transformation inherent in things. Matter, on the other hand, persists in itself and is renewed without being transformed, like the living stream whose waters are renewed every minute but nevertheless are always the same. This power comes, according to Azriel, from the sefirah of Mercy, by means of which God renews and preserves at the same time, every day, his Creation. However, according to him, form is a potency inherent in matter, by virtue of which matter receives an influx of ever-new forms. It is similar to the source from which the pool expands.

Accordingly there exist three degrees of prayer in which these three principles are reflected. The lowest is prayer without spirituality, the prayer that is not pervaded by the life of the soul flowing from the source of *binah.* This, according to Azriel, is the "fixed prayer" mentioned in and rejected by the Mishnah (*Berakhoth*

---

133. Thus in Abraham bar Ḥiyya, *Megillath ha-Megalleh* (1924), 5, in whose Nought, *'efess,* it is already difficult to recognize the Aristotelian *steresis:* "When in the pure Thought there arose [the idea] to bring matter, form, and the Nought into reality, he made the Nought ascend from them and united the form with matter, and thus was born the substance of the world." The idea is found in an authentically Aristotelian context in Al-Ḥarizi's translation of the *Moreh* 1:17. The Tibbonite translation of *steresis* by *he'ader* (literally: *privatio*) does not lend itself to a mystical reinterpretation of this kind.

14:2), because it is like the stagnant water of a pool into which no life flows from any source. Above it, there is the prayer that the Mishnah defines as the "imploring of grace," *taḥanunim,* in which the vitality of the source gushes forth with great force. This is the prayer of the "form." The highest prayer, however, is that of the devotee who casts off everything that impedes him and who leads the word whose origin is in the Nought back to its Nought. Here, we can easily follow the transformation of the concept of the Nought or Nothing into a mystical category. This prayer is named *tefillah,* in the proper sense of the Hebrew term, which the author derives from *pillul,* "judgment." So too must the prayer rise from the petition for the fulfillment of bodily needs to that of the needs of the soul, and from there to the pure spirituality of the life of the future world.

Here we see very clearly how the mystics took up philosophic concepts and transformed them to suit their purposes. Already Ezra related the "very good" in Genesis 1:31 to the *communio* of all things with the Nought *('ayin),* this communion being precisely the true principle of the good and at the same time the "Cause of the renewal of the generations."[134] The source of this idea apparently lies in Yehudah Al-Ḥarizi's translation of Maimonides' *Guide,* which was widely used by the kabbalists of Gerona. "All good and evil," it is said there (*Guide* 3:10),

> has only the reality of privations [literally: noughts] . . . and thus he [the Creator] had called matter, according to its nature, to reality, this nature resting upon its [matter's] permanent link with the Nought. And this is why the Torah says [Gen. 1:31]: "He saw, and behold: very good"; even the reality of this lower matter, according to its nature, which comes from its link with the Nought, which causes death and all evil—all this is good for the existence and the duration of the real, despite the transformation which occurs in the accidents.

From Al-Ḥarizi's and Maimonides' philosophic interpretation of the Bible it was only a step to the mystical misunderstanding of the terminology employed there; and thus arose the kabbalistic interpre-

---

134. Cf. Ezra's *Commentary on the Song of Songs,* fol. 27a, according to the better version of the manuscripts. The concept of generations, *doroth,* is interpreted in Azriel's *Commentary on the Prayers,* Ms. Oxford 1938, fol. 223a, with reference to the Romance translation, *generaciones,* as meaning the primordial depths of becoming, "the supreme causes of everything temporal."

tation, according to which the world is perpetually renewed by the goodness of God, which is realized in a permanent contact of reality with the Nought, conceived here as the highest potency. But this misinterpretation was only possible because the kabbalists had already read their texts with the eyes of Neoplatonic mystics for whom "creation out of nothing" had already evolved from an orthodox theologoumenon to a mystical paradox. This leads us to the symbolic style of expression by which Azriel, more than any other member of his circle, dealt with the question of the origin of Creation.

It is already possible, today, to follow clearly the history of the reinterpretation of the orthodox theological formula of a creation ex nihilo in the direction of the Neoplatonic doctrine of emanation, as a creation out of the indeterminate being or nature of God himself, which precisely for that reason can also be called Nought.[135] It can be shown that this kind of reinterpretation took place at almost the same time in all three monotheistic religions. In Christian thought it can be found in the doctrine of Scotus Erigena concerning God's descent to the primordial origins and depths of all things, which is none other than his descent into his own Nought, whence everything stems. "But when he descends to the primordial depths of things, He begins, creating Himself in this manner, as it were, to be a something." For it is not, in fact, out of nought in the usual sense of the term that God created the world, but from a Nought that he is Himself, the Nought of the superessentiality of the divine goodness. Maimonides' aforementioned Aristotelian interpretation of the biblical "very good" in the account of Creation comes surprisingly close to Scotus Erigena's definition, the sources of which must be sought in the totally different world of the Neoplatonic mysticism of Dionysius the Areopagite. The same reinterpretation appears simultaneously in Isaac Israeli, the Jewish Neoplatonist in North Africa, and among the Ismailites, the Neoplatonic mystics of Shiite Islam. Always, it is either God Himself or one of his determinations that, in its all-embracing void, is designated as Nought and interpreted as

135. Cf. Harry A. Wolfson, "The Meaning of ex nihilo in the Church Fathers, Arabic and Hebrew Philosophy, and St. Thomas," *Mediaeval Studies in Honor of J.D.M. Ford* (1948), 350–370, reprinted in H.A. Wolfson, "The Meaning of ex nihilo in Isaac Israeli," *JQR* 50 (1959): 1–12; G. Scholem, "Schöpfung aus Nichts und Selbstverschränkung Gottes," in *Über einige Grundbegriffe des Judentums* (Frankfurt, 1970), 53–89; Jürgen von Kempski, "Die Schöpfung aus Nichts," in *Merkur,* vol. 14 (Munich, 1960), 1107–1126.

such, albeit with all kinds of qualifications as *causa materialis* of the Creation.

The kabbalists therefore were not the first to equate creation and emanation. It is still not possible to say with certainty whether it was under the influence of Israeli or Erigena that the kabbalistic terminology of the Nought, which we already encountered in the preceding chapter, evolved. To be sure, many elements in the language of the kabbalists argue in favor of a dependence on Erigena, especially Azriel's use of a Hebrew equivalent of the term "superbeing" of God. Azriel's Hebrew term is more likely than not an awkward rendering of Erigena's Latin *superesse* and cannot be explained on the basis of any Arabic terminology.[136] A determination of the supreme being as higher than anything that can be counted and therefore higher than the sefiroth (as primordial numbers), that is, as the "absolute Nought," is also found in Naḥmanides' commentary on *Yeṣirah* 1:7. The context there leaves no doubt that he is not speaking of the Nought of the philosophers but of the deity itself, or at best the first sefirah.[137] Creation out of nothing in the kabbalistic sense therefore represents the transition from this *superesse* of God, which is at the same time his Nought, to the archetypal being of his Wisdom. This definition was generally adopted in kabbalistic literature, mainly through the Gerona circle. The orthodox formula masks a point of esoteric doctrine. Azriel writes:

> "If someone asks you: What is God? answer: He who is in no way deficient. If he asks you: Does anything exist outside of him? answer: Nothing exists outside of Him. If he asks you: How did He bring forth Being from Nought, for there is a great difference between Being and Nought? answer: He who brings forth Being from Nought is thereby lacking in nothing, for the Being is in the Nought after the manner of the Nought, and the Nought is in the Being after the manner [according to the modality] of the Being.[138] And of this the author

---

136. Hebrew: *yather min ha-kol,* in the Gulak and Klein memorial volume, 207. *Yithron* is used in the same sense, also ibid., 208, and in section 8 of the *Sha'ar ha-Sho'el.*

137. Cf. *Kiryath Sefer* 6 (1928/1929): 404, 408.

138. This remarkable sentence is doubtlessly modeled after the similar formulation in the *Liber de Causis,* a Neoplatonic text, that was probably known to the kabbalists in an early translation. It is said there in section 11, ed. Bardenhewer: "the effect is in the cause in the manner of the cause, and the cause is in the effect in the manner of the effect." Azriel applied this thesis to the relation between Being and Nought.

> of the Book *Yeṣirah* said: He made his Nought into his Being, and he did not say: He made the Being from the Nought.[139] This teaches us that the Nought is the Being and the Being is the Nought. However, the Nought is called "bearer" *('omen).* But the place at which the Being is linked to the point where, from the Nought, it begins to have existence is called "faith" *('emunah).* For faith is not related to a visible and apprehensible Being, nor to the invisible and unknowable Nought, but precisely to the place where the Nought is connected to Being. For Being does not stem from the Nought alone; Being and Nought together represent that which is meant when the phrase "Being from Nought" is used. Being is therefore nothing but a Nought, and everything is one in the simplicity of the absolute indistinctness and it is to this that the warning refers [Eccles. 7:16]:[140] Do not take on too much in your speculation, for our finite intellect cannot grasp the perfection of the Impenetrable which is one with *'en-sof.*[141]

It is interesting to observe that precisely the decisive sentences of this passage on the Being and the Nought were quoted without a word of polemic or criticism by Johannes Reuchlin, a great admirer of Nicholas of Cusa, in the first fairly accurate Latin account of the Kabbalah. To be sure, Reuchlin did not know who was the author of this quotation, which was undoubtedly close to his own way of thinking. Being and Nought therefore are only different aspects of the *superesse* of the divine reality. There is a Nought of God that gives birth to being, and there is a being of God that represents the Nought. There is one manner in which things exist in the Nought of God; and a very different manner in which they exist in his being. Yet both are modalities of *'en-sof* itself that constitute the indistinct unity of "Ought" and of "Nought."

Azriel uses the same passage of *Yeṣirah* 2:6, which deals with creation ex nihilo in the literal sense, in order to read his own mystical conception into the text. The passage says, literally, "He fashioned from the *tohu* the real and made what-is-not into what-is." The words *'asah 'eno yeshno* could signify equally well "he made the nonexistent into an existent," without the nature of this nonexistent being in any way prejudged—indeed, this determination could also apply to the primordial matter of Platonists—as also: He made the

---

139. For the explanation of this sentence, see below.

140. The verse is translated here in the sense in which the kabbalists interpret it.

141. Cf. the Hebrew text in the Gulak and Klein memorial volume, 207.

Nought into Ought. Azriel, however, took advantage of the particular structure of the Hebrew sentence, where *'eno,* "it is not," can also be understood as a possessive pronoun: "his Nought." He thus states that God made his Nought into a being, and Being and Nought are defined as two different aspects of the divine itself. The nought is not THE Nought, independent of God, but HIS nought. The transformation of the nought into being is an event occurring in God himself; it is, as Azriel understands it, the act through which the divine wisdom is manifested. Nought and Being are both merely aspects of the one undifferentiated *superesse.*[142]

Naḥmanides, in his commentary on the Torah, disguised the same idea so skillfully and, to all appearances, so deliberately mixed the exoteric with the esoteric, that the reader fails to notice how much his description was in accord with the doctrine of the origin of the *ḥokhmah* from the mystical Nought. As a matter of fact, he expounds his doctrine, to which he also alludes in other passages, in the specifically exoteric part of his interpretation, without clearly isolating the kabbalistic element or defining the kabbalistic meaning hidden behind the plain words. This led many authors to the fantastic error of asserting that on the subject of creation Naḥmanides' views were diametrically opposed to those of the kabbalists.[143] Obviously everything sounds different in the context of nonkabbalistic discourse, and any kabbalist would undoubtedly offer to the uninitiated exactly the same traditional version of the theory of creation ex nihilo that Naḥmanides also gives in the passage in question. The choice of words and images, however, as well as a brief but highly significant kabbalistic observation at the beginning of his remarks on Genesis 1:1 indicate that he had in mind an esoteric theory that more or less coincides with, or at least comes very close to, that expounded by Azriel and Jacob ben Shesheth. Without entering into the details of the kabbalistic understanding of the first verse of the Torah, Naḥmanides declares that the word *bereshith* alludes to

---

142. Jacob ben Shesheth speaks of the Nought in the same spirit; cf. *Meshibh* chap. 19, fol. 52b, as well as *'Emunah u-Biṭṭaḥon,* chap. 12.

143. Thus, for example, B. M. Ehrenpreis, *Emanationslehre,* 32, and M. Grajwer, *Die kabbalistischen Lebren des Moses ben Nachman in seinem Kommentar zum Pentateuch* (Breslau, 1933), 31–36. The latter work is utterly inadequate and absolutely wrong on essential points. The kabbalistic passages in Naḥmanides require an altogether different interpretation, for which it is necessary to take into account the entire literature of this circle.

the *ḥokhmah,* in which lies the foundation (in Hebrew also: the element) of the entire subject of creation, as it is written (Prov. 3:19): "The Lord founded the earth by *ḥokhmah."* At the end of his exposition he again emphasizes that Genesis 1:1 has a kabbalistic meaning: "It speaks of that which is below and makes allusion to that which is above," and that *ḥokhmah* is the "beginning of the beginnings," the foundation or the element of all creation.

In the course of his exposition, however, he explains that God created in the beginning from the absolute Nought, as also indicated by the verb *bara',* a very subtle immaterial element—he employs the same expression as he had previously used for the *ḥokhmah* considered as "foundation" or element—that he defines as being "a power that brings forth [that produces]." This element, he says, is disposed in a manner to assume forms and to assure the transition to actual being. It is, in fact, the primordial matter that the Greeks called hyle and from which everything emerged. Without accounting for his leap Naḥmanides immediately goes on to explain, in what is evidently a purely exoteric line of reasoning, that the matter of heaven as well as of earth or the sublunar world were both directly created out of Nothing. But then, reverting to the aforementioned hyle, he identifies it with the *tohu,* whereas the form that causes it to appear is the *bohu* of Genesis 1:2, for which he refers to *Bahir,* section 2. *Tohu,* according to Naḥmanides, is not an actual existent, but the primordial element behind the nought and underlying all existence—his authority for this view being *Yeṣirah* 2:6. This primordially created element, the hyle, which comes from the nought and is differentiated in some way into two distinct matters—that of the higher and that of the lower world—is compared by him to a "very subtle and immaterial point" that, however, already contains everything it can become. Naḥmanides emphasizes that this is the literal sense of the verse, which, by implication, lies on a different level from the kabbalistic one. Nevertheless, there can be no doubt about this second meaning either. The verb *bara',* which on the exoteric level means "create from nothing," signifies, on the esoteric level, "emanate." This much we learn from Naḥmanides himself, in the aforementioned fragment of a kabbalistic commentary on Genesis 1.

On the esoteric plane, the absolute Nought corresponds exactly to the concept already encountered in the aforementioned commentary on *Yeṣirah* as a supreme determination of God himself. It is the first sefirah, from which *ḥokhmah* originates as the primordial beginning of all that is. It is itself the hyle and the indeterminate *tohu,* to which corresponds the image of the primordial point that flashes up from the Nought and in which every sefirotic being is potentially given or prefigured. Heaven and earth, which come from this point, are nothing but symbols, as we already learned from the *Bahir.* In connection with *Yeṣirah* 1:8, Naḥmanides names the *ḥokhmah* the "place of the world," a midrashic expression that is given the meaning of substratum of the world, foundation, and primordial element. God is the "place of the world," insofar as he manifests himself in the sefirah of *ḥokhmah* as its substratum.

The same determination of *ḥokhmah* by means of formulas that are identical to the philosophical definition of matter as the substratum of the potentiality of all things is also found, though more explicitly than in Naḥmanides, in Jacob ben Shesheth and Azriel.[144] The image of the primordial point,[145] too, is already adumbrated by Jacob, since he describes *ḥokhmah,* the "first-emanated," as a "very subtle being, from which the straight line extends in the emanation." Jacob expounds this idea precisely in a controversy concerning the error of those who believe that the world was created from something that existed eternally alongside God, because they "do not understand the secrets of the Torah"! Not from some Being, he seems to say, but from the mystical Nought symbolized by the *'alef,* has the *ḥokhmah,* the beginning of all essences *(hawwayoth),* been created, that is, emanated.[146] Nevertheless, Jacob refrains from speaking in this context of a primordial matter that would be the *ḥokhmah,* although such a definition would seem to be suggested by his own exposition; he substitutes for it—as does Naḥmanides—the notion of a double primordial matter whose transformations he describes in greater detail regarding the matter of heaven.[147] It is here

144. Cf. Jacob ben Shesheth, *Meshibh,* fol. 28a–b, who defines the *ḥokhmah* as *nosse koaḥ she'ar ha-debharim.* Similarly, Azriel, *Perush 'Aggadoth,* 84.

145. On the doctrine of the primordial point, cf. also *Fons Vitae* 2:22, where this image serves to describe the emanation of multiplicity (line) from unity (point). Similarly in the ibn Gabirol quotations in Isaac ibn Latif and in other authors. In fact, the image is a Neoplatonic commonplace, as has been shown by H. Wolfson in *HTR* 45 (1952): 118–119. Cf. A. Altmann, "The motif of the 'Shells' in Azriel of Gerona" in *JJS* 9 (1958): 73–80.

146. Cf. Jacob ben Shesheth, *Meshibh,* fols. 28 and 53a.

147. Ibid., fols. 30a–32b. The interpretation of Abraham bar Ḥiyya in *Hegyon ha-Nefesh* 2a–b is explicitly quoted here, fol. 32a, as the source for a further division of hyle and form, respectively, into two subdivisions each. The passage shows in a

that we should probably look for Naḥmanides' source. The comparison of *ḥokhmah* and the "formless hyle" is advanced without hesitation by Naḥmanides' master Yehudah ben Yaqar in his commentary on the prayers.[148] The fact that Naḥmanides identifies the hyle, on the one hand, explicitly with *tohu,* and on the other hand, implicitly with *ḥokhmah* is by no means as surprising as it might seem. In fact, Azriel already had clearly established the same relation between *tohu* and *ḥokhmah* in his commentary on the aggadoth, whereas other kabbalists, in the *'Iyyun* circle and in Gerona, identified *tohu* with *binah.*[149] In Barzilai's treatise on the sefiroth, the Platonic symbol-

---

very instructive manner the adoption by the Kabbalah of Platonic exegesis. Perhaps Jacob's paraphrase served as the direct source for Naḥmanides. Jacob too says, fol. 35a, that the *ḥokhmah* is the foundation of Creation, which "takes place by means of this essence [the *materia universalis*], which precedes everything and encompasses everything."

148. *JQR* 4 (1892): 249; the *ḥokhmah* is *kemo golem bli ṣurah.*

149. Cf. *Perush 'Aggadoth,* 89, 92, 103, 105. On 103 he explains the *tohu* and *bohu* as having their foundation in a place that is itself called *tehom,* abyss, "the infinite, boundless, and unfathomable abyss, which reaches to the pure Nought." The abyss is therefore not something that is really dark and devoid of God, but the symbol of a moment in God Himself. Scotus Erigena, *De divisione naturae* 2:17, similarly explains the dark abyss of Genesis 1:2 as the unknowable world of the undifferentiated, unformed, and simple *causae primordiales.* For Azriel the abyss is also the *belimah* in the expression *sefiroth belimah* in *Yeṣirah* 1:1, the "WHAT-less," the indeterminable, where question and answer are extinguished, the place "where the questioner and the questioned cease" (103). Ezra has a different explanation, Ms. Vatican 185, fol. 13b:

> Everything that the Torah explains up to the end of Genesis 1:2 refers to the essences which were in the Sophia, and when God enveloped Himself in the primordial light, this primordial light, *('or bahir)* shone forth, and in it were all these essences, as they are found in the Sophia. . . . And *tohu* is the quintessence of all the essences without limitation, form and matter, and *bohu* is imprinted and hidden in the *tohu* as the soul in the body.

Here too the *bohu,* the element of form, is therefore inherent in the *tohu.* Although the description of the *tohu* necessarily elevates it above ordinary matter, the description given is nevertheless that of the immaterial primordial hyle. As the sequel shows, Ezra clearly had recourse to Abraham bar Ḥiyya's notion of the double *tohu,* in *Hegyon ha-Nefesh.* The coordination of hyle and *binah* probably goes back to a symbolism that was penetrated—for completely different reasons far removed from philosophical considerations—by a conception that was incompatible with the aforementioned definition of the notion of form, to wit, that of the *ḥokhmah* as the masculine principle, which belongs to the seed, and of *binah* as the feminine principle, which unfolds the seed and gives birth. This conception formulated by Plato in the *Timaeus,* where hyle is called mother and the form is called father, exactly corresponds to the symbolism commonly used among the kabbalists for *ḥokhmah* and *binah. Binah* as mother pulled the symbolism in the direction of the hyle, to which should be added the Neoplatonic depreciation of matter in relation to form—which was hardly compatible with its superiority in the realm of the sefiroth. Maimonides, *Moreh* 1:17,

ism of the hyle as mother is linked to *ḥokhmah* as primordial beginning, "and the *ḥokhmah* is named by the masters of the language [sic!] the *materia prima,* in which all the other matters are contained."[150]

This conception, which identifies *ḥokhmah* with the hyle, though in esoteric symbolism only and by no means in everyday language, represents a philosophic speculation projected upon an earlier one existing independently of it. This follows quite strikingly from the terminology, which is indeed exactly the opposite of that employed normally for *ḥokhmah* in the circles of Jewish Neoplatonists discussed here. Abraham ibn Ezra already calls the quintessential notion of the forms *ḥokhmah*, no doubt following ibn Gabirol, who, though arranging the symbols differently, designates, in his *Fons Vitae,* the *sapientia* as will, form, and intellect, but never as hyle.

It is to the Neoplatonic tradition that one must attribute the identification of this sefirah with the Active Intellect, the "giver of forms," as adopted by Jacob ben Shesheth and other kabbalists.[151] Among the kabbalists, the two motifs of the *ḥokhmah* as bearer and giver of the forms seem to have become intertwined. The Gerona circle, in any case, held the opinion represented in philosophy particularly by Averroes, according to which the forms, by their origin, are inherent in the hyle. God did not produce the forms separately from formless matter in order to unite them subsequently, but he "drew them forth" from the *ḥokhmah*-hyle, in which they preexisted in pure potentiality, as still undifferentiated essences. *Bohu* is a product of the development of *tohu* and not a totally separate prin-

---

however, attributes to Plato the less determined designation of the masculine and the feminine for matter and form; cf. Munk, *Mélanges,* on this passage.

150. Ms. Christ Church College 198, fol. 73b.

151. Cf. Jacob ben Shesheth, *Meshibh,* fol. 20b (against its localization as the last of the ten intelligences by Maimonides), 28b: "If you wish, name the essence [to which allusion is made in *Bereshith*] Sophia, and if you wish, name it universal intelligence, which corresponds in the language of the philosophers to the *intellectus agens."* The identification of the two intelligences is also found repeatedly in ibn Gabirol. In the *'Emunah u-Biṭṭaḥon,* chap. 12, Jacob relates the divine will to the *'alef,* the Active Intellect to the *yod* which, in kabbalistic letter-symbolism, is correlated with the Sophia. Similarly, also in *Kether Shem Tob,* in Jellinek's *Auswahl kabbalistischer Mystik,* 33. In the Neoplatonic tradition of the Pure Brethren and of Al-Kindi, the Active Intellect of the Aristotelians is identical with the universal intellect of Plotinus; cf. M. Wittman, *Zur Stellung Avencebrols im Entwicklungsgang der arabischen Philosophie* (Münster, 1905), 41–48, and G. Vajda, *Juda ben Nissim,* 63, 74.

ciple. In this sense, Azriel explained the *ḥokhmah* as "the power of that which has a possible being, a simple power, which forms the forms of the changing substances"; this agrees perfectly with his definition of form in his theses on prayer,[152] and it may also be related to the curious explanation of the hyle as the "productive force," advanced on several occasions by Naḥmanides.[153] Whether this is a systematic misunderstanding of the concept of hyle or a reversion to the doctrine of the inherence of the forms remains a moot question. The conception of the *ḥokhmah* as the primordial Torah might, at a pinch, be combined with such an idea. It seems more reasonable, however, to assume that various motifs met and combined here, rather than to seek a single origin of these different determinations. Azriel's quotations from Pseudo-Plato and Pseudo-Aristotle on the subject of primordial matter (so very close to ibn Gabirol's concept of a *materia universalis*) and of substantial form, both inherent in the divine idea and uniting in the Intellect, indicate that his speculations could well have been nourished from very diverse sources.[154]

4. The Doctrines of Azriel and Naḥmanides on the Process of Emanation—'En-sof, *the Primordial Will and the Primordial Idea—The Sefiroth*

The preceding account took as its starting point Azriel's prayer-mysticism, which, of course, already reflects his conception of God. This conception merits closer analysis if we want to understand

152. Cf. *Perush 'Aggadoth,* 84, as well as Tishby's remark there, and the text in the Gulak and Klein memorial volume, 215.

153. In his commentary on the Torah, Genesis 1:1, as well as in a passage on the formation of the embryo, Leviticus 12:1; also in his *Sermon on the Torah* (1873) 16–17, 26. In a tract on the thirty-two paths, from the *'Iyyun* circle, the hyle (*golem*), is also described as a power "that places all things in their proper order and emanates from power to power in order to bring forth all things." Naḥmanides seems to have been acquainted with this text, for his doctrine concerning the *Ṣimṣum* originates there; cf. p. 450. Naḥmanides' explanation of the formation of the embryo through the power of the hyle has its correspondences in Alfarabi and in the *Picatrix* of Pseudo-Mağriti; cf. the German translation by H. Ritter and M. Plessner (1962), 354 (Arabic text, 338). Cf. also Meister Eckhart, *Die lateinischen Werke,* vol. 2 (1966), 416–417.

154. *Perush 'Aggadoth,* 82–83. The Pseudo-Aristotle is, in fact, Isaac Israeli, as Alexander Altmann has demonstrated, *JJS* 8 (1956): 31–57. The sources of the Pseudo-Plato remain to be established.

more accurately the evolution of the Kabbalah in Gerona. The formulations of this school mark the course taken by the early Kabbalah in its further development and above all also render possible a comprehension of the potential contradictions in some of the fundamental kabbalistic positions that began to emerge at that time. From 1250 onward, a degree of uncertainty existed among the kabbalists with regard to such important questions as whether the first sefirah itself was not to be considered as the transcendent deity, or whether the sefiroth were to be regarded as identical with the substance of the deity, or merely as organs of its manifestation. The history of these problems is beyond the scope of this book; but the fact that their very emergence was due to the elaboration of kabbalistic material in this circle will be demonstrated here.

If, as was shown in the preceding chapter, there was at first a great deal of uncertainty about the use of the term *'en-sof,* no such ambiguity exists any longer in the mystical vocabulary of the school of Gerona. *'En-sof* there is a technical, indeed artificial, term detached from all adverbial associations and serving as a noun designating God in all his inconceivability. Here it is well to remember that the determination of God as the Infinite served for the thinkers of antiquity and the Neoplatonists (as Jonas Cohn has demonstrated) precisely as a symbol of his inconceivability, and not as an attribute that can be grasped by reason (such as it became with the Scholastics).[155] Among the kabbalists, God is regarded as Infinitude no less than as the Infinite One. The inconceivability of the hidden God and the impossibility of determining him, which occasionally seem to point to a neutral stratum of the divine nature, are nevertheless those of the infinite person on the whole, the latter being the theistic reinterpretation of the Neoplatonic "One." Azriel himself introduces him as such at the beginning of his questions and answers on the sefiroth, for he identifies *'en-sof*—a word he employs often and without hesitation—with the leader of the world and the master of creation.

Asher ben David, too, expresses himself clearly in a theistic and personalistic vein, identifying *'en-sof* with the personally conceived supreme primordial cause. His primordial will, which is apparently the first sefirah and the "innermost power" of everything

155. Jonas Cohn, *Geschichte des Unendlichkeitsproblems* (Leipzig, 1896), 71.

real and which is also called the Nought, acts in the different *middoth,* within which it expands or in which it is "implanted," since the six days of creation, insofar as it is active within creation. The *middoth* and the sefiroth, starting at least from *ḥokhmah,* are nothing but the organs through which it acts. If its power is withdrawn from them, they have no being of their own; but where it acts in them, their being, which is nothing but the different stages of emanation, is inseparably united with the power that acts in them and that comes from the source and from *'en-sof.* So far there is no hint of a possible identity of the sefiroth with the substance of *'en-sof.* But it is precisely Asher ben David who abetted this development by occasionally applying to the first sefirah phrases that were normally reserved for *'en-sof.* This is particularly striking in his explanation of the sefiroth of the Book *Yeṣirah* where the first sefirah, "the pneuma of the living God" is interpreted (following Isaac the Blind), as the *ḥokhmah.* If the two realities situated above it are not clearly separated, it is apparently because the will of *'en-sof* is uncreated and has no beginning in the emanation either, but simply existed all along in the *'en-sof.* For this reason, as Asher himself said, it should not be called a sefirah.

> Because it is only from there that the sefiroth extend and everything exists through the primordial will which is implanted in them, the highest degree—*rom ma 'alah,* the only name which [after the primordial will] can be attributed to this degree of the will—is also called a sefirah.[156]

Asher likes to speak of the "effluence," *meshekh,* that flowed from the *'en-sof* and extended itself into the *ḥokhmah* and all the other sefiroth. However, this effluence itself is the first sefirah, which he represents with the symbol of the *'alef.* It is for him the "source of life," "life" itself being identical with the *ḥokhmah*. But that which comes from the *'alef* also comes from the *'en-sof.* In the juxtaposition of such expressions, the boundaries between the *'en-sof* and the Nought can easily become blurred. The different readings of these passages in the manuscripts of Asher's treatises prove how easily the transition could be made. *'En-sof* is above the One and the Source of Life; it remains entirely without determination, and all

156. Asher ben David, 6, as well as in various other passages, 11–13.

personal elements of its effects are within its Will, conceived as its Essence. *'En-sof* never appears, in Asher's writings, independent of the above, as the subject of a predicative sentence. There exist therefore, strictly speaking, two different sefiroth: one which is known only as "height," "supreme degree," or *"'alef,"* whose will extends everywhere, like a source, in the "garden" of the sefiroth, and which therefore cannot be numbered together with the other sefiroth;[157] and another that really figures, as Sophia, at the beginning of the enumeration.

However, a more impersonal conception of *'en-sof* could also somehow be fitted into the framework of such considerations, as we learn somewhat to our surprise from Naḥmanides' commentary on *Yeṣirah* 1:4:

> Ten and not eleven [sefiroth]: this is to exclude from the enumeration that hidden thing that stands at the beginning of *kether.* For if we behold an end [of *kether*] at the beginning of the paths of *ḥokhmah,* one might think that *kether* too has a beginning. Hence that which is above it is a hidden thing beyond all thought and speech, and which does not enter into any enumeration.

The ambiguity of the kabbalistic terminology is evident here. The highest essence in God is a "hidden thing"—a strange determination, indeed, of the infinite person of the Godhead, if indeed it is meant as such. No matter how much he spoke of God in his writings, Naḥmanides managed extremely well without the term *'en-sof,* using a strictly orthodox language in spite of the fact that everything he had to say about God's actions really referred to his sefirotic manifestations only. Azriel, on the other hand, did just the opposite: he spoke of *'en-sof* as the God whom the philosophers had in mind and whose sefiroth were but aspects of his revelation and of his activity, the "categories of the order of all reality." Precisely the most hidden element in God, that which the mystics had in mind when they spoke of *'en-sof,* he transformed into the most public. In doing so he already prepared the personalization of the term *'en-sof,* which from the designation of an abstract concept begins to appear here as a proper name. Whereas in general, and even in Azriel's own writings, *'en-sof* still has much of the *deus absconditus,* which attains an

157. Most clearly, ibid., 4–5 (according to the pagination of the text edited in *Ha-Segulla*).

apprehensible existence in the theosophic notion of God and in the doctrine of the sefiroth only, the commentary on the ten sefiroth already presents the *'en-sof* as the ruler of the world, which certainly suggests an image of the government of the world that is very different from that of the theosophy of the Infinite and its sefiroth. For Azriel the highest sefirah is evidently the unfathomable or unknowable and especially the divine will, which in this circle is elevated above the primordial idea. In the abstract the latter could be distinguished from *'en-sof*, but in the concrete it constitutes a real unity with it. The hidden God acts by means of this will, clothes himself in it, as it were, and is one with it. In order to express this, the kabbalists of Gerona readily speak of the "will up to the Infinite," the "height up to the Infinite," the "unknowable up to the Infinite," by which they evidently mean the unity in which the supreme sefirah, represented in each case by the corresponding symbol, extends up to the *'en-sof* and forms with it a unity of action.[158]

This may also explain the remarkable terminology used by Azriel in his profoundly speculative commentary on the aggadoth. Here, in fact, he says almost nothing about *'en-sof,* which appears only once in an independent construction and twice in adverbial combinations of the known kind,[159] which, for their part, are entirely absent in his commentary on the sefiroth. Instead he speaks of the will in the same figures of speech (such as "outside of which there is nothing," etc.) that are usually applied to *'en-sof.* Sometimes the two notions are easily interchanged,[160] and such confusion of terminology is indeed attested as early as 1250. In fact, however, underlying this discourse on the will there is precisely the aforementioned "will up to the Infinite," which takes *'en-sof* as the last transcendent reality contained in this will without, however, explicitly identifying the two. Such a conception presented no major difficulties as long as the coexistence and coeternity of the will with God as *'en-sof* could be either presupposed or explicitly taught. The difficulties began at the moment when the first sefirah itself was viewed as a beginning in the emanation. Henceforth expressions like those mentioned previously became problematic and could cause offense by the

158. Cf. these expressions in Jacob ben Shesheth, *Meshibh,* fols. 28b and 57a; *'Emunah u-Biṭṭaḥon,* chap. 12.

159. *Perush 'Aggadoth,* 24, 90, 116.

160. Ibid., 107, is particularly characteristic in this regard.

link they established between that which came into being primordially and that which, properly speaking, never "came into being." It is therefore not surprising that these expressions disappeared from kabbalistic literature.

Azriel, like the other kabbalists of Gerona, lowers the *maḥshabah* by one degree, identifying it with the Sophia itself—contrary to the *Bahir* and Isaac the Blind. Above it there is the "will,"[161] and both spheres interpenetrate in the concept of the *reṣon ha-maḥshabah,* the "will of the primordial idea," which appears with some frequency for the first time in the writings of Azriel and signifies "the will hidden in the primordial idea." It is indeed hidden there, like the cause in the effect. All things are hidden not only in the primordial idea, but already, in "the depth of the will of the primordial idea," and they stand out, as in a relief, in the actual accomplishment of the emanation.[162]

The formula employed in the prayers: "May it be acceptable [to you]," or the words of the Psalmist [19:15]: "May the words of my mouth be acceptable [literally: to the will]," are interpreted by Jacob ben Shesheth as signifying the unity of all the logoi in *'en-sof.* "For the will," he continues,

> is the cause of everything, is entirely hidden and is only to be understood through another [medium through which it communicated itself] and from it extends an essence, which is apprehensible, and this is the Sophia, which differentiates and clarifies the will; it is through her that [the will] becomes knowable, and not by itself.[163]

Azriel is fond of referring Job 11:7: "Can you find out the depth of God?" to this primordial depth in God, which can signify both the fathomable as well as precisely that in the will that is unfathomable

---

161. In the subsequent post-Geronese development (for example, in ibn Gikatilla's *Sha'are 'Orah*) the will is similarly lowered, at least partly, to the Sophia: "the highest *maḥshabah,* which is called the limitless will (!) and which is the second sefirah."

162. Cf. ibid., 92–94, 107. On p. 101 the creation of the primordial Torah is explained by the emergence of the incessantly acting will into the actuality of the idea. The curious combination of the two notions is also found in Scotus Erigena's work on predestination, where the author speaks of the *voluntas rationabilis;* cf. J. Huber, *Johannes Scotus Erigena* (Munich, 1861), 74.

163. *'Emunah u-Biṭṭaḥon,* chap. 5, and in part almost verbatim, in *Sha'ar ha-Shamayim,* 155.

and beyond the grasp of all thought. From this primordial depth flow all the paths of wisdom and it is this primordial depth that in the "Chapter on the *kawwanah*" is literally called "the perfection of the depth that is one with *'en-sof*," a phrase that can also be translated equally literally as "that unites itself with *'en-sof*," that is, that extends up to its infinity. Thus the terminology of *ḥeqer,* the primordial depth, at which all contemplation of the divine is aimed, changes at the same time into that of the "undepth" (Hebrew: *'en-ḥeqer*), this primordial depth proving to be precisely the unfathomable, and thereby a perfect analogy, in its linguistic form as well, to the Infinite, *'en-sof.*

The will as primordial depth thus becomes the source of all being, and the deity, insofar as it can be envisioned from the point of view of the creature, is conceived entirely as creative will. The intellectualist element of *maḥshabah*-mysticicm is relegated to a second degree. The fact that this creative will is then understood by Azriel, in the context of the ideas analyzed in the foregoing, as the Nought is by no means an isolated instance in the history of mystical terminology. Jacob Böhme, whose *Ungrund* is reminiscent of Azriel's formulations, considers the will that eternally emerges from this *Ungrund* as the Nought.[164] It is therefore no wonder that in these writings the will never appears as something emanated, but rather as that which emanates. In fact Azriel speaks repeatedly of three lights or potencies, which for him apparently correspond to the three supreme sefiroth situated below *'en-sof.* They are called the light of that which emanates, the light of the emanation, and the light of the emanated. This triad is often associated by him with another: the potency of the divine, of the angelic, and of the prophetic, which is at the same time the highest human level.[165] For Azriel it is perfectly clear that the lowest of these lights or potencies is the sefirah *binah.* The essence of the highest human level is the prophetic, the spark of the divine intellect that illuminates it. The idea that the intuitive power of prophecy originates in *binah* seems

164. Cf. H. Grunsky, *Jacob Böhme* (Stuttgart, 1956), 75–76; Alex Koyré, *La philosophie de Jacob Böhme* (Paris, 1929), 328–330, 340–342.

165. In the "Chapter on Faith and Heresy," Gulak and Klein memorial volume, 208–209, as well as in the *Commentary on the Prayers,* Ms. Parma, fols. 75a–76b. The first triad, by itself, is frequently mentioned by Azriel. Cf. also *Sha'ar ha-Sho'el,* section 14, fol. 4b.

to be part of the traditions this school inherited from Isaac the Blind.[166] This view was by no means held by all later kabbalists. Azriel mentions two bearers of the revelation of these lights: God revealed to Moses the innermost three sefiroth, defined previously. The other is the Messiah, at whose advent the spirit of wisdom and intelligence that rests upon him (according to Isaiah 11:2) will draw nourishment from these three potencies.[167] The "potency of that which emanates" is not, as one might think, *'en-sof* itself; it proceeds from the *sether ha-ta 'alumah,* the mysterious darkness of the primordial unity, from which these three principles derive.[168]

A state in which *'en-sof* would be without the will accompanying it is thus inconceivable. This again raises the problem of the necessity of the emanation versus the freedom of *'en-sof* in the primordial act of the creation. Have we not returned to the position of Plotinus? Azriel offers two answers to this question, different in their formulations but essentially connected. He teaches that the first sefirah was always, potentially, in *'en-sof.*[169] But this does not mean that there was ever a situation in which it, and it alone, was actualized before the other sefiroth. God's "freedom" lies with the second sefirah! The actualization of the first sefirah, the Will, is precisely the emanation of the Sophia, and nothing else. An actualized Will exists, therefore, only in the medium of the emanation and of

---

166. An old text, immediately after the *kawwanoth* of Abraham Ḥazan in Ms. Munich 92, fol. 216b, says: "The power of prophecy comes from the sefirah named 'Return' *(teshubah).*"

167. On Moses, cf. Azriel's exposition in *Madda 'e ha-Yahaduth* 2:231; on the Messiah, see "Chapter on Faith," 211.

168. Cf. ibid., 208. The same term also in Azriel's Epistle to Burgos, ibid., 233, and in the chapter on the *kawwanah.*

169. *Sha'ar ha-Sho'el,* section 8. The same idea is also found in Jacob ben Sheshetb, *Sha'ar ha-Shamayim,* in *'Oṣar Neḥmad* 3:155–156: the first sefirah is united with the Infinite and it is, in fact, its will.

> And with it, at the same time, is indicated the Supreme above all the Supreme, the God of Gods and the master of masters, the first cause and the highest pool, which no thought can grasp. And because it [this Supreme] is removed from all thought, no limited name whatsoever can be attributed to it, and all things and allusions found in relation to it in the words of the Bible refer to the realities [sefiroth] which come from its cause.

In *'Emunah u-Biṭṭaḥon,* chap. 3, the various kinds of destruction of the divine unity, the "devastation of the plants," are defined; among them also is the separation of the first sefirah from *'en-sof,* as if these were two really different essences. It follows that for the author, while not being identical in the abstract, they are inseparably united in their reality.

the emanated essences. The act of creation does not consist, as with later generations of kabbalists, in the establishment of the Nought but is in that of "something that is": the Sophia. The "idea" is the Will realized in God. There was therefore a state in which this realization had not yet taken place. The "leap" of creation does not consist, therefore, in the transition from *'en-sof* to the first sefirah, but in the unity of both with the second sefirah. It is this leap that constitutes God's free decision to emanate. The discerning reader will find this idea present among all the representatives of the school of Gerona, including Naḥmanides, and it appears to be part of the heritage this circle bequeathed to the author of the *Zohar.* Many other kabbalists abandoned this view in order to safeguard the emanated character of all ten sefiroth; but this of necessity compelled them to modify the character of the first sefirah, as we have sought to define it here.

It can be said of *'en-sof* as well as of the Will that nothing exists outside it.[170]

> All beings come from the incomprehensible primordial ether, and their existence [*yeshuth*] comes from the pure Nought. However, this primordial ether is not divisible in any direction, and it is One in a simplicity that does not admit of any composition. All acts of the will were in its unity, and it is the will that preceded everything. . . . And that is the meaning of [Job 23:13]: "He is One"—He is the unity of the will, outside of which nothing exists.[171]

The will still embraced the indistinct unity of all opposites and of all possible acts of will.

> The order of all reality was given in the potency of the will, but did not emerge into visible manifestation until the time had come for its visible existence. The sefiroth, however, had their essence [*hawwayah*] in the will without recognizable distinction that might enter into the

---

170. Whereas in the commentary on *Yeṣirah* 1:7 Azriel explains *'eḥad* in the sense that *'en-sof,* in its absolute indistinctness, is called "One," the parallel passage in his Epistle to Burgos says that it is called "One" because nothing exists outside of it. Similarly on *Yeṣirah* 2:6: "The One is the foundation of the multiplicity, and the [multiple] things [or perhaps the sefiroth, which could be meant by the word *debharim*], have no existence outside the One." The same formula in *Sha'ar ha-Sho'el,* sections 1, 2, 7, 12; in the *Commentary on the Prayers,* Ms. Parma, fol. 86a and in the text I edited in the Gulak and Klein memorial volume, 218. The formula also occurs frequently in Scotus Erigena; cf. Huber, *Johannes Scotus Erigena,* 169: *praeter eum nihil est.*

171. *Perush 'Aggadoth,* 107.

contemplation of thought; from them derives the emanation of the logoi through which the world was created, logoi that are connected with the will, outside of which nothing exists.[172]

Neither in *'en-sof* nor in the will is there any differentiation; both are designated as the indistinct root of the opposites. For this indistinctness, which corresponds to the Latin term *indistinctio* or *aequalitas,* the *'Iyyun* circle and Azriel use the Hebrew *hashwa'ah;* unseparated and indifferent is there called *shaweh,* literally "equal," a word that is never used in this sense elsewhere in the Hebrew literature. *'En-sof* as well as the will are "indifferent with regard to the opposites." They do not conjoin the opposites, as does for example the *res divina* of Yehudah Halevi,[173] but no distinctions are admitted at all; since the opposites in these supreme principles are "equal," that is, indistinct, they coincide in them. It is in this sense that mention is often made of the "indistinct unity" or of the "indifference of unity" in which apparent opposites coincide.[174] Whereas in the commentary on the ten sefiroth this mystical indifference is attributed to *'en-sof,* the commentary on the aggadoth ascribes them to the will, which, as we have seen, almost replaces the *'en-sof,* in this text.[175] The opposites are abolished in the infinite. The Kabbalah

172. Ibid., 110, as well as in a paraphrase of the same idea, 116.

173. Cf. *Kuzari* 4:25, ed. Hirschfeld, 274–275.

174. The term *hashwa'ath ha-'aḥduth,* which occurs already in the *Sefer ha-'Iyyun,* is almost certainly a translation from the Latin. Thierry of Chartres, one of the most illustrious philosophers of Europe in his time and a teacher of the School of Chartres, 1120–1150, several times uses the expression *aequalitatis unitatis* for the "Word of God" in his commentary on the account of creation (*verbum igitur deitatis unitatis aequalitas est*). The text is given by N. Häring in *Platonismus in der Philosophie des Mittelalters,* ed W. Beierwalter, in the series Wege der Forschung, vol. 197 (Darmstadt, 1969), 248. But here the expression is not used in the sense of the kabbalists but rather in a mathematical-theological sense (see Häring, *Platonismus,* 195, 198–199). Azriel in *parashah* 2 of his commentary, says: "'En-Sof is the *hashwa'ah gemurah* in perfect unity," that is, absolute indistinction. Flavius Mithridates translates the passage: "Ensof id est sine fine, et est equalitas perfecta in unitate perfecta," Ms. Vatican 190, fol. 166b. The concept belongs to the vocabulary of the Neoplatonic schools and plays a central role with Meister Eckhart: "In Gott sind alle Dinge gleich [*glīch*] und sind Gott selber" (Pfeiffer, 311). In Eckhart's usage, Latin *similis* corresponds not to "similar" but to "equal [Germ. *glīch*]." The Hebrew *hashwa'ah* is thus an exact rendering of Latin *similitudo* (or *Verglīchunge,* in Eckhart's German.)

175. Cf. on the subject of this usage of *'aḥduth shawah* and *hashwa'ath ha-'aḥduth* my remarks in the Gulak and Klein memorial volume, 204, and Tishby's references in his study on the writings of Ezra and Azriel, 8 of the offprint. Jacob ben Shesheth says that the contraries in the divine will are "leveled," *yesharim,* instead of *shawim.*

could hardly have found this concept in the Jewish philosophical tradition, and one must ask where its source is to be sought.

It is interesting to note in this connection that as early as 1415 Johannes Reuchlin, referring explicitly to the "Treatise on Faith and Heresy" that we have already come to know as a work of Azriel, gives an excellent definition of the indifferent *'en-sof:*

> Nominatur *Ensoph,* id est infinitudo, quae est summa quaedam res secundum se incomprehensibilis et ineffabilis, in remotissimo suae divinitatis retrocessu et in fontani luminis inaccessibili abysso se retrahens et contegens, ut sic nihil intelligatur ex ea procedere, quasi absolutissima deitas per ocium omnimoda sui in se ipsa clausione immanens nuda sine veste ac absque ullo circumstantiarum amictu, nec sui profusa, nec splendoris sui dilatata bonitate indiscriminatim ens et non ens, et omnia quae rationi nostrae videntur inter se contraria et contradictoria, ut segregata et libera unitas simplicissime implicans.[176]

Reuchlin next refers the reader to the doctrine of the *coincidentia oppositorum* in God, "as a certain eminently philosophical archpriest of the Germans bequeathed it to posterity, as representing his decided opinion, about fifty-two years ago." Cardinal Nicholas of Cusa died in 1464, fifty-two years before Reuchlin wrote these lines. Understandably surprised by the agreement between the two mystical philosophers, Reuchlin did not suspect a common source. But it seems to me that such a common source exists in Scotus Erigena's *De divisione naturae* 1:72, which contains a clear formulation of precisely this doctrine, adopted, among others, by older contemporaries of Azriel such as David of Dinant, whom the Church rejected as a heretic.[177] Among the deviations from the true faith that Azriel enumerated in this treatise, we find:

---

176. J. Reuchlin, *De Arte cabbalistica;* at the end of Book 1 (Hagenau, 1517), fol. xxia, Reuchlin's definition goes right to the heart of Azriel's conception. The essence of this statement is, as Chaim Wirszubski was the first to recognize, almost literally Pico's thirty-fifth thesis on the *Cabala secundum propriam opinionem.* It is thus Pico who deserves the credit for intuitive insight.

177. Cf. G. Théry, *David de Dinant: Étude sur son panthéisme matérialiste* (1925). Azriel's and Scotus Erigena's agreement on important ideas and concepts appears so striking and so powerful that the hypothesis of possible historical links between the two thinkers, which I have already discussed here many times, must be seriously taken into consideration. Of course, attenuations, qualifications, de-Christianizations, and even misunderstandings must have occurred; nevertheless, the Christian Neoplatonist remains Azriel's closest possible model on too many points of detail for the resemblance to be accidental. The relationship of Azriel's Hebrew to

The eighth erroneous path is that of him who believes that he [*'en-sof*] has a *superesse* above everything and that nothing exists outside of him, but that he is not indifferent [indistinct] in relation to everything, and also that he draws the substance of the effluence that comes from him only as far as the potency of the emanating, which always preexisted, but not to the potency of the emanation, which originates from it, and still less to the potency of the emanated; and in this way he posits a lack in his power. For if he wants to explain the power of the emanating as indistinct from the mysterious darkness from which it comes, he is unable to do so since he does not recognize this principle according to which, both in the visible and in the hidden, he [the *'en-sof*] is without distinction "equal" in relation to Nought and to Being, in the complete simplicity and nondifferentiation that is called unity.[178]

One could say that the predilection for neutral predicates of the primordial being, as we have come to recognize it here, reflects the influence of Neoplatonism on this mystical theology. Only with the penetration of Neoplatonic thought into the older gnostic stratum do such conceptions acquire a dominant position. The infinite, the incomprehensible, the hidden, the *superesse,* the indifferent—all these are determinations deriving from the same spiritual climate of "negative theology." In fact, Azriel himself explicitly takes his position on this ground.

'En-sof is the absolute indistinctness in the perfect unity, in which there is no change. And since it is without limits, nothing exists outside of it; since it is above everything it is the principle in which ev-

---

Erigena's Latin is sometimes clearly evident from the choice of words as well. *Hashlamah,* as a variant for *shelemuth,* renders the two nuances of the Latin *perfectio.* Scotus' indications relating to the world of the logos and of the Son, identical according to him with Wisdom, coincide in the most surprising manner with the determinations of the earliest kabbalists regarding the *ḥokhmah;* cf. Huber, 201–206. These go far beyond the detailed interpretations of biblical terms and notions, which could also be the result of the inner logic of the mystical interpretation of the Bible (for example, the days of creation as intelligible primordial days, an idea that Scotus 3:24 and the kabbalists had in common); this does not prove very much. The transition from the world of the *sapientia* and the Word to that of the Spirit corresponds, among the kabbalists of Gerona, to that from the second to the third sefirah, which was conceived by them in a completely analogous manner, with the obvious elimination of the christological element. The notion of *ḥayye ha-ruaḥ* for *binah,* which Azriel frequently likes to use but which has no foundation in older Jewish terminology, is likewise easily explained by reference to Erigena's doctrine of *spiritus* and to the relation between it and Wisdom. If these relationships could be raised from the level of an hypothesis to that of certainty, it would be an important and far-reaching advance in the study of the Kabbalah.

178. Cf. Gulak and Klein memorial volume, 208.

> erything hidden and visible meet; and since it is hidden, it is the [common] root of faith and unbelief, and the investigating sages [the philosophers] agree with those who say that our comprehension of it can take place only through the path of negation.[179]

There is a tension, no doubt, in the coexistence of the impersonal type of discourse with the more personalist manner of speaking of God as ruler and Creator; but the kabbalists seem to have come to terms with it. For it is not only, as might logically be supposed, in his actions and manifestation in the sefiroth that God appears as the Creator, but also in the context of the discourse on the *superesse* of the Creator who stands above being and nonbeing, and in whom the two coincide. It is difficult to decide to what extent this should be seen as merely an accommodation to the usual style of biblical language, which is, however, avoided whenever the authors strive for greater precision. In the writings of Azriel in particular the coloring of his language oscillates between the personal, the impersonal, and the neutral, and the reader gains the impression that it really does not greatly matter to the author. Thus, the general mood of his "Questions and Answers Concerning the Sefiroth" and of his commentary on *Yeṣirah* is significantly different from that of his commentary on the aggadoth and his epistle to Burgos. It is therefore not surprising that in the first two of these writings *'en-sof* is mentioned often and without restraint as the Creator God (with utter disregard of Neoplatonic definitions) and, as the God who is the subject of theology.[180] However, in his other writings *'en-sof* is barely mentioned at all, though there is a faint suggestion that it is the primordial foundation of the will. Naḥmanides seems to stay the furthest from the language of the Neoplatonic schools, and hence the tension between the gnostic heritage of the *Bahir* and the new speculation is weakest in his case. He manages to avoid even mentioning *'en-sof* in his commentary on the Torah, precisely because it is nothing but the dark ground from which the God of revelation, who is the unity of the ten sefiroth, arises. In other words, *'en-sof*

179. *Sha'ar ha-Sho'el,* section 2. The image of God as the root of belief and unbelief comes from Yehudah Halevi, *Kuzari* 1:77.

180. This is related to the fact that Azriel, in his commentary on *Yeṣirah,* identifies *'en-sof* with other concepts of a positive nature. He is the pure quiddity, *mahuth,* and the "Lord," as he is symbolically understood in *Yeṣirah* 1:5; this rather unusual identification can only be explained in the context of the exegesis of this text.

plays no active role in religion; it is the abyss and *Ungrund* hidden in the absolute Nothingness of which we have only a vague intimation. From here the road leads directly to the position of the anonymous kabbalist who wrote around 1300: "*'En-sof* is not even alluded to in the Torah or in the prophets, in the hagiographers or in the words of the sages; only the mystics received a small indication of it." The corresponding positive statement would be to the effect that the deity, the God of religion, is nothing but the dynamic unity of the emanation of the ten sefiroth.[181]

The vacillation between images and concepts that were almost the same for *'en-sof* and the first sefirah or that could be used interchangeably led to the explicit identification of the two by the disciples of the kabbalists of Gerona around the middle of the thirteenth century. The first sefirah is itself the bearer of all the others, and no hidden primordial essence is situated above it. That which, from one perspective, is called *'en-sof* is, from another perspective, the Nought or the primordial will. This conception, according to the testimony of some kabbalists, became very widespread at a later date;[182] it is emphatically argued for the first time in the book *Kether Shem Tob* of Abraham Axelrad of Cologne, a kabbalist who came from the school of Eleazar of Worms to Spain and whose work combined the numbers-mysticism of the German Hasidim with the sefirotic Kabbalah as taught most notably by Ezra ben Solomon and Naḥmanides.[183] The author quotes the doctrine of Naḥmanides that we cited above as an oral tradition but does not, however, name Naḥmanides.

> I have heard that there are many who add above the ten sefiroth another sefirah in the Infinite, which would lead one to suppose that there is at the beginning of the *kether 'elyon* something hidden in the Infinite, which is the Cause of causes . . . and this is not correct and does not make sense.[184]

---

181. Cf. in the anonymous work *Ma 'arekheth ha-'Elohuth* (Mantua, 1558), fols. 28a and 82b. Cf. also p. 437 n. 169, herein.

182. In the *Sefer ha-Shem,* composed around 1350 by a certain R. Moses (not Moses de Leon, as many kabbalists assumed) this conception is said to be that of most leading kabbalists; cf. ed. (Venice, 1601), fol. 4b, in the collection *Hekhal 'Adonai.*

183. Edited according to a bad text by Jellinek, *Auswahl kabbalistischer Mystik,* 29–48.

184. Thus the sharpest wording of rejection, in Ms. Paris 843. In the printed text, 44–45, the formulation is attenuated.

In one version, this passage is followed by the remark, added during Naḥmanides' lifetime: "However, the Rab [an honorific title for Naḥmanides], our master, may he live long, wrote that it is so.[185]

In a collection of old oral traditions written down by one of the disciples of this circle, the two conceptions are objectively juxtaposed and discussed:

> I have heard that *kether 'elyon* is not the Cause of causes . . . for if we count it as the first, it must have an end and a beginning. And if *ḥokhmah* is the end of the first sefirah, which is *kether 'elyon,* then it too must exist at its beginning and above itself a hidden and subtle being, called *'en-sof* and Cause of all causes, and it is to it that we pray. But others contradict this opinion and say that there is no other cause of any kind above *'en-sof.* And if we divide the sefiroth [in ten], this is not, God forbid, in order to destroy [the unity] in them. And if we count in reference to them one and two and so on, this is only in order to distinguish them by their names, while in reality they all represent an undivided union in which a separation is effected only in name. Thus we say, for example, of the light of a lamp, that it is called at its beginning light, in its middle candle, and at its end fire [sic!], and yet all is one, namely, light. So, too, God (making this comparison *salva reverentia*), is like the power of the fire that has at the same time the power to emit white and dark luminosity,[186] to fuse and to consume, and yet all is one. And if there is above *kether 'elyon* a supreme cause, how then could the Book *Yeṣirah* have said: ten and not nine, ten and not eleven?[187]

Our author decided against this last conception, which, to judge by the texts, seems not to have been shared by the masters of the school. The theory of the identification of the two degrees apparently does not recognize any real existence of the sefiroth.

Like Isaac the Blind, Azriel distinguishes three aspects in the first two sefiroth, the middle one, situated between *kether* and *ḥokhmah,* being likewise designated (see above, p. 272) as *haskel.* Here, too, it remains uncertain whether this *haskel,* God's *intelligere,* is closer to the first or to the second sefirah; Azriel seems to incline to the latter view.[188] The difference between the two hypostasized

185. Thus the text according to Ms. Milan, Bernheimer 57, fol. 21b.

186. Read *le-haqdir* instead of *le-haqrir.*

187. Cf. the Hebrew text in *Reshith ha-Qabbala,* 253–254.

188. In Ms. Vatican 441, fol. 53a, Ezra defines *haskel* as "*ḥokhmah* together with that upon which it depends." Azriel says in the *Perush 'Aggadoth,* 107, that "the

noetic acts of *haskel* and *histakluth* that are associated by him with the *sekhel* itself, the intellect, in order to form a triad, is not quite clear. Does *haskel* perhaps signify the pure *intelligere* that originates in the will, whereas *histakluth* (a reflexive form in Hebrew) would be the *intelligere* that relates to itself, that makes itself its own object? In favor of this interpretation one might cite Azriel's reference to precisely such an act, in which the divine idea arises, "in order to contemplate the inwardness of itself to the point of the extinction of its power of comprehension."[189] As against this it should be borne in mind that in medieval Hebrew usage this word has no reflexive sense and simply means contemplate. Hebrew *haskel* and *histakluth,* exactly as the Latin *intuitio,* unite thought and contemplation. It is not impossible that *haskel* denotes the process of *intelligere, histakluth,* more precisely contemplation in the Platonic sense of *theoria,* namely, the *intuitus* of ibn Gabirol's *Fons Vitae.* In his commentary on the prayers Azriel explicitly designates as *haskel* the effluence that comes from God to us and through which we have an *intuitio* of him.[190] Another aspect of the same effluence is called by him *da 'ath,* knowledge or gnosis of God. That which is, from the perspective of God's *intuitio* (namely, *histakluth*), a beginning is, from the perspective of man, the end of what can be grasped by thought or, more to the point, the goal and final aim of all knowledge. In this proposition the two definitions that Azriel gives to *haskel* can meet. On one occasion he defines it as the beginning of the *histakluth,* another time as the essence of the *ḥokhmah,* the final aim of all comprehension of thought.[191] Only in the union of these two acts of *haskel* and *histakluth* does the intellect itself, *sekhel,* arise as the diversity of all the ideal objects and essences in the divine intellect, which Azriel identifies with the sefirah *binah.* It is certainly not by accident that Azriel designates *ḥokhmah* as the beginning of both being, *hathḥalath yeshuth,* and the *intuitio* of God, *teḥillath histak-*

---

foundation of the essence of *ḥokhmah* is the *haskel,* the final goal of the comprehension of the thought," which doubtless means the final goal of that which the *maḥshabah* can grasp.

189. Cf. *Perush 'Aggadoth,* 116. The triad of *haskel, histakluth,* and *sekhel* corresponds in Azriel's Epistle to Burgos, 234, to the first three sefiroth, *kether, ḥokhmah* and *binah.*

190. Ms. Oxford 1938, fol. 226a.

191. Ibid., fol. 226b, and *Perush 'Aggadoth,* 107.

luth. He also explicitly states that this *haskel* exactly marks the passage from the will to the thought of the Sophia, and stands at that point where, in a different theosophic terminology, being emerges from Nothingness.[192] One wonders whether behind all this there lies the idea that the deity gives birth to things by thinking them. But even if this were so, the details of this speculation still remain unclear. The Sophia, in which more than anywhere else God thinks and contemplates himself, is explicitly distinguished from *haskel* and even equated in rank with the beginning of *histakluth,* without, however, being identified with it. It seems as if this entire sequence of ideas was only later added to the older Sophia-mysticism. In the order of the sefiroth, as conceived by Azriel, the potencies of *haskel* and *ḥokhmah,* though differentiated, nevertheless constitute a single sefirah.[193] Strangely enough, the triad of the intellect that we have encountered here is never connected by Azriel with the traditional triad of the knower, the knowing, and the known, although it is associated, in the "Prayer of Neḥunya ben Haqqanah," with the three first sefiroth.

Different views were current in Gerona concerning the process of emanation, *'aṣiluth.* The gnostic character of the aeons as found in the *Bahir* is replaced, above all in Asher ben David and Azriel, by the Neoplatonic conception of the sefiroth as intermediary beings. Azriel goes furthest in this direction, since he, at least in the commentary on the sefiroth, applies this view to all ten sefiroth. The emanation is for him the activity of the infinite power in the finite, the transition from the pure transcendence of the One to the manifestation of its diversity of aspects in creation. This is combined with the idea, as truly Platonic as it is in conformity with the Book *Yeṣirah,* of the numerical character of the sefiroth, which represent at the same time the ideal order of everything real. This transition to a definition of the sefiroth as "the quintessence of all reality that can be determined by numbers" and as "the order of everything created" had been prepared by older Neoplatonist authors writing in Arabic, such as Moses ibn Ezra, who had described the ten categories as the cause of all Being. Whether Scotus Erigena held similar views cannot be inferred clearly from his discussion. One cannot help wonder-

192. Cf. *Perush 'Aggadoth,* 84 as well as 81 and 107, on the will as origin of the *maḥshabah* and the *ḥokhmah.*

193. Thus, explicitly, in *Madda 'e ha-Yahaduth* 2:231.

ing whether some kind of iconographic representation of the so-called "Tree of Porphyry" describing the relationship of genus and species and widespread in the early Middle Ages—we do not know the date of its first appearance, but it certainly existed after about 1100[194]—might not have constituted one of the links connecting the notions of categories and sefiroth. We have in fact such a depiction of the ten categories in Ramon Lull's *Arbor Elementalis* (1295), where the trunk constitutes the substance or hyle and the leaves form the nine accidents.[195] Such images might well be much older.

In mystical reinterpretation, the sefiroth now become, above all in Azriel, a "pure medium," something that is not in itself an object but, according to its determination, exclusively a means: the means by which the boundless exercises its action in the measure of the *middoth,* and the infinite acts in the finite. God himself acts in and through the sefiroth as the soul acts in and through the body. God is "in them and outside of them and surrounds everything from within and from without, like the soul which is inside as well as outside of the body," as Jacob ben Shesheth puts it.[196] In this manner, certain other conceptions also become possible, such as that of the *middoth* as accidents of the supreme category, substance; such conceptions would accord well with the general tendency of this school,[197] for which, as we know, the sefiroth do not simply represent the substance of the deity itself, but—depending on the various formulations—its organs, aspects, or determinations.

The *'aṣiluth* is indeed emanation, but not in the sense of a diminution of that which emanates. The idea that the light is not dimin-

---

194. Such a picture can be found in a Porphyry manuscript written in Montecassino ca.1100 (Cod. Vatican, Ottobonianus latinus 1406, fol. 11a).

195. Cf. the extracts from Moses ibn Ezra, *'Arugath ha-Bosem,* in Creizenach's *Zion* 2 (1842): 118. This translation into Hebrew of an original Arabic text might have been known to Azriel. On Scotus Erigena, cf. above all *De divisione naturae* 1:34. For the tree of Porphyry and the descriptions by Ramon Lull, cf. Walter Ong, [*Petrus*] *Ramus* (Cambridge, 1958), 78–83, 234–235; E. W. Platzek in *Estudios Lulianos* (1958), 2:20–24; Frances Yates, *Journal of the Warburg and Courtauld Institutes* 23 (1960):22, as well as the illustrations on plate 15 of her earlier study, ibid., 17 (1954): 146. J. C. Schramm, *Introductio in Dialecticam Cabbaleorum* (1703), 53, already drew attention to the tree of Porphyry. Solomon Maimon, in his autobiography (ed. Fromm, 162) recounts that when he began to study Kabbalah he regarded the ten sefiroth as the ten categories of Aristotle, and proceeds (163) to elaborate on this idea. He also tells us that he got into trouble as a result of this interpretation.

196. *Meshibh Debharim,* fol. 60b.

197. Thus, for the first time, as far as I know, in *'Emunah u-Biṭṭaḥon,* chap. 3.

ished by its emanation is taken, as the terminology proves, from a parable in the *Midrash Tanḥuma* on Numbers 11:17, where the verb *'aṣal* is used. At the same time, it is also in full agreement with Plotinus, for whom the source of the emanation suffers no diminution of its power as a result of the transmission of its power to the product. But for the kabbalists of Gerona, the emanation always remains with God and does not move away from him. This esoteric conception may lie behind Naḥmanides' interpretation of the verse in question, where in discussing the notion of *'aṣiluth* he explicitly rejects its interpretation as an effluence and, on the contrary, derives the word from the Hebrew *'eṣel,* "near," as that "which remains with God." Very possibly his polemic was directed at translators who interpreted *'aṣiluth* in the sense of effluence. His protest may reflect an esoteric terminology, as can be seen in his commentary on *Yeṣirah*—where he himself employs this same notion of effluence *(hamshakhah),* which he rejected in the aforementioned passage of his commentary on the Torah, for the coming into being of the sefiroth.[198] The contradiction between the theosophic and Neoplatonic determinations of the concept of emanation is evident here. When Azriel defines the sefiroth as serving as an intermediary between the One and the many he nevertheless seeks at the same time to avoid the conclusion that these intermediary beings existed outside the sphere of the deity—a conclusion that would flatly contradict the decisive interests of the theosophic conception of God. The sefiroth are "der Gottheit lebendiges Kleid," the living garment of the deity, to quote a phrase from Goethe's *Faust;* but these "garments"—the image is very popular in this circle—are not of the kind that could be removed from the deity; they are the forms of its manifestation. In a more mystical sense, it is true, the *'aṣiluth* represents the name or the names of God, as has been shown in the preceding chapter. This theosophic conception was preserved in Gerona. Creation can subsist only to the extent that the name of God is engraved in it.[199] The revelation of the name is the actual revela-

198. Cf. *Kiryath Sefer* 4:403, 406. On Exodus 3:13, Naḥmanides says that the ten sefiroth themselves are the *'aṣiluth.* Grajwer's exposition, in his chapter "on the concept of the *Aziluth* in Nahmanides" must be corrected accordingly; cf. *Die kabbalistischen Lehren des Moses ben Nachman,* 45–56. Baḥya ben Asher later combines, in his commentary on Numbers 11:17, Naḥmanides' interpretation with the meaning of emanation rejected by him.

199. *Perush 'Aggadoth,* 99.

tion, and the Torah is not merely a conglomeration of the names of God, but, in its very essence, nothing but this one name itself. This doctrine, which transmuted an originally magical tradition into a strictly mystical one, was clearly expressed for the first time in Gerona, and from there reached the author of the *Zohar.*[200] Light-mysticism for the emanation and language-mysticism for the divine name remain the two principal means by which the world of the sefiroth could be described.

For Naḥmanides, the ten sefiroth are the "inwardness" of the letters. The beginning and the end of the Torah together form, according to a mystical pun, the "heart," לב, of creation; in terms of gematria, the traditional mysticism of numbers the numerical value of the word (thirty-two) also indicates the thirty-two paths of wisdom active in it. This "heart" is nothing other than the "will" of God itself, which maintains the creation as long as it acts in it. For it becomes the Nothing, בל (the inversion of the same two letters), as soon as the will reverses its direction and brings all things back to their original essentiality, "like someone who draws in his breath." But this return of all things to their proprietor is also their return to the mystical pure Nothingness.[201] The primordial beginning of creation consisted in the emergence of *ḥokhmah* from the infinite plenitude of the "supreme crown" or the will, in an act of limitation, *ṣimṣum,* in which the all-embracing divine *kabhod* was restricted. This restriction of the light at first produced a darkness, into which there flowed the clear light of *ḥokhmah.* We thus find in Naḥmanides the oldest form of the doctrine of a self-contraction of

200. More details on this subject in my book *On the Kabbalah,* 37–42, as well as the sources indicated in the notes there.

201. This is the apocatastasis of all things as understood by Naḥmanides; cf. *Kiryath Sefer* 6:401–402, as well as his hymn on the fate of the soul, in the final stanza, and in a quotation from Naḥmanides mentioned by Baḥya ben Asher, *Shulḥan 'Arba',* s.v. "Se'udath Ṣaddiqim," of which I cannot find the source. Also Naḥmanides' disciples speak of apocatastasis in the same sense, for example, Isaac ben Todros in his commentary on the maḥzor, Ms. Paris 839, fol. 209b, and the quotation of an unnamed pupil of Naḥmanides in Sahula, fol. 28a. It seems probable to me that the terminology is of Christian origin. Naḥmanides also used Christian sources elsewhere, as in the parallel drawn between the week of creation and the week of worlds (derived from Isidore of Seville) and in his doctrine of the purificatory nature of Purgatory (in *Sha 'ar ha-Gemul*). On Deuteronomy 17:14, Naḥmanides quotes a saying from the New Testament; it is therefore perfectly plausible that he could also have used Acts 3:21 for the idea of the return of all things to their origin in God.

God at creation, which, however, is not a contraction of the *'en-sof* itself, as taught by later kabbalists, but of the first sefirah.[202]

From here, the statements of Naḥmanides on *Yeṣirah* 1 converge with the received symbolism of the sefiroth. No doubt for him this *'or bahir* is, as we have seen, the *ḥokhmah,* whereas for Ezra it is rather *binah,* and for Azriel, even *tif'ereth.*[203] For the purposes of our analysis, the details of the symbolism of the sefiroth are no longer of decisive importance. Gnostic symbolism prevails over the philosophic definitions. The totality of the emanation is, especially for Ezra and Azriel—but also for the other kabbalists of this circle—as much the name as the Throne of the Glory of God. At the same time this determination is also frequently restricted to that which is between the first and the last sefirah. If the first sefirah, the will or the root of the Nought, is conceived as the "source of life," then the world of the emanation that flows from it up to the ninth sefirah is this "life" itself, exercising its action in the "tree of life," which irradiates the whole of creation.[204]

In their conception of the emanation, the kabbalists of Gerona unite the two motifs of the emergence from potentiality to actuality,

---

202. Cf. Naḥmanides commentary on *Yeṣirah* in *Kiryath Sefer* 6:402–403, to which may also be added his commentary on Job. 28:13. The oldest source of this idea of *ṣimṣum* in the kabbalistic sense is found in a work of the *'Iyyun* group, in the preface to one of the expositions of the thirty-two paths of *ḥokhmah,* Ms. Florence, Plut. II, Cod. 18, fol. 101a, as well as in the further development of the same passage, quoted from "the writings of the kabbalists" by Shemtob ben Shemtob in his untitled book, in Ms. British Museum, Margoliouth 771, fol. 140b. It is said there:

> How did He produce and create His world? Like a man who holds his breath and resticts himself [Ms. Florence: restricts his breath], in order that the little may contain the many. Thus, He restricted His light to a span, according to the measure of His span, and thus, the world remained in darkness, and in the darkness he chiseled the rocks in order to produce from them the paths, which are called the wonders of the *ḥokhmah,* and it is this of which Scripture says [Job 28:11]: The hidden things may be brought to light.

The span of God, mentioned here, naturally stands in contrast to the terrestrial span, upon which, according to the *Midrash Shemoth Rabba, parashah* 34, section 1, God descended in order to inhabit the Tabernacle and he "restricted his shekhinah to the square of an ell," namely over the cover of the Ark of the Covenant. In this context, Yehudah ben Barzilai on *Yeṣirah,* 150, already uses the same figure of speech employed here for the creation of the world, "in order that the little may contain the many."

203. Cf. Ezra's *Perush 'Aggadoth,* Ms. Vatican 294, fols. 27a, 31a, 48a, as well as his *Commentary on the Song of Songs* on 1:1 and fol. 27c; Azriel, *Perush 'Aggadoth,* 78.

204. Cf. Ezra's letter in *Sefer Bialik,* 157–158.

on the one hand, and of the maturation of the organic process, on the other. We have already found both, in other connections, in Isaac the Blind. The combination of ideas is expressed in characteristic fashion in a text on the sefiroth emanating from this circle:

> Before God created His world He was alone with His name, and His name is equivalent to His wisdom. And in His wisdom all things were mixed together and all the essences were hidden, for He had not yet brought them forth from potentiality to reality, like a tree in whose potency the fruit is already present, but which it has not yet brought forth. When he contemplated the wisdom, he transformed that which was in the root into mountains, and he cleft rivers [Job 28:9–10], that is: He drew forth all the essences that were hidden in the wisdom and brought them to light by means of His *binah* [discernment].[205]

The Gerona circle no longer knows any vacillation between the world of the sefiroth, which could be designated as the Merkabah only in a symbolic sense, and the world of the true Merkabah, located below it. The first or mystical Merkabah concerns the gnosis of the Creator, and it alone, according to Naḥmanides, is indicated in the Torah. The Merkabah of the prophetic and mystical vision, on the other hand, of which Ezekiel and the Hekhaloth speak, was at best the object of an oral tradition until Isaiah and Ezekiel spoke of it. It dealt with ontology, the knowledge of the true nature of creaturely things, and it is a vision that takes place, as it were, in the primordial light of Adam.[206] The prophets can contemplate only this latter Merkabah, which possesses its own ten degrees or sefiroth. The prophetic vision rises from below, and beholds, through the veils of this inferior decade, the reflection of the Shekhinah as the last sefirah of the deity itself.[207] Of all the prophets, only Moses penetrated even more deeply into the mystery of the deity. Other authors, such as Asher ben David, generally held that a prophetic vision of the five lower sefiroth was possible, according to the respective rank of the prophet.[208]

---

205. Thus in Ms. British Museum, Margoliouth 752, fol. 36a. A very similar passage also in *Kether Shem Tob,* in Jellinek, *Auswahl kabbalistischer Mystik,* 41.

206. Naḥmanides in *Torath 'Adonai Temimah,* 23, and *Sha 'ar ha-Gemul,* fol. 23a. The two passages complement each other perfectly.

207. Naḥmanides on *Yeṣirah,* in *Kiryath Sefer* 6:407–408.

208. Asher ben David in his commentary on the *Shem ha-Meforash,* Ms. Casanatense, Sacerdoti 179, fol. 91b.

The transition from the sefiroth to the Merkabah represents no new act of creation ex nihilo, in the strict sense of the term. The current of emanation indeed stops, as it were, at the last sefirah, and that which unfolds from there as created being is no longer "with God" in the sense of the theosophic *'aṣiluth,* which remains in the world of the deity itself. But after this caesura the creative power continues to flow into the realm of that which is created and separated from the unity of God.[209] The creative power of God, however, not only in the one world that we know, but all nine sefiroth—with the exception of the first, in which no contraries exist since it is the Nought—unfold in their double action toward the sides of Stern Judgment and of Mercy, and each produces a thousand worlds in each direction. The universe would thus contain a total of 18,000 worlds, a figure that once again takes up an old talmudic aggadah but that also has its counterpart in certain Muslim speculations, in Ismailite gnosis.[210]

Azriel, in his commentary on the ten sefiroth, absorbed the Neoplatonic hierarchy of being into the world of the sefiroth. The first three sefiroth form, according to him (section 10), the world of the intellect, the next three the world of the souls, and the last four constitute the corporeal world, identified in other passages with the world of nature. These and similar correlations, such as, for example in the same passage, the correlation of all ten sefiroth with the spiritual and physical powers of man, only prove that Neoplatonic traditions on the one hand and ideas completely independent of it on the other are combined in rather schematic fashion. For the kabbalists the three principles of the Plotinian sequence of all existence, always remain within the world of the divine *middoth,* and it is from within this divine world that the powers radiate into all that is terrestrial and creaturely.

We shall forgo a closer analysis of the views of this circle on the constitution of creation but shall nevertheless mention the im-

209. This transition is described most clearly, in addition to the exegesis on Genesis 2:10 discussed in the preceding chapter, pp. 281–282, in *'Emunah u-Biṭṭaḥon,* chap. 24.

210. The talmudic aggadah *'Abodah Zarah* 3b mentions 18,000 simultaneously existing worlds. In the thirteenth century these worlds became 18,000 successive aeons, both among the kabbalists (cf. Baḥya ben Asher on Numbers 10:35) and among the Ismailites; cf. W. Ivanow, *JRAS* (1931): 548, who quotes this figure for the number of the worlds, from a tract attributed to Nasr ud-Din Tusi.

portant contribution made by Naḥmanides, in marked opposition to Maimonides, with his doctrine of "hidden miracles." This doctrine, repeatedly expounded by him as the foundation of the whole Torah, sees the natural law in certain respects as mere appearance behind which is concealed, in reality, a continuum of secret miracles. Hidden miracles are those that give the impression of being nothing more than the effects of the natural course of events, although they are not.[211] In relation to man, the world is not "nature" at all but a perpetually renewed miracle. In fact, the blessedness of man depends upon his acceptance of this doctrine! Naḥmanides may thus well be described as an occasionalist of the purest stripe—at least as regards Israel's relationship to nature. The opinion of most authorities, including Maimonides, that God does not always act by means of miracles and that the world in general takes its natural course is, according to Naḥmanides, a major error, the refutation of which is the purpose and meaning of the revelation of the Torah. It is true that Maimonides himself in his *Treatise on the Resurrection* had already explained the coincidence of the promises in Leviticus 26 and Deuteronomy 33 on the one hand and the natural law on the other as a "permanent miracle," and as a "miraculous sign greater than all the others."[212] Baḥya ibn Paquda, too, and above all Yehudah Halevi, discussed this subject at length. They too teach that events appear to occur in an order conforming to the natural law whereas in truth they follow the religious order that regulates them in consonance with the Torah's promises of reward and punishment for Israel in accordance with its conduct. But the notion of hidden miracles is not yet formulated by these authors; Naḥmanides took it from the astrological theory of Abraham ibn Ezra and reinterpreted it in a kabbalistic spirit.[213] God acts in nature in secret ways and introduces into its course a supernatural causal chain that is linked to the moral order of the world and to its system of rewards and

211. Naḥmanides on Genesis 17:1, 46:15; Exodus 6:3, 13:16; the preface to the commentary on Job, and in his sermon *Torath 'Adonai Temimah,* 13–15.

212. Maimonides, *Qobeṣ Teshuboth ha-Rambam* (Leipzig, 1859), 2:fol. 10b. Cf. also Charles Touati in *Annuaire de l'Ecole Pratique des Hautes Etudes,* 5e section (Sciences Religieuses) (Paris, 1971–1972): 246–247.

213. Cf. on this subject J. Kramer, *Das Problem des Wunders bei den jüdischen Religionsphilosophen* (Strassburg, 1903), 29. Naḥmanides' commentary on Exodus 6:3 is particularly important for an understanding of his use of ibn Ezra in reference to this question. Ibn Ezra, he says, discovered the truth without knowing it.

punishments. The hidden miracles are not historical, local, or individual events that are directly recognizable as miracles; they represent the action of individual providence within the natural order. As YHWH, who suspends the natural order from outside, God brings about manifest miracles; as 'El Shaddai, he causes the hidden miracles for the Patriarchs and for all Israel through the power of the Shekhinah, the sefirah *malkhuth,* his "royal dominion," thanks to which Israel is removed from the causality of natural law and placed in a higher causal order of permanent miracles. Divine intervention, in the form of rewards and punishments, occurs at every instant; rain and sunshine do not come from the hidden harmony of creation but are, in this sense, hidden miracles. Since they are by no means inherent in the inner necessity of the course of nature, these hidden miracles must be announced explicitly in the Torah, whereas doctrines such as the immortality of the soul or retribution in the beyond after death necessarily follow, according to Naḥmanides, from the natural course of things and therefore need not be explicitly mentioned in the Torah. This doctrine may well be expressed in the words of the eighteenth-century German poet and thinker G. E. Lessing: "The greatest miracle is that the true, the genuine miracles can and should become so ordinary to us."

5. Man and the Soul

Together with his specific form of theosophy in the Epistle to Burgos, Azriel also developed his anthropology. His conception of the nature and destiny of man is closely bound up with his theosophy. The possibility offered to man was that of a perfect analogy between creature and Creator. Like the Creator, the creature was to be one in its organic unity. If the fall of Adam had not interfered, the higher will would have acted in Adam, Eve, and all their descendants as a single, collective will, although under three different aspects. Man is defined by the same formula as the deity; he is the one in whom the power of the many is enclosed. But this formula, applied to man, implies his freedom to choose between good and evil, between unity and multiplicity, which is the nature of sin. Adam's fall was his abandonment of contact with the higher will. Without original sin, there would not have been any individuality, which comes into being only through separation and through multiplicity becoming independent. Likewise there would have been no dialectic of extreme opposites acting upon man, but only relative differences in the intensity with which the various *middoth* would have taken effect. The paradisiacal state therefore would have remained a nonindividual and undialectical condition. Life would have developed its rhythm not through contraries but in slight fluctuations. There existed a supreme state of conduct, *hanhagah,* by virtue of which man would have behaved in perfect conformity with the higher will. Adam violated this supreme state, which also would have represented a living unity of opposites, and as a result lost the possibility of such a truly mystical conduct.

Only an eschatological perspective allows us to contemplate again as a possibility the state that today the mystics alone anticipate in their *kawwanah.* This is the supreme aspect of God, by which he is called *'elohe 'amen,* the God of faithfulness, namely, confirmation. By this aspect of divine action, God constantly renews the creation of nature. Only when He becomes visible again can there be a restoration of the connection of all things interrupted by the Fall, and especially of all opposites. Everything that was defective must draw from the possibility of perfection disposed in its contrary and be united with it. To this highest possibility in man, which is grounded beyond the intellectual in the most hidden sphere, corresponds the possibility of his participation in the unity and holiness of God and the plenitude of his benediction. The participation of man in the divine realm, at present attainable only in mystical prayer and *kawwanah,* will be fully represented and realized in the messianic kingdom.[214]

The soul of man is created out of nothing only in an exoteric sense. In a mystical sense it comes from the *'aṣiluth* and is of a divine nature. It does not derive its origin, like the souls of the animals, in the elements, nor in the separate, angelic intelligences alone. The latter idea, which doubtless was known to Naḥmanides from a work by Isaac Israeli, was rejected by him as an "opinion of the Greeks."[215] The human soul is essentially different from the animal

214. All this according to *Madda'e ha-Yahaduth* 2:234–237.

215. Naḥmanides on Leviticus 17:11. What is said there concerning the origin of the souls of animals is taken from the pseudo-Aristotelian "Chapter of the Elements," which is in reality the work of the Jewish Neoplatonist Isaac Israeli; cf. the text in A. Altmann, *JJS* 7 (1956): 42.

soul;[216] Naḥmanides adopts, along with other kabbalists of the earliest period, the Platonic view of the soul, according to which there exist different souls in man and not only different faculties of a unitary soul. According to Naḥmanides, man's *anima rationalis* unites the rational and the mystical-intuitive, and hence he sees no need for further distinctions. Nevertheless, the weight shifts imperceptibly to the second side: the highest soul, *neshamah,* which comes from *binah* and *yesod,* is the mediator of prophecy, and through it man, in the state of *debhequth,* attains communion with the deity as a result of the longing for its origin implanted in it.[217] Enoch and the three Patriarchs, Moses, and Elijah had achieved this supreme state already on earth;[218] however, it is not a full *unio mystica* with the deity but rather a *communio,* as we have argued at length in our discussion of the subject of *kawwanah.* In the prophetic vision, during which the soul is united with the objects of its contemplation, it is in this state of *debhequth,* that it obtains a "knowledge of God face to face."[219] In this longing for its origin, the highest soul of man becomes capable of penetrating all the intermediary spheres and rising up to God by means of its acts—which, strangely enough, are united here with contemplation.[220]

The eclectic manner in which the kabbalists adopted philosophical doctrines concerning the soul is also apparent in the fact that Azriel, for example, accepts the Aristotelian definition of the soul as the form of the body, seemingly unaware of the contradiction be-

---

216. Cf. Naḥmanides on Genesis 2:7.

217. Cf. on Numbers 22:23. On the sefirotic origin of the *neshamah* cf., e.g., Exodus 31:13 and Naḥmanides' sermon on Ecclesiastes, 16.

218. Cf. on Deuteronomy 5:23, 11:22, 21:18, as well as in the *Sha'ar ha-Gemul,* fol. 21b.

219. Cf. on Numbers 22:41 and above all Deuteronomy 34:10. Naḥmanides defines this status of *debhequth* in his commentary on Deuteronomy 26:19. Cf. also above, p. 303, n. 206.

220. Thus above all in the psychological passage of Naḥmanides' halakhic work *Sefer ha-Ma'or,* to which Isaac of Acre, Ms. Munich 17, fol. 143a, already refers, with good reason, in order to explain Naḥmanides' psychology. In his responsum to his cousin, Jonah Gerondi, on the creation of the souls, Naḥmanides explains that the soul was born at the same time as the sefirotic world of the primordial days, invoking on this point a verse of Yehudah Halevi to which he gives a mystical interpretation. This well-known poem, which glorifies the emanation of the soul from the Holy Spirit, is also mentioned approvingly by Naḥmanides in other passages, cf. on Numbers 11:11.

tween this idea and important kabbalistic doctrines.[221] The contradiction results from the adoption and further development of the doctrine of metempsychosis. While this doctrine is rather openly propounded in the Book *Bahir,* as we saw on p. 188ff., it is treated, strangely enough, as a great mystery in Provence and in Gerona. The authors without exception speak of it only in hints and in veiled allusions. They make no attempt to account for this idea but presuppose it as a truth handed down by esoteric tradition. The term *gilgul,* generally used at a later date for the transmigration of souls, seems to be as yet unknown among these early authors. Instead, they prefer to speak of *sod ha-'ibbur.* This term, literally "secret of impregnation," is used in the Talmud for the methods of computing the calendar, handed down only orally for a long time, the idea being that the leap years were impregnated, as it were, by the addition of an extra month. But *'ibbur* can, if necessary, also be understood as "transition," and it is doubtless in this sense that the term was picked up by the kabbalists. The "secret of the *'ibbur*" is that of the passage of the soul from one body to another and not, as among the later kabbalists,[222] a real phenomenon of impregnation through which, after birth an additional soul sometimes enters into the one originally born with a person.

We still do not know what led the kabbalists of the first generation to treat this doctrine in such a strictly esoteric manner and what danger they saw in exposing it to the public. It is most unlikely that fear of the Catholic Church, which had officially condemned this doctrine, was a factor. Where no christological elements were involved, Jewish theology generally had no inhibitions. The polemics directed by the philosophers against this doctrine should likewise have stimulated controversy rather than secrecy. Naḥmanides had no lack of opportunity to denounce the philosophic criticism of this doctrine. Instead, he retreated into extremely prudent, and for the uninitiated, often impenetrable statements in his com-

221. Azriel, *Perush 'Aggadoth,* 33.

222. Thus, for the first time, in Shemtob ibn Gaon, *Kether Shem Tob* on Leviticus 18:6, and Isaac of Acre, *Me'irath 'Enayim,* Ms. Munich 17, fol. 100a and above all 139b. [See now also M. Idel "No Kabbalistic Tradition," in I. Twersky (ed.) *Rabbi Moses Naḥmanides,* (1983), 53 n. 8. There now seems to be evidence that Naḥmanides (and not only his disciples after 1300), had already distinguished between transmigration and impregnation. Z.W.]

mentary on the book of Job, the key to which, according to the kabbalists of Gerona, lay precisely in the doctrine of metempsychosis. According to the kabbalistic view, Job had to suffer in order to make amends for sins committed in an earlier life. Undoubtedly basing himself on traditions passed down to him, Naḥmanides discovered in the words of Elihu (Job 33) a clear indication and a great number of proof texts for this doctrine, in which all the problems of theodicy find their solution. Certain prescriptions of the Bible, above all the institution of levirate marriage (Deuteronomy 25), according to which the brother of a man who dies childless must marry his widow, are explained with reference to this doctrine. The son of such a marriage bears within him the soul of the deceased and can therefore fulfill in this life the commandment of procreation, the fulfilment of which had been denied to him in his previous life. Also the sterility of women is explained by substitution of souls: when a male soul inhabits a female body, the woman remains childless.[223] The Gerona School still knew nothing about a migration through the bodies of animals. It should also be noted that although the doctrine of metempsychosis serves primarily to explain the sufferings of the righteous and the prosperity of the wicked and presupposes a very wide and inclusive nexus, it appears in Gerona as very limited in scope and as concerned mainly with the phenomenon of childlessness. Not all sins lead to a further migration of the soul, only those connected with procreation. These migrations are as much a punishment and an increase in suffering as a renewed chance for the reparation of previous wrongs. The transmigration of souls therefore constitutes an arrangement through which the divine Mercy and Stern Judgment are held in equilibrium.[224] Azriel and other authors apparently also combine the mystery of *'ibbur* with other processes in the world of emanation that, however, are not clear. This mystery, it is repeatedly emphasized, has its root in the sefirah *ḥokhmah*

223. Thus, for the first time, in Ezra, *Perush 'Aggadoth,* Ms. Vatican 441, fol. 53a, printed in *Liqqute Shikhḥah* (Ferrara), fol. 14b. An interpretation of the book of Job on the basis of the doctrine of metempsychosis is still offered as representing the literal sense of Scripture by Jacob Zlotnik, *A New Introduction to the Book of Job* (in Hebrew) (Jerusalem, 1938).

224. Azriel, *Perush Tefilloth,* Ms. Parma, fol. 84a. In this sense the transmigration of souls is strictly distinguished, among the kabbalists of Gerona, from the punishment of hell. To the question whether the righteous too return in new bodies, not as a punishment but for the salvation of the world, Ezra gives an affirmative answer.

and is somehow grounded in the "transition" of the powers united in the divine Sophia to the lower sefiroth.[225] Occasionally even the mystical illumination produced by the effluence of the divine power from one sefirah to another is designated as *sod ha-'ibbur.*[226] In general, the kabbalists of Gerona restricted the transmigration of souls, on the basis of Job 33:29, to three rebirths following the first entry of the soul into the human body,[227] though they admitted the existence of exceptional cases. An important detail has been transmitted from the school of Naḥmanides. In the famous disputation with the ex-Jew Paulus Christiani, the monk invokes the well-known aggadah according to which the Messiah was born at the hour of the destruction of the Temple. To this Naḥmanides replied: "Either this aggadah is not true, or else it has another explanation according to the mysteries of the sages."[228] Although the wording of this reply clearly points to kabbalistic teaching, it has not been understood until now. Naḥmanides does indeed give a plausible—literal and exoteric—explanation of the aggadah, to the effect that the Messiah was currently biding his time in the terrestrial paradise, but his true opinion can be gleaned from the questions of his disciple Shesheth des Mercadell concerning metempsychosis, where this aggadah figures as a proof text for this doctrine.[229] What the aggadah means to say is, therefore, that since the destruction of the Temple the soul of the Messiah is in the process of *'ibbur.* On this point, Naḥmanides and his school depart from the older idea of the *Bahir* section 126, according to which the soul of the Messiah does not inhabit a human body before.

On the other hand, this text already exhibits the transition to the doctrine, first attested shortly after Naḥmanides, to the effect that the name of Adam is an abbreviation (ADaM) of the three forms of existence of this soul in Adam, David, and the Messiah.

---

225. Cf. Azriel, in *Madda'e ha-Yahaduth* 2:232 and 237, as well as the obscure allusions in *'Emunah u-Bittaḥon,* chap. 4. On Deuteronomy 3:26, Baḥya ben Asher explains that the notion of *'ibbur* represents the power of the generations, impregnated as it were by the inner power of the sefiroth. Cf. also herein, p. 421.

226. Cf. in the very old glosses of Ms. Parma, de Rossi 68, fol. 16a.

227. This verse must, in fact, have appeared very suggestive to the kabbalists: "All these things does God work twice or thrice with a man: To bring back his soul from decay, that he may be enlightened with the light of the living." This verse later became the standard kabbalistic proof text.

228. Cf. *Wikkuaḥ ha-Ramban,* ed. Steinschneider (Berlin, 1860), 8.

229. Cf. *Tarbiz* 16 (1945): 144.

This would imply that the Messiah has to pass through various stages of incarnation so that his essence "always lives among us" in one form or another. The idea that also arose shortly after Naḥmanides and according to which "soul sparks" can fly off from a central soul and thus pass simultaneously through many bodies is not yet attested in Gerona.[230] This doctrine was also used in the school of Solomon ibn Adreth in order to eliminate the difficulty that would arise at the resurrection of the dead for the different bodies through which one single soul had passed. The different bodies of the resurrected would be inhabited by sparks of the same soul, thus providing a solution to the problem.[231] According to Azriel there also exist souls of such exalted rank that they do not return to the world of bodies, but remain in the "world of life" and thus do not participate at all, or only in a purely spiritual sense, in the resurrection.[232] In this manner the kabbalists seem to move, at least as regards a privileged category of superior souls, in the direction of a denial of bodily resurrection—precisely the view for which the radical Maimonideans were so bitterly rebuked. It should be added, however, that this idea appears only in strictly esoteric contexts describing the eschatological progress of the souls after their departure from the terrestrial world and was never formulated in a dogmatic manner.

6. The Book Temunah *and the Doctrine of World Cycles or* Shemiṭṭoth

By way of conclusion of this investigation, one more very important doctrine should be discussed that is frequently alluded to in the school of Gerona but expounded in detail in a separate tract that has achieved a considerable significance for the development of the Kabbalah. This is the doctrine of the *shemiṭṭoth,* or world cycles, as expounded above all in the anonymous Book *Temunah.*[233] This book

230. Cf. the important text, ibid., 143.

231. Ms. Parma, de Rossi 1221, fol. 186b.

232. Cf. the prudent, but unequivocal, formulation in *Madda'e ha-Yahaduth* 2:238.

233. The research of my students and subsequent colleagues Moshe Idel and the late Ephraim Gottlieb have rendered highly improbable the view, previously also defended by me, that this text was composed before the *Zohar.* A closer examination of the manuscripts has shown the alleged quotation in Abraham Abulafia to be erro-

provides a kabbalistic explanation of the letters of the Hebrew alphabet. The title signifies "Book of the Figure," that is, the figure or shape of the Hebrew letters. In contrast to all other kabbalistic writings from Catalonia, this work carries no indication of the author's identity. The attribution to the mishnaic teacher and hero of Merkabah-mysticism Ishmael ben Elisha, common since the sixteenth century and also found in the printed editions of the book,[234] is late. All early manuscripts are anonymous and make no pseudepigraphic claims. The author's mode of exposition is entirely different from that of the other kabbalists of Gerona known to us. There is no discursive development of an argument nor any reference to real or alleged sources; on the contrary, everything is presented in an authoritative tone that excludes any further discussion. The style is, however, one of uncommon brevity and rich in obscure images and expressions. It is obvious that the author deliberately chose an epigrammatic, often semipoetic, and in any case highly allusive style that conceals more than it reveals in matters of detail.

If the text really originated in Gerona, it is by far the most difficult one produced in this circle. The early dating (ca. 1280), based on a mistaken quotation in Abraham Abulafia, must now be abandoned (cf. n. 234). On the other hand, its symbolism of the sefiroth, militates against an early date. Perhaps the book was composed not in Catalonia, but in Provence; the spelling of foreign words of Romance origin occurring in the text could just as well be Catalan as Provençal. The author's kabbalistic universe of discourse is already very richly developed, and the doctrine of the *shemiṭṭoth,* which is at the center of his system, is propounded as a matter of course and as if it were by no means a new idea.

As a matter of fact, doctrines relating to cosmic cycles in the

---

neous. It seems that the book was written around 1300. There is, however, no gainsaying that the writings of the Gerona school do indeed propound for the first time the doctrine of *shemiṭṭoth,* albeit in a simpler form; cf. p. 470. [Whilst the fully articulated doctrines of the *Temunah* cannot, therefore, be said to reflect Gerona teaching in every detail, it may not be illegitimate to use the evidence of the *Temunah* to illustrate the notion of cosmic cycles as they began to emerge and crystallize in the school of Gerona. See also Editor's Preface, pp. xiii–xiv. Z.W.]

234. Korez, 1784 is regarded as the first edition. I quote from the second edition (Lemberg, 1892), which is better. But the real editio princeps seems to have been printed in Cracow in 1599. Daniel Janotzki attests that he saw a copy in 1743 in a Jewish library; cf. Steinschneider, *Hebräische Bibliographie,* vol. 14 (1874), 81. This printing seems, for the time being, to be completely lost.

evolution of the world were also known in Jewish medieval literature outside the Kabbalah. Through the intermediary of Indian and Arabic sources, rather than under the influence of Platonic thoughts, ideas of this type slipped into astrological writings in particular. Abraham bar Ḥiyya in Aragon was familiar with them around 1125 as the "teachings of certain philosophers," for he informs us that some of them say:

> After all the creatures have passed from potentiality to actuality, God once again returns them to potentiality as in the beginning and then brings them back to actuality a second and a third time, and thus without end. . . . Others again say that the days of the world are 49,000 years and that each of the seven planets reigns 7,000 years in the world. When at the end of 49,000 years they have completed their reign, God destroys His world, leaves it for 1,000 years in a state of *tohu,* and at the end of the fiftieth millennium He renews it as in the beginning.[235]

This is an astrological cosmic theory also known from Arabic sources, and the author adds that we are not permitted to accept such ideas, which are nothing more than mere suppositions. Ideas of this kind must have been known to other scholars also and no doubt circulated in other Jewish groups as is proved by the testimony of Muṭahhar al-Maqdisi. Writing in the tenth century, he reports that a Jewish scholar—evidently in the Orient—assured him that certain of his coreligionists believed in a perpetual process of the re-creation of the world.[236]

Here is how this doctrine is presented in its kabbalistic version: the hidden creative power of God is expressed not only in the sefiroth, but also in the succession and sequence of creations, in each of which the various sefiroth unfold their power. Everything that is interior must be expressed in that which is exterior, and thus the creative power of each divine potency must be fully actualized. But such realization is only possible if this power exercises its action in a cosmic unit, the laws of which are determined by the specific nature of the respective potency. On this point, however, the kabbalistic

235. Cf. *Megillath ha-Megalleh* (Berlin, 1924), 10. Related ideas also are mentioned by Saadya in his commentary on *Yeṣirah* (French translation by Lambert, 19), as well by Yehudah ben Barzilai, 174.

236. Cf. the French translation of the *Kitāb al-bad'i wa'l-ta'riḥi* (French translation by Cl. Huart) 2:44.

doctrine distinguishes between the first three sefiroth and the seven lower ones. The first three are hidden potencies that are not, strictly speaking, *middoth* like the other sefiroth. This is illustrated, for example, by the fact that in the symbolism of the primordial man the seven lower sefiroth correspond to external members, whereas the three higher ones correspond to hidden powers of the brain, localized in the three cerebral cavities. They do not act in the visible sphere and do not build worlds like the other sefiroth, but constitute as root, material, and formative power the substratum of the cosmic process. If (as the Book *Temunah* seems to assume) there exist hidden structures in which they are expressed, these escape the knowledge of even the kabbalists.

The seven lower sefiroth, on the other hand, which correspond to the seven primordial days of creation, are expressed in seven cosmic units, each of which represents a separate creation. Each is a complete world, organically formed out of chaos; each is formed according to the character of its dominant sefirah and lasts 7,000 years, that is, one cosmic week of God whom, according to the psalmist, a thousand years are like one day. Subsequently, this creation returns to the state of *tohu* and, having lain fallow for one cosmic Sabbath, is only reconstructed through the activity of the next sefirah. Having discovered an allusion to this idea in the biblical prescription concerning the sabbatical year (Deuteronomy 15), during which the fallow field renews its powers, the adherents of this doctrine designated every one of these units of creation with the term *shemiṭṭah,* used in this context in the Torah. Although each sefirah stamps its cosmic *shemiṭṭah* of seven millennia with its specific character, nevertheless the other sefiroth cooperate with it, as a kind of concomitant accessory motif, helping to vary the effect of the principal sefirah. In each millennium, one of these contributing sefiroth stands out a little more prominently than the others. After six millennia, the sefirah that contains the power of the Sabbath and of rest takes effect, and the world celebrates a Sabbath at the end of which it returns to chaos. Seven of these *shemiṭṭoth* exhaust the productive power hidden in the seven "sefiroth of construction." After 49,000 years, in the "great jubilee year," the entire creation returns to its origin in the womb of *binah,* the "mother of the world," just as according to the biblical ordinance concerning the jubilee year, after fifty years "liberty is proclaimed throughout the land," and all things return to their original owner. The cosmic jubilee of 50,000 years is therefore the most comprehensive cosmic unit; in it the power of the Creator takes full effect in the sequence of the seven fundamental units of *shemiṭṭoth,* which together constitute the *yobhel,* the cosmic jubilee.

In a broader framework, this doctrine displays a certain structural similarity to the ideas of Joachim of Fiore, who at the end of the twelfth century gave an historico-metaphysical twist to the Christian doctrine of the Trinity that attained considerable historical importance. The fundamental idea was that the deity expresses itself not only in the three persons of the Trinity, but that its hidden power also acts in external creation and in the history of the world according to a sequence of three periods, each of which receives its character from one of the persons of the Trinity. The hidden plenitude of the deity manifests itself therefore in the totality of the successive historical periods or states *(status).* In every *status,* the divine revelation assumes a different form. The period of the Father was characterized by the revelation of the Old Testament and the reign of the Mosaic law. In the period of the Son, there began the reign of Grace, as expressed in the Catholic Church and its institutions. In the third period, on the other hand, whose advent he considered imminent, the Holy Spirit would reign alone; the mystical content of the Gospel would be completely revealed and either penetrate the external institutions of the Church or render them redundant. This doctrine played a considerable role in the history of the Franciscan order and the sects of "spirituals." It is not our purpose here to discuss in detail the historical implications of this doctrine, to which much scholarly attention has been devoted in recent decades, but merely to draw attention to an interesting kabbalistic analogy to Joachite doctrine with its strong utopian elements and explosive power. Direct historical connections between the two systems seem to me most unlikely although chronologically not impossible. Joachim developed his doctrines between 1180 and 1200 in Calabria, and by the time it had spread to France and Spain, the kabbalistic doctrine of the *shemiṭṭoth* was already known in Gerona. The Book *Temunah* was composed at the end of the period that saw the composition of the great Joachite pseudepigrapha (the commentary on Jeremiah). Of more immediate relevance to our discussion is the fact that the assumption of an inner dynamic and mystical structure of the deity led, in both cases, to similar consequences. But what for Joachim is one process of world history, divided into periods from creation up to the end of time is divided by the kabbalists according to a rhythm of the world-process as a whole and its cosmic units of creation. It is precisely the utopian and radical element, still lacking in the astrological forms of this doctrine, that connects the kabbalistic version with the Joachite one. I do not believe that the issue of Joachim's possible Jewish ancestry, recently raised, is of any relevance to our subject.[237]

The historical origins of this doctrine remain to be examined. It is entirely conceivable that it came from the Orient to Provence, where it became associated at a later date with the doctrine of the sefiroth. The penchant for great numbers in the cosmic cycles, which quickly led beyond the 50,000 years of a cosmic jubilee, corresponds to similar tendencies in India and the Ismailite gnosis. As early as the thirteenth century (as Baḥya ben Asher attests), the single *yobhel* had become 18,000 and the seven *shemiṭṭoth* had mushroomed to thousands.[238] The view that the slowing down of the revolutions of the stars at the end of every period of creation took place in geometric progression led to an extension of the 7,000 years of every single *shemiṭṭah,* reaching prodigious numbers. On the other hand these ideas may also have roots, however tenuous, in the Aggadah. Several old rabbinic dicta were quoted by the kabbalists in this context for example, the epigram of R. Qaṭina in *Sanhedrin* 97a: "Six millennia shall the world exist, and in the following one it shall be desolate," deduced, paradoxically enough from Isaiah 2:11. Apparently the idea of such cosmic weeks arose independently of any scriptural foundation. Similarly, the same talmudic text declares: "As the land lies fallow once in seven years, the world too lies fallow one thousand years in seven thousand," and only later, in the eighth millennium, the new aeon, which is the "world to come," will begin. The midrashic text known as *Pirqe Rabbi Eliezer* speaks in chapter 51 of a periodic opening and closing of the cosmic book or, to be more exact, of an unrolling of the celestial scroll, indicating a similar notion of continual creation. Another motif that later attained great importance among the kabbalists was provided by the dictum

---

237. Cf. Herbert Grundmann, *Deutsches Archiv für Erforschung des Mittelalters* 16 (1960): 519–528.

238. Thus in the treatise of an anonymous kabbalist from the end of the thirteenth century, quoted by Meir ibn Sahula in his supercommentary on Naḥmanides, fols. 27d–28b.

of R. Abbahu (third century) in *Bereshith Rabba,* section 9 (and the parallel paraphrase in *Shemoth Rabba*), who deduced from Ecclesiastes 3:11 that "God created and destroyed worlds before creating this one; He said, these please me, those do not please me." Here the motif of the worlds that succeed our creation is combined with that of previous worlds, a motif that also plays a role in the doctrine of the *shemiṭṭah.* The destruction of the world is explained by the kabbalists of Gerona as the interruption of the current of the emanation, which no longer flows toward the lower worlds, toward heaven and earth, but remains closed in on itself. Creation, then, remains in a chaotic state, and only when the current is once again renewed is new life formed.

In the Book *Temunah* the doctrine of the *shemiṭṭoth* is elaborated in great detail and closely linked, above all, with the mystical conception of the nature of the Torah. There exists a supreme Torah, which we have already encountered on page 287 as *torah qedumah.* This primordial Torah is none other than the divine Sophia, containing within itself in pure spirituality, the traces of all being and all becoming. Its letters are "very subtle and hidden, without figure, form, or limit." But when the lower sefiroth emanate, they act in every *shemiṭṭah* in a different manner, according to the particular law of each one. No *shemiṭṭah* is by itself capable of manifesting all the power of God, expressed in the Sophia and in the primordial Torah. Rather, the timeless and self-enclosed content of this primordial Torah is distributed at the time of the cosmic and historical creation in such a way that each *shemiṭṭah* unveils a particular aspect of the divine revelation, and with that, the intention pursued by God in this particular unit of creation. This means, in effect, that the specific causality of each *shemiṭṭah* is expressed in a corresponding revelation of the Torah. The spiritual engrams hidden in the primordial Torah certainly do not undergo any change in their essence, but they are manifested in various permutations and forms as constituted by the letters of the Torah, and as combined in different manners in accordance with the changing *shemiṭṭoth.*

The presupposition of the one Torah that is at the same time the highest and most all-embracing mystical essence thus serves as a justification of the existence of the most diverse manifestations in the changing *shemiṭṭoth.* The fundamental principle of the absolute divine character of the Torah is thus maintained, but it receives an interpretation that renders possible a completely new conception. It is necessary, in this connection, to emphasize that such a pillar of contemporary orthodox Judaism as Naḥmanides saw no deviation from the doctrine of a single divine revelation in this idea. In the preface to his commentary on the Torah he draws attention to the difference in principle between the absolute nature of the Torah and its modes of appearance to us. The Torah exists in itself as a unitary organism of divine names—that is of manifestations of his power or energies—without there being a division into "comprehensible words." In this state, the Torah is not "legible" for human beings. At the Sinaitic revelation, God taught Moses how to read the Torah by a division into letters and words, in such manner that it yielded a meaning in the Hebrew language. These considerations also opened the door to the possibility of alternative mystical readings, and it is precisely this notion that the Book *Temunah* presents in such a radical fashion.

In fact, according to this book, the world in which we live and which we know as the creation that began so and so many thousand years ago is not the first. It was preceded by another *shemiṭṭah:* the aeon of Grace, in the course of which all the sefiroth acted under the determining regime of this principal sefirah. The world "built by Grace" at that time—according to the interpretation given by the kabbalists to Psalms 89:3—bears some resemblance to the Golden Age of Greek mythology. This *shemiṭṭah* was entirely bathed in light. The spheres of the heavens were simple and not composed of four elements; men stood at the highest spiritual pinnacle and possessed a pure body. Even the cattle and other animals stood as high then as the animals that bear the Merkabah in our *shemiṭṭah.* The cult practiced by the creatures resembled the adoration of God by the angels in the present aeon. There was neither an exile of the body, as that of Israel, nor an exile of the souls, which is the transmigration of souls.[239] Man looked like the celestial man whom Ezekiel saw upon the throne. The manifestation of the primordial Torah as beheld by the creatures of that *shemiṭṭah* came exclusively from the side of Grace. Since there existed no evil inclination and no tempting serpent, the Torah of this *shemiṭṭah* (that is, the manner in

239. The Book *Temunah* is one of the oldest texts to use the technical term *gilgul* for the transmigration of soul; the term must be a translation of either Arabic *tanāsuḥ* or Latin *revolutio.* Cf. on the subject of this terminology my discussion in *Tarbiz* 16 (1945): 135–139.

which the mystical letters were combined) contained nothing concerning impurities or prohibitions. Even those letters had a simple form and were not in large measure composite, as at present.[240]

It is altogether different with our present *shemiṭṭah,* the aeon of Stern Judgment. All the powers of judgment are concentrated here, and just as every organic process leaves a residue, waste, and sediment—generally designated as dregs by the kabbalists since the Book *Temunah*—so also the present *shemiṭṭah* is a collection basin for all the residues.[241] No wonder, then, that in this aeon gold is the metal most sought after, for in its red color it symbolizes the power of judgment—in contrast to the whiteness of silver, which represents grace. From the regime of this sefirah come the exiles and migrations of the soul. This also explains the particular character of the Torah, which is designed to show the way to the worship of God under the specific conditions of this aeon. The present aeon is ruled by the evil inclination that stems from the power of Stern Judgment and that seduces man to idolatry, which had no place during the preceding period. At present, the Torah aims to conquer the power of evil, and that is why it contains commandments and prohibitions, things permitted, things forbidden, the pure and the impure. Only a few souls, originating in the preceding aeon, return in order to preserve the world through the power of grace and to temper the destructive sternness of judgment. Among them are Enoch, Abraham, and Moses. At present, even the perfectly righteous must enter into the bodies of animals; this is the secret reason for the special prescriptions relating to ritual slaughter.

The doctrine of the passage of the souls into the bodies of animals appears here for the first time in kabbalistic literature; it may reflect a direct contact with Cathar ideas (as suggested on p. 238) and serve to support the argument for the Provençal origin of the *Temunah.* But among the Cathars as also in India this doctrine led to vegetarianism whereas here, on the contrary, it led to a more meticulous observance of the prescriptions concerning the consumption of meat; the slaughtering of an animal and the eating of its flesh are related to the elevation of the soul confined there from an animal to

---

240. Cf. the description of this *shemiṭṭah* in *Temunah,* fol. 37b, and, in a better text, in David ben Zimra, *Magen David* (Amsterdam, 1713), fol. 10a.

241. Cf. ibid., fol. 40a. In addition to the description offered there, fols. 38b–40a, the author also adds a parallel description, fol. 29a.

a human existence. A distinct concept of hell, which would compete with the notion of the transmigration of souls, seems to be outside the purview of our author. For the rest, the book deals with this doctrine only with great reserve, in spite of its almost unlimited validity; the old commentary, printed together with the editions of the text, was to be much less discreet.[242]

The author even knew that in the present aeon the letters of the Torah had refused to assemble themselves into the particular combinations that would compose the form in which it was to be given to Israel at Sinai. They saw the law of Stern Judgment and how this *shemiṭṭah* is entangled and ensnared in evil, and they did not wish to descend into the filth upon which the palace of this aeon was erected. But "God arranged with them that the great and glorious name would be combined with them and would be contained in the Torah."[243] Apparently this signifies more than the direct mention of the name of God in the Torah. Rather, the name of God is contained everywhere in the Torah, in a mystical mode; as ibn Gikatilla put it: "It is woven into" the Torah. All the laws and mysteries of this aeon are inscribed in secret language in this Torah, which embraces all ten sefiroth, and all this is indicated by the particular form of the letters. "No angel can understand them, but only God Himself, who explained them to Moses and communicated to him their entire mystery" (fol. 30a). On the basis of these instructions, Moses wrote the Torah in his own language, organizing it, however, in a mystical spirit that conformed to these secret causalities. The present aeon must obey this law of Stern Judgment and the Torah that corresponds to it, and only at its end will all things return to their original state. The author proceeds from the assumption that there also exists within the *shemiṭṭah* an internal cyclical system. The human race, born from the one Adam, developed into millions of individuals. After the redemption, which will take place in the sixth millenium, humanity will perish in the same rhythm in which it began. "In the manner in which everything came, everything passes away." "The doors to the street are shut" (Eccles. 12:4), and everything returns home to its origin, even the angels of the Merkabah corresponding to this aeon, the heavenly spheres, and the stars. Ev-

242. Cf. ibid., fols. 16b, 29a, 39b.
243. Cf. ibid., fol. 29b.

erything goes back into its "receptacle," and the world lies fallow until, through the power of the next sefirah, God calls forth a new *shemiṭṭah.*[244]

The next *shemiṭṭah* seems, in comparison with our own, like a return to utopia. Instead of the differences of class that now prevail, there will be complete equality. The Torah will deal solely with things holy and pure, and the sacrifices will not be animals, but offerings of gratitude and love. There will be no transmigration of souls and no defilement, neither of the body nor of the soul. The entire world will be like a paradise. No evil inclination will exist and no sin. The souls will walk like the angels, with God in their midst. The face of men will be of great beauty and will reflect a divine light "without the slightest veil" such as Moses had to wear in our aeon, covering his face because men would not have been able to bear this brilliance. The descriptions of these three *shemiṭṭoth* greatly stimulated the imagination, and kabbalistic literature of the following generations is full of speculations concerning the conditions prevailing there, whereas the other *shemiṭṭoth* are only vaguely outlined. Nowhere does the Book *Temunah* go beyond the cosmic jubilee year, to which our *shemiṭṭah* belongs. What comes afterward remains unclear. According to Joseph ben Samuel of Catalonia, all things return to the hiddenness of the divine wisdom, and Jacob ben Shesheth seems to have entertained similar ideas.[245] Only later kabbalists seem to have assumed a return of all things to *'en-sof,* to be followed by a new creation out of the mystical Nought. Naḥmanides' successors already put forward far-reaching speculations concerning subsequent cosmic jubilees, but these were rejected by other kabbalists as sheer fantasies. In the opinion of Menaḥem Recanati, speculation beyond our present cosmic jubilee is strictly forbidden. The oldest Kabbalah, in any case, remained within these limits.

But more important than the details of this doctrine—elaborated tirelessly above all by fourteenth-century kabbalists such as Isaac of Acre, the anonymous author of the books *Peli'ah* and *Qanah,*[246] and others—is its underlying principle. I have in mind here especially the combination of apocalyptic mysticism of history

244. Cf. ibid., fols. 57a–59a.

245. *Meshibh Debharim,* Ms. Oxford, fol. 63a; Joseph ben Samuel's view is quoted by Isaac of Acre, *Me 'irath 'Enayim,* Ms. Munich 17, fol. 18b.

246. But see later, n. 250.

on the one hand and cosmogonic theosophy on the other. The doctrine of *shemiṭṭoth* enlarged the perspective of the Kabbalah to an extraordinary degree, since it viewed the development of creation not solely within the narrow framework of a cosmic week. It did not, of course, neglect further speculations within this framework. Following the example of Abraham bar Ḥiyya (or possibly that of his Christian sources, for example, Isidore of Seville), Naḥmanides and others posited a parallelism between the content of each day of creation and the millennium in the history of the world that corresponds to it. As a result, all of history appears as the manifestation of a content implicit from the very beginning in each day of creation. Using the framework of this historical construction within the cosmic week, the kabbalists sought to understand the history of Israel and its place in creation. The representatives of the *shemiṭṭah*-speculations, by way of contrast, attempted to explain the fate of Israel by means of a more comprehensive symbol. The very nature of the aeon of Stern Judgment has a compelling effect on the fate of Israel and its vicissitudes. These kabbalists wrestled no less than Yehudah Halevi in his *Kuzari* with the problem of the history of Israel, and they emphasized no less than he its national aspects. But their speculations on the activity of the sefirah of Stern Judgment within the deity and its impulse to externalize itself actively in its full force provided a powerful symbol that enabled them to associate the historical existence of Israel with the very essence of creation. The representatives of this doctrine, too, awaited with impatience the great messianic revolution, but their expectations transcended the limits of the traditional conceptions of redemption—as if the idea of the cosmic Sabbath in the last millennium and of the redemption preceding it were no longer sufficient to satisfy the utopian urge. Hence the author of the Book *Temunah* transfers his interest from the redemption at the end of the current *shemiṭṭah* (about which he has little to say anyway) to the vision of the following one. The vision of the end of the present *shemiṭṭah,* of the gradual extinction of humanity, and of the slowing down of the rhythm of life in the entire creation—of which older Jewish messianism knew nothing—already forms part of this newly erupting sense of utopia. In this conception of redemption, the Messiah himself no longer plays a visible role; interest is completely focused on the cosmic processes.

For the historian of religion, the most striking aspect of the doctrine of *shemiṭṭoth* resides in the close link between a rigorous

Jewish piety that maintains the revelatory character of the Torah and the vision of a change in the manifestation of the Torah in the other *shemiṭṭoth.* We have a clear case of utopian antinomianism. The assertion of the *Temunah* that "what is forbidden below is permitted above" (fol. 62a) entails the logical inference that what is forbidden according to the reading of the Torah in our present aeon might be permitted and even required in other aeons, when some other divine quality—Mercy, for example, instead of Stern Judgment—governs the world. In fact, in both the Book *Temunah* itself and writings that follow in its footsteps we find astonishing statements regarding the Torah that imply a virtual antinomianism.

Two ideas should be stressed at this point. Several passages suggest that in the current *shemiṭṭah* one of the letters of the Torah is missing. This lack can be understood in two ways. It could signify that one of the letters has a defective form, contrary to its past perfection, that would of course be restored in a future *shemiṭṭah.* However, as the book indefatigably asserts, since each letter represents a divine potency, the imperfection of its form could mean that the sefirah of Stern Judgment that predominates today effectively restricts the efficacy of the divine lights, which are therefore unable to reveal themselves perfectly. According to this view, one such "defective" or incomplete letter of the alphabet is *shin,* which in its perfect form should have four heads, but which is written at present with three: ש . But the statement also could signify that today one of the letters of the alphabet is missing completely: it has become invisible in our aeon but will reappear and become legible once again in the future aeon. Such a view evidently implies a thoroughly changed attitude toward the received Torah. In fact, it can (and did) lead to the supposition that all the prohibitions we read in the present text of the Torah are due to this absent letter.[247] The alphabet, and with it the complete Torah, are actually based upon a series of twenty-three letters; if we find in the Torah positive and negative commandments, it is only because this letter has dropped out of the present text. Everything negative is connected with the missing letter of the original alphabet.[248]

According to another and no less audacious idea, the complete

---

247. Cf. *Temunah,* fol. 61b on the figure of the *shin* in the future aeon.

248. Cf. Ms. Vatican 223, fol. 197a and the quotation from a tract of the *Temunah* circle in David ben Zimra, *Magen David* (Amsterdam, 1713), fol. 47b.

Torah contained in reality seven books, corresponding to the seven sefiroth and *shemiṭṭoth.* It is only in the current *shemiṭṭah* that, through the restrictive power of Stern Judgment, two of these books have shrunk to the point that only a bare hint of their existence remains. The proof text of this assertion was a passage in the Talmud (*Shabbath* 116a), according to which the book of Numbers actually consists of three books. A tradition from the school of Naḥmanides specifies that the power inherent in the Torah will manifest itself in the future aeon in such manner that we shall again perceive seven books.[249] The Book *Temunah* itself (fol. 31a) avers that the first chapter of Genesis is merely the vestige of a fuller Torah revealed to the *shemiṭṭah* of Grace, but which has become invisible in our *shemiṭṭah,* as the light of this earlier book has disappeared. Within the framework of the doctrine of the *shemiṭṭoth,* and based on the premises of a Kabbalah that regarded itself as perfectly orthodox, the most diverse possibilities of spiritualizing as well as antinomian mysticism could thus present themselves. Once one permitted the assumption that a new combination of the letters of the Torah, in themselves unalterable, might yield a new meaning, or that by keeping open the lacunae left by missing letters or lost parts of the Torah a complete transformation of its physiognomy was possible without requiring any essential modification of the Torah, then a decisive step was taken in the direction of relativizing the validity of the Torah. At the same time, however, the defenders of this doctrine passionately insisted upon the absolute authority of the Torah in the respective *shemiṭṭah.* They were by no means disposed to limit the validity or authority of the commandments of the Torah as given at Sinai within the period of the present *shemiṭṭah.* A very old commentary on the *Temunah* that incorporates excellent traditions and is often indispensable for an understanding of the book polemicizes against Jews who would restrict the authority of the Torah to the Holy Land, claiming that its commandments were not obligatory abroad. Such tendencies as well as apostasy in general, are viewed by the commentator as a characteristic sign of this aeon, a symptom of the "harshness of the [present] *shemiṭṭah*" that leads to such revolts against the authority of the divine law. The excess of evil due

---

249. Thus in Joshua ibn Shu 'eib, *Derashoth* (Cracow, 1573), fol. 63a. On the seven books of the Torah, cf. *Temunah,* fol. 31a.

to the harshness of the *shemiṭṭah* also generates these seditious and impious ideas.[250]

In any case, the Book *Temunah* is without doubt the most radical product of the Kabbalah in its early period. One is amazed at the degree of freedom with which kabbalistic speculation attempted to combine its conception of the deity with a new understanding of the world, not only as a natural or cosmic entity, but also a historical one. The history of the world unfolds according to an inner law that is the hidden law of the divine nature itself. Every gnosis transforms history into a symbol of cosmic processes. But one can also invert this principle and say, as has happened here, that the cosmic process, unfolding according to the nature of the divine potencies, necessarily acquires historical forms. In this instance the historical sequence of events loses none of its meaning, unlike most other cases of symbolic explanation where the historical retains its value only as a projection on a new, supratemporal dimension. In kabbalistic doctrine, it is precisely in the noninterchangeable sequence of epochs that the true mystery of the deity is unveiled. The author of the Book *Temunah* was undoubtedly gifted with an original mind. He was able to construct his kabbalistic historiosophy on the basis of ideas that for his colleagues, and perhaps also for his unknown masters, were of secondary importance only. For the rest his book attests, with a wealth of detail that do not concern us here, to its relations with theosophy and the comtemplative ideal of *debhequth,* which even in this harsh *shemiṭṭah* is capable of leading man back to his true origin.

I have described in these chapters the different currents that the present state of our knowledge enables us to discern among the oldest kabbalists, from the first appearance of the Kabbalah in the

250. Cf. the commentary on *Temunah,* fol. 39a. Sharply polemical remarks assuming a relationship between the law of this *shemiṭṭah* and the current impious "enlightenment" type of ideas are also expressed, in a similar context, by the anonymous author of the Book *Qana* (Poritzk, 1786), fols. 15d–17d. [Whẹn writing the original version of this book, and for many years subsequently, Scholem held the view, shared also by his eminent colleague, the historian Yitsḥak F. Baer, that the *Qana* and *Peli'ah* were composed in Spain during the middle or the second half of the fourteenth century. More recent research suggests that these books were written early in the fifteenth century and not in Spain but rather in a Greek-Jewish (Byzantine?) environment. Z.W.]

Book *Bahir* up to around the middle of the thirteenth century. I have sought to summarize the current state of research concerning this complex of problems and to set forth its results. In the process we have come to see the diverse religious as well as general historical factors that moved the generations in which the Kabbalah struggled to crystallize. At the end of the period described in this book, the Kabbalah already appears in full flower and in all its vigor. The different currents that developed from around 1250 onward could already draw on a rich heritage bequeathed to them by the three or four preceding generations. From that period on the kabbalists began to compose major works and to elaborate their conceptions in increasing detail. But all the trends discernible in the further evolution of the Spanish Kabbalah are rooted in the profound religious ferment of the first generations.

Also the question of the foundations of the Kabbalah that so preoccupied subsequent generations was already prefigured in this heritage. I have analyzed in considerable detail the earlier stages of this development which are of particular importance for the history of religion, and have dealt much more briefly with the achievements of the last generation falling within the purview of this book. Here our information is so varied and rich that today it is already possible to offer a summary as well as a detailed presentation. I chose the first method in order to bring out more clearly the most salient factors and the essential lines of development, and thereby to determine the historical framework that is significant not only for the further study of the Kabbalah itself, but also for historians in general. The hundred years leading up to Naḥmanides may be regarded as the youth of the Kabbalah that in the subsequent period of the *Zohar*—a period of "splendor" in a double sense—reached its full maturity.

Index